吴承明全集

第六卷

未发表的论述

通信

诗话

外文论著

附录

社会科学文献出版社

SOCIAL SCIENCES ACADEMIC PRESS (CHINA)

目　　录

未发表的论述

通　　信

诗　话

外文论著

附　录

未发表的论述

关于中国的 Guilds

引　论

　　在中国经济史学家中，有一个中国有没有 guilds 以及何时出现 guilds 的争论。只要有众多的商人和手工业者，就会有他们的某种组织。但是，中国学者间的争论，不是指商人和手工业者一般的组织，而是指有特定含义的 guild 这个词，即指欧洲中世纪晚期城市中的那种 guilds（gilds），或在不同国家被称为 zunft，metier，arti，company 的组织。在讨论中，又着重研究 craft guilds。因为在 craft guilds 中，它的 protectionism，exclusiveness，apprenticeship 和 monopoly tendency 最为明显。

　　西方学者到中国来，看见中国的工商业组织，就立刻把它们都称为 guilds。John Steward Burgess 的 *The Guilds of Peking*（New York，1928）也许是第一本研究中国 guilds 的著作。在 Burgess 以前，还有 D. J. Macgowan 等人的论述。后来，仁井田陞对清代北京的工商业组织作了详细的调查，他的书《北京工商行会资料集》（Guilds）则是在他死后才由东京大学于 1979 ~ 1981 陆续出版的。[①]

　　在西方学者把清代工商业组织称为 guilds 以后，中国学者也都这样做，

---

① 根岸结：《上海のギルド》，东京，1951；《中国のギルド》，东京，1953。

并且大部分人把宋代以来的工商业组织都看成是像欧洲中世纪那样的 guilds。中国学者特别感兴趣的是，马克思和恩格斯对欧洲中世纪的 craft guilds 有精湛的分析和论述，而这种分析是有理论上的普遍意义的。研究中国手工业史的彭泽益，收集了清代一些手工业组织的行规（regulations），这些行规有力地证明了马克思论述的普遍意义。不过他所收集的行规都是18 世纪晚期和 19 世纪的。但同时，也有经济史学家如傅筑夫，从更早的文献研究中，证明在 18 世纪以前的工商业组织中，不存在像西方中世纪那样的 guild system。这就在经济史学家中引起了争论。

Regulations（hanggui，行规）是研究工商业组织的性质和功能的最有力的资料。在欧洲，也没有发现早期的 guild regulation，因为 guilds 最早是秘密组织，后来才被当局批准。在中国，工商业的组织很早就是政府批准的，那么为什么没有行规遗留下来呢？这是一个谜。近年来，中国学者做了大量的史料发掘工作。除了从档案中收集资料外，还发掘出不少碑刻资料。许多碑刻是民间的，也有半官方的，都是确实的记录。上海博物馆编辑了《上海碑刻资料选集》，① 人民大学的李华编辑了《明清以来北京工商会馆碑刻选编》，② 南京大学的洪焕椿编辑了《明清苏州工商业碑刻集》。③ 这都非常有利于对中国工商业组织的历史的研究。遗憾的是，至今我们还未发现清代以前工商业组织的行规。

中国的工商业的组织，在宋代以前都称"hang"（行），宋代称"tuan-hang"（团行），明代称"pu-hang"（铺行），清代称"hui-guan"（会馆）和"gong-suo"（公所）。下面我就按照这个顺序作一些讨论，当然，重点是放在清代上。

HANG

Hang 的字义是 line，row。中国古代城市实行居民区和市场严格分离的体制，叫作 fang-shi（坊市）制。这种制度可上溯到公元前 7 世纪，一直流行到唐代，即 8 世纪。在这种制度下，居民区（fang）内不准开设店铺，商人只能

---

① 上海人民出版社，1980。
② 文物出版社，1980。
③ 江苏人民出版社，1981。

在市场（shi）做生意。市场有墙围起来，有官吏管理，早晨开市门，下午关闭市门。在市场里，卖同一种商品的商人都集中在一起，排成一个 line（hang），因而一个 hang 也就成为一种 profession。这种办法显然是为了便于官吏们管理（尤其是价格管理）和收税，大概也便利消费者选择和购买商品。

至于一个 hang 是否有 membership 或有什么样的组织，我们不知道，因为没发现过有关记载。不过可以肯定，hang 的组织，如果有的话，是限于本市场的。大的城市常有几个市场，如汉代的长安有九个市场，各市场大小悬殊，hang 的数目也大不相同，各市场的同一 profession 的商人之间并无联系。这时的商人都有市籍，他们被登记为商人就不能再转换别的职业，但是我们没听说过有 hang 籍。这一点和欧洲的 guilds 不同。在中世纪欧洲的一些城市里，一个人要先取得某 guild 会员的资格，才能取得市民的资格。

在 fang-shi 制下，在市场里做生意的人都是商人，但是也包括手工业者，因为那时手工业者都是自己出卖自己的产品，从文献中所见 hang 的名称，几乎有半数是手工业者的 hang，不过都是人数很少的 hang。手工业者的家中制造商品，然后拿到市场里去卖。他们的家是在居民区（fang），市场里是不准住家的。于是，手工业者就有一个比商人优惠的条件，即他们除了在市场出卖商品外，还可以在家里接待顾客，接受顾客的订货。从这一点也可看出，市场的 hang 的组织，如果有的话，是没有什么像西方的 guilds 那种限制生产规模的功能的。

在市场里做生意的都是零售商，即小商店和摊贩，也有茶馆、饭馆、酒店之类。从事地区间贩运贸易的大商人或 traders，并不进入市场。商业资本是集中在这些大商人手里，有些大商人非常富有，他们同高级官员甚至同宫廷往来，但他们既不进入市场，也就和 hang 没有关系。这些贩运商也没有自己的组织，至少我们没见过他们组织的文献。这就说明 hang 的组织，如果有的话，也不是一种 exclusive 组织。

TUAN-HANG

随着商业的发展，在唐代晚期 fang-shi 制就维持不住了，到宋代即 10 世纪时已完全打破这个制度，也就是说在居民区各处都可以开设店铺，都有商人活动。这么一来，商人的组织才真正有了 professional 的意义。

宋代的商人组织有的称"tuan"（团），多数仍称 hang。Tuan 的字义是 group，与 hang（line）没有什么区别。称 tuan 的多是较小的 professions，如卖花的、卖水果的，为数不多。Tuan-hang 的组织也和以前一样，包括手工业产品。不过，到宋代，又有了一个手工业者的名称，叫"zuo"（作），字义是 workshop。文献中有各种的 zuo，如刀 zuo、玉 zuo 等。但是有没有同行业的 zuo 的组织，我们不知道。Tuan 和 hang 则确实是有同行业的组织的。

宋代的 tuan-hang 是怎样组织起来的呢？我们有两个当时代人笔记的材料：

> 市间所说的 hang 是由于政府征税和勒索（商品）而来的。不管（商人经营的）商品大小，只要是有用的，都要建立 hang（见附录 1）。
>
> 市间所说的 tuan-hang 是由于政府收买（商品）而来的。不管（商人经营的）商品大小，都要建立 tuan-hang（见附录 2）。

第二例所说"收买"是一种政府征购制度，在宋代叫"huimai"（回买）或"hemai"（和买）。实际是由商人供应政府和官吏所需的物品，从肉、茶叶以至布匹、绸缎等。政府和官吏只给很低的价格，有的不给代价。

从这二例可见，宋代的 tuan-hang 并不是商人自己组织起来的，而是政府把他们组织起来的，为了收税和勒索物品。在有关宋代法令的文献中，有个法令说："不加入 hang 的人不准在街上卖东西……不到政府去登记入 hang 的商人是有罪的，别人可以告发他。"（见附录 3）又说：自这个法令公布后，在首都（开封）连卖茶的、挑水的小贩也都参加 hang 了。

这种 tuan-hang 由商人轮流值班来收税和供应政府的需要，或者承担政府的差役。值班的人就是这个 tuan-hang 的临时的首领。例如开封的米 hang，是十天一轮班。商人对这种制度非常反对，有些官员也认为弊病太大。1073 年，开封的肉 hang 发起不供应政府肉了，要求改交钱；以后各 tuan-hang 都改为交钱。据 1085 年的记载，在开封的各 tuan-hang，共有 6400 多家商户，每年交钱 43300 多 wen（文）（见附录 4）。但是在其他城市，官吏向 tuan-hang 勒索的情况还很严重。有的地方官就向中央政府提出，要求取消 tuan-hang，说"不取消 hang 的名义，它始终要害人的"（见附录 5）。但我们不知道以后的结果，大概是并未取消。

宋代的 tuan-hang 是政府组织起来的，它也就和欧洲中世纪的 guilds 完全不同。西部欧洲在日耳曼人入侵时，原来西罗马帝国的城市大部分被破坏了；接着发生一个乡村化的过程，有势力的领主都住在乡村，而城市荒废了。到 11 世纪以后城市复兴时，城市的居民主要是手工业者和商人。他们利用 guilds 组织向乡村的领主争取自治权，以至组织军队夺取城市政权。这在历史上是一个特殊的情况。中国并没有这样一个乡村化过程，城市一直在发展着，并且一直是各省、各州县（prefecture and county）的政治中心。手工业者和商人并不是城市的主要居民，他们的组织 hang 或 tuan，丝毫不具有争夺政权的作用，反而是政府控制的组织，这是很自然的。

欧洲中世纪的 guilds 有一个均等主义（equalitarianism）的原则，因而争取限制经营规模、限制工作时间和人数，统一价格，避免竞争等措施。在宋代的 tuan-hang 中，这些都不存在；一个 hang 中有大户、有小户，大户兼并小户的事是常见的。有个 1072 年的记载，说在茶 hang 里，有十几家大户，他们操纵价格，侵夺小户的利益，最后说"其他的 hang 也是这样"（见附录 6）。

然而，tuan-hang 虽然是在政府强制下建立的，但它既成为商人（包括手工业者）的组织，就多少也要争取他们本身的利益。首先是排斥外地来的商人，上述这个 1072 年的记载中就透露，外地来的茶商，都要到当地茶 hang 去，由当地茶 hang 评定他们贩来的茶的价格。一般说，外地来的商人只能将商品交给当地的 hang 去卖，不能自己设店出售。其次，tuan-hang 也为着同业的利益，同政府进行交涉，其中最重要的是政府"收买"商品时，要争取个较好的价格。从上述 1073 年的事例中也可看出，要求不再供应政府商品，改为交钱，也是由 hang 发起的。

PU-HANG

到明代，商人的组织叫 pu-hang。pu 的字义是 shop。pu-hang 和宋代的 tuan-hang 一样，也是由政府组织起来的，叫作"bian hang"（编行，enroll in hang）。有个当时代的人的笔记说：

Pu-hang 的名称不知怎样来的。大约因为商人的职务不同，所以叫 pu-hang。（明王朝）建立时，城市内外的居民都按所住街道编组，同时注明他们的职务或所营商品。政府遇有典礼需要时，按所注明的职务叫他们供差役，给以报酬……或需要一个 hang 的商品时，都要有一个人负责供应。这个人每年轮换一次，叫作 dang hang（当行，即负责人）（见附录 7）。

明代的手工业户，大约也没有单独的组织，而是包括在 pu-hang 之内。南京的地方志，在讲 pu-hang "罗纱 hang" 时下面有个注："并机户"（loomers），机户是织绸的手工业者。到明代晚期，广东佛山的"炉户"就单独列出，不在 pu-hang 之内了。炉户是制铁锅的，广东的铁锅很出名，他们有了独立的组织。

到了明后期，pu-hang 的组织发生变化。大约因为商人和手工业者极力反对政府给他们组织 hang，在 1582 年有个中央政府给首都（北京）地方政府的训令，说以后大的商户，如典当、布匹、粮食等，有资本 300 两、500 两以至 1000 两的，才把它们 "bian hang"（enroll in hang）；"其余的都不许骚扰他们"（见附录 8）。大约到了明末期，政府就不再强制工商业户组 hang 了，而是由工商业者自己组织团体。他们也抛弃了自古传下来的 hang 这个名称，而改用新的名称了。Hang 的历史到明末遂告终结，这当然是工商业发展、力量增大的结果。

HUIGUAN（MERCHANT HOUSES）

新的组织叫"huiguan"（会馆）。会馆最初并不是由商人组织的，而是由在北京做官的外省人建筑房屋，供他们的同乡到北京来参加皇家考试的举子（candidates）住的。它很像老式的 lodging house，所以叫它 house 很相宜。后来商人也建立这种 house，我们就叫它 merchant houses（商人会馆）。但要注意，不只是商人，各种民间团体都建有这种 houses。huiguan 这个词在中国和日本是很熟悉的，现在日本还有很多会馆。Ping-ti Ho 详细地研究了中国会馆的历史，据他考察，四川会馆最多，有 662 个，因为那里

immigrants 多。中国现在有不少学者研究商人会馆，像人民大学的李华、南京大学的吕作燮，都有成果。还有我的同事汪士信，他也研究了宋代的 tuan-hang。我的这个 lecture，很多就是取自汪士信的研究。

商人会馆（Merchant houses），最早是明后期建立的。北京有个歙县会馆，是明代嘉靖（1522～1566）时安徽商人所建，但它的章程上说该会馆是供考试的举子住的，并说不准商人住。北京还有个延平邵武会馆，是明代万历（1573～1620）时福建商人所建，但最初也是供考试的举子住用。我们所见最早的供商人住用的会馆，是在万历时建在苏州的岭南会馆和三山会馆，这两家的捐款名单中都主要是商人。

商人会馆的大量出现是在清代，而以在嘉庆朝（1796～1820）以前为多，因为这以后商人就不常用会馆这个名称了。其情况见表1。表1主要根据碑刻材料，可谓十分确实，但并不完全。并且我们只选有建立时间记载的，例如苏州碑刻中有近40个商人会馆，但有时间记载的仅28个。

表 1 有建立时间记载的商人会馆数

时　期	北　京	苏　州	上　海	佛　山
明代（1643 以前）	3	2		
康熙（1662～1722）	4	8	1	
雍正（1723～1735）	3			1
乾隆（1736～1795）	3	8	3	3
嘉庆（1796～1820）	4	2	1	
道光（1821～1850）				
咸丰（1851～1861）			10	12
同治（1862～1874）	1	3		
光绪（1875～1908）		5		
合　计	18	28	15	16

商人会馆的组织原则和过去的 hang 大不相同，它不是按照行业而是按照地区的原则建立的，并多用地区作名称。如北京的潞安会馆，即山西潞州的商人在北京所建。因而它有增进同乡友谊和互助，类似 fraternity 的作用。但下面立即看到，这一点不能强调过分。重要的区别是，hang 是一个城市的商人、主要是零售商的组织，而商人会馆则是外地来的商人，主要是贩运

商的组织。一个地方的贩运商往往经营同类的商品。山西潞州的商人大都是经营铜、铁、锡的，所以北京的潞安会馆实际是个经营金属产品的商人会馆。同样，像建于苏州的汀州会馆，乃是福建汀州纸商的会馆；建于苏州的钱江会馆，乃是浙江杭州绸商的会馆。苏州还有一个叫作"全山西"的会馆，实际上只是经营汇兑业务的山西票号的会馆。另外，会馆也有不少是用行业做名称的，如药材会馆、桐油会馆等。因为既是商人的组织，尤其是贩运商，总是有一定的行业性的。

但是，会馆和 hang 的更重要的区别是，它已经和政府没有什么关系，而完全是商人自己的组织了。它的功能就主要是谋求商人的利益，如评定价格、评定利润、排斥别的商业集团、要求减轻税课等等；有时就会同政府发生冲突，用集体的力量和政府办交涉。有的会馆还设有仓库和交易市场。这样，会馆就更多地具有西方 guild 的功能了。有的学者认为，中国的 guild 性质的组织，实在是从清代开始的。不过，我觉得这种论点似乎又有点过分了。

前面说过，hang 是包括手工业的。商人会馆也包括手工业者。如北京的帽行会馆，包括制帽子和卖帽子；有个长春会馆（Ever Spring），是做玉器和卖玉器的。但这种会馆很少，几乎找不到几个。我们只能假定，手工业者资本很小，他们拿不出多少钱来建立会馆；又因他们都是本城市的居民，用不着去建立 lodging house。

GONGSUO（PUBLIC HALL）

18 世纪末期，工商业的组织开始不叫 huiguan 而叫 gongsuo 了。这两个词最初没有什么分别。我们见到一个碑刻，题目上用的 huiguan，文内则用 gongsuo；还有一家会馆（merchant house），碑文上称 huiguan，门上挂牌却是 gongsuo。有趣的是一个碑文写道："huiguan 就是同乡人建立的 gongsuo"。不过从后来发展的情况看，两者的区别是很大的。gongsuo 的 gong，字义是 public，因而我想把它译成 public hall，以区别于 merchant house。在读它们的区别以前，先看一下 public hall 建立的情况。也和前面一样，表 2 主要是根据碑刻的材料，并不完全。从表 2 可见，公所的数目是随着时间前进而增多的。

表 2　苏州、上海的公所数

时　　期	苏　　州	上　　海
乾隆（1736～1795）	1	6
嘉庆（1796～1820）	5	2
道光（1821～1850）	15	4
咸丰（1851～1861）	5	2
同治（1862～1874）	16	8
光绪（1875～1908）	15	14
宣统（1909～1911）	1	4
不明	56	26
合　计	114	66

商人会馆（merchant houses）大部分是以地区命名的，公所（public hall）则绝大部分是用行业命名了，如鞋业公所、铜锡器公所等。公所也有以地区命名的，但差不多都属于某一行业，如建于苏州的七襄公所，实际属于绸缎商人；建于上海的星江公所，实际属于浙江的茶商。因此，到了公所时期，地方性减弱了，行业性加强了，更近于西方的 guilds 了。

前面说过，会馆是类似 lodging house 的组织，房租收入是会馆的一项经常收入。公所则绝少供住宿的，完全是一个会议、办事的机关，所以我想译成 hall 比较合适。公所的职能也更着重在营业方面。我们曾见到一些碑文，有的说是为了公议价格、避免跌价竞争而成立公所，有的说是为了防止外地人的竞争而成立公所。有个苏州酱坊业公所的碑刻很有趣味。酱坊是手工业，碑文说：近来酱坊的酱卖不出去，生意困难，通过查考，原因是政府开办的酱店太多了。这些酱坊冒用他们的牌号，偷着造酱。为了"禁止政府的酱店作不合法的经营"，他们创建这个公所，并立这块石碑。我将这个碑的原文放在附录 9。

商人会馆主要是商人的组织，而公所则有商人的，也有手工业者的，并且愈到后来手工业者的公所愈多。表 2 中，在同治（1862～1874）、光绪（1878～1908）两朝苏州建立的公所有一半是手工业者的。另外，还有一些手工业者的组织不叫公所，而叫 tang（堂），它们主要在上海。这样，我们就可以从手工业者留下的碑刻中发现一些行规。

前面提过，行规是研究工商业组织的性质和功能的最好的材料。在商人会馆时代,很少见行规。我们只找到三件,即北京的颜料会馆、靛行会馆、皮行会馆。其中皮行会馆存有一件 1883 年由 43 名手艺人公议的行规,它是关于招收学徒和雇工的:全行业每年招收学徒 2~4 人,不准多招。学徒的工作,有些人被准许做某些皮货,有些人则不被准许。学徒三年满期,给八分银工资,无论在哪个店,都不准多给,也不准少给。各店要雇人时,应该平均分配。不在本行业名册上的任何人,都不准在本行业工作。如果有店主招收非本行业的或是张家口的人工作,他就是个强盗或娼妓(张家口是生产皮货的地方)。这个行规可说是十足的 guild 精神,原文见附录 10。

到了公所的时代,我们就可以看见更多的行规了。不过,从碑刻中收集到的行规,大部分是规定会员登记的办法、会议章程、捐款的办法以及轮流负责管事的办法等,另外还有一些是工艺操作规程。真正具有 guild 精神的条文并不多,除了统一价格、统一工资外,就只有限制开业和限制收学徒两项。

限制开业,一般是从征收入会费上限制。凡本行业的人开业,收费低些,非本行来的人开业,就收较高的入会费。上海典业公所的一个章程限制较严,它规定新开的典店必须设在已有的典店 1400chi(尺,370 米)以外,并且要几家已有的典店担保。这个规定原文见附录 11。

限制收学徒的规定,多数是三年招收一次学徒。有的行业公议从某年起停止招收,从某年起开始招收。学徒的年限从三年到五六年,各行业不一样。又多数规定,一个店有一个学徒满期,才能招进一个,这叫作“一出一进”制度。不过,也有些行规对招徒没有什么限制。有一个苏州染坊业的行规,记入附录 12。

前面提到,彭泽益曾从文献材料收集了一些行规;这些行规被编入《中国近代手工业史资料》第 1 卷和第 2 卷。该书比较容易见到,我就不再重述。这样,加上我们从碑刻到中发现的,就有 50 个左右的行规了。从这些行规看,它们确有类似西方 guilds 的条款,有一种 guild 精神。但是,无论在 protectionism 或 exclusiveness 上,都没有欧洲 guilds 那么强烈,它的 equalitarianism 很不明显,处罚条款也不很严。但是,应当注意到我们所见到的中国的行规是 19 世纪初期的,而和它做比较的却是中世纪晚期欧洲的 guilds。事实上,在 19 世纪末期,上面说的那些商人会馆和公所,就逐渐变成 trade associations（同业公会）和 chambers of commerce（商会）了。

以下 12 个附录用中文，毋需英译。[①]

附　录

1. 市肆谓之行者，因官府科索而得此名。不以其物之大小，但合充用者，皆置为行。

（耐得翁：《都城纪胜·诸行》）

2. 市肆谓之团行者，盖因官府回买而得此名。不以物之大小，皆置为团行。

（吴自牧：《梦粱录·团行》）

3. 元不系行之人，不得在街市卖坏钱纳免行钱争利（原文"坏"字有误——笔者按）。仰各自诣官投充行人，纳免行钱，方得在市卖易。不赴官自投行者有罪，告者有赏。此指挥行，凡十余日之间，京师如街市提瓶者必投充茶行，负水担粥以至麻鞋、头发之属，无敢不投行者。

（马端临：《文献通考》卷二〇《市籴考》）

4. 在京诸色行户，总六千四百有奇免轮差官中只应，一年共出缗钱四万三千三百有奇。

（李焘：《续资治通鉴长编》卷三五九"元丰八年九月乙未"）

---

① 　参见增井经夫《会馆公所》，《历史教育》13.9，1965，第 26 - 31 页。

5. 州县官凡有需索，皆取办于一镇，（黄池镇）之内，诸般百物，皆有行名。人户之挂名籍，终其身以至子孙，无由得脱。若使依价支钱，尚不免胥吏减克，况名为和买，其实白科……行名不除，终为人户之害。

（真德秀：《真文忠公集》卷七《罢黄池镇行铺状》）

6. 兼并之家，如茶一行，自来有十余户。若客人将茶到京，即先馈献设燕，乞为定价。比十余户所买茶更不敢取利，但得定为高价，即于下户倍取利，以偿其费……余行盖皆如此。

（李焘：《续资治通鉴长编》卷二三六，熙宁五年闰七月丙辰）

7. 铺行之起不知所始。盖铺居之民各行不同，因以名之。国初悉城内外居民，因其里巷多少，编为排甲，而以其所业所货注之籍。遇各衙门有大典礼，则按籍给值使役，而互易之，其名曰行户。或一排之中，一行之物，总以一人答应，岁终践更，其名曰当行。

（沈榜：《宛署杂记·铺行》）

8. 其铺行果有典当、布行、杂粮等项，三五百两至千两的方许编行，其余再不许骚扰。

（沈榜：《宛署杂记·铺行》）

9. 《苏州府为酱坊业创建公所禁止官酱店铺营私碑》："窃坊等酱坊一业，共有徽、苏、宁、绍四帮，计共八十六家。在长、元、吴三县各都图开张，均经请照、请烙在案。上年因酱货不销，几至所定额盐，不能按缸秤领。坊等推源其故，悉由官酱店过多，漫无稽查。往往借牌营私，偷造酱货。再四思维，当邀同业妥议章程，由盐公堂商人禀案举办，将城乡各酱店，一律严查。责令愿拆某坊酱货者，出具认销切结。并令承认之坊，加具保结，按户造册。呈送在案。试办经年，酱店既易稽查，酱销亦渐起色。第恐日久弛废，酱店复萌故智，今复集议，设立公所……俾能垂诸永久。"

（苏州历史博物馆等编《明清苏州工商业碑刻集》，江苏人民出版社，1981，第 260~261 页）

10. 学手艺者，徒也，以三年为满。不许重学，不许包年；谁要重学包年者，男盗女娼。公同商议：每年本行学徒弟者，二、三、四个人，不许多学。在沟者，许作银鼠皮、红狐皮腿；不在沟者，不许。不遵行规，男盗女娼。学满，给捌分；诸位宝号，通同工头，不分两样，毫厘不爽。到春天，够捌分工，就写工账。有存欠，写账俱要言明。众手艺人自家来时，诸号匀对添人。在行名者，行中吃也；不在名者，不能吃也。如果添外行者，或口外之人，大众不容；准要相容，男盗女娼。不准瞒心昧己，俱是一样也。

〔仁井田陞：《北京ギルド资料集（三）》，昭和五十三年版，第 543 页〕

11. 《上海典业公所章程》（无年月）："上海典铺，星罗棋布，已遍城乡。倘再有创新之典，必须同业集议，基址离老典左右前后一百间外，方可互相具保。以营造尺一丈四尺一间，一百四十丈为一百间。如在一百四十丈以内，非但同业不能具保，需要联名禀官禁止……"

（上海博物馆编《上海碑刻资料选辑》，上海人民出版社，1980，第 405~406 页）

12. 谨启：吾行洋蓝咈布染坊一业，向有成规：
一、议原布对开。
一、议详标对开。
一、议斜纹布三开。
一、议粗布三开。
一、议每匹酒资四十二文。

一、议改色陈修蓝底，每匹酒资二十一文。

一、议管缸司长，每月工俸钱三千文。

一、议蓝头司长，每月工俸钱二千六百文。

一、议洋头司长，每月工俸钱二千六百文。

一、议石头司长，每月工俸钱二千二百文。

一、议帮司长，每月工俸钱一千八百文。

一、议众司工俸，准加不准减。

一、议徒弟一年，每月钱五百文，三年准工俸全工，领照行单，一低为凭。

一、议徒弟五年准满，六年准留，不准私留。

一、议每月准三十天，每日贴小菜钱二十文。

一、议众司公议，司长到绍（兴）至家，不准分取酒资。

一、议徒弟不准捐入乱规。

一、议倘徒弟捐入乱规者，罚洋一百元，捐入公所。

一、议如有外坊染司，不准存留在坊混做。

一、议吾同行汇议勒石恪守遵规，不得紊乱。勒石刻碑之后，凡司长众友等并力同心，永远长生。

一、议同行汇议各项条规，不准乱规。

特此勒刻石碑，在浙绍长生公所内布知。

浙绍哔布染司同业公启

同治九年四月二十八日示

（苏州历史博物馆等编《明清苏州工商业碑刻集》，第83~84页）

从经济理论和历史上看
社会主义市场经济

经济增长，社会进步，最终要看一国资源的利用是否合理，亦即资源配置是否优化了。全部优化，所谓帕累托最优，恐不可能。部分地、逐步地优化，则历史上常见。当然，资源配置劣化，导致经济衰退，也是常有的。

资源配置主要有两个途径：一是主权者或政府制定计划，命令行之；一是通过交易，由市场调节。二者在历史上常并存，以一为主。以欧洲而论，古希腊城邦间交易颇繁，其手工业生产尝受市场节制。古罗马的大地产庄园产品输往各地，其生产和劳动力（奴隶）配置亦受市场调节。古代村社和中世纪的领主庄园属封闭型经济，生产和劳动由主权者计划支配，市场极不重要。其后城市兴起，16 世纪重商主义滥觞，开辟世界市场，以至工业革命，其间欧洲有三百年繁荣，可谓市场经济之功。第一次世界大战后，德国以集中的计划指导经济复兴，一时颇见成效。苏联以严密的指令性计划调配全国资源，迅速建成工业化基础，世人为之瞩目。第二次世界大战后，东欧数国实行计划经济，成效各异。而原来实行市场经济的国家，亦皆加强国家干预，以致含有计划性的社会党政策盛行。到 20 世纪 60 年代以后，情况又为之一变，下文可见。

在马克思主义理论体系中，资源调配被归结为劳动时间（包括劳动和物化劳动）的节约和在各部门间的比例分配；这是"自然规律"，无论资本主义社会或社会主义社会都是一样的。市场调节是由价值规律作用，计划调节亦应按价值规律行事，这也是在资本主义或社会主义制度下都是一样的。不过，决定价值的"社会必要劳动时间"或"抽象劳动"无法计量。因而,市场调节是用生产价格(成本加平均利润)来解释;在计划经济中,因废除要素市场,只好用主观的政策性的计划价格来计值。20 世纪 30 年代,苏联学者 Π. B. 坎特罗维奇曾提出用线性规划求"最优计划价格"的方法,可按资源稀缺程度定价,未能应用。在中国则有经过国家批准,实行"幅度浮动价格"的办法。

西方经济学以主流派新古典主义为准,认为资源配置是由市场上的相对价格形成的均衡价格调节的。均衡价格即生产要素的边际收益相等时的价格。例如各生产主体均按收益最大化原则配置劳动力,以致劳动的边际收益相等,表现为工资水平大体一致,劳动力的配置即属优化了。在新古典模型中,人力以外的各种资源都是包括在资本变量中,如资本的边际收益率达到均衡,资源配置趋于完善。当然,西方经济学尚有许多其他流派,如主张用产权制度或经济结构来解释资源配置的优化或劣化,用不平衡发展战略来观察资源配置的状况。在市场价格上,主要是对垄断价格、价格加价(make-up pricing)的争议,也有人主张用反映资源使用最佳效果的影子价格来评价投资效果。

西方经济学者一般认为市场调节的效果优于计划调节,有"消费者剩余""多种帕累托最优""公共选择""自愿行为"等论点。但对市场上由于不完全竞争和垄断造成的后果,特别是对市场经济导致的分配不公平问题,难获结论。又市场调节资源配置并非完全是通过价格,如价格信号系统之外尚有非价格信号系统,平行交易之外尚有垂直交易、等级交易。故近年来日益注意对市场上"看得见的手"的研究。原来,过去和现在,都不曾有过完全自由贸易的市场,资源配置也不仅限于计划和市场两途,人们的选择常据历史条件而定。下面,我们再从历史上作些探讨。

人类受个人能力和环境的限制,只有通过交换才能获得经济上的增益。故亚当·斯密的交换导致分工,分工和专业化增进社会生产力的观点,至今为多数经济学家奉为圭臬。不过,自法国重农学派以来,在经济发展理论上生产导向的思想常占优势,供给创造需求的萨伊定律深入人心。德国历史学派的先驱者 F. 李斯特批评斯密的理论是"交换经济学",提出工商协调的"生产力经济学",并认为历史发展的顺序是农业经济、农工业经济、农工商业经济。19 世纪 70 年代,边际效用学派兴起,从需求即物品的稀少性和效用上来说明价值和价格决定。到 19 世纪晚期,历史学派的经济发展观点也有所改变。如 B. H. 希尔德布兰德按交换方式提出实物经济、贸易经济、信用经济的发展阶段论。K. 毕歇尔更从变换的过程上提出家庭经济（包括村社和中世纪庄园，无须依赖交换）、城市经济（中世纪城邦，生产者与消费者直接交换）、国民经济（生产者为市场而生产，商品须经许多环节才到达消费者手中）的发展阶段论。

众所周知，马克思曾提出人类社会相继出现的五种经济形态或生产方式，而在封建社会向现代化生产过渡中，他是十分注意市场和商业资本的作用的。在《德意志意识形态》中，有一篇题为"交往与生产力"的史论，讲中世纪后期"商人阶级"的出现和世界大市场的开辟怎样导致工场手工业的兴起以至大机器工业的建立。在《资本论》中，他指出商业资本是最早的资本自由存在方式，在前资本主义社会它"支配着产业"，因而，"它在封建生产的最早的变革时期，即现代生产的发生时期，产生过压倒一切的影响。"①

19 世纪末，新古典主义的奠基人 A. 马歇尔提出"需求理论"和均衡价值论；此后，西方经济学就大都是从需求讲起了。不过，马歇尔的重点仍在生产，并认为短期内是需求起作用，而长期看仍是供给起主要作用。马歇尔的均衡是局部均衡；同时期洛桑学派提出一般或全部均衡理论，又在此基础上提出帕累托最优效率，成为资源配置的理想模式。然而，直到凯恩斯主义兴起，西方经济学都是探讨微观，不注意整个经济发展问题。唯 J. A. 熊彼特于 1912 年出版《经济发展理论》，提出创新论，是理论上一大创造；但其发展观仍是生产导向的。

20 世纪 30 年代，出现所谓凯恩斯革命，经济学转向宏观分析，重新与历史研究结合。并因 J. M. 凯恩斯彻底批判了萨伊定律，需求和有效需求成为讨论中心。第二次世界大战后，对经济史特别是从传统经济向现代经济转变的看法发生变化。过去，大多是强调工业革命，现在则认为欧洲经济的变革始于 16 世纪的重商主义，二百年后的工业革命乃是市场扩大和一系列政治社会变革的结果（其实，马克思早就提出欧洲的资本主义制度是 16 世纪建立的）。这种新思潮可以 C. M. 奇波拉主编的六卷本《欧洲经济史》为代表，它每篇都是从分析总需求开始。也可说，经济发展观由生产导向转为需求导向。

---

① 马克思：《资本论》第 3 卷，人民出版社，1975，第 369、376 页。

1969 年，以一般均衡价值论闻名的 J. R. 希克斯出版《经济史理论》。他认为，迄今世界经济的发展是有共同趋势的，即由习俗经济和命令经济过渡到市场经济，尽管这种过渡在世界各地是不同步的，并且在历史上是有反复的。欧洲中世纪的封建主义是习俗、命令两种经济的混合，它向现代经济转换的起点是商业的专门化。专门商人要求保护财产权和保护合同，于是出现了一个长达二三百年的"市场渗透"时期，即适应市场经济的货币、信用、法律制度的确立，政府财政和行政管理的改造，农业的商业化劳动力市场的建立。这一切，导致工业革命。20 世纪 80 年代兴起的以 D. C. 诺斯为首的新制度学派经济史理论，实际是以希克斯的理论为基础。不过强调了产权（不光所有制）制度和交易费用，产权制度是否有效，实现这种制度的交易费用能否降低，是经济发展的关键。

从上述经济理论和经济史理论历史看，我国社会主义经济要实现现代化，转向市场经济是不可避免的。社会主义经济的基础在于它的所有制体系和分配制度，不在于用什么方法来配置资源。从社会主义经济学的历史看，可以得出同样结论。用指令性计划调配资源，可收一时之效，但时间一长必然导致效率低下、资源浪费和比例失调。20 世纪 30 年代，O. 兰格即提出用模拟市场办法确定生产货料价格的意见。到 60 年代，先后有 W. 布鲁斯的企业分权引进市场机制、O. 锡克的计划调节与市场调节相结合模式；70 年代以后，有 J. 考斯塔将农业、消费品生产、第三产业纳入市场调节的方案，A. 阿甘别江和 Π. 阿尔巴金的中央计划改为指导性、用合同等市场形式实施计划的方案，以及比较彻底的 J. 科尔内的"短缺经济学"理论。我国在改革中也经过计划为主、市场为辅，计划与市场相结合等考虑，最后决定逐步建立社会主义市场经济，这是十分英明的。

市场经济并不废除国家计划、国家干预或宏观调控，即使西方国家，这也成为常例。在我国又有其特殊性。这不仅因为我国市场尚在发育中，尤其要素市场和抵御风险的市场尚待建立，还因为市场的功能不仅是资源配置，还对实现价值分配产生很大作用，为保证社会主义原则，国家的管理和干预就更为重要了。

1994 年 7 月

关于土布的材料

土布史

唐代在岭南已产棉布，并输入宫廷，文宗（827～840）曾服用。又新疆织布甚早，已有四处遗物出土，并出土棉籽，鉴定为一千年前至七世纪遗物。宋代织布传入闽、粤、松江。元代改进纺织技术。而棉纺织之发展实自明代始。明代棉布已代替大麻布，并代替部分苎麻布，成为人民衣被之主要材料。不过明代棉纺织中心在松江一带，余则福建，略及山东。北方虽产棉，但不精纺织，所谓"吉贝则泛舟而鬻诸南，布则泛舟而鬻诸北"。①

棉纺织的普遍化实在清代。清松江府包括华亭、娄、奉贤、金山、上海、南汇、青浦七县及川沙厅，都有土布生产，仍为最大产区，据《江南土布史》估计，年产在1800万匹至3000万匹。由此区扩大，常熟、无锡、嘉兴、嘉定、平湖、均生产土布，而以苏州为贸易和加工（染、踹）中心，即江南土布产区。全区产量，估计年约4500万匹。

此外，湖北、湖南、河南、山东、河北也有了土布产区。湖北产量较多，集中在中部汉阳、孝感、应城一带，而以沙市为贸易中心，盖销西南也。其南端监利产区，则与湖南相接。湖南产区在洞庭湖南岸，即巴陵布或都布，亦销西南并广西。河南产区一在北部孟县，主销西北；一在南部南

---

① 徐光启：《农政全书》卷三五《木棉》。

阳，即陇布，也主销西北。山东产区在中部历城、章丘、齐东、蒲台，主销东北。河北产生一在北部滦县、乐亭，主销东北；一在南部元氏、南宫，主销西北。再山西榆次、四川江津、广东潮阳、福建邵武，也有较小之产区。

以上所谓产区，指有大量商品布销往外省者。实则土布为农民家庭纺织，主要为自给布，有余则在地方市场出售，遍及各省，不以产区名之，尽管如此，也绝非家家都纺纱织布，"男耕女织"之说是象征性的。据估算，农村织布户最盛时（18世纪末）不过占全国总农户的45%，一半多一点的农户是买布穿，或衣麻、丝、皮毛。至18世纪末，棉布代替麻布的过程大体完成。此时苎麻、葛、蕉主要用于织造夏布、麻纱等高级品，非棉布所能代替，然仍有自给性之苎麻布以至大麻布充衣料。估计全国棉布产量约6亿标准匹，半数为商品布。详见"中国土布产销估计"。

土布技术

元代黄道婆引进黎族纺织技术，文献、碑刻确凿，殆非虚语。其改进一在轧花，这是过去丝、麻纺织所没有的工序，所引进大约即为王祯《农书》中之搅车，系用双木滚轴相对转动，挤出棉籽，须用三人操作。至明末，已改为一人操作。清代改进，称轧车；加三脚架，高3尺（原只1.5尺），人可坐操作。用径3寸和1.5寸滚轴一对，水平装置，大轴木制，手摇，外旋；小轴铁制，脚踏转，内旋；利用压力和转速差，将棉籽内落，棉花外扬。一人操作。"日可轧百十斤"。太仓是棉花转运站，太仓式轧车尤精，"两人可当六人"，"一人当四人"。但在一般植棉户，自轧自用，则仍用明代式搅车，或用杆棍将籽扦出。

纺的过程包括弹棉、搓条、纺纱、成纤四工序。弹棉用弹弓，大约是明代遗制，清无改进。搓条用竹管卷上花衣，抽去竹管即成条，比较简单。成纤是将纺成的纱用缕车绕在架上，这是利用过去缕丝技术，也比较简单。最重要的是纺纱，系利用过去的麻纺车。

中国麻纺车宋代已颇先进，已有5锭纺车，又有水力、畜力传动的32锭大纺车，但不适于棉纺。因麻是韧皮纤维，拉力强，纺时主要是加捻（twist）；棉纤维短，拉力小，纺时不仅是加捻，更重要的是牵伸（draft）。当时的木棉，纤维比今棉更短，自撚度少，纺来不易。3锭、5锭麻纺车均是摩擦转动，不适于纺棉；32 锭大纺车是皮带转动，水平置锭，该车系集体用，家庭户置备不起。黄道婆引进的棉纺车是单锭小车，直径 30 ~ 40 厘米，另有大轮者，径亦只 61 厘米。清代农家所用均为此种单锭纺车，但已大于 40 厘米，纺锭在轮下，左高右低（麻纺车纺锭在轮上，水平装置）；一人坐操作，左手执棉条，右手摇车，皮带传动。这种纺车效率很低，一个工作日（10 ~ 12 小时）通常产纱 5 两。技术高者，能左手握三管（棉条），减少换条时间，但"捷则不坚"。在松江区，高技术者可日纺 8 两，起早贪黑延长时间，可得 10 两以上。所纺为 7 ~ 10 支粗纱。这种单锭手摇纺车的劳动生产率约为 19 世纪前期英国纺纱机的 1/80。

为增进纺纱效率，在上海曾有三锭棉纺车出现；由于增加纺锭，又必须改手摇为脚踏，以解放右手，帮助理棉条。这种三锭脚车虽有文献记载，我们却未见过实物。记载始于乾隆《上海县志》，使用限于上海，道光时郑光祖曾买了一架带回常熟，却不会使用。在上海也限于少数人家，据说日可出纱十余两，但需"少壮"劳力。而一般农家都是壮年妇女织布，老幼劳力纺纱。上海最著名的纺车金泽谢家车，有百年历史，亦系单锭手摇车。

织布是利用过去丝织技术，用投梭机。中国丝织机在唐宋已属世界先进，以后递有改进和专用化。这种织机用于织布，绰绰有余。因丝织所用经线在 5000 根以上，以至 17000 根，而棉织宽幅土布不过用径 800 ~ 1200 根。丝织须将丝纺成双经；棉纱则不需加纺，但作经线要浆。有上浆（浸浆）、刷浆二法，刷浆较费工力，须一定技术。棉织因经线根数少，牵经、穿综、穿筘都比丝织省工，也不需专门技工（丝织有专业）。当时用手投梭，同时打筘，断头不多。织法也比丝简单，不用拉花机，主要是平织，也可纹织。又均织本色布，不像丝织有熟货（先染后织）。效率大体是一个成年女劳力，每个工作日（10 ~ 12 小时）产布一匹。这种投梭机的劳动生产率约为 19 世纪前期英国织布机的 1/16。

显而易见，纺纱效率远低于织布。大体是为供应一个工作日的织布，须有 3.5 个工作日来纺纱；或 3.5 人纺纱供 1 人织布之用。但在农家是成年劳动力织布，老幼劳动力纺纱。总计成布一匹，须 5 ~ 6 个劳动日，其中纺纱 3.5 日，织布 1 日，其余用于拣料、弹花、搓条、成纤、浆纱、接头（新机穿综、穿筘）等。

规格品种

农家自用土布（自给布）无须统一规格，多为小布，幅宽 1 尺以内，长 15 尺以上。集中产区之商品布，各地规格也不一致。江南土布大体有标布、稀布二类，前者较厚实，销北方，后者较细，销南方。近代上海标准土布，每匹宽 1.2 尺，长 20 尺，合 3.633 平方码；重 20 两，合 1.455 磅。乾嘉时，幅稍狭，或稍长，重 18 两左右；但亦有大布幅宽约 1.5 尺，长达 32 尺者，为特殊用途，不多产。

松江著名品种，有丁娘子布，即飞花布，因弹花工细、洁白精软著称。有紫花布，选用紫木棉织成，色淡赭。有兼丝布，以丝或夹丝为经，棉纱为纬织成。有绒布，亦夹丝起绒，径剪者称剪绒布。南京亦产紫花布，后出口之布西人统称南京布（Nankeen），实不只南京所出，其中销欧洲者加宽幅面，称公司布，为英东印度公司规格。青浦所出尤墩布，最细薄，做暑袜用。松江有象眼布，据称新创，可能有孔，但织法未详。又有称斜纹布、三梭布者，则显系仿丝织斜纹、换梭之法，可能有暗花。但无论如何，棉织在绞经、成孔、浮花、显花上逊于丝织远甚。苏州、松江均染布中心。染布以青蓝为大宗，亦有深浅单色布，光绪初称有"七十二种"，恐夸大。印花布始于明末，有二法，用灰遮花，或木刻板印花。清代有发展。有称药斑布者，亦称浇花布，大约是小图案。总之印花并不普遍，色彩单调。唯嘉庆以后，蓝白条织或格织已颇普及。

湖北布，用棉较佳，销外省者为大布，质较薄。湖南布以都布出名，较粗糙，但耐湿。河南布，棉花质好，北部孟布，南部陡布，均驰名，属质地较厚之布。山东布，有平机、阔布、小布等规格，质亦粗厚。阔布供军士用，小布销边塞，其耐穿。又章丘染青蓝布，工精色艳，驰名京师。河北布亦属厚质，北部滦州、乐亭产尤佳，适销东北。中部冀县、赵县、深州、定州之布，织工精细，并销朝鲜。又有特粗厚之大布，销蒙古供帐幕用。

土布出口

土布出口甚早，18 世纪 30 年代英东印度公司收购南京布，始有记录，年均万匹，80 年代增至数十万匹，90 年代增至百余万匹。进入 19 世纪，年在一百数十万匹，1819 年达 300 万匹最高，以后衰落。但同时美国船运出土布增加，年在 100 万匹以上。截至 1830 年，中国土布输英价值始终超过英国纺织品输华价值。这以后英国纺织品输华剧增，纺织品贸易变为入超。然 1870 年以后，土布出口又增加。这时有海关统计，用关担计，年均数千关担。80 年代达数万关担，90 年代增为 10 余万关担（1 关担约合 91.6 匹）。进入 20 世纪，土布出口仍不断增加，至 1921～1925 年，年达 30 万关担，以后衰落。土布生命力强，于此可见。国内消费，1920 年土布仍占 70%，不过这时的土布已大量使用机制纱织成。

附：1840～1936 年中国土布产销估计（摘要）

本估计系上海社会科学院经济研究所的同行（徐新吾主编）为《中国资本主义发展史》第 2 卷所作。摘要仅录估计结果，各项说明及资料来源从略。该书尚未出版。摘要数字可引用，但请勿发表全文。

估计方法：以 1860 年为基准，调查棉布和棉花人均消费量、农村织布产所占比重、生产土布所需工时，以此测算出棉花及土布应有产量。其余各年，根据人口、消费率变化、进出口、国内纺织工业变化等因素估算。

名词解释："棉花"均指皮棉。"机布"即机制布，包括进口机布及国内中外纺织厂所产机布。"土布"指农村纺织户手织布，包括少量城镇居民家庭手织布，但不包括改良土布（即用手拉机或铁木机所织布）。

"匹"为标准土布匹，其规格为 1.2 海尺 × 20 海尺；每匹合 3.6337 平方码，重 20 会馆秤两。

折算法：所有土布、改良土布、机布均按重量折成标准土布匹。重量用海关秤：

1 关担 = 100 关斤　1 关斤 = 1.2096 市斤 = 1.3333 磅

1 会馆秤斤（16 两）= 0.8731 关斤　1 码 = 2.57 海尺

进口机布（幅阔 1 码，长 40 码），原按关担计者，依上述折算率折为标准匹。原按机布匹计者，在 1840～1860 年按每机布匹重 7.5 磅计；1894 年按每机布匹重 10 磅计；1913～1936 年按每机布匹重 12 磅计，即：

$$\frac{磅数}{1.3333 \times 1.0914} = 标准土布匹 \quad 1\ 机匹 = 8.247\ 土匹 = 13\ 土匹$$

皮棉手工弹成絮棉，损耗率 4%；在纺织厂清花车间梳成机纱用棉，损耗率 6%。絮棉纺成土纱或机纱，损耗率免计。土布重量，包括上浆重 5%；机布重量，包括上浆重 12%。故

土布重量扣除 5% ＝用纱量

用纱重量回收成絮损耗 4%（即除以 0.96）＝用棉量

机布重量扣除 12% ＝用纱量

用纱重量回收成絮损耗 6%（即除以 0.94）＝用棉量

表 1　江苏、松江、闽广及全国土布生产（1860）

	单　位	江　苏	松　江	福建、广东	全　国
棉花产量	千关担	2070.00	600.00	50.00	8119.76
加:外区运入棉花	千关担			50.00	
进口棉花	千关担			571.78	571.78
减:供应外区棉花	千关担	410.00	250.00		
出口棉花	千关担				71.58
棉花消费量	千关担	1660.00	350.00	671.78	8619.96
减:棉花成絮损耗 4%	千关担	66.40	14.00	26.87	344.80
絮棉产量	千关担	1593.60	336.00	644.91	8275.16
减:非纺织耗用絮棉	千关担	240.00	19.80	60.00	2250.00
纺织用絮棉(＝土纱量)	千关担	1353.60	316.20	584.91	6250.16
加:进口洋纱	千关担			35.38	35.38
纱总量	千关担	1353.60	316.20	620.29	6285.54
加:棉布上浆 5%	千关担	67.68	15.81	31.01	314.28
用于织布的花纱总重量	千关担	1421.28	332.01	651.30	6599.82
土布产量	千　匹	130225.40	30420.56	59675.65	604711.38
各地区占全国比重	%	21.54	5.03	9.87	100.00

	单位	江 苏	松 江	福建、广东	全 国
完成土布产量所需劳动日	千 日	781352.40	182523.36	358053.90	3628268.28
从事纺织户数	千 户	4680.00	459.00	3150.00	34263.00
每纺织户平均年产土布	匹	27.50	66.25	19.19	17.58

表 2 农村纺织户及各类户消费水平

	单位	1840 年	1860 年	1894 年	1913 年	1920 年	1936 年
全国人口	千人	400000.00	405000.00	415000.00	430000.00	440000.00	450000.00
城镇及非农业人口	千人	20000.00	24300.00	33200.00	38700.00	44000.00	54000.00
农村人口	千人	380000.00	380700.00	381800.00	391300.00	396300.00	396000.00
农村户数	千户	76000.00	76140.00	76360.00	78260.00	79200.00	79200.00
农村纺织户	千户	34200.00	34263.00	32835.00	31304.00	31680.00	23760.00
占农村户数	%	45.00	45.00	43.00	40.00	40.00	30.00
农村土布应有产量	千匹	597327.39	604710.36	589157.79	497421.36	552317.03	352980.07
农村纺织户平均每户年产土布	匹	17.47	17.65	17.94	15.89	17.43	14.86
城镇及非农业人口消费棉布	千匹	36000.00	44712.00	65736.00	83592.00	100320.00	129600.00
人均消费水平	匹	1.80	1.84	1.98	2.16	2.28	2.40
农村纺织户消费棉布	千匹	282150.00	287809.00	298799.00	309910.00	331056.00	261360.00
人均消费水平	匹	1.65	1.68	1.82	1.98	2.09	2.20
农村非纺织户消费棉布	千匹	281850.00	287129.00	320215.00	380498.00	404624.00	509040.00
人均消费水平	匹	-1.35	+1.37	+1.47	+1.62	+1.70	-1.84

表 3 农村植棉纺织户与非植棉纺织户

	单位	1840 年	1860 年	1894 年	1913 年	1920 年	1936 年
农村纺织户中植棉户比重	%	80.00	80.00	78.00	76.00	78.00	72.00
农村纺织户中植棉户数	千户	27360.00	27410.40	25611.30	23791.04	24710.40	17107.20
农村纺织户中非植棉户数	千户	6840.00	6852.60	7223.70	7512.94	6969.60	6652.80
植棉而不纺织户户数毛估	千户	1000.00	1000.00	1000.00	900.00	1300.00	1500.00
全国植棉户总数	千户	28360.00	28410.40	26611.30	24691.04	26010.40	18607.20
全国植棉户人口	千人	258200.00	262948.00	281943.50	306544.80	309948.00	356964.00

表 4　农村土布产量

	单位	1840 年	1860 年	1894 年	1913 年	1920 年	1936 年
全国棉布应有消费量	千匹	600000.00	619650.00	684750.00	774000.00	836000.00	900000.00
加:出口	千匹	59.04	4944.57	1495.67	4594.91	6946.50	10421.54
全国棉布应有产量	千匹	600059.04	624594.57	686245.67	778594.91	842946.50	910421.54
减:进口机制布	千匹	2731.65	19884.21	91696.90	253612.72	203993.55	107771.13
减:国内机制布	千匹			5390.98	17560.83	36635.92	409670.34
全国手织布应有产量	千匹	597327.39	604710.36	589157.79	507421.36	602317.03	392980.07
减:改良土布	千匹				10000.00	50000.00	40000.00
全国农村土布应有产量	千匹	597327.39	604710.36	589157.79	497421.36	552317.03	352980.07
全国棉布应有产量中:							
机制布所占比重	%	0.46	3.18	14.15	34.83	28.55	56.84
手织布所占比重	%	99.54	96.82	85.85	65.17	71.45	43.16
内农村土布所占比重	%	99.54	96.82	85.85	63.89	65.52	38.77

表 5　农村土布消用机纱量

	单位	1840 年	1860 年	1894 年	1913 年	1920 年	1936 年
农村土布应有产量	千匹	597327.39	604710.36	589157.79	497421.36	552317.03	352980.07
农村土布用纱总量	千关担	6208.79	6285.53	6123.87	5170.34	5740.94	3668.98
进口机制纱	千关担	25.00	35.38	1159.60	2685.36	1325.38	108.75
国内机纱	千关担			342.17	1678.58	3052.28	8582.34
机纱总量	千关担	25.00	35.38	1501.77	4363.94	4308.01	8463.64
非织布用机纱	千关担			15.02	349.12	516.96	1269.55
机制布用机纱	千关担			52.53	171.12	357.00	3992.09
改良土布用机纱	千关担				103.94	519.71	415.77
农村土布消用机纱	千关担	25.00	35.38	1434.22	3739.76	2914.34	2786.23
占农村土布用纱总量	%	0.40	0.56	23.42	72.33	50.76	75.94

表 6　棉花消费量和产量

	单位	1840 年	1860 年	1894 年	1913 年	1920 年	1936 年
全国人口	千人	400000.00	405000.00	415000.00	430000.00	440000.00	450000.00
每人每年平均消费棉布	匹	1.50	1.53	1.65	1.80	1.90	2.00
	方码	5.45	5.56	6.00	6.54	6.90	7.27

	单 位	1840 年	1860 年	1894 年	1913 年	1920 年	1936 年
全国棉布应的消费量	千 匹	600000.00	619650.00	684750.00	774000.00	836000.00	900000.00
折合棉花消费量	千关担	6496.43	6709.19	7414.05	8380.39	9051.69	9744.64
每人每年平均消费絮棉	关 斤	0.50	0.50	0.52	0.53	0.54	0.55
全国絮棉消费量	千关担	2000.00	2025.00	2158.00	2279.00	2376.00	2475.00
折合棉花消费量	千关担	2083.33	2109.38	2247.92	2373.96	2475.00	2578.13
非织布用纱消棉量	千关担			15.65	363.67	538.50	1322.45
工业、卫生、军需用棉量	千关担			112.40	237.40	371.25	644.53
棉花消费总量	千关担	8579.76	8818.57	9790.02	11355.42	12436.44	14289.75
加：出口棉花	千关担		71.58	755.14	794.92	445.77	723.49
出口机纱、机制布折棉花	千关担					79.35	322.74
出口土布折棉花	千关担	0.64	53.54	16.19	49.75	68.42	27.02
减：进口棉花	千关担	500.00	571.78	43.10	134.74	678.30	1056.53
进口洋纱折棉花	千关担	26.04	36.86	1207.91	2797.25	1380.60	113.28
进口洋布折棉花	千关担	29.58	215.29	992.84	2745.96	2208.72	1166.88
全国棉花应有产量	千关担	8024.78	8119.76	8317.50	6522.14	8762.36	13026.31
折合市秤	千市担	9706.77	9821.66	10060.85	7889.18	10598.95	15756.62
参考华纱联《中国棉花统计》	千市担					7897.97	16974.63
参考华纱联《中国棉花统计》，加前一年平均数	千市担					9230.59	13250.92

表 7　自给土布与商品土布

	单位	1840 年	1860 年	1894 年	1913 年	1920 年	1936 年
全国棉布应有产量	千匹	600059.00	624595.00	686246.00	778595.00	842947.00	910422.00
农村土布应有产量	千匹	597327.00	604710.00	589158.00	497421.00	552317.00	352980.00
其中：自给土布	千匹	282150.00	287809.00	298799.00	309910.00	331056.00	261360.00
商品土布	千匹	315177.00	316901.00	290359.00	187511.00	221261.00	91620.00
自给土布在农村土布中所占比重	%	47.24	47.59	52.72	62.30	59.94	74.04
商品土布在农村土布中所中比重	%	52.76	52.41	49.28	37.70	40.06	25.96
自给土布在全国棉布中所占比重	%	47.02	46.08	43.54	39.80	39.27	28.71
商品土布在全国棉布中所占比重	%	52.52	50.74	42.31	24.08	26.25	10.06

表 8　自给棉与商品棉

	单　位	1840 年	1860 年	1894 年	1913 年	1920 年	1936 年
织造农村土布消用棉花量	千关担	6441.45	6510.57	4885.05	1490.19	2944.38	919.53
其中:消用自给棉	千关担	5173.99	5237.94	4885.05	1490.19	2944.38	919.53
消用商品棉	千关担	1267.46	1272.64	—	—	—	—
国内机制纱消用棉花量(商品棉)	千关担	—	—	356.43	1748.52	3179.46	8939.94
絮棉消用棉花量	千关担	2083.33	2109.38	2247.92	2373.96	2475.00	2578.13
其中:植棉户消用自给棉	千关担	738.54	739.85	720.72	681.58	731.54	533.02
非植棉户消用商品棉	千关担	1344.79	1369.53	1527.20	1692.38	1743.46	2045.11
工业、卫生、军需等用棉(商品棉)	千关担	—	—	112.40	237.40	371.25	644.53
自给棉总量	千关担	5912.53	5977.79	5605.77	2171.77	3675.92	1452.55
占全国棉花消费量	%	69.36	69.35	73.71	37.05	40.87	10.87
商品棉总量	千关担	2612.25	2642.17	1996.03	3678.30	5294.17	11629.58
占全国棉花消费量	%	30.64	30.65	26.24	62.75	58.86	87.05
商品棉中纺制土纱占	%	48.52	48.17				
纺制机纱占	%			17.86	47.54	60.06	76.87

洋务派经济活动补遗[*]

洋务运动是晚清统治阶级为挽救王朝倾覆、维持封建制度的一个政治运动。洋务派经济活动是这一运动的产物，而非其目的，所以是"末"，而不是"本"。但是，它一旦形成经济实体——机、船、矿、路，就要受经济规律，尤其是生产力本身发展规律的支配。因而它未随王朝消逝，我这一代还见过它的某些原型。

时贤大都肯定洋务派引进和建立了一些新生产力，但内容如何，多不屑一论。本文想在此作点拾遗补阙。分别考察钢铁、煤、电力、机器、造船、棉纺、铁路、电信八项基本生产力，其生产能力和技术水平，下限到1911年。

有比较才有鉴别。我主要同当时外国在华经济活动比较，也同当时国际水平和日本比较。钢铁、煤、铁路的新生产力都是中国人建立的，外国资本比洋务派晚20~30年，棉纺晚7年。机器、造船外资较先，但外厂是装配进口机械，华厂则专攻制造。中外厂都有造2000吨级船能力，但外厂用进口主机，中国厂因造兵船，力求自造主机，锅炉和铁甲舰均成功，1911年升至万吨级，超过外厂。国内第一台蒸汽机、康邦机、火车头、内燃机均中国厂造。洋务派培养了大批科技人员，外商只培养买办。

19世纪70年代国际已进入钢铁时代。中国在生产力结构、进口替代、

＊　此为未完成文稿，约写于1987年春。缺文部分用双省略号表示。——编者

生产力布局上基本适应。但动力水平落后约 30 年，机械工艺水平落后 20～30 年，电讯迟于莫尔斯 30 余年，造成效率低、质量次，加以分工少、服务环节差、中转成本高，不能和进口货竞争。

然而，发展速度最大的障碍还是官办、官督商办形式和管理腐败。日本移交民营后，中国与日本制造业的差距迅速加大，铁路的差距增至 5 倍，钢铁起步稍早，差距亦达 1 倍。

补遗内容：

1. 造船
2. 机器
3. 钢铁
4. 煤矿
5. 纺织
6. 铁路
7. 电信

…………

3. 钢铁

直到 1911 年，不曾有外国资本在中国设钢铁厂。中国的近代钢铁工业完全是洋务派创建的。按投产次序是贵州青溪铁厂、江南制造局钢厂、汉阳铁厂、天津机器局钢厂。到甲午前共有炼铁炉 3 座，日产能力 125 吨；炼钢炉 8 座，日产能力 95 吨；1895 年实产生铁约 5000 吨，钢 1342 吨。青溪厂早夭，天津厂毁于八国联军，汉阳铁厂则扩大为汉冶萍公司。1910 年（1911 年因战争停产）共有高炉 3 座，日产能力 450 吨，平炉 6 座，日产能力 280 吨；实产生铁 119396 吨，钢 50113 吨。这点产量在国际上还无足挂齿，但已相当于进口钢铁量的一半，在以后 10 年，就超过进口量了。就是说，如果没有汉冶萍，进口钢铁要增加 1 倍以上。

1889 年，中国国土上，是在贵州首先出现了高炉和贝色麻平炉。创办青溪铁厂的潘露可称中国钢铁事业的先锋。该厂大约未用洋工程师，而日出生铁 20吨，经营略有盈余。但潘露是个学化学的知识分子，无法应付官场的重重阻碍，没等到出钢，竟忧愤而死。贵州竟找不出一个人来接替他，厂遂停办，生存期不到三年。当青溪炼铁时，"黔省无一识者"，只张之洞表示关怀，送电垂询。

张之洞办汉阳厂，历时九载，耗资五百余万，誉少毁多。据人揭发，当初向英国订机时，英厂谓须先化验煤铁，方知配何式炼炉。"张大言曰：以中国之大，何所不有……但照英国所用专购一份可耳"。结果购来贝色麻炉二副，而大冶铁多磷，竟不适用。此事并选择厂址事，均未做可行性研究，遗为笑柄。但也正像揭发人叶景葵所说："然当时风气锢蔽，昏庸在朝，苟无张之卤莽为之，恐冶铁萍煤至今尚蕴诸岩壑。"这是句公道话。

张之洞办钢铁厂直接目的在筑钢轨、修铁路。而1889年他给李鸿章电中说："晋铁如万不能用，即用粤铁，粤铁如亦不精不旺，用闽铁、黔铁、楚铁、陕铁，岂有地球之上独中华之铁皆是弃物？"按大周期（康德拉捷夫周期）理论，这时正当西方资本主义进入钢铁时代（熊彼特定为1842～1897年，恰好是鸦片战争到甲午战争），当时立国确是以钢为纲。张之洞不自觉地捉捕到时代脉搏。而李鸿章之流则否，李复电说：炼钢铁需巨款，"岂能各省同开"，又说，日本铁路日增，"惟钢轨等项仍购西洋"。的确，1893年汉阳铁厂和大冶铁矿建成，不仅在中国是第一个钢铁联合企业，在远东也是第一个大型钢铁企业。印度还没有，日本的八幡制铁所也是在1895年才建厂，1901年才出铁，比汉厂晚七年。

1896年盛宣怀接办汉厂，解决了炼钢去磷和煤焦供应两大难题。到1909年，该厂日出85磅标准钢轨及附件28500吨，经岳汉铁路工程师验收，"其质极佳"。津浦、京汉、南浔、广九、浙江诸路均已购用，"而定轨之单甚多，仍有接应不暇之势"。同时，盛宣怀也造成大擘，引进日本借款，以平价铁输日，成了八幡制铁所的原料基地。为此，辛亥革命后，盛宣怀变成通缉犯。不过，从生产力来说，1909年该厂产生铁74000吨，其中自用炼钢只占40%，余运销上海等地16800吨，销美国3800吨，输日本23700吨，即32%的生产力为日本占用。炼钢和轧钢的生产力，则全为国内服务。也因此，汉口出现了周恒顺、扬子等一批民营机器厂，加工铁路配件，并在辛亥前首先制成30马力抽水机、80马力起重机及其他矿山机械。重型机器业之出现在汉口，即因有汉厂钢铁，而在上海系用进口原料，太贵。

4. 煤矿

西方列强早谋在中国开矿，但未得逞。新法采矿技术是中国人引进的，也不限于洋务派。矿属国家资源，开矿要清廷给予矿权，商人开矿也多要挂个官督商办招牌以应付地方势力。甲午前开办过 29 个官督商办的各种矿,其中除 5 个洋务派插手经营外,其余 24 个都是真正的民办矿。

差不多所有新法煤矿都是在原来手工民窑的矿区兴办的。不少民窑已进入工场手工业即资本主义阶段。有些民窑已用三井或二井制,即竖井提煤、戽水,深可达 50 米以上,畜力辘轳卷扬;斜井进出工人,有矿柱,也有掌子面。当时所谓新法只是在井口卷扬和排水上用蒸汽动力而已,井下操作还完全是手工。

不过,土法勘探不行。洋务派开矿都是请洋矿师勘探。有的勘而未采,如李鸿章倡办的磁州煤矿。有的西法勘探后仍用手工窑开采,如盛宣怀办的广济兴国煤矿。有的虽用机器,但限于排水,卷扬仍用辘轳,如张曜开办的淄川煤矿。民办矿也不少是这样:今天买架抽水机,明天改造井筒,赚了钱再添部卷扬机。这也正是 18 世纪英国煤矿所走的道路。技术是有继承性的。沈葆桢开办的基隆煤矿,全部新式机器,但从 1878 年出煤到甲午台湾沦陷,年产量从未达到原来当地民窑的水平,中外轮船用煤仍部分靠民窑,中法战争后更基本上靠民窑。

开平、萍乡都是洋务派经营比较成功的煤矿,并引进洗煤、炼焦技术。开平的产量由 1882 年的 3.8 万吨增至 1898 年的 73.2 万吨(后沦入英人之手)。萍乡产量由 1898 年的 1 万吨增至 1911 年的 61 万吨。两矿都已达日产 3000 吨能力。开平的井上运输较好,萍乡则已用电动机车在井下运输,当时属最新设备。和机器、造船不同,洋务派没有注意在矿业上培养中国工程师,两矿都一直用洋人,萍乡还有永远用法国人之约。

甲午战争以后,外国资本大量侵入矿业。外国资本经营的煤矿,几乎都是原来中国人已开采的、有些是中国人已用新法开采的矿。他们所引进的生产技术,决不高于洋务派。俄国人在东北开煤矿不下 10 处,都是手工挖煤。最大的抚顺、烟台,只是派兵占领,添点排水机而已。日本人以战利品接收后进行改造,日产能力达到 3000 吨,1911 年产 129.2 万吨。本溪湖煤矿到 1911 年还设备有限,炼铁高炉还来完工。德国人经营的山东各煤矿,规模不大,但设备较新,大部机器已用电力,1911 年产 78.8 万吨。最大的仍是开平,英人攫取后,将日产能力提高到 5000 吨,继又提高到 8000 吨,1911 年产 152.7 万吨。但装备也只是量的扩大,卷扬仍用蒸汽动力,井上运输有改进，井下只是添用驴子而已。

由于大矿陆续沦入外人之手，1912 年外资和中外合资矿产煤约 410 万吨，华资只有 40 余万吨了；但是，手工开采仍有约 390 余万吨，民窑的力量不可小估。

…………

6. 铁路

中国有铁路，始于李鸿章于 1881 年修筑的唐胥路，比日本的第一条铁路横滨东京线晚一年。当然，这以前有 1865 年英人在北京宣武门外敷设的"铁道一里"，1876 年英人在上海修建的吴松铁路。前者说不上是铁路；后者只是一条 13 公里的、2′6″窄距和 60 磅轻轨的小铁道，进口一辆小机车拴上几节车厢，招人游览，根本不是一条实用的运输铁路，旋即拆毁。中国修铁路时外国人曾建议用窄轨或米轨，幸未采纳，毅然决定用 4′8 $\frac{1}{2}$″标准轨距和 85 磅标准钢轨，是足称道，否则将贻害后世。不仅如此，第一条铁路用的是第一台中国自造的机车，即 1881 年胥各庄厂造的 0 - 3 - 0 型蒸汽机车"中国火箭号"；后来运务繁忙，才进口英国机车。

洋务派诸经济活动中，遭受顽固派反对最烈的就是铁路，有所谓"三不可""五大害""九不利"等说，这是中国铁路出现晚、发展极其迟缓的原因之一。唐胥路的兴起只比日本的第一条铁路横滨东京线晚一年。此后，1888 年完成津沽铁路，1893 年完成基隆到新竹的台湾铁路，1894 年完成唐山出山海关的关东铁路。到 1894 年，连同大冶矿区铁路，中国还只有铁路 477 公里，这时日本已有铁路 3300 余公里了。铁路须有一定长度才有经济效益，否则只是专用铁路性质。

甲午战争以后，情况大变，列强猛烈争夺铁路权，中国自筑之铁路亦被外国借款控制。到 1911 年，中国共有铁路 8895 公里，内外国资本修筑 3766公里，外国借款修筑 4006 公里，中国自筑仅 1123 公里。中国自筑路中，有民办铁路 508 公里，而清政府或说洋务派所办者仍只有 500 余公里（余为矿区等专用路）。民办铁路大值得注意，在热烈的利权收回运动中，各省铁路集资达 6000 万两，可修铁路 4000 公里；若不是清政府或说洋务派的蛮横"国有"政策，中国铁路必将大有发展。

铁路是生产力，但要看其地区分布、客货比率、运输密度，更要看铁路质量。1910年，39%的铁路在东北。东北日本人所筑铁路中有1800多公里不合格，后来都经改筑。而中国建筑的津沽关东（京奉）路，运输密度居全国第一（1918年统计）。正太路有1.84%坡度，法国人经修，用米距、56磅轨，结果使每公里运输成本增加60%（1916年统计）。稍晚，京绥路有3.33%坡度，杰出的工程师詹天佑在路线设计和机车牵引上出奇制胜，坚持用标准制，与京汉、京奉接轨，花钱不多，运输称便。经过多年培训，中国铁路工人形成一支经验丰富、技术高明、组织性强的无产阶级队伍，在抗战时期表现的卓越成绩尤为世所称道。

7. 电信

李鸿章于1879年敷设中国第一条电报线时，目的还是在"号令各营，顷刻响应"（该线由天津通大沽炮台）。但这以前，早有英国人敷设通香港的电报线和丹麦大北公司敷设的香港上海线，都是海底电线，并于1873年从吴淞口登陆，通至上海租界。他们的业务已是商电为主了。电信作为生产力，当时主要是商业信息。

中国国内电信是洋务派创建的，计有津沪、苏浙闽粤、长江、川滇、陕甘五大干线，连同支线2.3万余公里，即所谓"商线"。另在东北、西北、西南和沿海军事重镇架设"官线"，全长亦2.3万余公里。到1895年，全国各省，除西藏外，都已通电报。

电报是洋务派经营得最成功的事业，这和商线、官线分开颇有关系。商线官资商办，由电报局统一经营，靠收取资费营运，而年有盈余，股票市价常超过面值，投资踊跃；郑观应、经元善为此做出贡献。1884年赎回大北公司在中国的陆线，1886年自行敷设汉口武昌水线，同年敷设福州台湾海底线。商业繁忙区和洪险区设辅助线和平行线。电报收发迅速、准确，制度完备，博得社会信誉。电报学堂培训严格，毕业生分配电台后，仍由学堂考绩、升级。1902~1908年收归官办，就少有建树了。

中国的封建主义

1840 年鸦片战争前，中国是一个封建社会。封建土地所有制的农业经济在国民经济中占统治地位，手工业也是农民家庭生产占最大比重。商品经济有了发展，但自给自足的自然经济仍居绝对优势。已出现资本主义生产的萌芽，但在国民经济中没有什么地位。

我国封建经济较早地由领主制过渡到地主制，农业生产力发展较快。11 世纪以后，随着水田的开发，铁犁畜耕的传统农业发展到世界先进水平；食物供给状况优于欧洲，人口开始长期性增长。16 世纪以后，转向集约化耕作。到 18 世纪，南方一些省份精耕细作，单位面积产量达到传统农业可能有的高度，加以东北的开发，19 世纪初，人口达到 4 亿。到鸦片战争前，估计年产约有粮食 2320 亿斤，棉花 970.7 万担，茶 260.5 万担，丝 7.7 万担，蔚为农业大国，除满足国内需要外，茶、丝都大量出口。[①]

不过，在我国租佃制度下，是以一家一户为生产单位，平均每户耕作面积原比欧洲农民的份地为小，随着人口增长，就更趋零细。16 世纪以来，生产工具甚少改进，生产的发展主要靠每亩地投入更多的人力，因而劳动生产率（平均每人产量）有下降趋势。我国畜牧业本来不够发达，为供应众多人口衣食，更趋向种植业单一化，影响培养地力和生态平衡，这都给农业

---

① 本节关于封建的中国所用资料，除另有标注者外，均取自许泽新、吴承明主编《中国资本主义发展史》第 1 卷《中国资本主义的萌芽》，人民出版社，1985。

带来隐忧。

农业生产关系方面，也经历了一系列变化。地主阶级力图把土地集中在自己手中，但由于农民战争和王朝变动，也交替着有地权分散的趋势。到18世纪，最集中的地区如江苏南部，大约有80%的农户是无地户；最分散的地区如甘肃，无地户只占20%～30%。一般地区，无地和少地户大约占50%～60%，中等农户（自耕农）占30%～40%。地主占不到人口的10%，其所占土地则差异很大。如在直隶获鹿县，地主约占有全部耕地的34.5%，在湖南则占到50%以上。不过，这时大地主已不多，大约北方数百亩、南方一二百亩就算大户，千亩以上的地主已少见了。

14世纪以来，世族地主逐渐为缙绅地主所代替，到18世纪，庶民地主已占绝对优势。同时，除少数民族和个别地区外，依附农制逐渐消失，基本上都是租佃关系了。到18世纪末，仍是以实物地租为主，货币地租约占30%。实物地租率通常为产量的50%左右，唯定额租已逐渐代替分成租，成为主要形式。同时，在南方和四川，押租制相当盛行，南方一些地区并兴起永佃权。押租制和永佃权加重了佃农的负担，但也反映土地耕作权和土地所有权在一定程度上的分离。它们连同定额租的流行，都可以增加佃农在生产上的独立性。所以，这一系列变化有利于缓和租佃制本身的矛盾，客观上看，实际是为巩固封建土地所有制所进行的自我调整。

我国手工业早以工艺精练见称。11世纪以后，科学技术有较大进步，生产也有较快发展。1050年代生铁产量年达12.5万吨，相当于全欧洲17世纪的水平。丝织、陶瓷，造船以及有色金属和水力和利用，都是很先进的。16世纪以后，棉纺织成为最重要的手工业，同时，手艺人逐渐向小商品生产者转化。到18世纪，漂染、制糖、酿造、制纸等都有较大发展。鸦片战争前，估计年产约有生铁20万吨，棉布近6亿匹（按每匹3.633平方码计），丝织品4.9万担。棉布、丝织品及糖、瓷器等均有出口。但是，采矿业相对不足，煤铁资源未能充分利用，铜依靠进口。并且，自16世纪以来，生产工具没有什么改进，水力的利用反不如前，技术保守，已日益落后于欧洲了。

我国原有官手工业传统，到十四五世纪发展到巨大规模。官手工业属皇族自给经济，又是一种封建垄断制度。它曾经对技艺起过促进作用，但具垄断性和相应的匠籍制度又日益成为发展生产力的障碍。16 世纪以后，官手工业衰落，城市手工业才有较快发展。手工业行会制度在我国并不发达，又由于城市是各级封建统治的中心，手工业者不是城市主要居民，城乡对立不尖锐；因而，没有像西欧的城市那样发展成为反对农村封建主的力量，也没有形成像西方那样的市民阶级。

我国城市手工业发展不足，农民家庭手工业却十分发达，除农民家用外，并从事商品生产。如丝织、陶瓷、制糖、造纸等都有农民家庭生产，单商品棉布一项即超过全部独立手工业者的产值。小农业与家庭手工业相结合，原是我国封建经济的基本的生产结构。16 世纪以来，随着农村人口增加而耕地日趋狭小，以及生活负担和租赋的加重，农民更需以副养农、以耕助织，小农业与家庭手工业的结合就更加紧密、更加牢固了。农民家庭手工业本来是自然经济的基础，现在竟成为市场上商品的主要提供者。这实际是封建的生产结构，通过一定的商品货币关系，巩固和加强了自己。

我国较早地结束领主割据局面，实现大统一的国家，商业一向比较发达。但在十四五世纪以前，除作为自然经济补充的墟集和盐铁等贸易外，主要是发展了城市商业和珍奇宝货等奢侈品的贩运贸易。这种城市商业主要是供封建统治阶级其仆从、士兵等消费之用，而非生产者之间的交换。16 世纪以后，贩运贸易渐以民生用品为主了，商路扩充，沿江、沿河出现一批新兴商业城市。18 世纪进一步发展，商业专业化，商人会馆林立。估计到鸦片战争前，国内市场主要商品流通额约达 3.88 亿两，其中粮食占 42%，棉布占 24.4%，盐占 15%，以下依次为茶、丝及丝织品、棉花等。

这时商业虽颇发达，但在整个国民经济中比重不大。上述市场结构表明，当时的流通主要是粮食同经济作物和手工业品相交换，农村有多少余粮可以运出，是市场大小的一个界限。据估计，当时流通的粮食约 245 亿斤，除去无交换的漕粮丁赋等，约 208 亿斤，还占不到产量的 9%。[①] 并且，粮食不是作为商品生产的，无论农民或地主出卖余粮，都是为买而卖，为了使

---

① 1820 年美国农业的商品率约为 25%，1890 年日本农业的商品率为 20% ~30%，这都属自给性生产。1870 年美国农业商品率超过 50%，开始进入商品性生产。

用价值。市场上最大量的交易是粮与布的交换。布虽已有松江等商品布产区，但长距离贩运只占全部商品布的14%，就是说绝大部分商品布仍是织户自用有余的布，在地方市场上与非织布户交换口粮。这实际是"男耕女织"的另一种结合形式。占第二位的粮与盐的交换，更是自然经济所固有的。盐民虽是商品生产者，但他们是"只缘海角不生物，无可奈何来收卤"，[①] 和渔民、猎户一样，是一种靠山吃山、靠水吃水的自然经济。所以整个说来，当时的中国仍是自然经济占绝对优势。事实上，当时商业网是偏在某些区域，广大内地"商贾罕至"，"几无外货入境"，农民"白首不至城市"，记载屡见。

16世纪，已出现徽商、山陕商等大商人资本。到18世纪，大商人的资本积累由数十万两进入百万两，以至千万两。这本来会形成一种革命的因素，因为，正如马克思所说，资本"起初到处是以货币形式，作为货币财产，作为商人资本和高利贷资本，与地产相对立"。[②] 欧洲的封建社会，即在这种对立中，以货币权力最后战胜土地权力而告终。在我国，这种对立原来也很尖锐，历代的抑商政策即其反映。但16世纪以后逐渐有了变化。土地买卖已完全自由，在两种权力之间建立了桥梁。清王朝基本停止抑商政策。地主大量经商，商人大量购买土地。18世纪的粮价陡涨和地主城居潮流加强了这一过程，终于形成地主、商人、高利贷者"三位一体"的剥削结构，共同分猎农民和手工业者的剩余劳动。"三位一体"的剥削结构可以使地租、利润、利息互相转化，而封建商业利润率和利息率是以地租率为最低界限的，因而，实际上是地主阶级通过商品货币关系加强了自己。

我国在16世纪出现了资本主义生产的萌芽，18世纪有了发展。据我们考察，到鸦片战争前有资本主义萌芽的有丝织、染布、踹布、陶瓷、制茶、制烟、榨油、酿酒、造纸、印刷、铜矿、煤矿、冶铁、铁器、木材、井盐池盐等16个手工业行业和沙船运输业。主要形式是工场手工业和商人雇工生产，仅个别行业有包买商。在农业中，则仅有一些佃农或自耕农雇工从事商品性生产，地主雇工从事商品性生产和商人租地经营农业的个别事例。

---

① 林正清：《小海盐场志》。
② 马克思：《资本论》第1卷，人民出版社，1975，第167页。

　　然而，这些手工业的资本主义萌芽只是出现在某地区的某些户中，在全行业中无代表性，有些在本地区本行业中也无代表性。工场手工业，除四川井盐业具有先进技术和较大规模外，多属简陋，甚少内部分工。有些行业虽然雇工众多，但因存在封建性的分业分帮，在一个资本支配下的劳动者并不多。总之，直到鸦片战争前，资本主义萌芽还极其微弱。尤其是最重要的手工业部门棉纺织业仍停留在农民家庭生产，使整个资本主义萌芽黯然失色。农业中的资本主义关系，就更微不足道了。

　　我国封建社会较早地过渡到租佃制，较早地实现大统一，比之中世纪欧洲，农民有较多的独立性，生产力有较高的发展，商业繁荣，堪称发达的封建经济。但也正因为是发达的封建经济，它的生产结构比较坚固，自给性比较完整，上层建筑对旧制度的维护力量比较顽强。因而，新的经济关系不容易产生，产生后不容易发展。在我国地主制经济中，土地可以买卖，城乡之间、商品货币与土地之间的矛盾不尖锐。因而，当封建社会达于成熟、进入腐朽阶段后，它能在一定程度上容纳和利用商品经济调整和加强自己，延长寿命。正是这样，16 世纪当我国出现资本主义萌芽时，西欧已进入工场手工业阶段；18 世纪，我国资本主义萌芽刚有发展，西欧已开始产业革命；19 世纪，西方资本主义大规模入侵中国时，中国还是一个封建社会。

1983 年 7 月 4 日在经济所讨论

社会主义商品经济试析

1984 年元旦中央发出一号文件，大力发展农村商品生产。年来成绩斐然，农村专业户增至 2500 余万户，粮食商品率由 20 世纪 70 年代以前的 20% 左右增至 30% 以上。其他作物和林牧副渔业商品率达 90%，农村一片生机勃勃的兴旺景象。

此事发人深思。我国商业素称发达，或谓春秋战国已进入商品经济。20 世纪 30 年代外国人和国民党的调查都说农民收支已半数以上依赖市场。何以到今天才提出"变自给经济、半自给经济为商品经济"的口号，明确社会主义是"有计划的商品经济"？我想这涉及一些历史和理论问题，试作浅析。

分工论

马克思说："产品之所以成为商品……仅仅因为有其他商品成为它们的等价物，仅仅因为有作为商品和作为价值的其他产品同它们相对立……生产劳动的分工。使它们各自的产品互相变为商品，互相成为等价物，使它们互相成为市场。"① 列宁根据这个论点，提出"社会分工是商品经济的基础"的命题。② 指出不仅是一个个生产部门从农业中分离出来，一个生产中各部

---

① 马克思：《资本论》第 3 卷，人民出版社，1975，第 718 页。
② 《列宁全集》第 3 卷，人民出版社，1959，第 17 页。

分、各工序的分工，也都互相成为商品和市场。他还用图式说明个体生产者彼此分工造成商品经济的过程。①

这种理论似乎尽美尽善。但求之史实，却不尽然。人类最初的交换是出现在原始公社"和其他公社接触"的"边界"，交换的主要是"奴隶、牲畜、金属"等。② 既是相邻的公社，生产条件略同。就不会有什么分工；不过是这个打了胜仗，奴隶多了；那个闹瘟疫，牲畜少了。③ 后来，在农村日益发展的集市贸易，也是这种余缺调剂的性质。在这种地方小市场上交易的东西，正如恩格斯所说，原是每个农户都能生产的，并不需要分工。宋代商税的一半是出在地方小市场。宋代以后，它的性质有所改变，到近代已部分地转化为大宗商品的初级市场。但余缺调剂仍是它的主要内容，并且直到1980年以前，还是社会主义计划流通的"补充"。

的确，春秋战国商业已盛，那是指城市商业："临淄之途，车毂击，人肩摩……举袂成幕，挥汗成雨。"④ 城市市场一直是我国最发达的商品市场。《清明上河图》中的汴京，《梦粱录》中的临安，繁华眩目。这种城市商业的出现，不是由于分工，而是由于剥削。王室、贵族、官僚（和他们的仆从、军队）都要在城市购买生活品和奢侈品，于是商贾云集，店肆栉比。这里不是商品和它的对立物相交换，而是如马克思在论亚洲城市所说的"收入同自由人手（斯图亚特的用语）相交换"。⑤ 当时剥削阶级的收入。无论何种，都不外是地租的转化形态。生产发展，地租量扩大，城市商业也更繁荣。直到国民党时代，消费性的城市贸易仍是当时所谓商品经济的主要部分；不过，那时剥削阶级（包括外国人）的收入已不限于地租了。

看来，对于"商品"和"商品经济"可以有不同的理解。最早的交换，是使用价值的直接交换。它们"在交换之前不是商品"，⑥ 后来的集市贸易，

---

① 《列宁全集》第1卷，人民出版社，1955，第78~79页。
② 《马克思恩格斯全集》第13卷，人民出版社，第39页。
③ 原始社会后期有所谓第一次社会大分工。不过，近年来学者对世界范围落后民族的考察，对这次大分工有些怀疑。即使是渔猎部落，食物也主要靠采集或种植。恩格斯在《家庭、私有制和国家的起源》中也说过："纯粹打猎民族……是从来没有过的。"《马克思恩格斯选集》第4卷，人民出版社，1972，第18页。
④ 《战国策·齐策》。
⑤ 参见《马克思恩格斯全集》第46卷上册，人民出版社，第465~466页。
⑥ 马克思：《资本论》第1卷，第105页。

尽管称为贸易，但其余缺调剂的部分，性质还是这样。因为每个生产者都是为买而卖，它们是为使用价值，并不是为价值而生产出来，在交换时才表现为价值。不仅如此，进入商人大宗收购、长距离贩运的农产品，即农村的余粮、余棉等，它们也是已生产出来的东西，是商业活动"使产品发展成为商品"。① 至于剥削所引起的商品流通，是一种没有商品交换的流通。例如，粮赋年额3000万石，折色征银，市场上就出现3000万石商品粮。但是，从农村说，无论征实或征银。每年都要输出3000万石粮到城市，却没有回头货来补偿。在20世纪30年代的调查中，是把上述余缺调剂、单向输出以及农民临时出卖而后来必须买回的口粮（即返销粮，在20世纪50年代约达出售总量一半）都算作商品，因而粮食的商品率达50%左右。

马克思在讲分工时说："我们这里所指的分工……是表现为交换价值生产的分工。"② 又说，这里所说分工，"仅仅把它看作同交换价值是一回事"。③ 按照这个含义，可以说农村无论有多少农产品参加商品流通，只要没有专业户，即没有为交换价值生产的分工，都不能算商品经济。马、列的分工论没有错，是符合史实的。我曾估算，鸦片战争前我国国内商品流通额的合3.9亿两，人均近1两，已不算小，其中粮食居第一位，占42.1%；布（土布）居第二位，占24.3%。④ 但是，粮基本上都是余粮，基本上没有专业户，而布，即使在商品布的集中产区松江，也还是农家副业，没有从农业中分工出来。农村缺乏专业户的情况，直到1980年以前无何改变。1984年一号文件的伟大意义在此。

不仅如此，粮和布这两项最大"商品"的生产，恰恰是我国"男耕女织"的自然经济的基础。马克思说："家庭手工业劳动和工场手工业劳动，作为农业（它是基础）的副业……就是这种自然经济赖以建立的生产方式的条件。"⑤ 又说，中世纪的城市手工业，目的在换取使用价值，其生产也"不是作为交换价值的交换价值"。⑥ 于是，我在《什么是自然经济?》一文

① 马克思：《资本论》第3卷，第376页。
② 《马克思恩格斯全集》第46卷下册，第471页。
③ 《马克思恩格斯全集》第46卷下册，第470页。
④ 参见拙作《论清代前期我国国内市场》，《历史研究》1983年第1期。
⑤ 马克思：《资本论》第3卷，第886页。
⑥ 《马克思恩格斯全集》第46卷上册，第516页。

中提出自然经济的第四个含义，即广义的含义："凡是以使用价值为目的的生产，或以获取使用价值为目的的交换，都属于自然经济范畴。"① 这个含义把手工业包括进去，主要是从理论思想上说的。那时我正学习孙冶方同志对"自然经济论"的批判。"自然经济论"的基本论点就是：社会主义经济是使用价值的生产，不应受价值规律的作用。因此孙冶方把国营工业不讲求经济效率、"复制古董"、不更新技术设备都作为自然经济论。其实，从思想理论说，像金融业的慢周转，商业的大库存政策，也都是"自然经济论"，因为使用价值是不妨积存以至窖藏的，还都与商品经济大相径庭。

劳动论

分工为什么导致商品生产呢？通常都强调了所有制。在私有制下，分工造成商品交换，是不言而喻的。在公有制下则未必然。列宁曾设想全社会成为一个辛迪加，分工变成内部分工，那就无须商品交换了。但他很快发现这是不可能的，因此在1921年提出"自由贸易"。而在1952年，斯大林正是根据工业的全民所有制，不承认苏联的生产资料是商品。其实，所有制并不是个严格界限，实际的占有权、使用权、经营管理权、产品支配权更为重要。苏联是土地国有的，那时拖拉机、收割机也全部国有，就是说，农业基本生产资料也是全民所有制，但集体农庄是一个联合劳动的独立生产单位，它们"只愿把自己的产品当作商品让出去"，② 斯大林也只好承认农产品是商品了。

"在原则上，没有产品的交换，只有参加生产的各种劳动的交换。"③ 研究商品，我们不如从劳动、劳动和生产资料结合的方式上去探讨。

马克思曾把产品交换的历史（到他那时的历史）分为三个阶段。第一个阶段，"例如中世纪，当时交换的只是剩余品"，基本上没有专业户，劳动的交换主要是在家庭内部和领地内部进行的。第二个阶段，有了专业户，

---

① 吴承明：《什么是自然经济？》，《经济研究》1983年第9期。
② 斯大林：《苏联社会主义经济问题》，人民出版社，1952，第12页。
③ 《马克思恩格斯全集》第4卷，人民出版社，第116页。

应当是简单商品生产的交换了。① 这以城市手工业最典型，它是劳动者的"特殊技能使他成为工具的所有者"。这种生产资料是不能转移的，"就象蜗牛和它的甲壳互相结合一样"。② 马克思曾把这种结合叫"行会所有制"。在这种直接结合方式下，劳动者只能通过商品，即通过物化劳动互相交换自己的劳动。在第三个阶段，蜗牛的壳被打掉了，生产资料变成"他人的财产"，劳动者的技能（已不需要"特殊技能"）变成商品出卖给资本——也就是资本主义所有制。这时，"双方仅仅以物化劳动的形式交换自己的劳动，这种关系就不可能存在"了。③ 劳动者的个人劳动要经过迂回曲折的道路才能转化为社会劳动，互相交换。

现在要说到第四个阶段（如果可以这样说的话），即社会主义的交换。社会主义否定了资本主义，劳动与生产资料重新直接结合。但不是恢复蜗牛式的结合，而是"在一个集体的、以共同占有生产资料为基础的"结合。马克思在《哥达纲领批判》中指出这个特点后说，这时"个人的劳动不再经过迂回曲折的道路，而是直接地作为总劳动的构成部分存在着"。这样，就不需要商品交换这种物化形式了。但劳动交换仍然存在，它是凭一张劳动"证书"交换的。不过，"这里通行的是商品等价交换中也通行的同一原则"，调节劳动交换"是调节商品交换（就它是等价交换而言）的同一原则"，即等量劳动互换的原则。④

马克思在《哥达纲领批判》中所设想的，不是指共产主义，而是指"刚从资本主义社会中产生出来的"社会主义社会。从几十年来社会主义的历史经验看，情况并非如此。所有制可以利用革命运动迅速改变，劳动和劳动组织却不能。社会主义社会分工日益发达，劳动也日益专业化，并有质的不同。它只能在一定范围里联合劳动，因而也是在不同程度上共同占有、使用生产资料；过大过公、人海战术，并无好处。这种在一定范围的联合劳动，对于社会劳动来说是一种局部劳动；它不能直接表现为社会劳动，仍然要通过物

---

① 《马克思恩格斯全集》第 4 卷，第 79 页。马克思在《哲学的贫困》中所说的第二阶段已不限于简单商品生产，我这里是按照他在《政治经济学批判》中的划分，那里他叫"第二个历史阶段"，见《马克思恩格斯全集》第 46 卷上册，第 501 页。

② 《马克思恩格斯全集》第 46 卷上册，第 501 页；马克思：《资本论》第 1 卷，第 397 页。

③ 《马克思恩格斯全集》第 46 卷上册，461～462 页。

④ 《马克思恩格斯选集》第 3 卷，人民出版社，1972，第 10、11 页。

化形式进行交换。同时，在社会主义社会，劳动还是谋生之道，劳动者之间存在着因劳动而产生的物质利益的差别；这种差别也只能用"调节商品交换的同一原则"，即抽象劳动等量交换的原则来调节。这就是在"联合劳动、共同占有"这种劳动和生产资料结合的形式下，还必须有商品生产和商品交换的根本原因。

但是，在社会主义社会，也不是所有的劳动都是为了谋生。为了谋生的，也不是都必须通过物化形式进行交换。物化的劳动，也不必都是商品。马克思曾经谴责那种"普遍贿赂，普遍买卖……用政治经济学的术语来说，是一切精神的或物质的东西都变成交换价值"的现象。① 土地、矿山、银行、铁路等不是商品。这也不都是从劳动性质上说，而是从整个国民经济上考虑的。从整个国民经济上考虑，这张单子还不妨长一些。至于精神产品是否都是商品，那就更值得考虑。反对吃大锅饭，不一定要商品化。马克思曾特别提到知识商品化的问题；把应该"传授"的东西变成"买卖"，意义何在呢？待价而沽的知识分子，是在创立一个人力市场吗？

实现论

凡是商品生产，都有一个如何在交换中实现其价值的问题，不能实现也就不能完成劳动的社会化，乃至成为无效劳动。马克思的实现论是从分工上说的："只有当全部产品是按必要的比例进行生产时，它们才能卖出去。"② 而这也就是价值规律的要求，"商品的价值规律决定社会在所支配的全部劳动时间中能够用多少时间去生产每一种特殊商品"。③ 最重要的比例即生产资料和生活资料两大部类生产的比例，因而可以归纳为一个公式：$I(V+M) = IIC$。列宁专门研究了实现问题，他用复杂的计算论证了在扩大再生产中实现的条件，即生产资料的生产应大于其当年消耗，或：$I(V+M)$

---

① 《马克思恩格斯全集》第4卷，第80页。
② 马克思：《资本论》第3卷，第717页。
③ 马克思：《资本论》第1卷，第394页。

> ⅡC。① 马、列的这个理论可适用于各种社会，但是，这种比例关系又是怎样保持下来的呢？是单纯靠那只"看不见的手"在冥冥中支配吗？为此，又要回顾一点历史。

事实上，实现问题是古已有之的，如"屡贱踊贵""谷贱伤农"之类，不过在扩大再生产以前不那么严重罢了；而封建政府已在采取均输、平准、市易等办法略作补救。进入资本主义，魁奈的《经济表》可说是第一个系统的实现论。《经济表》有个谜，即年产50亿（利弗尔）的农产品中，有20亿没有实现。对此，"有一千零一种解释"，马克思也至少有三次解释。② 看来，这20亿至少一半，也许全部是交给表中居中央地位的地主了，由他去实现。60年后，马尔萨斯的政治经济学就出现了一个只买不卖的"第三者"，没有他，商品就不能全部实现。这个"第三者"就是地主和政府。从这以后，直到凯恩斯就都把政府看作实现商品价值、解救危机的支柱。从"谷物法"到罗斯福"新政"，政府也确实日趋经济主义。第二次世界大战后，发达国家都进入国家垄断资本主义。当代的宏观经济学的"三大块"模式，第一大块就是政府，无论是对付滞销或滞胀，又无论是货币主义或供应学派，在这一点上并无二致。

总之，从历史上看，直到资本主义，商品经济的发展并不完全是靠那"看不见的手"的自发作用来调节；所谓市场机制、经济杠杆，早已为人们所利用了。人们也不完全是跟在市场波动后面修修补补，利用信息，市场预测，也已有之。至于比例关系，如农业劳动力的转移，新工业部门的出现，以至由劳动密集向资本密集的发展等，又多半与人们对科学技术的研究成果攸关。而这些，自始就有国家干预其事，并愈来愈多地依靠政府这个最大的购买者，以至利用财政担保、补贴等办法来实现。

社会主义是自觉地利用价值规律的、有计划的商品经济，这是它不同于资本主义商品经济的地方。但是它仍然有个实现问题，如比例失调、货不对路等，在社会主义国家在所难免。这是因为：

第一，所谓"自觉"是个相对概念，由不自觉到比较自觉，否则就

---

① 《列宁全集》第1卷，第66～72页。
② 《马克思恩格斯全集》第26卷上册，人民出版社，1972，第352、406页；《马克思恩格斯全集》第20卷，人民出版社，1973，第270～271页。

再没有进步了。价值规律并不是一个系统方程，即使我们能建立一个（我们应该能建立一个）系统方程或宏观模式，它也不能像自然界的方程或模式那样精确，而是一种模糊方程或经验模式。并且，许多现象，如比例失调，涉及面太广，只能在一定的时间之后，进行系统的"调整"。有些现象，如价格背离价值，虽老早就"自觉"了，也只好等待时机，小步改革。改革后的价格结构也不能完全服从价值规律，因为还要服从政策和策略。

第二，"有计划"也是一个相对的概念。今天的资本主义也不完全是"无政府"。由于废除私有制，社会主义的经济计划比资本主义国家的计划，基础广泛得多了，并且可以直接计划，可以用指令执行。但是，如果除去非商品生产，专就商品部分而言，所谓有计划是指战略决策、宏观计划，不是指微观计划。因为既是商品生声，微观计划（它可以十分精密）就应该是企业的事了。这种宏观计划定不能包罗万象，也不能严丝合扣，而"只能是粗线条的和有弹性的"。① 制定这种计划，虽可利用预测，但只能根据经验数据，或回归分析，而不能像自然科学那样进行模拟测算。因此，这种计划要经过"综合平衡和经济手段的调节"，才能"保证重大比例关系比较适当，国民经济大体按比例发展"。这种调节，恐怕也不是事前计划好了的，仍然是利用信息反馈，然后拨动杠杆，或等待着为时尚不太晚的"调整"。为了保证实现，计划亏损或财政补贴，自是不免的。

这样看来，社会主义的实现论似乎又和资本主义的实现论无大区别；其实不然。历史上的实现论，从均输、平准到供应学派，其目的都是为了地主阶级、后来是资产阶级、最后是垄断资本集团的利益，根本不是从等量劳动交换这个原则出发的。社会主义的商品实现，则是个人劳动转化为社会劳动的完成。等量劳动交换的实现，这话并不是虚论，而是有它具体内容的。剥削阶级的消灭，劳动力不再是商品，按劳取酬原则的确立，都是具体的内容；正是在这些条件下，劳动交换（物化为商品交换）才真正成为劳动人民内部的交换，才能在全体劳动人民中进行。

---

① 《中共中央关于经济体制改革的决定》，1984 年 10 月 20 日，下引文同。

至于保证实现的手段,诸如经济杠杆以至计划等,常是由手段本身技术性的特点决定的,并不一定反映交换的性质。实现的成果,既受技术手段的限制,又受社会以至国际条件的限制,而不能用一个标准(如人均收入之类)论成败。

附记:本文为1985年5月2~6日"中国社会主义经济理论的回顾与展望"讨论会论文。该讨论会系《经济研究》编辑部为《经济研究》创刊三十周年纪念而组织的。

1985年1月完稿

儒家思想的发展变化

儒家思想是古代中国的主流思想，儒学长时期居于官学地位。学校教学、科举考试都用儒家经典。外国人就常把中国古代文化称为儒家文化。其实，二千多年来，儒家思想是不断发展变化的，在发展中它吸收了非儒家的以至外国的思想因素，充实自己，它才能长期保持主流地位。

春秋末期，孔子创建的儒家学派，是一种以"仁"为核心的伦理道德思想体系和一套讲礼教、德治的社会规范。后来，孟子提出性善说、修养论，并以仁义礼智信的价值观补充孔学。但在先秦时代，儒学仍然主要是讲伦理道德，没有完整的本体论和认识论，不是一个完整的哲学思想体系。

汉武帝罢黜百家，独尊儒术，儒学成为官学。汉代的儒生考究"五经"，即《诗》《书》《礼》《易》《春秋》，用它们来注疏孔子、孟子的学说，被称为经学。"五经"原都不是儒家的著作，其中有丰富的社会、历史、文化和哲学材料。汉代经学把这些思想材料吸收进来，使儒学大大地丰富起来。

汉以后，从魏晋到隋唐七百年间，老子、庄子的哲学和外国传来的佛学接连兴盛起来，作为官学的儒学反见沉寂，非改造不可了。到宋代，儒生们吸取老庄和佛学思想，把旧儒学改造成新儒学，即理学，重新获得生命力。

理学的发展又分为两个阶段。先是宋儒吸取老庄的自然观建立理气论，吸取佛教、道教若干观点建立心性论，由朱熹集其大成，完成了以理（客观规律）为宇宙本元的本体论，以格物穷理为要略的认识论，将孔孟的伦理道德原则理性化、哲学化，成为系统理论，并以"存天理、灭人欲"作为社会行为准则。

朱熹理学自发轫到明初历四百多年，声势日隆，但也日益教条化、僵化。《明史·儒林传》说明初的学子只是"笃践履，谨绳墨，守先儒之正传，无敢改错"。错了都不敢改，这种思想还能有生气吗？到明中叶，就出现了王守仁理学，很快就代替了朱熹理学，成为主流。王守仁理学又称心学，认为"心即理"，心是宇宙本元，又创致良知说，即知善知恶、去恶存善，人人都可以致良知，即人人都可成为圣人。王守仁的心学崇尚自我，提高个人存在和思考的价值。这就鼓舞许多学者打破教条，创立新说。例如晚明的泰州学派以及李贽，都说受王守仁心学的启发，提出许多反传统的新思想。

但是王守仁的理学大量吸取佛学，讲心灵养性，脱离实际，流行一百多年也愈来愈空虚。到明朝要亡的时候，许多学子还是闭门"明心见性"，不问世事。这样，可说理学已走到它的尽头，再向前就非根本改造不可了，于是，在明清之际，出现了以顾炎武、黄宗羲、王夫之为代表的启蒙思潮。这种启蒙思潮反对空谈心性，主张治学要"经世致用"，提出"天下兴亡，匹夫有责"，提倡功利主义，有的学者还吸取了明末从西方传来的科学思想，一时生气勃勃，统称实学。

这种经世致用的实学，本来可以成为儒学发展的新方向，使儒学更加理性化和科学化，与时代合拍，变成新学。但是，顾炎武等人在提倡经世致用之学时，采取了复古的方法，回到"五经"中去找理论根据和治世之道。同时，清王朝建立后厉行文化专制主义，立朱熹理学为官学，大兴文字狱，不准有违反"三纲五常"的思想。而学者们对朱子理学"存天理、灭人欲"的教条早已厌恶，既然不准发挥新思想，只好回到经学中去，特别是与政治无关的训诂考据之学，有很大发展。所以这次启蒙运动虽蓬勃一时，然而不到五十年就戛然而止，清代的儒学反而像汉儒一样，走上经学之路。

清代经学在发掘"五经"的现实性含义上，特别是在经文的训诂考据方面有很大成就，但未能改造儒学，使之成为新学。直到鸦片战争前后，以龚自珍、魏源、林则徐为代表的第二次启蒙思潮才有转机，儒家思想又重新向经世致用发展。接着，在清末民初出现以严复、康有为、梁启超为代表的再一次启蒙思潮，则主要是传播西方民主、科学和进化论思想，只还带着公羊学等儒家的外衣。这以后的发展，如孙中山的革命思想，以至五四运动，就不属于儒家思想范畴了。

1998 年 10 月 20 日

唐绢、布产量

绢：每匹阔一尺八寸，长四丈。唐尺 1 尺 = 0.295 米，即每匹 6.266 平方米。麻布，阔大约也是一尺八寸，长五丈，即每端 7.832 平方米。就使用价值说：1 匹绢 = 1 端布。

唐制，调每丁"随乡土所产绫绢绝各二丈，布加五分之一"。此"各"字应为"共"字，即绢 2 丈，或半匹；布 2.4 丈，作 2.5 丈，或半端。另外，绢加绵 3 两，布加麻 3 斤。根据税负均等原则（永业田均为每丁 20 亩），就价值说：1 匹绢 = 1 端布；1 两绵 = 1 斤麻。

天宝时，"约出丝绵郡县……输绢约七百四十余万匹，绵则百八十五万余屯，租粟则七百四十余万石。约出布郡县……输布约千三十五万余端，其租……折纳布约五百七十余万端……纳粟五百二十余万石"。[①]（按：开元时数与此略同，看来是定额）

上述绢调 740 万匹，布调 1035 万端，按等价计，即全国绢产值与布产值之比为 41.7% 比 58.3%，或 40% 比 60%（调占产值的比率即税率假定一致）。

绢产区，纳粟 740 万石，按每丁租二石，应有 370 万丁。每丁调绢半匹，共调 185 万匹，而实收 740 万匹，这是因为人民把庸（役）折绢交纳了。役每丁 20 日，日折绢 3 尺，共 60 尺，即 1.5 匹，370 万丁共 555 万匹。

---

① 杜佑：《通典》卷六《食货六·赋税下》。

185 万 +555 万恰好为 740 万匹。又，收绵 185 万屯，每屯 6 两，共 1110 万两。375 万丁，每丁应纳 3 两，恰好 1110 万两。

布产区，《通典》明言"四百五十余万丁"，每丁调布半端，应调布 225 万端，而实收 1035 万端，这是因为人民不但将庸折布，还将应纳之麻也折布交纳了。庸每日折布 3.75 尺，20 日共 75 尺，即 1.5 端，450 万丁共 675 万端。麻每丁纳 3 斤，450 万丁共纳 1350 万斤，应折布 x 端。225 万 + 675 万 + x 万 = 1035 万。x = 135 万端。也就是：1 斤麻 = 0.1 端布，这指价值。但也可设想 10 斤麻织 1 端布，或一端布重 10 斤（似乎重了些）。但不能说 1 两绵 = 0.1 匹绢，因织绢用丝，绵则废丝。也不能说 1 匹绢重 16 两，没有那么重的绢，大约 10 两左右。

上面，绢产区有 370 万丁，布产区有 450 万丁，共 820 万丁。按天宝十三载（754）在籍有约 900 万户，5300 万口，按丁占全人口 20% 计，应有 1060 万丁，即每户 1.2 丁，这是合理的。但，唐不课户占 85%，天宝十三载课户共 7662800 口，这个"口"实际是"丁"，即 766 万丁。调查课户总是少报，故纳课之丁应以《通典》820 万为准。实际还多，因《通典》都有"余"字。

按丁计，则绢产区为 370 万丁，布产区为 450 万丁，即 45% 比 55%。或说，穿绢的占 45%，穿布的占 55%。然而，绢的商品率远比布大，看来，还是 40% 比 60% 为宜。这说明穿绢的不只贵族，像绌是很粗的，民家也用。另方面，官府需布孔殷，依上引，不但应交的麻折成布，应纳的租粟也部分折成布了，有 570 万端，比调布大一倍。就官府说，共收绢 740 万匹，布 1605 万端，为 32% 比 68%。官府需布是因为兵多于官。

参考官府给奴婢的口粮（《唐六典·尚书刑部》）及园丁口粮（《唐会要》），韩国磐计算，一家五口，年需食粮 26 石。一家缴租粟、地税共约 3 石（按 1.2 丁，30 亩地计），即赋粮合民食用粮的 8.7 倍。这是指吃的。如果穿的也是这样（即税负相等），每丁纳半匹（或端），则自穿应为 4.35 匹（或端），按每户 1.2 丁计，则每户需 5.5 匹（或端）。

李伯重根据《天宝六载四月交河郡佛寺给家人春衣历》，用复杂的算法计算五口之家，每年需用布 4.6 端，加上被褥帐帘等，"总计一年约用布

5.5 端略多"。① 但他算了衫、裤，没算裤，不知何故？

唐布每匹 7.832 平方米，这很大。棉布初流行，明洪武二十六年（1393）定纳税布每匹阔一尺八寸，长三丈二尺，明尺等于今尺，合 6.4 平方米，也相当大，大约受麻布影响。清松江土布，每匹只 3.036 平方米。据徐新吾考算，1840 年平均每人年消费 1.5 匹，五口之家合 7.5 匹，即 22.77 平方米，合唐布只 2.9 端。唐衣宽袍大袖，费布，但古人消费大于今人，终不可解。徐估计偏低，严中平及外国人估计都要高。又，按徐估计平均每人消费棉花为 2.86 磅，而国际棉业咨询会估计世界标准都在 5 磅以上。

看来每户 5.5 端之数可用，天宝 900 万户，即每年需 4950 万端（或匹），可作 5000 万端（匹）。这是民户消费量，不是产量。开元政府收绢布共 2345 万端（匹）。是供那些（主要）不在 900 万户籍中人之用。两数相加可作产量，即 7300 万端（匹）。其中，绢约 3000 万匹，麻布约 4300 万端。

两税法后，绢价由 3200 文跌至 1600 文（每匹），因税额以货即定，纳税交实物，故政府收绢增一倍（布价未详，大约亦同）。跌价是因通货紧缩（粟价亦跌），与生产无关。但绢（布）征收增一倍，则与生产有关。例如由 2345 万端（匹）增为 4690 万端（匹），就有 426 万户人家没衣穿了。可见，生产有发展。到唐末，至少增产到 9500 万端（匹）。

贞观初，大体 1 匹绢价 = 1 石米价。到开元，1 匹绢 = 1.5 石米。但开元末，1 匹绢 = 0.6 石米。以后无记录，大约绢价下落快于米价，故反映两税法负担太重多用绢为例。这说明绢（布大约同）的增产快于米。

---

① 李伯重：《略论唐代的"日绢三尺"》，《唐史论丛》第 2 辑，陕西人民出版社，1987，第 101～117 页。

轮船招商局

1873 年以前，是外国公司垄断着中国沿海和内河轮船航运业。1873 年轮船招商局成立，冲破了外国公司的垄断，收回了部分航权。到抗日战争前夕，沿海和长江航线，中国轮船的吨位已超过外国轮船，占总吨位 60% 以上，这是不容易的。而中国轮船中，招商局一直是最大的一家，是与外轮抗衡的主力。

招商局创建初期，有轮船 4000 余吨，连同地产、码头、仓库等，财产值 100 余万银两。到 19 世纪末，轮船增至 4 万余吨，财产增至 1000 万两。到抗战前夕，有轮船 7 万余吨，财产 3000 余万两，它还对其他企业投资，连同贷款，高时达 800 万两。所以，招商局在发展中国航运业方面，在促进贸易和近代企业的发展上是有功绩的。

招商局在旧中国有 76 年历史，走的却是一条艰难曲折的道路。它有发展，但发展很慢，在 19 世纪，27 年中船只吨位的年增长率不到 1%，比英商太古、日商日清慢得多。进入 20 世纪，49 年间轮船吨位年增长率只有 1‰，比新兴的华商三北、民生慢得多。生产效率低，19 世纪平均每吨轮船的年产值不到 70 两，到 20 世纪，除第一次世界大战几年外，降为 60 两，许多生产力被浪费了。经营效益也低，19 世纪平均每年盈利由 30 余万两增至 60 余万两，这是最好时期，但按资本（股本加借款）利润率算，不到 10%，最好时平均只有 15% 左右。进入 20 世纪，除世界大战几年外，年平均利润只有 20 余万两，利润率更低，1921 年以后，连年亏损，由每年亏损几十万两增到 150 万两。

生产效率低、经营效益更低的原因很多，有外因，也有内因。我想说，其中一个重要原因是体制不健全。招商局是一家官督商办企业。官督商办有老传统，如盐商、矿商、茶商，但多是招商承办后放手商营。招商局不同，没有明确的权力界线。同是官督商办，前后不同。唐廷枢承办时期，商人还有些权力，经营较好。盛宣怀承办时期，则官权在握，商董形同虚设，股东叫苦连天，郑观应所谓"官督商办势如虎"。1909 年改为完全商办，但仍"隶部"，由邮传部主管，后来成立股份公司，实际仍是官权膨胀。

招商局是全部商股，是第一家股份制的大企业。但是，它始终未能自主经营、自贸盈亏，产权不明确，没有法人应有的财产占有权、使用权、收益权、处分权。尤其北洋政府时期，袁世凯、政府各部、各界要人都要插手招商局，都要从招商局中分肥，以至 1926 年，招商局发表宣言，全部停航。1927 年起，国民党政府整理招商局，1932 年以 200 余万两购买价值 2000 余万两的招商局，改为国营。但政府内部矛盾、局内派系斗争，仍是乱纷纷。一度大力整顿局务的赵铁桥，最后被暗杀。一度大力改革制度的刘鸿生，处处掣肘，愤而辞职。

招商局的新生命，是在解放以后。上海招商局残存财产，接管后并入社会主义企业。香港招商局起义，遵周总理指示："社会主义企业，资本主义运作。"体制明确了，产权也清晰了，按市场经济原则经营，发展壮大。1979 年受中央委托，建立中国第一个经济特区——蛇口工业区。十几年来，吸引外资，完全按照市场经济原则营运，成绩昭著，为国为民，做出重大贡献，也为国有企业的改革创立模范。

1996 年 12 月 12 日

（为中央电视台录制专题片撰写的解说词）

近代封建主义

1982 年日本"中国近现代史研究会"组团访华，9 月 1 日在中国社会科学院经济研究所召开"中国近现代经济史学术座谈会"，会上我提出"近代封建主义"的观点。提纲无存，仅奥村哲在《近きに在りて》（《近邻》）第 6 号（1984 年 11 月）文中有简介。1982 年 11 月 26 日在南开大学讨论《中国资本主义发展史》书稿时，我作"近代封建主义"的讲话，《南开经济研究所季刊》1983 年第 1 期刊出要点。1983 年 1 月 19 日我在经济所与经济史同志讲"近代封建主义"，有个提纲。

下面是根据上述三次残存材料整理。主要讲"近代封建主义"的消极作用。1989 年我发表《谈封建主义二题》（《中国经济史研究》1989 年第 4 期），其第二题有"近代封建主义"，则谈了其积极作用。

1999 年 8 月 10 日识

1979 年我提出研究近代中国经济史的四点意见，其一就是要研究封建主义。那是鉴于在近代史研究中，对帝国主义的侵略压迫论述綦详，而对封建主义的制约注意不够。我认为，封建主义的长期延续，是中国近代经济落后的根源，是内因。18 世纪中国就落后了，那时还没有帝国主义特权。帝国主义压迫是外来的，打倒它，它就倒了。封建主义是土生土长，不是一场土改或政治革命就能肃清的，"文革"中还几乎出现封建主义复辟。在经济上，废除地主制经济，必须有新的东西代替它，否则在一有条件时它就会复活。在政治和文化上，更是这样。经济上，封建主义不单表现在地租剥削，很重要的一点是市场狭隘，不能发展社会化大生产。

毛主席说："封建时代的自给自足的自然经济基础是破坏了；但是，封建制度的根基——地主阶级对农民的剥削，不但依旧保持着，而且同买办资本和高利贷资本的剥削结合在一起，在中国社会经济生活中，占着显然的优势。"[1] 一个"基础"，一个"根基"，基础破坏了，根基反而因与买办资本和高利贷资本相结合，仍占着显然的优势。这是毛主席对近代中国社会经济的论断。

基础破坏，指自然经济变成商品经济。20 世纪 30 年代中国社会性质论战中，争的就是这个问题。王宜昌等认为中国已是资本主义经济了，被打成托派。苏联的马札亚尔、拉狄克也是这样，受斯大林批评，作了检讨。陶希圣提出中国已是商业资本主义。70 年代，国外如罗友枝（Evelyn Rawski）研究福建、湖南农村，马若孟（Ramon H. Myers）研究山东、河北农村，都认为地主所有制没什么作用，农民生产已是依靠市场，佃农等于租地农业家，"家庭资本主义"。奇怪的是，日本左派也有类似观点。里井彦七郎（东京大学教授，日共）提出中国农民"半フロ"理论，着眼洋货下乡，农民变成半无产者。狭间直树（京都大学教授）提出"资本隶农"论点，农民种棉为出口，而穿衣要买洋布，一进一出都受资本剥削。出口农产品，进口工业品。这是从左的方面否定封建主义的根基，起码江南无封建。

我们在《中国资本主义发展史》（以下简称《中资史》）中研究"自然经济的解体"，花了很大工夫，主要是徐新吾。结论是解体很不彻底，农业和家庭手工业结合十分顽固。土纱土布一有机会就要复活；在丝织业，凡是小农与之竞争激烈之处，工场手工业就发展不起来。小麦是商品化较高的，大约有 60% 出卖，但主要是土磨坊加工，留给机器面粉厂的不过 18%。徐新吾说：中国近代封建束缚主要表现为自然经济解体缓慢，封建经济结构十分顽固，扯不开、切不断。

---

[1] 《新民主主义论》，《毛泽东选集》第 2 卷，人民出版社，1991，第 630 页。

然而，商业和商品经济确实发展了。《中资史》列有"农产品商品化"专题。1920 年比之 1894 年，按不变价格计算，粮食的商品值增加 40% 强，其他五种农产品商品值增加 64%。1936 年比之 1920 年，按不变价格计，农产品商品值增加 56%，工矿业商品值增加 54%。进口商品另有海关详报，勿论。

用毛主席的话说，封建主义的"基础"即自然经济，不说"破坏了"，也是"破坏着"，而封建制度的"根基""依旧保持着"。这就发生一个问题，封建制度能否建立在商品经济的基础上呢？奴隶制有建立在商品经济之上的，如迦太基，以至雅典、罗马城邦。封建经济，如中世纪威尼斯、热那亚，作为个小王国，也可这么说。但一个大帝国就不能这么说，东罗马、拜占庭、阿拉伯哈利发，商业发达，但还不能说是建立在商品经济"基础"上的。同样，近代中国，商业资本主义，半フロ、资本隶农，以及前述马若孟、罗友枝等论点，恐怕是不能成立的。其实，这些理论都是否定封建主义，把近代中国看成是资本主义的，历史证明这是不对的；因为直到"文革"，封建主义还几乎复辟。

毛主席说，在近代，封建剥削不但依旧保持着，而且同买办资本和高利贷资本的剥削结合在一起，在中国社会经济生活中占着显然优势。似乎有更加重的味道。不知这话是否受斯大林的影响。斯大林说，帝国主义"到处致力于保持资本主义以前的一切剥削形式（特别是在乡村），并使之永久化"。斯大林这话不对，因为西方列强是"按照自己的面貌创造一个世界"。近代中国不能说更封建了，而是半殖民地半封建社会。单就地租剥削说，也不是更厉害了，而是相对削弱了。地主的剥削与买办资本、高利贷资本结合则是事实，乃至与外国资本、外国银行资本结合也不奇怪，洋务派就首开其例。

其实，地主与商人、高利贷结合，即三位一体说，老早就有了，方行同志有深入研究。这是中国的地主制经济使然。西欧的领主制经济与商业、高利贷资本是完全对立的；商品经济发展必然导致领主制灭亡。这就是马克思所说的货币权力战胜土地权力。中国的地主制经济，能容纳一定的商品经济，与之并存，乃至与之结合，加强自己，延长封建寿命。宋以后，尤其明后期和清前期，这已是明白无误的事情。问题是走入近代，有了强大的外国资本主义,有了自然经济的解体,有了官僚资本和民族资本,地主制经济不但与商品经济共存,简直是与资本主义共存。用西欧经验来看,几乎是不可能的。这种共存看来是长期的,如果不是土改和1956年的改造,还会继续共存下去。

我把这种与资本主义共存的封建主义,称为"近代封建主义",它是我国封建主义发展的一个新阶段,有了新的质,新的质就是它能与资本主义共存。这当然是由我国半殖民地半封建条件造成的。所以近代封建主义也可称为半封建主义,不是列宁所说的半封建主义,那是指解放农奴后的俄国封建主义。我国的"半封建"原是"半资本主义半封建主义",也就是两者并存的意思。"半半"当然不是指50%对50%,而是指并存,长期共存。不只经济上,或剥削方式上,也指政治上、文化思想上都是两者并存。这种观象说奇怪,也不奇怪。目前第三世界,有的国家还是封建统治,但靠石油贸易,经济已资本主义化了。因而,近代封建主义也不是中国独创,在一定的社会条件下有普遍意义。

质的变化,不仅表现在与资本主义共存上,封建本身也有所变化。如地主本身,原由世族地主、绅衿地主转变到庶民地主为主;在近代又有新地主出现。所谓新地主,主要是另有职业的、城居的,投资于土地而已,实即商人地主。当然也有军阀、官僚、豪劣等新地主。潭仪父调查1935年川西、川东、川南、川北十个县,新地主占70%,有的县旧地主全消灭了。这个调查大约是不可靠的。广东有的县,一半以上的地主是海外华侨,则是可靠的。地租制度原由分成到定额,又有押租和永佃,近代以来似无大变化,但货币租确有增加,佃权有增大,尤其太平天国后。小农经济的格局没有改变,但因部分家庭手工业解体和农产品商品化,经营似乎更单一化。

我不大相信近代地租剥削愈来愈重的说法,但农业经营零碎化、亩产量降低、劳动生产率降低,恐怕是真的。在《中资史》中研究资本主义萌芽,始终不能肯定,尤其从效益上说,富农效益甚低,规模生产建不起来,最后,把农业资本主义萌芽全部取消了,这也是近代封建主义的罪过。

历史学与社会学

前些时候有一种议论，说你们搞历史的，特别是搞经济史的，不研究社会问题，这是不对的；近来才注意社会问题的研究。我想这话有理，但不完全是这样。我作学生的时候，即 20 世纪三四十年代，史学界是注意社会研究的。郭沫若的《中国古代社会研究》，侯外庐的《中国古典社会史论》，都是热门的书。陶孟和主持的社会调查所发行《中国社会经济史研究集刊》，从 1932 年直到 1949 年，是历史最长的史学期刊。陶希圣主编的《食货》半月刊风行一时，其中社会学文章更多些。不过确有一个时期，大体是 1949～1979 年三十年间，历史学与社会学完全脱钩了。这时大学取消社会学课程，社会学成为禁区，史学界也不敢涉及社会问题了。揆其故大约是，当时我国是在社会主义革命中，一切以阶级斗争为纲，而西方的社会学，除冲突论各家外大都是进化论者，他们主张社会要和谐稳定，才能发展。如当时流行的结构功能学派，即认为社会各系统的功能都在于维护整体的均衡，而社会的功能即在于整合各系统的作用。冲突论者认为冲突是社会发展的动力，但不是以阶段斗争为纲，阶级斗争只在工业化早期有效，诸如人口冲突、亚族群、地区、文化等冲突问题都要和平解决。1979 年党的十一届三中全会以后，实行改革开放政策，也讲安定团结了。社会学解禁，史学界尤其是经济史学者又重新研究社会问题了。

这是中国的情况。其实在西方，历史学者与社会学者之间也不是亲密无间的。社会学晚出，19 世纪 30 年代才正式建立。早期的社会学家都是实证论者，他们有点看不起历史学。因为他们主张用自然学同样的方法来研究社会发展的普遍规律，乃至是"与历史无关的"（ahistorical）的社会规律。而当时的历史学是研究个别的、民族的乃至是"一次如此"的事情，没有普遍规律可言。在孔德的学术体系中就没有历史学，历史学是附属于社会学的，目的在为社会学提供社会研究资料。又社会学是研究整个社会，并着重基层组织，如家庭、社区、行会等，而当时流行的历史学即兰克学派史学，主要是研究政治史，研究上层人物。社会学家不屑于谈政治，斯宾塞说，那些君主们的传记，对社会研究没有任何启示。另一方面，历史学家也有点看不起社会学。历史学是老大，有两千几百年传统，而社会学才出襁褓。兰克学派的史学这时正由编年史进入新开放的国家档案的检索研究，认为这是大事，是严肃的工作，而那些社会现象只是琐闻杂记。著名的史学理论家，如德国的狄尔泰、意大利的克罗齐，则直称社会普遍规律的研究是"伪科学"，因为它是从外部关系研究人类有意志的活动，用机械论来研究精神现象。

19 世纪末 20 世纪初情况有了很大改变。这时出现了两位社会学大师，他们也都是历史学家，即涂尔干（杜尔凯姆）和韦伯。涂尔干是实证社会学的奠基者。原来孔德、斯宾塞都是从概念上研究社会关系，涂尔干主张要研究社会事象本身，并强调事象的客观性，这就直接进入历史。韦伯的社会学叫诠释社会学，即阐述和理解社会行为，并用因果关系来说明它，这也必须进入历史。同时，历史学家也不满于单纯的政治、军事、外交史，转而注意社会、经济、文化。特纳提出要写"全方位考虑人的活动"的历史。鲁滨孙著《新史学》，主张从人类学、社会学、经济史吸取历史事实。经济学方面，自李嘉图起与历史脱钩，边际主义兴起后更摒弃历史研究。进入 20 世纪，则有桑巴特、熊彼特等大师重振经济史，并吸收社会学成果。20 年代，法国布洛克、费弗尔创办《社会经济史年鉴》，把社会学融入历史研究，经布罗代尔完成"总体史观"，成为当代最负盛名的社会经济历史学派。

然而，20 世纪前期历史学与社会学的合作主要是历史家主动的，社会学方面则有周折。涂尔干于 1917 年去世，韦伯于 1920 年去世，社会研究中心由欧洲转移到美国。美国人是实用主义者，不注意历史（美国历史很短）。美国的社会学研究注重当前的社会问题，特别是人口问题、劳工问题、社会福利问题、家庭和妇女儿童问题等。这种研究当然也涉及历史，但属行业史，他们更着重的是社会调查，成为社会学的专业。1937 年帕森斯发表《社会行动结构》，力图调和涂尔干注重环境和集体行动与韦伯注重意向和个体行为两派观点，并引进当时流行的结构主义，成为一种新的社会行动理论。50 年代帕森斯又以一系列的著作，完成他的结构功能主义理论，一时成为社会学的主流。而在帕森斯的理论中，历史是相当被忽视的。

20 世纪 30 年代我国流行的社会学就是主要是从美国传入的，注重研究社会问题，设立社会调查机构和开展农村调查，以至国情普查，都卓有成果。理论方面，也主要帕森斯的结构功能主义，不过按照中国传统，更重历史实证研究。例如我们今天会议讨论的家庭人口问题，即是应用家族、基干家庭、核心家庭的历史框架，研究家庭功能的分化，以及它与社会分工、流动性加强的关系等。

这里，我想提出的是，帕森斯的社会学理论虽然风行一时，但为时甚暂。第二次世界大战以后，思想界进行反思，社会学界震动尤大，出现了各种冲突论和主观社会学派，以及后现代主义思潮。20 世纪 80 年代以来，定型为三大学派，即以美国亚历山大为首的新功能主义，以英国吉登斯为代表的“社会结构化”理论，以德国哈贝马斯为代表的“交往行动”理论，三者成鼎立之势。这三派有个共同特点，就是他们都力图综合各家的长处，尤其是吸纳自己对立面的某些论点以求充实，并且，都在不同程度上吸纳马克思主义的理论，以符合时代要求。如亚历山大吸纳了阶级冲突论；吉登斯批判资本主义全球化引起的危机，要求“政治解放”；哈贝马斯则自称要“重建”历史唯物主义。这里要说明的是，原来马克思的历史唯物主义提供了丰富的社会学原理，再如结构论、交往概念、异化理论也是马克思首先提出的，被称为“批判的社会学”。但在 19 世纪，马克思的社会学受到抵制，第一次世界大战后才逐渐受到重视，而于 20 世纪中叶广为流行起来。当然，这时流行的已不是“原教旨主义”的马克思，而是经过修正解释（特别是卢卡奇的解释）的后马克思主义了。任何伟大思想都是与时俱进的，而不能是“原教旨主义”。

哈贝马斯的《交往行动理论》以马克思主义的批判社会理论为基础，综合了实证主义、诠释社会学、主观社会学和帕森斯的结构功能主义，创立了一种新的社会批判理论。他以交往（communication，或译沟通）为人类社会存在和再生产的基本要素。在部落制时代，人们通过自由的合理的交往，组成家庭、部落等社会系统。到阶级社会和国家出现后，各种系统（经济系统、法制系统等）不再以生活交往为中介，社会系统与生活世界分离了。到现代资本主义社会，所有社会系统（包括生活系统）都是由金钱和权力支配，不再通过交往协商，生活世界殖民地化。这种情况是工具理性凌驾于交往理性，人们的策略行动战胜交往行动的结果。而这种情况并不是不可避免的，历史并未规定只有一条道路。在西方严重的资本主义危机下，突破金钱与权力体制，恢复系统社会与生活世界的统一是可能的。

为此，哈贝马斯讲述了六项社会批判的任务，包括家庭的社会化和自我发展问题。他认为，家庭原是"主体间"性交往的产物，夫妻原无主客之分。在现代资本主义制度下，这种主体间关系被"物化"了；在传统的主客体模式的行动中，出现婚姻、家庭结构、儿童抚育等不合理现象。我们从这点出发，就会给家庭问题和自我发展问题的研究开辟一条新的思路。

我还想提到，在吉登斯的"社会结构化"理论中，针对社会学中存在的主观论与物质论、价值与事实、理论与实践等"二元"观点，他提出"双重性"的概念，认为这些对立观点原是互相包容的，因而是可以调和的。而他的双重性的论点，就在于取消主体与客体的对立，把事物间的关系看成是主体间的关系。这种主体间关系的认识论，有点像中国宋儒的"体用一源，显微无间"论点，以及禅宗"主看主"的说法。西方一直是主客对立的传统，以至出现自我主义的史学理论。西方主客统一的认识肇始于20世纪早期胡塞尔的现象学，经过存在主义和海德格尔、伽达默尔，成为历史学和社会学中新的思维方法，而盛行于后现代主义思想家。这种新的认识论和思维方法，是值得我们注意的。

通信

1992 年 10 月与张宗植的通信

宗植学长：

早奉九月八日来示，旋得宏世　兄寄《樱花岛国余话》，连夜读竟，未能释手也。缘五月间弟去港澳，内子以病躯暂寓女儿处，旧居无人，致退邮，而重劳公及世　兄，歉甚，并谢。

几年前于《何凤元》集得见《竹骡记》，睹　兄少年风华正茂，倾心感佩。今拜读《樱花岛国余话》，更见　兄洞察世事，知著见微，而以游逸笔墨出之，袅袅读来，酣畅舒漓，所谓文章老更成也。至于经商有道，乐成大业，义利之说，似在其中矣。弟昔在上海时曾接触广大华行，在南京时一度参与日本业务，吴半农、魏文翰诸公皆旧识，是以读来倍觉亲切。

又有闲事一桩，可否请教：1980 年春弟曾携女访尊府，一出地铁即见大木牌"洗足池"，大喜，即池拍照一张，并口占云"昔闻沧浪水，今见洗足池；高人挂衣去，云路渺愁予"。此次理《濯足偶谈》稿拟用作首页（因我们"五七干校"是从来不拍照的）。但是，对于洗足池故事弟全然不晓，旁木牌有记，弟又不通日文，"挂衣"全凭猜测，滥用《湘夫人》眇眇笑话。谨请教，不知　兄可否将洗足池典故略示一二，俾无笑话。此固闲事，请勿以为意，他日有闲，回复片纸而已。顺颂

俪祺

弟吴承明上

1992 年 10 月 14 日

张宗植（1914~2004），日籍华人企业家，曾任清华大学顾问教授、清华大学海外校友会日本分会名誉会长等。

1993～2007 年与何炳棣的通信

一

承明兄：

元旦惠书三日前收到，立即捧读一通。今日重读，喜同曷胜！（可憾的是在清华时，由于政见不同，反不如今日亲切）我们今日回忆六十年前事物，无不出于至诚（当然曾做过坏事的一定讳饰到底），这正是回忆之所以可贵。数年前读我级毕业五十年纪念册后，有此志愿：如可能当请若干位老同年做尽可能忠实详细的追忆，以丰富我自己的追忆，并渴望因此而为三十年代历史留下有价值的参考资料。我国传统传记不值得读，主要原因在不坦白，不翔实，缺乏第一性（手）经历与情趣。吾　兄高才（在北平时我衷心以为你的头脑最明白，分析力极强，口才极佳，为我级有数高材之一，决非虚誉！），如诚恳谈家世，早年家庭、学校教育（你古文根基甚好，想象中未必完全得自学校）等等，最所欣闻。传统传记最大缺点之一是对真正的家世不肯具体讲出。如"家贫"，究竟如何贫；"家富"，究竟如何富；喜读书，究竟如何启蒙，如何逐步了解学问……如黄诚兄及其姊黄珮之例，想象中不但黄系书香之家，而且必定相当富有，否则姊弟二人不能皆去北平读

何炳棣（1917～2012），美国艺文及科学院院士，美国亚洲学会会长。

书，而黄珮更无机缘取得了解公平的知识。如系地主之家，田产大约多少。凡此诸端，皆为社、经史重要参考资料（三句话不离本行，一笑）。

再：清华共开除了多少学生？从事革命究竟还不是正面违犯校章，当初究竟怎样才被开除的，这点直至今日我还不是真明白。

提到黄氏姊弟，我好像在入清华之前只见过姐姐，进清华后反而完全未曾注意。周永升南开开除后似并未考进清华，而且自 1932 冬即未曾再见过他。不日当给他一信。

大作 萌芽之部已经拜读，分析诠释当然与尚钺等等不可同日而语。夏间当细读近代之部，如有问题当再请教。我正在初步筹划试写一本 Intellectual autohagiography，只就生平学习、研究、写作第一性经验感受方面入手，亦当及当年学生运动。因亲老家衰，我在北平三年至少自修了一般人五年的课程，自入清华之前即立志考留美，与 兄及姚依林兄等所走之路将将相反。今后我们自两个不同方向做共同回忆，应该比较真切有趣。

敬颂

新春一切如意！

弟炳棣
1993 年 1 月 31 日

二

承明学长：

旬前喜获《濯足偶谈》，充分证明了我对 兄早年国学基础坚实的推测是正确的。 兄之 versatility 使人倾服，使我惭愧——因为亲老家衰，我初中毕业后读书就不得不"功利"了，美的东西都成为我的"禁脔"了，我真正变成一个"prosaic"的人了。试想：多年为准备考留美，清晨气象台前朗读（不能用诵字）英国史家论述式的散文，生平从来未好好读过英国诗人。中国的诗词，包括《诗经》和《离骚》，南开开除之后即从不再问津。虽然在北平的三年，自信读了相当一般人五年的书，但都是"洋八股"（极广义的，包括欧战前 pre-1914 的欧洲外交史），都是与美无关之物。Gibbon 的《罗马帝国衰亡史》倒是大气磅礴，不愧英国的太史公，以至在某一阶段，我的英文散文已达不可救药的地步了，婴儿要在奥运会里赛百米！遇到奇人杨善荃先生（由何廉的弟弟何基——清华历史系助教介绍的），经他一顿"痛击"之后，我英文才"近代化"。回忆起来，我国内的教育多由自修，但极功利。对广义的美要等到五十年代末才开始自修，如对中国传统绘画及瓷器等等，对诗词等已悔不当初了，换言之连平仄都未学过，遑论其他！但为教书起见，我也戏译过律诗及宋词以为中国通史班上用。如所附拙译柳耆卿的《八声甘州》（律诗的对偶和结构西方一般人译不出，或译不好）。

《八声甘州》
Autumn Nostalgia（英文译名我加）

A late rain has rushed over sky and river,

Autumn is washed clear and pure.

Gradually frost and wind tighten thick hold,

Passes and fords are deserted.

While windows upstair's flush in evening glow,

Here the red decay and the green fades,

Soon life will come to a repose,

Only the waters of Yangtze River

Without a word, eastward flow.

Now can I bear climbing high and looking afar

In the direction of my native land—

Nostalgia without end!

I pity my drifting of late years,

And wonder why I still tarry.

My beauteous lady, gazing from her bower,

Must have mistaken— how many times—

The homecoming boat emerging from sky's very edge.

But how can she know

That I too lean on a railing,

Congealed in sorrow?

当时在 British Columbia，同事诗人 Earle Birney（曾两度获英帝国诗金奖），看到"是处红衰翠减，苒苒物华休"，拍案叫绝。世上竟有用如此脱俗之字写出秋（的最基本）义、意！同样，他对钱起的"浮天沧海远"亦是叫绝。也许是年龄，近年每多感伤，对我们这一代，特别是依林兄等从事革命者的感叹，当初我们怎能料到祖国会产生出这样一个人呢!? 我理智与情感方面都在"号召"我自己，还是追索这巨龙文化的多种"根"吧，还是尽有限的才力做古今整合工作吧！一笑。

祝

健康长寿！

乞代我问候嫂夫人！嫂夫人书法宗王而有骨，胜于乾隆之无骨赵。

弟炳棣

一九九三年二月廿晨

附言：不久当以杂作（中文近作）另行邮奉。

三

炳棣学长：

前奉 1 月 31 日华翰，今又接 2 月 20 日来示并英译《八声甘州》。倩词丽句，信达柳公原旨。而纯以西人思路及用语出之，艺术上所谓再创作者，今见之，感佩莫名。文史一家，盖非只中华传统，西方以历史入 Art 久矣，古之 Gibbon，今之 Arnold Toynbee 亦然。吾 兄以史学大师，追索美学境界（绘画、瓷器、诗词），实树模于来者，不可以老来养生之道视之也。弟原习经济，于计量经济学亦有兴趣。曾有人约讲计量史学 cliometrics，勉应之，实不以为然也。

弟实在没有一点国学根底。缘先父为中国第一代律师，母为第一代女学（北洋女子师范）毕业生。然当时北方保守，弟曾入私塾二年，略识古文而已。《濯足偶谈》是当时"干校"产物，"文革"中要求是手足劳动，头脑休息，在干校只能"我思故我在"。《偶谈》游戏文字，不能登大雅之堂，但有"争生存"的味道，当时身处逆境，唯未曾悲观，可说 sanguine disposition，是以尚未尝悲观。可说 sanguine disposition，非故作豁达也。至于英文，弟可谓一窍不通。在学校既未学习，仅敷衍考试，在 Columbia 三年，记专业名词而已。一种文字，若只能应付生活，等于文盲。美国就有这种文盲（还能用英语打架）。

再读吾 兄前函（读忆旧事），倍受感动。老年怀旧，原不足取。而所论传记、往事必须真实、具体、有第一性经验等等，则非只怀旧也。 兄计划中之大作，有需弟回忆帮助之处，自当奉命。对当时国内形势，看法不同，不妨兼听，或事非一说，亦不妨兼纳。弟近查清华同学录，确无周永升。缘我留有大礼堂前照片一张，黄诚、杨成生、闫家旗及弟，凡北洋来者均在内。周永升亦在照内，是以误会。他也许是伴黄氏姊弟来清华。惟弟从未见黄氏在清华照片，为憾。

弟吴承明

1993.3.5

四

承明学长：

惠赠航寄 大著《市场·近代化·经济史论》旬前收到，至为欣感！

景洛病情上周经医生当面详告，一切大有进步，注射及内服两种药效均佳，全部疗程走完以后 C 型肝炎有可能根本控制。这才使我们放心，最近才有心情对大作仔细拜读反思。

弟读史六十余年，始终对各学派理论未曾精读细敲过。大著有关经济史理论部分对我大有裨益。 兄思维锐敏而又周密平衡，所论例皆允当。这又再度证明我在三十年代认为 兄是我级头脑最清楚之一是正确的。因此，我恳切要求 兄对我"明清人口及社会"敝书惠予严肃评价（有空的话），待我与景洛明年初秋访京时当面聆教不迟。因我个人早晚也必须做一番自我评价工作。 兄与我专长不同。我人口、土地、农业、移民等等类皆只能在定性方法做出原创性贡献（偶尔也有定量工作），因我一向感到传统史料无法统统量化。五口通商、海关建立之后，统计始较传统官方数字，大为优越，计量工作才有可能。我相信我对明代"鱼鳞图册"的考证是今生最精细的考证。但其贡献是 iconoclastic（破除偶像的），而不是积极建设性的。我感到国内了解我工作性质的人不多，因我书、文的作用是警告式的，不是肯定性的。后者才受人欢迎，如张仲礼的著作。事实上，张极聪明，但对史料不负责任。绅士（生员以上）定义大有问题，穷秀才在社会小说中往往极为卑劣，贡生（张认为是 upper gentry），事实上多数不能入仕，生活往往仍甚清苦。洪杨后人口总数已不可靠，"绅士"人口更无法确知。"绅士"的田产也无法知其约数，收入如何能估？每年占全国总产值 22%，竟高到 6 亿之多——请问全国每年税收才多少!？再如黄宗智，他的史料几乎是 void。华北农村经济"商业化"始于清初植棉，而不知明代直隶、山东、河南棉花已大批输入松江，明末肃宁棉纺已成松江劲敌；他又说下江一直是"小农"经济，事实上江南一向是大地主最集中区域，太平天国之后，因业主死亡，田园荒芜，省方、私人方面才大批吸引河南等省移民，此后才变成"小农"区域。此外，他的过密化在理论上兜圈子，而道理本极简单。而这种书居然在美国得奖，上海社科院立即出汉译本。我《人口史》一书至今国内未有评介，而其史料之结实，远非张黄等作所可同日而语。拙作 *The Ladder of Success in Imperial China* 用功如此之勤，也至今除你一提外，也未曾有系统评介。我《土地》一书在《中国史研究》本年第 6 期有王锺翰和韦庆远等译，王兄奖誉指出我的《中国会馆史论》和《黄土与中国农业的起源》，竟不知我一生最坚实之作是《人口》（《明初已降人口及其相关问题》——编者）和《社会》（《明清社会史论》——编者），隔阂竟有如此者！

此二书自七十年代初即由 Cipolla 选入意大利文的经、社、史一系列专著，而我竟不知奇氏的背景（读　兄书才较清楚）。我俩书是仅有的该 series 中的非欧洲的研究。难怪我要把我自己列为"历史学派"了，一笑，一叹！

你所谓国史中早、晚两种"封建"和我的看法并不冲突。我觉得战国至秦由封建而变成统一大帝国，两千年帝制时期，深层"意识"是"宗法"的，国是"家"有的。

兹寄上去年苦思困撰出的长文，请特别注意我所指出的"宗法基因"。我即将写儒家（甚至所有名家）的深层意识都是宗法的。宋代理学的本体宇宙论深析起来是宗法模式的，汉代董仲舒当然是宗法模式的。

寄上拙文（上），p. 99，及（下）pp. 98 - 99，请特别严肃评正！

拉杂写来，就以此搁笔。1986 颈部脊椎骨手术后，右二手指麻，写字吃力，写不成书，乞谅一二。

　　敬颂

撰祺！

弟炳棣拜

Nov. 11，1996

儒家无论新、旧、当代，都绝写不出民主和科学的！

　　国内所译西方著作（尊著所引，理论章内），我在海外从未见到过。不久当有书单寄上，请代我设法购置。

五

承明兄：

　　近月前芝大的学生　雷鼎鸣博士（现任香港科技大学经济系教授及经济发展研究所所长）有意于本年十月下旬（Oct. 25 以后）召开一严选的国际中国经济发展问题研讨会（此会对中国历史及文化相当注意，盖否则研讨可能深度不够）。他托我推荐被邀请学人，我立即想到你，不知你今秋有意参加此会否。

　　详细计划尚在商讨中，但主要 target 是历史上和今后中国经济（极广义）发展问题。

　　国内专才，希望先向我出荐（先提一二人为宜），我再向雷推荐。报酬及招待应该是上乘的。

　　此会之所以订在十月 25 日以后（大概三天）是因为我将于本年十月 22 日在香港商务印书馆百年馆庆会上做一大规模的学术演讲。23 日馆宴（亦大规模），24 日我和景洛休息一日，25 或 26 日起再在科技大学活动。

　　余不一一，即颂

新春佳胜

弟炳棣

一九九七年一月十七日

六

炳棣学长：

去年 12 月 18 日函并大作《华夏人本主义文化：渊源、特征及意义（上）》和今年 11 月 17 日来示均经奉悉。得知景洛学长已告安吉，并将伉俪远游，曷胜忻忭，值公杖朝之年，福乐莫过于此也。

先说十月下旬香港之会。弟于文化史完全不懂，于中国当代经济发展，身受而已。然若能参加盛会，得聆 兄等宏论，固所夙愿。惟中央研究院中山人文社科所并经济所邀弟于 10 月 15～11 月 15 日往台讲学，时间恰抵牾，或者弟届时抽若干日由台之港，或访台时间稍提前，尚待与中山所商量，惟恐怕无暇"造"论文了。

至嘱推荐"专才"事。国内这方面当以"国务院发展研究中心"（D. R. C）为权威，有智囊团性质，但领导者吴敬琏等皆我所（社科院经济所）去的。又我所编《中国经济发展研究论丛》，本月（二月）问世十种，著者刘国光为首，均属知名之士（不限本所人）。又北京大学"中国经济研究中心"，11 位成员全部是美英博士，林毅夫（芝大）为首，可谓英才荟萃。以上三中心，弟不敢评甄人物。盖皆知名之士，雷鼎鸣教授当已熟知，其中尚有学派问题（香港乃新制度学派天下，张五常名重泰山，曾在诺贝尔授奖大会上评介获奖主 Ronald Coase），弟不敢推荐也。

但弟想请吾 兄考虑两位小子（年青不宜说余子）：李伯重和陈其广。伯重吾 兄已悉，他近年来转治文化史，盖在法国时受年鉴学派影响（从文化角度看经济发展是对的）。他将于 4 月初去美国，9 月初返北京。陈其广是弟的博士生，治物价史，留学剑桥应用农业经济系，作大陆与台湾土改后农业发展研究，现在我所微观经济研究室，课题是"技术成果转化（应用）"问题，亦偏重农业方面，所论不乏创见。弟以为"有心人"也。

大作《华夏人本主义文化》，已读三通。弟于古史毫无根柢，但见宏文卓识，璇玑星空（新观点），歆羡无已。黄河流域农业，自始即属定居，国人已成共识。即江南河姆渡文化，亦多以为"相对稳定的定居"，主要据"长屋"构造之坚固，新见解是东北、内蒙古原始亦是农业，后来才转入游牧，与恩格斯说不同，弟曾有文论及。

太史公"究天人之际"是治中国史的关键问题，这也是中国哲学的优势所在。吾 兄"人本"之说，道其实质，令人信服。而人本至于"理性"，当为量子式跃进，义莫大焉；论周公、孔子一节，尤见创造，总之，全文四节，迄周孔，弟皆完全折服。所盼者后文，有论中古及明清文化问世。盖"人本"与"宗法"并非自然相等。秦汉以降，宗法递有变化，大作亦有范仲淹"近代型"家族之说。缘"宗法基因"有遗传、继承含义，若仅限于皇族（家天下，立太子），只是政治专制制度。而我们治社会经济史者，最苦恼的是多子继承制和析产制（西欧"原始工业化研究"亦以为凡多子继承地区总是不成气候）。专制制度与民间社会制度有别。

章太炎自叙治学经过：初，"程朱以下尤不足论"；中年，"程朱陆王诸儒，终未足厌望"；晚年则谓宋儒"虽不见全像，而谓其所见之非像，则过矣"。先师陈寅恪谓"华夏民族之文化，造极于赵宋之世"；先师冯友兰揭橥"理在事先"，常萦心怀。汉学宋学之争，弟以天资愚鲁，转成困惑，望兄有以教我。

敬颂

俪祺！

弟吴承明

1997 年 3 月 3 日

七

承明学长：

晨间接奉本年 3 月 3 日四页惠复，非常高兴。先谈要事，①十月事先保留下 26～29 这四天。26（Sunday），故十九会开在 27～29 这三天。 兄如尽早以此事通知经济所，应无问题。②其余人选稍后始能初步决定，不过我一定要你参加（是否撰文，再说，我也是不知其详）。③与雷鼎鸣通话后将再函通知。

雷虽属新派（我其实不解新派意义），但他有芝大好的传统，不固执于单一学派（当然芝派意志最坚，立场最极端的是 Friedman，我和 Ted Schultz 最熟，最谈得来）。

远古"黄河流域农业，自始即属定居，国人已成共识"，可喜但也小小可惊。1960 年代《西安半坡》，1970 年代《姜寨》等报告（专册）的作者们都是游耕说者，更不要提海外张光直辈等。即使一般推许的 Ester Boserup（Dwigth H. Perkins 等皆根据他极泛而淡之说，最初游耕……）也无不认为最初是游耕。我《东方的摇篮》稿成于 1970～1991，那时何处有此"共识"？自信拙文并非曲解事实以自大，因我吃游耕之苦已多年矣！一笑。现中、美合作的考古、人类……等 50 人已坚实证明长江流域是亚洲水稻的摇篮，而且 10000 年前已经"定居"。国内对东北原始农牧的看法很有意思。Eurasian Steppe：1500BC. 以后的农、牧并行，或多少有些参考价值。

"人本"拙文对《廿一世纪》而言是特长了，在力求紧缩及其他考虑下，"结语"拼命浓缩。指出范冲淹即已说明全部社会已非宗法。宗法之"基因"有遗传及继承含义，　兄此语极精深旨要。我最早扬州盐商（1952 撰成，1954 刊于 Harvard《亚洲学报》）中已略阐分产之不利于资本主义式的发展。但"人本"一文结语中强调而无空间发挥的是它对现在国人深层思维、观念、行动方面的 linkage effect……文中不便明指某些事例。我和杨振宁开玩笑，指出虽经我屡次劝促，杨仍不愿和我或其他人文学者共同发表对祖国的愿望，这是宗法基因作祟。

我十月 22 日香港的大型演讲就是想，撒出些"酵母"，希望能多少能引起一些促进你所谓由"人本至于'理性'"的"量子式"的跃进。

By the way，我不同意寅恪、芝生师等对宋儒的崇拜。Genially，张载"天人合一"的命题可能是中国思想界中最佳提法之一，可是他本体宇宙论的深层意识是宗法的。"宗法"一词是他创的，古称"宗子之法"。在极力希望复建西周式宗法制度的同时，他深刻感到："夫宗法不立，则天下无世家，天下无世家，则朝廷无世臣"（近代葛守礼 rephrased it）已深知财产不集中于宗子之弊！我在拙作 *The Ladder of Success in Imperial China，1368 - 1911* 第四章中有详尽的阐发。

即此结束。敬颂

健康，继续创作！

弟炳棣

1997 年 3 月八日傍晚

台中院近史所出了一本很好的书《从清华学堂到清华大学》，我已叫作者寄一本给黄明信，此书应先供你、陈宝仁、嵇国权等级友阅读。

八

承明学长：

月前收到中国社会科学出版社庆祝吾　兄九十寿辰纪念论文集，装潢雅丽，内容充实，且有宋瀛名家之派，足征吾　兄学术成就，早已为国际所公认。日前又收到尊著《经济史：历史观与方法论》，列为"十一五"国家重点图书。自 1934 年秋入清华，弟一直认为　兄乃吾级头脑最敏锐级友之一；近年拙作《读史阅世六十年》中重申此一观察与信念。盖实望始克名归，信哉斯言也！

弟小　兄三个月，今年亦值九十。本月中清华历史系为此举行一小型座谈会。此外考古学家石兴邦以及古文字历史地理家黄胜璋（二人皆中央大学出身），不顾弟多度劝阻，坚决筹出祝寿论文集，盛情可感。

日内即嘱台湾中研院近史所将拙著《有关〈孙子〉〈老子〉的三篇考证》及《从〈庄子·天下〉篇首解析先秦思想中的基本关怀》寄呈我　兄，尚望严格评正为祷。全力集中于此类基本翻案，似亦防老之良方也，一笑。

敬请道安

弟炳棣敬上

（2007）丁亥 4 月 22 日

九

炳棣学长：

暌违多年，接奉 4 月 22 日大教，曷胜欣慰。4 月 29 日清华校庆，我级例会甲所，到级友 6 人，凋谢之余矣。乃有一位一级（1928 级）的大长者吴宗济先生莅临，99 岁，声如洪钟，谈清华往事如昨，举座惊奇。

5 月 9 日社科院为弟 90 岁召开学术讨论会，有南开、复旦、武大、中山、云南大学（均经济史名校）同仁参加，约七八十人。学术讨论乃胡说，实际是讲故事。弟因讲了参加经济史耆宿巫宝三 90 岁、李文治 90 岁"讨论会"（假）的故事。还有经济史祖师爷陈翰笙 100 岁"讨论会"的大故事。皆十年前的事，尚能记忆。年老喜谈往事，不能如吾　兄《读史阅世六十年》之"学术"也。今年初，又有王一鹤（清华六级，思想史）庆 100 岁，以在上海社科院，弟不能赴会，寄诗一首为贺。

弟有一事不解：美国治宋史尤其治明清史学者（包括华裔）两学派之争，近年加剧。由笔墨官司转至"不同席"（开会）、不讲话，听说还诉诸法院，去年并各有人驻北京，一派驻清华大学，一派驻人民大学，以至我们（社科院）接待为难。出版社为弟 90 岁出论文集，我嘱编者千万勿邀美国学者文章，怕得罪人也。此事我的主张是遵循 A. 孔德：肯定自己，但不要否定别人，特别是古人。

弟自 2003 年（85 岁）以来，体力陡衰。目疾、耳背，以至行动不便，过目即忘，提笔前言不搭后语。《历史观与方法论》一稿不得不偷工减料，勉强杀青，供　兄一哂耳。然亦是绝笔之作，今后不敢握管矣。

弟以老伴去沪省亲，生活不能自理，暂住女儿家，即蓝旗营清华大学宿舍，在成府路。每天到照澜园、近春园散步。原住处仍保留，有时回去，两栖动物。

　　顺颂

道安

弟吴承明敬上
2007 年 5 月 15 日

1966 年 4 月与徐新吾关于 "中国橡胶工业" 的通信

新吾同志：

看到你给铁文同志的信，提到橡胶工业一稿。现将关于此稿的情况，和你商量一下。

橡胶一稿，我们早就看过，也送中华书局看过。这稿是早期较完整的一部，原打算早付印。但也正因其完成较早，对改造部分写得多，历史部分材料少些，文字上有些重复，章节划分过细。后来看到你们送来的其他稿子，就把橡胶压下来了。当时我们不知道上海橡胶组的同志是否还在，决定由我们加工整理一遍，借资学习，然后请你们核对。一经整理，当时的要求和目前行业史的要求很不相同，因而变动很大，有些地方等于改写了。后来我又看了第一至第三章（整理以后的），又作了很大改动，有些章节又改写了。由于改写多了，自己更觉没有把握。一则恐怕失掉原稿的论点，因而对材料的运用也就变成予取予求，不科学。二则加工愈多，愈有可能失掉原来材料的真实性，由外行处理，出现曲解。我们觉得这样做很有盲目武断之弊，所以从去年十二月起，就停下来了。打算在其他几本资料出版后，再同你们商量。

见来信，承询及此事，我们考虑，上海搞橡胶一稿的同志，可能还可以组织一下力量，把原稿再加工一遍。这样内行熟手来加工，是最理想的了。

徐新吾（1921.10～1997.10），上海社会科学院经济研究所研究员。

同时，也将我们外行硬手加工的东西寄给你们，作为参考。但仅是作参考而已，其中一定有很多曲解、误解和失实之处，是不足为凭的。

下面谈一下我个人意见。

这部稿子，由于我们当时要求不同，在历史材料上是少一些。但在当时几部稿子中，又是多的一个。从这些材料中，看出一个新兴工业的变化，则是很有典型性的。我觉得特别注意的是以下几点：（1）商业资本转入工业，在本业最多，而且是经营外国商品的商业资本转入，其转入方式也很值得注意，原因很值得分析。（2）工业与商业的关系比较突出，商品销售的包销形式，很值得研究。（3）在本业发展上，对外国商品让路，但确实抵制一部分外国商品，而且是比较有成绩的，外国资本主要是从原料上垄断。成品的市场，有农村支持。（4）业内大小资本的关系很突出，大资本靠牺牲小资本而发展，非常典型，但小厂又有自己存在的条件。（5）资本积累的材料，虽还不多，但很能说明问题，积累是比较迅速的。我觉得，对于研究中国资本主义发展来说，这部资料提供了很多东西，有许多是别的行业资料中没有或很少涉及的。

分章来看（按我们加工后的分章）：第一章，即发展过程，主要是中期和后期材料少了一些，多只举几种报刊记载，记载也比较简单。这方面能补充些行业内部或档案材料最好，否则也可以了。我们在加工时，这部分压缩最多，为了突出变化过程。如果补充材料较多，则可以不限于一章，而扩充为二、三章。

第二章，即生产经营和资本利润。生产经营部分，如果有内行同志来加工，想来还可更充实些。资本利润部分，是事例少了一些，变成以分析为主。如果能有更多事例，就会更好。新的事例，也许会改变原来论点，这要实事求是，千万不要受原来分析的约束。

第三章，工商关系，显得单薄一些。但问题是很重要的。

第四章，文字可再简练些。这章可不作为重点（这章我没修改过）。

解放以后部分，我意见可改写为一章或两章。这样，有些材料只好割爱，但特点会更突出些。

以上意见，供你参考。首先看力量组织如何而定。力量大，大加工，多补充些材料；力量小，小加工，核对一下材料。你觉得怎样？

上海棉布，我准备再看一遍，即送印。希望机器、大生（或加上橡胶）都能今年出版。造纸、面粉我还未看，可晚一步。

目前各机关都在学习，半月工作，你们那里想也一样。讨论会恐怕要延期一些时候。我们希望把这个会开好，准备充实一些。我们只准备了一些参考资料，论文也在进行，但题目还没定下来。大家以为，主要"看上海的"了。你们人才多、力量大、准备早、题目也好。这也包括向上海看齐之意。盼你们抓一下，大家把会开好，真正能获得些收益。

许局长因患肺炎在南方休养几个月。休养期间，他嘱咐我们写资本主义发展史提纲给他看，准备考虑这问题。我们已准备了一些材料和问题。我估计他这期间比较有空闲，可能对许多学术问题加以考虑，给我们指示。这样，我们的讨论会可能开得更好些。

我们在编辑资料中，感觉规格需要统一。附注的形式，照出版社意见，一律改为每页之下用脚注。最困难的是数字。像上海毛纺一稿，我们已按《红旗》规格，一律改称汉字，仅百分数仍用"20.5％"，年代仍用"1958年"。但《永安》一稿，因原来是以阿拉伯字为主，故一律改用阿拉伯字。仅不宜用者（如"一次""十几家""数十户"）仍用汉字。这两种形式都可以，但一部稿子中，要统一（橡胶也是用阿拉伯字的）。希望你们在加工时也注意一下。

祝

健康！

诸同志请代致候！

附上：我们加工的一、二、三、四章供参考。

原寄来的"补遗"一份，"勘误表"一份。

吴承明

一九六六年四月廿七日

吴承明教授关于传统经济的若干论述

——1987~2005 年与方行的通信

引言：新中国成立后不久，我就在吴承明教授领导下工作。六十余年的言传身教，使我获益终生。1978 年，我开始研究清代经济史，有时提出一些问题和意见向吴老请教，有些文章也呈请吴老指正。他每次总是回复我一封信，对我提的问题和观点以及文章中论述不足之处，一一作答，并从理论上引申，以求题无剩义。从1982 年至2004 年，这类信函共达23 件，约3 万余字。这充分体现了他诲人不倦的崇高美德，也体现出他与我之间一种诚挚的师生般情谊。遗憾的是，有些重要问题未能按吴老要求做出改正，或进一步深入研究，有负厚望，至今深为愧悔。在这批信函中，吴老有许多真知灼见，我一直妥为保存。如今哲人已萎，睹物思人，眼泪潸然，悲伤难已。为寄托我的怀念和感激之情，特将全部信函，汇编成《吴承明教授关于传统经济的若干论述》的学术资料，加以发表，以惠同仁。此次整理，信函中开头一段中的繁文客套，一律删除，只保留与后文有直接关联的文字。结尾部分也都删除，只保留全部正文。信函按时间先后排列。不妥之处，请读者指正。

方行　2011 年 7 月 25 日

方行（1926~2014），中国社会科学院经济研究所研究员。

一

商人支配生产"成了真正的资本主义生产方式的障碍",是专指包买商制度而言的,因为它不破坏而是竭力保存旧的生产方式,即小生产。"真正的资本主义"是由小生产者分化而来的,即"两条途径"中的第一条。这是由于商业资本(脱离生产)"独立"发展的性质决定的。列宁说,这种独立发展"阻碍着农民的分化"(《列宁全集》第3卷,第154页)。

包买商制度下,生产仍然是简单再生产,不是扩大再生产。生产者的目的是求生不是求富。并且,由于商人资本的多变性,在一个地方一个行业变为不利时,商人可迅速转入别的地方别的行业。

只是在有一个不断扩大的大市场的情况下,商人才要求改变生产方式。但第一步只是在商品加工过程中,如棉布流通中的染、踹。在有新生产方式的竞争的情况下,这一步可走得较远;例如由于有外国机器缫丝业的竞争,丝商才由收购生丝改为收购生茧,然后租厂雇工加工。茶也是这样。

不过,在商人雇主(或商人雇工)的形式下,就谈不到"障碍"了,因为它已改变或部分改变了旧的生产方式。然而,如原稿中所分类,那种临时性的、季节性的农产品加工和贩运商设立的作坊是不同的。前者,劳动者仍是小生产者,不是无产者。后者,已多少具有工人身份。这条路一发展,就是三重过渡中的第一重:"商人直接成为工业家",原是很好的一条路。

可是,这条路很难。在欧洲,照马克思说,这条路特别是在"奢侈品工业中","这种工业连原料和工人一起都是由商人从外国输入的"(《资本论》第3卷,第375页)。在中国,最典型的是后来(20世纪30年代)的橡胶业。在早期,只有丝厂。所以,实际上这条路多是半通不通的。

(至于盐商、鸦片商、钱庄老板投资开纱厂、面粉厂,那不是上述意义的"商人直接成为工业家",而是在商业"积累货币资本"意义上的作用。)

商人雇主(商人雇工)虽谈不到"障碍",其积极作用也很有限。这是由前资本主义商人资本的性格决定的。其性格是"独立存在"、独立运动(独立于生产),而关键是这种独立运动是以不等价交换为基础,有较高利润。尽管商人已有雇工,乃至开设加工作坊,他主要还是商人,这种性格未变。这种性格和利润结构，实际是扼制资本主义生产方式的。这种扼制，在橡胶业中非常明显。现代化大橡胶厂，几乎都是橡胶商号创办的。但在创办后，他们要求由商号控制厂的生产和分配，在控制不了时，仍要求由商号包销或独家经销，到最后才不得不结束商号，并入工厂，这时商人才成为工业家。

"在资本主义生产中，商人资本从它原来的独立存在，下降为一般投资的一个特殊要素，而利润的平均化，又把它的利润率化为一般的平均水平。"（《资本论》第3卷，第366页）这就是困难之所在。显然，当商人资本不只是经营商业，并且支配了生产时，这种"下降"和转化就尤其困难了。在有支配生产的商业中（各种包买主、附有作坊的中药商、有砻坊的米商等），大约到1936年也还没下降多少。

总之，商人资本的存在和发展到一定的水平，本身就是资本主义生产方式发展的前提（《资本论》第3卷，第365页）这是不容怀疑的。商人资本所以有这种积极作用，在于（1）它积累货币财富；（2）它开拓大市场，而不是因为它必然采取新的生产方式。商业资本的发展，使生产朝着交换价值发展，对旧生产方式起着或多或少的解体作用，这也是不容置疑的，但是这种解体作用有多大，首先并不取决于商业资本本身。至于用什么生产方式代替它，更是不取决于商业本身。

何以阻碍过渡？首先是分析（前资本主义）商人资本的本质，它是古老的资本形式，但它只有资本剥削的形式，没有生产的形式。封建社会商人资本的发展，是以小生产为基础的，这种商人资本的发展，不反映生产方式的改变。商人支配生产仍是剩余农产品的交换，而不是（像资本主义商业那样）全部商品的交换。

其次，商人资本支配生产，一般并不要求改变（它所支配的生产的）生产方式。这是因为它有广泛的活动余地来剥削小生产者，在这些生产（农产品加工）中，利用农民家庭和农闲劳动最有利。并且在一个行业或一个地方变为不利时，商人资本多变的本性，可以迅速转移到别的地区和别的行业。只是在有一个不断扩大的大市场（如海外市场）的条件下，商人资本才要求改变生产方式，由小生产变为扩大再生产（工场手工业），以满足这个大市场的需要。即使在这种条件下，也往往是因为有外在的竞争，商人才不得不如此。例如，由于海外市场上丝厂所产丝的价格远高于手工缫丝，丝商才由收购生丝改为收购生茧，再租厂加工。

前资本主义商业原是独立生产、独立活动的。商人支配生产并不改变，并且加强了它独立活动的力量。而资本主义则是产业资本支配商业资本，商人变成奴仆。"在资本主义生产中，商人资本从它原来的独立存在，下降为一般投资的一个特殊要素。"（《资本论》第 3 卷，第 366 页）转变为产业资本的分离部分。显然，商人支配生产愈厉害，这种下降和转变就愈困难。

前资本主义商业，是从不等价交换中获取利润的。资本主义则要求等价交换，"把它（商人资本）的利润率化为一般的平均水平"（同上）。在商人支配生产的情况下，它会用不等价交换保护落后的生产方式，这也造成过渡的困难。

"起初是商业利润决定产业利润，只是在资本主义生产方式确立，生产者自己变成商人之后，商业利润才被归结为"平均利润（《资本论》第 3 卷，第 320 页）。这个过程恐怕到 1930 年代还未完成。商人支配生产在这里起着推迟的作用。

商人雇工（作坊）的形式，在一定程度上改变了旧的生产方式。其改变程度，决定于雇工的数目和雇佣形式。在主要是临时性、季节性的情况下，生产者仍然是农民，而不是无产者。在主要是农产品加工的情况下，加工的价值是有限的，商人基本上还是商人。但是不同商品情况是不同的。例如酿酒、制纸已不是简单的加工，而是制造了。

从支配形式说，丝织业和踹坊是不同的。丝织业中，（1）商人支配个体机户、络工、手艺人（这三种人都是家庭劳动者），这是主要的一类。不过支配这三种人的有的不是商人，而是工场手工业主。（2）商人支配小作坊（有雇工的机户）。（3）商人自设作坊，雇工生产。

对丝织业，应说明此已有了雇工生产的小作坊、工场手工业，但仍以商人支配生产为主，即以（1）为主，因为，机户大都是一户一机。

至于踹坊，不是独立作坊，不同于（2），也不是商人所设，不同于（3）。它是介乎这两者之间的"包头"制。还应说明，染坊大概也类此，因无材料，从略。

踹坊，很有点像"（五）贩运商人兼营生产加工"一类，只是它已不是农产品加工了。

注：对讨论商人支配生产问题的来信。1982 年 2 月，系吴老来函时间，下同。

二

什么是市镇？第 9 页讲市镇的功能，它是农村产品外销的起点，又是输入农村商品的终点，即集散市场，以下三页都讲这种功能。我赞成这个看法。这是从商品流通理论上讲的，商品流通需要各级市场，各级市场功能不同。由于市镇的主要功能是集散商品，故趋向专业化。市镇专业化趋向比城市大得多，大城市多不专业化。台湾刘石吉研究了江南 395 个市镇，有桑蚕丝织市镇 25 个，棉花棉布市镇 52 个，米粮市镇 13 个，铁市 3 个，陶、靛各 2 个，刺绣 1 个。

但本文第 6 页所下市镇的定义却不是这样，而定义为"商贾贸易"。这是"商贾所集谓之镇"（正德《姑苏志》）的说法，用店铺多少来区分市镇与墟集。我不赞成这个定义。集散商品不完全靠坐商，而店铺不一定是集散作用。

另外还有两种市镇理论。

一是以人口（户）数为断，所谓"人烟凑集之处谓之市镇"（弘治《吴江县志》）。因市镇之设本为治安收税，地方志书载市镇始于《元丰九域志》，前此无有。唐以 500 人为上镇，300 人为中镇，原指军；宋废军将，留镇监，其职务就是"主烟火征商"了。这个定义的好处是把市镇和建置联系起来，事实上我们统计市镇数只有依靠建置，历朝发展情况也靠建置。按人口定义，似与经济无关。其实不然。因经济学上有个城乡关系，城市经济与乡村经济大不同，两者对立矛盾，现代化就是城市化。但两者之间还有个中间层。晚近社会学家称为"似城聚落"（City-like Settlement），它半似城市，半属乡村；生活文化上如此，经济上也是半城半乡。现在我们讲社会主义市镇经济学，多是从这个观点出发。用于研究经济史，如吴柏均研究江南，取 100～500 户市镇 6 个，1000～5000 户市镇 12 个，万户以上的 6 个。因他研究粮食供销，与人口关系密切。

另一理论，是把市镇作为一定范围（区域）的经济中心，它多在交通枢纽，有经济集中和向边区扩散的功能。这是根据"中心地理论"（Central Place Theory），是晚近经济地理学通行的理论，演化为卫星城理论。台湾的沙学俊、张秋实，我们的詹小洪都是用这个理论研究市镇。其好处是把市镇的作用同区域经济联系起来。不能全国去任意挑选例子，而要一个大区、一个大区地去研究本区市镇的作用，研究其水平。我们现在打破条条块块，建立以大城市为中心的经济协作区，就是根据这个理论。

本文第三节封建政府扶持小农一节，与全文不甚协调。本文是讲小农再生产的市场条件，这些市场，无论是墟集、市镇或雇工、资金市场，都是自发形成的，不是政府部署的。政府只是治安收税，以至和买勒索，恐怕利少弊多。至于政府的仓储、救灾等，不构成"市场条件"，也不是为了小农的再生产。讲市场条件，可提到政府的干预（收税等），在清代，干预不太大。

本文结束语不够明确。结束语主要作了反面文章，说上述种种不可夸大。而未说明市场在农民再生产中究竟起多大作用。文中说："市场是小农经济再生产实现的必要条件"（2 页 8 行），小农是通过市场"以实现需求和供给的平衡，持续自己的再生产"（3 页 1～2 行），好像没有市场，就不能再生产，农民就只能活一年了。本来，所有农业生产都是再生产，因为小农经济中，再生产的条件，即 I（v＋m）＝Ⅱc 根本不存在，不必要，有了市场，才有这个条件。因此，在结束语中，就应明确，到了清代，小农经济已是市场经济了，或是半市场经济了，或是以自给生产为主、市场为辅的经济了。在国外，马若孟（河北农村）、Evelyn Rawski（湖南、福建）都认为是依靠市场的经济。黄宗智（山东、河北）是分为市场、半市场、自给三类。地区不同，一地区内作物品种不同，其情况也是不同的。

注：对拙作《清代前期农村市场的发展》的意见，文载《清代经济论稿》（本书 2010 年由天津古籍出版社出版——编者）。1987 年 3 月 19 日。

三

本文的基本论点是"封建经济是自然经济和商品经济的结合"。基本方法是把生产者划分为自给型、半自给型、交换型甲、交换型乙四种类型。四种类型户的消长或"分配比例",决定"结合"的程度,即封建早期和后期自然经济与商品经济的发展变化。

从方法论上说,划分四种类型是从微观上来考察,四者有不同的质。进一步是上升到宏观层次,考察全社会经济是什么质,这里只提"结合",未明确中国封建社会究竟是什么质,是什么经济占统治地位。

从方法论上说,宏观的质,不是微观相加的和。宏观系统的运行,决定于各微观的行为。在这里,微观中的自给性生产(包括赋税生产)是宏观层次的稳定因素;而其商品性生产(交换行为)是宏观层次的变动(振荡)因素,它给予宏观新的质。一般说,变动因素到了宏观领域,有加强趋势(放大效应)。例如第四类农户占 10%,到了宏观,其行为效果也许是20%。但另一方面,稳定因素有很强的惰性,而上层建筑是保护稳定因素的。这是控制原理,微观上自发的东西(受自然规律支配),到了宏观,就变成受控的东西。封建上层建筑(政府和学者们)犹然,所以总是重本抑末、重农轻商。

自然经济和商品经济,在微观生产上是互补作用,缺一不可。但两者的质不同。自给性生产是旧质,在宏观上表现为土地权利,在上层建筑上表现为封建主义,其代表是地主阶级。商品生产是新质,在宏观上表现为货币权利,在上层建筑上是"钱神论",其代表是商人。所以到了宏观领域,特别是上层建筑中,两者的互补作用成为次要的,矛盾变成主要的。

生产是决定的因素,因而任何封建社会不能取消商品生产,而是不同程度地容纳商品生产。所谓不同程度,同制度(控制)有很大关系,领主制下小,地主制下大;分裂地区小,统一帝国大;保守派政权下小,开明派政权下大;等等。但是,容纳商品生产到一定程度,新质超过旧质,货币权利超过土地权利,尽管君主、大臣仍然存在,它已不是封建社会,至少不是典型的封建社会,而是资本主义或半资本主义社会了。

从方法论上说，划分类型的办法是可用的。20 世纪 50 年代农业合作化时，即将合作社按经营情况分为三类。60 年代考察农业经济，也是分为三类，一类户增多，三类户减少，表现进步。近年来仍有万元户、贫困户的用法，不过更多是引进了一些纯宏观的概念，如人均产值、人均国民收入、积累率、投资率等。这些是"纯宏观的概念"，因为用在微观上毫无意义。阶级社会，贫富悬殊，何来"人均"？许多部门或单位，没有积累，或没有投资，何来"率"？它们纯是社会（宏观）指标。这类指标的运用，是根据"整体不等于部分之和"这一原理。再如"粮食商品率""农产品商品率""农村消费结构"这些概念也是纯宏观的，用在微观上没有意义，如独立手工业户，根本不发生"率"的问题。

现在问题是，中国封建社会，例如乾隆（十八世纪）时究竟是自然经济还是商品经济？我的看法是由近及远。我认为，鸦片战争后，农村自然经济解体这一过程是确实存在的，为此，在《中国资本主义发展史》中设了两节，一节讲 1840～1920 年的解体，一节讲 20 世纪 30 年代的解体。30 年代初，发生一次中国社会性质论战和一次中国农村社会性质论战，我认为，两次论战的结论是正确的，其结论之一即农村仍是自然、半自然占统治地位。解放以后，（十一届）三中全会决议直到最近赵紫阳的报告，仍是这种看法。1952 年，征购粮食 665 亿斤，返销 102 亿斤，商品粮约占产量 3088 亿斤的 18%。30 年代到 1952 年，人口是低率增长，所以 30 年代粮食的商品率也不过如此。30 年代经济作物产值约为粮食的 37%，以 80% 作为商品，全部农作物的商品率不过 40%。乾隆年间到 20 世纪 30 年代人口也无大膨胀，经济作物远不及 30 年代，故商品率会更低。

注：对我一个讨论提纲的意见。此提纲未形成文章。观点在其他文章中引用过。1987 年 11 月 12 日。

四

文章我反复读过，文章写得很好，用过深思。文章的最大好处是贯彻辩证唯物主义。所提各项观点，我都同意。下面是我自己的一些想法，供参考。

全文是论封建社会中自然经济和商品经济的结合，两者的互补作用和发展过程。因此，题目似可放宽，改为"封建社会的自然经济和商品经济"。

这还有一层意思：在五六年前，即孙冶方同志批我们社会主义理论中的"自然经济论"时，自然经济是个重要问题，目前已不是重要问题。目前，商品经济的研究是重要问题了。历史研究总是为现实服务的。

第2页说，自然经济"本身不具有特定的社会性质"，可存在于各种社会。商品经济更是这样，从奴隶社会到社会主义社会都有。历史家的任务在辨明其不同的质，不是说有买有卖就是商品经济。

第2页说，在历史过程中，"自然经济具有一系列阶段性的部分质变"。商品经济更是这样。但是，现在要研究的不是在不同社会中的质变（如社会主义的商品经济不同于资本主义的商品经济），而是在同一社会，即封建社会中，它有什么"部分质变"。

文中对自然经济的部分质变并未讲清楚。按照第6～10页"三层次"和"四种类型"的说法（我同意这种说法），自然经济在各层次或类型中的作用是不同的。如在自给型中起主导作用，在交换型中仅是辅助作用了。这也可说是部分质变，但究竟是量变。商品经济就不同了，它变化很明显，以商品论：物物交换、剩余品交换、小商品交换、大商品（＝资本主义商品）交换，是截然不同的，是质变。

第12～13页一段似乎说，在封建社会中，随着生产力的发展，自然经济有一个发展或完善的过程。这点我还有点怀疑。这是从以家庭为单位的生产说的，生产力发展，可生产更多样的东西。但从社会上说，自然经济是否发展了？就商品经济来说，则无疑问，是发展的，日趋完善的。

我认为，研究封建社会中自然经济的发展或衰退，已经不是很重要的问题；重要的是研究它的反面，即商品经济，究竟发展到什么程度，更重要的是什么性质。我提出"不完全意义的商品"，强调剩余品生产、小商品生产、大商品生产之不同，原因在此。

我觉得，大商品生产即资本主义生产，才是商品经济史上的分水岭，或大的质变。那就是资本主义了，但未必是机器大工业；在西欧，16世纪已进入真正的商品经济，也就是工场手工业和重商主义时代。这有两个意义：(1) 不要以为市场上农产品多了，就是"变自给经济为商品经济"了，还要看那些农产品是怎样生产出来的。（2）不要以为机械化才是商品经济，粮食专业户还是手工为主，已是完全意义的商品生产了。

文中把独立手工业户（包括城乡）和小农并论，其区别在于自然经济成分或补充之大小。这点值得商榷。西方的行会（＝封建）手工业者在城郊都有小块地种粮种菜，但他们已是小商品生产者。我国的手工业者在家乡有地，现在的专业户定义是70%收入靠专业，并非100%。封建社会独立手工业者马克思称为生产的"第二个历史阶段"，"第二所有制"，以区别于农户、农民家庭手工业。自给经济在这里已无足轻重，其"补充"作用限于生活资料。当然，文中用"痕迹"还是很好。总之，小商品生产者与农户大不相同。

第21页"大量出现的不是典型的小商品生产者"和下句"具有一定的专业分工的小商品生产者"，分别何在？我看，独立手工业者是典型的小商品生产者，尽管没脱离土地。

第28页的地方小市场，所谓使用价值的交换，不排斥经商人之手。没有商人经手的交换，在封建社会墟集上怕已是很少见了，有无商人中介似不重要。当然，地方小市场上的交换有不同性质，有的是剩余品，有的只是余缺调剂、品种调剂，是所有农户都能生产、因偶然原因而未生产或少生产的。这见恩格斯在《资本论》第3卷中的跋。

文中把自然经济和商品经济看作是互相结合、互相补充的（指在封建社会），共同促成封建经济的协调和发展。从历史上看是这样。不过，自然经济和商品经济究竟是不同质的，对立的。前者基于土地权利，主张使用价值生产；后者基于货币权利，注重交换价值生产。两者并不是完全和谐的。我们说：中国地主制经济（比西方领主制经济）能"容纳"更多的商品经济，这正是宋元以前中国封建社会发达的原因之一。但这"容纳"并非有意地调和、利用。历史上，人们不是抑商，就是轻商，究竟是末，不是本，因为它对封建经济来说是异质的东西。系统论的理论，有异质的东西才能进步。商品经济代替自然经济是历史的必然，问题在于代替的程度和时间早晚，包括量的比重，也包括质的变化。马克思说，"中世纪"是剩余品的交换。"中世纪"一般指9至14世纪，这以后已不是中世纪了。15世纪，地理大发现，海外殖民，已是完全的商品经济。在中国，即弘治、嘉靖，还不能这么说，商品经济还不算发达，恐怕还是以剩余品为主。这也是中国封建社会长期延续的原因之一。

注：对拙作《封建社会的自然经济与商品经济》所提意见，文载《中国封建经济论稿》。1987 年 10 月 25 日。

五

封建领主的家庭消费，不限于生存、享受、发展资料。分封土地的前提是提供军事义务。军队是领主家计中首要的支出，而兵器、甲胄、车骑也是较早商品化的东西。领主愈小（如骑士级），军费在其家计中所占比重愈大。较大领主都是一级政权。因而，教会、司法、行政以及官吏、牧师的费用都列入领主的家计簿。领主剥削农民，同时也向农民提供一定的服务：社会治安、宗教生活、评议诉讼以至交通、货币、市场等便利；这些服务都可计价（当然远小于地租量）。这是领主经济内部的交换（非物质交换）。

经济学用抽象法，把物质的生产、交换、消费从整个社会生活中抽象出来考察。于是治经济史者也只研究地租和生存、享受、发展消费，未免把领主经济"简单化"。若从历史学、整体论、系统论的观点考察，情况就不同了。

地主制经济中，地主作为一个阶级，也负有军事、司法、行政的义务和同样的服务。不过，这种功能和行为已脱离地主家庭，而社会化了，不见于地主的家计簿。孤立地研究地主家庭生活，就看不见。宏观经济学的兴起，就是要补足这个缺陷。经济史就其本来意义说，应是以宏观经济为基础。

总之，我的看法是：生产和交换是人类经济生活的基本行为（恩格斯）。从历史看，交换早于生产。生产和交换不仅是物质的，还有非物质的，随着社会进化，非物质的愈来愈重要。任何社会，物质的和非物质的生产的商品化、社会化，都是社会进步的标志。中国地主制经济中，这种商品化、社会化的程度高于西欧领主制，这是古中国人的骄傲。不过，商品化、社会化的发展，主要的不是决定于生产关系，主要的是决定于生产力。资本主义社会，商品化、社会化程度很高，那是由于生产力很高。社会主义社会，如果生产力不高（初级阶段），也还得致力于商品化、社会化。

注：对拙作《封建社会地主的自给经济》所提意见，文载《中国封建经济论稿》。1988 年 2 月 15 日。

六

一、湘川粮食生产的小农与江南织布桑蚕的小农是两种类型，完全正确。但孰优孰劣，未可厚薄。作者似有厚此薄彼之意。如第 13 页谓江南小农"其商品量是有限的"，未必是。按理，粮食生产是有限的（土地限制），手工业则可无限（如从北方运原料棉花来）。作者主要是从积累着眼：湘川小农有积累，江南小农则无。此亦无征。按理，同样劳动投于加工业能创造更大价值。事实上，江南小农还是比湘川小农要富些。并且，湘川余粮之能运出，正因为江南从事手工业（本来江南粮食是自给的）。以湘川之米易江南之布（和盐），优势在后者。依第 38 页，江南小农原也可上升为地主，后来不行了。湘川是开发较晚，也有这一天。江南小农手工业始终是副业，有种种原因，是须另外探讨。所以，本文专研川湘，似不必同江南比较优劣。

二、川湘是押租最发达地区，文中论押租非常精彩。押租有两重性，本文似乎偏重它是"地租之外的又一层剥削"（第 28 页）、"使佃农的积累转化为剥削农民的资产"（第 39 页）这一面。对其另一面论述不够。这另一面是它保障佃权，减轻常租负担。文中也指明，"押重租轻"在押租"初起之时"就是如此（第 30 页）。也提到对缴大额押租的佃农等于"买田"（第 33 页）。据我看，对缴小额押租的佃农，也是因祸得福。地主即田主，按年收租，这是封建古例。今要押租，减常租，表示地主地位没落了。急需钱用，只好减少经常收入；等于借债，每年所减之租即债息。从佃农说，地位上升了，等于有钱放债，年取其利。

押租不是永佃。永佃制行于江南，四川没有，湖南似也没有。但，湖南有换约之例，即缴押租，一佃十年，或二十年，或三十年，到期换约（《湖南通志》卷四九），这与永佃何异？有 10～30 年的佃权（我们现在仅给 15

年），佃农即可垦荒、水利、改良土壤，增加生产。永佃是个进步，因为土地所有权和使用权分离。文中也有佃农转佃他人之例（第 35 页），以及"有押无租"之说（第 31 页），这不就是永佃吗？我看，此曰押租，彼曰永佃，其实有共同之处。具体建议是：论押租，可提到永佃。

注：对拙作《清代前期湖南四川的小农经济》所提意见，文载《中国史研究》1991 年第 2 期。1990 年 8 月 1 日。

七

地租率是租额占产量的百分比。西方则用租额占土地投资（地价）的百分比。刘克祥讲近代，是两者并用（租额占地价 5% ~ 10%）。本文已有定义，自可不管地价。但由于中国早就土地自由买卖，地价确会影响地租率。证明材料是太平天国战争时。清前期，似未见。

本文（一）节的概念是：由地主供牛种发展到佃农自备牛种，对半分的地租率实际是提高了。第（二）节的概念是：由于复种、春作增加，对半分的地租率实际上是降低了。这个降低是写在"定额租"一节中，实际上分成制地区春花也是不交租的，也应降低。

那么，清初到乾嘉，地租率究竟是提高趋势还是降低趋势呢？

地租率提高或降低的原因何在？本文屡提农业生产力提高了，它是地租率增加的原因（第 13 页），也是地租率降低的原因（第 18 页）。农业生产力的提高没有证明。

生产力的提高可作分析（如无证明的话）：（1）投入增加了，即劳动力、肥料、排灌（水浇田）的增加。这主要在南方（北方仅增井灌）。这应该反映为南方地租率的提高或降低大于北方。（2）复种指数提高，经济作物扩大，高产作物推广（包括麦田变稻田）。这应该反映为地租率下降，因为地租是按正田粮食计算的。

还有一节，（3）清代农业生产力的增长得力于湖南、湖北、江西等丘陵地、山地和湖田的开发，四川的开发，西北的放垦和东北的放垦，因而耕地面积增大。这种增大不都是劣等土地，但即使有 1/3 是劣等地（新垦地相当于劣等地），也要增加级差地租Ⅰ。另外，江南原有的好地的改良，尤其是施肥，也会增加级差地租Ⅱ。这都是理论，未经证明。级差地租的存在以农产品有生产价格为前提，我以为，乾嘉时多少有了一些生产价格，因为粮价的变动是全国性的。四川、湖南、东北粮食流往江南。

第23～24页一段，押租增加了地租率。我想这种增加有保障佃农佃权的作用（十年到二三十年），农民可以投资土地，对农民不一定是不利的。

第（四）节的结论，我完全同意，地租率的变动十分复杂，要用种种影响地租率的因素去分析，不能用地主阶级的贪婪来说明一切。

最后还有一个问题。对半分的地租率似乎从古到今没什么改变（尽管实际地租率有变）。并且，似乎也是中外一律，尤其像法国这种小农经济占优势的国家，也是对半分。那么，究竟是什么原因造成一半对一半呢，难道只是为了简单易算吗？我的想法是，在手工劳动的农业中，土地价值和劳动价值大体相当，而资本投入并不重要，主佃双方都投入一点。大的资本投入是由国家或领主用徭役或赋税执行，与地租无关。

注：对拙作《中国封建地租率》所提意见，文载《中国封建经济论稿》（商务印书馆，2004）。1992年2月14日。

八

大作从封建制度特别是赋役制度和租佃制度的演变上，解述农民逐步获得经营的独立性，论证完整清晰。

在"自由迁徙"一节，尚有历代移民实边、徙富豪等强迫迁徙，其数甚大。此虽非由于"制度"，但是由于"政策"，同样妨碍人民的居住自由。在"自由占有土地"一节，对于定额租、押租、永佃权之作用，论述綦详，而于三者的史实，介绍简单。此三者为中国所独有。西方佃农之自由，来源于货币租之出现，中国则在实物租形式内部，完成了西方货币租的功能和解放农民。其妙即在于定额、押租、永佃。定额不知始于何时，但乾隆时已占主流（60%以上）。押租起于明中叶，由于押租是付货币，其意义不下于定额。永佃有谓始于宋者，不可靠。永佃在西方亦早有之

（99 年租期），而中国独有者为田面权之买卖，这才有了革命的意义，非西方可比。

本文主要是历述史实，农民经营自由是破除种种制度上限制之结果。至于何以有种种限制性的制度，非本文研究范围。第 3 页中有"封建社会中，农民处于被统治、被剥削的地位……"数语，含有种种限制农民自由的制度在加强剥削之意，我意未必然也。如限制迁徙自由，恐怕以 50 ~ 60 年代的"农转非"更为典型。又"均田制"有保证赋役的作用，但非主要目的。"征实"制度是市场不发达情况下的必然效果。国家或政府在历史上有不同的功能，统治者制定的制度和法令，或社会习俗，主要是适应这些功能的，而秩序和稳定常是第一位的考虑。"凡是存在的都是合理的"，黑格尔这话是从客观上说的。"凡是存在的都是不合理的"，马克思这个意思是从发展上说的。恩格斯比较全面："今天是真理的东西都有它将来是错误的方面，今天是错误的东西都有它从前是真理的方面，因而它从前是合理的。"（所有引文都非原文，大意而已）这个问题非常复杂。我建议本文不去讨论历史上各种制度产生的原因或目的，只讲其演变对农民自由的关系。因而，第 3 页这几句话可删改。

历史的发展是有曲折（或周期）的。以农民的自由来说，也不是逐步自由的线性过程，而是有起伏的，当然总的说是进步的。魏晋南北朝就是一个大的起伏，每个朝代又有小的起伏。本文既是研究农民自由化的全过程，对于大的起伏似应提及，表明农民之获得独立性经营并不是一帆风顺。有些具体的自由，好像是得而复失、失而复得。事实上，统观全文就有这种感觉，细心的读者也会领悟，不过未点明而已。我觉得不妨点明。

本文的结论，即第 43 页，"农民自主经营的能力越强，就越有利于农业生产资料配置的优化。清代前期……（农业高峰）就与……自由私有者的地位完全分不开的"。我完全赞成这个结论。不过，这个论点，以至本文全篇，都是从农户，从微观经济上立论的，而制度，往往是宏观的。这就是矛盾。从本文主旨说，不必涉及宏观（因不是论整个农业的发展），论制度时也仅取其限制或解除农民自由的条款。但第 44 页最后一句，"与西方产权理论在这个问题上是相通的"，似可不提。因西方产权理论，属于当代制度学派，是一种新古典（微观）与凯恩斯（宏观）相结合的理论，而且其所谓"产权"与马克思所说的"所有制"不是一回事。这里虽加上了"在这个问题上"的限制词，也可能引起一些名词解释上的麻烦。

注：对拙作《中国封建社会农民的经营独立性》所提意见，文载《中国封建经济论稿》。1994 年 10 月 23 日。

九

拜读新作，大开眼界。湖南、四川农户之"规模经济"优于江浙之农工结合，户均收入多于江浙三四成，读之令我震惊。这样看来，江南"优势"造成劣势，整个中国小农经济的理论都须从新考虑。

其中，有个粮价问题，文中比较农户收入每石米的价格：浙江为 1330 文，江苏为 1750 文，湖南为 2000 文，四川为 1700 文（按二谷一米计）。湖南米价高于江浙，令人莫解。因湘米东运也。若将湖南米价与江浙相等计，则湖南优势略失，四川米价系用道光时价，道光时苏州米价在 2500 文以上，若江浙亦用道光价，四川的优势也很小。湖南、四川米运江浙，运费及其他费用不会少于 30%。若将江浙米价减 30% 作为产地价，则湖南、四川农户的收入均小于江浙农户，结果就反过来了。

比较农户收入，自以净收入即净产值为佳，文中已多次提及。这就需要计算成本。章谦存、顾炎武称每亩需千文，这不包括劳力投入，而劳力投入最重要。江南劳力投入已有人研究过。江南丝、布的成本，似不难估计。只是湖南、四川农业成本，不知是否有资料可用。

所谓规模经济，是指扩大生产规模可以降低成本。这在同一地区较易比较。如上户田多，可生活裕如。有材料说，富户农产有余，不从事副业，与其自织，不如买布。若在不同地区，因土地、气候、价格不同，很难作规模比较。所谓适度规模，指超过一定规模，需雇工生产，成本反会增大。也是同一地区，较易比较。湖南、四川种稻 20 亩，是否适度，要有当地比较材料才好。

总之，我觉得说江浙农户调整生产结构是对的。说湖南、四川在农户是规模效益，似乎理由不够充分。

若设经济发展或进步，应是由于分工和专业化提高了劳动生产率，而分工和专业化则是由于在市场交换中可获得比较优势的收益。江南农户治丝织布，仍是副业，并未专业化。但丝布商品性强，能从市场上获得比较优势的利益（尽管乾隆以来这种优势已下降）。也有少数是丝、布专业户，但属无地的贫困户。湖南、四川的农家，恐怕不能说是种稻的专业户。文中（第36页）说"其粮食生产已基本上商品化，并已实现了专业化生产"，似乎勉强。这两省产米总在1亿石以上，运往江南者最多不超过1500万石，其中不少可能是租谷。即使农户能在市场上获得优势收益，那也是很少的。地区专业化不等于农户专业化。地区专业化可能由于自然条件，农户专业化指从市场上获得额外收益。

江浙农户力农致富买田者，确实不如湖南、四川之多。这是因为江浙人稠地少，而湖南、四川尚有余田可开发。从经济上说，是江浙田价高，农家即有积蓄，亦难置田。但是，我只有乾隆朝江浙田价近30个数据，同朝湖南田价30多个数据，而湖南田价平均高于江浙近一倍，大惑不解。又四川田价几乎无数据可寻。不过，据钱咏所说，无锡田价增长速度大于粮价增长速度。如果湖南田价真是高于江浙一倍，那么，有20亩地的湘农，比有10亩地的江苏农民，资产要大四倍，富裕得多了。至于缫丝、织布等设备，价值有限，算不上什么家产。

也可得出这样的结论：18世纪，江南农业已达到或接近古典经济学所说"增长终极"，农民只能过着黄宗智所说的"糊口经济"。而在湖南、四川，农业仍能增长，农民仍可发家致富，扩大再生产。

不过，就18世纪而论，江南仍是全国最富庶之区，所以赋税甲天下。若说当时的江南，社会最富而农民最穷，似有点说不过去。就是工业化国家，富了城市，农民也非更穷。江南是商品经济最发达的地区，农民从市场上所获额外收益肯定高于他省。农民治丝织布，终岁劬劳，未必没有剩余。有剩余不买地，因为地太少，且地价上涨速度高于粮价上涨速度，买地不如买粮。他们不能买地向扩大农业发展，但可向扩大工业，尤其是向商业发展，商帮迭起。或向仕进及文教等业发展。社会史研究（主要是日本人），18世纪江南士绅阶层膨胀，掌握了部分政治和经济权利，被称为"江南模式"。若说官富、商富、绅富，而农民愈穷（比湖南农民还穷），用阶级剥削理论也说得通。不过长期看，官、商、绅还是由农分化出来的。

本文引起我震惊，但一时脑子还转不过弯来。但无碍。本文是篇创新之作，也是实证文章，一论惊人，重新检讨小农经济理论将自兹始。因此，我主张应急发表，在学术论坛上可起一石激起千层浪的作用。发表时题目（原稿无题）可小些，如"江浙与湖南、四川农民收入"之类。小题大做、由实入虚，是谓之"史笔"。

注：对我关于"江浙与湖南、四川农民收入研究"的意见。1995 年 6 月 10 日。

十

结论部分，第 8 页"自工业革命以来"，似可改为"明清以来"（在西方是重商主义以来），又第 9 页"随具体条件而定，并无规律可寻"一语，建议删去。

弟还建议，文末还可加上一段，讲经济史研究的任务。弟以为，所谓"市场经济的萌芽"当自嘉万开始。嘉万以来流通的作用，应为经济史研究的一个重点。所谓流通的作用，又集中表现在资源利用的合理化，或资源配置的优化。也就是说，在没有技术革命（工业化）的条件下，仍有改进资源配置的可能，这种可能的实现，主要是通过流通驱动或市场机制。桑基鱼塘是出口贸易拉动。陈春声研究乾隆时广东耕地只要有半数种稻，即足够全省人口食用；但广东却成为缺粮省，因种植经济作物（乃至葵）有更大的市场效益，这非是由于出口，主要由于内贸。江南尤其苏南的资源利用有所改进，主要是内贸拉动。西南尤其东北的开发亦然，东北大豆主销关内。弟以为，类此的研究，应为经济史一个重点。但是，直到外国入侵，中国迄未能完成向市场经济的转变，则是因为诸多"逆流"，阻碍了市场经济萌芽的发展。"逆流"主要出在政治性制度和文化思想方面，尤其是康雍乾三朝。三朝属盛世，愈是盛世愈保守。制度尤其是产权和商法方面毫无改变，观念上重本抑末回潮，明末的启蒙思潮被扼杀，至嘉道时才复兴。这应是经济史研究的又一重点。不过。吾兄"漫谈"自不能讲具体史实，只提出把这段流通作为经济史研究的重点而已。

经济学理论是概括"一般",寻找规律。这样概括下来,只能得出明清以来中国社会"停滞",至多是"有增长而无发展"的结论。经济史要讲具体过程,包括一般,也重视特殊,要找出原因,而不去套规律。若就"规律"说,嘉万以后的中国本应走向市场经济的,像桑基鱼塘、丝织手工业的发展才是真正的"一般"。然而,它们却成了"特殊",皆因种种"逆流"所致。

注:对拙作《应当重视对流通的研究》所提意见,文载《中国经济史研究》1997 年第 1 期。1996 年 11 月 16 日。

十一

对大作《提纲》,有不同看法。

《提纲》是论"地主经济",唯有二处称"地主制经济"(第 1 页倒 3 行,第 11 页第 1 行)。中国地主制经济概指租佃制,第 1 页述其特征为"土地买卖,农民经营,实物地租",极精当。而"地主经济"为何?未详。通观全文,是把"地主经济"与"农民经济"相对立而言。"农民经济"当指自耕农经营和佃农经营,那么,"地主经济"应指地主自营(用奴仆或雇工)。那就太小了。第 1 页说"地主经济是主导,农民经济是主体",地主自营太小,主导不起来。第 12 页说"地主经济是封建经济的主体,是决定社会性质的经济形态",这对西欧的领主经济来说是对的,对中国则不合适。

"地主制经济"则不是一种形态,而是一种制度,今称"体制"。制度良窳对经济盛衰有决定性作用。个人或阶级(地主、佃农)的行为受制度约束,制度包括成文的典章也包括不成文的社会规范和礼俗习惯。中国地主制经济的最大特点是它能不断地革新,即第 11 页所说"自我完善"。这应归功于中国的传统文化。西方领主制不能革新,因为他们没有苟日新又日新的传统,只能用休克疗法,使之崩溃。这一点是中国史家应大书特书的。但,这种制度的改革不能归功于地主。其中如税制的由丁而地,劳动之由人身依附而自由择佃，所有者之由贵族地主而绅衿地主而庶民地主，地租之由分成而定额而与所有权分离（永佃），所有这些变革都是违反地主利益的。改革家或体改委中不少出身地主，但他们不是代表地主行事，而是以天下为己任的开明人士。

从国家（政府）的功能来说，中国政府一般是有效率的。无论是维持社会秩序，或是劝农桑、兴水利，或是教育英才、平准赈灾，都是西方神圣罗马帝国或王权时代的君主所不及的。这也要归功于中国传统文化所形成的政治制度，而不能归功于地主。非地主出身的君主一旦掌权，也要实行仁政。否则，西方的君主都是地地道道的领主，为什么政府无能呢？

在社会发展中，会出现一种非政府的社会力量，参与治理国家。在西方，称为 public sphere，兴于 16、17 世纪，在中国即"乡绅"，始于宋，明渐兴，乾隆为盛。这些人今称"社会精英"，虽多出身地主，但必有较高文化，一般是有功名者，而不是收地租最多者。他们有所成就，不能归功于地主（出身），而要归功于知识，知识就是力量。

《提纲》所列地主四大功绩：垦辟土地；兴修水利；发展商品经济；建立社会保障制度。其中兴修水利和社会保障制度二项属于上述"社会精英"的活动。他们先是辅助政府官吏之不足或失职，如汶上老人之类，继之，有些地方甚至团练代替守备，义学代替官学，义仓代替官仓（西方因官吏大都失职，故社会力量特别重要）。不过，如前所述，他们有所成就不能归功于地主，而要归功于知识。垦辟土地、发展商品经济二项，则属地主的功能。因二者皆需资本，唯地主有资本。但二者又有不同情况。

垦辟土地是地主分内之事，地主就是治地。地主将地租（积累、储蓄）用于垦辟土地（而非用于奢侈消费），功莫大焉，史家应大书特书。至于垸田、山田棚户破坏生态，当另论。至于发展商品经济，不在于第 7 页所说拥奴"千指"或"指千"生产商品，那太小了，而在于经营盐茶丝木和开典当。但这里发生一个资本转化问题，即土地资本转化为商业资本和高利贷资本，转化为货币财产。如第 9 页所说，货币财产和地产是对立的。在西欧，转化为货币财产，地主也变成商人，组织辉格党，或第三等级，与地主阶级对立，实行革命。最后，货币财产战胜土地财产，封建崩溃，实现市场经济。中国则不然，没有出现对立，而是形成"三位一体"，结果，封建没有崩溃，没有近代化。其故，仍在于中国地主制经济能"自我完善"，能容纳商品经济，延长自己的寿命，阻碍革命性变动。这里，好事变成坏事，这也是中国史家要深入追究、大书特书的。

总之，在土地经济上我有点制度学派，论制度不论人，制度有良窳，人则无好坏。租佃制优于领主制，但好的制度中也有利有弊，今日之利，他日成弊，不但要自我完善，而且到一定时候要全面革新。人无好坏，因为人作为经济人都是趋利的。地主得利，不同于其他经济人的，是在平均利润或边际收益之外，还可以多得一些，即级差地租。但级差地租是个客观存在，在资本主义社会、社会主义社会都存在，至于在分配上如何处理，那仍是个制度问题。我国地主制经济也已注意这个问题，如三等九则、折亩等，目的在抵消级差地租，抵消得好，便无所谓剥削。

马克思经济学讲生产、消费、交换、分配，恩格斯经济学讲生产、交换、分配，都不讲剥削。西方经济学也不讲剥削。剥削不是个经济范畴，是个道德范畴。经济学中只有分配制度的合理或不合理，而更多是在再分配上。因为初次分配，无论是按平均利润原则，或按边际收益原则，都是合理的，没说过地主不准收地租，除非是在革命或土改中。

注：对我关于地主制经济论文提纲的意见。1997 年 8 月 15 日。

十二

《清代商人的预买（提要）》第 2 页称：预买"利润最高，实源于投资风险最大"。此语正确，因预买利润高于现货贩运的利润即由于它特有的预买风险。不过，不宜一上来就这样讲。因读者的"利润"概念是指预买的价格与现货价格之差很大。此差价很大，是因为它包括：（1）预付价款的利息；（2）预买风险；（3）利用农民青黄不接、急需现金时的额外压价。这需要先讲明，否则读者会出误会。

过去论述，强调第（3）项剥削。在我看，这种剥削确实存在，但非必是主要的，因为就农民说，解救燃眉之急，不只预卖一途，还有替代方法（如借贷）。否则，不能解释何以到"清后期"预买少了，而为现货交易取代。

其实，这三项都是由于市场不发达而来。如果是现代化市场经济，则（1）商人可在期货市场上买商品，不支付利息，因为期货是到交割时付款，买时只付5%～18%的保证金。（2）买期货的风险可转移给专负担风险的期货商即投机商。对贩运商或生产者来说，期货市场的功能正在于"锁定价格"即避免（转移）风险。（3）买卖双方平等竞争，谁也不能"乘人之危"。

大作指出，清代预买，乾隆间臻于鼎盛，清后期，除造纸外，农产品的预买日益走向衰微，逐渐为现货交易所取代。这点我原来无知，我想应作为历史论文的重点，分析其何以兴，何以衰。

所谓"预买风险"，指一般现货贩运风险（水火、盗贼等）以外的风险，只有一项，即价格预测。农产品价格预测包括年成丰歉和未来市场供需，在现代都是用概率论，以及所谓蛛网理论等；在古代都是凭经验。古穰旱之说用岁星（木星）宫位，不科学，商人也不懂，但商人都知道不会年年丰收。供需之说，包括生产和货币量两个变量，商人也不懂（文人也事后才懂），但也可由经验推测。总之，预测价格，变量很多，即使用概率论，仍风险颇大，凭经验，风险更大。在现代，可在期货市场上转移给别人，在古代则不可避免。故大作"实源于风险最大"之说是正确的。

不过，我们写历史文章，可以事后诸葛亮。大作"清后期"，不知指何时，或指嘉庆以降。我以为，乾隆一朝，市场扩大，人口繁滋，物价虽有波动，总趋势是上升的。物价尤其粮价上升，自有利于预买。嘉庆开始波动，进入19世纪，粮价大跌，我称之为"道光萧条"。跌价自不利于预买。银钱比价大变动亦自嘉庆时始，由于银贵，也不利于预买，因大商人是银本位。再有利息，我据黄冕堂378个案件计算，也是19世纪初陡降，这会使农民不去预买，而转向借贷。我有《十八与十九世纪上叶的市场》一文，尚未发表，辑粮价资料较多，兹附上，供您查阅。又利息卡片二份，亦附上。用毕均请赐还。

至于造纸预买仍盛，不知何解。《史记》《越绝书》范蠡条有文，大意是粮价上升则它物价下降，粮价下降则它物价上升。设货币流通量不变，此说可通。19世纪初是银贵，而非银荒。我无纸价资料，不能证实。一般说，纸的需求弹性远大于粮食，价格下跌当不如粮食之甚。

注：对拙作《清代商人对农民产品的预买》所提意见，文载《中国农史》1998 年第 1 期。1997 年 4 月 28 日。

十三

拜读大作，悉兄对地主制经济的全面观点，我无异议。另有两点意见，供参考。

一、第 3 页下段。自耕农与佃农都有"余额"，差别只在"赋轻租重"。作者认为，先有自耕农，等到有"更高的生产力发展水平"时，才出现佃农。这在历史上无法证实。"令黔首自实田"甚早，秦始皇三十年左右。"耕豪民之田，见税什五"，则不知"始"于何时。"豪民"是最早的地主，而奴隶或农奴变为佃户是很自然的。又作者认为，佃农比自耕农"具有更高劳动生产率"，这一点也无法证实。劳动生产率是按"时均"计算，很难说佃农更强，若说因"赋轻租重"，佃农必须付出更多的劳动，也许合理，那就不是劳动生产率更高了。

二、第 8 页说土地是"一种积累""一种储蓄"，这在常识上说是对的。但用经济学术语说则否。经济学上"积累"指一年的国民收入中用于扩大再生产、基本建设和物资储备的部分，只有这年新垦辟的土地费用才属积累。"储蓄"专指货币形态的非消费部分，也是就一年的国民收入来说的。又据马克思劳动价值论，土地非劳动创造，无价值（只有价格），也难说积累。又"生产基金"是社会主义（苏联）经济学术语，不是对"消费基金"而言，而是对"流通基金"而言，指投入生产领域部分（"流通基金"指投于货币和商品形态部分）。下面，"土地买卖已是……"一句是对的，因为"土地买卖"指一年国民收入的流向，指买卖行为属积累，非指土地本身。

注：这是对我关于地主制经济讨论提纲所提意见。1997 年 12 月 8 日。

十四

此文虽以"经济强制"为题，实际讲了中国地主制经济的发展史。结构严整，论据精当，是吾兄多年研究的成熟之作。提不出什么意见。下面都是题外之话。

文中提出地主对佃农的经济强制，始于宋"不立田制""不抑兼并"，完成于清定额租和押租制的普遍化。我非常赞赏这个提法。任何制度的发展都会有阶段性，每个大的阶段都是新的。这个阶段的特点是"佃农人身自由"，也就是"经济强制"的地主制经济，而这种经济乃是"典型的地主制经济"（第10页），即"地主制经济"达于典型、达于成熟。

从历史上来说，宋代确实有个大变动。宋以前的地主制经济和宋以后的地主制经济，有个划时代的变动，相应的封建主义（不只是经济），也有个划时代的变动（到近代，鸦片战争以后，有个更大的变动）。这需要另文研究，不仅在经济上（田制、租佃制、佃农择主、迁徙自由等等），在社会上（特别是在宗法制度上，范仲淹式新家族之兴起），在文化思想上（特别是浙东学派的兴起），都应加以研究。

（仅就"不立田制""不抑兼并"来说，曾受到学者猛烈攻击，以为不如均田法、占田法有效。都是因为没有"新时代"的观点。）

我还想提一个另外的题外之话。本文说，中国地主制经济的核心是租佃制，因为它是土地所有权与使用权的分离，调动了农民的生产积极性（第1页）。这要看条件。所有权和使用权分离，在经济学上是个普遍现象，租赁、借贷、委托、承包都是，是生产资料或资本与劳动者或经营相结合的便当形式，不是为了调动使用者的积极性，也不一定能调动使用者的积极性。以土地租赁说，即使在定额租和契约制下，地主可随时铲佃，佃农就没有改良土地的积极性，甚至造成短期行为，竭泽而渔，反而是有害的。所以我们家庭承包制要30年不变，现在又加30年，声明以后还要加。租佃制下，农民都要争取固定佃权。欧洲有过30年、60年、90年佃权，不仅在货币租，在分成制下就有。清代押租制下，有订10年、20年、30年者，还不够长。永佃制才根本解决问题。所以，所有权与使用权分离不能说就使佃农有积极性，那是有条件的。

注：这是对我一篇未刊稿的意见。1998 年 10 月 20 日。

十五

希克斯没有给"命令经济"（厉以平译"指令经济"）下个完整定义。依《经济史理论》，它起初总是军事性质的，出现在"习俗经济被彻底扰乱"的时候，"除了在危急的情况下，一般是难以存在的"（第 16 页）。但是，一旦军事目的完成，就需要建立官僚制度，这时，"制度又恢复到习俗，指令成分所剩无几"。

希克斯又说，封建制度就是军事征服之后，"恢复到习俗"的新制度，它是习俗经济和指令经济的"混合类型"。而习俗经济"居于领导地位"。只是当社会受到汤因比所称"挑战"压力时，"制度转向指令方向"（汤因比所称"挑战"，主要是指外部压力，特别是军事压力）。

还有一点，指令经济"在原则上并不依赖市场制度"，逻辑上"与市场无关"。

这样，我以为，指令经济只存在于军事行动时期，一切听指挥。而在封建官僚体系中，只有指令的"成分"。真正的、全面的指令经济，是在"计划经济"中。俄国革命，"军事共产主义"结束后，斯大林没有执行列宁的新经济政策，而实行了完全按指令行事的计划经济。中国在征公粮、供给制的军事经济结束后，没有按计划实行新民主主义，匆忙地转入计划经济。计划经济是不要市场的，但不能持久，60 或 30 年后又转入了市场经济。

公有制经济，公田或官田，百工食官，官盐铁，均输平准，都是历史悠久，非源于军事，与其视为命令经济，不如视为传统（习俗）经济。而在封建时期，公有制经济是逐渐削弱的。殆均田不行，小农为主，公有制经济在 GDP 中大约占不到 10%。但鸦片战争后，公有制经济是发展的，洋务派企业、官僚资本、国家垄断资本，尤其解放战争后，全民所有制、集体所有制，几乎囊括整个 GDP。公有制的削弱是制度问题，很难说是"命令"经济削弱了。其后的大发展，尤其是全民所有制和集体所有制，倒可说是

"命令经济"加强了,因为它们属于"计划经济",计划经济是典型的命令经济。

国家干预经济,也是自古即有,迄于今天,非必起源于军事。干预有直接的,如令民植桑种榆枣,效果未详,因为农家种地要受家庭需要限制,实际不是按命令行事。在长期内,地主干预大于国家干预。间接的干预,有财政、金融两途。封建社会,信用制不发达,金融如利息率、投放等干预不行,主要靠财政。故希克斯有"岁入经济"之说,岁入经济先于市场经济。在中国,即赋役制。我以为,赋役制实际上支配中国封建经济的运行,成为国民经济运行的机制(当然也有市场机制,很小),而田制(所有制)并不重要。盐茶禁榷均属财政,纳入赋役制研究。

赋役制的演变,总的说是趋向合理化。而此种演变,很难说是"命令"削弱了,也难说是"命令"加强了,它是制度的演变(不是体制的演变)。不过,演变不是直线的。如田赋,秦汉都是据地出税,而西晋计丁,北魏按户,隋及唐前期收丁租,即丁税。这又与本时期的占田、均田制有关。但由税地变为税丁税户,总是一种倒退。又赋役由征实物到货币化,是个进步;而明初实物制泛滥,甚至叫农民直接送税粮给对口的军户,废除统收、统支、会计,显然是个倒退。大约一条鞭以后,赋役制的合理化演变才成为"不可逆"的。但直到民国,也没有完全废役、废人头税,也没有完全货币化。不过,后来,在抗战后方改为征实和抓壮丁,在解放区收公粮和"动员",又有倒退。抗战后方和解放区都是军事经济、命令经济,不得不尔。

希克斯的书,重点是讲由传统经济向市场经济的转变。我们通常说由封建经济向资本主义经济转变。希克斯肯定马克思"封建主义""封建社会"的说法,他自己也用"封建社会""封建制度"等词。但他另提出一个"指令经济"来。马克思的"封建主义"在经济学、社会学上都有明确的涵义,在历史上有封建时代,这是人所公认共识的,封建主义是个科学概念。"命令经济"则不是个科学概念,历史上有国家即有命令,没有个命令时代。希克斯的书,在第三章以后就不提"指令经济"了,而改用封建制度、封建社会了(全书共十章)。值得注意的是,希克斯1969年发表"指令经济"论后,在史学界和经济学界都未引起波澜,至少我没见到讨论它、赞成或反对这个提法的文章，不把它当回事。有人（如我）撷拾"命令经济"一词，只是作为一个描述性的词，不是当作科学范畴。我说："计划经济是真正的命令经济"也是这样，是指主观决定、命令行事而言，有幽默（或忧默）味道。因为按希克斯所举的例子，即成吉思汗、亚历山大，他们可形成一个"时代"，但没有经济计划。

写得太啰嗦，歉甚。

《读书》1989年第3期有厉以宁写的一篇《希克斯的经济史研究》，主要讲希克斯的经济增长论和周期论，也提到《经济史理论》一书，但根本未提"命令经济"。

注：此信是讨论对希克斯"命令经济"一词的看法。1999年1月25日。

十六

拜读大作前稿，我曾说多种资源配置机制的理论是一大创造。这次修订稿，提出各种机制之间及其主体利益之间的协调发展问题，是又一创造。市场机制显然是最主要的调节器。这样，整个中国封建经济的运行，有了一个系统的理论。这个理论的框架已形成，至于其完整化，恐怕要等发表后，听取时贤评论，再作修正补充。

在"通古今之变"上，本文以唐中叶（两税法）为界，分为两大阶段。前此，国家干预占据主导地位；后此，地主干预占据主导地位。这点恐怕会引起争议的。在西方，中世纪庄园制是地主干预的顶峰，此后，王权兴起，民族国家形成，地主干预式微了。中国，早是中央专制国家，国家干预一直是强的。而中唐以前，即陈寅恪所谓"南北朝相承之旧局面"，也是地主干预的顶峰。那时是依附农盛行，庄园和坞壁经济，地主决定一切。唐中叶以后，国家干预松弛了，地主干预也松弛了，依附农变为契约佃农，分成租变为定额，等等。不过，降至明清，恐怕还是国家干预大于地主干预。因为国家干预经济运行，除田赋外尚有军工杂役，禁榷及法令限制；地主干预则除地租外，已没有什么了。地租大于田赋，但地租干预限于佃农，只有50%的耕地；田赋干预则为100%的耕地。地租大于田赋，也大得有限。张仲礼估计1887年GDP，出于政府者占6%，出于地主（绅士）者占8.7%，其绅士收入估计过高，已成公论，且地租之外，包括薪俸等多项。至清代，地租是否大于国税，还可研究。

注：参阅拙著《中国封建经济论稿》第22～27、32～33页。1999年4月26日。

十七

我完全同意大作各节的观点和论点。下面是题外的话。

江南雇工没问题，难处在给"市场"定性，因市场资料太少。市场定性通常有二：一是自由度，在本文即劳动的流动性。二是价格，在本文即工价。城乡流动，可用城镇人口增长来观察。外地流动更为重要。江南外流劳动很少，而外地流入很多，表明市场发育。工价在于整合化。城乡工价、各府州工价都无材料，整合程度不知。黄冕堂收集了长工工价120多件，独少江南。大约江南长工不多，犯刑案者更少。不过，江浙与东北都是高工价区。

关于小农经济，我同意大作的结论，对分工与专业化是个障碍。其原因，过去归之于市场不够发达。近年来我读了点社会学，按结构—功能学说，可归之于家庭这种群体组织的功能。但我还不能评价。因为我现在还相信斯密型动力，即通过市场分工和专业化导致经济发展。并且，从长距离贸易看，这种家庭功能与市场并无矛盾。我现在还不能评价，因为还没有深入研究（将来也不能，因"恐年岁之不吾与"）。这与劳动力市场无关，完全是题外话。不过我觉得，我们搞经济史，单读经济学不行，最好也读点社会学。

注：对拙作《清代江南市镇的劳动力市场》所提意见，文载《清代经济论稿》。2003年2月20日。

十八

大作《中国封建经济发展阶段述略》，几经拜读，所有三阶段论、赋役与租佃两大制度论、资源配置和商品经济两大指标，我完全同意。

封建史分阶段，在于"部分质变"。大作以晋、宋、清代表三大阶段。[①]其未惬人意者，晋（连同魏南北朝不过 400 年）代表不了从秦汉到中唐这个大阶段（长达 1000 年）。秦"黔首自实田"，就是自耕农世界了（"耕豪民之田"还是少数）。西汉是侯王天下，还是自耕农占优势吗？少数自由佃农忽然变成漫山遍野的依附农，说不清楚。魏晋南北朝像是插入这个大阶段的曲折、反复。我以为，只能从田制上来解释。中唐两税法以后（第二、三大阶段），就比较顺理成章了。我以为，讲制度经济史，在废均田或土地私有制真的确立以前，田制是最重要的制度。土地私有制确立后，户调、丁调才能土地化，以至摊丁入地。同时，分成到定额才有可能，以至永佃（土地私有制的否定）。

讲制度经济史，以某个或某两个制度为代表，未尝不可，因为是说明某某指标。但制度经济史原意是制度体系，因为各种制度都互相关联。文中对田制（但是从土地资源配置上立论）、币制（从实物到货币）都很注意，其实雇工制（从人身到自由）、社会良贱和等级制、选举（隋科举才除门阀）也都很重要。当然不必事事专论，只是在论三大阶段时，要着眼于制度体系的变化。

制度经济史原意是制度体系，因为来自结构主义历史观。原来无论中国外国，都是线性历史观。历史发展是线性的（承认起伏曲折，即曲线），因而史学家的任务在找出其因果关系（因果链）。20 世纪 30 年代，法国人提出结构主义历史观，50 年代，经济学的增长（发展）观也以结构主义代替

---

① 我在一篇《中国封建经济发展阶段》的文章中，曾提出中国封建经济有发展变化，大致经历了如下三个阶段：自秦汉魏晋南北朝至唐代中叶，为第一个阶段；自唐代中叶经过宋元至明代中叶，为第二个阶段；明代中叶至鸦片战争前清代前期，为第三个阶段。从吴老的前封来信中，说明他是同意这个意见的。但他在本封来信中却提出"大作以晋、宋、清代表三大阶段"，与我的原意不同，恐为老人善忘，一时疏忽所至。特此说明。——方行

线性增长论。历史的发展根本不是线性的，而是结构的变迁。其表现之一是资源配置的优化，但还有部门、规模、地域、整合等结构的变迁（方向是结构合理化）。结构变迁是整体性的，很难说什么原因，没有单项原因。除个别事件（如战争、政变、通货膨胀、市场危机）外，史学家不再纠缠于因果论，放弃了因果链。制度经济史，奠基在这种新的历史观上。

话说得远了，也太空了。因为对大作提不出意见，只好空言。但空言无益，就此打住。

本文框架已立。今后的工作，是充实实证分析；必须有实证（尽可能定量实证），框架才能定论。实证分析仍是定论框架，即宏观大略，不能涉及枝蔓细节。上面的空论可供思路参考，实与实证无益。本文出笼后，必会引起一场讨论或争论，那时再解决枝蔓细节问题。

注：对拙作《中国封建经济发展阶段述略》定稿的意见，文载《中国封建经济论稿》。2000 年 8 月 25 日。

十九

《中国封建赋税与商品经济》稿，是您"中国封建经济三阶段论"的续篇，是第一阶段的实证。"三阶段"论是个伟大的创新，实证是史学第一要义；创新尤需实证，否则不能成史。本文实证丰实，功力很高，说服力强，对文章全无异见，下面所谈均题外之话，可不看。

把政府作为支配市场的第一力量，始于凯恩斯。对封建政府，重农学派把它看成支配市场的第二力量，居地主之后。封建政府的收入主要是租，凡凭权力得来的收入都是租，马克思视之为地租转化形态，因为主要凭土地权力得来。资本主义政府的收入也有凭权力得来的租（今称寻租），但不大，主要是税。税是政府以服务（防卫、治安、教育、公用等）与居民交换而来的，一般是等价交换（契约论）。凯恩斯之重视政府，不仅因为它是最大的购买者，还因它是最大的提供服务者（卖方）。

秦汉以后，中国封建政府异于西方，其收入不限于租（凭土地权力），而日益多是税，由服务得来。就治安服务说，远优于西方，水利、驿运、漕运、德化教育等服务，西方没有。本文只讲商品经济，不讲服务市场，故未涉及。

中国封建政府的财政不仅是机构的收支（官吏士兵俸饷只占赋税半数，第 13 页），而且是一种大财政，包括政策和资源调配。所以对前文（三阶段）我建议增论土地政策。本文中，又看出许多政策内容，除产业政策（尤其桑蚕茶）外，还有平准、和籴等。不过，我觉得更重要的是货币政策。

最大问题是汉以后赋税的实物化。赋税实物化何因？是进步还是退步？本文把它看作是提高市场"丰度"的"机制"（第 2 页），是积极的看法。不过就贡禹的思想说是保守的。"机制"说，本文的实证是，因为粮食，尤其桑蚕丝织发达了，征实，尤其征帛有可能了。专就布帛说，不如看作是货币。有个地方说征粮改为征帛，实际是货币化了。西汉为什么有那么多金银，始终是个谜。东汉至中唐，生产发展，市场扩大，赋税也增大 2.5 ~ 4 倍。赋税（购买力）增大 2.5 ~ 4 倍，市场交易至少增大 5 ~ 8 倍（倍数效应），金银铜不足，只好征实。通货不足，文中屡见，恐怕是实情，因为中国没有金银铜大矿。这就是货币政策问题，好像到北宋才解决。我始终谴责朱元璋的赋税实物化是个历史的倒退。但对曹操的租调令、司马炎的户调令，不敢说，因没弄清楚。

注：对拙作《中国封建赋税与商品经济》所提意见，文载《中国封建经济论稿》。2001 年 5 月 21 日。

二十

大作《中国封建地租与商品经济》稿，实证丰富。

第一节：全文骨干，目的在论证宋代地租量超过赋税，成为需求推动生产的主力。所有量化处理和论地租的营运，都无懈可击。本文是论地租，不论赋税。但于宋代商税超过田赋的现象（第 4 页）仍不妨略作申论。因这是前所未有、后世亦无之事。它不仅反映宋代商品经济的发达（历史上第二个高峰），而且反映服务市场的空前扩大。盖商税多来自服务业，并且，商税不同于田赋，主要不是凭权力征敛，而是政府以服务与商民交换。

第二节：高消费，资料淋漓尽致，但显得有点堆积。如写法以论带史，就不显堆积了。本节论在第18～21页，讲高消费推动了手工业的发展。这十分重要，因高消费是享受性消费（生存性消费推动农业是有限度的），自然落在手工业上。本节还有一个论点，在第22～23页，即高消费不仅在贵族显宦（人数太少），而且在地主尤其是城居地主（人也不多）和商人、手工业户、广大市民。这点很重要，惜所论太少（不到一页）。从这点看，第21页说《东京梦华录》《梦粱录》《都城纪胜》不必引证，是不对的。三书代表宋代市民生活，不能不引证。不能把所有新的消费都直接和地租挂钩。

此外，我想还可补充一个论点，即高消费反映服务业的发展，服务市场的扩大。文中所谓精神产品、文化消费和大部分发展性消费，都是服务。商品经济包括物质和服务两大部分，宋代服务开始占重要地位，是一大特点。服务比之商品，是高一层的消费，衣食足而后的消费，它的消费弹性大，是促进生产的新力量。龙登高有篇长文《南宋杭州娱乐市场分析》，从经济上分析文化消费，有见地。

第三节：宋代的城市化、镇市开始网络化，城居地主成趋势，这都是宋代的特点，很重要。宋代恐怕是城市化水平最高的，或谓达20%，而明清还不过5%～6%。这有偏安江南、人口等多重原因，不去管它，而城市化是扩大需求、发展商品经济的最重要因素。第一个商业高峰战国和希腊，即因是城邦制。文章不能把需求的扩大都抠死在地租量上。地租是根子，地租转化为需求、转化为购买力，也有个再分配过程，有扩散和倍数效应，城市化是其转换和扩散的工具。

宋代城市还有个结构革新问题。不仅破除坊市制，大城市还表现为金融业与贸易分离，批发与零售分离，形成专业街，达400行，以及邸店等服务业兴起，乃至有出租车马、桌椅、婚丧用具的专业。这都是前所未有的。斯波义信有典型考察。

注：对拙作《中国封建地租与商品经济》所提意见，文载《中国封建经济论稿》。2002年1月6日。

二十一

粮食，我向来重视高产量，不问劳动生产率，因农民人均收入不能只计粮食。亩产量，清前期略高于宋，这是因宋代北方辽金太低，若就江南说，清实低于宋。至于劳动生产率，清大大低于宋，可能低30%～40%，但不是由于地力（自然）原因，而是由于人口增加太快，要承认人口压力。因而，人均占有粮食低于宋，但还是够吃饱；因嘉道民国人均占有量更低，也没饿死人，不过人口增长慢了。这是我对粮食的粗略概念，因未作专业研究，不敢自信。此生也来不及研究了。

粮食加经济作物，加农家手工业，清前期的农业经济大大高于宋明。从农业生产力说，清是封建社会的高峰，这点我不怀疑。

一国经济评价，有两方面：一是生产力和消费水平，人们爱用居民生活的舒适度和安全性来衡量。另方面是制度，包括政府效率、经济制度、市场功能、社会和文化。记得在一次座谈会上，我说清代经济发达，制度落后。林甘泉似乎表示同意。不过，当时是说比18世纪欧洲落后，不是同宋代比。说清代制度比宋代落后，不合逻辑。不过，我说比乾隆时应有的制度落后，则有我的道理。

我以为16世纪中国已有现代化因素，即向市场经济转变的萌芽。但清人入主中原，把这些因素打断了。首先，消灭了明末的启蒙运动，中断理性思维，回到汉经学。其次，闭关自守，拒绝贸易，也中断中西交流。其三，经济制度，除摊丁入地外，无建树。其四，市场，只是商品量和地域有扩大，无质的变化。这一切，要到1840年后吸收西方思维，才有转机。我文章中用"文化逆流""经济逆流"字样，结论是"愈是盛世，愈是保守"。"盛世"指生产，"保守"指制度。合起来就是物质发展，制度落后，比这种物质条件下应有的制度落后。

关于市场多说两句。商品经济不是市场经济。市场经济主要表现为市场调配资源，即每种资源的边际收益等于其边际成本。市场商品量扩大不能使市场达到这种功能，这种功能是个制度问题。正如生产增长不能自动使制度达到生产力的要求一样。制度变革是人为的，要有先进思想的人去变革。理性主义是制度变革的动力。到今天，中国还未完全实现市场经济（即现代化），因为曲折太多。如计划经济就是一次曲折，一次逆流，因为计划经济直接调配资源，不要市场。清前期是凭租和税调配资源，市场调配只是很小部分。1840 年后市场扩大，但直到 1950 年，市场还未能调配占国民经济 70% 的农业资源（即土地与劳动的配置）。

市场量当然也有关系。我研究 1840～1936 年的市场商品量，结论是 1840～1908 年增长太慢，1908～1936 年增长也不快。1840 年我估 3.5 亿两，偏低，用吴慧 5.25 亿两，也不高。对比生产来说太低，例如粮食商品率只有 10%。10% 怎能调配资源？到 1936 年，粮食商品率提高到 30% 以上，经济作物达 80% 以上，但市场仍未能调配农业资源；因为没有制度变革，土地、劳动、资本都不是市场配置的，而是小农制配置的。制度变革要有有先进思想的人去变，不会自变。

注：对我一个讨论提纲的意见。2003 年 5 月 4 日。

二十二

大作所有论点，我完全同意。

耕织结合的小农经济，有它积极的作用，优于西方领主经济；也有它消极的一面，它妨碍新生产方式的建立。这在您 80 年代的论文中就已明确了。这个结论并不鼓舞人心，但似乎无可奈何，必须接受。但不是说就没有研究的余地了。

耕织结合的小农经济可以说是一种习俗经济，因为自元代发展棉纺织以来已有六百年了。不过，希克斯所说习俗经济指希腊以前，而自罗马征服欧洲和中亚以来，就有了命令经济。中世纪是习俗和命令经济的混合体，因为中世纪是僧侣和武士的社会，基督教代表习俗，武士代表命令。

现在流行新制度学派经济史。有正式制度和非正式制度。正式制度即法律，相当于命令。非正式制度首先是意识形态，其次是家庭家族，相当于习俗。意识形态，在西方是基督教，在中国是儒学，都与经济活动有关。

总之，新经济史研究，不能就经济谈经济。我们过去对小农经济的研究，都有只重经济关系分析、忽视非经济因素的毛病。

耕织结合的小农经济是一种经济结构，也是一种社会组织。它的形成、发展以至解体，与传统的义利观、本末论、家庭观念、多子继承，以及国家巩固自耕农的政策、榷关制度等都是分不开的。对小农经济的研究，从经济学方面转入社会学方面，加上非经济因素的分析（当然都需要实证），就大有可为了。说不定会多少修正原来的评价和结论。

注：对我一个论文提纲的意见。2004 年 10 月 25 日。

二十三

拜读新作第三部分，唯第 2 页宗族关系，康熙圣谕不过重申嘉靖十五年夏言上疏，没有新的限制。我以为清代宗族关系仍是继晚明以来"松解"的趋势（李文治看法）。康熙圣谕 16 条中反动的是对知识分子的"黜异端以崇正学"（朱学），"讲法律以警愚顽"（文字狱）。又，下面"多子继承"一节，说"增强农民经济活力"，我看不然。此"习俗"（当然非始于清）分散家庭财产，使小农不能成大农，为害匪浅。

总之，问题又回到农业与家庭手工业密切结合的小农经济，新论似乎增加了它的负面作用。回忆 70 年代末我们写《中资史》第一卷时，徐新吾提出"小农经济万恶论"，因为它阻塞了资本主义萌芽的发展。当时我觉得过分了，改为"自然经济的分解"。为造 1840～1936 年耕织结合的分解表，徐公花了三年时间，全文见第二卷第二章附录。这以前，30 年代，梁漱溟曾提出，小农经济工农结合很好，中国工业化的道路应当是在农村复兴中发展工业，工业与农业"合作"生长。90 年代，乡镇企业兴起，费孝通写了篇文章大加赞扬，说这就是中国传统的工农在家庭结合转化为社会上的结合，是完全正确的道路。我同意费公的看法。

我的想法一直是：中国现代化必须利用传统经济，特别是小农经济的"能动因素"或积极因素。因而有《中国近代化过程中的内部因素和外部因素》（1987）、《中国工业化的道路》（1991）二文。怎样利用呢？我的意思是通过市场，而不是大企业（大企业是科斯定理，那时我还不知科斯定理）。通过市场也就是通过分工，也就是自然经济的分解。现在看来，农业与手工业密切结合的小农，能不能不分解，直接过渡为工农结合的现代化经济呢？那样最好，但恐怕不能。

　　注：对我一个未刊稿的意见。2004 年 11 月 26 日。

1994年3月与方行关于
"西汉封建经济" 的通信

方行兄：

　　拜读大作《读〈货殖列传〉》，获益良多，至深感佩。我完全同意尊兄：司马迁卓越的经济思想反映了以使用价值为目的的和以剩余价值为目的的两种商品经济的发展。唯论汉初至汉中期，后一种商品经济的发展速度超过前一种，似论据尚有不足。

　　在前资本主义社会，以剩余价值为目的的生产一般限于大奴隶制。如希腊之矿业（有达万人者）、大作坊（百人左右）、罗马之大庄园（数十至数百人）。西汉已是封建社会，但司马迁所举与千户侯等富的大产业都是使用奴隶的。

　　他列举了近50个这样的大产业。其中属于"农"的都是畜牧业和经济作物，唯一例外是"带郭千亩亩钟之田"。按吴慧，这种田是特高产，超常产三倍，这种田是很少的，因铁犁进步，至汉大田产大都小农化了，千亩之家改为收租。经济作物之中，若千亩卮茜、千畦姜韭等，似是按值计收益，未必实有，至少不会普遍。属于"工"的，仅四业，即酒、酱、浆、①屠宰。因为"百工"这时已不属官，变成小手工业者了。属于"虞"的最突出（大富），但只盐、铁二业（铸钱已于元鼎四年禁私铸，司马迁赞成）。

---

① 浆不知是什么，但有"卖浆，小业也，而张氏千万"。引车卖浆，不会是使用奴隶的剩余价值生产。

属于"商"的至少有27业，占一半以上，包括贩卖农产品和手工业品的，但要谷千钟、布千钧、文采千匹以上的才行，而这些货源大都来自小农和农家手工业，不是剩余价值的生产。

看来司马迁所说与千户侯等富的产业主要是指商业（贩运商）。他写的"传"也以商人为多。陶朱公、计然、白圭最受推崇，因他们各有经商技术。冶铁卓氏、程郑、宛孔氏、曹邴氏也是商人，畜长乌氏、任氏、卜式也兼商。所谓"无财（资本）作力，少有斗智，既饶争时"，都是指经商。"能者辐凑，不肖者瓦解"，"巧者有余，拙者不足"，也是指经商。因为当时在矿业上未见技术改进记载，技术改进最大的是丝织，但那是家庭生产。"货殖"包括实物和货币，而在司马迁行文中，实物都货币化了，故有各行业都有100万本钱20万利润的比较，这种平均利润的概念只能从商业中得出。我曾以为，商业资本（和高利贷资本）是封建社会"异质"的东西，属资本主义。司马迁在那时有后来资本主义初期的经济放任主义思想也就不足为怪。

"汉兴，海内为一，开关梁，弛山泽之禁，是以富商大贾周流天下"。商业资本大发展，但不一定是剩余价值生产的发展。整个商品流通中，是以农产品为主，布帛次之，盐铁占比重不大。小农种植作物有50%以上的剩余，连同他们的副业纺织品都可转化为商品。小手工业者本是商品生产，但在没有自由雇工的条件下不是剩余价值的生产。商人20%的利润主要不是生产过程中的剩余价值，而是从交换中得来，所谓"富者必用奇胜"，大商人都有奇术。元狩以后，盐铁改为官营，官营后是否产量增加了，我不知道。至于商品国营，如均输平准，则肯定不会增加剩余价值的生产。从大趋势说，封建代替奴隶，剩余价值生产相对是减少的（当然也有逆转的时候）。而汉初至西汉末，人口约增2.5倍，粮食（使用价值的生产）至少也是这样。

吴承明

1994 年 3 月 5 日

《清代前期小农经济》一文容再详读（已读过）。

吴老：

您好！

我那篇东西写于春节前，仓促从事，既粗糙而又多谬误，承蒙赐教，实深感荷。

对西汉经济，有如下看法，简述以就正于您。

（一）西汉为封建社会初级阶段，封建社会还不发达，劳动者与生产资料结合的方式遂纷然杂陈。吴王濞 "招致天下亡命者盗铸钱，煮海水为盐"。邓通亦如此，故 "山东奸猾咸聚吴国，秦雍汉蜀因邓氏"。卓氏、程郑冶铁用 "僮"。《盐铁论》说，豪强 "采铁石鼓铸煮盐，一家聚众或至千余人，大抵尽收放流人民也"。《平准书》说，富商大贾 "蹛财役贫……冶铁煮盐"。又说，他们 "擅管山海之货……役利细民"。铸钱、冶铁和煮盐为当时最重要的工矿业，固不足为奇。其他手工行业亦如此，如大官僚张安世，"夫人自纺绩，家童七百人，皆有手技作业，内治产业，累积纤微，是以能殖其货，富于大将军光"。

农业中，陈涉 "尝为人佣耕"，季布在朱家家中，是 "田事听此奴"。地主与商人经营农牧业，当是奴隶与佣工杂用。范文澜说："田客要月钱一千，两汉奴价普通是一万五千钱，耕作技术最高的奴隶，买价不过二万钱，用奴比用客便宜得多。" 所以，"西汉地主确实使用巨大数量的奴隶"。"汉武帝曾经没收商人的大量田地与田僮"。

从上可见当时豪强大家役使的劳动者，除佃农之外，还有奴隶、佣工，以及诸如 "放流人民""亡命者" 之类的具有依附性的劳动者。故容易出现较大规模经营，与后世雇佣关系发展之后的情况有所不同。

（二）正是由于西汉还处在封建社会的初级阶段，农业生产力还不发展。农民除自用与交税之后，能出售的产品不多。城市中大量需要的农产品、畜产品，特别是一些重要经济作物，难以靠农民来满足，这就给封建地主与达官贵人经营农牧业留下了广阔余地。估计有些经济作物是主要靠地主们来供给的。《货殖列传》中所述当是实情。千亩田地，按小亩计，约合三百市亩；按大亩计，约六七百市亩，与当时农民一夫 "耕百亩" 计，并不算过多。晋人说："秦汉以来……公侯之尊，莫不殖园圃之田，而收市井之利。"当可信。

（三）在工农业中出现一批较大规模的经营，是当时一个重要经济现象。这引起了司马迁的关注与热情。他在《货殖列传》中"略道当世"的大商贾，列有事迹者九人，其中冶铁四人，"力田畜"二人，"逐渔盐商贾之利"一人，大商人和大高利贷者各一人。

虽近在咫尺，亦难常受耳提面命，聊借笔谈，以求明教。顺颂

春安！

方行

三月十一日

2005 年 12 月与方行关于
"清代江南经济"的通信

方公老兄：

拜读大作《清代江南经济：自然环境作用的一个典型》，立言均切实际，论证綦翔，至为钦佩。唯以自然环境为题，嫌窄，实已论及人文环境。尚有地理环境，其事有：

①江南粮食不能自给，仰仗江西、湖南、四川供应。

②肥料（豆及饼）仰仗华北、东北。

③牛力短缺，价过昂，过于人力。

④木材靠福建、西南诸省输入。

⑤煤、铁、有色金属全靠外省以至南洋、日本输入，使江南工业只能是"超轻型"的。

以上各条非均自然条件，而有人为，故称地理环境。①～④是因扩充棉、桑而然。⑤是交通运输落后，如有海运、铁路，即可解决。

对这五条，有三种理论解释：

1. 李伯重持"发展与制约"论。而江南经济发展，受这五条制约。我在给李书的序中说："江南给予外区的大约还多于它所取的……而这种不平衡也正是江南经济的主要制约。只有外区经济有了进步，江南在能源、原材料和粮食上得到保证，它才能进一步发展。"

2. 法国年鉴学派 F. 布罗代尔在《地中海》一书中说：环境（构造）史决定了地中海政治史、经济史、文化史的"边界"。他的环境（构造）有三：自然条件、地理条件、人们心态（宗教信仰、生活习惯）。这三者都变迁很慢，以 100 年计，政治、经济、文化变迁虽快，但不能逾越构造的"边际"。例如在 18 世纪晚期，江南只能有"超轻型"工业；19 世纪晚期，上海即成为机器、造船业中心；20 世纪晚期就有了宝钢。

3. 拉美学派 I. 华勒斯坦以"核心—半边缘—边缘"理论来解释这种现象。江南处于全国经济核心地位，它的发展靠剥削边缘、半边缘省份，积累了大量资本，但基本上被清廷的赋税囊括去了。不过，清廷这种抽肥补瘦的再分配政策，至今还是正确的。

此外，文化环境，江南人确实因为富有而多读书、科举盛。但主要是出了大儒商和小官僚。张居正以降，至曾、胡、左、李、张之洞，都非江南户。历数清代学术巨子，除顾炎武外，黄梨洲、王船山、颜李学派、阎百诗、孙诒让、戴东原、章学诚、龚自珍、康有为、梁启超、黄遵宪，都不是江南人。真正的人材与财富无关，古今皆然。

以上皆漫谈，请哂阅。严寒稍杀，祝

伉俪大安！

2005 年 12 月 18 日

方公老兄：

来示敬悉。尊稿拟加地理环境一段，我看似不够妥当。因煤、铁等问题不是环境问题（不是江南变得没有煤铁了），而是区域经济的发展问题。我的那句话也是指区域经济史研究，而不是指环境史研究。

"地理构造""地理时间"是 F. 布罗代尔创造的名词，实指生态结构的变迁，这种变迁总是有人为因素。后来如斯波義信、K. 彭慕兰用布氏理论，都径称"生态史"。这是对的。

环境史是研究环境变迁与经济发展的关系。明清江南的环境变迁主要是：人们追逐布、丝绸之厚利，广植棉、桑、破坏了江南原来的生态循环，进入新的生态结构，即粮食、肥料、木材要靠外地输入，牛不能利用（牧草消失，全要喂羊）的生态结构。问题是如何使这种新的结构良性循环（用经济学术语）即"平衡"。至于这种变迁与江南经济发展的关系，就出现多种论点。看得最重的是黄宗智的"过密化"；其次是王国斌、彭慕兰认为"面临但尚未达到"斯密"极限"（也就是布罗代尔的"边界"）；看得较轻的是李伯重的"制约"说；还有"中心—边缘"论。再从进一步发展看，则有徐新吾的"小农经济万恶论"，张忠民的"小生产、大市场"论，林刚的"农工副业密的结合"论，等等。

总之，要讲江南环境史，就不能避免这些问题。正因有这些问题，研究江南环境史才有意义。祝
大安！

吴承明

2005. 12. 27

吴老：

　　谢谢您给我这多教诲，可惜我经济学理论根基太浅，一时难以从江南地区经济环境变化中悟出什么想法。但我仍在文章最后加了一小段（见下）。本来不应该再麻烦您了，但事关诠释您的思想，不敢不送您过目。好在文字不多，只有三百字。如果无大错，您就不必回信了。尚此，敬问

冬安，并祝您和文老师新年快乐。

方行 28/12

　　江南地区通过发展棉、丝、棉布、绸缎生产，与全国各地建立了广泛的经济联系。从江南赋税占全国之半和北洋商船往往回空，可见其区域间贸易实处于一种出超和顺差的优势地位。吴承明教授认为："这种不平衡正是江南发展的主要制约。只是有外区经济发展，江南在能源、原材料和粮食上得到保证，它才能进一步发展。"我想他这是说，外地区也应当像江南一样，充分利用本地的自然条件，发展优势产业，生产比较成本相对有利的产品，实行专业化分工，然后通过交换，优势互补，在地区之间建立起一种整体的经济均衡，以互利共赢。这才是外地区经济发展的出路所在，也是江南地区经济进一步发展的出路所在。

1989～2003 年与
斯波義信的通信

January 29，2003

吴承明　教授：

I hope this letter finds you in good health, and I would like to thank you again for your continuing interest in and cooperation with The Toyo Bunko.

I am writing to you today to inform you that as part of the activities surrounding our upcoming 80th anniversary on19 November 2004, we are in the process of compiling an eighty year history of The Toyo Bunko (about 300 B5-size pages) and also to request that you, as a person who has been deeply involved with The Toyo Bunko, contribute a short piece to the volume. We will leave the subject of your contribution up to you and only ask that it be no longer than 4 double-spaced pages (about 1000 words) in length. Please submit it in either typewritten (word processed) manuscript form or on a floppy disk no later than September 2003.

We look forward to hearing from you on this matter at your earliest convenience.

斯波義信（1930～），日本历史学者，宋代经济史研究专家，大阪大学名誉教授。

Thank you again.

Sincerely,

斯波義信

SHIBA, Yoshinobu

Director General

The Toyo Bunko

INSTITUTE OF ECONOMICS, CHINESE

ACADEMY OF SOCIAL SCIENCES

August 15, 2003

Dear Professor Yoshinobu Shiba:

I hope this letter will meet you in good health and at a royal time. I want to tell you that all the academic circles were fine in the Beijing SARS spring, but we are now in a hot summer.

In replaying to the letter of January 29, 2003 in which you requested me to write a short piece on celebrating the 80th anniversary of the Toyo Bunko, I would like send you an eight-line-in-seven as follows. Please oblige me with your comments and dispose it at will.

Sincerely,

祝东洋文库八秩庆典

石室金匮俱往矣　　花魂柳眼望东洋

八十万卷藏国宝　　两库真经尽琳琅

有教琼林文郁郁　　无涯学海路茫茫

莫公岩公宏图在　　仰止风高水山长

September 1st. 2003

Dear Professor Wu:

Most appreciative thanks for your cordial letter of August 15 and for a most excellent eight-line-in-seven poem written by yourself celebrating the eightieth anniversary of our Toyo Bunko. Indeed, we people of the Toyo Bunko are impressed deeply by the sonorousness and the gracefulness of the poem which was composed personally by such a world-renowned scholar like yourself. We are very happy to carry it in our commemorative volume. Thanks you most heartily again!

Well, I have no word to say in excuse to express my heartfelt thanks to yours gift of a Collection of Works of Professor Wu Cheng-ming, which you so kindly sent me early in May, in such late. I just hope you will forgive my rudeness generously. Your articles collected in this volume are all condensed fruits of your tireless engagement in major themes of the economic history of China for many years. Therefore, each word and each line reveal your virtuoso discernment on the topic under discussion. By now I have read the book carefully, and have gained a good deal of enlightments from it. I also got a number of stimuli from your essays on the overall trends of the market economy in China in sixteenth through nineteenth centuries. Further, it is my great honor to find in it your kind review on my small piece of work.

I am pleased to hear that you along with other scholars in Beijing had been safe and sound during the SARS spring. Here, we had an unusually cool summer because of a lot of rainfall. The Toyo Bunko is happy to tell you that our application to the government for our inauguration of the new project, the Supra-disciplinary inquiry into modern Asian issues, were approved in last July. This means that in addition to the continuation of our collection of sources and the research on them for pre-1949 China and Asia, we now are able to expand our activities to include the contemporary problems in Asia, that of China in particular.

Thank you so much again for your contribution!

With warmest best wishes, as ever,

Sincerely yours,

Yoshinobu SHIBA

斯波義信

2010年1月与赵德馨的通信

德馨、秀鸾学长：

去岁末接来示，即在家门口报亭购贺年卡寄上。不意今天忽接邮局退回，批示"邮资逾期"。原来报亭老板竟以前年存货卖给我，卡封邮资印"牛"而非"虎"，亦奇事也。

愚近年来先是目疾，继而耳聋，行动不便，等于报废，秋忽患肺炎，医药缠绵月余。不过到年末已暂勿药，头脑尚清晰，不致不辨虎牛也。又，新春接通知，九十岁（愚今年93）以上老人补贴翻一翻，又学部委员退休待遇改为副部级，皆社会主义早期阶段之功也。

大作《经济史学概论》早已收到。弟搞了几十年经济史，尚未见经济史学，此书乃创见，弟以视力不佳（需要吊灯的放大镜），尚待仔细研读也。祝

新春幸福！

吴承明

2010.1.27

赵德馨（1932.3～），中南财经政法大学教授。

2004年与刘福寿关于《中国经济学患有"贫史症"》的通信

福寿同志：

昨天，有人带回你7月30日信和《中国经济学患有"贫史症"》一文。拜读了两遍，初步感觉是：此文立意极佳，切中时弊，但就全文看，尚感不足，恐难符孙冶方奖的要求，我也不便推荐。

该文不足处主要是：从经验上以二例说明历史知识的重要性，而未从理论上阐明经济学应以历史为根据。理论上作此阐明的，首先是施穆勒的《国民经济学》，继之是熊彼特的《经济分析史》，均属巨著。索洛的《经济史与经济学》主要是批评福格尔。该文是我首次介绍到中国的，因1986年我参加福格尔召开的计量史学会议，见此文，这时，诺斯、戴维斯已离开福格尔，另创新制度学派了。

在中国，对这个问题的讨论是集中在章学诚的"六经皆史"一句话上。此话宋代已有（刘因）。宋代陈亮、叶适的"事功"之学是以历史为根据的，朱熹等讲治国也是以历史为根据，不过陈、叶重现汉唐，朱熹专尊三代而已。至清，"六经皆史"争论加剧。1898年设"经济专科"，科场命题仍重历史。西方经济学输入，对边际主义反应迟缓，梁启超拟作《中国生计学史》，大约新古典主义兴起后，中国经济学者不谈历史了，"贫史症"约始

刘福寿（1944~），河北经贸大学经济学教授、副校长。

于 20 世纪 30 年代（西方始于李嘉图，实际在边际主义兴起后）。

孙冶方奖颇重理论，单国有企业、农村劳力转移二例，显得单薄。亦可以二例为主，唯宜有调查材料和数据证明，始具"学术"性。我的《经济学理论与经济史研究》一文获孙冶方奖，是该文由《经济研究》转载后，《经济研究》提出的，我并未申请。

来信以快件专递寄来，知事急迫。乃初读大作，立即作复，皆"直言"无讳，未及多思也。仓促命笔，容有未当，或不当言者，祈谅！顺颂
大安

吴承明

2004. 8. 4

吴老师：

听太昌说先生身体硬朗，甚感欣慰。

近两年在《中国社科文摘》和《经济学家茶座》上读了先生的几篇近作，直感先生的学问深不可测，吾辈虽终生努力，也难得其一二。先生已年高米寿，尚如此勤奋，吾辈汗颜无地，当以锥梁之功，趑步前行，以不辜负先生教诲。

最近遇一疑难，特请教先生。

报上公布今年评选孙冶方奖。学生多年学业荒废，拿不出什么像样的东西，本不敢问津。但对当前我国经济学研究中忽视历史的问题感触颇深，写了一个《中国经济学患有"贫史症"》的小东西，发表在《经济学家茶座》上。比起《经济研究》类权威刊物上的万言巨制来，恐怕连一碟"六必居"的小菜都谈不上。但我觉得这个问题又非常现实，特别是在西方经济理论已成为我国经济学圭臬之时，提出这个问题当有现实意义。只是因为它分量太轻，底气不足，不敢贸然登大雅。所以特别请教先生：

1. 请先生直言，这个东西拿得出手不？如果先生不以为然，那就算了。丑学生不怕见先生，还是怕见外人的。

2. 如果先生觉得尚可，学生斗胆请先生赐一500字左右的推荐信如何？

请先生明示。

伏祈

暑安！

学生　刘福寿

2004.7.30

2000～2005年与
方健的通信

　　说明： 吴老致我的大示约有十余封，但今只找到四通，其中三封是关于我应北大邓广铭教授之嘱，为日本著名宋史专家、东京大学荣誉教授、原东洋文库理事长斯波义信教授的大著《宋代江南经济史研究》翻译成中文本，于2000年完成，遂向吴老求中文版序言，吴老慨然应允，很快寄来大序，我请示可否先到刊物上发表，吴老亦同意。遂交刘东教授主编为《中国学术》创刊号（2001年6月）书评版头条始刊。记得还有讨论吴老大序及斯波书中存在问题的数信今则未能找到。斗室容数万藏书，杂乱无章，实在难觅。另一封则为2005年我退居二线时作学术论著规划时向吴老求教时吴老的复信。另有数通我因撰写《中国茶书全集校正》申报"国家出版基金资助项目"时于2010年请吴老写"推荐书"，吴老慨然应允，但这几通吴老大示也遍寻未获。

方健

2016年11月18日

方健（1947～），苏州市经济贸易委员会高级经济师，宋史学者。

一

方健兄：

二月十四日来示歉意。承赐大作各件，至为感谢。弟拟先作我所项目及讲学事，"序"之执笔略迟，唯当于四月底奉上拙稿。

顺颂

大安！

吴承明

2000 年三八节

二

方健先生：

遵嘱为斯波义信先生《宋代江南经济史研究》中文版作序。兹奉上拙稿，不知合意否？谬误之处，请改正后告我。

即颂

大安！

吴承明

2000 年 4 月 21 日

三

方健兄：

示悉。"序"稿奉还，承指正谬误，至感。至于该稿是否发行发表，悉听尊意。盖另行发表须加题目，有些文字也应修改。我前为王国斌书作序在《读书》发表，都是他与编者商定的，我不知道。因为我只管作序就是了。

顺祝

大安！

吴承明

2000 年 4 月 29 日

四

方健兄如晤：

　　顷接春节来示，及大作多篇，并自述小品，披览之琳琅满目、目不暇接。唯以视力障碍，尚容暇时拜读也。吾　兄即将退居二线之际，而宏图远略，有十年二十年计划，潜心致力于学术，自强不息，令人仰止。

　　弟之九十岁文集，蒙　兄允赐宏文，感激无已。至以何篇为宜，自当悉听尊意，弟毋庸置喙。吾　兄退居二线后，若有意去上海之大学教授，需荐书时，弟当遵嘱，其内容立请草定，以副要求。至于为尊著《茶书集成》作序事，自忖或力有未迨。盖弟于宋史素无研究，于茶事更是完全无知之门外汉。而近年来目疾日益加剧，经查系老年性玻璃体混浊，非若水晶体之可置换，尚无救治之方，阅读、执笔俱有困难，又不会电脑，是以踟蹰也。此乃实情，只有赧求谅鉴。

　　敬颂

春祺！

吴承明
2005 年 3 月 15 日

1994年8月与林刚关于 "长江三角洲近代工业与 小农经济"的通信

林刚同志:

奉7月31日来信及《长江三角洲近代大工业与小农经济的相互关系及协调发展》博士论文,拜读一遍,至为感佩。

尊著目的,似在探讨一条大工业与小农经济在利益互补的基础上协同发展并利用大工业改造、重构传统农业的现代化道路。我也有这种思想,但功夫不够,所作皆属空论。尊著从专题入手,资料丰富,用宏取精,许多是罕见的和档案文献,全用实证方法,实为治史正途,令人信服。分析綦详,每篇均有创见。此论文属成功之作,盼能组织成一篇或数篇较简短文章,以利发表,为经济史研究做出新的贡献。

所论南通棉纺、无锡桑蚕、淮南盐垦,最后不免失败,至末章以"一损俱损"为题,未免令人沮丧。这里有微观与宏观问题;专题研究是治史要略,结论则需要全面些。窃意尊文对于大工业与小农经济互补一面考察入微,而于两者矛盾一面甚少言及,盖有矛盾才有互补,哲学谓之对立统一,经济学即无差异曲线原理。我国小农经济生产效率很高,舒尔兹所谓"没有一种生产要素不被有效利用"。但农工副在家庭形式下密切结合并非最佳的组织形式。社会经济发展与否最后要看生产要素的配置能否优化,哪怕是

林刚(1948~),中国社会科学院经济研究所研究员。

一点点的优化，这种配置与其说在组合（家庭）之中，不如说在部门和地区之间。这就必须招致经济组合的某些变动，哪怕是一点点的变动。

斯密以分工和专业化为经济进步之源，实为至理。以今观之，我国传统农业的改造、再构，即在于生产的商品化和专业户与乡镇企业的出现。专业户和乡镇企业都不是通过家庭，而是通过市场使农工副结合了。尊文中论无锡农村经济，初以手织布而盛，殆织布衰而桑蚕兴，进一步发展；到1929年丝业危机，农家只好"毁桑改茬"。不过，据吴柏均所辑11个村的逐户调查，1929年无锡农村就业人口中，已有19%的人从事商业、运输、灌溉等，11%的人从事佣工及家务劳动，11.8%的人从事工厂劳动，就是说有41.8%脱离农工副家庭结合，成为类似"专业户"了。到1936年，这种"专业户"增至43.1%，所以无锡农村经济并未"一损俱损"，而是劳动力人均收入以1.5%年率递增。

无锡仅是个别事例。不过我以为，从近代化或现代化角度看，分工、专业化，以市场结合替代家庭内的农工副结合恐怕是不可避免的。换句话说，终于要走上市场经济的道路。当然，这是长期的道路，历史研究只是见微知著。并且，即使在没有帝国主义和政治腐败的情况下，仍是道路曲折的（例如大而全、小而全的曲折）。

以上是个人拙见，未必恰当。仅供参考。

祝

撰安

吴承明

1994年8月29日

吴老：您好！

我叫林刚，在江苏社会科学院从事中国近代经济史研究工作。我以在职人员身份到南京大学历史系攻读博士学位，现已通过答辩，冒昧地将论文呈您，望得到您的批评指正。

认识、探讨中国从"传统"向"现代"的演变特点、规律，我个人虽有兴趣，并作过一些初步探讨（1983 年我的硕士论文《南通土布生产与新式资本主义企业——大生纱厂》，摘要发表在《历史研究》1985 年第 4 期，题目为《试论大生纱厂的市场基础》），但无论从认识问题的深度还是从资料的掌握上都很不够。您在南京张謇国际学术研讨会上的论文及以后发展的一系列文章，均给我以很大的启发。这篇论文的一些基本观点都与这些启发有关。也正因为如此，我非常希望您能在百忙中对拙文加以过目，指出其中不足，以便我今后继续努力，不知能否如愿？

知您非常忙，贸然打扰，惶恐不安，请原谅。

致礼！

林刚

94.7.31

1999年6月与林刚关于"中国围墙与早期现代化"的通信

林刚兄：

拜读大作《中国围墙与早期现代化》，获益良多。文中观点，就近代中国即"早期现代化"来说，我完全同意。我一向重视传统经济中的积极因素。我还重看你95年8月给我的《再论中国现代化道路的民族性特征》，对农民家庭纺织业与机器大工业关系的分析至详。

不过，文中从第6页起就谈到当前农业的现代化问题。当前我国农业是否仍应以劳动力代替资本投入？这不是个理论问题，而应从现代经验，特别是近20年的经验入手。我没有作过研究，不过我感触最深的几件事是：

①乡镇企业及农民运输业的发展。

②80年代专业户的兴起，其中粮食专业户最具重要意义。

③90年代初，机耕机收已不可缺，今天更重要了，否则不能应付夏粮收、播和秋收。

④展望前途，农业产业化似乎是唯一出路。

当前的农业现代化，还有没有"传统经济的积极因素"？我觉得还是有的，我没有研究过。我想可从这些方面考虑：①传统思想文化，特别是非个人主义的价值观；②家族互助精神；③教育传统，培育子女，人力资本。

在历史上（近代），近来对小农经济的研究有些新的看法，可以注意：

①"人口爆炸说"基本被否定。对 18～19 世纪人口增长速度的新估计，人口行为的研究"人口压力"并不是那么严重（严重在解放后）。

②小农很精明，不会在土地上浪费劳动力，决不会搞"人海战术"。有人计算，江南每亩稻田的用工量，从宋到明到清，没有什么改变，都是 11 个，顶多 12 个工。剩余劳动力是投在经济作物和副业上去了。反之，清代每亩的资本投入（主要是肥料）是增加颇大。

③尽管人均土地不断缩小，以致有人均不到 2 亩。但实际耕作之中，农场面积有个常数，从明到清，江南总是"一夫十亩"（夫妇二人），北方是 20～30 亩。过大过小都会造成浪费，农民不取。

④18 世纪以后，亩产量确有下降趋势。主要由于生态破坏和恢复地力的资本投入不足。20 世纪以来亩产量有上升，但未恢复到乾隆水平。

这些看法，我都未深入研究，不知确否。但研究近代农业的现代化，应该考虑。因为从经济史角度说，我们的研究是建立在实证上，不是建立在理论上。

1999 年 6 月 16 日

1989 年与 Tim Wright 的通信

Dear Professor Wu,

We met briefly last autumn when I was visiting your Institute. I remember then that you expressed some reservations about the history. Peter Nolan, who, as you know, is the editor of the series, has nevertheless encouraged me to go ahead: we think it will be many years until your fully worked conclusions as in *Zhongguo zibenzhuyi fazhan shi*, vol 3, will be available in translation for Western readers. So it might still be worthwhile to provide for a Western readers. So it might still be worthwhile to provide for a Western audience some feeling for the changes in the field in China over the past ten years. I hope this is agreeable to you.

I enclose a copy of the letter I am sending to the authors of all the articles we want to translate, which outlines the project and its timetable. I know not all of the articles are in full agreement, but that is part of the intention: to show that it is (I hope still) possible to have open and free debate between different views in a way that was not possible during the Cultural Revolution.

I will be visiting China later this year, and hope to be in Beijing from 2 to 5

Tim. Wright（1948～），澳大利亚莫多克大学教授。

December. If it would be convenient I would like to visit the Institute and perhaps talk briefly with you. I realize that that will depend on the situation, however, and will not disturb you unless I hear that my visit would cause no problems.

With best wishes,

Yours sincerely,

Dr Tim Wright

September 23, 1989

Dr. Tim Wright

School of Humanities

Murdoch University

Murdoch Western Australia, 6150

Dear Dr. Wright:

I was delighted to receive your letter of September 6, 1989 and I am so glad to know that you will be visiting Beijing in December. From the table enclosed in your letter I see in advance the well picked contents of the proposed book you will be editing. I expect it to be a success.

You reminded me that I had expressed reservation on my article "An outline of the development of Chinese capitalism" to be appeared in your project when we met last autumn. The case is that my article was published in 1981, and from then on lots of new materials and studies are available, therefore many figures in the article are pending revision. I have been planning to make a detailed and more comprehensive estimate on the historical capital formation and GNP which will be appeared as Appendices in *Zhongguo zibenzhuji fazhan shi*, Vol. II and III. I did raced most parts of the calculation, but still far from completion. As to my viewpoints in the article, there will be no variation of importance. Considering the article has been reprinted in some collections and in Japanese version, and that the "fazhan shi" will not be available in English for many years, I would agree to include my article in your project. For the extraction, however, I suggest that you may add table 9 in page 135.

I will look forward to renewing our acquaintance in December, of course depending your programme in Beijing. Maybe you would call me on tel. 592191 (home) at your arrival.

With best wishes,

Yours sincerely

1999年6月与许檀关于
"明清传统市场"的通信

许檀同志：

　　拜读《明清时期传统市场的发展》书稿，获益良深。它集中了你多年研究调查成果，精华荟萃，蔚为大观。

　　全书重点，似在第二编"城乡市场网络体系之形成"。网络说似应以相互（互补）关系为主。本书按枢纽城市、中等城镇、农村集市三级编写（层次、枢纽较中心地理论灵活适用）。其中第五章农村集市网写得最好，无懈可击。第三、四章按沿运河、沿长江、沿海安排了32个大中城镇，在设计上是网络的，但具体写时，也许受地方志影响，像是商埠志。商埠志的内容，如沿革、范围、行业、商户、会馆、商税等，是完全必要的，但显得孤立，冲淡了网络意义。给人印象，微观分析强，中观、宏观不足。

　　其实，第一编的大区域分析是极好的。到第二编因32个城镇是重头戏，读者忘怀了。第三章改写时，最好呼应第一编，在"网络形成"上下点笔墨，使每个城镇在网络中定位。第四章以山东、江西为例，有中观分析，就比较好。其中山东一节内容丰富，笔调精彩，你最熟悉，得心应手。但在网络分析上，江西一节更佳，也许因为四大镇关系，江西网络本来清楚（龙登高的《中国传统市场发展史》也是以江西为例，另一例是福建）。

　　清代的市场整合，本来包括在网络形成之中。一个大区网络形成完了，

许檀（1953～），南开大学历史学院教授。

也是整合完了。因不讲价格，整合过程难以量化，只好在网络形成中带出来。这个含义，是否可在改写时表现一、二。

网络最好用地图表现。我读你书稿时就常要用地图对照。如果能配上一些地图，会方便读者多多，并加强网络概念。这要花很大功夫，可考虑少作一些，如大区，沿运河、沿江、沿海。外国人喜欢用图，施坚雅有近百幅幻灯片，我看过他演示；斯波义信讲宋代市场，也有不少图。我们也应改变学术风气，多用图表，由你倡导。当然，要花力气。

经济研究有个"统筹"指标，即人口。有时不能计量，就用人口代替，因有个"人均"概念。市场网络，与人口（密度、移民）关系更大。本书在讲各城镇时已有人口史，在中观、宏观以至长江流域等上也以人口为统筹要素，就显得更科学。市场的发展以需求为主，供给次之；而需求的首要指标是人口，因为传统市场的主体是农户（近现代是企业）。人口用梁方仲，可修正，现在修正已不难，用章有义、姜涛都可，移民用曹树基。

第三编"传统市场在近代的转型"，你打算删去。我对这编最有兴趣，这编也最具现实意义。删去是因为材料积累不足，但已有了不少，删去可惜。已有材料，毛病在于都是典型城镇，看来有"举例子"之嫌，而这个时期，已有条件作宏观考察了。

如果删去，本编最后一页总结的思想却不能删。其思想是：鸦片战争后列强入侵，不是创建一个新的市场体系，而是利用和部分改造既有的市场体系，而传统市场的真正改造，是随着中国近代化过程逐步发展的，是内因为主。这是个卓越的思想。这思想，在你 1997 年 6 月一篇《明清时期农村集市的发展》论文中写得更好。该文最后一页总结中说：明清市场网络的形成"是中国近代化过程的一项重要内容"，这个过程"至少从明代中叶已经起步，到清中叶已具相当规模，且卓有成效"。把城乡市场网络的形成同中国经济近代化联系起来，我完全拥护。在成书时，第三编尽管删除，这个思想却要发扬，表现在全书中。

1999 年 6 月

2000 年 3 月与许檀关于 "市场网络体系" 的信

许檀同志：

拜读 "市场网络体系" 大作，受益良多。我没什么意见。文已付梓，毋需改动。唯我对 "网络" 有些遐想，或供以后研究参考。

一，网络是门新学问

过去我们讲商路，明清不少 "士商便览" 之类，刘秀生有 "清代商业交通考" 甚详，但非网络。西方讲 "市场一体化" （integration），以价格为指标，可计量，但与网络含义不同。施坚雅的 8 级市场，各形成 "市场圈"，是垂直体系（hierarchy），而网络是平行体系，不同。滨下武志的东亚 "贸易圈"，有对抗性，而国内网络是互助的，无对立，不同。所以，网络是门新学向，有些理论问题可探讨。

二，网络论

网络是由不同地方（网址）之间的商品流通组成的。你的枢纽城市、中等城镇、集市，都是网址。考察每个网址的输入输出，即得网络。各类网络与其说层次（级别），不如说范围，即 "覆盖数省或数十省" （大网），"覆盖一两个府，十来个府" （中网），集市（小网）。施坚雅重级别，忽视面，因而得出 "独立性" （autarchy）概念，这是错误的。网络从来不会独立。

我主张用输入输出观察，因两者覆盖面不同，作用也有异，一般说输入以集中好，输出以多路为佳。一个网址的作用，就看其覆盖面大小和输入输出情况，而不由级别决定，例如周村作用大于县城。集市网作用小于城镇网，城镇网作用小于枢纽网。"集市是基础"是从层次论说的，不是从网络论说的。从网络论说，集市网不会有"调整经济布局、优化资源配置"的作用，下举江南、珠江三角洲二例，都不是集市网。

彭泽益有篇长文，考证清前期广州的输入输出，有数十个品种，并有各商品的来源地或输往地，是个很好的网络图（枢纽网）。他给我一份，黄皮16开繁体字，可惜我没找到。我在论近代市场一文中，有几个纽枢城市间流量（价值），因是1936年，明清资料无数量，但有时有大量少量概念。网络有出入地点、数量最佳。

三，网络史

施坚雅从农村市镇市场（standard market town）讲起，因人口增加，出现中间市场；人口继增，出现中心市场；然后进入县、府、道、省、京师市场。这与历史不符。农村集市，战国以后才有；农村市镇，宋以后才发达。而商代贩运贸易已活跃，西周城市市场已颇发达（《左传》为据，《易系辞》《周礼》或晚出）。

城邦时代（西周、希腊、罗马）地区间贸易都盛。农村市场要村社（井田）废后，小农出现才有。魏晋南北朝商业衰退，首先是农村市场，因小农变成依附农。宋以后，尤其明嘉万后，市场发展的顺序是枢纽第一，城镇第二，农村第三。网络的发展也是这样。最大的发展，或网络的形成，如你另文所讲，是在中国近代化过程中。

以上是我的遐想或瞎想，请批评。

吴承明

2000 年 3 月 2 日

1993～1994 年与
王玉茹的通信

玉茹：

接 2 月 28 日来信，知你近日已摆脱一些杂事，转入学问，甚慰。所论世间事有可得者有不可得者，唯事业可努力求之，确属灼论，有此怀抱，我深为欣佩。

我前提及诺思等著作，以是经济史的一种最新理论，应该知道，非必遵行也。制度关系经济发展至巨，马克思所说生产方式，实即制度。这是从客观而言，具体研究资源配置，恐怕还是从看不见的手或相对价格入手。科斯等新制度学派把它完全归之于产权问题，未免绝对化。又将经济效益完全归之于交易费用，也未免绝对化。盖其立足点是当代大资本集团，如跨国公司，能将市场交易置于集团内部调配，即钱德勒所说《看得见的手》（有商务中译本）。这在历史上并非如此。试看诺思的两书，其论当代资本主义的厂商行为，一般有理，而其用产权、交易费用论领主制经济一章，则难令人信服。以我国近代而论，最大的生产是农业、手工业，这有什么产权问题呢？开厂、转业、改变生产品种都有自由，也不需要产权保护。他们生产什么（也就是资源配置）主要还是看何者有利，也就是相对价格，市场交易费用（运费、风险、利息、税、佣金等）倒是重要的，交易费用高（尤其运费）阻碍发展，而将政府支出都看作交易费用，则无足取。

王玉茹（1954～），南开大学经济研究所教授。

相对价格指商品比价，以及工资、利息（钱价）、金银比价、汇价等。最重要的是工农业产品比价，长期不利于农业，故农业落后，但有利于工业发展，最明显的是原料与成品比价，如棉花与棉纱，小麦与面粉，研究者多，效果立见。各产业之间的比价，如黄金（资源）是流向何种产业，还很少有人研究。新产业何以兴，何以衰，即产品与进口货比价，也较显见。工资与产业关系，未见系统论述，涉及劳动或资本（都代表资源）密集问题。农业内部比价，如经济作物与粮食，经济作物之间，也很少有人研究。金银比价、汇价在近代中国特别重要，盖半殖民地关系。而利息不甚敏感，因基本上是农业国。

相对价格变动有长期、短期之分，就中国近代史说，最缺乏的是长期趋势，用以解释宏观变动。而短期的，往往影响几业兴衰，比较易见，但未必改变产业结构和发展模式。

但价格不是唯一因素。经济发展和资源配置还有其他经济因素和非经济因素。非经济因素中传统习惯、道德取向等在某些方面有决定性，往往被忽视；战争也有决定性，而政府政策不是很重要，因政策多半行不通。经济史和经济学不同。经济学是把其他因素都抽象掉，只讲价格和最优化，即看不见的手。经济史却是要发现那些看得见的手，不能抽象掉。经济学是把价格作为内生变量，价格决定资源配置和发展模式。经济史是把经济发展作为已成事实，从已成事实出发，去找看不见的和看得见的手。只有在没有历史事实记载时，才用价格作推论。如西方推论15～17世纪农业兴衰就是这样，因为这时期仅有一些教会的价格材料，因而，粗粮价格上涨快于细粮，推论农业衰败；葡萄酒价上涨快于谷物，推论农业兴旺，等等。

就市场研究说，不仅相对价格，还有价格结构、价格是怎样形成的，这又涉及商品流向问题。就市场商品量来说，洋货仅占很小比重（10%左右），但进出口价却有决定性作用。这看来不通，但事实恐怕是如此。

以上是我个人一些看法。你写博士论文，不要以我的看法为准。因为我没有专门研究过市场价格问题，一些新的价格理论也不懂，我的看法必不免错误。即使不错，你也不必采用，因为博士论文要有创见性，有自己的观点。还有个根本的理论问题没有解决，即今天西方价格理论，大都是新古典主义，基本上是立足于边际效率价值论。而斯密的看不见的手，是以劳动价值论为基础的，不会有什么无差异曲线。以旧中国农业的、落后的市场来说，也确有劳动价值决定价格的道理。究竟价格与价值的关系如何，我看我们只好不论。把价格看成是市场上存在的一个可计量的东西，它是个客观存在的东西，经济史也就不问他的实质是什么了。不过，有些商品，中国市场上还没有，但它的国外价格也对中国经济有影响，这可作影子价格看待。

附上《中资史》第三卷中关于 1936 年市场的一节。又导论中总结了这个问题，也附上。所附上的不是给出版社的定稿，在那个定稿中又有少许改动。第三卷我去年秋末就看过校样，现在还没出版，我也没去催问。因为校样看完，编辑部就不管了，何时开印是出版科的事。出版科讲生意经，怕赔钱就要拖。出版科我不认识人，也不想去催。我已交稿，就算交代了。收到请赐复。

祝

健康！

吴承明

1993 年 3 月 4 日

玉茹同志：

两封来信及转来的信都收到。知你的学位、职称、论文出版诸事均妥，甚慰。下学期将讲授外经史，这对你研究大有好处。至于采用发展经济学方法，其实就是注重近代（15～20世纪）一段，过去也是这样。西方的经济史学思想，二次大战后有转变。过去强调生产力，如对工业革命特别重视。现则强调需求，以16世纪重商主义为变革起点。这是受凯恩斯主义影响，从总需求—总供给上看经济发展。此种新思潮可以奇波拉主编的六卷本《欧洲经济史》为代表，每阶段都从总需求讲起，可参看。

我这里一切都好，天热很少出门，看看闲书而已。近有二元经济一文，系《历史研究》四十周年纪念约文，奉上一份，你是行家，请指正。

祝

暑祺

吴承明

1994年7月30日

1989 年与 Jae-Dong Han （韩宰东） 的通信

October 27, 1989.

吴承明教授榻下，

I am currently writing the thesis on the Hyperinflation under the Kuomintang government from 1946 – 49. The main hypothesis I put forth there is that the cetral KMT regime might have used the multiple currency-areas （Fapi ［法币］, and Taipi ［台币］, and Dongbei Liutongjuan ［东北流通券］） to maximize the revenues from money creation or seigniorages combined from these areas in the process of financing budget deficits.

Professor Brandt and I share the view that it will be of great importance to clarify the institutional channels through which the seigniorages extracted from Manchuria （Dongbei） and from Taiwan were transferred to the central KMT government. The data or materials about the Dongbei of the time seem to be scarce and hard to obtain here. We have only come across sketchy and brief references. For instance, We have found a reference that the Central Trust came to Manchuria with Dongbei Liutongjuan and bought a huge mount of soybean, and that the proceeds were channeled into political funds of the KMT.

Jae-Dang Han （韩宰东, 1957 ~ 2016）, 加拿大国王大学学院经济系教授。

Your advice or suggestion on this matter will be greatly appreciated. Looking forward to hearing from you, I remain,

With best regard,

sincerely yours,

韩宰东顿首

Jae-Dong Han.

November 20, 1989

Dear Mr. Jae-Dong Han:

I was pleased to receive your letter of october 27, 1989, which was mailed by professor L. Brandt.

I think it is a reasonable hypothesis that the kuomintang government might have used the multiple currency system in financing its budget deficits. I have not, however, gone into this problem and have had no reference about the postwar financial situation in Dongbei, therefore I am not in a position to answer your questions. I think, however, the issue of Dongbei Liu-tongjuan had its historical backgrounds. Xiong Shi-Xui in Dongbei as well as Chen Yi in Taiwan, might have kept somewhat seigniorages as you suggested in your letter. But judged from the charactor of Chang Kia-ngau, the former Director-general of the Bank of China, I do believe that one of the main subjects of the scheme was "to avoid the impact of Eapi" （see enclosure）. Therefore, the rate to Eapi was set at 1 : 10, and its rate of inflaiion （27. 5billions in 1946 and 319. 2 billions in 1948 July）was in fact lower than that of Eapi.

The Central Trust did buy huge amount of soybeans from Dongbei. So far as I know, one of the major business of the Central Trust at that time was handling the barter trade under the government contracts with foreign countries, and soybeans were the most important goods to be bartered. I do not know, however, how the proceeds there of were channeled into political funds of the KMT.

with best wishes.

Sincerely,

Wu Cheng-Ming

December 1, 1989

Dear professor Wu:

Your letter of November 20 is gratefully acknowledged. Your advice is well heeded, The paper you kindly enclosed surely enhances my understanding of the political sentiment and perhaps economic compliance by the DongBeiRen with the KMT regime.

In fact, in the magazine 传记文学, I have been given some references to the disposal of the proceeds from soybean operation by the KMT. It was a sort of memoir by 田雨时. It was in the library that an old gentleman gave me a list of references containing the tale of Mr. Zhang Jiao Ao in Dongbei. Surprisingly he turns out to be a Chinese teacher of my former supervisor, Professor T. G. Rawski of the University of Pittsburgh.

As I put forward a hypothesis which is somewhat radically different from the conventional wisdom surrounding the multi-currency system, I am happy even with your partially approving remarks. To my mind, it is a worthy intellectual exercise. I have been emboldened by Plato's following aphorism about usefulness of intellectual risk:

(After talking at length about his theory of souls, Plato added) "Of course, no reasonable man ought to insist that the facts are exactly as I have described them. But that either this or something very like it is a true account of our souls and their future habitations-since we have clear evidence that the soul is immortal – this, I think, is both a reasonable contention and a belief worth risking, for the risk is a noble one. We should use such accounts to inspire ourselves with confidence, and that is why I have already drawn out my tale so long." (Plato, *Phaedo*, 114d, E. Hamilton and H. Cairns ed., *The Collected Dialogues of Plato*, *Including the Letters*, Princeton University Press, 1961, pp. 94 – 95)

Although occasionally feeling like I am trying to build a house (hypothesis) out of small fragments （scattered evidence） or to level-up a lake with a crate of earth each time, it is my sincere wish to pursue this theme of research, which I dare to believe will, upon completion, shed some light on the characteristics of monetary policy of the KMT in the 1940's.

Please find my preliminary paper enclosed herewith. I will be very much honoured if you can read it at your leisure time and give me your advice. If in the future you come across related materials or scholars interested in it, would you be so kind to let me know about them? It is my belief that fellowship is the essential part of scholarship. Also, if there is anything I can do for you here, it will be my pleasure to do so.

Thanking you warmly fou your wisdom and scholarship shared in this matter, I remain,

Respectfully yours,

韩宰东顿首

Jae-Dong Han.

Encl.

诗　话

濯足一谈

序

我原无每晚濯足的习惯。"文革"中，我机关同人都于 1969 年秋下放到商业部"五七干校"，地在辽宁省盘锦县南部，属退海平原，风狂雪暴，号南大荒。我们主要的劳动是开荒种稻，赤足下田，往返多经泥沼；每晚必浸泡双足良久，才能登炕就寝。而每到濯足，就表示一天的劳动和批斗任务已告结束，于是三五聚谈，满舍叨叨。闲谈中亦偶及诗词，有时也作点笔记。1971 年冬，我们迁往粮食部"五七干校"。地在河北省固安县的永定河畔。这里的劳动以治沙为主，也是种稻田，兼事基建；而每晚濯足、闲谈、偶尔笔记如故。1973 年秋我被借调到北京，恢复坐办公室。离开干校了，但那四年激动心魂的岁月却总是萦绕心怀，时刻难忘。"暖汤濯我足，剪纸招我魂"，因将所记所忆写成一册，名曰《濯足偶谈》，并请我妻洪达琳题签。

离开干校后，生活方式完全变了。然"文革"未已，激情仍在，每晚濯足也已成习。于是再弄纸笔，成《濯足偶谈续集》，迄 1977 年我转入现职工作为止。

我是搞经济工作的，不懂文学，更从未学过诗。但是在干校的风雨情怀

165

中，也不免有所吟咏。遂连同旧稿并离干校后所作检抄一遍，题名《一锄集》。

1992年春，我的主要工作任务已经完成，人则年满七十五周岁。回忆往事，不能自已。因将原草《濯足偶谈》、《濯足偶谈续集》及《一锄集》作些删剪，汇成此册。文中原有"文革"时语言并干校术语则都保留原貌，连同谬论，供老友一哂。

1992 年 4 月

再版序

十年前，我将这本小册子分赠给"五七干校"十一连同窗和经历了"文革"的一些学长。反应出乎意外的热烈：黾勉外，或唱和，或赐新作，乃至有国外学长以英文《八声甘州》见赠。原共"偶谈"的老友，或作长篇评论，或逐条签批，重现当年炕头论坛。还有我不曾拜识的前辈，为之逐页校正错字，并指出用事、声韵之误。这种热情洋溢的反应可概括为"文革"情结，《濯足偶谈》供矢的耳。年来索阅者仍不绝，已无存，而我已85岁，因再版留念。

再版于《濯足偶谈》增《死不改悔》等二篇，《濯足偶谈续集》增"无题诗"等五篇，都是旧稿中原已论及，经检出重写者。《一锄集》未动。

在干校无人敢带照相机，整个"文革"中我无留影。1980年3月往东京大田区南千束访张宗植学长，出地铁站忽见"洗足池"，留一影，置再版篇首，并题一绝：

> 昔闻沧浪水，今见洗足池。
> 高人挂衣去，烟波渺愁疑。

承宗植兄详示故事，盖弘安五年（1282）日莲宗宗主过此洗足，竟圆寂于千束，后人因名洗足池，日语洗足与千束同音也。唯所见松树非日莲上人挂袈裟原株，而为换植之第三代矣。

2002 年 1 月 3 日

"不薄今人爱古人"

"不薄今人爱古人"。杜甫这话比传统文人的厚古薄今大为进步。不过，他所说的"今人"并不是他同时代的那些伟大诗人，而是《戏为六绝句》开头所说的庾信以及王杨卢骆诸子，或齐梁诗坛。对杜甫说原属近代，应称之为"近人"。"不薄今人爱古人，清词丽句必为邻。窃攀屈宋宜方驾，恐与齐梁作后尘。"近人有清词丽句，学诗若一定攀古，反会落到近代人后面了。

据我看，《六绝句》与元好问、王士禛的论诗绝句不同，它不是一组诗论，而是针对一件事，即针对当时对六朝以来诗风的批判和改革思潮而言的。历史上的革新都是打着复古的旗号。陈子昂所谓"前不见古人，后不见来者"，也许是首倡这种改革的。李白叹"大雅久不作"，认为"自从建安来，绮丽不足珍"，要求"圣代复元古"，"重辉映千春"。这种文艺复兴也是个否定之否定，是合乎辩证法的。

杜甫也是从齐梁绮丽中解放出来的一位创新主将。但是在诗学上，他不讲辩证法，而是讲进化论。

照杜甫看，六朝选体并不坏。他曾"颇学阴何苦用心"。他非常推崇庾信和鲍照。鲍照刘宋人，严格说不属齐梁，但琢字研声实自鲍始，故称"才兼鲍照愁绝倒"。杜甫对唐初诸子沈佺期、宋之问迄乃祖杜审言也是十分肯定的，因为他们是继承齐梁的。

《六绝句》说的"递相祖述"，可视为杜甫进化论的原则。唐初诸子祖述齐梁，齐梁祖述汉魏，汉魏祖述风骚。因而，学诗要由近及远，从近代可通达古代。"纵使卢王操翰墨，劣于汉魏近风骚。"但此语并无贬义。因为"别裁伪体亲风雅，转益多师是吾师"。似是说，历代的诗都有继承而来的精彩的东西，但也有伪造的古董，只要裁去假古董，就接近风骚了。因而，历代诗人皆为我师。

杜甫一生是以前辈诗人为师，而不批评任何前辈，顶多说有些人（如何刘沈谢）"力未工"而已。但在《六绝句》中却严厉批评了某些人，说他们"嗤点流传赋"，"轻薄为文哂未休"，称这些人为"尔曹"。这是些什么人呢？我前面说，是指对六朝诗风持批判态度者。但可断言，绝不是指从陈子昂到李白的那些伟大诗人。我想，大约是指一些爱发议论、根本不创作或很少创作的文人，故称"为文哂未休"。我举不出名字，不过，每个时代都有不少"真正的"批评家。像我们这些炕头的评论家也包括在内。

杜牧和数字

杜牧七绝善用数字。"南朝四百八十寺，多少楼台烟雨中"；"二十四桥明月夜，玉人何处教吹箫？"都是数字上见功夫。汪士信云，后者可解为二十四个歌女在桥上弄箫。

"东风不与周郎便，铜雀春深锁二乔"。"二"字分外轻巧。"一骑红尘妃子笑，无人知是荔枝来"。这里"一"字出色。送荔枝的原不止一骑，但如用"数骑"就没有诗味了。这首，我看又是咏杨妃最好的诗，短短四句，意味深长。其前联"长安回望绣成堆，山顶千门次第开"，生动明朗，也用数字。

可与杜牧这类句子相比的有温庭筠的"雁声远过潇湘去，十二楼中月自明"。两句给人以寥廓之感，读者的意境好像也随雁声远逝。其全诗则没有什么意思。

温庭筠有"万顷江田一鹭飞"，李商隐有"万里云罗一雁飞"。温句比李句美。但李诗是说写好情书，却无法寄去。温诗则除一片澹然水景外，没说什么。杜牧"分司一语惊四座，两行红粉尽回头"；用的是数字，讲的是故事，也许不仅仅是风流故事，与"十年一觉扬州梦"同工。

徐凝的"天下三分明月夜，二分无赖是扬州"，简直是杜牧风味。但前面两句很难堪，这两句是"萧娘脸下难胜泪，桃叶眉头易得愁"，所以苏东坡称之为"恶诗"。

杜牧"娉娉袅袅十三余，豆蔻梢头二月初。春风十里扬州路，卷上珠帘总不如"；连用三个数字。当然，像张祜《河满子》："故国三千里，深宫二十年。一声河满子，双泪落君前"；句句用数字。又《正月十五夜灯》："千门开锁万灯明，正月中旬动帝京。三百内人连袖舞，一时天上著词声"；则未免有堆砌之感了。

一般说，诗中用数字并不难，有时还以数字取巧，尤其在对偶中。白居易"在郡六百日，入山十二回"属此。黄庭坚的外甥徐俯有联："一百五日寒食雨，二十四番花信风。"用典属对都极轻巧，陆游曾摹用。李白咏杜鹃："一叫一回肠一断，三春三月忆三巴。"乍看有点堆砌，但并看上联"蜀国曾闻子规鸟，宣城还见杜鹃花"，便会忘其属对之工，反而是啼血溅花之感，令人泪下。

聂夷中和杜荀鹤

今人选唐诗颇称颂皮日休、聂夷中、杜荀鹤，认为他们的作品有人民性，称晚唐三杰。我没读过《皮子文薮》，他的《正乐府》提出了一些社会问题，但无解答。聂夷中诗留有三十七首，杜荀鹤有《唐风集》，都很好读。

聂诗中为选家称道的《伤田家》。《伤田家》确实生动反映了社会矛盾，提法尖锐，不像皮日休那样啰唆。"二月卖新丝，五月粜新谷。医得眼前疮，剜却心头肉"；确实深刻。但他所提的疗法却令人失望："我愿君王心，化作光明烛。不照绮罗筵，只照逃亡屋。"据说皮日休曾参加黄巢起义，皮是不会有这种提法的。

余如《赠农》《勉客》等只是讲大道理，劝人力耕，莫谈国事。《公子行》等写贵人骄奢生活，已是唐人老话。聂诗中我看《行路难》一首倒很出色："莫言行路难，夷狄犹中国。谓言骨肉亲，中门如异域。出入全在人，路亦无通塞。门前两条辙，何处去不得。"这诗的好处是有辩证观点。

杜荀鹤的诗，不少写得很深刻，如"桑柘废来犹纳税，田园荒尽尚征苗"；"因供寨木无桑柘，为点乡兵绝子孙"等。有特色的是《再经胡城县》："去岁曾经此县城，县民无口不冤声。今来县宰加朱绂，便是生灵血染成。"又，《题所居邨舍》尾联云："如此数州谁会得，杀民将尽更邀勋。"这种思想还少人言出。不过，杜所写的是军阀混战。有的如"握手相看谁敢言，军家刀剑在腰边"；但仔细一看，诗题乃是《旅泊遇郡中叛乱示同志》。

读《唐风集》还有个障碍，即投赠达官贵人和赠僧谈禅的诗太多了，令人生厌。

有人说"杜诗三百首，惟在一联中，正谓'风暖鸟声碎，日高花影重'也；《唐风集》以之压卷。"（毛晋跋）我看《春宫怨》中这一联并不怎么样，倒是前一联"承恩不在貌，教妾若为容"颇有意思。我最喜欢的是《送人游吴》一首："君到姑苏见，人家尽枕河。古宫闲地少，水港小桥多。夜市卖菱藕，春船载绮罗。遥知未眠月，乡思在渔歌。"其中除"春船载绮罗"一景外，我皆亲见。

有人说杜荀鹤是杜牧的微子，诗风相近。此决不可靠。我看杜荀鹤是学白居易的，语言平易一点比白诗又进一步。白《百花亭》诗有"佛寺乘船入，人家枕水居"。白居易说他和元稹都是"外服儒风，内宗梵行"。可是元稹愈老愈官迷，白居易愈老愈风流，而诗中绝无梵刹之声。杜荀鹤的《唐风集》则兼而有之，真是知识分子的末世唐风。至于杜牧，似另有哀怨者在。1960年我在民族宫参加编写《历史唯物主义》时读《樊川诗集》，曾题一律，有句云："君诚有策歌河朔，命自无常哀杜秋。欲罢一麾浮江海，还思十载梦扬州。"

诗词人事（一）

诗中最好有人有事。我不是说叙事诗、咏史诗，而是说无论写景或抒情，都要内中有人的活动，感染力才强。

贾岛"鸟宿池边树，僧敲月下门"；动人景象是下一句。李白"长安一片月，万户捣衣声"；"暮从碧山下，山月随人归"。也是这样。没有人，便成死景。

"春风又绿江南岸"，把自然写得生气勃勃。但终不若柳宗元"欸乃一声山水绿"来得活泼，这句并有人改造大自然的意味。"池塘生春草"，"远峰隐半规"。吐语自然，都是好句子。但比起"采菊东篱下，悠然见南山"就显得黯然了。谢灵运的山水诗就是山水，陶渊明笔下的田园总有个种田的人。

柳宗元："千山鸟飞绝，万径人踪灭。孤舟蓑笠翁，独钓寒江雪。"用蓑翁独钓写出一派《江雪》景象，闭目思之，如入其境。元稹："寥落古行宫，宫花寂寞红。白头宫女在，闲坐说玄宗。"用宫女闲话，抒尽今昔之感，闭目思之，如闻其语。

杜牧的"清明时节雨纷纷"一首，有欲断魂的行路人，问酒家何处，又有个牧童，遥指代答。这恐怕是用人事写景抒情最好的绝句了。人最熟悉的是人，最关心的是人的活动，所以能给读者最深刻的印象。

也可以虚写。张继："姑苏城外寒山寺，夜半钟声到客船。"人的活动是隐藏在钟声里。陆游："伤心桥下春波绿，曾是惊鸿照影来。"这时唐琬已去世四十年了，但在这首诗中真是音容宛在。

李商隐善用人物形象。他的《无题》诗，每首都有一对情人的影子在活动，这是它吸引人的原因之一。或谓乃政治诗，就是政治吧，人的活动还是存在的。

"昨夜星辰昨夜风，画楼西畔桂堂东"；这首是点出时间、地点后，写人们相聚的热闹场面中的寂寞心情，最后几声漏鼓，催人离去。若说是叙事诗，谁也不知道叙的是啥事。《无题》都不是叙事诗，而是思想感情依托人物活动而出的诗。

"扇裁月魄羞难掩，车走雷声语未通"；这首确实写了一段故事，但是借故事人物抒发感情。"斑骓只系垂杨岸，何处西南任好风"；这首是虚写或暗写人物的活动。"蓬莱此去无多路，青鸟殷勤为探看"；这首简直是用物的活动写人了。

有意思的是这一首："飒飒东风细雨来，芙蓉塘外有轻雷。金蟾啮锁烧香入，玉虎牵丝汲井回。贾氏窥帘韩掾少，宓妃留枕魏王才。春心莫共花争发，一寸相思一寸灰。"这里有烧香人、汲井人、窥帘者、赠枕人，当然还有被窥者、受枕人以及他们的故事。"轻雷"暗用典，所以又有乘车人和等候乘车人的人。诗人是想抒发自己错综复杂的思想情绪，在诗中则是纷奇的场面相继出现，恍如《仲夏夜之梦》。

虽然如此，我想这首算不上一首好诗。它立意不高，一切都谈不上了。笔法是好的，但我想最好的笔法应是爽朗明了，而不是绕圈子。

诗词人事（二）

用人事活动写情，在词中更为突出。李清照："试问卷帘人，却道海棠依旧。知否，知否，应是绿肥红瘦。"通过与同样爱花的人的问答，写出更深一层的惜春情绪。这比黄庭坚的《清平乐》"春归何处"一首有味得多。黄庭坚是去问黄鹂，黄鹂不会说话，"嘟"的一声飞走了。

晏几道《临江仙》："记得小蘋初见，两重心字罗衣。琵琶弦上说相思。当时明月在，曾照彩云归。"有了这些形象故事，才见得上边两句"落花人独立，微雨燕双飞"的感情所在。这比之柳永那首"多情自古伤离别，更那堪冷落清秋节"，给人印象更深刻。柳词长篇铺叙，情节单调，虽有"杨柳岸晓风残月"等佳句，但感染力不强。可是其上阕"执手相看泪眼，竟无语凝噎"两语，给人以真挚感，极佳，正因有人事活动。

张先《木兰花·乙卯吴兴寒食》结句："中庭月色正清明，无数杨花过无影"；朱彝尊说"工绝"。其实并无可取，倒是其开头四句："龙头舴艋吴儿竞，笋柱秋千游女并，芳洲拾翠暮忘归，秀野踏青来不定"，写得十分活泼。张先自称"张三影"。这种影子词本来无聊，如"云破月来花弄影"，并没什么意思。倒是他在《青门引》中的"那堪更被明月，隔墙送过秋千影"较好，这里暗示有个打秋千的人。

苏轼的"花褪残红青杏小"这首《蝶恋花》，几乎全用故事写内心感情，很动人，并耐人寻思。"老夫聊发少年狂"那首《江城子》，豪迈胸怀全用故事写出；不过，可能人都把它看成记事词了。"大江东去"那首著名的《念奴娇》，就是因为穿插了一段人物活动，格外提神："遥想公瑾当年，小乔初嫁了，雄姿英发；羽扇纶巾，谈笑间，强虏灰飞烟灭。"有了这几句，真叫人"故国神游"，全词都跃跃活动起来。

辛弃疾的《摸鱼儿》"更能消几番风雨"，是写自己做闲官、悲国难的心情。中间插入一段故事："长门事，准拟佳期又误。蛾眉曾有人妒。千金纵买相如赋，脉脉此情谁诉。"这属于用典，使全词活跃起来，但这个典掺了水，因为陈阿娇并未与汉武帝拟准佳期，可是这样才见曲折。

辛弃疾的《永遇乐·京口北固亭怀古》，借用孙权、刘裕、刘义隆、廉颇等一连串历史人物事迹，抒发他抗敌的壮怀和决心。后人批评这词"用事多"，有道理。不过我想说，后人对元嘉北伐这种小的战役已无足重视，而在辛弃疾时代，乃是近代史上的惨痛教训，耿耿于怀的。故云："元嘉草草，封狼居胥，赢得仓皇北顾。四十三年，望中犹记，烽火扬州路。"结尾："凭谁问，廉颇老矣，尚能饭否？"这种襟怀，就不觉其"用事多"了。

有人有事，也须有些意思，才算好词。像前述晏几道、张先的那几篇，思想无所取，只是讲其手法。可是，如像冯延巳的《谒金门》："闲引鸳鸯芳径里，手挼红杏蕊"；"斗鸭栏干独倚，碧玉搔头斜坠"；可以说是写最无聊的人的最无聊的事。也称名作，却不堪一读。

拟人化

由于用人事活动写景最感人，人们也常把自然物写成人，即拟人化。这在《楚辞》中已很突出，而宋人在这方面最成熟。

"春风又绿江南岸"，即把风拟人化了，有意志，有行动。王安石很善这种手法。如写杨湖阴的书斋："一水护田将绿绕，两山排闼送青来。""排闼"是推门而入，把山写成大力士。而最好的是《元日》："爆竹声中一岁除，春风送暖入屠苏。千门万户曈曈日，总把新桃换旧符。"这诗充满不断更新的积极精神。"春风"句是风把暖送入酒中，从前后文看，也可说是人饮了元日酒，暖洋洋的，知道春天来了。饮这种屠苏酒还有个规矩，就是年少者先饮。这又是青春的人格化了。

苏轼的《新城道中二首（之一）》："东风知我欲山行，吹断檐间积雨声。岭上晴云披絮帽，树头初日挂铜钲。"前两句说风有思维，能知我意。后两句看上去只是描写山上云、树上日；但仔细一想，似是说山像个戴白帽子的老头，树像个手执铜钲的战士。铜钲是军乐器。

拟人化在苏诗中真是神奇。"沙平风软望不到，孤山久与船低昂"。这诗本是题唐人李思训画的长江绝岛图，却超出画面，把山写得随人意动起来了。"峨峨两烟鬟，晓镜开新妆"，这是把孤山拟人化。黄庭坚写君山"缩结湘娥十二鬟"，也是这种手法。苏轼在此诗中称小孤山为"小姑"，本民间"小姑嫁彭郎"传说，小孤山在民间早已拟人化了。

拟人化最简单的是用比喻；山比作眉，水比作眼，已是老生常谈。如王观词："水是眼波横，山是眉峰聚。"但是，要把西湖比作西子，才达到最高水平。"欲把西湖比西子，淡妆浓抹总相宜"。此诗一出，即成千古定论。

不过，苏轼原有西湖诗："云山已作歌眉浅，山下碧流清似眼。"可见，他的西湖比西子，也是从山比作眉、水比作眼发展来的。

把花比作美女，太普通了，以至庸俗。秦观："有情芍药含春泪，无力蔷薇卧晓枝。"可谓庸俗典型。但苏轼的《海棠》："只恐夜深花睡去，高烧银烛照红妆。"写海棠有起居生活，并且精神饱满，令人振奋。白居易也有《惜牡丹花二首（之一）》："明朝风起应吹尽，夜惜衰红把火看。"不过若拟人化，就变成老太婆了。苏轼还有篇古风：《寓居定惠院之东，杂花满山，有海棠一株，土人不知贵也》。这是他谪居黄州时作，洪迈因以之比白居易的《琵琶行》。但苏诗以海棠自况，却充满积极乐观精神。写海棠"嫣然一笑竹篱间，桃李漫山总粗俗"；"朱唇得酒晕生脸，翠袖卷纱红映肉。林深雾暗晓光迟，日暖风轻春睡足"。全是拟人手法，不故弄风雅，不避俗字，是以感情充沛。

拟人化要拟得自然。黄庭坚有首诗写竹："程婴杵臼立孤难，伯夷叔齐采薇瘦。"这和竹子有什么关系？任渊注曰："言竹之劲且瘦如此。"这是字谜，不是诗。

声音人事

诗不是乐谱，用诗写音乐只能是打比方，最常用的是风呀、雨呀，莺啼、鹤唳之类。只能写声音，很难表现曲调、曲式和旋律。不过，比方中多半是听者感情所在，因而用人事活动打比方会更生动和富有想象力。

李颀写董庭兰弹琴，有一段是"幽音变调忽飘洒，长风吹林雨坠瓦。迸泉飒飒飞木末，野鹿呦呦走堂下"。写出变调后的节奏，以至音色。最后一句最富想象力，因为呦呦鹿鸣本来是"食野之苹"，现在走到堂下来了，进入人们的思路。这显然是反用《湘夫人》。

黄庭坚有首《听宋宗儒摘阮歌》，描绘阮的声调："楚国羁臣放十年，汉宫佳人嫁千里。深闺洞房语恩怨，紫燕黄鹂韵桃李。楚狂声歌惊市人，渔父挐舟在葭苇。"用不同的人事典故表现不同的音感。"渔父"句不是用《楚辞》，是用《庄子》。渔父刺船从芦苇中 Nü……的一声滑走了，孔子"待水波定，不闻挐音"，才敢离开。不过，这许多音响颇为零乱，看不出曲调。

李贺的《李凭箜篌引》有一段是："十二门前融冷光，二十三弦动紫皇。女娲炼石补天处，石破天惊动秋雨。梦入神山教神妪，老鱼跳波瘦蛟舞。"前两句是说弦调清凄，若冷光遍入长安十二城门，又直上太清紫皇宫。次二句是说音调突破幽抑，急转直下，若秋雨骤倾。后二句总说声调感神人、动万物。"神妪"大约指成夫人，能箜篌，见《搜神记》。这里用神人神话，格外生动，属浪漫主义。黄庭坚不懂浪漫主义，他用的屈原、王嫱、接舆、孔丘都是正人君子。

振衣和濯足

左思《咏史》有"振衣千仞岗，濯足万里流"。意气豪迈，正是锺嵘所说"左思风力"。不过这个振衣，并非高岗上风吹衣振，而是故意抖动衣衫，是古代上层阶级男人显示自己地位的一种姿态，所以是可厌的。若韩愈的"当流赤足踏涧石，水声激激风生衣"，才是真正的风吹衣振。

左思出身寒门，拙于仕进，《咏史》是谴责魏晋的门阀政治。上引诗的前联是说他看不惯城中的峨峨高门、蔼蔼王侯，才"被褐出阊阖，高步追许由"的。可见他是穿粗布衣服上山冈的，本来没有什么可振；这振衣大约是出于习惯。

谢灵运《述祖德》有"高揖七州外，拂衣五湖里"。这里"拂衣"即振衣，并且是从左思那里套来的，因为《述祖德》中大段袭用《咏史》的句子，有的只改动一两个字。谢灵运出身豪门，宰相世家。这诗是夸耀乃祖谢安、谢玄的。序中说谢玄"拂衣蕃岳"，在其他诗中还有"拂衣遵沙垣"。而此诗绝无"风力"。据说谢灵运每出游都有"四人掣衣裙"，当然不会随便脱下鞋来濯足了。谢集中有"缘流洗素足"，但那是看农女洗脚。

陶渊明《归园》有"山涧清且浅，遇以濯我足"。陶渊明曾倒穿衣服去迎客——"清晨闻叩门，倒裳往自开"，大约没有振衣的习气。这里的"濯足"也不是为表示什么"风力"，而是走了山间小道，偶尔遇见清且浅的水，洗洗脚。我们在干校也有此经验。

晞发和濯足

《离骚》："夕归次于穷石兮，朝濯发乎洧盘。"按上文，是写宓妃。宓妃是洛水神，怎么跑到西极的洧水洗头发？郭沫若说，是后羿迁居西极穷石山，宓妃来和他私通。根据是《天问》：后羿"妻彼雒嫔"。雒嫔即洛神宓妃。"次"宿也，她与后羿睡一觉起来，到洧水去洗头。

《九歌·少司命》："与女沐兮咸池，晞女发兮阳之阿。""女"即汝，指司命女神。咸池是日神洗澡的地方，不过"沐"专指洗头，"浴"才是洗身。所以女神洗头后在太阳底下晒头发，不是与日神同浴。

张孝祥《水调歌头·泛湘水》，全篇用《楚辞》。起句"濯足夜滩急，晞发北风凉"。这里晞发即用《少司命》，不是用宓妃故事。濯足是用《渔父》："沧浪之水浊兮，可以濯我足。""浊"（音独）不是脏，"水涨则浊，水落则清"，故曰"夜滩急"，涨水也。把濯足与晞发并用，比濯足与振衣并用，命意要高。不过，《渔父》还有"新沐者必弹冠，新浴者必振衣"，也把振衣扯进来了。

陆云有一首《九愍·行思》："朝弹冠以晞发，夕振裳而濯足。"把几件事都堆在一起，活画了一个腐儒。

我之濯足成习，是因为在"五七干校"每日劳动，下田种稻，每晚必洗脚才能上炕，因而引起《偶谈》。陈煤在浙江"五七干校"，闻之来信说："我原也无濯足习惯。因偶患失眠。好心人劝我每晚以热水洗足。"这很对。苏东坡有"主人劝我洗足眠，倒床不复闻钟鼓"；陆放翁有"洗脚上床真一快"句。看来，濯足就是濯足，"偶谈"倒是多余的话了。

死不改悔

大批斗时常用"死不改悔"，不知何出？唯《离骚》有"虽九死其犹未悔"；又有"虽体解吾犹未变"，变训改。

前一句是说我有两件事，朝夕为人们指责，而此二事乃"余心之所善兮，虽九死其犹未悔"。哪两件事呢？一是"蕙镶"，就是把蕙兰镶在衣服边上。二是"揽茝",就是把白芷串起来挂在身上。据说这两件事都是"法夫前修",即效法古人的,所以受到人们"朝谇(骂)而夕替(打)",但九死不悔,真顽固极了。

后一句也是说我有两件事,受到人们指责。一是"制芰荷以为衣兮,集芙蓉以为裳",穿绿色上衣,粉红色下衣。二是"高余冠之岌岌兮,长余佩之陆离",戴个大高帽子,佩一把怪模怪样的长剑。这两件事不是学古人,而是"民生各有所乐兮",我就喜欢这样。虽受批判,但不改("吾犹未变")。可是,下面又加上一句"岂余心之可惩"?虽行为反常,难道心坏了?这句加得不好,因为批判的正是心,不联系思想实质,哪能行!

《离骚》还有一联:"阽余身而危死兮,览余初其犹未悔。""阽余身",即临近我身,指现在;"览余初",则指检查过去。这联前面是大段历史,从大禹讲到西周,即当代。但是只讲事,没有触动思想实质,所以到临危要死了,"其犹未悔"。

王安石《明妃曲》

王安石的《明妃曲》是咏昭君最好的诗,好在立意新。这诗前半部只写昭君的美,但不是从形象上写,而是从故事上写。昭君出来,泪湿鬓角,自顾"无颜色",但元帝见了,竟不能自持。原来昭君美不在容貌,而在精神,即"意态"。而画师又是个画肉不画骨的,所以"意态由来画不成,当时枉杀毛延寿",二句成为千古绝唱。

后半部写昭君在蒙古仍是关心祖国的,但是,"家人万里传消息,好在毡城莫相忆"。就是说,安慰来自家人,而非宫廷。宫廷呢?"君不见,咫尺长门闭阿娇,人生失意无南北"。这才是诗的主题。玩弄、遗弃女子,历代帝王皆如此,古今中外,概莫能外。"南北"者即中外。

这样,王安石就提出一个社会制度问题,虽然他没有解答。这层意思,比"和亲事却非"的论点高得多了;而白居易的"黄金何日赎娥眉"则简直不像话。居然有人作考证,说蔡文姬是被俘,可赎;王昭君是官派的,不可赎了。真是腐儒。不过,有人匿名作了首《反明妃怨》,说"昔日画图金不足,今日天涯以金赎",讽刺得痛快。此人大约是清代的蔡尚翔。

郭老（沫若）在一篇文章（可惜我记不清是那篇文章）中说，王安石闯了诗祸。这是指王安石的另一篇《明妃曲》，今选本皆不录，不知何故？其诗曰："明妃初嫁与胡儿，毡车百两皆胡姬。含情欲语独无处，传语琵琶心自知。黄金捍拨春风手，弹看飞鸿劝胡酒。汉宫侍女暗垂泪，沙上行人却回首。汉恩自浅胡自深，人生乐在相知心。可怜青冢已芜没，尚有哀弦留至今。"

所谓诗祸，当然是指"汉恩自浅胡自深，人生乐在相知心"一联。此语一出，议论汹汹。或谓"今之背君父之恩投拜而为盗贼者皆合于安石之意"；或谓"苟心不相知，臣可以叛其君，妻可以弃其夫乎？"为王安石辩护的人也只好说，"汉恩自浅胡自深"的"恩"是专指男女关系，无关君臣之义。我想，王安石这里所说的恩，确是指男女关系。但不是一般的男女关系，而是从更高的角度，即从社会的角度来看这问题的。也可说，此语即对前一首所提问题的答案，即男女结合应以"相知心"为准则。这思想非常近代化，有资本主义萌芽味道。不过，男女关系也要从政治上看问题，例如我们在大批判中就是这样，那情况就有所不同了。

还有，王安石这诗的结尾是错误的。陈煤告诉我，曾经拜访过明妃的青冢，而明妃的"哀弦"却并未"留至今"（留下的是词）。

《长恨歌》和《连昌宫词》

郑畋《马嵬坡》："玄宗回马杨妃死，云雨难忘日月新。终是圣明天子事，景阳宫井又何人。"注家说"咏杨妃诗殆皆讽刺，唯此诗敦厚"。我看未必，问题在后二句怎么解。我以为这是反话：圣明天子都是一样的，还有景阳宫井里的人呢！似是说李隆基还不如陈叔宝，因陈还能和张丽华共患难。

咏杨妃诗确实殆皆讽刺。敦厚如杜老，《丽人行》中也有"炙手可热势绝伦"之类的话。唯一例外恐怕就是《长恨歌》，通篇是歌颂杨李的情思绵绵。

《长恨歌》脍炙人口，主要因为它那轻松、畅利、极易上口的歌行体词句。如"遂令天下父母心，不重生男重生女"，就比杜老的"信知生男恶，反是生女好"容易上口。但杜诗命意是反对乱征兵，是为人民打算。《长恨歌》的重生女是因为"姊妹弟兄皆列土",是为了卖女求荣。这难道是"父母心"吗?

《连昌宫词》的主旨是"努力庙谟休用兵",这原是唐诗一般的内容。但诗中讽刺深刻,也很坦率。如"百官队仗避岐薛,杨氏诸姨车斗风";"禄山宫里养作儿,虢国门前闹如市";"弄权宰相"点名"杨与李"等。文字有独到处。如叙乱后行宫荒凉,有句"蛇出燕巢盘斗拱,菌生香案正当衙"。试想,皇帝宝座前香案上长出个大蘑菇来,是何等景象!又如"力士传呼觅念奴,念奴潜伴诸郎宿";"飞上九天歌一声,二十五郎吹管逐"。二十五郎即邠王,"诸郎"这些王爷就更拆烂污了。

其实,杨玉环进宫在天宝三载,这时岐王、薛王、邠王和李隆基的另三个兄弟都已死了。李商隐:"夜半宴归宫漏永,薛王沉醉寿王醒。"寿王瑁即杨玉环的前夫,还活着。诗人叙事泰半虚构,不过这家人的荒唐是说不完的。

论文字,《连昌宫词》之流畅一如《长恨歌》。抗日战争时我曾住凤翔虢镇。一日,去西安,夜半车坏,在卡车上曲宿。次晨起视,见一碑,书曰"马嵬坡",遂想到此二诗。解放后,一次出差,旅途中方行说,近人论《长恨歌》百二十句仅用"小玉双成"一典,足见作者之才。我说,《连昌宫词》百句一个典也不用。因戏成一律,有句"长恨千言唯一典,连昌百韵一典无。后来居上新乐府,无论元轻与白俗"。

白居易《琵琶行》(一)

白居易《琵琶行》的小序中说,这位琵琶女曾"快弹数曲";但诗中点明的只是"初为霓裳后绿腰"。《霓裳》是个宫廷舞曲,元稹说"霓裳羽衣偏宛转",意为太宛转了。《长恨歌》中也说它是"缓歌曼舞凝丝竹",决非"快弹"。《绿腰》是个流行歌曲,也是闲婉的。元稹说"管儿还为弹六么,六么依旧声迢迢"。《琵琶行》中说两曲的弹法都是"轻拢慢捻抹复挑",可见都不是快弹。

拢是扣弦,捻是揉弦,都是左手技巧。轻拢慢捻,是用于委婉轻松的调子。抹是下拨弦,挑是反手回拨,都是右手技巧。据说唐代琵琶名手,善拢捻的如裴兴奴不大会下拨,善抹挑的如曹纲不大会叩弦。《琵琶行》中这位女士倒是全才。

《琵琶行》的主题是白居易借琵琶女哀叹自己被谪的飘羁生活，所谓"同是天涯沦落人，相逢何必曾相识"。因此选曲应以幽怨为主，《霓裳》《绿腰》都与主题不合。《霓裳》据说原为印度婆罗门（贵族）舞曲，经西京节度使杨敬述献给玄宗，玄宗把它改谱，并加上了一个散序。元稹说"明皇度曲多新态，宛转浸淫易（替换）沉着；赤白桃李取花名，霓裳羽衣号天落"。即原来曲中比较沉着的部分也换上浸淫的调子了，因而是"春风荡漾霓裳翻"。《绿腰》内容稍异，元稹说它有"猿鸣雪岫来三峡，鹤唳晴空闻九霄"的音色，有"霜刀破竹无残节"即一通到底的音调。但这是说其高亢、明澈，并非哀怨。为弥补选曲的缺陷，诗人钻了一个空子，即在曲中一个全音休止符（这几乎每曲都有的）时写道："别有幽愁暗恨生，此时无声胜有声。"休止符无声，诗人可随意解释。但试想明皇为杨妃度的曲，真会有"忧愁暗恨"的内容吗？

但是，《琵琶行》在开头一段写的音乐，却是完全符合全诗主题思想的。这段是："转轴拨弦三两声，未成曲调先有情。弦弦掩抑声声思，似诉平生不得意。低眉信手续续弹，说尽心中无限事。""掩抑"是按弦和遏弦的手法，使出声吞咽幽抑，但也和曲调有关。白居易说"蕤宾掩抑娇多怨"。蕤宾一般相当于变徵，略如今天的F调，听起来有抑制感。白居易又说"第五弦声最掩抑，陇水冻咽流不得"。这是讲五弦琴，在琵琶上即小弦。

这是一段什么音乐呢？有两种可能：一是琵琶女的即兴表演，自抒感慨；那最好，这位善才又是作曲家。另一可能，它是《霓裳》或《绿腰》的散序。《霓裳》十二遍，前几遍是散序，无拍。中序以后开始入拍，照沈括说，中序即第六遍（后为第七叠），故这个散序颇长。散序不受节奏限制，比较自由，故白居易说"曲爱霓裳未拍时"。但如前所说，这个散序是玄宗加制的，恐怕难以表现哀怨。《绿腰》也有散序，而且很出名。元稹说"六么散序多笼捻"，适于掩抑。王建《宫词》："琵琶先抹绿腰头，小管丁宁侧调愁。""头"即散序。原来唐乐皆以丝声起调，管声次之（后世则相反），乐家称"细抹将来"。奏曲都先"细抹"一段，这其中最能表现奏曲家的再创造。看来，这段序曲以《绿腰》的散序可能性较大。

琵琶女演奏后，白居易要求 encore，《琵琶行》中只写了三句："却坐促弦弦转急，凄凄不似向前声，满座重闻皆掩泣。"这段 encore 确是段"快弹"。

白居易《琵琶行》（二）

《琵琶行》如果只写开头那段音乐，其诗就成全璧了，因为"心中无限事"已在此"说尽"了，但看全诗，却是以写不合主题情调的《霓裳》为主。这是因为白居易太喜欢《霓裳》了。他曾说"我爱霓裳君合知，发于歌咏形于诗"，并说他在杭州曾教杭州妓女演《霓裳》，到苏州又打算教苏州妓女演此曲。这次琵琶女奏《霓裳》，很可能是白居易"点拨"的——那时弹琵琶用拨，不像后来用五指。

不过，《琵琶行》确是写音乐的一篇佳作。我说过，诗不是乐谱，写音乐只能打比方，本诗则不仅打比方，还写出一些曲调、曲式来，虽然是片断的。"大弦嘈嘈如急雨，小弦切切如私语"一段，好像是说有粗犷、婉细两个主旋律。因唐乐不用和弦，这两个旋律是分别由低音部和高音部奏出。白在《五弦》中说"大声粗若散，飒飒风和雨；小声细欲绝，切切鬼神语"。大声小声即大弦小弦，是说音阶，不是音量。"嘈嘈切切错杂弹"，似是两个旋律在对比，模进。以下"莺语""泉流""冰下滩"似是说曲调由舒畅转入细缓，又像出现了琶音或涩音（"冰下滩"或作"水下滩"，非）。休止后的"银瓶乍破""铁骑突出"，好像又是由两部声调竞奏，繁音促节，达于高潮。最后，"四弦一声如裂帛"，曲终。这是一般乐曲的结构，即把高潮放在曲尾。《霓裳》却不是这样。白居易在《霓裳羽衣舞歌》中说"翔鸾舞了却收翅，唳鹤曲终长引声"；自注："凡曲将毕，皆声拍促速，惟霓裳之末长引一声也。"霓裳舞是用管弦乐队伴奏的，"长引一声"在琵琶上很难表现。因此改用了一般收尾，或者是写《绿腰》的收尾。

以上都只是我自己的想象，恐非原义。不过，这诗的好处即在给人以丰富的想象，也可说能给人以丰富想象的就是好诗。各人想象不同，因而解诗可以百家争鸣，也可说能引起百家争鸣的都是好诗。

元、白《五弦弹》

元稹和白居易都有一首《五弦弹》。元诗把五弦附会成"五贤",说与其听五弦不如去求贤臣,陈寅恪说他"迂远"(《元白诗笺证稿》)。白诗自注曰"恶郑之夺雅也",说五弦是邪声,不如古调。

但元诗所写五弦名手赵璧的琴音是很美的。所弹是徵调,才绝清峭,像白鹤在破晓时喷叫。然后转入细腻的旋律,"风入春松正凌乱,莺含晓舌怜娇妙"。再转入快奏,有"珠幢斗绝金铃掉""万片清球击虞庙"等节奏。

白诗也是写赵璧弹五弦,却把琴音写得十分可怕:"铁声杀,冰声寒。杀声入耳肤血惨,寒气中人肌骨酸。"接着说:"吾闻正始之音不如是。正始之音其若何?朱弦疏越清庙歌,一弹一唱再三叹,曲淡节稀声不多。"这种论点可谓"迂腐"。

值得注意的是,白居易批赵璧弹五弦,并批起五弦琴本身来了。他说由于五弦琴流行,"古琴有弦今不抚",这是指七弦琴。又说"更从赵璧艺成来,二十五弦不如五"。这是指瑟。白居易在《秦中吟》组诗中还有一首《五弦》,更把五弦琴批得不像样子,说它"十指无定音,颠倒宫徵羽"。

五弦琴今不传。但知它是"北国所出",类似琵琶,但不用拨,而用指弹。这应是个进步,后来琵琶也废拨用指。白居易所说"十指无定音",可能是五弦琴不像琵琶那样按格,而可以"抚"。若然,则更是个进步,可出滑音;不过需加长弦长,也许正因此改为五弦。"颠倒宫徵羽",可能是大小弦的排列与琵琶相反,这在乐器中是常有的事。

唐代音乐的大发展得力于外国(当时的西方)音乐和乐器的传入。据白居易说,当时奏《霓裳》主要用觱篥、笛、笙、箜篌。觱篥来自龟兹,笛出于羌,笙和琵琶都来自印度。箜篌说法不一,但乐队用的大箜篌(二十三弦)大约是创于埃及,经中亚到中国。令白居易叹息的琴和瑟是中国的古乐器,所谓"农瑟羲琴",但据郭老(沫若)考证,也都是西周时由外国传入的。

白居易酷爱《霓裳》,盛赞琵琶,也有诗赞赏觱篥,但我未见过他写琴或瑟的诗。他是个新音乐的爱好者。那他为什么反对五弦呢?他真的讨厌五弦吗？白居易住在庐山时，于香炉峰下盖了个草堂，并《咏怀题于石上》："左手携一壶，右手挈五弦。傲然意自足，箕踞于其间。"原来他也爱弹五弦。

元、白《华原磬》

元稹和白居易都有一首《华原磬》。原来磬是用山东泗水浮石做的，叫泗滨磬。天宝中改用华原石，于是元、白大加批评。元诗说华原石"不辨邪声嫌雅正"，"钟律参差管弦病"。白诗更提到政治标准："宫悬一听华原石，君心遂忘封疆臣。"他们又都把此事归罪于乐工、乐胥。元诗："弃旧美新由乐胥，自此黄钟不能竞。"白诗："今人古人何不同？用之舍之由乐工。"乃至谩骂"工师小贱牙旷稀"，"长安市人为乐师"。

为什么泗滨磬改为华原磬呢？白诗有个注："询之磬人，则曰，故老云：泗滨石下调之不能合，得华原石考之，乃和。"这是因为古乐调低，后来逐渐增高，唐受胡乐影响，当时流行调已比黄钟下四律，即高四个音阶。磬是定调的标准器，所谓"依我磬声"。流行调已高，标准器也要改变。磬人说"下调之不能合"，即需提高，故改用华原石。元、白都是音乐家，完全懂得这个道理。又晋代荀勖即提高过一次（那时标准器是管），元、白也是知道的。那他们为什么要反对呢？

汪士信听我议论，笑曰：元、白所写的磬实际是指人。完全正确。《新乐府》本来都是"刺美见事"的，包括前述《五弦弹》，都是借题发挥。《华原磬》自注中更说"刺乐工非其人也"。这是指当时的当权派。"弃旧美新由乐胥"，"用之舍之由乐工"；元、白都是被弃、被舍者，因有此大批判。

元、白的新乐府中还有《法曲》《立部伎》《胡旋女》等篇，也都是借音乐之题的大批判。唐王朝有十四国乐曲、八国舞伎，主要是西方来的，统称"胡乐"。天宝十三载，诏道调、法曲与胡部新声合作。这事元、白大为恼火。更使他们恼火的是"选坐部伎无性识者退入立部伎，又选立部伎无性识者退入雅部乐"。坐部伎奏宴乐，几乎全是外国乐，所谓"胡部新声锦宴座"。立部伎变成给杂伎伴奏，"立部伎，鼓笛喧。双舞剑，跳七丸，袅巨索，掉长竿。"而"后土郊祀"的雅乐，因一再选退，都是些聋子、傻子了，"工师尽取聋昧人"。

元、白的这种借题发挥的手法实在不高明。因为谁都知道，元、白都是十分迷恋新乐胡乐的；也知道，要提倡"一唱三叹""曲淡节稀"的古乐是不可能的，元稹也说雅乐是"九奏未终百僚惰"。因而这些诗，没人当作"刺美见事"来读，只欣赏它对音乐的描写。批判失效，文学永存。

《听颖师弹琴》

欧阳修问苏轼在写琴的诗中哪首最好，苏轼说韩愈的《听颖师弹琴》最好。欧阳修说"此诗固奇丽，然自是听琵琶诗，非琴诗"。于是苏轼用心作了一首《听贤师琴》，正想寄给欧阳修，欧阳修死了（《东坡诗话》）。

韩愈的《听颖师弹琴》前几句："昵昵儿女语，恩怨相尔汝。划然变轩昂，勇士赴敌场"等，确是像琵琶。但后面一段："浮云柳絮无根蒂，天地阔远随飞扬。喧啾百鸟群，忽见孤凤凰。跻攀分寸不可上，失势一落千丈强"；这就是琴音了。后两句是泛音、滑音，琵琶弹不出的。

我说过，诗写音乐都是打比方。就打比方说，李贺的《听颖师琴》想象更丰富："芙蓉叶落秋鸾离，越王夜起游天姥。暗珮清臣敲水玉，渡海蛾眉牵白鹿。谁看挟剑赴长桥，谁看浸发题春竹。"前两句写琴音凄切、悠扬，像夜登天姥似的。中间两句是叮叮当当之声，渐远渐缈，如入大海神境。最后两句说，听了琴音，就没人去看长桥比剑或钩连书法了。不过，越王巡天姥，仙女骑白鹿，都不见经传，大约是李贺杜撰的。

颖师是当时著名琴手，大约是个和尚，故不称"师颖"。但韩愈所写"颖"从水，有人说应是姓不是名，那就是个道士。不管是僧是道，李贺诗其后说"竺僧前立当吾门，梵宫真象眉棱尊"；形象可憎，使全诗大煞风景。韩愈诗的结尾则极好："自闻颖师弹，起坐在一旁，推手遽止之，湿衣泪滂滂。颖师尔诚能，无以冰炭置我肠。"生动白描，十分感人。

至于苏轼的《听贤师琴》，我看只有四句是写琴音："大弦春温和且平，小弦廉折亮以清。平生未识宫与角，但闻牛鸣盎中雉登木。"前两句写琴音，但未写内容，好像在调弦。后两句本《乐记》。《乐记》说宫调如牛鸣，角调像鸡叫，这是根据律管，律管是定调子的。但若说听贤师琴只是识别了宫调与角调，那未免太糟遢人了。

或者，苏轼是善于写管乐的，《赤壁赋》有："客有吹洞箫者……其声呜呜然，如怨如慕，如泣如诉；余音袅袅，不绝如缕。"也是打比方，但非常形象，非常生动，而且余意深长。

《锦瑟》

"一篇锦瑟解人难"。一次去南开大学，郝世峰示我一文，谓《锦瑟》非悼亡诗，论甚是。这里不去解《锦瑟》，只谈"锦瑟无端五十弦"一句。既非悼亡，不存在二十五"断弦"为五十之意；并且，实际上没有五十弦之瑟。瑟每弦有柱，将弦一分为二，看去就像五十弦。李商隐此句是说弦多，喻心绪繁赜。辛弃疾："八百里分麾下炙，五十弦翻塞外声。"五十弦喻众多乐器，状兵勇之众。

近因马王堆出土汉瑟，《文物》载文考证，可证我言。我国原已出土楚瑟十六具，一具二十三弦，一具二十四弦，余均二十五弦。其二十四弦瑟边弦密迹，不能弹，恐是明器，非真瑟。马王堆汉瑟极完整，亦二十五弦，分为三组：中央七弦为低音部，外九弦和内九弦完全相同，均高音部。盖高音柱位向瑟首递移，有的有效弦长仅十余厘米，音弱，故重复一组以加重音量，并便于上下游弄指法。由此可知，如用五十弦，只能高低音部再重复一遍，否则高音有效弦长仅一二厘米，根本不能弹。又弦太多不能用轸木调弦，只有取消轸木，类西方竖琴，那就不是瑟了。

二十三弦瑟，《吕氏春秋·古乐》说是将瞽叟的瑟"益八弦，以为二十三弦"。我想原瑟大约只有一组高音部，"益八弦"，即重复一组高音部以增音量。据马王堆汉瑟，高音部第九弦为升半音，很少用，故重复八弦已足。

诗中讲五十弦瑟盖本《乐书》引《世本》："庖羲作瑟五十弦，黄帝使素女鼓之，哀不自胜，乃破为二十五弦。"这纯属神话。说破为二十五弦就不哀，毫无道理。李商隐"逶巡又过潇湘雨，雨打湘灵五十弦"，是用湘灵鼓瑟故事，并且是雨打瑟，自不怕弦多。黄庭坚"风鸣娲皇五十弦"，也是神瑟，并且是风吹瑟，当然更不怕弦多。总之，人弹的瑟不能超过二十五弦。

《锦瑟》非关悼亡，但李商隐另有悼亡诗："忆得前年春，未语含悲辛。归来已不见，锦瑟长于人。"寥寥数语，而真挚纯朴，溢于言外。我看是悼亡诗之最好者。

元好问《论诗》

元好问《论诗》三十首，有许多卓越见解。这里只讲他论诗的演进一点。

"只知诗到苏黄尽"，似太武断。但我怀疑这是专指苏门学士和江西诗派而言。"苏门果有忠臣在，肯放坡诗百态新"。似说苏门学士未能发挥苏诗的特长，否则肯定会百花齐放，推陈出新。"古雅难将子美亲，精纯全失义山真。论诗宁下涪翁拜，未作江西社里人"。这是肯定黄庭坚而批评江西诗派。黄自谓诗法自杜甫，而江西诗派谨守"无一字无出处"教条，把杜诗的古雅全忘了；又注重声韵和用典师自李商隐，而将李诗的"真"全丢了。

批评苏门学士和江西诗派，都是说他们只继承形式，缺乏创造性，或墨守成规，失掉精神。"传语闭门陈正字，可怜无补费精神"。这批得很重。"闭门"不仅实指（陈师道作诗时把老婆孩子都赶出门外），也有关门主义的意思。

这是论宋诗。元好问论唐诗也有类似见解："论功若准平吴例，合着黄金铸子昂。"陈子昂是首开有唐一代新诗风的，对开拓者应该立纪念像。李、杜当然是唐诗的最高峰。晚唐呢？"风云若恨张华少，温李新声奈尔何？"看来绝非贬低温、李。温、李虽不及李、杜那么高，但对李、杜说，他们是"新声"，即推陈出新了。

陆游在一首《示子遹》中说："数仞李杜墙，常恨欠领会。元白才倚门，温李真自郐。"这么说，唐诗是每况愈下的。也许就高度或成熟度来说是这样，但就新或创造性来说并非如此。元好问总是希望后来者推陈出新。

赵翼《论诗》

王士祯有《戏仿元遗山论诗绝句三十五首》。我借得万有文库本《渔洋精华录》只见三十二首。方行说，大约"风流不见秦淮海，寂寞江南五百年"等说得过分，删去了。但集中实有此诗，而不在《论诗》之例。其《论诗》，有些我看不懂，不知什么意思；有些看懂了，又好像没什么意思。只好不谈。

赵翼的《论诗绝句》七首，却颇有见地："李杜诗篇万口传，至今已觉不新鲜。江山代有才人出，各领风骚数百年。"诗也和其他文化一样，一代有一代的思想风格。这诗无所指，鉴于王士祯五百年之说，我看等于是批评王的。王倡神韵，专找妙语，就找到了秦淮海。赵翼又有："羚羊眠挂角，天马奔绝尘。其实论过高，后学未易尊。"这回肯定是指王士祯了。神韵说是不讲内容的；"论过高"，我看是讽刺语。

"满眼生机转化钧，天工人巧日争新。预支五百年新意，到了千秋又觉陈。"这是陶钧人才，日新又日新的思想。又说"自身已有初中晚，安得千秋尚汉唐？"诗不能永远宗汉崇唐。"自身已有初中晚"句在《瓯北诗话》中有解说。他说杜甫自夔州以后的诗，只《秋兴》《咏怀古迹》较好，其他则"意兴衰飒，笔亦枯率"了。又说陆游诗风凡三变，戎驻南郑一段最好，"及乎晚年，则又造平淡"。

然而，赵翼所推崇的"新"是什么呢？他说："意未经人说过则新，书未经人用过则新，诗家之新正以此耳。"这未免有点形式主义。又说韩愈开李、杜之新，因有"创体""创格""创句法"；白居易之新在于"和韵""次韵""新体律"。这就更形式主义了。元好问说"一语天然万古新"，新在自然。赵翼说"天工人巧日争新"，新在造作。这点我不敢苟同。

赵翼论苏轼，说他自乌台诗案入狱后，"不敢复论天下事"，"故其诗止于此"。一向从形式、技巧上评诗的赵翼，这次忽然政治挂帅了。赵翼是反对宋代的变法的。他称赞苏轼当年抨击新法"口快笔锐"，而乌台诗案以后，"不敢出其不平之鸣"，深以为憾。

赵翼论诗可归纳为：形式要新，思想要旧。

宋诗坛

唐诗炉火纯青，是诗的高峰。但宋诗题材广，风格多样化，格律较自由；也可说好处在于不那么炉火纯青。元好问《论诗绝句》："奇外无奇更出奇，一波才动万波随。"说的就是这种情况。

宋代派系斗争厉害，是在政治上，而在诗坛上则是互相尊重的，这正是宋诗多样化的好处。"讳学金陵犹有说，竟将何罪废欧梅？"元好问这话过分了，至少我没见过批欧梅的诗，也没见过批王安石的诗。

王安石罢相后居钟山，有首《题西太一宫壁》："柳叶鸣蜩绿暗，荷花落日红酣。三十六陂春水，白头想见江南。"黄庭坚次韵曰："风急啼乌未了，雨来蚁战方酣。真是真非安在，人间北看成南。"任渊注黄诗，说是用《庄子》"彼亦一是非，此亦一是非"。我看黄诗这里有一分为二的味道。所以他另和一首曰："短世风惊雨过，成功梦迷酒酣。草玄不妨准易，论诗终近周南。"他对王的人品才学是十分欣佩的。

苏轼与王安石唱和也是在王罢相以后。王有《北山》："北山输绿涨横陂，直堑回塘滟滟时。细数落花因坐久，缓寻芳草得归迟。"苏轼次韵："骑驴渺渺入荒陂，想见先生未病时。劝我试求三亩宅，从公已觉十年迟。""骑驴"指王心爱的一幅骑驴图，王曾就图咏志。"求宅"是苏轼曾想买金陵田。

我谈过王安石的《明妃曲》，据说此诗一出，连司马光都有和作。又苏轼读王安石《寄女诗》中"积李兮缟夜，崇桃兮炫昼"曰："自屈宋殁世旷千余年，无复离骚句法，今乃见之。"（《西清诗话》）

王安石死后，敕赠太傅。这个敕是苏轼起草的："罔罗六艺之遗文，断以己意；糠秕百家之陈迹，作新斯人。"这是深知安石之言。

王安石与欧阳修相见较晚。欧阳修赠王诗云："翰林风月三千首，吏部文章二百年。老去自怜心尚在，后来谁与子争先。"王答曰："欲传道义心虽壮，强学文章力已穷。他日若能窥孟子，终身何敢望韩公。"这事引起后人许多议论，我看多半出于对王的偏见。清人蔡尚翔在《王荆公年谱考略》中说：欧阳修诗好李白，文宗韩愈；"三千首""二百年"分别指李、韩。又欧阳修寄苏子美诗："韩孟于文词，两雄力相当……寂寥二百年，至宝埋无光。"总之，欧阳修的赠诗只是以长者身份称赞王安石的文才，并无他意。王的答诗，我看是比较认真的。似是说，我心在道义（指政治），若就文章说，终身比不上韩愈。结语还有"只恐虚名因此得，嘉篇为贶岂宜蒙"。似是说，我若真以文章出名，那就不好了。都是真心话。

隐 括

宋词中常用唐诗名句，叫"隐括"。这有如用典，可启人联想，增加兴味，但用得不好，反见累赘。

姜夔《扬州慢》，用"杜郎俊赏""豆蔻词工""青楼梦好""二十四桥仍在"，连用这么多杜牧，只为说在扬州，变成堆砌。王安石《桂枝香》咏金陵："至今商女，时时犹唱，后庭遗曲"；反将杜牧句化简为繁，颇不值得。而秦观《风流子》："算天长地久，有时有尽，奈何绵绵，此恨无休"；用白居易，不但化简为繁，而且弄巧成拙了。

张炎《八声甘州》："问谁留楚佩，弄影中洲？"八个字使人联想到《湘君》"捐余玦兮江中，遗余佩兮澧浦"与"君不行兮夷犹，蹇谁留兮中洲"两段故事，思想立刻丰富起来。秦观《鹊桥仙》："两情若是长久时，又岂在朝朝暮暮？"用宋玉"朝朝暮暮，阳台之下"，因有一段故事在内，所以吸引人。不过这都不是用唐诗，一般视为用典。

杜甫《一百五日夜对月》："斫却月中桂，清光应更多。"是他被困在沦陷后的长安怀念家乡妻子所作，和"今夜鄜州月"感情相同。辛弃疾《太常引》："斫去桂婆娑，人道是清光更多。"虽用杜句，但命意不同了。这词前面"把酒问姮娥"，是说在天上看人间被敌人践踏的山河，结句有砍掉黑暗的影子，才有更多的光明的意思。用"婆娑""人道是"都使杜诗原意转化的效果。

李贺"天若有情天亦老"，是说天和人一样也会（为铜人被劫走）悲伤的。孙洙《河满子》："天若有情天亦老，遥遥幽恨难尽"，仍是原意。石曼卿"天若有情天亦老，月如无恨月常圆"，只顾凑对，把李贺的原意给糟蹋了。秦观《水龙吟》："名缰利锁，天还知道，和天也瘦。"这是暗用李贺，改"老"为"瘦"以叶韵而有了新意，但仍不能超脱悲天感觉。只有到

"天若有情天亦老，人间正道是沧桑"，才把原意彻底翻过来了。

宋诗中也用隐括。杜甫《曲江对雨》："林花着雨胭脂湿"；没说什么花，但后人常称海棠为胭脂。王安石的儿子王雱《倦寻芳》："海棠着雨胭脂透"，即偷用杜句。陈与义《雨中对酒庭下海棠经雨不谢》："燕子不禁连夜雨，海棠犹待老夫诗。天翻地覆伤春色，齿豁头童祝圣时。"这也是偷用杜甫，偷得好，把"胭脂"替换掉了。并且，"伤春色"是指金兵渡江，朝廷反复，正杜甫"国破山河在，城春草木深"之意；海棠经久不谢则自况。

《醉翁吟》

欧阳修的《醉翁亭记》驰名遐迩。乐官沈遵博士就抱琴到滁州去，谱了一曲《醉翁吟》。沈遵把此曲弹给欧阳修听，请他作词。欧阳修随即作了首《醉翁引》，"然调不主声，为知琴者所惜"。过了三十年，欧阳修、沈遵都死了。有个沈遵的朋友崔闲，拿《醉翁吟》去请苏轼补词。崔闲边弹琴，苏轼边听边作词，顷刻而就，都合音律（王辟之《渑水燕谈录》卷七）。

欧阳修作的词"调不主声"，就是唱不出来。琴操用字要合律。如诗的同韵字，在律有宫、商等五音之分；又诗用字分平仄，而律则重清浊。但是，一个曲词要字字入律是不可能的。沈括说乐家常是"随律用之，本无定音。常以浊者为宫，稍清为商，最清为角，清浊不常为徵羽"（《梦溪笔谈》卷一五）。这话极是。如我们唱《义勇军进行曲》："前进！前进！前进进！"七个字中没有一个字是合律的，必须唱成"浅今！浅今！浅今今！"才行。好在国歌是只奏曲不唱词的。

《醉翁引》是宫声三叠。苏轼补的词是："琅然，清圆。谁弹，响空山，无言。惟翁醉中知其天。月明风露娟娟，人未眠。荷蒉过山前。曰有心哉此贤。醉翁啸咏，声和流泉。醉翁去后，空有朝吟夜怨。山有时而童巅，水有时而回川，思翁无岁年。翁今为飞仙，此意在人间。试听徽外三两弦。"

平心而论，这词作得并不怎样，有几处显然是凑宫声字。并且，我敢说，它全然不合曲的原意。沈遵是抱着琴到滁州去，面对琅琊酿泉作的曲，而苏词中前二叠全然未提滁州风物，难道曲中没有志在高山流水的音调吗？下面全是悼念已死的欧阳修。试想，沈遵曾把此曲弹给欧阳修听，这曲中能有悼念欧阳的音调吗？能在颂曲中填悼词吗？

然而，"试听徽外三两弦"却有意思。大约《醉翁吟》是以高音作结束，还有两三声尾音，可能是舒畅的羽弦或变宫。这种作曲手法和苏轼这句词都有"醉翁之意不在酒"的味道，就是说，余音袅袅，其味无穷。

无弦琴

萧统《陶渊明传》说陶"不解音律，而蓄无弦琴一张。每酒适，辄抚弄以寄其意"。我很怀疑这个说法。

陶集中提到琴的很多，如"少学琴书""委怀琴书""衡门之下，有琴有书""曰琴曰书，顾盼有俦""乐琴书以消忧"。这些都可看成是其读书而琴是陪衬语。但有诗："觞弦肆朝日，樽中酒不燥"；"清琴横床，浊酒半壶"。这就真有琴了，不过也许是无弦的，没说弹。《拟古》："知我故来意，取琴为我弹。上弦惊别鹤，下弦操孤鸾。"这个弹琴人其实就是陶渊明自己，因为这诗是用第三人口气写的。

陶诗《咏荆轲》："渐离击悲筑，宋意唱高声。萧萧哀风逝，淡淡寒波生。商音更流涕，羽奏壮士惊。"是说宋意唱的是悲怆的商调，商是高音调；然后高渐离又奏了个更高的羽调，荆轲也惊住了。羽调是一种高亢奇特的调子，调式大约是 d，e，f，g，a，b，c，在西乐中也很少用。当时史书不记乐调，这诗是陶渊明的构思，说明他是很懂音律的。

陶在《闲情赋》中写美人鼓瑟："曲调将半，景落西轩。悲商叩林，白云依山。仰睇天路，俯促鸣弦。"也说明他懂音律。陶在绝笔作《自祭文》中说："欣以素牍，和以七弦。"我看这是生活写实，他那张琴是七弦琴。

无弦琴我见过。一次越南音乐家访华演出，奏科龙布琴，是一排竹筒，用手拍奏，浑厚深沉。又奏德郎琴，是一排竹管，音色悠扬。两者都以节奏见长。

陶渊明和诸葛亮

辛弃疾《贺新郎》："把酒长亭说。看渊明风流，酷似卧龙诸葛。"这词是在长亭送陈同父时写的，大约二人议论了国事。后来他又有首《玉蝴蝶》说："往日曾论，渊明似胜卧龙些。"这是补充前次长亭之论。辛弃疾还有首《贺新郎》："渊明重九，晚岁凄其无诸葛，惟有黄花入手。"似是说陶渊明没有诸葛亮那样运气，老来只有采菊自颐。

陶渊明《述酒》篇确是评刘裕篡晋事，不过用语隐晦。刘裕把晋恭帝关起来，送毒酒给他，恭帝不饮，被杀。黄庭坚有首《宿旧彭泽怀陶令》："司马寒如灰，礼乐卯金刀。岁晚以字行，更始号元亮。凄其望诸葛，肮脏犹汉相。时无益州牧，指挥用诸将。""卯金刀"指刘裕篡晋事，说渊明因此改字元亮，自比诸葛亮，余如辛词意。这大约是当时流传的一种说法。我以为，《述酒》篇的政治见解并不可取。因为偏安江左的东晋小朝廷已腐烂透顶，如果诸葛亮再生，恐怕也不会出来保恭帝的。

到清代，龚自珍的一首诗我看说明白了："陶潜酷似卧龙豪，万古浔阳松菊高。莫信诗人竟平淡，三分梁甫一分骚。"陶渊明酷似诸葛亮在一个"豪"字，不是豪放的豪，是豪杰的豪。他并不是平淡成性，即鲁迅所说陶并非"浑身静穆"。末句"三分梁甫一分骚"是说他比之诸葛，还多点屈原气质。这也就是辛词所说"胜似卧龙些"。"些"，音，无义。

事实上，陶渊明的归隐远在刘裕篡晋之前，与《述酒》无关。据说是因为他作彭泽令时，督邮来了，他不肯为五斗米折腰，于是归田。他没有像张飞那样怒鞭督邮，而是写了篇《归去来兮辞》，这是知识分子的软弱性。不过，如果是武侯诸葛，恐怕也不会怒鞭督邮，而是吟几句《梁甫吟》算了。

陶　谢

杜甫："安得思如陶谢手。"其实，陶渊明和谢灵运完全不同，尤其是在"思"上。

陶渊明的情况上面谈过。谢灵运呢？他在刘裕篡晋前就在《戏马台》中称刘为"圣"；后又勾结刘的次子谋取夺权；失败后又和掌兵权的檀道济结党，又失败；最后被捕，被徙，被杀。《南史》说他"猖獗不已，自致覆亡"。这样一个野心家，在诗中却是位隐士，真希奇。这就是诗的欺骗性。

然而，诗中也会透露消息。陶渊明说"代耕本非望，所业在田桑"。"代耕"指做官。谢灵运则说"庐园当栖岩，卑位代躬耕"。后句说以做官代耕田，与陶思相反。前句又有讲究。原来他在《山居赋》中把隐士分为四等："巢居穴处曰岩栖"，岩栖，这是第一等；山居、在林野、在郊区就是二、三、四等的了。谢灵运要当隐士，当然要当头等的，但又吃不了岩栖的苦，便以"庐园"代之。这个庐园即始宁墅，是谢的私人庄园，内有山川湖泊，亭台苑囿，僮仆千人。

隐士中，陶渊明最赞赏长沮、桀溺，在《扇上画赞》中说："辽辽沮溺，耦耕自欣；入鸟不骇，杂兽斯群。"后句是针对孔子说他们"鸟兽不可以同群"而发。谢灵运则说："既笑沮溺苦，又哂子云阁：执戟亦已疲，耕稼岂云乐？"长沮、桀溺多苦啊，种地有什么好处呀。这谢灵运真该下干校十年。又拉上个扬雄。扬雄曾执戟站岗；后在天禄阁校书，王莽派兵捉他，他想跳楼自杀。"又哂子云阁"，是讥扬雄投阁，简化汉语到可笑地步。

谢灵运《道路忆山中》："采菱调易急，江南歌不缓：楚人心昔绝，越客肠今断。"用《楚辞·招魂》，用得极好。这里以屈原自况，但又说"存乡尔思积，忆山我愤懑"。你想你的家乡，我想我被没收的大庄园。其实，屈原想的不是家乡，而是祖国。谢灵运的思想和为人有哪点和屈原相像呢？不过谢灵运是最善于用《楚辞》的。这就是诗的欺骗性。

"池塘生春草"

元好问在《论诗绝句》中赞陶渊明"一语天然万古新"，称谢灵运的"池塘生春草"是"万古千秋五字新"。

谢灵运这句诗确是吐语天拔。其下联"园柳变鸣禽"也非常好，柳树变成歌唱的鸟。两句都说春天来了，生气勃勃。但除这两句外，全诗再设一句"天然"的话了。这首是谢灵运的自叙诗，几乎句句用典，以穿凿雕琢为工。但有两句还算真实："进德智所拙，退耕力不任。""进德"用《易·乾卦》："君子进德修业，欲及时也。"这里指谋掌握朝柄失败，故云"智所拙"；像陶渊明那样"退耕"吧，又吃不消体力劳动，故云"力不任"。

谢灵运还有一句"芙蓉始发池"也很天然。这是用《楚辞·招魂》：

"芙蓉始发，杂芰荷些"，用得好，不露痕迹。此外就没有什么天然的东西了。他的山水诗，有人评"繁芜"，锺嵘说"富艳难踪"，本是渲染、雕琢手法。但在破东晋玄言诗风上，还是个革命。

陶渊明的天然，如"今日天气佳，清吹与鸣弹"，"桑麻日已长，我土日已广"等，到处皆是。最好的当然是"采菊东篱下，悠然见南山"。不过我确信陶公采菊是当药吃。像"酒能祛百虑，菊解制颓龄"之类的话，陶集中屡见。因此，有的本子作"悠然望南山"，恐怕更好。一面采菊，一面望山，默祝长寿，盖用《诗》"如南山之寿"意。采菊并非故作闲适，而是和他种豆植麻一样，是生活中一件事。这句诗也就和"相见无杂言，但道桑麻长"一样，是生活写实，也就更觉自然了。

偏义复词

诗中常用偏义复词，大约因为诗有格律，要凑字。偏义复词多半是偏定了的。好像我们说"能上能下"是专指下放干校，"能上"是凑字。"契阔"一般指"阔"，即分离，如杜甫"白首甘契阔"。唯曹操《短歌行》的"契阔谈宴"是指"契"，即相聚。这正是曹操慷慨之处。

不过，有些偏义复词需要动动脑筋。有首送别诗："请为游子吟，泠泠一何悲。丝竹厉清声，慷慨有余哀。"《游子吟》是琴操，琴一般不用管乐伴奏，"丝竹"偏指丝。又有首送别诗："安知非日月，弦望自有时。"月有弦望，而日总是圆的，是拉来给月作陪衬。如果说是日月相望，即每月十五的望日，那么"弦"字又是拉出来给"望"作陪衬了。古诗《艳歌行》说兄弟在外，"故衣谁当补，新衣谁当绽？"旧衣是要补的，新衣为什么要撕裂呢？整个后句都是作陪衬的，这叫偏义类举。

古诗《白头吟》："沟水东西流"，是东流还是西流呢？李商隐解为"沟水分流西复东"（《代应》），把事情搞混了。其实，这诗是写男女双方在御沟办离婚手续，以后男婚女嫁各不相干，故曰"东西流"。《孔雀东南飞》中焦仲卿陪葬在刘兰芝墓，"东西植松柏，左右种梧桐"。墓穴总是南北向的，东西就是左右。不过这里不是凑字，而是为了加重。《木兰辞》：木兰回家后，"开我东阁门，坐我西阁床"。这是办不到的。但这两句把回家后的木兰写成蹦蹦跳跳的女孩子，这正是民歌的好处。同诗先是说"可汗大点兵"，战胜后又说"归来见天子"。这大约因为可汗与天子本是同类，可称"同义类举"。

《天问》和《天对》

屈原的《天问》提出关于宇宙万物的一百七十多个问题，真了不起。鲁迅说它是"放言无惮，为前人所不敢言"（《摩罗诗力说》）；又说它是"呵而问之，以抒愤懑"（《汉文学史纲要》）。怀疑、愤懑，以"问"的形式出现，而实际是批判。后来仿《天问》的文章很多，但就博大精深来说，恐怕只有柳宗元《天对》可与比拟。

《天问》："斡维焉系？天极焉加？八柱何当？东南何亏？"拴天伞把子的绳子的另一端拴在哪里？天的边（极）是怎样加上去的？八根擎天柱支在哪里？东南方为什么塌下去？这是怀疑当时流行的盖天说，屈原的问其实包含着答，即对所设定问题本身的否定。

《天对》回答说，何必系上绳子才能定天的位置呢？天本"无极""非垠"，如果有形体可以加上去，怎么算大呢？天宏大，运动不息，不相连属，何必要八根柱子支持它呢？柳宗元的答很得屈原原意，又有发展。宇宙无限论很彻底，而天运动不息、不相连属的思想，已打破天穹是一块整体的概念，超过托勒密，接近牛顿了。但是，柳宗元的天体观仍是传统的盖天说，而当时中国已经有了比较先进的浑天说和宣夜说了。

《天问》："九天之际，安放安属？隅隈（边角）有多，谁知其数？"这里的"九天"不是指九重天（那是有一定道理的，天体不在一个球面上），而是指中央钧天、南方赤天等九天——这是完全没有道理的。《天对》正确地回答说，这都是"巧欺淫诞"。又说："无中无旁，乌际乎天则？"如单独看这句话，那就超过哥白尼，赶上康德了。但是，他实际只是说天没有中央，不是说宇宙没有中心。柳宗元恐怕还是地心论者。

最高明的一段是屈原问太阳起落的原因，柳宗元答：太阳哪里有起落，不过像车轮向南转、车轴就好像在它北边，是你跟太阳的方位在变动而已。有人说，这指地球的自转或公转。我看未免走得太远了。他只是用轮转则轴平移作比方，柳宗元仍然是扁平大地和弓隆天穹的盖天论者，不过这个答很富辩证思想。

柳宗元的答，有些很妙。如问黄道周天十二辰是谁给划分的？答是用天自言的口吻："非余之为，焉以告汝！"很多"学说"都是人造的，天怎么知道呢？诗意盎然。

《天问》和《天对》都是诗。这种诗是说理的，但和玄言诗、理学诗不同。怎么不同？我看就在于玄言诗、理学诗看了使人头痛，而《天问》和《天对》看了使人感兴趣。用锺嵘的话说，这种诗虽也"理过其辞"，但决非"淡乎寡味"。

"三星在户"

顾炎武在《日知录》中说："三代以上人人皆知天文。七月流火，农夫之辞也；三星在天，妇人之语也……后世文人学士，有问之而茫然不知者矣。"的确，有了日历、手表和天气预报，现代文人就更不知天文了。

观察星位可以定季候、定时间。先说定季候，我国古代是看昏星，即傍晚某星的位置。古代西方是看晨星，即日出前某星的位置。而在整个长夜里，星是不断移动的，不足为据。王安石《田漏》："占星昏晚中，寒暑已不疑。"李壁注王诗，以"昏晚"重复，改为"昏晓"。这就闹笑话了。昏晓星位大异，怎能定季候呢？

观星位定时间，则是另一回事。《召南·小星》："嘒彼小星，三五在东。""三"即参宿，它有七颗星，四颗在四角，以中间横列的三颗亮星为代表。西方人看猎户座，也是以猎人腰带上的这三颗亮星为代表。"五"即昴宿，也是七颗星，有两颗较暗，遂以五为代表。三星很亮，但在黄昏时看，它和五还是嘒（暗淡）的小星，挂在东方天边。到午夜，三星就在天中央了。半夜过，它又偏西隅。天快亮时，它更低垂，以至从门里都可望见。

《唐风·绸缪》："绸缪束薪，三星在天。今夕何夕，见此良人。子兮子兮，如此良人何？绸缪束刍，三星在隅。今夕何夕，见此邂逅。子兮子兮，如此邂逅何？绸缪束楚，三星在户。今夕何夕，见此粲者。子兮子兮，如此縶者何？"午夜了，我这爱人真好呀；下半夜了，我这爱人真聪明呀；天快明了，我这爱人真漂亮呀。赞赏了一夜，还不知怎么办才好。我看这是写新婚的最好的一首古诗，真诚、淳朴、简洁。尤其是把夫妻比作一束薪、一束柴、一束草，难解难分，真正的农民诗。

杜甫："人生不相见，动如参与商。"他显然是用《绸缪》，因为下面也是"今夕何夕"。但这个"参"却不是参宿，而是启明星，"商"则是长庚星。启明总是天未亮时在东方出现，长庚总是黄昏时在西方出现，两者绝不能相遇，故曰"人生不相见"。

这个启明星，也有首极好的夫妇诗，即《郑风》的"女曰鸡鸣，士曰昧旦。子兴视夜，明星有烂！"女：鸡叫了。男：天还没亮呢。女：你起来看看吧，启明星都那么亮了。"明星"，即启明星简称。

《小雅·大东》有几章专讲星的缺点，如织女星不会织布，牵牛星不会拉车，簸箕星不能扬糠，北斗星不能酌酒。唯独"东有启明，西有长庚"两句，没说缺点。但仔细一想，东有启明的时候，西天怎么会有长庚呢？这不是异想天开吗？诗的妙处就在这里。

后来人们经过观察，知道启明和长庚原来是一颗星，即金星。

屈原《九歌》

《九歌》是《楚辞》中别具风格的作品：健康、积极，表现一种淳朴的乐观主义，与《骚》异趣。

《九歌》作为祭神乐歌，里面却没有一点神诛鬼罚的东西，所有的神和鬼都和蔼可亲，这点超过希腊神话。只有管人寿命的大司命是幅冷酷面孔，但人们还是"结桂枝兮延伫"，愿和他交朋友。因为他告诉人们"愿若今兮无亏"，"固人命兮有当"，只要不自损毁身体，是会有正常寿命的。少司命则是位多情的女子，专和人类讲恋爱。《山鬼》一上来就说它是个"人"，而且是个含睇宜笑的少女。

《九歌》绝大部分是爱情故事，结局是悲剧。但情调不是悲伤或哀怨，而是一种真挚的情操，带有狂热追求和乐观精神。他究竟爱不爱我呢？还在犹豫吧——"君思我兮然疑作"。她不来了，怎么办呢？对着风高歌吧——

"临风恍兮浩歌"——"时不可兮骤得，聊逍遥兮容与"。凡事都不能一下子成功，要在从容中去追求。

《九歌》的词极美。它的音乐如何呢？词中有两段是提到乐的。一段在《东皇太一》："扬枹兮拊鼓，疏缓节兮安歌，陈竽瑟兮浩倡。灵偃蹇兮姣服，芳菲菲兮满堂。五音兮繁会，君欣欣兮乐康。"这乐分三段：先是鼓奏。然后一段节拍疏缓、韵调安详的歌唱，大约是无伴奏的独唱。接着是管弦乐队伴奏的大合唱。这时，服装美丽的巫女高低起舞，香气满堂。最后是一段音调繁赜的交响乐。礼成。

另一段在《东君》："缊瑟兮交鼓，箫钟兮瑶簴，鸣篪兮吹竽。""缊瑟"是急弹瑟；"交鼓"是二人对打一面鼓，使鼓声有力；"箫钟"是猛击钟，连架子都摇晃起来了。篪和竽想也是使劲地吹。这都因为所迎的是日神，日神是"乘雷"来的，非常威武。这个乐队显然是个 band，瑟作打击乐器用。下面写有大合唱和群舞，都"应律兮合节"；节奏强，日神动作应该如此。

《九歌》的乐舞究竟如何，没人知道，我却看见过。那是 1942 年，郭沫若的《屈原》在重庆抗建堂首演，楚王宴张仪，郑袖背对观众下令："奏《九歌》之歌！"于是，钟鼓齐鸣，诸神一个接一个在天幕边上场，但随即落下大幕。虽然只是走过场，我却印象很深。

《湘君》《湘夫人》别解

楚辞中我最喜《九歌》，尤喜《湘君》《湘夫人》。诵读之余，有所得，乃作别解。戏为耳，只述拙见，不敢垺前贤大家。

《湘君》《湘夫人》在《九歌》中篇幅最长，例多按文意分段，长短不一。缘《九歌》乃祀神乐曲，章节应有规矩。屈原以原词鄙俚改写之，当不动原曲。原曲如何，不得而知。我试将《湘君》按四句一段，共得九段，余结语"时不可兮再得，聊逍遥兮容与"。又将《湘夫人》按四句一段，刚好也是九段，余结语"时不可兮骤得，聊逍遥兮容与"。这颇合乐理，即九个乐章，每章四小节，二篇同用一乐谱，符合二神同祀假说。兹将分段编号列于文末，以便解说。

这样分段，无碍文意，且如Ⅰ2、Ⅰ4、Ⅰ6、Ⅰ7都更合我的解释，下详。还有个好处，若Ⅰ5、Ⅱ5之第二联通常编入下段，致韵脚不叶；按四句一段，皆叶（"盖"古音"记"）。

唯乐曲九章同式，未免呆板。不过，祭乐庄穆，少变换，九叠亦非太过。设想若四女、八女或两队往复对舞，"缓节兮安歌"，"翱游兮周章"，也就不呆板了。

《湘君》《湘夫人》取自舜与二妃故事，述死别恋情未了之悲剧，除韩愈、朱熹外，殆少异议。唯解者多以二妃及舜死后皆湘水之神，以至有些词句难解。我以为，二妃溺湘水，为水神，能令沅湘无波，出入不离舟楫。然舜死苍梧山，葬九嶷山，若为神，只是山神，与水无涉。其行也，驾"飞龙"，或"鹜"，我以为即《东君》中之马拉龙车，腾空而行，故止处曰"弭节"；总之，与舟楫无涉。只因他是湘夫人之君，故称"湘君"，实与湘水无关。明乎此，则诗中暧昧之处迎刃而解。

试解《湘君》。此诗为夫人独白（巫女唱），而文中一段写其君，一段写自己；一句写其君，一句写自己。反复置换，生动活泼。这是女性思路，自叙总忘记不了加几句"他"。

Ⅰ1节是写君，约好来洞庭与我相会，却又犹豫不行，"沛吾乘兮桂舟"是派船去接他。Ⅰ2写自己，久等不来，第一次约会失败。"谁思"，意"思谁"？

Ⅰ3第一联写君，"北征"指很远的北方，因舜的统治中心在黄河流域，但他答应北征时绕道来洞庭湖看望夫人。"薜荔柏兮蕙绸"以下和Ⅰ4全节都是写夫人自己，而重点是船上高插绸帜旌旗，向乘飞龙的君发信号，即"扬灵"。结果信号失灵，"未极"意未达目的，第二次约会失败。

Ⅰ5是夫人伤感，不是痛哭，所以"横流涕"，泪水浸在眼帘里。接着，"桂棹兮兰枻"写自己，夫人离不开船。"斫冰兮积雪"写北征的君，想他那里是冰天雪地。这句前人多解为飞船浪花，实说不过去。

Ⅰ6是夫人回忆他第一次爽约，Ⅰ7是回忆第二次爽约，从"告余以不闲"可知。有意思的是这里也插入两句，"石濑兮浅浅"指自己，"飞龙兮翩翩"指他，有上舒、下困之意。

Ⅰ8前两句写他，这次是真的真的走了，不回来了。后两句写夫人自己的心情，"鸟次兮屋上，水周兮堂下"，极其清冷寂寞，就像屋中没有生命一样，写得好极了。

Ⅰ9 也是妙笔，旧解都是。不过，我以为"下女"是指夫人的下女，或即婵媛。

而最好的是结语，"时不可兮再得"，完全绝望了，但不是要自杀，也不痛哭，而是逍遥一番，且散散心，这正是夫人所以为神。

再看《湘夫人》。此诗是湘君自叙，称已故的夫人曰帝子、公子、佳人，有如"对象"，有大男子气；笔法亦全写自己，不像夫人之诗念念不忘男人。

Ⅱ1 写景极美，含愁意。是想象夫人来到北渚，故Ⅱ2 有"佳期"（约会）的设想，随即有"鸟何萃兮蘋中"二句，意不可能。这种以比喻作完全否定的句法楚辞中屡用，大约是一种习惯。

Ⅱ3 是君独思。"远望"意二人南北相距甚远，"观流水"含她离不开水意。

Ⅱ4 乘马西行一节我不能解，因"闻佳人召予"应是南下。又"腾驾偕逝"则不是马，而是马拉飞车。"筑室兮水中"以下，我意皆想象之词，并未与夫人同居。Ⅱ6 讲房屋构造；Ⅱ7 讲床帷；Ⅱ8 讲庭院。中插有"芷葺兮荷屋"二句与Ⅱ5 重复，或谓衍文。郭沫若说："屋"应为"幄"，"葺"应为"茸"，颇勉强。去此二句，则本诗恰好九章，与《湘君》同。故以衍文为是。

按Ⅱ8，此房有庭院、花圃、厢房、大门，不会是在"水中"，而是在个岛上。所以说"水中"，因夫人是水神，其实夫人原居处"水周兮堂下"，并不在水中。又Ⅱ8 说九嶷山的诸神像云一样来了，但没说夫人没来。这是因为整个筑室事都是想象，用不着说了。

Ⅱ9 一如Ⅰ9，构思绝妙，旧解皆是。

结语佳处，在于不用"时不可兮再得"，而用"时不可兮骤得"，男人不像女人那样悲观，还有一线希望。

湘 君

Ⅰ1　君不行兮夷犹，蹇谁留兮中洲？

美要眇兮宜修，沛吾乘兮桂舟。

Ⅰ2 令沅湘兮无波，使江水兮安流。
望夫君兮未来，吹参差兮谁思？

Ⅰ3 驾飞龙兮北征，邅吾道兮洞庭。
薜荔柏兮蕙绸，荪桡兮兰旌。

Ⅰ4 望涔阳兮极浦，横大江兮扬灵。
扬灵兮未极，女婵媛兮为余太息。

Ⅰ5 横流涕兮潺湲，隐思君兮陫侧。
桂棹兮兰枻，斫冰兮积雪。

Ⅰ6 采薜荔兮水中，搴芙蓉兮木末。
心不同兮媒劳，恩不甚兮轻绝。

Ⅰ7 石濑兮浅浅，飞龙兮翩翩。
交不忠兮怨长，期不信兮告余以不闲。

Ⅰ8 朝骋骛兮江皋，夕弭节兮北渚。
鸟次兮屋上，水周兮堂下。

Ⅰ9 捐余玦兮江中，遗余佩兮澧浦。
采芳洲兮杜若，将以遗兮下女。

结语　时不可兮再得，聊逍遥兮容与。

湘夫人

Ⅱ1 帝子降兮北渚，目眇眇兮愁予。
袅袅兮秋风，洞庭波兮木叶下。

Ⅱ2 登白薠兮骋望，与佳期兮夕张。
鸟何萃兮薠中，罾何为兮木上？

Ⅱ3 沅有芷兮澧有兰，思公子兮未敢言。
荒忽兮远望，观流水兮潺湲。

Ⅱ4 麋何食兮庭中，蛟何为兮水裔？
朝驰余马兮江皋，夕济兮西澨。

Ⅱ5 闻佳人兮召予，将腾驾兮偕逝。

筑室兮水中，葺之兮荷盖。

Ⅱ6　荪壁兮紫坛，播芳椒兮成堂。

桂栋兮兰橑，辛夷楣兮药房。

Ⅱ7　罔薜荔兮为帷，擗蕙櫋兮既张。

白玉兮为镇，疏石兰兮为芳。

衍文　芷葺兮荷屋，缭之兮杜衡。

Ⅱ8　合百草兮实庭，建芳馨兮庑门。

九嶷缤兮并迎，灵之来兮如云。

Ⅱ9　捐余袂兮江中，遗余褋兮澧浦。

搴汀洲兮杜若，将以遗兮远者。

结语　时不可兮骤得，聊逍遥兮容与。

濯足二谈

无标题

近来报刊文章大批西方的无标题音乐，我看不懂，若说一首乐曲总有自己的意境，似没什么可说；若说一个名家的几百号 Opus 都要加个标题，实不可能。鸣奏曲、小鸣奏曲、回旋曲一般无标题，因为曲式就代表了标题，三个乐章代表三种意境。协奏曲常有标题，但批者各异。如贝多芬的命运交响曲挨批最多；英雄交响曲有人说是写拿破仑，有人说不是，于是又有批派、保派。总之，我看不懂，因而下面只谈无标题的诗。

王国维在《人间词话》中说，诗三百篇、古诗十九首都无标题，五代和北宋的词也都无标题，标题是后人加上去的。这不错。但又说："诗有题而诗亡，词有题而词亡"，这就奇怪了。他又说，严羽讲兴趣，王士禛讲神韵，"不若鄙人拈出境界二字，为探其本也"。"落日照大旗"是一种境界；"宝帘闲挂小银钩"也是一种境界。这种境界，最好是无标题了。我曾说过，冯延巳的"闲引鸳鸯芳径里，手挼红杏蕊"，写的是最无聊的人的最无聊的事，若加标题只能标《无聊》。

然而，无标题诗却曾发挥很大的威力。

最好的无题诗，古有李商隐，近有鲁迅。李的无题诗晦涩难解，因有难言之隐，或谓政治，或谓婚外恋，近来讲儒法斗争，政治论又占上风。

不管怎样，"楚雨含情皆有托"，大家公认这些无题诗是有丰富的思想内容的。

鲁迅的无题诗有十余首，加上原无题后来许广平在编入《集外集拾遗》时加上题目的，和一些有题等于无题如《赠人》之类，就更多了。这些诗，虽然许多具体人和事需靠专家注释（有题诗也是这样），其思想内容则是非常鲜明的。它是革命的号角，投向敌人的匕首，爱的大纛，憎的丰碑。正因如此，可以说无题胜有题。

这是鲁迅先生最有代表性的一首《无题》："万家墨面没蒿莱，敢有歌吟动地哀。心事浩茫连广宇，于无声处听惊雷。"

《湘灵鼓瑟》

鲁迅在《题未定草》之七中批判了所谓"静穆"的诗境，说那种欣赏"曲终人不见，江上数峰青"的境界的心理，就像道士所说"至心归命礼，玉皇大天尊"一样，眼前不见，只有想着远处在。

这两句诗是钱起《湘灵鼓瑟》的尾联，而全诗并非"静穆"。鲁迅指出，这是"摘句"之过，"历来的伟大的作者，是没有一个'浑身是静穆'的"。

鲁迅似乎很喜欢钱起这首《湘灵鼓瑟》，他曾手书全诗，题"仲足先生教"，手迹现存。这诗全文是："善鼓云和瑟，常闻帝子灵。冯夷空自舞，楚客不堪听。苦调凄金石，清音入杳冥。苍梧来怨慕，白芷动芳馨。流水传湘浦，悲风过洞庭。曲终人不见，江上数峰青。"曲调高亢，清怨浑然。

1931年鲁迅还手书钱起的《归雁》给日本友人长尾景和。我在历史博物馆所办鲁迅展览会上看到这个条幅，原题"义山诗"，其实是钱起诗，内容也是讲湘灵鼓瑟的："潇湘何事等闲回，水碧沙明两岸苔。二十五弦弹夜月，不胜清怨却飞来。"这时正是鲁迅为柔石等五烈士被捕事避居花园庄，心情宛见。

大约在写这个条幅后，鲁迅自己写了一首《湘灵歌》，并手书条幅，题"偶作奉应松元先生雅嘱"，手迹现存："昔闻湘水碧于染，今闻湘水胭脂痕。湘灵妆成照湘水，皓如素月窥彤云。高丘寂寞竦中夜，芳荃零落无余春。鼓完瑶瑟人不闻，太平成像盈秋门。"显然是说国民党白色恐怖，杀人如麻，湘水为赤。而湘灵鼓瑟，应代表革命歌声；尾联用钱起笔法，钱起诗是激情变为静穆，这里是零落变成国民党的"太平成像"。

1933 年，鲁迅又有诗题赠日本友人土屋文明："一枝清采妥湘灵，九畹贞风慰独醒。无奈终输萧艾密，却成迁客播芳馨。"这里播送的应是革命福音。

湘灵鼓瑟是个动人的故事，她鼓的是什么曲子，可由诗人自裁。诗人没有不喜欢她的。只有秦始皇过湘山祠，大发脾气，"使刑徒三千人，皆伐湘山树，赭其山"。

李商隐的《无题》

李商隐有《无题》，尾联是"刘郎已恨蓬山远，更隔蓬山一万重"。又有首《无题》，尾联是"蓬山此去无多路，青鸟殷勤为探看"。同是刘郎游蓬山会神女故事，而这个蓬山说远就远，说近就近，可谓用事随意性。

原来第一首起句"来是空言去绝踪"，是写久别无音信，忽梦里相见，故叹蓬山太远。第二首起句"相见时难别亦难"，是写两情相聚，难舍难分，告别时以蓬山在迩且通信使为慰。

第一首颔联"梦为远别啼难唤，书被催成墨未浓"，情真意切，真是清新佳句。但下面腹联"蜡照半笼金翡翠，麝熏微度绣芙蓉"，写梦醒后闺房寂寞，落入俗套，未免笔弱。第二首颔联"春蚕到死丝方尽，蜡炬成灰泪始干"，千古绝唱，脍炙人口。而腹联"晓镜但愁云鬓改，夜吟应觉月光寒"，亦见笔弱，并且说回去了，像是补笔。

李商隐《无题》诗腹联常有笔弱毛病。如另一首："昨夜星辰昨夜风，画楼西畔桂堂东。身无彩凤双飞翼，心有灵犀一点通。"其颔联也是惊人之笔，绝世之作。而腹联"隔座送钩春酒暖，分曹射覆蜡灯红"；补述宴会情景，字句平平。

这是因为，律诗一上来无论写情或写景，到颔联已达高潮，接下去必须转述他事，此即"起承转合"之童子课也。续写高潮，常致笔弱。

杜甫的登高诗

我作学生时曾听一代大师刘文典（叔雅）的诗课，第一课即讲起承转合。他说：今天我在清华大学讲起承转合，人家都会笑话我，难道大学就不要起承转合了吗？

杜甫有两首登高的诗，一是登台，一是登楼，都是安史乱后漂泊西南时作。

登台的诗云："风急天高猿啸哀，渚清沙白鸟飞回。无边落木萧萧下，不尽长江滚滚来。"气势磅礴，把登高所见雄伟景象写到家了，不能再加一词；下面即转入写事："万里悲秋常作客，百年多病独登台。""百年多病"有点问题。杜公此时约五十五六岁，说不上百年，且身体素健，只是这时偶患上呼吸道感染。我疑这是指国事，即《秋兴》"百年世事不胜悲"，《登楼》"万方多难此登临"之意。

尾联"艰难苦恨繁霜鬓，潦倒新停浊酒杯"，乃本诗主旨所在。对诗人说，没有什么比停止饮酒更悲伤了。注家争论"潦倒"二字，实属无味，"潦倒"正是诗人本意。

《登楼》云："花近高楼伤客心，万方多难此登临。锦江春色来天地，玉垒浮云变古今。"玉垒山在成都西北。这两句雄浑壮阔，天地古今，整个宇宙都入胸怀，不能再置一词了。于是腹联转入时事："北极朝廷终不改，西山寇盗莫相侵。"或谓这二句不类史诗笔法，不如"羯胡事主终无赖"，我倒觉得很新鲜，可称时论笔法，开宋诗新风。

尾联，即结语，却令人吃惊："可怜后主还祠庙，日暮聊为梁甫吟。"把当今皇上（代宗）比作刘禅，难道不怕杀头么？杜甫是被肃宗罢官的，罢官后还说"君诚中兴主，经纬固密勿"（《北征》）。代宗继位，收复两京，写此诗时已平安史之乱，故曰"北极朝廷终不改"，何得以后主视之？

还有，就祠庙论，诸葛亮已死，阿斗不会吟诗，这个"日暮聊为梁甫吟"的是谁呢？这就不如李商隐的"他年锦里经祠庙，梁父吟成恨有余"了。附带说，李商隐这首《筹笔驿》，起句"猿鸟犹疑畏简书，风云常为护储胥"，绝妙之笔。颔联"徒令上将挥神笔，终见降王走传车"，高超史诗笔法，二句概括一部《蜀志》；而腹联"管乐有才真不忝，关张无命欲何如?"未免流俗笔弱了。

《咏怀古迹》（一）

杜甫有五首《咏怀古迹》，都是大历初出蜀到江陵时所作。

第一首咏庾信。但全诗是讲自己，结尾时才有"庾信平生最萧瑟，暮年诗赋动江关"。庾信是由南京避乱到江陵，说不上"支离东北风尘际，漂泊西南天地间"。他根本未入蜀，大约没到过三峡。"三峡楼台淹日月，五溪衣服共云山"。只有亲自经过瞿塘峡、一线天的人（杜公，还有我）才能悟及"楼台"假象，才能领会"日月忽其不淹"的真景。"五溪"句更绝妙。武陵有五条溪，会于辰州，各居不同的少数民族；听不懂他们的话，唯见各民族服装不同，赶集时熙熙攘攘，"共云山"。多好啊！旧注"五色服"，全失诗意。

这首诗完全没说古迹。大约庾信在这一带没留下什么遗迹，只是住过宋玉的故宅。

第二首咏宋玉。起句"摇落深知宋玉悲"。前首用"萧瑟"二字概括庾信，取自《哀江南赋》；这首用"摇落"二字概括宋玉，取自《九辩》。太好了！两个字说出全部人生性情。这种概括法，后世无人。

这首下阕全是古迹。宋玉在这里有三大遗迹：故宅；陪襄王游云梦时讲神女故事的台；每天上班去的楚宫。"江山故宅空文藻，云雨荒台岂梦思？最是楚宫俱泯灭，舟人指点到今疑"。故宅不见了，只有到文章中去找。那个神女出没的台本来就是幻想的，"岂梦思"应译为"难道不是做梦吗？"最有意思的是楚宫，雇舟往访，舟人指点说，这里就是，那里就是；其实哪里都不是。所谓古迹大都类此。

《咏怀古迹》（二）

第三首咏明妃。这篇也没古迹。"群山万壑赴荆门，生长明妃尚有村"。明妃村在秭归县，但村不是古迹，如张家村、李家店都不是古迹，要有明妃故宅才是古迹。杜公有《将适江陵》四十韵："神女峰娟妙，昭君宅有无"，意思是没有宅。但方行曰，此诗有一大古迹，"一去紫台连朔漠，独留青冢向黄昏"。不错，青冢是个大古迹，但它在呼和浩特，杜公根本没去过，不能算。

这首尾联："千载琵琶作胡语，分明怨恨曲中论。"《琴操》说，昭君"恨帝始终不见遇……心念乡土，乃作旷怨思惟歌"。《乐府诗集》："琴曲有昭君怨"，即（避晋帝讳）《王明君》。既是琴曲，又怨元帝、思乡土，其词大约不会用胡语。其词起句"秋木凄凄，其叶萎黄"，类乐府，不会是胡语译文。"千载琵琶作胡语"应为"作胡声"，指其曲掺用胡音以至胡调。唐代这种情况常见，汉代也有，如《胡笳十八拍》。

蔡文姬的《胡笳十八拍》也是琴曲，掺用胡音，尤其节奏和曲式上。但《十八拍》不能用笳来奏，因不是鼓吹曲；《昭君怨》则是用琵琶演奏。唐代清商乐部用琴，也用琵琶，胡乐部用琵琶不用琴。清商乐用传统琵琶，亦称秦琵琶，胡乐部用五弦琵琶。宋欧阳修《明妃曲》（和王安石）："身行不遇中国人，马上自作思归曲。推手为琵却手琶，胡人共听亦咨嗟。"推、却，出自汉刘熙《释名》，"推手前曰批，引手却曰把"，是指秦琵琶，欧阳公以批把为琵琶。宋代已无秦琵琶、胡琵琶之分。宋人常用"推、揉"，即唐代所称"拢、捻"，指左手技法，推或拢可出滑音。白居易"轻拢慢捻抹复挑"；"抹"，宋人曰"却"，是右手技法。

《咏怀古迹》（三）

第四首咏刘备。"蜀主窥吴幸三峡，崩年亦在永安宫。翠华想象空山里，玉殿虚无野寺中。"永安宫在奉节县，这个古迹看不见了，只见野寺，至于刘备的仪仗更只能去想象。

第五首咏诸葛亮。这首也没说古迹。尾联"运移汉祚终难复，志决身歼军务劳"。"志决身歼"有如大批斗中"下定决心，不怕牺牲"，而"军务劳"三字笔弱。诸葛亮"功盖三分国"，岂止军务劳。然而这里是用典。诸葛亮的使节误向司马懿泄密："诸葛公夙兴夜寐，罚二十以上皆亲览焉"，司马懿知道"亮将死矣"。故"军务劳"实为"鞠躬尽瘁，死而后矣"八字。省了字，但不响亮，不如《蜀相》结语："出师未捷身先死，长使英雄泪满襟。"

这首没讲古迹，但起句"诸葛大名垂宇宙，宗臣遗像肃清高"，暗含有个祠堂在。这里确有个武侯祠。前首有"武侯祠屋常邻近，一体君臣祭祀同"，自注："庙在（永安）宫东。"永安宫已不见，而武侯祠仍有香火，祭武侯兼及刘备。

1962年我到成都，游《蜀相》所叙丞相祠，当地人称武侯祠。进大殿，不见武侯，而是刘、关、张高座中央，环众百官，皆有帏帐、塑像、碑记。武侯乃在后殿，空寂无华。内外题咏殆遍，多摭拾杜句。因成一律：

> 丞相祠屋天下奇，君王窃居武侯祠。
>
> 黄鹂早去无新语，翠柏犹存发旧枝。
>
> 历数兴亡皆往事，检查功过费心思。
>
> 骚人到此枯肠尽，一半文章是杜诗。

剑器浑脱

杜甫《观公孙大娘弟子舞剑器行》传诵至今。但其序中所说"剑器浑脱"是什么，各家注均无确解。

《正字通》：剑器，武舞，用女伎，雄妆空手而舞。这是对的。唐代健舞如柘枝、棱大、胡旋、胡腾，都是用女伎，空手。《文献通考》等以剑器为刀剑，错了。

这个舞是状英勇战士，我想是两手连续、曲折而有强节奏的动作，所谓"浏漓顿挫"。"燿如羿射九日落"是由下向上的手势；"矫如群帝骖龙翔"是双手横空挥荡；"来如雷霆收震怒"是两臂合抱；"罢如江海凝清光"是两手推开。

这是据杜老诗想象的舞姿，可是一看《曲子剑器词》又黯然失色了。这曲子词是在敦煌石窟中发现的，前人注唐诗还不知道。词曰："丈夫气力全，一个拟当千。猛气冲心出，视死亦如眠。率率不离手，恒日在阵前。譬如鹘打雁，左右悉皆穿。"真是气壮山河。不过，舞蹈舞成这样，似也不必。

剑器舞原是民间舞。杜甫曾在郾城看过公孙氏此舞，这诗则是他后来看公孙大娘的弟子临颍十二娘舞时写的。又张旭曾在邺县看过公孙大娘"舞西河剑器"。郾城、临颍、邺县都在河南，但此舞并非产于河南，而是来自西河。陕西、山西、内蒙古都有西河。子夏居西河，吴起为西河守，都是陕西的西河。剑器舞大约也产此，今有西河大鼓。唐代健舞是用鼓伴奏的。张祜："舞停歌罢鼓连催"；白居易："连击三声画鼓催"；杨巨源："大鼓当风舞柘枝。"

那么，浑脱又是什么呢？

浑脱照字义说就是黑羊。长孙无忌用黑羊皮做帽叫浑脱帽，彝人用黑羊皮充气骑着过河叫浑脱舟。这都是唐诗注家引用了的。

但唐代有浑脱曲。《明皇杂录》讲诸公主等争学吹箫，唯公孙大娘（这时已由民间入宫）"能为邻里曲……西河剑气、浑脱"。《乐书》："唐自天后末，剑气入浑脱，为犯声之始"，"剑气宫调，浑脱角调，以臣犯君"，故有犯声。所谓犯声，就是转调，由宫调转入角调。浑脱又可作"解"用。《梦溪笔谈》："柘枝旧曲遍数极多，如《羯鼓录》所谓浑脱解之类。"解是大曲中一段快速乐段，表示分章处。

剑器曲是伴剑器舞的，浑脱曲想也是伴浑脱舞。浑脱舞未见记载，如果有，我想是模仿黑羊的动作，踊跃，比较轻快。

杜甫"于郾城观公孙氏舞剑器浑脱，浏漓顿挫，独出冠时"。我想可以有二解。公孙氏（不一定是大娘）舞了一段雄壮的剑器，又跳了一段快舞浑脱收场。或者是剑器舞舞到转调时，就改为轻快，用浑脱曲伴奏。乐和舞都讲究对比，乐不能从头到尾都是"时代最高音"，喊破嗓子；舞也不能一直雄壮，像要杀人。

诗与乐（一）

古诗都是唱的，三百篇皆被弦歌。但若说三百篇（据说原有三千篇）每篇都有个曲调，我却不信。大约雅、颂有几个标准曲，各国国风有几个习惯曲，唱时把诗套进去。至于用琴或瑟伴奏，有些可能是即兴，或者只弹个过门。清乾隆间收集民歌不下千首，而所用曲调主要只有西调、岔曲、寄生草三种。

并且，我以为古代是先有曲，后有词即诗，诗是从属于乐的。像"断竹，续竹，飞土，逐肉"以及《易》中那些几乎都是二字句的诗，是从劳动中的哼唷或行军中的呼应来的。这种二音阶的乐在反复歌唱中经拖长、急过等技法变化，也使词即诗发生变化。如写夫妇剪羊毛的"女承筐，无实；士刲羊，无血"。大约就是将两个二分音符变换为一个二分和两个四分音符来的。又如《候人歌》，传说是涂山氏女等候大禹时所唱，应该唱很久，但只有"候人兮猗"四字，实际只有"候人"二字。唱时用重叠、拉长、变位等来适应情绪。这也是诗从属于乐之证。

在古代，乐、舞、诗常是结合在一起的。但我想，最初是乐和舞的结合，诗是后加的。如《韶》《大武》都有乐有舞，无诗。《乐记》说《大武》六个乐章，在第一章末段"咏叹之，淫液之"，即加了点词，也许只是哼哼一阵，还未成诗。又说"武乱皆坐"，即奏到"乱"的时候，两个舞队都坐下了，这时就只有乐了。孔子说："关雎之乱洋洋乎，盈耳哉！"（《论语·泰伯》）这是指乐，在诗中却不见。因为"乱"是一段热烈、急速、音量大的乐段，用以区分乐章，奏到"乱"时，就不唱诗了。

但是《楚辞》中却有"乱"。《离骚》"乱曰：已矣哉！国无人，莫我知兮……"慷慨悲愤。我想这是因为《楚辞》比《诗》晚出二三百年，加以屈原文才出众，就把乐曲中"乱"的部分填上总结性诗句。由于"乱"的节奏不同，《楚辞》中的"乱曰"也都用变文，即改变句法，无韵。以后乐府仿此，也有了乱文，或叫"趋"。有的乱文很长，达十数句；大约此时乐曲中的"乱"也不只是"钟鼓齐鸣"一阵，而有点旋律了。这也是诗从乐。

诗与乐（二）

我国古代无乐谱，只凭口传，日久就失传了。到了汉代，最受人推崇的《韶》已无人会奏，《诗》除列入典礼乐的几首外也唱不出来了，歌诗变成吟诗。

对音乐来说，这是件好事。因无乐谱，乐曲总是不断更新。"古调虽可爱，今人多不弹"；成为发展规律，而诗因有文字记载，一直保留下来。礼坏乐崩，诗没有崩，也就很少更新。

汉代，由于古乐亡，都是新乐。李延年"善歌，为新变声"；又把司马相如等所作诗颂"为之新声曲"；又"因胡曲更造新声二十八解"（《汉书·李延年传》《晋书·乐志》）。反之，汉代除乐府外，没什么好诗。像《古诗十九首》，题材狭隘，情调低沉，千篇一律；秦嘉、蔡邕等的五言诗更是这样。

汉乐府很好，因为它是从民间采来的。其中，鼓吹曲占很大势力，这是因为经李延年等加工作为皇家军乐，但仍保留了民间采来的词。故如《铙歌十八曲》，其词大部分是讲爱情的，《有所思》《上邪》都是极好的情诗。只有《战城南》的词有关军旅，但是反战的内容。什么道理呢？我想大约当时皇家乐队（有三百多人）是只奏曲，不唱词，因军乐是以节奏为主。或者是曾由御用文人改了词，但未流传下来。例如后来魏文帝时将《有所思》改名《应帝期》，《上邪》改名《太和》，仍用原曲，词则改为颂登位、颂改元。又如孙吴时将《战城南》改名《克皖城》，词改为颂战功。但没人去读这些改词，至今人们还只知道《有所思》《上邪》是极好的情诗，《战城南》是反战诗。

若说情歌曲子可填上颂辞，反战曲子可改成战歌，似乎奇怪，其实不怪。因为这种短曲，旋律不是主要的。例如北伐时一首"打倒列强，除军阀"的歌流传极广，它的曲就是利用外国一首儿歌。

汉乐府中的相和歌，很有感染力。这种诗，原是无伴奏的清唱，叫"徒歌"；后加上帮腔，叫"但歌"；最后用管弦伴奏，叫"相和歌"，所谓"丝竹更相和，执节（打拍）者歌"（《晋书·乐志》）。故相和歌原来是以词即诗为主。

但是，相和歌进一步发展为大曲，音乐复杂化，又增加舞，诗就变成次要的了。有的大曲如《碣石》，后来变成《拂舞》，废词；有的大曲如《黄老弹》，大约创作时就没有词。大曲中的"解"，一般是没有词的。今所见乐府诗中注有"一解""二解"等，即指这里有一段快板乐曲，没有词。说明乐曲进一步发展，诗就跟不上去了。像近代的交响乐，都无法配词。

《汉书·艺文志》"乐六家，百六十五篇"，这都是有乐无诗的。"歌诗二十八家，三百一十四篇"，这是有乐又有诗的。我相信汉代还没有乐谱，这些乐都失传了，但有诗的，有些保留下来。乐失传是因为有新乐替代了它。从这点说，是坏事变好事。

诗与乐 （三）

唐代是个诗的伟大时代，也是音乐大发展时代。唐诗名气太大了，盖过了音乐，但我以为，推其原，唐诗仍是随着乐发展起来的。

唐代音乐繁盛，主要得力于外国音乐输入。而这种输入，实际在唐建国以前。唐十部乐中，龟兹、西凉、高昌、康国、疏勒、天竺、安国、高丽八部都是南北朝时输入的。乐是跟着人走的。这时不仅北方民族大融合，还有南北人民大迁徙，开发了民间的西曲和吴歌，给乐坛添上绚丽色彩。外国乐和南乐都是当时的新声。老调子没人听了。永嘉南渡后，太常贺循奏称：原来的雅乐乐工亡散，"又无识者"，只好将乐器封存库中，"遂至朽坏焉"（《晋书·乐志下》）。

魏晋南北朝，诗除曹氏和陶渊明两个奇峰外，多属平平。至于玄言诗、齐梁体，实不足论。至唐，诗却极盛。这与经济繁荣、政治开放、以诗取士等是分不开的。不过我看，魏晋以来音乐的发展也是重要原因。唐诗还是注意唱的。李白的《清平乐》大约是按曲造词。王维的《渭城曲》大约是依词配曲。李贺诗称奇峭，但他的乐府"云韶诸工皆合之弦管"；李益的乐府"每一篇出，乐人辄以重赂购之"。据说，王昌龄、高适、王之涣在酒楼偷听妓女唱歌，听到唱自己的诗都沾沾自喜。有个妓女说"我是唱白居易《长恨歌》的，岂同凡响哉！"唐诗就这样受到鼓舞。把诗的评选权从官府移到乐工、歌妓之手，单这点民主就是了不起的。

唐在音乐上是拿来主义，有十四国乐队。天宝十四载，诏道调、法曲与胡部新声合作，而实际上新乐或胡乐占绝对优势。"梨园弟子调律吕，知有新声不如古"。诗上则没有拿来什么，即使拿来，限于翻译和格律限制，也没什么成就。

诗受格律限制，乐也有乐律，而且更严。所谓乐律，是包括绝对音高的一套十二个半音体系，用三分损益法定出，本不科学。但古人把它看成是"万事根本"（《天官书》），风雨节令、人世兴衰都要受这个律的支配，所以是绝对不能改变的。但随着时代风尚的变化，标准音逐渐提高，十二音阶都不能合黄钟宫调的古律。晋代荀勖因造新的律管，而受到阮咸等保守派攻击。荀勖是当权派，就把阮咸下放了。可是，不知什么人发掘一根周代玉尺，拿来一量荀勖所造律管，果然不合钟律，只好将阮咸官复原职。

虽然如此，真正的音乐家即乐师、乐工、歌妓、民间艺人等是不受律的限制的。隋高祖令雅乐只准用黄钟宫调，但演奏时乐工偷偷地改用蕤宾之宫，满朝官员只觉好听，"竟无觉者"（《隋书·音乐志》）。到唐代，流行调已用夹钟宫了，比黄钟宫高四个半音，乐工称"倍四"，并将标准音器泗滨磬改为华原磬，已如前述。

此外，音乐家还有种种方法突破律的限制。如前述将宫调《剑器》转入角调《浑脱》叫"犯声"。元稹："能唱犯声歌，偏精变筹议"，犯声或改调视为技巧。又如《绿腰》羽调，段善本用枫香调来弹，听者赞赏，叫"移调"。有的曲如《凉州》可以一下子移几个调。还有"改调"，吴歌："初歌子夜曲，改调促鸣筝。"又有"侧声""正杀""寄杀"等手法，都部分地摆脱律的限制。乐的自由化主要来自民间，因为好听，皇帝也赞赏，"新声变律，深惬上旨"（《唐会要》卷三四）。

诗却不能这样自由。并且到了齐梁，沈约、谢朓等音韵学家出来，又给它加上"四声谱"的约束，动不动就得"病"。白居易的"四弦不似琵琶声"，"忽闻水上琵琶声"，都应改作"屁琶声"，才不得病。不过，真正的诗人，包括音乐家白居易，是不去纠缠这些声病的。在这方面，李、杜尤有气魄。但是，像五七格律，定下来后就一直到今天，很难改变。

西方作曲学上有一条原则：凡是不合规则的旋律、节奏或和声，只要把它重复或模进（在较高或较低音段上重复）一两遍，就视为合法了。作诗就没有这种便宜。律诗破律只能用"拗"，但拗后必须"救"。

所以，乐比诗进化快，诗比乐保守。

诗与乐 （四）

到了宋代，诗完全脱离了乐，只吟不唱了。然而，又有唱的东西出来，即词。

因敦煌发现曲子抄本，知词（即曲子）在隋唐已流行民间。只是那时文人醉心于诗，未予注意。到宋代，民间曲子已有八百多个曲牌，文人按曲牌填词，就是宋词。词是从曲子来的，正如乐府是从民歌来的一样。

可是文人总想自成正统，把词说成"诗余"，来自诗；甚至说来自长短句的《南风》《周颂》（《词综序》）。朱熹倒是看到了诗与乐的关系，但又造了一个学说，说古人唱诗有许多泛声，"后来人怕失了那泛声，逐一声添个实字，遂成长短句"。这样，词不是"诗余"，而是"诗添"了。怪论。

有人承认词是跟着曲牌来的，但又认为这些曲牌是截取唐代大曲而来，因为很多用引、序、慢、近、令等，标明是取大曲的一部分。我看这是说不通的。引、序、慢是指节奏，都属慢板。近是"近拍"，即将入破，节奏加快。令是快板短调。还有捉拍，则是急板。这都是曲本身的标记。大部分词牌并无这种标记，因原曲为中速。

当诗在文人的手中僵化了的时候，他们从曲子中找到了词。这是一个进步。但词在文人手中也逐渐僵化起来，特别是音乐部分。原来民间曲子是随时代风尚变化的，固定为词牌，就不能变了。像前谈犯调即转调或换调，在乐师手中视为等闲，在文人手中就不敢动了。只有像姜夔那样的词人兼乐师，颇用犯调和"自度曲"。纯文人则只敢"减字""偷声"或"摊破"，即在原词牌上增减一至三个字，而不敢改动曲调或曲式。

填词，都是像刘禹锡所说"踏曲兴无穷，调同词不同"。无论是欢乐的、哀怨的、说英雄的、谈恋爱的，都可填入一个词牌。如果只是长短句，倒没有什么，如果是和乐来唱，那怎么行呢？因此，词入文人之手后，逐渐与音乐脱节，大约宋以后的词，多半也只吟不唱了。

譬如《念奴娇》，原曲大约是适合念奴唱的，"念奴九天歌一声"，也许是花腔女高音。那么，怎能填入"大江东去"，由"关西大汉，铜琵琶、铁绰板"来唱呢？后来，我真看见苏轼这首《念奴娇》的曲谱了（杨荫浏译自《九宫大成南北词宫谱曲》）。我请洪达琳用钢琴奏了一遍，可以说不怎么雄壮，也绝非靡靡之音。好像是词的曲到了文人手中后中性化了。

当宋代文人竞相就曲填词的时候，这些曲子在民间已不时髦了。而是流行起多调式的缠令、诸宫调了；一个诸宫调的套曲甚至可以有一百五十个基本调、四百多个变奏。因而，后来文人又放下填词，去追求这种新音乐，这就是元曲。所以，诗和乐比，总是乐比诗进化快，诗比乐保守。

清 商

在乐书中，东晋以后的民间乐曲通称清商。《晋书·乐志》中的清商乐几乎都是吴歌或荆楚西曲。

但诗中所谓清商，含义不同。《古诗十九首》："清商随风发，中曲正徘徊。一弹再三叹，慷慨有余哀"；"被服罗裳人，当户理清曲。音响一何悲，弦急知柱促"；《黄鹄一远别》："长歌正激烈，中心怆以摧。欲展清商曲，念子不能归。"这是汉代的清商。

汉代乐曲通行三调：平调以宫为主，清调以商为主，瑟调以角为主（《魏书》陈仲如语）。"为主"可解为基音，那么，汉代的清商大约相当于唐代的商调，或以太簇为首音的 sol 调式。宫调以黄钟为首音（Fa 调式），较低，声平和。商比宫高两个半音，古人称高曰清。又把商声训为金、为秋、为杀，用于悲怆乐章。

汉代的官乐（乐部）是相和歌，由管弦乐队伴奏，多达几百人，只有宫廷才能演奏。从上引诗看，清商是在家中唱的，用琴或瑟伴奏（《黄鹄》中有"丝竹"，恐是偏义复词，专指丝）。因而，它是室内乐，文人发牢骚、闺妇思离人，常用清商。

但是，到了魏晋，发生变化。王僧虔上表《论舞并三调歌》曰："今之清商，实由铜雀。魏氏三祖，风流可怀，京洛相高，江左弥重。"曹氏父子都是诗人和音乐家，他们把清商用于宴乐，同他们的性格和他们的时代是相符的。曹丕《燕歌行》："援琴鸣弦发清商，短歌微吟不能长。"曹植《正会诗》："悲歌厉响，咀嚼清商"；《弃妇篇》："慷慨有余音，要妙悲且清。"

王僧虔又说，三曹以后，"情变听改，（清商）稍复零落，十数年间，亡者将半"。这"情变听改"四字真好。政治社会情况变了，人们的喜爱也变了，清商亡掉一半，只有铜雀台上还"秋风木叶落，萧瑟管弦清"——而这只是想象（何逊《铜雀妓》）。

前面引《晋书·乐志》所说的江南清商乐，有人说是晋马南渡的结果。《乐府诗集》清商曲辞题解说后魏孝文帝"得江左所传中原旧曲……总谓之清商乐，至于殿庭飨宴则兼奏之"。我很怀疑。江南的清商原是民间乐曲，又主要是诉爱情不自由等，与政治变动无关，像《子夜歌》《乌夜啼》《西乌夜飞》等也决非中原之韵。它们应是早已存在，只是大批文人南渡后才把它们拉进诗坛。其所以总称清商乐大约因为吴音较高之故。郭茂倩又说隋文帝平陈，收其乐，于太常置清商署，"此华夏正声也"。这是可能的；唯"华夏正声"可能是文人把它和汉代清商联系起来说的。

不过，隋的清商乐已不限于南曲，也包括北朝流行的外来音乐了，其音调也是高亢的。

含 嚼

李贺《申胡子觱篥歌》："颜热感君酒，含嚼芦中声。"白居易《小童薛阳陶吹觱篥歌》："指点之下师授声，含嚼之间天与气。"有的注家说觱篥有个芦制嘴子，吹时含在口中。这是怪论。吹觱篥何必把嘴子含起来，嚼烂了就吹不响了。

含嚼是指音调。诗人首先用于写声乐。曹植《正会诗》："悲歌厉响，咀嚼清商。"鲍照《白纻舞歌词》："含商咀徵歌露晞。"李贺《许公子郑姬歌》："转角含商破碧云。"元稹《何满子歌》："犯羽含商移调态。"这都是指唱歌，也用于写器乐。温庭筠《李相妓人吹觱篥歌》："含商咀徵双幽咽。"宋葛胜仲《水调歌头》："谁吹尺八寥亮，嚼徵更含宫。"尺八指箫，怎能含下去？

唱歌有所谓"圆腔"，说把字嚼碎了，入于声，所谓"声中无字，字中有声"，也好像是含着声。诗人喜欢悲切的商调，故常用含商（葛胜仲诗用"含宫"，因是写箫，箫曲多宫调。不过《水调》原是南宫商）。清商调中，主音商和徵是纯五度，用现代说法即徵是商的属音。把主音唱得圆熟，就叫"含商嚼徵"。梁简文帝《笔赋》"含商触徵之奇"，亦此意。

不过，我觉得更好是把它解释为转调（或犯调），"含商嚼徵"即商调转入徵调时转得圆滑、自然。上引例中，李贺的"转角含商破碧云"，显然是商调转入角调，是转入高调，故"破碧云"。他是用"响遏行云"典，改"遏"为"破"，这是李贺聪明处。元稹的"犯羽含商移调态"，更明白指出是商调转羽调。羽调更高，其下句是"留情度意抛弦管"，是说转得这样高明，伴奏的弦管都跟不上去了。这是"丝不如竹，竹不如肉"的概念。而更常用的是商调转入徵调，因徵是属音，单唱徵调者很少，多是由商调转入。

管乐转调其实比唱容易。觱篥九孔，可吹两个八度以至更高。李颀《听安万善吹觱篥歌》："龙吟虎啸一时发，万籁百泉相与秋。忽然更作渔洋掺，黄云萧条白日暗。变调如闻杨柳春，上林繁花照眼新。"这里有两次转调。先是悲壮慷慨的曲子转入凄凉萧疏的《渔洋掺》，然后又转入明媚的抒情曲。《渔洋掺》，原鼓曲，即京剧《击鼓骂曹》中祢衡所奏，《后汉书》说它"声节悲壮"；不过，我听过言菊朋的，是由慢而快，不觉悲壮。

温庭筠《经五丈原》

近来常听人谈温庭筠的《经五丈原》，尤其是尾联："象床宝帐无言语，从此谯周是老臣。"或谓谯周劝刘禅投降是免得二次投降。又以"中原得鹿不由人"，是说大势已定，有法家思想。我都不懂。我只知谯周是经学家，据《三国演义》，他是夜观天象决定投降的。

问题不在谯周，因为诗是温庭筠作的。温本人似非法家。"下国卧龙空寤主"，等于给诸葛亮盖棺论定，有的本子还写成"误主"。鞠躬尽瘁，难道就是这样吗？杜甫有"三分割据纡筹策"，李商隐有"徒令上将挥神笔"，叹息已矣，但情调和温庭筠完全不同。

"铁马云雕共绝尘，柳阴高压汉宫春"。"压"字何意？温庭筠喜讲柳，有不少柳诗。有首是"卓氏垆前金线柳，隋家堤畔锦帆风。贪为两地分霖雨，不见池莲照水红。"这诗是送给杜悰的，大约是希望得到一官半职。杜娶了公主做老婆，一路高升，入相封公，是个炙手可热的人物。温之为人可见。

然而，温庭筠终因得罪首长，困顿一生。他有首《过陈琳墓》："曾于青史见遗文，今日飘蓬过此坟。词客有灵应识我，霸才无主始怜君。""霸才"是自指，还是指曹操？温庭筠好像对曹操也不满意。不过，曹操若见温庭筠，恐怕也不会见怜。陈琳虽然骂曹操祖宗，但魏王粲有首《从军诗》说："从军有苦乐，但问所从谁。"温庭筠好像没有解决"从谁"的问题，而对于知识分子来说，这是最重要不过的。

李贽

年来法家兴时，出版了一些古人文集，都一售即罄。唯李贽的《藏书》

《焚书》等积压书店，我因得全套。

袁中道说李贽"诗不多作，大有神境"。我所见李集中诗近三百篇，不算少，却看不出"神"。李贽文章有战斗性，如论王安石变法议，连批"胡说""不是"。其诗却写得规规矩矩，一点没有浪漫主义。

李诗中最重"义"字，如连赞关羽及桃园三结义。又如《咏史》中有"荆卿原不识燕丹，只为田光一死难。慷慨悲歌唯击筑，萧萧易水至今寒！"他在《读史》中也说："荆卿何曾识燕丹哉？只无奈相知如田光者荐之于前，又继以刎颈送之于后耳。荆卿至此，虽欲不死不可得矣。"《咏史》中又有三诗赞美侯嬴。都是为了一个"义"字，而不必讲是非。这次死了四个人，包括一位断腕女士，但不知是否法家精神。

李贽的诗，我看其狱中八绝句最好："名山大壑登临遍，独此桓中未入门"；"杨花飞入囚人眼，始觉冥司亦有春。"这不是故作旷达，而是有无畏精神。所以无畏，因为他是因著书入狱的，他相信他的书会得到皇帝的青睐；"但愿将书细细观，必然反覆知其是"，因而，"自思懒散老何成，照旧观书候圣旨"。可惜的是，圣旨还未下来，他就用剃头刀自杀了。所以，狱中又有《书能误人》一绝："年年岁岁笑书奴，生世无端同处女。世上何人不读书，书奴却以读书死。"

"沉舟侧畔千帆过"

"沉舟侧畔千帆过，病树前头万木春"。刘禹锡这两句诗近来很流行，尤其在红卫兵文献中，还常加上"长江后浪推前浪，一代新人换旧人"。

这诗是刘禹锡谪居湘蜀二十三年后，在去洛阳途中见白居易所作。诗哀怨欲绝，但结尾变了调子，说"今日听君歌一曲，暂凭杯酒长精神"。

我说他改变了调子，因为前联即"沉舟"一联乃是反映自然界变化规律的。刘禹锡是个唯物主义者，《天论》三篇提出天人相胜的学说，又"空者，形之希微者也"；否定空虚，这是相当彻底的唯物论。彻底的唯物主义者是无所畏惧的。他的诗中有"在人虽晚达，于树似冬青"；"莫道桑榆晚，为霞尚满天"；又有"芳林新叶催陈叶，流水前波让后波"等。这都是看到了自然界的规律。

这种精神集中见于他的玄都观桃花诗。刘禹锡在革新派失败后被贬连州，十年后回京师，写下"紫陌红尘拂面来，无人不道看花回。玄都观里桃千树，尽是刘郎去后栽"。不意此诗得罪了新的当权派，刘又被贬连州、夔州。十四年后回来，玄都观一棵桃树也没有了。于是他又写："百亩庭中半是苔，桃花净尽菜花开。种桃道士归何处？前度刘郎今又来。"但这诗又以"讥权近"，刘被再度下放，"分司东都"（《旧唐书》本传）。"桃花净尽菜花开"不过是个希望，但它是合乎自然规律或辩证法的，所以诗中有"我又来了"的凛然气魄。

杨柳枝词

刘禹锡《杨柳枝词》第一首："塞北梅花羌笛吹，淮南桂树小山词。请君莫奏前朝曲，听唱新翻杨柳枝。"《梅花》是晋笛曲，小山词是汉代作品，故曰"前朝"。由于批林批孔，这几句话大受赞扬。

但我看，人们把这一点夸大了。刘是和白居易一起搞创作的，白的《杨柳枝》第一首也是"六么水调家家唱，白雪梅花处处吹。古歌旧曲君休听，听取新翻杨柳枝"。白诗比刘诗先出，而白居易决非政治革新派。

《杨柳枝》原是隋代宫词，对刘、白说也是前朝。但《杨柳枝》这个曲却是民间的，并且在唐代改了调。刘、白《杨柳枝》词并无隋宫词遗迹，而是按唐杨柳枝曲"新翻"的。鲁迅说："唐朝的《竹枝词》和《柳枝词》之类，原都是无名氏创作，经文人的采录和润色之后，留传下来的。"（《门外文谈》）可是，"文化大革命"中出版的刘、白诗选，注《杨柳枝》仍说是隋宫词。可谓善于泥古。

诗体的新和内容的新是两回事。白居易说"诗到元和体变新"，是指次韵、和答之类，不关内容。我看，刘、白的《杨柳枝》其新也在体制，即突破七绝格律，能唱能舞。至其内容，不过寄情杨柳，抒写儿女情怀。至于把杨柳写得袅袅多姿，桃李反见庸俗，乃是文人常弄的把戏，算不上"新"。这种《杨柳枝》后来仿作的多了，也失掉体制的新颖性，到袁枚、查初白手里，变成陈词滥调。

刘禹锡在四川作的《竹枝词》，确是少数民族的民歌的改编，但在改编中也只保留下"东边日出西边雨，道是无晴却有晴"之类的儿女情怀。他从民间"曲子"改制的《浪淘沙》，开后来长短句之始，其中有些好句子，如"流水淘沙不暂停，前波未灭后波生"等，确是内容的新。

柳宗元

柳宗元在政治上也是革新派。元和十年（815）他和刘禹锡一同奉诏进京，后又一同被黜。所以他在《重别梦得》中说"二十年来万事同，今朝歧路忽西东"。若从二人同登进士算起，实有二十三年。

柳宗元的牢骚比刘禹锡多。他在另一别刘诗中说："直以慵疏招物议，休将文字占时名。今朝不用临河别，垂泪千行便濯缨。"可说泪如沧浪。《登柳州城寄四州》："城上高楼接大荒，海天愁思正茫茫。惊风乱飐芙蓉水，密雨斜侵薜荔墙。岭树重遮千里目，江流曲似九回肠。共来百粤文身地，犹自音书滞一乡。"真是一字一泪。还有"一身去国六千里，万死投荒十二年"等。

不过这些诗情调虽悲，却不是哀，倒有愤意，即悲愤。"惊风""密雨"一联，读之心惊肉跳。有首《岭南行》后半段点明了："射工巧伺游人影，飓母偏惊旅客船。从此忧来非一事，岂容华发待流年。"意深沉而不是无所作为，较之杜甫"魑魅喜人过"，尤为有力。

柳宗元也是个唯物主义者。我在《天问与天对》中说他的宇宙无限和"无中无旁"的思想超过哥白尼。人说柳宗元文章"寄至味于淡泊"。但他的自然观会使淡泊中有实际内容。我曾谈过他的《江雪》，"独钓寒江雪"有积极意义。又如"烟销日出不见人，欸乃一声山水绿"，呼唤大地，万象生春。这种诗情实为罕见。

贾谊和鬼神

批林批孔中，人们谈论李商隐的《贾生》："宣室求贤访逐臣，贾生才调更无伦。可怜夜半虚前席，不问苍生问鬼神。"此诗全是议论，但使人不觉是发议论，而是叙事，这是李诗的长处。议论不说清楚，这是李诗的短处，也正是人们谈论之由。我想，此诗不是讽，而是赞，赞贾谊及其文章——古人说"怜",是指"爱"。

司马迁说文帝问贾谊"鬼神之本,贾生因具道所以然之状"。道了些什么没有说。但文帝所问不是鬼神,而是鬼神之"本",而贾谊能道出"所以然",即其道理、规律。要知,神学家是不讲"所以然"的,儒家或法家也不讲。追究"所以然"是科学问题,在当时是自然哲学的命题。

文帝不像武帝那样喜欢神仙,贾谊也不是方士。我以为这次讨论的是科学问题,是"天";因为是在祭天之后吃冷猪肉时的一次谈话。李商隐在《异俗》中说"贾生兼事鬼,不信有洪炉"。"洪炉"是天地这个大炉子产生万物的学说,这是道家的学说。贾谊不信,而有自己的创世纪,刘恒愈听愈有兴趣,所以靠近坐,"虚前席"。贾谊的创世纪如何?不知道。但我想,非法非儒非道,那么,与批林批孔何关?

贾谊"杂阴阳五行之学",这就是古代的科学。汉代文人不少是兼攻科学的,尤其是天文学,张衡、扬雄、桓谭、王充、蔡邕都是,有很高成就,浑天说、宣夜说都产生于此时。像司马相如那种纯文人,只能是"当年赐帛娟优等",与妓女同级。

贾谊《服鸟赋》

文帝很喜欢贾谊,大约因他建议削藩。据说因周勃、灌婴反对,把贾谊下放到长沙当老师去了。他在长沙写了《服鸟赋》。

后人把《服鸟赋》认作贾谊谋高官未成的牢骚经,其实不对。严复说:"古人名位心原淡,绛灌何能沮贾生?鹏鸟深情人不解,只言未得作公卿。"王安石说:"一时谋议略施行,谁道君王薄贾生?爵位自高言尽废,古来何啻万公卿。"王安石也是这样,他虽被罢相,其新法却大部实行了。因为贾谊的建议和王安石的新法是合乎历史发展规律的。

《服鸟赋》其实是一篇哲学论文。司马迁说"读《服鸟赋》,同生死,轻去就,又爽然自失矣"。

赋曰:"且夫天地为炉兮,造化为工;阴阳为炭兮,万物为铜。合散消息兮,安有常则?千变万化兮,未始有极。"这里是用《庄子》,但不是《庄子》原意,而提出造物的能源即炭和原料即铜的问题。能源即动力,就是阴阳这对矛盾，原料就是物质，万物是由物质在矛盾运动中产生的。庄子说"人之形千变万化，未始有极"，说的是"形"，例如庄子变蝴蝶，那是玄学。贾谊说"千变万化"是指物质，所以千变万化是因"合散消息"不同，即化学方程式不同，没有"常则"。这是科学。

又说"万物变化兮，固无休息。斡流而迁兮，或推而还。形气转续兮，变化而嬗"。这就不是《庄子》，而是《老子》了。所以下面讲"祸兮福所倚，福兮祸所伏"。这是讲辩证法。

《服鸟赋》在讲自然界时蛮好，但在讲到人类社会时就不行了。"命不可说""道不可谋"，只好"养空而浮""知命不忧"了。在马克思以前，最伟大的唯物主义者遇到社会历史问题也会变成唯心论者。看来，文帝"不问苍生问鬼神"倒是问对了。

沧海桑田

储光羲："独往不可群，沧海成桑田。"（《献八舅东归》）

《诗·十月之交》："高岸为谷，深谷为陵"，恐怕是最早的辩证自然观。但这里所写的是公元前 780 年发生在陕西岐山的一次大地震，与通常所说的沧海桑田是两码事。

地震造成的地表变形是突然变化。诗称："烨烨震电，不宁不令；百川沸腾，山冢崒崩。"（"不令"是不合时令）写得有声有色。这种突变，如果不考察地应力的消长，就会得出居维叶式的"突变说"，或"词句上是革命的而实际上是反动的"结论（恩格斯语）。但《十月之交》的作者比居维叶高明，其结论是"下民之孽，匪降自天；噂沓背憎，职竞由人"。这是颇为唯物主义的。有人（晋国史墨）还因此得出"社稷无常奉，君臣无常位"这种十分革命的判断。

至于沧海桑田，乃是地壳长期的、缓慢的垂直运动的结果，要经历万年的时间。大陆下降最快的地方如荷兰海岸，上升最快的地方如珠穆朗玛峰地区，平均每年升降都不过二毫米。《神仙传》中麻姑能总结出这种变化，真了不起。不过，她所说的东海（即渤海）三变为桑田并不是地壳升降的结果，而是黄河流沙入海所致，有王方平所说"海中行复扬尘也"可证。"三变"为桑田，大约是黄河三次改道所致。这与真正的沧海桑田也是两码事。

首先发现这一点的是李贺。他的《天上谣》："东指羲和能走马，海尘新生石山下"，即用王方平的理论。他的《梦天》写得更好："黄尘清水三山下，更变千年如走马。遥望齐州九点烟，一泓海水杯中泻。"九州之大，四海之广，从天上看，点烟杯水而已。

尽管诗人喜欢用沧海桑田的故事，但大多是慨叹人世多变，骨子里是"最好不变"的思想。李贺比较超脱些。但要到王安石的"山川在理有崩竭，丘壑自古相虚盈"（《九井》），才把它提到物质运动规律上来。

李贺《金铜仙人辞汉歌》

我在《拟人化》中谈的都是宋诗。其实，李贺的《金铜仙人辞汉歌》乃是拟人化的最佳手法。这里，刘彻吟着《秋风词》从墓中出来，三十六宫长满了青苔，望着魏家的官赶着拉铜人的车队到来，酸风射进他们的眼睛。铜人被砍倒，捆在车上。汉家的月亮凄凉地看着，泪如铅水一样落地。悠悠咸阳古道，只有衰老的兰草来给铜人送行。天哪！天若有情天亦老！——这里，死人、活人、铜人、酸风、寒月、衰兰、古道，还有天，都是活的。

李贺对魏明帝拆走汉武帝所造铜人非常反感。杜牧看出这点，在序李贺诗集中特意指出。魏明帝拆走的还有汉宫诸钟簴、铜驼等多种文物，李贺为什么专咏铜人呢？若说工程大，那武则天所造铜人更大，而且是造在铁山上。原来汉武帝这个铜人是手捧承露盘，接云表之露，供武帝冲服玉屑以求长生用的。李贺对此屡有讽咏。《拂舞歌词》："全胜汉武锦楼上，晓望晴寒饮花露"；《苦昼短》："何为服黄金，吞白玉？……刘彻茂陵多滞骨"；《昆仑使者》："昆仑使者无消息，茂陵烟树生愁色。金盘玉露自淋漓，元气茫茫收不得"。《金铜仙人辞汉歌》实际是讽汉武帝的，写得故事栩栩，不见批判字样，这是李贺的高明处。

这个铜人高二十丈，大七围，高的是铜人下面的铜柱。这个铜柱很重要，杜甫《秋兴》："蓬莱宫阙对南山，承露金茎霄汉间"，只讲铜柱，不讲铜人。李贺说拆迁时，"携盘独出月荒凉"，只讲铜人，不讲铜柱。铜柱哪里去了？

李贺在《古悠悠行》中有交代："海沙变成石，鱼沫吹秦桥。空光远流浪，铜柱从年消。"它和秦始皇为求神仙所造入海三十里的世界最长的桥一样，销蚀了。

铜人承露盘现在北海的瀛台。陈煤和我在此流连过，果然没有铜柱，而是一根石柱。"文化大革命"后北海公园就封闭了，不知何时能开放。

韩愈《蓝关》

韩愈诗多枯燥，唯那首传说最多的《蓝关》极有味道。他的侄孙韩湘子几次想度韩愈成仙，总因官瘾太大未成。韩湘子用魔术在花叶上显示出"雪拥蓝关"联句。后来韩愈被贬潮州，就写了《左迁至蓝关示侄孙湘》："一封朝奏九重天，夕贬潮阳路八千。欲为圣明除弊事，肯将衰朽惜残年。云横秦岭家何在，雪拥蓝关马不前。知汝远来应有意，好收吾骨瘴江边。"这诗哀痛欲绝。这次罢官是为谏迎佛骨，诗中未作检讨，有死不改悔之意。

出长安先过蓝关，再过武关。韩愈又有过武关诗："我今罪重无归望，直去长安路八千。"简直绝望了。

韩愈还有首入蓝关的诗，那是元和元年进京当博士时写的（出京在元和十四年）。诗是咏马："岁老岂能充上驷，力微当自慎前程。不知何故翻骧首，牵过关门妄一鸣。"虽想谨言慎行，终还大叫一声，遂有"雪拥蓝关马不前"的下场。

我看出《蓝关》在韩愈的诗风上是个转折点。韩的格律诗以选字雕句、用僻典为能，出关后的诗则比较平易有感情。张籍是韩愈的老朋友，韩有许多赠张籍的诗，逞奇斗险，以至有"座暖销那怪，池清失可猜"等哑谜式的句子。出蓝关后，又有许多赠张籍的诗，我看《早春呈水部张员外》二首恐怕是韩诗中最好的了："天街小雨润如酥，草色遥看近却无。最是一年春好处，绝胜烟柳满皇都"；"莫道官忙身老大，即无年少逐春心。凭君先到江头看，柳色如今深未深？"

我不说他的《山石》等，因这里只谈律诗。

韩愈赠和尚诗

韩愈无疑是个大儒，他谏迎佛骨是为了保卫儒道，怕被佛道侵蚀。但他有不少和尚朋友，有不少赠和尚诗，并在这些诗中大骂和尚。

《送灵师》诗，一上来就大骂佛教，又写灵师斗棋聚赌，"醉花月""罗婵娟"。这位灵师大约是个风流和尚。

《送惠师》写惠师不愿做官，"太守邀不去，群官请徒频"，而且"囊无一金资，翻谓富者贫"，是个高人。但笔锋一转："吾非西方教，怜子狂且醇。吾嫉惰游者，怜子愚且谆。"大约风流派和惰游派是唐代和尚两大派。

另外还有忙忙碌碌的和尚。《送僧约》："早知皆是自拘囚，不学因循到白头。汝既出家还扰扰，何人更得死前休？"

照韩愈看，这些和尚朋友最好还俗做官，才是正果。《送僧澄观》骂他造僧迦塔靡费愚民，然后说"向风长叹不可见，我欲收敛加冠巾"，劝他脱掉迦裟，改服儒冠。《送文畅师北游》诗中不写文畅，而写自己如何得官晋升，洋洋得意。这大约是身教之意。

只有《送无本师归范阳》这首没有骂佛，也没有骂和尚。原来这个无本师就是贾岛，他听了韩愈的话，后来还俗了。这首诗佶屈聱牙，适合贾岛的口味，但肯定不适合读者的口味。

在韩愈批佛评儒的诗中，没有赠尼姑的，但有首《谢自然》。谢自然是个贫家女子，一心学仙。贞元十年十一月十二日，坐在家中，真的"须臾自轻举，飘若风中烟"，上天去了。郡守来调查，"入门无所见，冠履同蜕蝉"。韩愈把此事写得非常真实，无懈可击。结尾叹道："噫乎彼寒女，永托异物群。"她确实成仙了，但永远变成"异物"。

《阳关曲》

王维《渭城曲》："劝君更尽一杯酒，西出阳关无故人。"高适《别董大》："莫愁前路无知己，天下谁人不识君？"王维送的是出使的官员元二，与老百姓无缘。高适送的董庭兰是个著名的琴师，当时虽然没有广播电台，但天下人都知道他。

董庭兰的琴后人听不到了。王维的诗被谱成《阳关曲》，送别时都要唱，所以留传下来了。《东坡志林》："旧传阳关三叠，然今世歌者每句再叠而已……及在黄州偶读乐天《对酒》诗云：'听唱阳关第四声'。自注云：

第四声'劝君更尽一杯酒'。以此验之，若第一句再叠，则此句为第五声。是首句不叠审矣。"

东坡看出第一句不应叠，但没说出三叠的道理。我想三叠是指乐谱上的三个乐句，不是指诗句。重唱诗句时不一定重复乐句，反之亦然。今天唱歌也是这样。

《阳关曲》大约在唐代就不止一个谱，即不止一个唱法。李商隐"唱尽阳关无限叠"，是说唱了又唱，反复唱，因是诉别情。陈陶"歌是伊州第三遍，唱着右军征戍词"。有人说这是把《阳关曲》作为《伊州》大曲的第三乐章。《伊州》本是别离曲，白居易《伊州》"老去将何散老愁，新教小玉唱伊州"。《伊州》也有多种唱法，所谓"七商调"，收进《阳关曲》也是可能的。

《阳关三叠》并曾谱成琴曲，有的流传至今。这个歌，近代还有唱的。徐新吾告诉我，他小的时候就唱过，其词在"西出阳关无故人"后还有"霜叶与霜痕，历苦辛，历苦辛，宜自珍，宜自珍"。"西出阳关无故人"句和所加的一段，都重唱三遍。

这加的句子是惜别时反复叮咛之意。不过我看有点蛇足。王维这诗的好处就是"劝君更尽一杯酒"，没有伤感气。不像江淹《别赋》那样"黯然销魂"，而有点像李白"汪伦踏歌送我行"那样豪迈。

张衡《四愁诗》

张衡的《四愁诗》文词自然，感情洋溢，流传广远，直到近代，鲁迅还戏为仿作。

但《四愁诗》究竟是什么意思，却搞不清楚。诗中思念的人，忽在山东，忽在广西，忽在湖北，忽在山西。我的孩子景先儿时读此诗，问："我所思兮在哪里？"问得好。《文选》序此诗，说是张衡作河间王相时不得志，效屈原芳草美人之意所作。我颇怀疑。张衡原为太史令，《五臣传》说他"不乐久处机密"才出为河间王相的。我想张衡所思的不是一个人，而是一种思想，投赠之间代表社会差距。

张衡是个科学家。他的水运浑天仪是个追踪天体运行的装置，不仅设计精巧，还表现他时间、空间统一的伟大思想。他在《灵宪》中说，圣人本没有什么理论，是观察天体运动的规律后才有了理论。又说我们观察的只是个小天地，还有看不到的才是宇宙。"宇之表无极，宙之端无穷"。张衡有篇《思玄赋》，人们把它当作游仙诗看。其实，这是一篇描写在太阳系以外的太空旅行的幻想曲，是以他的时空观为基础的。这篇《四愁诗》则是写小天地，或者说是写人类社会关系的一个侧面。

《四愁诗》的特点是思境奇绝，而所述皆常见事物，从小刀到饭碗，互相投赠代表人际关系，又不出一个"愁"字。鲁迅大约看到这点。据许寿裳说，连同鲁诗中的猫头鹰、赤练蛇都是鲁迅所喜爱的东西。鲁迅的仿作中，对方所赠的都是金表链、玫瑰花等高级物品，我回赠的则是糖葫芦、发汗药等低级物品。这大约是说两个阶级的不同表态。张衡没有阶级观点，但用"路远莫致兮"表明社会距离是很大的。正因如此，他的结论是"烦劳""烦伤""烦纡""烦惋"四种愁，而鲁迅的结论则是"由他去吧！"

举逸民，招隐士

批孔运动深入，有评"举逸民，招隐士"之说。

什么是逸民，没有定义。《论语·微子》："逸民：伯夷、叔齐、虞仲、夷逸、朱张、柳下惠、少连"，共七位。为首的伯夷、叔齐和"兴灭国，继绝世"有牵连，不过已饿死五百年，举不起来了。柳下惠大约与孔丘同时代，他有反帝言论，但没有像他弟弟柳下跖那样挺身批孔。

什么是隐士，也没有定义，不过《论语》中有长沮、桀溺、荷蓧丈人、石门的晨门、荷蒉唱歌者、仪封人、楚狂接舆，也是七位。奇怪的是，此七人都是当孔子面批孔的，招隐士大约也招不到他们。

《招隐士》是淮南小山作的。小山是谁，无人知道。招的是谁，也没人知道。诗中有"王孙游兮不归，春草生兮萋萋"；又有"王孙归来兮，山中不可以久留"。看来这位隐士不是寻常人，历来文人怀念的也是这两句"王孙"，像白居易的"离离原上草"就是。

我觉得这首诗中最好的乃是两句"桂枝"。诗一上来就讲"桂树丛生兮山之幽"；接着就是深山老林里的孤寂、荒凉；继而虎狼成群，人生险境，心里恫慌，登木战栗。然而，"猿狄群啸兮虎豹嗥，攀援桂枝兮聊淹留"；"攀援桂枝兮聊淹留，虎豹斗兮聊熊罴咆"。险境变成诗人的胸怀，恐怖变成沉思。

小山不知何许人，但总是淮南王刘安府中一个或几个词客的笔名。据《汉书·艺文志》，刘安门下献赋不下四十四篇，都亡佚了，偏偏留下这篇《招隐士》，也是奇事。

开天窗

近读《亭林诗集》乾隆刻本，见开有许多天窗，唯大都一两个字，没有整句开掉的。较多的是指明皇室的"君""御""诏"等字，如"天颜"作"□颜"，"君父"作"□父"之类；差不多都可猜出，等于没有开掉。

然而有些颇为费解。如《感事》中"须知六军出，一扫定神州"作"须知□军出，一□定□州"。著名的《京口即事》："河上三军合，关中一战收"，"关中"二字开去；"两河通诏旨，三辅急王师"，"诏"字并未援例开去；"转战收铜马，还进饮月支"，却把"月支"两字开去了。看来审查官也是马马糊糊。

除开天窗外还有改字。顾炎武诗中称清人为"虏"，在诗集中大都改了，如"虏骑"改为"牧骑"，"冬虏"改为"北边"，没有改的"虏"字则开天窗。

这种改动多半是潘次耕给顾炎武编诗集时搞的。潘是顾的好友，南下时顾赠他一诗云："知君心似玉壶清，未肯缁尘久雒京。若到吴闾寻旧迹，五噫东去一梁生。"可是后来潘次耕经不起考验，做了叛徒。顾炎武写诗骂他，说你到北京，少不得"分题赋淫丽，角句争飞腾"，"定有南冠思，悲哉不可胜！"但潘到北京做官后，竟写信拉顾炎武下水，说京中贵人想看顾的著作。顾炎武又写诗给他："年来行止类浮萍，虽有留书未杀青。世事粗谙身已老，古音方奏客难听。儿从死父传楹语，帝遣生徒受壁经。投笔纵然成一笑，春风绿草满阶庭。""楹语"指晏子临死凿楹纳书留示其子事，"壁经"是预计清廷会焚书。

潘次耕编《亭林诗集》时还删掉十几首。这比清政府的检查官厉害得多。因为开天窗有心人可按窗索引，而删除就等于灭迹了。唯顾炎武骂他的诗没有删，这点可说还能"正确对待自己"。又幸亏顾炎武晚年改名蒋山佣，有个《蒋山佣诗集》传世，于是删、改、开天窗之处都被人给一一查出来了。此人即孙毓修。

"眉来眼去"

辛弃疾有首《满江红·赣州席上呈太守陈季陵侍郎》。词一上来就讲江景，"落日苍茫，风才定，片帆无力"；接着说"还记得，眉来眼去，水光山色"。

这里"眉来眼去"是指山山水水。因诗人常以眉喻山，以眼喻水。王观《卜算子》："欲问行人去那边，眉眼盈盈处"，也是这种用法。

但接下去又说"倦客不知身远近，佳人已卜归消息"；这个"眉来眼去"又像是真个调情了。还有"便归来，只是赋行云，襄王客"。《高唐赋》中的行云是"忽兮改容"，靠不住的。

这首词，据说是当时茶商造反，攻赣州，辛弃疾率兵剿平后，陈季陵为他设宴时作的。茶商造反，是因朝廷实行茶专卖，茶贩茶农不堪压榨，起来反抗，事在淳熙二年。又过二年就是连州、柳州的农民暴动；再一年又是湖广农民大起义。茶商造反时，辛弃疾是江西提刑，自有职责去剿平，但他的心情是很为难的。这词下章："些个事，如何得？知有恨，休重忆"；说的就是上章"眉来眼去"之事。实际又何所指呢？本词结尾："过眼不如人意事，十常八九今头白。笑江州司马太多情，青衫湿。"总之，全词都是以风月论政局。湖广农民起义时，辛弃疾是湖南转运判官，他上书孝宗，历数人民疾苦，说"臣以谓斯民无所诉，不去为盗，将安之乎？"

"眉来眼去"的真正意思是：话不好讲，你皱皱眉，我挤挤眼，就是了。

濯足三谈

序

我原无每晚濯足习惯。"文革"中，所在中央工商行政管理局同仁于1969年下放"五七干校"，劳动以种稻为主。赤足下田，往返泥沼，每晚必浸泡双足良久，始能就寝。战友濯足闲谈，偶及诗词，或笔记之，后整理为《濯足偶谈》。1973年我被借调到人民出版社。工作改变，而"文革"未已，每晚濯足如故，因又有所记，至1976年"四人帮"垮台为止，后集为《濯足偶谈续集》。偶谈及续集曾于1992年印成小册子，并于2002年增订再版，分赠有过干校及"文革"经历的学长，以博一哂。

1976年我转到中国社会科学院经济研究所从事经济史研究，迄今已三十年，我也成为眼花耳背爱忘事的九十岁老人。这三十年来未触及诗词，但每晚濯足则一直坚持下来，并且向长者、医师和足疗房师傅请教，有一套足底按摩程序，大受裨益。因自2006年我最后一个科研项目完成之日起，濯足时再做一些诗词小记。并将原《濯足偶谈》改称《濯足一谈》，原续集改称《濯足二谈》，此记定名为《濯足三谈》，分赠学长一哂。是为序。

《黄鹤楼》与《登金陵凤凰台》

崔颢《黄鹤楼》诗，高唱入云，读者无不心折。传李白过黄鹤楼，曰"眼前有景道不得，崔颢题诗在上头"，无作而去。但后来李白还是写了一首摹崔颢《黄鹤楼》的诗，即《登金陵凤凰台》。然而白诗只是摹仿崔诗的格调，即所谓"龙池体"，而其主题和命意，则二诗完全不同。试比较来看。

前四句，崔诗曰："昔人已乘黄鹤去，此地空余黄鹤楼。黄鹤一去不复返，白云千载空悠悠。"白诗曰："凤凰台上凤凰游，凤去台空江自流。吴宫花草埋幽径，晋代衣冠成古丘。"

崔诗的"昔人"，有人说是指仙人王子安或费祎乘鹤过此（据《齐谐志》等），有人说指名士祢衡被黄祖杀于黄鹄矶。我到过拆迁前的黄鹤楼，确在矶上。李白有《望鹦鹉洲怀祢衡》赞之。不过我以为"昔人"乃泛指高人，即陶潜所说"高尚士也"，毛泽东所说"高尚的人"。又鹤去有仙逝之意，此语也可指哲人已逝，只剩下空空的楼和悠悠的云。

白诗意境完全不同。凤凰是天上飞来的，或谓指吴大帝迁都金陵，惜未能久留。因而他所感慨的不是哲人其萎，所怀念的只是吴宫繁华、晋廷权贵。白又有《金陵》诗，慨叹"六代兴亡国"，有"古殿吴花草，深宫晋绮罗"句，都是宫廷感情。

五、六句例讲究对仗。崔诗"晴川历历汉阳树，芳草萋萋鹦鹉洲"。白诗"三山半落青天外，二水中分白鹭洲"。皆写景，俱工。

结句即主题。崔诗"日暮乡关何处是，烟波江上使人愁"。继哲人其萎之慨，转念自身离乡别井、奔波俗务（包括当官僚之苦），而以诗的语言"烟波江上使人愁"出之。此所以令人心折也。

白诗"总为浮云能蔽日，长安不见使人愁"。回应前面宫廷之恋，希望破除仕途障碍，到朝廷去当高官。李白的这种感情，详见于他的《梁甫吟》。

《梁甫吟》

世传诸葛亮作《梁甫吟》,误。《梁甫吟》是个古琴曲,楚调,其声悲。诸葛亮依其调,"好为梁甫吟"(《蜀志》)。大约诗因人而出名,《乐府诗集》乃录亮作为代表。这种古曲都很简单,大都只二个或四个乐句,诗人用之反复吟唱。诸葛亮的《梁甫吟》是五言十二句,大约是依调反复三遍。这甚合古风,《诗·周南》《召南》就是反复三遍或四遍。但到唐,李白的《梁甫吟》长达四十余句,且改为七言,间三、五言,是否仍能按原曲吟唱,已属可疑。不过,白诗仍说"梁甫吟,声正悲",基调未变。

"长啸梁甫吟,何时见阳春。"诸葛亮和李白的诗都是希望能做大官,施展抱负。但二人抱负不同,诗的内容也迥异。诸葛亮是在汉室倾衰,群雄并起之际,希望找到一位英主,推行他三分天下之策。但在诗中,他完全避开主题,只讲了一个小故事,即齐景公的三位心腹,"一朝被谗言,二桃杀三士";并明确谴责:"谁能为此谋,相国齐晏子。"暗示为相之道,不能像晏婴那样用权术。

李白当然读过诸葛亮的诗,但他在自己的《梁甫吟》中淡化了这个故事,只说"力排南山三壮士,齐相杀之费二桃"。反之,他标榜"吴楚弄兵无剧孟,亚夫咍尔为徒劳";又竭力推崇郦食其:"高阳酒徒起草中,长揖山东隆准公。"原来李白曾任侠,又在《代寿山答孟少府移文书》中说自己的志向是:"申管、晏之谈,谋帝王之术,奋其智能,愿为辅弼,使寰区大定,海县清一。"换言之,李白急于为官,不是像杜甫那样为了"置君尧舜上,再使风俗淳"(《奉赠韦左丞丈》),也不是像诸葛亮那样为"三分割据纡筹策"(杜甫《咏怀古迹》),而是想以权术家和侠客的精神,建功立业。

李白的《梁甫吟》用了惊人的妙笔来批判阻碍他仕途的权贵和奸佞:"我欲攀龙见明主,雷公砰訇震天鼓,帝旁投壶多玉女";"阊阖九门不可通,以额叩关阍者怒。白日不照吾精诚,杞国无事忧天倾。"他在《远离别》中有同样的控诉:"日惨惨兮云冥冥,猩猩啼烟兮鬼啸雨。我纵言之将何补?皇穹窃恐不照余之忠诚,雷凭凭兮欲吼怒。"显然学《离骚》,而与他"长安不见使人愁"的感情是一致的。

李白的长安梦迄未实现，而在兵荒马乱之际错投了永王璘，几遭杀身之祸。

扁　舟

李白《谢朓楼饯别校书叔云》："人生在世不称意，明朝散发弄扁舟。"一提扁舟，人们便想到范蠡。李白也确实是此意，他在《古风》十八中直说："何如鸱夷子，散发棹扁舟。"在《代寿山答孟少府移文书》中说，他"事君之道成，荣亲之义毕，然后与陶朱、留侯，浮五湖，戏沧州"。

然而，范蠡的扁舟，并非"一叶之扁舟"，而是一艘大商船，内有粮食、百货仓库，有账房和伙计，水手、厨师之外，有人说还载有西施和她的宫女们。这是需要很大的资本的。范蠡以相国下海经商，不乏官僚资本，所以经营灵活，"三致千金"。诗人之中，恐怕只有李白有此资格。李白的父亲是个蜀锦贩运商，他自己大约也有经商经验，所以《将进酒》说："天生我材必有用（一本作'天生我身必有财'），千金散尽还复来。"

杜甫原来也有"道不行，乘桴浮于海"的想法。但隐居江海，比经商还需要更大的本钱，因为那是只出不入的。杜甫自知无此资格，所以使用否定的语气来说："非无江海志，潇洒送日月。"（《自京至奉先县咏怀五百字》）杜甫在《秋兴》中说："关塞极天唯鸟道，江湖满地一渔翁。"鸟道指皇廷高远，天意难问；渔翁则是自况，知道自己没有本钱，只能扁舟垂钓，自食其力。杜诗中还有"独把鱼竿终远去"，"天入沧浪一钓舟"等句，都是此意。

永王璘起兵江淮，征聘江南名士入幕。李白应召，孔巢父跑掉了去钓鱼。杜甫作《送孔巢父谢病归游江东兼呈李白》赞之曰："巢父掉头不肯往，东将入海随烟雾。诗卷长留天地间，钓竿欲拂珊瑚树。"奇怪的是，这诗尾部却加上了一句"南寻禹穴见李白，道甫问讯今何如？"不知何意。

再论韩愈《听颖师弹琴》

韩愈有篇《听颖师弹琴》，写了几段琴音，惟妙惟肖，苏轼说是写琴诗中最好的（《苕溪渔隐丛话》前集卷一六）。唯其结语称"推手遽止之"，"无以冰炭置我肠"。殊不能解。

琴曲一般用正宫调，沉着和谐，不会有高分贝的噪音、嘈音，何以会听了难以忍受，以至"推手剧止之"呢？韩愈写颖师的琴音："昵昵儿女语，恩怨相尔汝"，其声柔细。"划然变轩昂，勇士赴敌场"，转调慷慨。"浮云柳絮无根蒂，天地阔远随风扬"，其音空旷自然。"喧啾百鸟群，忽见孤凤凰，跻攀分寸不可上，失势一落千丈强。"这段写琴的指法，抑扬顿挫，高低自如，有泛音、滑音，为琴之独长。"失势"是韩愈想象，非必险境，如《平沙落雁》，即高空平落，极其自然。

李贺也有篇《听颖师弹琴歌》："别浦云归桂花渚，蜀国弦中双凤语。芙蓉叶落秋鸾离，越王夜起游天姥。暗珮清臣敲水玉，渡海蛾眉牵白鹿。"桂花渚言其音落地清幽。蜀国弦即琴，唐代琴以成都雷氏所制者最佳，今尚传其品。双凤语，指两弦和鸣，古乐无和声，但有合鸣。秋鸾离，状音之散落。夜游天姥，叙其声凌空缥缈。暗佩水玉，状音调清亮。渡海蛾眉，写其声飞扬欲仙。最后说"凉馆闻弦惊病客，药囊暂别龙须席"。旅馆中的病客闻颖师琴声，霍然病愈，把药囊也丢掉了。与韩愈的感觉完全相反。

琴音量较小，音程"埤"，意沉着。嵇康《琴赋》说："琵琶筝笛，间促而声高……故更（使听者）形躁而志越"；"琴瑟之体，闻辽而音埤……是以静听而心闲也。"间，指两个音位中的间隔；在琴就是弦上的徽，琴徽较宽。"间辽故音埤，弦长故徽鸣。"颖师所用的琴，据李贺说是"古琴大轸长八尺"（按汉制应为八尺一寸），属大琴，其弦长，有十三徽。这种琴不会弹出尖噪之音（后来的小琴长三尺六寸五）。

然而，琴曲中多悲声。今人所能知的最早琴曲有二，即《广陵散》和《胡笳十八拍》，均声悲。《广陵散》是叙聂政为报父仇，刺杀韩王故事。但曲中无铁声、杀声，只是悲凉。《胡笳十八拍》叙蔡文姬被俘及归汉事，声哀怨，但更多是生离死别之怨。与之相近的是王昭君之曲。《王昭》亦列入《琴赋》，但广为流行的是琵琶曲，其曲怨而恨，听之令人泪下、断肠。但正是因此，人们对之恋恋不舍，百听不厌。欧阳修《明妃曲和王介甫作》，说此曲传入汉宫，"汉宫争按新声谱"，就因为它"遗恨已深声更苦"。不仅宫人，在民间也是"纤纤女手生洞房，学得琵琶不下堂"，就是因为"此声能断肠"。不仅是弱势群体喜爱，男人也是一样，白居易要求琵琶女再弹一遍，"满座重闻皆掩泣"（《琵琶行》）。

琴（以至琵琶）音无论是悲怨、苦恨、下泪、断肠，都使人愈听愈要听，不会"推手遽止之"。

咏明妃诗

咏明妃诗多矣，名家亦均有作。李白《王昭君》结语曰："生乏黄金枉图画，死留青冢使人嗟。"枉图画犹图画冤，后来咏明妃者亦多以画工伪造图画事发表议论，实在很肤浅。

杜甫《咏怀古迹》之三，将此事淡化处理，说"画图省识春风面"，省识者不可认真也。而把重点放在"千载琵琶作胡语，分明怨恨曲中论"，这就深刻得多了，成为千古绝唱。这里胡语指《昭君怨》琵琶曲，非指其词，其词（不知是何人所作）"秋木凄凄，其叶萎黄"是汉语，非胡语。原来，曲调亦可称"语"，如白居易《琵琶行》："今夜闻君琵琶语，如听仙乐耳暂明。"

白居易有首《昭君怨》："自是君恩薄如纸，不须一向恨丹青。"可谓得杜老意。但白又有首《王昭君》提出一个怪论："汉使却回凭寄语，黄金何日赎蛾眉？"黄金也许是受李白诗启发，但以黄金贿赂画工，明妃尚不屑为，怎么可以赎身呢？这个论点简直市侩。李商隐咏明妃："毛延寿画欲通神，忍为黄金不为人。"回到浅俗的图画论去了。

至宋，王安石有两首《明妃曲》，我在《濯足偶谈》中说过，是咏昭君最好的诗。其一，以"意态由来画不成，当时枉杀毛延寿"，结束了历来画图的议论。同时，把昭君事提到一个社会问题上来："君不见，咫尺长门闭阿娇，人生失意无南北。"整个地球上都有这个弱势群体的问题。在第二首，进一步发挥了他的社会学理论："汉恩自浅胡自深，人生乐在相知心。"接着回到杜老意："可怜青冢已芜没，尚有哀弦留至今。"

王安石的诗引起轰动。司马光和王诗曰："妾身生死知不归，妾意终期寤人主。"寤作动词，与重耳事不同，作觉醒解。司马光是政治家，不懂社会学。

欧阳修和第二首王诗曰："耳目所及尚如此，万里安能制夷狄？"也是政治家的言论。但欧阳修和第一首王诗,走了杜甫的路子,只谈琵琶曲,却是十分高明。"身行不遇中国人,马上自作思归曲。推手为琵却手琶,胡人共听亦咨嗟。玉颜流落死天涯,琵琶却传来汉家。"下面就是我在《听颖师弹琴》中所引的两段,凸出了此曲声调的苦和怨。把社会学意义寓于美学之中,也是咏明妃最好的诗。

较晚,吕居仁有首明妃诗:"人生在相合,不论胡与秦。但取眼前好,莫言长苦辛。君看轻薄儿,何殊胡地人。"深得荆公之意。

音 书

诗中常用"音书",通指信息,特别是家乡亲友的信息。宋之问《汉江》:"岭外音书绝,经冬复历春。"在没有长话和手机的时代,所谓音只能是家乡来人带个口信,那是靠不住的。杜甫《宿府》:"风尘荏苒音书绝,关塞萧条行路难。"行路难,口信靠不住。所以音书实际是个偏义复词,实指书信,音陪衬而已。

不过,音书还另有含义。杜甫《阁夜》:"卧龙跃马终黄土,人事音书漫寂寥。"这里音书是指人事记录或档案。在没有录音带和光盘的时代,音不能记录,实指文书档案。杜老此语是说贤愚同归于尽,文书档案没有价值。这是反历史的,史学家不会同意,群众也不会同意。丞相祠堂香火不熄,公孙虽称帝,却无人记得,怎能说都是寂寥呢?

柳宗元《登柳州城楼》:"共来百粤纹身地,犹自音书滞一乡。"这里音书也不是家乡书信,而是指官府公文。此诗是"寄漳汀封连四州刺史",即韩泰、韩晔、刘禹锡、陈谏四人,若是家书,与四人何干?原来柳宗元与四人皆王叔文党,永贞元年王罢相,柳与四人皆遭贬;元和十年均召回京师,旋又下放为闽粤边区刺史。此诗是企望朝廷发来再度召回的公文。

柳宗元此诗写得好极了。"城上高楼接大荒,海天愁思正茫茫";海天愁思指王党改革朝政的计划。"惊风乱飐芙蓉水,密雨斜侵薜荔墙";写党争起伏,惊涛骇浪。"岭树重遮千里目,江流曲似九回肠";言不见长安,愁肠满怀。"共来百粤纹身地,犹自音书滞一乡";是说召回的圣谕被朝中的权宦和乡原们扣留了。

在没有长话和手机的时代，通讯只有书信，没有声音。但人们偏爱声音，要称音书。这是因为书信是写在纸上，是间接的；而声音乃口述，有真实感、亲切感。接到对方来信，要说"亲聆"雅教。王安石《明妃曲》："寄声欲问塞南事，只有年年鸿雁飞。"鸿雁传书，但偏要说"寄声"。《胡笳十八拍》第五拍："雁南征兮欲寄边声，雁北归兮为得汉音。"要说寄声寄音，若实事求是说寄书，就没有情意了。《诗·郑风·子衿》："青青子衿，悠悠我心。纵我不往，子宁不嗣音？"嗣，郑笺作传解。要传来音，才对得起我的心。

但音，也还有个表情问题。这在语言学中就是韵律问题。有中性语言，有感情语言。中性语言，如新闻联播，可以用文字表达（广播稿）。播音员绷着嘴念稿，不能动感情。感情语言，其感情是由音色、音高、音频、音强四个韵律要素表达，不能由文字代替。而诗，却是要用文字表现韵律，就是在选词造句时注意声调、平仄和韵脚，诱使读者（唱诗者）按所需韵律去读（或唱），这是不容易的。

屈原《九歌》别解

我在《濯足偶谈》再版中有《屈原〈九歌〉》《〈湘君〉〈湘夫人〉别解》二篇，甚简，意未尽，因重作，并增《河伯》《山鬼》别解。

我所谓别解，并无新道，只有两点小意思：其一，《九歌》原是沅湘一带民间祀神曲，有乐有舞有歌，三者配合。王逸说屈原以原歌"其词鄙陋"，另作新词（《楚辞章句》）；朱熹说原歌"词既鄙俚"，屈原"更定其词，去其泰甚"（《楚辞集注》）。所以屈原是按原来的乐舞曲作词的，若能了解一些原曲情况，对解释《九歌》必有裨益。

其二，《九歌》大部分是讲爱情的，神与神恋爱，神与人恋爱，而结局都是悲剧。其中《湘君》《湘夫人》《河伯》《山鬼》四篇不是泛谈爱情，而是有眉有眼，必是根据当时民间某个神话故事写的，但作者没有指明。若能探求这些神话故事梗概，对解释这四篇必大有裨益。

关于神话故事，将于下面四篇别解中再说，这里只谈乐舞曲。

对于战国时楚国的民间乐舞，我们一无所知。今年（2006）六月，报载湖北南漳县有家农民能作"端心舞",据说是楚巫舞遗裔,共十六场,中央广播电台曾予播放,据称有《东皇太一》味道。我未见广播,但见报载照片,舞者皆穿八卦衣,这就肯定它与楚国的巫舞无关,所以不去管它。

楚国的民间乐舞我们一无所知,只能借助于略有所知的《韶》《武》和《诗经·国风》作些推测。

《韶》《武》是周天子"六乐"中最常演的节目,属宫廷乐,但演出有群众性,启"舞九韶于大穆之野"(《竹书纪年》)。九招即《韶》,因韶有九大段,故称九招,其歌称九歌,舞称九辩(遍)。屈原《离骚》有"启九辩与九歌兮""奏九歌而舞韶兮",《天问》有"启棘宾商,九辩九歌"。实际是说,演了好几个《韶》体的乐舞之曲(启指夏禹之子启,喜音乐)。所以屈原写了十一篇词而称《九歌》,宋玉写了一篇长赋而称《九辩》。

《韶》的具体内容不详,《武》则略知一二,见《乐记》。《武》有六个成,每成都完成一个独立情节,合起来是武王伐纣故事。《武》没有歌词,所有故事都用音乐和舞蹈表现出来,栩栩如生。音乐以打击乐器为主,重节奏,但在第一成也有段抒情曲,需要有人哼哼。舞是分成两队的集体舞,两队互相进退,大约也有圆场。在第二成和第五成尾部各有一个"乱",是总结性音乐。"武乱皆坐",舞者都坐下不舞了,由乐队奏"乱"。

《诗经·国风》是民间歌曲,但限于北方。十五国音乐各有特色,吴国季札观看演出能一一辨认(《左传》襄二十九年)。今人却不能辨认,因无乐谱,只能从诗词中考察其节奏、调式。音乐史家杨荫浏等考察的结果是:它们大多是一篇只有一个曲调,反复使用;有的是两个曲调交叉使用;或是加个头或尾,或是加些拖长、急过等修饰。这些都是民歌的特点。《荀子·成相篇》是个说唱曲,一曲节奏重复了五十六遍。

孔子说:"师挚之始,关雎之乱,洋洋乎盈耳哉!"(《论语·泰伯》)我们在诗《关雎》中却看不见这个热情洋溢的"乱",因为《国风》的"乱"都没有词,又没有乐谱,不可考。屈原的作品中有六篇写有"乱曰",那是有唱词的"乱"。《橘颂》的末段写:"曰:吾怨往昔之所冀兮……"显然是"乱曰",脱漏了一个"乱"字。《离骚》末段有"乱曰",而中间有段"曰:吾怨往而狐疑兮……"我看也是脱漏了一个"乱"字。《抽思》

在一个曲调重复了十遍之后，有段"少歌曰"，看词意是小结语，又有几句"倡曰"，词意是开头语。以下原曲调再重复五遍，最后是个很长的"乱曰"。少歌和倡相当于乐曲中小的"乱"，如《武》有两个"乱"。以上所论曲调结构都适用于解释《九歌》。

《诗经》提到有二十九种乐器，但复杂的乐器是用于雅和颂。《九歌》中只提到八种乐器，都是打击、吹奏乐器，弦乐只有瑟。《仪礼》中燕礼和乡饮酒的节目中，有乐工演奏的三首，皆小雅；有群众合唱的六首，皆《周南》《召南》。我推测，《九歌》是由巫主唱，但参加祭祀的群众能唱者和之。至于舞，是由女巫来舞，设想是分两队交叉进退，并作圆场，这就会有"灵偃蹇兮姣服，芳菲菲兮满堂"的气氛。

《湘君》《湘夫人》别解

《湘君》的词句非常规则，若按四句一组分段，刚好九段（九遍），最后两句结束语。我猜想屈原是用一个四句式曲调，重复九遍作词，最后两句是"乱"。这种四句式的曲调，大约包括两个乐句，十六个音节，曲式比较简单，节奏比较抒缓，白居易所谓"调少情多"，适于咏叹。《离骚》全部都是用这种曲调。再设想是两队巫女交叉圆舞，就会出现"疏缓节兮安歌"，"聊翱游兮周章"的场景。

《湘夫人》的词句与《湘君》相同，只是中间多了"芷葺兮荷屋，缭之兮杜蘅"两句。这两句与前面"筑室兮水中，葺之兮荷盖"重复，解者多视为衍文。郭沫若说"屋"是"幄"之误，"葺"应为"其"，指室内装置（《屈原赋今译》）。我看以衍文为是。除去这两句衍文，《湘夫人》也是同一曲调重复九遍，最后一个"乱"，与《湘君》完全相同。我猜想是，人们祀湘君与湘夫人是用同一个乐舞曲，同样的舞步，可能还是在同一个庙内，唱词不同而已。这就是"合祀分献"说。

按照上述看法，我将《湘君》《湘夫人》的词重新分段如下。这种分段法与时贤的分段法不同，对词义的解释也有异，下面分述。还有一点，按时贤分段法，《湘君》第五遍和《湘夫人》第五遍的下联皆分入另段，以致韵脚不叶，按我的分段法，则韵脚皆叶。

湘　君

1　君不行兮夷犹，蹇谁留兮中洲？

　　美要眇兮宜修，沛吾乘兮桂舟。

2　令沅湘兮无波，使江水兮安流。

　　望夫君兮未来，吹参差兮谁思？

3　驾飞龙兮北征，邅吾道兮洞庭。

　　薜荔柏兮蕙绸，荪桡兮兰旌。

4　望涔阳兮极浦，横大江兮扬灵。

　　扬灵兮未极，女婵媛兮为余太息。

5　横流涕兮潺湲，隐思君兮陫侧。

　　桂棹兮兰枻，斫冰兮积雪。

6　采薜荔兮水中，搴芙蓉兮木末。

　　心不同兮媒劳，恩不甚兮轻绝。

7　石濑兮浅浅，飞龙兮翩翩。

　　交不忠兮怨长，期不信兮告余以不闲。

8　朝骋骛兮江皋，夕弭节兮北渚。

　　鸟次兮屋上，水周兮堂下。

9　捐余玦兮江中，遗余佩兮澧浦。

　　采芳洲兮杜若，将以遗兮下女。

乱　时不可兮再得，聊逍遥兮容与。

湘夫人

1　帝子降兮北渚，目眇眇兮愁予。

　　袅袅兮秋风，洞庭波兮木叶下。

2　登白薠兮骋望，与佳期兮夕张。

　　鸟何萃兮薠中，罾何为兮木上？

3　沅有芷兮澧有兰，思公子兮未敢言。

　　荒忽兮远望，观流水兮潺湲。

4　麋何食兮庭中，蛟何为兮水裔？

　　朝驰余马兮江皋，夕济兮西澨。

5　闻佳人兮召予，将腾驾兮偕逝。
　　筑室兮水中，葺之兮荷盖。

6　荪壁兮紫坛，匊芳椒兮成堂。
　　桂栋兮兰橑，辛夷楣兮药房。

7　罔薜荔兮为帷，擗蕙櫋兮既张。
　　白玉兮为镇，疏石兰兮为芳。

8　合百草兮实庭，建芳馨兮庑门。
　　九嶷缤兮并迎，灵之来兮如云。

9　捐余袂兮江中，遗余褋兮澧浦。
　　搴汀洲兮杜若，将以遗兮远者。

乱　时不可兮骤得，聊逍遥兮容与。

《湘君》《湘夫人》是用舜与娥皇女英二妃生离死别故事，自王逸以来，殆无疑义。全篇是讲舜与二妃死后成神之事，不及生前。既成神，则永生，因屡谋再聚而失败，成永生的悲剧。故李白以《远别离》咏之，可谓深得屈原之意。后来朱熹《楚辞集注》以湘君为娥皇，湘夫人为女英，毫无道理。顾炎武承认湘君与湘夫人原是夫妇关系，却否认了二妃事（《日知录》卷二五），也不足取。

但是，王逸以来，虽认为屈原所咏为舜与二妃神间爱情故事，却以湘夫人为湘水女神，湘君为湘水男神，则大误。二妃自投湘水，为湘水女神。舜则前此已死于苍梧山，葬于九嶷山，他只能是山神，不能是水神。再看屈原诗中，讲湘夫人时处处不离船棹。讲湘君时则说他"驾飞龙"，乘"鹜"和"马"，这鹜"弭节兮北渚"，应是飞车；这马能"济"水偕逝，应是飞马。诗称他为"湘君"（也只是在诗题上），只因他原是湘夫人的夫君，与湘水无涉。明乎此，则诗中一些暧昧的话迎刃而解。

《湘君》的句法还有个特点。此诗是夫人独自（女巫唱），而文中一段写其君，一段写自己，一句写其君，一句写自己，反复置换。这是女性的思路，自叙心情时总是忘不了加上"他"。

《湘君》第一遍是写君，你约好了来看我，怎么又犹疑不来？谁留住了你？末句"沛吾乘兮桂舟"是说湘夫人派船去接他。第二遍全写湘夫人，令沅湘、长江安排好行程，却久等不来，第一次约会失败。"谁思"意"思谁"？

第三遍前半段写君，君要北征，但答应绕道来洞庭见夫人一面。下半段和第四遍全写夫人，最重要的是装饰一只好船，船顶高悬绸织旌旗，向乘飞龙来的君发信号，即"扬灵"。但"扬灵兮未极"，未达到目的，第二次约会失败。

第五遍是夫人伤感，不是痛哭一场，而是"横流涕兮潺湲"，泪水含在眼帘里，所以横流。这和李白"恸哭兮远望"（《远别离》）的描述不同。屈原的悲剧人物精神上都是健康的，勇于承受，哀而不伤。最后两句，"桂棹兮兰枻"写夫人自己，"斫冰兮积雪"写北征的君。舜的事业在黄河流域，南人看来是冰天雪地的北方，兼状君之勇于职守。前人多将此句解为船急行浪花飞溅，误。

第六遍是夫人回忆君的第一次爽约，第七遍是回忆第二次爽约，从"告余以不闲"可知。此语屈原常用（见《山鬼》），怨而不怒。有意思的是这里也插入了"石濑兮浅浅，飞龙兮翩翩"二句，前句指自己，后句指君。二句有南北远隔、上舒下困之意。

第八遍，上联写君真的走了，驻节北浦，不回来了。下联写夫人清冷寂寞的心情，却只用"鸟次兮屋上，水周兮堂下"二语，屋中就像没有任何生命一样，写得好极了。前人多以此为夫人与君再次约会之地，误。

第九遍也是绝妙笔法：把男人送给她的信物丢到水里去了，但不是就此决绝，回过头来还是到洲中去采集信物，只是已不可能送给最心爱的人，就送给下女（大约即婵媛）吧。反映夫人的爱是何等真诚，不以物喜，不以己悲。

爱既如此坚贞，精神也不会被任何逆境击垮，因而有坚强的结束语："时不可兮再得，聊逍遥兮容与"。我把这个结束语作为"乱"，因为它需用另一种顿挫而拖长的音调唱出，也许是领唱者独唱，停止舞步，甚至不要伴奏，以示坚定。

现在再来看《湘夫人》。

《湘夫人》是湘君的独白，自称予，称夫人曰帝子、公子、佳人，若直呼其名，而不像夫人诗对爱人概称君。本篇也是叙离别之苦，谋聚会而不得，但全是自叙心境，不像夫人诗那样处处要提到君。这都是表现男子的气概。有人说此篇应是男巫独唱，我怀疑。朱熹《楚辞集注》小序说"使巫觋作乐歌舞"，据我所见，九歌中概未有用觋（男巫）者。

又本篇情节似乎都是湘君的设想，有类《河伯》。第一遍是设想夫人来了，但只写景，不写人，其景极美，而含愁意，表现人的心情。这是非常高明的笔法。第二遍是设想一个安排好了的"佳期"（约会），但旋成泡影。第三遍是沉思，用"远望"和"流水"（近观，因夫人是水神）表现内心的矛盾，也是极高明的笔法。第四遍，"麋何食兮庭中，蛟何为兮水裔?"不甘久困，决心骑马去寻夫人。

这以下，用了很长篇幅描述湘君设想与夫人同居的住处；而对此，楚辞学者解释颇多分歧，我只谈我的别解。

第五遍，"闻佳人兮召予，将腾驾兮偕逝"后，马上说"筑室兮水中，葺之兮荷盖"（盖音记，叶逝），这是临时想到的，因夫人是水神。下面详述其建筑规划，就不同了。第六遍：这房子是桂木做梁，兰木橼子，白芷墙，荃草饰壁，紫贝铺地。第七遍：室内有薜荔帐子、蕙兰幔子，用白玉压好，洒石兰放香气。第八遍：庭院里栽满了花草，周围建有厢房，还有一个大门。于是，九嶷山的众神都来祝贺新居了。这样一幢房子，岂是在"水中"？其实，湘夫人原来的住处，"水周兮堂下"，也不是在水中的。《河伯》是黄河之神，诗中问"灵何为兮水中?"河伯有龙堂珠宫，不该漂浮水中。我是说，屈原作品中的神都是人性化的，要用纯粹的、完全的人性去理解他们。

第九遍：丢弃了和再采集爱的信物，一如《湘君》诗。但在结束语或"乱"中，将夫人的"时不可兮再得"改为"时不可兮骤得"，表现男人的气概，机会还是有的，不悲观。

《河伯》别解

河伯是黄河之神，男性。禹治水，黄河除干流入海外，在南岸别开八条支流，统称九河。故河伯实是九河之神。《九歌·少司命》中有"与女（汝）游兮九河，冲风至兮水扬波"句，洪兴祖《楚辞补注》断为《河伯》篇之错简，完全正确。宋以后《河伯》篇起句遂改为"与女游兮九河，冲风起兮水扬波"（又本作"冲风起兮横波"）。

今人马茂元注《楚辞选》（人民文学出版社，1958）提出《少司命》中"与女沐兮咸池，晞女发兮阳之阿。望美人兮未来，临风恍兮浩歌"四句，似亦讲河伯事，但他未作移动（沐是洗发，浴才是洗身）。《诗·小雅·采绿》："予发曲局，薄言归沐。"我径将这四句移入《河伯》，并出于乐舞曲考虑，把它另作一遍。这样，《河伯》就全文如下：

河 伯

A 曲

1 与女游兮九河，冲风起兮水扬波。

乘水车兮荷盖，驾两龙兮骖螭。

2 与女沐兮咸池，晞女发兮阳之阿。

望美人兮未来，临风恍兮浩歌。

3 登昆仑兮四望，心飞扬兮浩荡。

日将暮兮怅忘归，惟极浦兮寤怀。

B 曲

1 鱼鳞屋兮龙堂，紫贝阙兮珠宫，

灵何为兮水中？

2 乘白鼋兮逐文鱼，与女游兮河之渚，

流澌纷兮将来下。

A 曲

4 子交手兮东行，送美人兮南浦。

波滔滔兮来迎，鱼鳞鳞兮媵予。

我这样做的理由是：（1）《少司命》是赞美主管生育婴儿的女神，根本不涉及与什么人同游同沐的事，咸池一节显系错简。（2）这四句移入《河伯》后，河伯的恋爱故事就曲折婉转，有头有尾了（下详）。（3）这样整理，《河伯》就表现为一个完整的乐舞曲：先是一个四句式曲调 A，重复三遍，而最后一个乐句，已有延缓踌躇之势。接着，转入一个三句式的曲调 B，其节奏较缓，尾音拖长。曲调 B 重复两遍后，再转回曲调 A 作为结束，乐和舞都恢复原来的气氛。我这种设想，是以词意为根据的。同时，每遍都叶韵：螭，古音罗；怀，古音回；下，古音户。

按词意，《河伯》是黄河男神向一位女神求爱故事的自叙。直称对方为"女（汝）"，亲昵而不是很尊重。在同游九河时似乎很顺利，而约她洗发于咸池，她就没有来。河伯并不伤心，而是浩歌一番。河伯登上黄河发源地昆仑，心胸开阔，旷然忘返，但也知道回家后必然会彻夜思念她，难以忘怀。转念一想，自己（灵）有很好的住处，何必荡漾水上求爱呢？再约她河边（渚）遨游，似也顺利，但可怕的洪峰或冰块（流澌，可怕之物）就要冲下来了。最后，还是握手（交手）告别吧，送女南下，自向东行。总之，全篇都是一种离合不定，女方三心二意，男方不悔也不怨的心情，写得好极了。

那么，这位女神是谁，它是根据什么神话故事写的呢？关于河伯的故事，有三种传说。

一，人们最熟悉的是《史记·滑稽列传》中河伯娶妇故事。故事说，河南邺郡的三老、廷掾每年要赋敛百姓数百万钱，叫大女巫选民女沉河，为河伯娶妇。魏文侯时西门豹为邺令，投三老、大女巫于河，一举废除了此陋习；改发民凿十二渠灌田，民皆富足。依所记，河伯娶妇故事显然是三老、廷掾为敛钱捏造出来的。虽有"长老曰"其事"从来久远矣"，并无明证。《史记·六国年表》有秦灵公八年（前417）"初以君主妻河"，那是几十年以后的事，曰"初"，即与邺郡事无关。屈原又是百年以后的人，屈原大约不理会河伯娶妇的故事，因为这故事早已被西门豹揭穿，说也没人相信了。

二，《庄子·秋水篇》有很长一段河伯与北海神若的对话，涉及自然和历史许多问题，但都是讲哲学，没一句讲爱情。唐人赵德明在该篇释文中说："河伯姓冯名夷，一名冰夷。"《山海经》有"冰夷，人面，乘两龙"。《河伯》A曲第一遍中有"驾两龙"。又曹植《洛神赋》有"冯夷鸣鼓"，把冯夷和洛水女神联系起来，《河伯》中也有这种联系，见下。

三，河伯与宓妃的故事，其蛛丝马迹全部在屈原作品中。《天问》："帝降夷羿革孽夏民，胡射夫河伯而妻彼雒嫔？"这个羿不是尧时射九日、其妻嫦娥奔月的羿，而是夏代打败禹的第四代传人相（革孽夏民）自立为君的羿。这个雒嫔即洛妃，通称宓妃。或谓《天问》此语暗示宓妃是河伯之妻，误。宓妃是伏羲（宓羲）氏之女，溺死洛水为神，故称宓妃。不过《天问》此语暗示河伯与宓妃有恋爱关系，所以羿要射河伯，想娶宓妃为妻。据王逸注，羿射伤河伯左目，河伯诉于天帝，帝曰："尔何故见射？"河伯曰："我时化为白龙出游"；帝曰："使汝深守神灵，羿何从得犯汝？"这与《河伯》中B曲第一遍"灵何为兮水中"一致，河伯是在他最后一次"乘白鼋"出游时被射的。

《离骚》的最后部分，有一段是讲屈原到处去"求女"。首先就是"吾令丰隆乘云兮，求宓妃之所在"，"吾令蹇修以为理"。丰隆是云神，蹇修传说是为伏羲氏之臣，理是使者，此处相当于婚姻介绍人。结果"纷总总其离合兮，忽纬繣其难迁"，宓妃三心二意，离合不定，怪戾（纬繣）难改。最后还说了宓妃几句坏话："夕归次于穷石兮，朝濯发乎洧盘。保厥美以骄傲兮，日康娱以淫游。"穷石是羿的居处，宓妃夜里和羿私通去了。洧盘，《尚书大传·禹贡传》"洧盘之水出崦嵫山"。这段之前还提到"饮余马于咸池"，后面又提到"览相关于四极"。这些话在《河伯》中都有，特别是"纷总总而离合兮"的情调，与《河伯》完全一致。《河伯》无疑是根据宓妃的神话故事写的。

《离骚》中屈原向宓妃求爱未成，又去求有娀之佚女、有虞之二姚，亦都失败。屈原之求女当然不是真的求爱，而是求楚怀王的谅解，使他官复原职。所以他总结说"世溷浊而嫉贤兮……哲王又不寤"。那么，《九歌》中的恋爱诗篇，包括《河伯》，是否也如朱熹所说，乃是眷恋故主之意呢？不是。我的解释是，《九歌》包括《河伯》的产生，楚辞学者有多种说法，郭沫若说是屈原年轻得意时之作，有人甚至认为是承怀王之命而作。总之，作《九歌》时他还没有被冤，完全按照神话故事去写，有些"鄙陋"的部分，如宓妃与羿通奸，就删去了。到被冤后写《离骚》时，为了突出小人的谗妄，又加进去。

《山鬼》别解

《山鬼》是叙一个多情的山之女神追求恋爱的故事，称其追求对象为子、灵修、公子、君，应是个可尊敬的人。整理《山鬼》的词，最感困难的是"余处幽篁兮终不见天，路险难兮独后来"和"留灵修兮澹忘归，岁既晏兮孰华予"这两小节。按文意，这两小节与上下文都无直接联系，有独立性。若把它们都放入上文，则成两个六句式的乐曲，这在屈原作品中并不罕见。惟"独后来"的来古音里，与上文不叶韵，而与下文叶韵，直到"孰华予"的予。若把它放入下文，则成一个八句式的乐曲，太长，舞者怕亦太累。又，《山鬼》原是巫女唱叙故事，这两小节却改用了第一人称，与上下文不同，演唱时需改换口气或腔调。因此，我把这两小节作为"少歌"或"倡"，即承上启下的两个小的"乱"，演出时也许有歌无舞，巫女独唱或独白。这样，《山鬼》就全部是用四句式的乐舞曲，重复六遍。这是《九歌》最通用的形式。

还有一个问题。无论何种曲式，在第五遍"饮石泉兮荫松柏"下显然脱漏了一句话，否则凭空出现个三句式曲调，并在词意上与下句"君思我兮然疑作"接不上气。我们不能补作一句，但我觉得把上遍的"怨公子兮怅忘归"在这里重复一下，倒很合适，因为第四、五两遍本是对称的，两个"怅忘归"就更对称。

于是，《山鬼》全文便表述如下：

山　鬼

1　若有人兮山之阿，被薜荔兮带女罗。
　　既含睇兮又宜笑，子慕予兮善窈窕。

2　乘赤豹兮从文狸，辛夷车兮结桂旗。
　　被石兰兮带杜衡，折芳馨兮遗所思。

乱　余处幽篁兮终不见天，路险难兮独后来。

3　表独立兮山之上，云容容兮而在下。
　　杳冥冥兮羌昼晦，东风飘兮神灵雨。

小乱　留灵修兮澹忘归，岁既晏兮孰华予？

4　采三秀兮於山间，石磊磊兮葛蔓蔓。
　　怨公子兮怅忘归，君思我兮不得闲。

5　山中人兮芳杜若，饮石泉兮荫松柏。
　　怨公子兮怅忘归，君思我兮然疑作。

6　雷填填兮雨冥冥，猿啾啾兮狖夜鸣。

　　风飒飒兮木萧萧，思公子兮徒离忧。

从文意看，第一遍，山之女神是会见了她敬爱之人，但没说具体交往，也许是"去其泰甚"，只说"子慕予兮善窈窕"。第二遍，约会与恋人再次会面，神女车驾盛装，隆重出发，但似乎没有真的会见，因为她"路险难兮独后来"。第三遍，于是她爬上高山之巅，四下瞻望，沉思一番。只见白昼忽变昏暗、晴天忽变雨天，世情无常，难以捉摸。怎么办呢？结论（乱曰）："留灵修兮澹忘归，岁既晏兮孰华予？"坦然为他留下来吧，岁已迟暮，有谁来爱我呢？这个"澹忘归"与下面两个"怅忘归"是两种感情。怅忘归是失望、不痛快地留下来；澹忘归是安然、有信心地留下来；说明少女感情的变化。

这个"澹"字，原文是竖心旁，我在新华字典上查不到，就把它改成了三点水旁。根据是：司马相如《子虚赋》"泊乎无为，澹乎自持"，郭璞注曰：那个竖心旁的"憺"与三点水的"澹"同（《文选》卷七）。《子虚赋》是子虚先生与乌有先生的对话，原不作数。但这两句是神话中楚王游巫山会神女时说的，神话都是真的。又查宋玉的《神女赋》，干脆就用了三点水的澹（《文选》卷一九）。

第四遍，神女到山上去采灵芝，而"石磊磊兮葛蔓蔓"，受到阻力甚多，以至"怨公子兮怅忘归"了。第五遍，我自己是那样贞洁贡献，而公子你却还是"然疑作"，犹疑不决，于是又"怨公子兮怅忘归"了。最后，第六遍，雷雨猿鸣，风吹叶落，怨有什么用？我真是想念你呀，但不能见面，"徒离忧"而已。

那么，《山鬼》是根据什么神话故事写的呢？多数楚辞学者认为山鬼是泛称，如《云中君》的君，没有专属故事。我看不然。

王逸《楚辞章句》注此诗，以忠诚高洁的山鬼乃屈原自况，灵修指楚怀王，公子指公子椒，这都是附会，且不去管它。而在"留灵修兮澹忘归"句下忽说："言已宿留怀王，冀其还已，心中澹然，安而忘归"。这分明是把山鬼作为巫山神女了。

郭沫若在《屈原赋今译》中解"采三秀兮於山间"，说三秀就是灵芝，於山就是巫山。很有道理。《九歌》中如"捐余玦兮江中，遗余佩兮澧浦"、

"与女沐兮咸池，晞汝发兮阳之阿"（均见前），兮字下直书地名。而"於"字即古乌字，於戏，即鸣呼。於山即巫山，属于笔误，但女巫唱时谁也听不出来，笔误音却不误。

江淹《别赋》"惜瑶草之徒芳"句，李善注引宋玉集（今佚），神女说："我帝之季女，名曰瑶姬。未行（嫁）而亡，封于巫山之台，精魂为草，实曰灵芝"（《文选》卷一六）。就是说，"采三秀兮於山间"的乃是巫山女神。

据宋玉《高唐赋·序》，楚怀王在高唐昼寝，巫山神女来，"愿荐枕席，王因幸之"；又宋玉《神女赋·序》，顷襄王游高唐，夜寝，"梦与神女通"（《文选》卷一九）。两次相会是两个男人，但是父子，可以合二为一。又《神女赋》写神女"既娬媚（娴雅）于幽静兮，又婆娑（窈窕）乎人间"；与洛神之淫不同，而与《山鬼》的描述一致。所以，可以断定《山鬼》乃是写巫山神女求爱的故事。

《高唐赋》是宋玉的作品，有曹植的《洛神赋·序》为证。或谓《神女赋》非宋玉所写，那没关系，因为所述为神话，无论谁写或民间口传，都是真的。

元稹《连昌宫词》

《连昌宫词》是元稹继白居易《长恨歌》所作，亦系咏唐玄宗与杨贵妃故事。白居易在《自选诗集》卷末云："一篇长恨有风情，十首秦吟近正声。每被老元偷格律，苦教短李（李绅）伏歌行。"指此。其实，元稹只是形式上采用白居易"首句标其目，卒章显其志"的格式，内容则全然不同。《长恨歌》首句是"汉皇重色思倾国"，"其目"在"重色"二字；"卒章"是"此恨绵绵无绝期"。全诗主旨是宣叙玄宗与杨妃的爱情和马嵬坡生离死别绵绵的遗恨。《连昌宫词》首句"连昌宫中满宫竹"，是为了引起下文所叙宫境之兴衰；而卒章"努力庙谋休用兵"，并非全诗主旨。元稹有反战思想，有名作《夫远征》，但此时正值李锜、刘辟、吴元济等军阀叛乱，不能不用兵征讨；诗中也称赞"诏书才下吴蜀平，官军又取淮西贼"。《连昌宫词》全篇主旨在批判、讽刺玄宗皇室之荒淫腐败与杨氏兄妹之祸国殃民。

　　唐人咏杨妃诗殆皆持批判态度。即专就李杨爱情言，郑畋的《马嵬坡》人称最为敦厚，但我以为其结语"终是圣明天子事，景阳宫井又何人"，实在讽刺，说李隆基还不如陈叔宝，因陈尚能与爱妃共生死。李商隐的《马嵬》则直斥"如何四纪为天子，不及卢家有莫愁"。杜甫在《哀江头》中婉言"人生有情泪沾臆，江水江花岂终极"，有点离恨绵绵味道。但接着"黄昏胡骑尘满城，欲往城南望城北"，就是批判了。杜老在《丽人行》中点出"赐名大国虢与秦"，"慎莫近前丞相嗔"，在《北征》中就干脆说"奸臣竟菹醢，同恶随荡析"；奸臣指杨国忠，同恶则指杨氏姊妹也。白居易为诗素重讽喻，他自编文集以美刺比兴之讽喻诗列入首类，而《长恨歌》独乏批判精神。陈鸿惜之，欲为补救，作《长恨歌传》曰："不特感其事，亦欲惩尤物、窒乱阶，垂于将来也。"然至《连昌宫词》始完成此志，成为咏杨妃最佳的诗篇。

　　元稹是以连昌宫景物之盛衰，写唐王朝之治乱。连昌宫在河南今宜阳县境，为西京长安与东都洛阳间一所行宫。玄宗自纳杨妃后，从未行幸东都，自然并无与杨妃驻跸连昌宫之事。但诗中所咏故事并非虚构，皆有史籍可考。元稹是将在长安和骊山等地有关杨妃的活动都移植到《连昌宫词》中，丰富多彩，有类电影中蒙太奇手法。

　　诗是以天宝十三载（754）寒食夜为杨妃所开的一次盛大音乐会开始的：

> 夜半月高弦索鸣，贺老琵琶定场屋。

唐燕（宴）乐起乐皆以丝声，竹声次之，所谓"细抹将来"。细末用琵琶，故曰定场屋。贺老怀智是开元早期乐师。元稹《琵琶歌》曰："玄宗偏许贺怀智，段师此艺还相匹。自后流传指拨衰，昆仑善才徒尔为。"其实段善本、康昆仑名气都不在贺老之下，李善才稍逊耳。接着诗以大量篇幅讲念奴故事：

> 力士传呼觅念奴，念奴潜伴诸郎宿。
> 须臾觅得又连催，特敕街中许燃烛。
> 春娇满眼睡红绡，掠削云鬟旋装束。

飞上九天歌一声，二十五郎吹管逐。

这里元稹自注："念奴，天宝中名倡"，每歌，"万众喧隘"不能禁，"玄宗遣高力士大呼于楼上曰：'欲遣念奴唱歌，邠二十五郎吹小管逐，看有人能听否？'"按：二十五郎邠王已于开元二十九年（741）去世，杨妃天宝三载（744）进宫，与念奴何干？《连昌宫词》书此只为讽刺玄宗诸郎宿娼而已。诗于这场音乐会的主题则只讲了两句：

逡巡大遍凉州彻，色色龟兹轰录续。

《旧唐书·音乐志二》："自（北）周、隋以来，管弦乐曲将数百曲，多用西凉乐，鼓舞曲多用龟兹乐。"又称"西凉乐最为闲雅"，而龟兹乐"多擂大鼓"，"声震百里"。西凉乐中有三个大曲，即《霓裳》、《凉州》和《六幺》。凉州有大遍、小遍。大遍是将散序、歌头、破三大部分十几遍（段）全奏完。裁截奏之则谓之摘遍即小遍。元稹《琵琶歌》："霓裳羽衣偏宛转，凉州大遍最豪嘈，六幺散序多笼撚"，所以这次音乐会主题是一个最热闹的凉州大曲。"逡巡大遍凉州彻"，即将凉州大曲徘徊通奏了一遍。音乐会的配曲是"色色龟兹轰录续"。色指乐工角色。龟兹乐以鼓吹为主，有拍板色、大鼓色、杖鼓色、羯鼓色、笛色、笙色等。其声震耳，故曰轰。龟兹乐多短曲，把它们陆续轰完。真是一个热闹的盛大音乐会。

音乐会完了，第二天：

平明大驾发行宫，万人鼓舞途路中。
百官队仗避岐薛，杨氏诸姨车斗风。

岐王、薛王是玄宗诸王中最跋扈的两位，不过已分别于开元十四年（726）、二十二年死了，不能与杨氏三姨碰面。这两句主要是讽刺杨氏姊妹。玄宗称她们为姨，已属不伦；复封为国，更令人侧目。虢国夫人与秦国夫人斗车事，历来受到批判。她们斗的是豪华、气派，有如奔驰与宝马；而不是斗车速、车技，否则就属六艺之一，应予褒扬了。

"明年十月东都破"，以下诗就写连昌宫的荒废、凄凉悲惨，而插入一段：

> 尔后相传六皇帝，不到离宫门久闭。
> 往来年少说长安，玄武楼成花萼废。

玄宗以后，肃宗、代宗、德宗、顺宗，至元稹写此诗的宪宗元和十三年（818），共五皇帝，不是六皇帝。而"说长安"则有特殊含义。花萼楼是玄宗与宫女们嬉游之处，刘禹锡《杨柳枝词》所说"花萼楼前初种时，美人楼上斗腰肢"是也。为防丑闻外泄，自花萼楼筑有夹墙经芙蓉苑到大明宫，安禄山反叛报到，玄宗正在花萼楼畅饮，竟不置信。即杜甫《秋兴》第六首所说"花萼夹城通御气，芙蓉小苑入边愁"也。诗描叙连昌宫皇帝办公厅的荒废景象说：

> 蛇出燕巢盘斗拱，菌生香案正当衙。

皇帝香案上长出个大蘑菇，这是多妙的讽刺！又描叙杨妃的端正楼说：

> 晨光未出帘影黑，至今反挂珊瑚钩。

杨妃梳妆的端正楼在骊山华清宫，元稹把它搬到连昌宫来了。此句是讥杨妃娇慵，天亮不肯起来；"反挂"乃垂帘之意。

诗最后写唐王朝倾败之由，有句曰：

> 开元之末姚（崇）宋（璟）死，朝廷渐渐由妃子。
> 禄山宫里养作儿，虢国门前闹如市。
> 弄权宰相不记名，依稀忆得杨与李。

禄山句指杨妃与安禄山通奸。白居易有《胡旋女》作于元和四年："中有太真外禄山，二人最道能胡旋。梨花园中册作妃，金鸡障下养为儿。"与通常所说"浴儿"不同，元稹或是受白居易影响。虢国夫人句亦指夫人与杨国忠私通，趋炎谄佞之徒麇集门前，所以闹如市也。

六　幺

白居易《琵琶行》："轻拢慢捻抹复挑，初为霓裳后绿腰。"我在《濯足偶谈》中谈过白居易这首诗，其中谈霓裳多，谈六幺少，并有错误，兹为补正。

霓裳、六幺都来自西凉，与西凉大遍同为西凉来的三大曲，并被定为燕乐（宴乐）法曲。霓裳原是天竺（印度）婆罗门（贵族）乐曲，由西凉节度使杨敬述献给唐玄宗。玄宗把它改谱，又加上一个散序，于天宝十三年（754）令改称霓裳羽衣曲（《唐会要》卷三三）。六幺来源不详，我想也是外国来的，六幺是音译名，故又称绿腰、录要、陆要。外国来的东西总是多名，如番薯又称白薯、红薯、甘薯；番茄又称西红柿、洋辣子，茄、柿、椒都搞不清。

中国乐调低，外国乐调高。唐十四国乐中，南方乐天竺、扶南、骠国等乐调低，西方乐高昌、疏勒、康国等乐调高。霓裳调式未详。六幺，段安节《乐府杂录》云，贞元间长安琵琶比赛，康昆仑"弹一曲新翻羽调绿腰"，段善本也弹羽调绿腰，但移作枫香调，"声如雷响"。周密《齐东野语》卷八称，宋人奏六幺有中吕调、高平调、仙吕调，并称相当于唐二十八调中夹中羽、林钟羽、仙吕羽。羽属高调，仙吕羽是二十八调中最高者。霓裳恐怕调没有这么高。

法曲在入拍以后始有歌，而入破以后以舞为主，歌或消失。许多法曲没有歌，有歌者亦很少留下歌词。霓裳、六幺均未见词。霓裳的歌，我只见白居易《长恨歌》："缓歌慢舞凝丝竹，尽日君王看不足；渔阳鼙鼓动地来，惊破霓裳羽衣曲。""缓歌"二字可能是指霓裳，也可能不是。

六幺的则比较明确。白居易《杨柳枝》："六幺水调家家唱，白雪梅花处处飞。"白雪、梅花是笛曲。水调，宋王灼《碧鸡漫志》卷三引唐人语：水调有十一遍，前五遍有歌，后六遍有舞，其"第五遍五言，调声最愁苦"。白居易《听水调》："五言一遍最殷勤，调少情多但有因；不会当时翻曲意，此声肠断为何人？"白居易把六幺与水调并列，至少说明六幺的歌，"家家唱"，同时也使人设想六幺的歌不像霓裳那样"缓"，而有愁苦之音。

再说舞。霓裳、六幺在法曲中都属于软舞，与柘枝、剑器等健舞不同。健舞也是女伎、徒手，其不同在于手足动作。白居易《霓裳羽衣舞歌》有详细描写："飘然转旋回雪轻，嫣然纵送游龙惊。小垂手后柳无力，斜曳裾时云欲生（自注：四句，皆霓裳舞之初态）。烟娥敛略不胜态，风袖低昂如有情。上元点鬟招萼绿，王母挥袂别飞琼。"（按：上元夫人、萼绿华、许飞琼皆仙女）这真是慢舞。

六幺，《碧鸡漫志》称：宋时六幺中有一段花十八，前后十八拍，又花四拍，共二十二拍。这里指舞步，花拍大约是连拍两下，用碎步。相传五代画家顾闳中《韩熙载夜宴图》有一段画王屋山（女）舞花十八。我曾见印制的此图，伴奏只有大鼓和拍板，另有两人击掌，也是打拍，有点踢踏舞味道。

我在《濯足偶谈》中的错误是：认为霓裳和六幺都是悠扬宛转、缓歌慢舞的乐曲，与《琵琶行·序》中所说"快弹数曲"和弹者"漂沦憔悴"的感情不和。上面已说了霓裳和六幺在调、歌、舞方面的不同，现在还要从整个乐曲的结构和节奏来看。据近人研究，唐大曲一般分散序、中序、破三大部分。散序是器乐独奏、轮奏或合奏，无歌亦无舞；节奏自由，用散板，有若干遍。中序以歌唱为主，又称歌头，器乐伴奏；节奏固定，用慢板；从入拍起，演奏若干遍。破以舞为主，又称舞遍；节奏逐渐加快，以至极快；从入破起，有十几遍；歇拍然后曲终。[1] 霓裳有散序六遍，六幺有散序五遍，都是悠扬宛转之乐。元稹《琵琶歌》："霓裳羽衣偏宛转"，"六幺散序多拢捻"。拢是扣弦，捻是揉弦，使音闲婉。元稹《法曲》："明皇度曲多新态，宛转浸淫易沉着。"把沉着的部分也换成宛转的乐段，这是指玄宗改谱霓裳，加上浸淫的散序。王建《宫词》："琵琶先抹六幺头，小管丁宁侧调稠。"霓裳、六幺都是弦乐开场，陆续加入笛笙和鼓拨拍板。六幺头即六幺散序是宛转的；加入管乐器后，就变成浓稠的中序了。白居易"管急弦繁曲渐稠，绿腰宛转曲终头"，则是六幺由浓稠加快入破的描述。

霓裳的中序却令人怀疑。白居易《霓裳羽衣舞歌》："中序擘騞初入拍，

---

[1] 杨荫浏：《中国古代音乐史稿》，人民音乐出版社，1964，第230~231页。

秋竹竿裂春冰坼。"擘是用手掰开，骟是用刀劈开，连同竹裂冰坼，都是第三部分"入破"的声音，怎么说是"入拍"呢？并且这两句以下，紧接着就讲上引的舞姿，都是第三部分破的内容。我想霓裳大约没有或只有很短的歌，因而没有或只有很短的中序，白居易按大曲惯例把入破写成入拍了。白居易另有《卧听法曲霓裳》"宛转柔声入破时"，似乎是由散序直接入破，这就对了。

元稹《琵琶歌》："管儿还为弹六幺，六幺依旧声迢迢。猿鸣雪岫来三峡，鹤唳晴空闻九霄。逡巡弹得六幺彻，霜刀破竹无残节。幽关鸦轧胡雁悲，断弦砉骟层冰裂。"这里一二句是散序，其声迢迢。二三句写中序，猿鸣鹤唳都是歌声。六幺有歌，"家家唱"，但没说中序有几遍。以下四句写入破，也用了砉骟、竹破、冰裂等破裂音，还加上乌鸦轧、胡雁悲的声音。遗憾的是元稹没有写入破后的大段舞曲。

白居易写霓裳的舞曲也有个问题。如前所引，他写霓裳的舞姿，"飘然""嫣然""小垂手""斜曳裾"，以至"点鬟""挥袂"等都是轻盈慢舞，而总结说"繁音急节十二遍，跳珠撼玉何铿铮"。乐曲与舞姿不合。陈寅恪先生在《元白诗笺证稿》中也看到这一点，说"姑记此疑，以俟更考"。[1]

不过，白居易对霓裳的结尾却说得明白："翔鸾舞了却收翅，唳鹤曲终长引声。"自注："凡曲将毕皆声拍促速，唯霓裳之末长引一声也。"因此可知：《琵琶行》中"曲终收拨当心画，四弦一声如裂帛"；弹的是六幺，不是霓裳。

建 安

李白的《古风》，其一是一篇诗论。论中说："自从建安来，绮丽不足珍。"此语不包括建安，因李白是非常推崇建安诗风的。按现代语法，"自某某年以来"应包括某某年，有时还用括号注明"含某某年"。故按现代语法，"自从建安来"应改为"自从建安去"。

但建安不能去，它去而复来。建安是一场新诗运动，一场文学革命。我

---

① 陈寅恪：《元白诗笺证稿》，三联书店，2001，第 26 页。

们曾经历 20 世纪六七十年代的"文化大革命"。那是一场破坏文化的政治阴谋，借除旧之名以劫取政权。所以林彪沉沙，"四人帮"垮台，革命就过去了。建安的领导者曹操父子也是当权派，但他们和建安七子都是文学巨擘，能够建设新的诗风。建安七子都在建安二十二年（217）以前去世了，曹操也在建安末年仙逝。但建安精神不死，在晋太康时一次复兴，在刘宋元嘉时又一次复兴，到唐初陈子昂、李白时又一次更大的复兴，等于诗的又一次革命。

刘勰《文心雕龙》说建安诗篇"慷慨以任气，磊落以使才。造怀指事，不求纤密乏巧；驱辞逐貌，唯取昭晰之能"。这就是所谓的建安风骨。这种新的诗风在正始（曹芳）以后，就逐渐"诗杂仙心"（指入于黄老），"率多浮浅"了。但入晋以后，出现"张（张载兄弟）、潘（潘岳父子）、左（左思）、陆（陆机、陆云），比肩诗衢"。这几位就是钟嵘《诗品》中所称的太康诗人。钟嵘说他们"勃尔复兴，踵武前王，风流未沫，亦文章之中兴也"。前王指曹操父子，这就是建安精神的第一次复兴。不过，刘勰说这些诗人"力柔于建安"，复兴不到家，亦无新遒。

到了东晋，玄学盛行，出现玄言诗。钟嵘《诗品》说这种诗"理过其辞，淡乎寡味"；又说它们"皆平典似道德论，建安风力尽矣"。然而，"元嘉中有谢灵运，才高词盛，富艳难纵"，这是建安精神的第二次复兴。

钟嵘说陆机、谢灵运的诗"其源出于陈思"，即陈思王曹植（子建）。李白也说："蓬莱文章建安骨，中间小谢又清发。"（《宿州谢朓楼饯别校书叔云》）李白的小谢指谢朓，因此诗是在谢朓楼写的。钟嵘说"小谢才思富捷，恨其兰玉夙凋"；则指谢惠连，因惠连二十七岁去世，太小了。谢灵运、谢惠连、谢朓都是谢玄族人。宋濂说："三谢亦本子建，而杂参于郭景纯。"（《答章秀才论诗书》）郭景纯即郭璞，钟嵘说他"始变永嘉平淡之体，故称中兴第一"。

说三谢本于曹植，并没什么根据。谢灵运有《拟魏太子邺中诗八首》，是假借曹丕的口气歌颂建安七子，每人一首；其论人论事颇有"磊落以使才"味道。唯七子之中删去了孔融，不知何解。刘勰《文心雕龙》说："宋初文咏，体有因革，庄老告退，而山水方滋。"其实谢灵运之称雄诗坛，正由于其山水诗顶替了玄言诗，使人耳目一新，并为当时士人所好。三谢的山水诗确有诸如"池塘生春草""明月照积雪""澄江静如练"等佳句，直感直言，有建安度。但他们通篇文章，雕琢字句，务求奇巧，正如刘勰所说："俪采百字之偶，争价一句之奇，情必极貌以写物，辞必穷力而追新"，离大雅更远了。

至于齐梁，盛行骈文，纤细而乏味，工整而无意境。降及陈隋，流行宫体诗、艳情诗，诗风更等而下之。物极必反，唐初遂有建安精神的第三次复兴，即李白论诗中所说："圣代复元古，垂衣贵清真。群才属休明，乘运共跃麟。文质相炳焕，众星罗秋旻。"

这次复兴，群才济济，休明繁茂，而运动的旗手当推陈子昂。陈是唐高宗时人，比李白早半个世纪。陈在《与东方左史虬修竹篇序》中说："文章道弊五百年矣。汉魏风骨，晋宋莫传"，"齐梁间诗，采繁竞丽，而兴寄都绝。每以咏叹，窃思古人，常恐逶迤颓废，风雅不作"。五百年是从建安算起（实际四百六七十年）；汉魏风骨即建安风骨。所以陈子昂之志，即在于复兴建安风骨。他在复兴建安时的心境是："前不见古人，后不见来者。念天地之悠悠，独怆然而涕下。"（《登幽州台歌》）然而这次复兴建安精神已不只是复古，而是创新，有如西方的文艺复兴，使中国的诗学达于成熟，达于登峰造极的唐诗的高度。这种创新的旗手，当推李白。李白创新时的心境，已不像陈子昂那样孤独，因为在陈后半个世纪，中国诗坛已是"群才属休明"，"众星罗秋旻"了。李白说他的任务是"我志在删述，垂辉映千春"。这话未免过于自谦。不过他是自比孔子，所以说"希圣如有立，绝笔于获麟"。

王维《桃园行》

陶渊明作《桃花源诗并记》。陶《记》原是陶《诗》之序，然独立成文，叙渔父探桃源故事，栩栩如缕，而文词省净，善用三四字短句，音韵铿然，又妙语连珠，读者过目成诵，反而忘记陶《诗》了。

后人之咏桃花源者累累，亦皆本于陶《记》。而王维、刘禹锡将桃花源写成神仙世界，则以陶《诗》有"借问游方士，焉测尘嚣外"语。此语用《庄子·德充符》，以儒者方内之士，不知游方外之乐也。韩愈写《桃源图》，亦作神仙世界，而着意于秦汉魏晋之兴衰，则以陶《诗》有"奇踪隐五百，一朝敞神界"语，五百年斗争，再归于隐逸。不过，韩愈改为"听终辞绝共凄然，自说经今六百年"，完全正确。我计算秦嬴至晋太康中应为600.5年。陶《诗》作五百，也许如宋人王安石、苏轼之意，只算到晋义熙以前。此意在王、苏的《桃园行》中未言明，而是洪迈在《容斋三笔》卷一〇《桃源行》中揣测的，认为陶《诗》"嬴氏乱天纪"乃"寓意于刘裕"，刘裕夺晋祚，渊明耻于二仕，遂归隐田园也。这都是用政治解诗。到"文革"时，渊明被划入法家诗人，陶《诗》又变成一首反对封建剥削的诗，以其有"春蚕收长丝，秋熟靡王税"语也。这更是政治挂帅了。

我喜诗亦读史，但不懂政治挂帅，所以这里我只谈陶《记》，不谈陶《诗》。从陶《记》看，则著名诗人之咏桃源者以王维的《桃园行》最佳，因其最切于陶《记》。

王维是第一个把桃源写成仙境的，但完全是为了加强隐逸之乐。王维的桃源人毫无仙气，而充满人气。他们有"家"，有"田园"，穿"衣服"而非羽氅，住"房栊"而非云洞，见了渔父忙"问都邑"（乡里），人情味十足。

陶《记》说，渔父在黑暗极狭的山涧中摸索前进，"豁然开朗，土地平旷，屋舍俨然，有良田、美池、桑竹之属……"写得极好，但有个毛病，一出洞便是村落，像是平地上钻出来的，不近情理。王维的诗则是："山口潜行始隈墺，山开旷望旋平陆。遥看一处攒（钻）云树，近入千家散花竹。"上联已暗含"豁然开朗"名句，下联是遥望有一片丛林，跑过去看，果然是人家村落。合情合理。

陶《记》说，桃源中"男女衣着，悉如外人"。这不可能，他们既与世隔绝，怎能知外人的时尚？王诗作"樵客初传汉姓名，居人未改秦衣服"，完全合理。"汉姓名"者，对秦乱而言，实则晋姓名变动更大，因有五胡。

王诗写桃源中人，"月明松下房栊静，日出云中鸡犬喧"。写得美极了，苏轼说王摩诘诗中有画，指此。这里是用淮南王刘安仙去，鸡犬随之升天故事，红日刚出，云中鸡鸣犬吠，绚丽烂漫，与松下房栊静成对比。其实就是不用《神仙传》故事，作为田园中鸡犬喧，也许更好。

王诗写桃源仙境，"峡里谁知有人事，世中遥望空云山"；两句洒脱，超过陶《记》。但也因这两句意境，略去了陶《记》中"不知有汉，无论魏晋"的历史观和"不足为外人道也"等名言。原来陶渊明的归隐是有其历史观的，并非不问天下事，所以有"金刚怒目"式作品（鲁迅语）。"不足为外人道也"不是与世决绝，而是如孔子著《春秋》，"至天道命，不传；传其人，不待告；告非其人，虽言不著"（《史记·天官书》）。桃源真谛，能领会者不用你去说，不能领会者说也没用，故不足为外人道也。

这也涉及全文的结语或结论。王诗的结语："春来遍是桃花水，不辨仙源何处寻？"为仙之道不是人人可辨的，这就把话说绝了。陶《记》的结语是，刘子骥死了，"后遂无问津者"。这就引起一连串思考。刘子骥是南阳隐逸，见《晋书·隐逸传》，陶《记》称他"高尚士也"。难道除刘子骥外就再也没有高尚士了吗？陶渊明你本人就很高尚，又对桃源知之甚稔，怎么不去问津呢？引起一连串思考正是陶《记》的目的，也可说，不论《诗》或《记》，能引起人们一连串思考就是好文章。

咏　蝉

蝉生于初秋，死于冬，不为害庄稼，也不捕食飞虹，于人无益。其命甚短，其貌不扬，其声聒噪，而诗人不乏吟咏，亦奇。

汉诗人咏蝉，多以其居高而不巢，饮露而不食，独处而不党，因多颂其行为高洁，而少及其鸣声。如陆士龙《寒蝉赋》说蝉有五德，君子则之。傅休奕《蝉赋》赞其"忽神蜕而灵变兮，奋轻翼之浮征"。最著名的是曹植的《蝉赋》："栖乔枝而仰首兮，漱朝露之清流"；"盛阳则来，太阴逝兮"；"皎皎贞素，侔夷惠兮。帝臣是戴，尚其洁兮。"

唐宋诗人咏蝉则更多是写其鸣声。蝉之鸣也，有声无调，无节奏，更无旋律，只是一片杂乱的噪音。诗人歌咏它，都是和悲秋联系起来。如上官仪《洛堤晓行》："鹊飞山月曙，蝉噪野风秋。"杜牧《题扬州禅智寺》："雨过一蝉噪，飘萧松桂秋。"姚合（宰相姚崇之孙）《闲居》："过门无马过，满宅是蝉声。"是一种感伤处境。王安石《葛溪驿》："鸣蝉更乱行人耳，正抱疏桐叶半黄。"此诗是荆公晚年不得意时在旅驿所作，前有"病身最觉风霜早，归梦不知山水长"句，这里"叶半黄"即风霜早来之意。王昌龄《塞上曲》："蝉鸣桑树间，八月萧关道"，也是叹塞上秋风来之过早，喻人生之迟暮。韩愈有篇《荐士》，其篇头是一段诗论，说周三百篇最"雅训"，汉兴五言诗，至建安达于"卓荦"；而这以后诗"凋耗"，仅鲍、谢二家可读，迨"齐梁及陈隋，众作等蝉噪"。那些齐梁体、宫廷艳体的作品，等于蝉噪。批得狠。

蝉有一类体形较小，名蟪蛄，其特点是早鸣。寒蝉八九月鸣，蟪蛄七月就鸣，因此引起诗人注意。《楚辞·招隐士》有"蟪蛄鸣兮啾啾"句，喻士之及早归隐。储光羲《田家杂兴》（八首之六）："蟪蛄鸣空泽……衣裳苦不早"，也是说寒风早到，哀人之早衰也。李白反用其意，在《拟古》十二之八中曰："蟪蛄啼青松，安见此树老？"有积极精神，洵属佳句。

蝉声枯燥、聒耳欲聋，一旦停鸣，余空反而产生旷静寂寞感。故《楚辞·九辩》有"蝉寂寞而无声"句。王维《辋川闲居赠裴秀才迪》："倚杖柴门外，临风听暮蝉"，暮蝉即大地将一片沉寂之意。杜甫《秦州杂诗》有"抱叶寒蝉静，归山独鸟迟"句。黑夜将临，寒蝉犹抱叶静待，独鸟欲归山而迟迟。盖喻己道之不行，只能抱志而流连；干戈未息，欲归故里而不得。此杜公客居秦州之心情也。

唐人有两首著名的咏蝉五律，即骆宾王的《在狱咏蝉》和李商隐的《蝉》。骆宾王诗曰：

> 西陆蝉声唱，南冠客思侵。
>
> 那堪玄鬓影，来对白头吟。
>
> 露重飞难进，风多响易沉。
>
> 无人信高洁，谁为表予心。

西陆即秋也。日循黄道而行，行南陆谓之夏，行西陆谓之秋。南冠即楚冠，因人也，用《左传》成公九年晋侯见锺仪故事。客，骆宾王自指；思侵，感慨万端。

三、四句，玄鬓，即蝉鬓，薄如蝉翼发式。白居易《妇人苦》："蝉鬓加意梳，蛾眉用心扫"；薛道衡《昭君辞》："蛾眉非本质，蝉鬓改真形。"

骆诗前句已用蝉字，故改为玄鬓。白头吟泛称，《乐府诗集》相和歌有楚调白头吟、瑟调白头吟多种，均南曲，适合骆宾王自况。这两句意思是：我这个老头子不堪面对那些在朝中走红的文人（武则天喜爱的年轻文人）。

五、六句，蝉因露水重飞不起来，蝉声因风多而低沉；喻己之"失路艰虞"，"未摇落而先衰"（诗序中语）。张正见（字见赜）《寒树晚蝉疏》诗："叶迥飞难住，枝残影共空。声疏饮露后，唱绝断弦中。"其实，蝉声低沉与风多无关，问题在于自身之衰老，即张诗中"露后""断弦"之义。

七、八句明白讲：现在已没人相信高洁了，谁能为我申述冤情呢！

其实，骆宾王是在当侍御史（谏官）时，屡上疏讽谏武则天而被系入狱的。武氏知道这些老文化人没什么可怕，打算不久即释放他。骆宾王也会意到这一点，所以在本诗的长序中说："闻蟪蛄之流声，悟平反之已奏；见螳螂之抱影，怯危机之未安。"这里用螳螂捕蝉故事（见《后汉书·蔡邕传》）。果然，骆宾王出狱后，参加了徐敬业讨伐武氏的起义，写下了流传后世的《讨武氏檄》。徐敬业兵败，骆逃逸不知所终。

李商隐的《蝉》：

> 本以高难饱，徒劳恨费声。
> 五更疏欲断，一树碧无情。
> 薄宦梗犹泛，故园芜已平。
> 烦君最相警，我亦举家清。

"本以高难饱"，不可解。"饮而不食者，蝉也"（《荀子·大略》），蝉本不要吃饱的。只有将此句与下句合看才能解释。这两句咏蝉，实是喻人，讲李商隐自己；本来是曲高和寡，人们不理解我，还要费劲去呼叫，那不是徒劳吗？

三、四句，蝉声五更稀疏欲断，一旦断绝，万籁俱静，即前述《楚辞·九辩》中的寂寞感。"一树碧无情"，是这种寂寞感的最佳写照。这句很出名，人称"神句"。这句是以蝉写树，一片碧绿，却似无情之物。其实是以树写人，即像鲁迅所写老子，"好像一段呆木头"（《故事新编·出关》）。李商隐还有首《柳》诗，说春风得意，柳枝袅娜，"如何肯到清秋日，已带斜阳又带蝉"。芳年既逝，柳也变得无情了。

五、六句，"梗"，指桃梗雕成的演戏的木偶；遇大水则泛流漂泊，用苏秦（应为苏代）说齐王故事，见《战国策·齐策》。"薄宦梗犹泛"，我这样木偶小官也要宦海浮沉，到处流离。下句"故园芜已平"，用陶渊明"田园将芜胡不归"意。此句也应加问号：故园芜已平了吗？

七、八句，"烦君最相警，我亦举家清"。最相警，好意警告，用心提醒。举家清，完全清醒，有安于清寒，不事钻营之意。谢谢您（蝉鸣）善意提醒我，我完全明白，不会去营苟于宦途。

朱载堉与十二平均律

老友吴慧字天汉，赠我新刊《翰苑一室：天汉诗词存稿》，收他的作品千九百余首，内有《谒朱载堉纪念馆》云：

> 皇皇世子自前明，胸纳沧波笔掣鲸。
> 十二律中称乐圣，九峰山下号狂生。
> 萧疏独往谁人会，邃密群科旷代惊。
> 我亦黄钟曾探索，登堂今始谒先行。

旋又接吴兄新刊《简明中国度量衡通史》，置此诗于扉页，并称他曾亲自试演黄钟之龠容秬黍（黑黍）1200粒之说，以证周尺之长度。是知其所称"黄钟曾探索"指律管之度量，非其音高也。

关于十二律之起源，李贺有《苦篁调啸引》曰：

> 请说轩辕在时事，伶伦采竹二十四。
> 伶伦采之自昆（仑）邱，轩辕诏遣中分作十二。
> 伶伦以之正音律，轩辕以之调元气。
> 当时黄帝上天时，二十三管咸相随，唯留一管人间吹。
> 无德不能得此管，此管沉埋虞舜祠。

李贺所说伶伦故事纯属传闻，但也道出实情，即自西周以来，历代所定十二律都是由沉埋在虞舜祠的标准音高黄钟按"三分损益法"推演出来的。黄钟的管长或弦长加 1/3，其发音即林钟；林钟的管长或弦长减 1/3，其发音即太簇；太簇加 1/3 即南吕，南吕减 1/3 即姑洗。以此类推的律十二，由低到高排序为黄钟、大吕、太簇、夹钟、姑洗、仲吕、蕤宾、林钟、夷则、南吕、无射、应钟。

也许因为缺"德"，周王和历代帝王都没找到沉埋在虞舜祠的那根黄钟律管。并且如李白所说："九疑联绵皆相似，重瞳孤坟竟何是？"（《远别离》）连虞舜祠在哪里也不知道。但标准音高总是有的，否则乐队无法演奏。不过乐队定音不用律管，而是"依我磬声"，即敲一组有弯角的石头片，也就是"黄钟毁弃，瓦釜雷鸣"。民间所用的标准音高随时代而异，据说从汉到唐已提高了四个音阶，迫使官方的谯乐也不得不"下律"（因律是由低到高往下排，例如由黄钟下到太簇就是上调一个音阶）。天宝中，乐工制磬改用华原石，又一次调高标准音高，引起文人震动，元稹和白居易都作新乐府《华原石》来评论。李贺当时任协律郎，职责就是掌管十二律。上引他的《苦篁调啸引》可能就是为此而作。史称"李贺乐府数十首，流播管弦……每一篇出，乐人辄以重赂购之"（清王琦《李长吉歌诗汇解·卷首·事纪》）。看来李贺不是保守派，他此诗字面看是要求复轩辕之古，而实际是讽喻，认为要找到古黄钟标准音高是办不到的。题"调啸引"亦作"调笑引"，恐有此意。

音乐无国界。公元前六世纪，古希腊流行毕达哥拉斯（Pythagoras）创制的十二律。毕氏律也是由一个标准音高 C，按"五度循环法"推演出来的，即每隔纯五度音，产生一个律，重复十六次，共得十二律，由低到高，排序为 C，C#，D，D#，E，F，F#，G，G#，A，A#，B。文艺复兴时期，毕氏十二律流行于欧美。

中国和西方的十二律，理论上都应该是相邻的二律相差半个音阶。但无论用三分损益法或五度循环法所得的音高差，都不恰好是半个音阶，所以都是不平均的十二律。这在演奏时就发生转调或移调的困难（任何一个八度音阶的调式都有两处是半音阶，转调时常会出现某个半音阶过低或过高）。历代中西音乐家都试图推演出十二平均律，提出各种方案，未能成功。到明代，朱载堉在山中一土屋中精研 19 年，终于发明十二平均律，著《律学新书》，成于万历十二年（1584）。这比十七世纪初法国麦尔森（Marin Mersenne）的同类著作早半个世纪；比 1766 年德国威克麦斯特（Andreas Werckmeister）正式提出十二平均律早 180 年。

朱载堉首先批判了王莽、刘歆、班固等狭隘的音乐理论，解放思想；然后抛弃传统的三分损益法，用等比级数计算出十二律的公比即开 2 的十二次方（1.05946），将一个八度音程的管距或弦距平均分配给十二律。这就是吴慧诗中所说"胸纳沧波笔掣鲸"，"邃密群科旷代惊"。而值得注意的是，朱载堉的惊人成就实际是根据实验而来的。他的实验是依尺造管，集管为笙，吹笙验律，曰吹验；然后，吹笙定琴，弹琴定瑟，曰弹验。19 年反复用当乐工的经验数据，创造出十二平均律。

十二平均律在科学上是一大发明，但实际用处并不很大。因为原来的十二不平均律的毛病主要是转调困难，而这种困难主要是在琵琶、瑟、筝等弦乐器上，一转调或移调式就要重新调弦。管乐器则不然，如一个七孔笛可吹出三个调式，一个十三管笙可吹出十来个调式，全看吹的技巧。《唐会要》卷三四，文宗太和九年（835），"云朝霞善吹笛，新声变律，深惬上旨"。新声变律即突破律的约束，指转调、移调式技巧。至于声乐，好的歌唱家可完全自由地转调移调式，不受律的限制。元稹《何满子歌》："犯羽含商移调态，留情度意抛弦管。"犯调即转调，因原以为黄钟宫为君，转他调即以臣犯君。这也是"丝不如竹，竹不如肉"。

用典故和用前人成语（一）

诗中用典故或用前人成语，常有论者非之。锺嵘《诗品》称用典为"补假"，曰"古今胜语多非补假，皆由直寻"。他列举刘宋、齐、梁一些喜用典故的诗人，说他们的作品"殆同书抄"。至于用前人成语，则视同剽窃。北宋初流行"西昆体"，其诗大量引用李商隐成语，被讥为"挦扯"（撕裂摘取）李氏（见刘攽《中山诗话》）。这类批判的理论依据是：诗乃文学创作，不同于科学分析；科学分析可有共同结论，而诗之创作，即使咏同一事物，也必须有诗人自己的境界和情意，用自己的语言表达，避免雷同，更不能摹仿、依傍古人。

我看这种理论未必全是。大约除应制诗、酬唱和诗、没有真情只靠绮文丽句的爱情诗外，真正的诗人总是有自己的境界和情意的。他们借用典故成语，乃是为了扩大语言的艺术效果；借用之外还常化用以至反用，更好地表达己意。写诗要用形象思维，典故成语是前人凝固了的生动形象，诗人用它来描述自己的思想，可以丰富诗句的内涵，并引发读者联想；如"黍离"一语便会引发人们一连串的去国之思。当然，用典故或成语必须恰当，少用，不可多用，否则形成堆砌，读之扫兴。

唐初诗坛受齐梁骈体影响，用典嫌多。但自陈子昂首倡"汉魏风骨"，复古以革新，诗风大变；至于李白、杜甫，达于极盛。这些大家都很少用典故，偶用亦极恰当。唯于乐府、古风，叙事常用喻法，即用古典故事，喻写诗人所要写的感慨，颇引人入胜。如王维的《老将行》，分三大段，三十韵，几乎每句都用喻。写勇士少壮立功，以"少年十五二十时，步行夺取胡马骑"开篇，用"一身转战三千里，一剑曾当百万师"喻其战功，最后以"卫青不败由天幸，李广无功缘数奇"代替总评。写他们中年赋闲，以"自从弃置便衰朽，世事蹉跎成白首"开篇；以"路旁时卖故侯瓜，门前学种先生柳"喻其心情；结语"誓令疏勒出飞泉，不似颍川空使酒"，表示并不泄气。写老将复出："节使三河募年少，诏书五道出将军"，他们"愿得燕弓射大将，耻令越甲鸣吾君"；结语"莫嫌旧日云中守，犹堪一战立功勋"。这就把诗人所要表达的人世遭遇之感和勇士的爱国主义精神，全部变成生动的形象语言，符合美学要求，读之兴趣益然。李白的《梁甫吟》中抒发"何时见阳春"的苦闷，杜甫的《奉赠韦左丞丈》中写"儒冠多误身"的感慨，也是用这种喻的笔法，化抽象思维为形象语言，令人百读不厌。

进入中唐，除所谓"大历十才子"一派诗风婉丽，用典稍多外，大家白居易、韩愈、柳宗元、刘禹锡都是很少用典故或前人成语的。白居易诗力求平易，老妪能懂，《长恨歌》长篇，只用"小玉双成"一典，人以为难能可贵。韩愈"文起八代之衰"，要求"惟陈言之务去"，"词必己出"，因而诗句常奇峭险僻；又主张以文入诗，不免稍用故事。然其以文入诗，不是说理论证，而主要是写景或叙事。前者如《山石》，用事使人不觉察，后者如《石鼓文》，属于连续用喻之法。又因其诗气魄大，笔力足，感情洋溢，无堆砌感。柳宗元亦是古文大师，诗中偶用故事，乃是寓感慨于山水之间，使人不察觉，如《登柳州城楼寄漳汀封连四州刺史》，我前文已言及。刘禹锡兼采民歌，作《竹枝词》《杨柳枝词》，更不用典故。

中唐诗人用典故较多者唯李贺。李贺生不逢时，心怀愤慨，而想象力极强，天上人间，语多诡诞。如《浩歌》："南风吹山作平地，帝遣天吴移海水；王母桃花千遍红，彭祖巫咸几回死？"《秋来》："谁看青简一编书，不遣花虫粉空蠹"；"秋坟鬼唱鲍家诗，恨血千年土中碧"。然其体实出自《楚辞》，更加浪漫主义，非故意用典也。有些佳句，如"我有迷魂招不得，雄鸡一声天下白"（《致酒行》）；"衰兰送客咸阳道，天若有情天亦老"（《金铜仙人辞汉歌》），则是李贺的创造，而后人视为典故矣。

殆至晚唐，诗风有形式主义倾向，而诗人间有较大分歧。杜荀鹤、聂夷中等宗杜甫，坚持现实主义，不用典故。杜牧艺术修养成熟，抒情诗婉丽而明朗，善巧用典故，不同寻常。如"古往今来只如此，牛山何必泪沾衣"（《九日齐山登高》），慨叹今古，而齐景公牛山流涕事是在否定意义上用的。又如"一骑红尘妃子笑，无人知是荔枝来"（《过华清宫》）；"商女不知亡国恨，隔江犹唱后庭花"（《泊秦淮》），意在讽今，典故作反面教材。而杜牧这些佳句，后来人都引为典范。

李商隐大约是唐诗人中用典最多者。他善用形象思维，借典故以实写虚。如《寄令狐郎中》："嵩云秦树久离居，双鲤迢迢一纸书。休问梁园旧宾客，茂陵秋雨病相如。"叙离情，四句中用了两个喻、四个典，无一虚字，洵属佳构。他在悼亡诗、无题诗、爱情诗中用典尤多。情洋溢其间，故用事虽多，不觉堆砌。元好问责后之摹仿者曰："精纯全失义山真。"（《论诗绝句》）有了真情，便不怕假借。李商隐有首《无题》曰：

> 飒飒东风细雨来，芙蓉塘外有轻雷。
> 金蟾啮锁烧香入，玉虎牵丝汲井回。
> 贾氏窥帘韩掾少，宓妃留枕魏王才。
> 春心莫共花争发，一寸相思一寸灰。

此诗第三联贾氏偷看韩姓小吏，宓妃（甄妃）将枕头留给曹植，都明知道自身已属他人，这种爱情是可望而不可即的。第二联烧香的和汲井的女人，没说其所恋对象，但也是单相思、空相思而已。第一联"轻雷"句是用司马相如《长门赋》"雷殷殷而响起兮，声象君之车音"；宫女们都希望君车来临，但谁知轮到谁呢！所以尾联结论："春心莫共花争发，一寸相思一寸灰。"这诗也是把诗人要说的话全都化为形象语言，但用事过多，终觉得有点啰嗦。

李商隐的名篇《锦瑟》：

> 锦瑟无端五十弦，一弦一柱思华年。
> 庄生晓梦迷蝴蝶，望帝春心托杜鹃。
> 沧海月明珠有泪，蓝田日暖玉生烟。
> 此情可待成追忆，只是当时已惘然。

此诗中间二联用了四个典故，都属常见易懂。但与前首《无题》不同，前首《无题》是写一般女性的心理活动，而《锦瑟》是写李商隐本人的恋爱史。李商隐的恋爱史人们大体知道，但不能解释这四个典所指的是哪几件事，是一个人还是两个人、四个人。元好问所谓"佳人锦瑟怨华年"，"独恨无人作郑笺"。王世祯所谓"獭祭曾惊博奥殚，一篇锦瑟解人难"（《戏仿元遗山论诗绝句》）。李商隐诗中常有这种情况。用典而使人不能尽解，总是不好的。

用典故和用前人成语（二）

总的看，唐人用典故者并不多，用典故泛滥始于宋。至于用前人成语，唐人限于《诗经》、《楚辞》及赋，绝不用近人，宋人则视用唐诗为理所当然，甚至用本朝先贤。

宋初流行西昆体，以"挦扯"前人为能事。如杨亿的《梨》："汉苑谩传卢橘赋，骊山谁识荔支尘？九秋青女霜添味，五夜方诸月溜津。"卢橘赋用司马相如《上林赋》："于是乎卢橘夏熟。"荔枝尘用杜牧《过华清宫》："一骑红尘妃子笑，无人知是荔枝来。"青女霜用李商隐《霜月》："青女素娥俱耐冷，月中霜里斗婵娟。"方诸乃月下取露水之器，这里用陆龟蒙《自遣》："月娥如有相思泪，只待方诸寄两行。"堆砌辞藻，都与梨无关；这种诗真该打倒。

西昆体本来没什么生命力，到梅尧臣、苏舜钦及大文豪欧阳修兴起，就完全被打倒了。欧阳修诗用典不多，他自诩的佳作《戏答元珍》《芦山高》《明妃曲》都不用典。但他实是最会用典的，用得使人不觉。如《秋怀》："感事悲双鬓，包羞食万钱。鹿车终自驾，归去颍东田。"鹿车自是用刘伶故事。而前二句也有来历：第一句用王维"独坐悲双鬓"（《秋夜独坐》）；第二句用韦应物"邑有流亡愧俸钱"（《寄李儋》）。其中"包羞"出自《易·否》卦六三；而"食万钱"出自《晋书·何曾传》。但不劳笺注家费力，欧阳的诗原可自通。

更妙的是《啼鸟》，读者只注意其尾联："可笑灵均楚泽畔，离骚憔悴愁独醒。"这是用《楚辞·渔父》："屈原既放……行吟泽畔……颜色憔悴……曰众人皆醉我独醒。"短短两句包含半篇大文，而用得一字不差。其实欧阳公此诗三十六韵，用典故、成语和有出处之鸟名共十三处，人多不察觉。如"日暖众鸟皆嘤鸣"用《诗·伐木》"嘤其鸣矣"；"百舌未晓催天明"，百舌是一种鸟，立春后鸣声不已，夏至后则无声，见《本草纲目》卷四九。天明，此处意春天来了。大家王安石、苏轼、黄庭坚兴起，宋诗坛达于鼎盛，三公用故事各有自己的风格。

王安石"博极群书"，经、史、佛典、小说皆可入诗。但他反对直用，他说用书须"自出己意，借事以相发明"。此语见李壁《王荆文公诗笺注·窥园》。按《窥园》曰："策杖窥园日数巡，攀花弄草兴常新；董生只被公羊惑，肯信捐书一语真。"用董仲舒读书三年目不窥园事，而讥其为经所惑，这是王公己意。下句是用《晋书·范宁传》，范宁患目疾，求医于张湛，张湛告他医目之道，包括"捐读书"，即放弃读书。放弃读书是王公己意，不过"捐书"二字，未免牵强。

我看王安石用故事最好的是那些用又似不用，即使不知其出处照样能发明己意的诗句。如《北山》"细数落花因坐久，缓寻芳草得归迟"，用王维《过杨氏别业》"兴阑啼鸟唤，坐久落花多"；但亦可说不用，全为己意。又如《夜直》"春色恼人眠不得"句，化用罗隐《春日叶秀才曲江》"春色恼人遮不得"，但亦可说不用，全属己创。"借事以相发明"，最好的一首是王公的《书湖阴先生壁》（二首之一）：

> 茅檐长扫静无苔，花木成畦手自栽。
> 一水护田将绿绕，两山排闼送青来。

护田据《汉书·西域传序》："轮台、渠犁皆有田卒数百人，置使者校尉领护。"排闼据《汉书·樊哙传》："樊哙乃排闼直入。"这两句受到评论家高度赞扬，说是"史对史""汉对汉"的最佳诗句。其实，即使抛开所据，不查其出处，这一联仍是千古佳句。它的好处不在于根据史书，而在于是用生动的形象语言，表达出诗人创意。

苏轼诗风豪放，主张为文要如"行云流水"，挥洒自如。苏公遗诗四千余首，用典故成语者并不多，但因喜集中使用，曾引起人们用事多、獭祭之讥。如《和董传留别》："粗缯大布裹生涯，腹有诗书气自华。厌伴老儒烹瓠叶，强随举子踏槐花。"粗缯大布用陶渊明《杂诗》："御冬足大布，粗绨以应阳。"腹有诗书用韩愈《读书城南》："由腹有诗书。"瓠叶用《诗·小雅·瓠叶》："幡幡瓠叶，采之烹之。"踏槐花用《南部新书》卷一，言长安举子落第留京补课，曰"槐花黄，举子忙"。此诗七律，下四句也是句句用故事，显得拥塞。但也有用得很好的。如《有美堂暴雨》："游人脚底一声雷，满座顽云拨不开。天外黑风吹海立，浙东飞雨过江来。"顽云用陆龟蒙《苦雨》："顽云猛雨更相欺"。海立用杜甫《太清宫赋》："四海之水皆立。"飞雨过江用谢朓《观朝雨》："朔风吹飞雨，萧条江上来。"此诗亦七律，下四句也是句句用故事，但用得很恰当，都表现苏公本意，也不失"行云流水"之势。

苏轼的诗特长不在于用典，而在于用喻。如《百步洪》写洪流："有如兔走鹰隼落，骏马下注千丈坡。断弦离柱箭脱手，飞电过隙珠翻荷。"一连串的生动形象的比喻加强了文章行云流水之势。喻可用故事，也可不用故事。如《与潘郭二生出郊寻春》："人似秋鸿来有信，事如春梦了无痕。"笺注家可寻找"秋鸿""春梦"的出处，其实徒劳，它们完全是苏公的创造。"欲把西湖比西子"是苏公的一大创造，千年来人所驰誉。还有一首《和子由渑池怀旧》，也是苏公一大创造：

> 人生到处知何似？应似飞鸿踏雪泥。
>
> 泥上偶然留指爪，鸿飞那复计东西。

从此，"雪泥鸿爪"变成了文人经常引用的"典故"。

黄庭坚是宋大家中用典故和前人成语最多的。他的理论是："老杜作诗，退之作文，无一字无来处；盖后人读书少，故谓韩杜自作此语耳。古之能为文章者，真能陶冶万物，虽取古人之陈言入于翰墨，如灵丹一粒，点铁成金也。"（《豫章黄先生文集·答洪驹父书》）依此理论，作诗不必自创意境，只取古人陈言，加以改造，便成无一字无来处的佳构。这正是后来长期占据宋诗坛的以黄庭坚为宗主的"江西诗派"的纲领，但并非黄公本意。《江西诗社宗派图》是吕本中写的，吕小于黄公四十岁，《宗派图》问世时黄公可能已不在人世了。黄公诗宗杜甫也宗韩愈，韩愈是主张"陈言务去""词必己出"的。黄庭坚诗的特点就是始终坚持自己的见解，特别是他的政见和禅学见解。因而他所谓"点铁成金"，就是把古人的诗句转化成自己的见解。所以元好问说："论诗宁下涪翁（黄公）拜，未作江西社里人。"

黄庭坚有首《病起荆江亭即事》（十首之一）："翰墨场中老伏波，菩提坊里病维摩。近人积水无鸥鹭，时有归牛浮鼻过。"这是他被贬谪后病中之作，以政界中的老将、佛学中的维摩自况，不变初衷。末句用唐人陈泳："隔岸水牛浮鼻渡"，近人指当权的变法派，他们找不到真才，我只如老牛浮鼻而去。黄庭坚有首《寄黄几复》：

> 我居北海君南海，寄雁传书谢不能。
>
> 桃李春风一杯酒，江湖夜雨十年灯。
>
> 持家但有四立壁，治病不蕲三折肱。
>
> 想得读书头已白，隔溪猿哭瘴溪藤。

时黄几复在广州，黄庭坚在德州，故用《左传》僖公四年"君处北海，寡人处南海"，示分离而已，无他含义。"四立壁"用《史记·司马相如传》"家居徒四壁立"，三折肱用《左传》定公十三年"三折肱知为良医"，皆指家境清寒。黄庭坚在《几复墓志铭》中称几复治六经，喜庄老；作此诗时在广州任教授，故曰"想得读书头已白"。末句用杜甫《九日》（五首之一）"殊方日落玄猿哭"，瘴溪指广州，盖慰问之意。

黄庭坚又有首《登快阁》，用事颇工：

> 痴儿了却公家事，快阁东西倚晚晴。
> 落木千山天远大，澄江一道月分明。
> 朱弦已为佳人绝，青眼聊因美酒横。
> 万里归船弄长笛，此心吾与白鸥盟。

快阁在黄庭坚故乡江西太和县，临澄江，后人在此建黄庭坚祠。痴儿句用《晋书·傅咸传》，夏侯济与傅咸书曰："生子痴，了官事，官事未易了也，了事正作痴，复为快耳。"此属僻典，但语甚恰，与下联呵成一气。朱弦句用锺子期死，俞伯牙破琴绝弦事，佳人指佳士。青眼句用《晋书·阮籍传》，嵇喜来吊，阮籍白眼视之；嵇康赍酒来吊，阮乃作青眼视之。"白鸥盟"用杜甫《奉赠韦左丞丈》"白鸥没浩荡，万里谁能驯"。

金人占领中原，士子南渡，国破家亡，诗风转向现实主义。大家如杨万里、范成大、陆游，均摆脱江西诗派雕琢之习，用典不多。杨万里虽作《江西宗派诗序》，他本人的诗则新鲜活泼，力求平易，用俗语而不用典故。他有首《怀故园海棠》，以两年未见故园海棠为憾，曰"只欠翠纱红映肉，两年寒食负先生"。用苏轼海棠诗"朱唇得酒晕生脸，翠袖卷纱红映肉"。范成大喜用佛典，但行文明白，如"纵有千年铁门限，终须一个土馒头"（《重九日行营寿藏之地》），通俗易懂，为妙玉所欣赏（《红楼梦》六十三回）。

伟大的爱国主义诗人陆游在《示子遹》中说："我初学诗日，但欲工藻绘。中年始少悟，渐若窥宏大……汝果欲学诗，工夫在诗外。""工夫在诗外"，就是"纸上得来终觉浅，绝知此事要躬行"（《冬夜读书示子聿》）。诗要来自生活实践，不能资"书以为诗"。

然而，陆游的诗中用典用事还是有的，但不是为藻绘、寻来处，而是适应此情此景。又善用前人概念组成新词，令人不察觉出处。如《游山西村》："山重水复疑无路，柳暗花明又一村"；化用王安石"青山缭绕疑无路，忽见千帆隐映来"（《江上》），但全如己造。又如《临安春雨初霁》：

"小楼一夜听春雨，深巷明朝卖杏花"，笺注家也可找到"杏花"的来处，然实系陆公己造。唐婉被迫与陆游离婚后四十年，偶在沈园重遇，陆游作《沈园》（二绝之一）诗：

> 城上斜阳画角哀，沈园无复旧池台。
>
> 伤心桥下春波绿，曾是惊鸿照影来。

末句用曹植《洛神赋》"翩若惊鸿"，但没有人这样看，而是把"惊鸿照影"作为陆氏语当典故用。陆游有篇《书愤》：

> 早岁那知世事艰，中原北望气如山。
>
> 楼船夜雪瓜洲渡，铁马秋风大散关。
>
> 塞上长城生自许，镜中衰鬓已先斑。
>
> 出师一表真名世，千载谁堪伯仲间。

此诗中，瓜洲（采石矶）、大散关都是兵家重地，连同塞上长城，都可找出战役的典故，但又何必去找呢？诸葛亮的《出师表》以及杜甫对诸葛亮"伯仲之间见伊吕"的评语，人所共知。总之，名家的好诗，都是创造，若仔细寻求，又都可以"无一字无来处"，但费力去寻出处有什么意思呢？

宋词与檃括（一）

宋词家常剪裁前人尤其是唐人诗句入词，有如诗人之用典故，称檃括。这在婉约派、格律派词人，主要是用前人诗句来修饰词语，使之典雅华丽，取得艺术效果；然运用不当或用得过多，便成堆砌。而在豪放派词人，檃括是为表达复杂的思想感情，丰富词语的内涵，一般不多用。此外，度曲家创制词牌时缀拾前人遗韵，也称檃括，本文不论。

宋初百余年间，晏殊、欧阳修领袖词坛。他们远韶《花间》，近袭冯延巳，延续五代艳科词风，唯艺术表现上有所建树，则或得力于檃括。

晏殊有首《蝶恋花》，尾句"浓睡觉来莺乱语，惊残好梦无寻处"。此用金昌绪《春怨》诗："打起黄莺儿，莫教枝上啼。啼时惊妾梦，不得到辽西。"精简恰当，用得好。晏殊有首《山亭柳·赠歌者》，首言"家住西秦"，用曹植《侍太子坐》"歌者出西秦"。这歌者是位女高音，"偶学念奴声调，有时高遏行云。"用《列子·汤问》："声震林木，响遏行云。"写歌者少年得意，"蜀锦缠头无数，不负辛勤。"用白居易《琵琶行》："五陵年少争缠头，一曲红绡不知数。"然而歌者年长色衰，不得不奔走衣食，"数年来往咸京道，残杯冷炙谩消魂"。用杜甫《奉赠韦左丞丈》："残杯与冷炙，到处潜悲辛。"最后，她的歌已不合时尚，终被淘汰；"若有知音见采，不辞遍唱阳春"。用宋玉《对楚王问》："其为阳春白雪"，高级歌曲之意。这首词暗喻格调高者难容于世俗，有现实意义。但全词用事偏多，有堆砌感。

欧阳修古文大师，笔酣墨饱，不假雕饰，故其作词虽宗艳体，而不用檃括，偶用亦极自然，形同己句。他有首《南歌子》："走来窗下笑相扶，爱道画眉深浅入时无。"用朱庆余《闺意上张水部》："妆罢低声问夫婿，画眉深浅入时无。"而读者常视为欧阳己句。

使欧晏词风发生变革者始于柳永，中经张先、晏几道，至于大家王安石、苏轼，完成革新，也使北宋词学达于顶峰。

柳永发展了长调，创慢词，用铺叙手法。又不避俚语，而很少用典故檃括，偶有用时有如未用，人不易察觉。如《八声甘州》咏秋景："是处红衰绿减，苒苒物华休"，不细察不知是用李商隐《赠荷花》："翠减红衰愁煞人。"又如《蝶恋花·独倚危楼》："也拟疏狂图一醉，对酒当歌，强乐还无味。衣带渐宽终不悔，为伊消得人憔悴。"对酒当歌自是用曹操《短歌行》。衣带句脍炙人口，王国维《人间词话》亦大加赞赏，皆以为柳永自创，实则来自古诗"相去日已远，衣带日已缓"；人不觉耳。

王安石用前人成语较多，然用得恰当。他有首《桂枝香》：

　　登临送目，正故国晚秋，天气初肃。千里澄江似练，翠峰如簇。归帆去棹残阳里，背西风、酒旗斜矗。彩舟云淡，星河鹭起，画图难足。

　　念往昔、繁华竞逐。叹门外楼头，悲恨相续。千古凭高，对此漫嗟荣辱。六朝旧事随流水，但寒烟、衰草凝绿。至今商女，时时犹唱，后庭遗曲。

此词咏"故国"即金陵之兴衰。天气初肃，用《诗·七月》"九月肃霜"，人不察觉。澄江似练，直用谢朓《晚登三山还望京邑》"澄江静如练"，因谢诗原是望金陵，甚恰当。门外楼头句用杜牧《台城曲》"门外韩擒虎，楼头张丽华"，意内忧外患，陈后主亡国之由，用得不露骨。苏轼《虢国夫人夜游图》亦用此事曰："当时亦笑张丽华，不知门外韩擒虎"，用得不如王词含蓄。王词六朝旧事句用窦巩《南游感兴》"伤心欲问前朝事，惟见江流去不回"，流水二字恰当。结尾三句用杜牧《泊秦淮》："商女不知亡国恨，隔江犹唱后庭花。"两句变成三句，未免化简为繁。但用"后庭遗曲"似有意兼指陈后主原辞："玉树后庭花，花开不复久"，人以为是亡国之谶。

　　柳永、王安石的革新并未冲破"词为艳科"的藩篱，到苏轼则创豪放风格，为词学开辟一条新路。苏词又突破词牌音律的束缚，并倡"以诗为词"，使词兼有言志咏怀的功能，所以达北宋词坛顶峰。苏词既属大雅，并不多用前人诗句，每有所用皆有新意，概属创造。如他有首《水龙吟》咏杨花："抛家傍路，思量却是，无情有思。"此用韩愈《晚春》："杨花榆荚无才思，惟解漫天作雪飞"。但将无才思化为无情有思，完全是新意。又有首《浣溪沙》是苏公被贬黄州时作，结尾云："门前流水尚能西，休将白发唱黄鸡。"这是用白居易《醉歌》："黄鸡催晓丑时鸣，白日催年西时没。腰间红绶系未稳，镜里朱颜看已失。"不但化繁为简，而且含意全新了。白诗悲年未老而罢官，苏词则潇洒坦荡，仕途波折，如东水西流，安知非福。又有首《永遇乐》，叙彭城夜宿燕子楼梦盼盼事曰："纮如三鼓，铿然一叶，黯黯梦云惊断。"纮，鼓声，用《晋书·邓攸传》引吴人歌："纮如打五鼓，鸡鸣天欲曙。"一叶，轻微之声。梦云，用宋玉《高唐赋》，神女"且为朝云，暮为行雨"。全句用了三个典，但词意自明，直如未用。

　　苏轼有首《念奴娇·中秋》，其下阕曰：

　　我醉拍手狂歌，举杯邀月，对影成三客。起舞徘徊风露下，今夕不知何夕。便欲乘风，翻然归去，何用骑鹏翼。水晶宫里，一声吹断横笛。

举杯邀月句用李白《月下独酌》："举杯邀明月，对影成三人。"今夕何夕，用《诗·绸缪》："今夕何夕，见此良人。"何用骑鹏翼，用《庄子·逍遥游》："鹏之背不知其几千里也。怒而飞，其翼若垂天之云。"用了三事，恍如未用。

苏轼又有首《满江红·寄鄂州朱使君寿昌》，其上阕曰：

> 江汉西来，高楼下，葡萄深碧。犹自带、岷峨云浪，锦江春色。君是南山遗爱守，我为剑外思归客。对此间风物岂无情，殷勤说。

江汉指长江、汉水，楼指黄鹤楼，葡萄深碧用李白《襄阳歌》："遥看汉水鸭头绿，恰似葡萄初酦醅。"锦江春色用杜甫《登楼》："锦江春色来天地。"均是苏公故乡四川景物，故曰剑外思归客，用杜甫"剑外忽传收蓟北"（《闻官军收河南河北》）。四处用李杜，不觉堆砌，因用辞极简，且恰当。

杰出的女词人李清照，在语言艺术方面可与北宋和南宋所有词学大家媲美。她很少用故事，而每用必有新创。她有首《点绛唇》写一个"蹴罢秋千"的少女："见有人来，袜刬金钗溜，和羞走。倚门回首，却把青梅嗅。"原来李煜的"刬袜步香阶，手提金缕鞋"（《菩萨蛮》），靡语也；"佳人舞点金钗溜，酒恶时拈花蕊嗅"（《浣溪沙》），腻语也。到李清照手里完全变了，她仅用"袜刬金钗溜"五字写出天真烂漫少女和羞走的形态。青梅暗用李白《长干行》"郎骑竹马来，绕床弄青梅"，有同样效果。

李清照有首《渔家傲·记梦》：

> 天接云涛连晓雾，星河欲转千帆舞。仿佛梦魂归帝所。闻天语，殷勤问我归何处？
>
> 我报路长嗟日暮，学诗谩有惊人句。九万里风鹏正举。风休住，蓬

舟吹取三山去。

路长嗟日暮句用《离骚》"欲少留此灵琐兮，日忽忽其将暮"，"路漫漫其修远兮，吾将上下而求索"。但与通常用法不同，她是用来说明下句"学诗谩有惊人句"的，空有高超的才学，却路长日暮，没有用武之地。九万里风鹏用《庄子·逍遥游》："鹏之徙于南冥也……抟扶摇而上者九万里。"李词也不是用原意，而是要"风休住"，吹到三神山去。三山即蓬莱、方丈、瀛洲，见《史记·封禅书》。

宋词与檃括（二）

南宋词坛实由两大派分据。一派是发展了苏轼词风的爱国思潮派，拥有张元幹、张孝祥、陈亮、刘克庄等名家，并有杰出的大师辛弃疾领袖群伦，使宋词进入又一高峰。另一派是以姜夔为代表的格律派。他们讲究音韵，自度新曲，辞藻华美而严谨，工艳词而比较庄重。格律派才子众多，并有张炎等理论家，直延至宋末元初。

辛弃疾词喜用典故，檃括不多，而善于把前人诗句简化成故事，作典用。如《祝英台近·晚春》："宝钗分，桃叶渡，烟柳暗南浦。"宝钗分来自白居易《长恨歌》："钗留一股合一扇，钗擘黄金合分钿。"这里变成三个字的典。桃叶渡原是王献之诗："桃叶复桃叶，渡江不用楫；但渡无所苦，我自迎接汝。"这里也化为三个字的典。南浦来自江淹《别赋》："送君南浦，伤如之何。"这里化为二字典，作送别处解。这样做的好处是把要叙述的事情形象化，属美学原则。

辛弃疾有首《贺新郎》，也是送别的词：

绿树听鹈鴂。更那堪、鹧鸪声住，杜鹃声切。啼到春归无寻处，苦恨芳菲都歇。算未抵、人间离别。马上琵琶关塞黑，更长门翠辇辞金阙。看燕燕，送归妾。

将军百战声名裂，向河梁、回头万里，故人长绝。易水萧萧西风冷，满座衣冠似雪。正壮士、悲歌未彻。啼鸟还知如许恨，料不啼清泪长啼血。谁共我。醉明月？

琵琶句，用王昭君远嫁胡邦故事，见《李义山诗集》卷中《王昭君》诗。长门用陈阿娇被黜离宫故事。燕燕句来自《诗·邶风》："燕燕于飞，差池其羽。之子于归，远送于野。"其故事是卫庄公立妾戴妫之子完为世子，完继位后被杀，牵连戴妫被送归娘家。故毛传曰"送归妾"。辛弃疾此词是送别他被罢官的族弟辛茂嘉，却用了三个宫廷贵妇的故事，虽都属被迫告别，终觉有点不协。下面，向河梁，据李陵《与苏武诗（三首之三）》："携手上河梁，游子暮何之？"易水句据荆轲告别歌："风萧萧兮易水寒，壮士一去兮不复还。"这两处都是作典故用。

辛弃疾又有首《贺新郎》，是他独坐停云堂小酌，诵陶渊明思念亲友的《停云》诗，哀叹自己抗敌救亡同志大都凋零，曰：

> 甚矣吾衰矣！怅平生，交游零落，只今余几？白发空垂三千丈，一笑人间万事。问何物，能令公喜？我见青山多妩媚，料青山、见我应如是。情与貌，略相似。
>
> 一樽搔首东窗里，想渊明《停云》诗就，此时风味。江左沉酣求名者，岂识浊醪妙理？回首叫、云飞风起。不恨古人吾不见，恨古人、不见吾狂耳。知我者，二三子。

甚矣吾衰矣，用《论语·述而》："甚矣吾衰也，久矣吾不复梦见周公。"乃吾道不行之意。白发空垂句，用李白《秋浦歌》："白发三千丈，缘愁似个长。"都是引上句使人联想全联，用得好。搔首东窗句，用陶渊明《停云》："静寄东轩，春醪独抚。良朋悠邈，搔首延伫。"也是一句话带出陶诗全境。江左沉酣句用苏轼《追和陶渊明诗·饮酒（二十首之三）》："江左风流人，醉中亦求名。"苏诗"江左"指南朝，是陶诗原意。辛词"江左"则指南宋，士子们只热衷于名位。二三子语亦出《论语》，这里指抗敌救亡的同志太少了。

浙东的陈亮，主张抗战，词风亦与辛弃疾一致，属于二三子之列。陈亮来上饶访辛弃疾，拟留十日，并约同去鹅湖与朱熹论学，而陈亮竟提前回浙江去了。次日辛弃疾急追，以雪深路滑未果，乃作《贺新郎》寄陈亮，其下阕曰：

> 佳人重约还轻别。怅清江、天寒不渡，水深冰合。路断车轮生四角，此地行人销骨。问谁使、君来愁绝？铸就而今相思错，料当初，费尽人间铁。长夜笛，莫吹裂。

佳人指陈亮，这里佳人指佳士。车轮生四角，用陆龟蒙《古意》："愿得双车轮，一夜生四角。"意盼车轮转不动，把行人留下。行人销骨，用孟郊《答韩愈李观别因献张徐州》："富别愁在颜，贫别愁销骨。"这两事均用原意，但属僻典，似不足取。下两句解答愁字，用苏轼《赠钱道人》："不知几州铁，铸此一大错。"原是用铁来铸错刀，苏诗借用为铸成错误，错误大，要用几州铁。而辛弃疾又转借为铸成"相思错"，这个相思错更大，要费尽人间铁。辛陈莫逆之交，怎么成为"相思错"了呢，人多不解。

然而陈亮是完全了解的。陈亮接到辛弃疾的《贺新郎》后，写了一首《贺新郎·寄辛幼安和见怀韵》，说"只使君、从来与我，话头多合"，而结尾说："九转丹砂牢拾取，管精金、只是寻常铁。龙共虎，应声裂。"虽都是寻常铁炼出来的精品，但有如龙虎之异。原来陈亮有唯物论倾向，主张功利主义，与正统派朱熹在"义利王霸"问题上有严重的争论。辛弃疾思想比较保守，接近朱熹。陈与辛在抗战和词风上完全一致，而基本思想却犹如龙与虎，是不同的。

陈亮不久又有一首《贺新郎·酬辛幼安再用韵见寄》，结尾说："天地洪炉谁扇鞴？算于中、安得长坚铁。淝水破，关东裂。"洪炉语出《庄子·大宗师》："今以天地为大炉，造化为大冶。"而实用贾谊《服鸟赋》："且夫天地为炉兮，造化为工。"同一社会，陶冶出不同人才。所以虽有淝水之战，关东仍然四分五裂。

一年后，陈亮又写了一首《贺新郎·怀辛幼安用前韵》，结尾云："天下适安耕且老，看买犁、卖剑平家铁。壮士泪，肺肝裂。"不谈思想分歧，也不谈抗敌大业了，卖剑买犁去归耕吧。

格律大师姜夔，运用辞藻比较严谨，檃括简练而轻巧。他有首名篇《扬州慢》是自度曲，写两次被金兵蹂躏后的扬州：

淮左名都，竹西佳处，解鞍少驻初程。过春风十里，尽荠麦青青。自胡马窥江去后，废池乔木，犹厌言兵。渐黄昏，清角吹寒，都在空城。

杜郎俊赏，算而今，重到须惊。纵豆蔻词工，青楼梦好，难赋深情。二十四桥仍在，波心荡，冷月无声。念桥边红药，年年知为谁生？

竹西佳处，见杜牧《题扬州禅智寺》："谁知竹西路，歌吹是扬州。"寺旁有竹西亭，为一景观。春风十里，用杜牧《赠别》（二首之一）："春风十里扬州路，捲上珠帘总不如。"豆蔻词，指上述《赠别》中"娉娉婷婷十三余，豆蔻梢头二月初"一联。青楼梦用杜牧《遣怀》："十年一觉扬州梦，赢得青楼薄幸名。"二十四桥用杜牧《寄扬州韩绰判官》："二十四桥明月夜，玉人何处教吹箫。"

此词上阕写兵燹后的扬州，废池乔木，清角吹寒，有黍离之感，素受称道。用杜牧"春风十里扬州路，捲上珠帘总不如"，而将下句改为"尽荠麦青青"，实暗用《诗·王风》"彼黍离离，彼稷之苗"；化绮丽为悲壮，尤见工力。但下阕连用杜牧《遣怀》《二十四桥》，"青楼梦好，难赋深情"，又变成怀念扬州过去的繁华绮梦了。以致"犹厌言兵"一语令人莫解，是悲愤侵略者的猖狂呢，还是怀念升平厌谈兵事呢？姜夔的词常有这种暧昧不明之处，所以王国维说读姜词"如雾里看花"（《人间词话》）。而这些不明朗处又多半是檃括引起的。

姜夔有两首被张炎《词源》誉为"前无古人、后无来者"的咏梅词《暗香》与《疏影》；两首均自度曲，曲名出自林逋《山园小梅》（二首之一）："疏影横斜水清浅，暗香浮动月黄昏。"

暗　香

旧时月色，算几番照我，梅边吹笛？唤起玉人，不管清寒与攀摘。何逊而今渐老，都忘却、春风词笔。但怪得、竹外疏花，香冷入瑶席。

江国，正寂寂。叹寄与路遥，夜雪初积。翠樽易泣，红萼无言耿相忆。长记曾携手处，千树压、西湖寒碧。又片片、吹尽也，几时见得？

疏　影

　　苔枝缀玉。有翠禽小小，枝上同宿。客里相逢，篱角黄昏，无言自倚修竹。昭君不惯胡沙远，但暗忆、江南江北。想佩环、月夜归来，化作此花幽独。

　　犹记深宫旧事，那人正睡里，飞近蛾绿。莫似春风，不管盈盈，早与安排金屋。还教一片随波去，又却怨、玉笼哀曲。等恁时、重觅幽香，已入小窗横幅。

《暗香》唤起玉人句，用贺铸《浣溪沙》："玉人和月折梅花。"何逊句，用杜甫《和裴迪登蜀州东亭送客》："东阁官梅动诗兴，还如何逊在扬州。"南梁何逊做扬州法曹，有咏梅诗。竹外疏花，用苏轼《和秦太虚梅花》："竹外一枝斜更好。"寄语路遥，用陆凯《寄范晔诗》："折梅逢驿使，寄与陇头人。"路程遥远之意。此词是借咏梅怀念一位雪夜在西湖相识的故人。用何逊、路遥，也许是位文友；用玉人、翠尊红萼，更像是位情妓。这都是姜词"如雾里看花"处。

《疏影》"苔枝""翠禽"，笺注家曾找出所据，属僻典，无甚意义。无言自倚修竹，用杜甫《佳人》："天寒翠袖薄，日暮倚修竹。"昭君句用王昭君出塞事，但不知为何写"江南江北"，而非塞南塞北。想佩环句，用杜甫《咏怀古迹》："画图省识春风面，环珮空归月夜魂。"深宫旧事，指宋武帝女寿阳公主卧于檐下，有梅花落额上，成梅花妆事，见《太平御览·时序部》。盈盈，用《古诗》："盈盈楼上女，皎皎当窗牖。"指美女，与梅无关。安排金屋用汉武帝故事，金屋藏娇，亦与梅无关。玉龙哀曲，用李白《与史郎中饮听黄鹤楼上吹笛》："黄鹤楼中吹玉笛，江城五月落梅花。"玉笼指笛，哀曲指《梅花落》曲。这首《疏影》何意？历来论者多注意所引王昭君故事，并把"想佩环月夜归来，化作此花幽独"作为主题。昭君客死变成梅花，是从王建《塞上梅》推出，王诗云："天山路旁一株梅，年年花发黄云下。昭君已殁汉使回，前后征人唯系马？"但咏梅词变成哀王昭君又有何命意，仍不知道，只能雾里看花。

濯足四谈

苏轼的自然观和人生观

苏轼是李白以后第一个浪漫主义豪放派诗人。豪放，用苏轼的话说就是"常行于所当行，常止于不可不止"（《与谢民师推官书》）。而在诗文中，豪放不仅是一种风格，它也反映作者的自然观和人生观，尤其是在不得意时发泄感情的诗文里，用苏轼的话说就是"寄妙理于豪放之外"（《书吴道子画后》）。

苏轼 22 岁举进士，入仕太常博士。但在神宗时，新党得势，苏轼不得参与中枢决策，被下放为地方官，历杭州、密州、徐州、湖州、扬州等地，以致他在《龟山》中说"身行万里半天下"，而对汴京总是"地隔中原劳北望"。他每次下放都是从淮水东南行，故晚年作《淮上早发》，有"此生定向江湖老，默数淮中十往来"句（尚有一次去蜀也是往来淮上，未计入）。因而对淮山淮水很有感情，在《出颍口初见淮山》中说"平淮忽迷天远近，青山久与船低昂"，"波平风软望不到，故人久立烟苍茫"；都是他最得意的诗句（他在《李思训画长江绝岛图》中又作"沙平风软望不到，孤山久与船低昂"）。笔法绝妙，也反映他敞开胸怀拥抱自然，或寓己意于自然、天人合一的自然观。

神宗元丰二年（1079）的乌台诗案，苏轼以其诗"讪谤"新政，被捕入狱，几至死罪，最后"责授检校水部员外郎、黄州团练副使，本州安置，不得签书公事"（《续资治通鉴长编》卷三〇一，元丰二年十二月庚申）。就是说做一个不准离开黄州、不能批示公文的诏除散官。他写了一篇《初到黄州》：

> 自笑平生为口忙，老来事业转荒唐。
> 长江绕郭知鱼美，好竹连山觉笋香。
> 逐客不妨员外置，诗人例作水曹郎。
> 只惭无补丝毫事，尚费官家压酒囊。

水曹郎是指过去的诗人何逊、张籍等被贬后都做过水部郎官。压酒囊是说宋制对诏除散官发给一些实物如废弃的压酒囊以代替部分薪给。此诗用语戏谑，未免牢骚。但它把长江、茂竹写成享受实际的美，把做员外、水部郎看成享受生活清闲，表现了他的自然观和人生观；这就是：要适应环境，但不为物累；要自己驾驭生活，不让生活驾驭自己。

在苏轼眼中，大自然的美及其功能是多样性的，并因人而异。他有首脍炙人口的名作《题西林壁》，但人们多注意其下联："不识庐山真面目，只缘身在此山中"，而忽视其上联："横看成岭侧成峰，远近高低各不同。"其实，庐山的美或其真面目就是成岭成峰、多姿多样，就是要人们从不同角度去观察，去领会。他在杭州时有首《法惠寺横翠阁》也说："朝见吴山横，暮见吴山纵。吴山故多态，转侧为君容。"大自然提供了多样性的美，人们"游于物之外"，随缘自适，便可"无所往而不乐"（《超然台记》）。苏轼误以为"三国周郎赤壁"即在黄州，他写《念奴娇·赤壁怀古》是"大江东去，乱石穿空，惊涛拍岸，卷起千堆雪"，人们感到周公瑾雄姿英发的形象。但在《前赤壁赋》中，这里变成了"清风徐来，水波不兴"，游船的主人、客和歌者也都心平如水，与"造物者"共适。而三个月后的《后赤壁赋》，赤壁恬然，主和客都羽化而登仙了。三国周郎赤壁谁也没见过，写的都是作者自己的自然观。

社会生活方面，无论是下放、谪贬，以至充边海南，苏轼并不孤单，到处都有他同政见的"故人"、同命运的"客"，还有大批在文学艺术上追随他的"诸生"。因而他不颓唐、悲观，也不想退隐山林或乘桴于海，而是看透世俗，热乎乎地去享受生活，认认真真地修身养性，耻事干谒，以乐终年。元丰四年（1081），他在黄州有首《与潘郭二生出郊寻春》，其下阕表白了他这种旷世达俗的人生观：

> 江城白酒三杯酽，野老苍颜一笑温。
>
> 已约年年为此会，故人不用赋招魂。

末句是借用宋玉赋《招魂》希冀屈原回到楚国的故事（《楚辞章句》中王逸之说），意思是说：我已安于这里的饮乐生活，老朋友们不用可怜我而设法把我招回朝廷了。这和韩愈、柳宗元不同。韩愈以谏迎佛骨触怒唐宪宗，被贬岭南潮阳，他的侄孙赶到蓝关来送行，他作《左迁至蓝关示侄孙湘》曰："云横秦岭家何在？雪拥蓝关马不前。知汝远来应有意，好收吾骨瘴江边。"这里韩愈完全失望了。不过，后来他还是被召回，以吏部侍郎致仕。柳宗元因党争失败，被贬柳州，在《登柳州城楼寄漳汀封连四州刺史》中说："岭树重遮千里目，江流曲似九回肠。共来百粤文身地，犹自音书滞一乡。"这是说不见长安，愁肠满怀，召我们回朝的圣谕被朝中的权宦扣留了（解见《濯足三谈》"音书"条）。不过，他还是终死柳州，致劳韩愈撰《祭柳子厚文》和《柳子厚墓志铭》。

元丰五年苏轼47岁，在黄州东坡筑堂，自称"东坡居士"。同年作诗寄46岁就致仕作居士的吴德仁，称赞他"谁似濮阳公子（即吴德仁）贤，饮酒食肉自得仙。平生寓物不留物，在家学得忘家禅"（《寄吴德仁兼简陈季常》）。自身以外的事情，饮食、男女、做官以至拜佛，都是物；人总是在物中生活，即寓于物。但要按自己的意志寓于物，像吴德仁那样饮酒吃肉在家读经，才能得到物的乐趣。否则，留于物，即意志受物的支配，那就成为物累、物病。苏轼进一步解释说："寓意于物，虽微物足以为乐，虽尤物不足以为病。留意于物，虽微物足以为病，虽尤物不足以为乐。"（《宝绘堂记》）

尤物，一般指有特殊功能能使人大乐和使人大病的女人。陈鸿在《长恨歌传》中称杨贵妃为尤物，自不待言。荔枝是微物，而苏轼称它为尤物，则是因为杨贵妃爱吃，以至它能大病天下。苏轼在广东惠州作《四月十一日初食荔支》曰："不知天公有意无，遣此尤物生海隅。"不久又作《荔支

285

叹》："我愿天公怜赤子，莫生尤物为疮痏。"

　　哲宗时苏轼陷于元祐党祸，绍圣元年（1094）下放定州，落两职；迁英州，未到任；再贬惠州安置；绍圣四年，责受琼州别驾，渡海，到海南岛的儋州，那真是天涯海角了。元符三年（1100），哲宗死，徽宗继位，诏原来元祐谪官都迁回内郡居住。苏轼作《儋耳》，其下阕曰：

> 野老已歌丰岁语，除书欲放逐臣回。
>
> 残年饱饭东坡老，一壑能专万事灰。

这时苏轼已65岁，在儋州困守三年，眼光有点小了。此诗残年句借用杜甫"但使残年饱吃饭"（《病后过王倚饮赠歌》），意思说回大陆有饭吃就行了。"一壑能专万事灰"，通常是说专有一壑的渔产就不要别的东西了，眼光更窄小。但古人"一丘一壑"说的本意并非如此。晋陆士龙《逸民赋序》说："古之逸民，或轻天下，细万物，而欲专一丘之欢，擅一壑之美，岂不以身胜于宇宙而心恬于纷华者哉？"人老了，不管新皇帝上台后的大事，只看好我身边的微物就行了；一个人自身心灵的美好较之世界纷纷大事更为重要。这是苏轼晚年对寓于物而不留于物哲学一种新的理解。

　　得诏后，苏轼立即渡海去廉州，作《六月二十日夜渡海》：

> 参横斗转欲三更，苦雨终风也解晴。
>
> 云散月明谁点缀？天容海色本澄清。
>
> 空余鲁叟乘桴意，粗识轩辕奏乐声。
>
> 九死南荒吾不恨，兹游奇绝冠平生。

这诗写得好极了。参横斗转用曹植《善哉行》"月没参横，北斗阑干"，喻天亮了。苦雨，苏轼在黄州有《寒食雨》"今年又苦雨"；又《吴中田妇叹》"霜风来时雨如泻，杷头出菌镰生衣；眼枯泪尽雨不尽，忍见黄穗卧青泥"。还有多首与子由对榻叹连夜雨的诗。终风用《诗·邶风·终风》，毛传解"终日之风"；唯原诗喻卫庄公暴戾，此处亦有狂爆意。妙在"也解晴"三字，晴谐情，苦雨终风，自己也懂得该停歇了。第二联"云散月明谁点缀"，用《晋书·谢重传》，谢重以为夜月明净"不如微云点缀"。其实苏轼是反用或不用其事。云散去，月明净了，是谁主使的？答案是"天容海色本澄清"——我们本来是清白的，元祐冤案早该平反了。第三联，像孔子那种乘桴浮于海的想法变成多余的了，因为我已"粗识轩辕奏乐声"。轩辕黄帝的国乐是《咸池》，谁也没听见过。不过咸池是日浴出海处，屈原说："与女（汝）沐兮咸池，晞女发兮阳之阿"（《九歌·少司命》），那一定是个洋洋融融的大池子。苏轼是把渡海的感觉比作渡咸池，并以此喻《咸池》之声，所以说"粗识"。这段海路我去海口时曾见过，浩浩荡荡，而非波涛汹涌。我想作者意思是，我已浩然正气地回来了。最后一联"九死南荒吾不恨，兹游奇绝冠平生"，则有点儿不够真实。此游奇绝是不错，但若说因此就愿意老死海南，绝非苏轼本意。他是切盼回朝的，但次年走到常州，就不幸病逝了。呜呼！

一锄集

外五首

一锄明月种梅花，几度东风细雨斜。

老去应知疏影浅，金波淡扫亦清佳。

1946 年 3 月洪达琳与我结婚，父亲寄赠牙章一枚，文曰"一锄明月种梅花"，遂用以铃记达琳琴书。1973 年离开"五七干校"后，检抄旧稿，作此以名篇。外赘五首，追忆往事。

明月天边信有时，浮云万里偶然期。

难忘一奏摇篮曲，偏爱德西踏雪词。

偶然期在纽约华美协进社举办的清华校友会上，邀请洪达琳钢琴独奏。德西今译德彪西。

踏雪寻梅自逶迤，主人挥手笑余痴。

清明山下疑无路，曲径从来最逶直。

主人为 Rachel Sutherland 夫人，住 Moutclair，因作清明山。

288

万里挈归半琴书，金陵小住傍亲居。
能言十指心思事，无限心思在望舒。

1946 年秋回国。岳父家住南京慈悲社。洪家姊妹有"月"字排行。

十指铮铮击清节，泠泠直上千山月。
天风浩浩水漉漉，三地音书同一别。

1947 年初我独去上海。父母则在北京。

海上繁华舞千魔，健儿挝鼓过天河。
红旗万里开新宇，自是风流北地多。

1949 年 5 月上海解放，12 月我全家定居北京。

有　赠

十四年间霜露尘，重逢犹是玉华新。
滇南春雨长于柳，蜀道秋风扫落蓁。
曾寄浮云游子意，叮咛松柏故乡人。
喜看绿树成荫后，华发尊前笑语嗔。

1951 年夏。

一九六二年一月即阴历腊月
初十日值四十五周岁

今年立春早，梅花清欲绝。
煮酒羊蹄羹，临窗对残雪。
儿女争爆豆，笑我齿牙拙。

学剑复学书，少年颇激烈。
因未识工农，南辕尝北辙。
十年逐逆流，半生遽潦落。
鬼域夜沉沉，鸱枭鸣呱呱。

东方日已红，出海磅且礴。
须臾人间改，霎那妖氛豁。
坚冰暖欲溶，轻云高自白。
晴空召归鸿，润土唤惊蛰。
时年三十二，惊喜逢转折。
譬如昨日死，譬如今日活。
人生有二命，死生常契阔。

枯木再逢春，春来发几枝。
雨露同所濡，甘苦乃异实。
草木多二性，淮南枳作橘。
改造因乘势，移花还换骨。
十载见扶疏，穷年累日月。

执柯以伐柯，接枝先断枝。
除草除务尽，间苗间勿稀。
可爱堂前柏，何妨涧底松。
葵藿向太阳，女萝附菟丝。
四十尚云壮，五十犹未迟。
垦辛无老幼，执杖亦耘耔。
春来多娇丽，江山在一麾。

过秦岭

秦岭巍巍天路斜，全凭电气两机车。

觉来已是重峰过，回首方知道路赊。

碧垒层层皆陇亩，白云处处有人家。

天低地冷雄心壮，银杏培出大如瓜。

1962 年 7 月 8 日，乘首建电气化铁路客车过秦岭，凌晨抵站，有卖大银杏者，八角一斤。此行作《西行记事》，留七首。

杜甫草堂

青羊宫外笑声痴，万里桥西访故师。

千尺青松遮翠盖，百花潭水泛红蕖。

前人诗史事往矣，近作丹青意何之。

尚有令人不解处，先贤诸葛入家祠。

公共汽车止于青羊宫，一大集市也。步行过万里桥，数里至草堂。右有诗史堂，左新建杜诗画意馆，而近人作品皆摹古。草堂后为杜祠，供"诸葛先贤之位"木牌一，不知何意。

武侯祠

丞相堂屋天下奇，君王窃居武侯祠。

黄鹂早去无新语，翠柏犹存发旧枝。

历数兴亡皆往事，检查功过费心思。

骚人到此枯肠尽，一半文章是杜诗。

入武侯祠，而大殿高座者乃刘、关、张，环众百官，皆有塑像并碑记。孔明则在后殿，空寂无物。内外题咏殆遍，大抵皆摭拾杜句。

山　城

重庆重游二十年，嘉陵依旧换人间。

山城昔日悲国破，江槛今朝看月圆。

新辟狮园共鹅岭，重开北水与南泉。

巍然最是红岩馆，惭愧终生拜圣贤。

乘江泸轮自重庆到武汉

流火下渝州，江泸风满楼。

船行天上水，人在夏之秋。

日照朝阳甲，星悬舴艋舟。

川江昔百险，今作笑谈游。

江泸系我国新建大型江轮，行车平稳，履险如夷。二层曰照阳甲板，有大瞭望室。三层曰救生艇甲板，舵楼在。

瞿塘峡

才入瞿塘口，蜀天一线开。

江流山欲动，人去岸忽回。

白帝云间过，天都水上来。

夜航应别致，滟滪已无堆。

船上仰望白帝城，"天都津棣"四巨字刻江边崖下。解放后修整峡道，炸去滟滪堆，巨轮已可安全夜航。

过巫山

谁数巫山十二峰，江边矗立一烟笼。
猿声已矣机声轧，神女重来梦也慵。

巫山十二峰者，夹江二十里，殊难一一辨认。峰下有高大烟囱，上书"巫山县机器修配厂"，"大跃进"之功也。

种　茄

踏上五七路，学园到大荒。
种瓜勤理蔓，种菜细铲稂。
葱椒播勿早，莳茄在育秧；
茄苗娇且嫩，料峭海风霜。
移栽论气令，殷勤验土墒。
反青耐人久，惮寒复畏阳。
宽心苗转秀，又恐虫害伤。
岂知吐花日，杆枝紫劲长。
昂首迎风雨，叶肥刺亦钢。
门茄大如斗，层叠十四囊。
采撷移刀剪，日举百十筐；
筐篓不胜举，车载进食堂。
烹煎何能已，干晒满绳墙。
云有西番种，丹食多果浆。
其苗颇顽健，脱裤可栽秧。
枝繁叶也茂，支架成翠岗。
谁知一夜雨，小涝尽伤亡。
我非怨番土，改土须易俗。
实践出真知，逝者亦如斯。

1970 年春，商业部"五七干校"十一连，在辽宁省盘锦县大荒公社。汪士信与我司灌园。番种指番茄，此土不宜，栽数畦，皆涝死。"脱裤"即不带土栽秧。

菩萨蛮·除夕

狂飙落地吹折树，坚冰冻破盘山路。红日透尼龙，秧盘一色茸。

两灶兼八味，难买今宵醉。絮语话新规，春播大有为。

1971 年阴历除夕，张维常与我在实验尼龙房值夜。时十一连已迁鸭子场，改为服务连。西风凛冽，秧苗蔼然。是日食堂备四菜，维常属一连食堂，我属服务连食堂，共打得八味，饮间山白酒，有大曲味道。

西江月·盘锦鸭子场

未暑南风小咬，已凉西陆无蝉。泥足拔兮路嗟艰，更有雪封桥断。

着意惊雷破晓，心红沧海桑田。胸怀壮兮霜满天，夺得新粮十万。

小咬成群结队，为虐胜于蚊。1971 年我连开荒种稻五十亩，脱谷得十余万斤。

一剪梅·别鸭子场

九派末梢路难行，雨也泥泞，雪也飘零。一年难得半年晴，才罢南风，又是西风。

斗地战天逞豪情，文也能行，武也能行。稻香流脂好收成，来是匆匆，去又匆匆。

鸭子场盐碱低温，称九河末梢。1971 年国庆会演，我编一独幕剧。忽接命令：今年文艺节目必须战备题材。遂改编全武行对口词，我也登台。这年 11 月迁河北固安粮食部干校。

蝶恋花·别鸭子场

不到桃花柳无絮。头上青天，脚下泥泞地。敢道人间无奇迹？五七道路谁会意。

枯木朽株齐努力。稻香十里，都被风吹熟。坝上葵花高几许？鸡豚足、客人离去。

鸭子场地寒，有桃无花，有柳无絮。

永遇乐·干校记事

退海隰原，风狂雪暴，鸡起鸣舞。堕碱沉沙，参天换地，尽是奇男女。檐低炕暖，炉边茶熟，贫下中农细语。怅回首、田园篱舍，景物何曾应许。

轻装再卸，桑乾河畔，又是一番寒暑。穹顶圆仓，高屋建瓴，老去攀登处。峥嵘岁月，今冬明夏，几个人生三五。桃李无言蹊自就，凭谁留去？

固安县粮食部"五七干校"，在永定河畔。流沙成田，种稻外参加基建，以用一根无限长的粗秸缆盘造高耸入云的粮仓，最称绝活。在干校常有人问：何时毕业？答曰：三五年。明年再问，答如是。

浣溪沙·赠友

遥望南天楚江隈，东风吹送彩云来。梅花一曲唤春回。
坝上松枝犹童子，向阳花朵绣成堆。夕阳西下听轻雷。

1972 年春永定河畔。

插　秧

春兰九畹傍河栽，纫蕙千条次第开。
荷笠霜足涉水去，鼓盆携手踏沙回。
长堤暗柳梨千树，短袖宽鞋酒一杯。
我欲尊前歌半阕，芳邻喧笑为谁恢。

1973 年春。凡插秧，必携面盆一只。

井房值夜

莫道沙城月色浑，稻田如锦绿如簪。
愿得肥雨停车水，便唤长风扫暮惜。
堪笑牵牛不负轭，何如黄犬卧花阴。
两熟稻米人声远，一系孤舟寂寞心。

1973 年夏。"黄犬"友人赠句。

看　青

索索高粱叶，橙橙玉米堆。
扬鞭抬望鸟，平地一声雷。
听说鹦鹉劫，香稻粒有余。
南海何佳丽，阳天舞韶徐。

地多麻雀，看青儿常以爆竹驱之。客云海南岛患鹦鹉，稻农常放排枪，余未之信。

春　耕

百亩凤梨带雪吹，几株山杏绽胭脂。

群锄耕罢千支曲，对口吟成半头诗。

胃病何需三折臂，顽躯不卖五羊皮。

一杯难尽平章兴，水满沙畦月满枝。

半头诗即三句半，我为文艺演出所作。我长期患胃溃疡，到干校三年竟愈。

久　别

十年风雨旧文章，重到江南草木长。

海上友朋惊我在，饼摊巧遇故同航。

激情语咽三握手，热泪眶盈九回肠。

不是谁家多久别，樽前一座尽蒙霜。

1974 年春，为重定《旧中国的资本主义生产关系》旧稿到上海征求意见，老友见我惊呼"你还活着！""同航"，同船出国者。

一九七五年夏随岭南二老游杭州四首

岭上梅花留梦取，江南处处开新宇。

当年卒子志将军，转作楼头册工贾。

百战高温老变新，西湖应自嘲西姥。

江南干部下放劳动曰"战高温"。至杭州，主人仍任局长，热情接待。我们住新老兵中转站，设备甚佳。

倾倒湖天飞白羽，沙堤信步谈今古。

幽兰不见泪啼妆，水佩云裳仍起舞。

吐溜于今已无龙，竹林深处犹藏虎。

虎跑泉之吐溜龙头已不见，而竹林内有假虎一只，岂示警耶？

夏至孤山草木深，遍山游女爱高音。

"坟坛冷落将军岳，梅鹤凄凉处士林"。

市议纷纭争儒法，湖光依旧鉴忠忱？

云间苍狗成奇境，亭上风波何处寻。

欲访岳坟，岳坟已封闭。因忆鲁迅阻郁达夫游杭诗。

山之阳兮水之浒，潋滟空蒙谁是主？

桃李城中斗妍媸，西泠路上风和雨。

罡风吹老浙江潮，红藕婷立虾蟆咻。

次日雨中游湖，晚归宿舍，知今日城有事，主人亦罢官。

悼周总理

钧天霹雳巨星沉，八亿神洲痛失亲。

磊落胸襟怀远大，鞠躬尽瘁为人民。

山河大地埋忠骨，日月经天自在身。

帷幄无声通广宇，停车回顾后来人。

1976 年 1 月。

悼毛主席

五岳昆仑肃立，九河东海沉流。天风辘辘月低头，一代哲人辞世。
领袖英灵永在，思想经世弥真。如今世界正三分，亿万生民何去？

1976 年 8 月，调寄《西江月》。

一九七七年天安门清明节

烈士碑前白络缤，风云常为护斯民。
清明细雨成惊浪，扫荡妖氛挽巨轮。
继往开来应有主，无私无畏史无论。
重听一曲绣金匾，举国流泪最多人。

白松亭

亭外松犹白，山中叶未红。
崎岖有鸟道，绝顶待攀攻。

1978 年秋，《中国资本主义发展史》会议后与徐新吾、王水、卜英敏游
香山；时传诵叶老《攻关》诗，戏作五绝五首。

眼镜湖

昔人多短视，眼镜亦成湖。
如今天地大，放眼看宏图。

星火中学学生

星火争上游，红旗鬼见愁。

攻关输小将，俯首老黄牛。

松林餐厅所见

二女竖英眉，二士斗饭痴。

知是谁家子，我为哭路歧。

卧佛寺

仰望称"得大"，圆通自有余。

金身空自保，长卧欲何如？

一九三九年送阿野之沪

五年学士梦一回，寂寞休翻过来词。

山望有无云望渺，风如缠锦雨如丝。

景迁时过成追忆，事到临头总不知。

君自天南浮海去，空留旧语费心思。

1978 年春，阿野退休来京访旧，与任以沛、黄季方会餐展览馆餐厅，出示一纪念册，乃三十九年前在昆明西南联大同学送阿野去沪时所书。内有我赠诗一首，署 1940 年 6 月 17 日，我早忘记了，重抄如上。该纪念册原系阿诺所遗。

春 望

策马登峰极，边城看雪消。

含悲辞燕阙，饮恨建康桥。

国破云犹黑，情狂意转高。

大地新培血，明年一树桃。

1980 年初，魏东明至自湖南，别四十年矣。云尚记得抗日战争中我在西北从军时寄给他的诗数句，即一、二、六、七、八句。这是 1937 年冬我在凤翔试马时所作，因以意补上三、四、五句。建康桥是平津流亡同学会在南京遭镇压时我蛰居处。少年时之涂鸦已完全忘记，仅因挚友所记，得以上二首。

附

敬贺令仁教授八秩华诞

孔门八府一淑嫒，功成仍守杏坛隅。

近人开拓皆新史，锦瑟年华漫文郭。

乱世从来争霸业，升平大道还用儒。

有情岁月仁者寿，桃李芬芳半城湖。

2004 年 5 月

（原载王育济主编《岁月有情》，山东大学出版社，2004，第 30 页）

悼王永兴教授

少年清华老北大，西南联袂史学初。

寅师门第君入室，考异长编我不如。①

坎坷边城千里路，重来燕阙五车书。

满园桃李家锦绣，九五飞天寿有馀。

（原载《王永兴先生纪念文集》编委会编《通向义宁之学：王永兴先生纪念文集》，中华书局，2010，第 4 页）

---

① 徐高阮、王永兴和我皆在西南联大转入历史系侍陈寅恪先师，故云。

外文论著

War Borrowing Under The Federal Reserve System

编者说明：*War Borrowing Under The Federal Reserve System*（《美联储的战争借款》）一书署名 Cheng-Ming Wu，为作者在美国哥伦比亚大学商学院的硕士学位论文，写于 1945 年 10 月。作者在《财经评论》1947 年 1～2 月发表的《美国战时公债与金融政策评述》一文，是本书的概要。今据藏于美国哥伦比亚大学图书馆数据库的版本收入全集。

CONTENTS

TABLES

CHARTS

Foreword

It is never easy to write on current financing practice. Many facts are uncollected, much material may not be made accessible, and, above all, the phases of the war changed overnight and so did the war financing program. When this essay was being prepared in late 1994, the invasion of Europe was in its critical stage. Nobody believed then that peace might come within one year. On August 6, 1945, when the author was writing the outline of the final chapter, an atomic bomb was dropped on Hiroshima, and eight days later the war suddenly ended. That chapter, which was supposed to deal later the war suddenly problems, has never been finished. The nation has gone quickly into reconversion, and all the suppositions and estimates which the writer made in his draft became outdated. The end of the war has come so suddenly and dramatically that there was no time even to revise all the discussions and inferences in the earlier chapters.

Chapter I is a discussion of the general aspects of war borrowing. It is to be observed that the theories of taxation and deficit financing, though they appear in various places in that chapter, are not the main points of argument in this thesis. Chapter II is a critical analysis of the policies which the Treasury has adopted in its war borrowing program. Chapter III is an analysis of the effects of war borrowing, especially the War Loan drives, upon the banking system.

Chapters IV and V deal with the wartime Federal Reserve policy in regard to the supply of member bank reserve funds, the maintenance of Government security market, and the control of bank credits. These are the main problems to be discussed in this essay. Special attention has been given to the liquidity preference of the public, the reluctance of banks to borrow, the decline in interest rates, the short-term financing, the expansion of bank portfolio, the difficulties of credit control, the accumulation of liquid assets, and the over-all effort to restrain the development of inflationary potentialities. The various measures taken by the Federal Reserve System are briefly described in Chapter Ⅵ.

A summary of the inferences and conclusions is given in Chapter Ⅶ.

Chapter Ⅰ　The Theory of War Borrowing

Taxation Vs. Borrowing

Modern wars have always been largely financed by borrowing. Nevertheless, there are few economic questions upon which opinion has been so divided as the problem of borrowing for the conduct of war. For two centuries and a half statesman and economists have debated whether in time of war all funds should be raised by taxation or some reliance should be placed upon public debt. [1]

Great Britain financed through taxation about 63 per cent of the cost of the Napoleonic Wars, and about 39 per cent of the cost of the Boer War. [2] The inadequacy of taxation, however, was not fully exposed until World War Ⅰ, the first total war in its modern sense.

About 37.3 per cent of cost of World War Ⅰ was met by taxes in the United States. 28.7 per cent in Great Britain, and only 12.3 per cent in Germany and 4.2 per cent in France. [3] Taken as a whole, belligerent nations financed only about one-fourth of war expenditures out of taxes. Three-fourths of war costs were met by borrowing.

---

[1]　Cf. Jacob H. Hollander, *War Borrowing*, New York, 1919, p. 3.

[2]　Sir Josiah Stamp, *The Aftermath of War*, London, 1932, p. 41.

[3]　Based on Fisk's figures. War cost is defined as the excess of actual wartime expenditures over the peacetime level of government expenditures. H. E. Fisk, *The Inter-Allied Debts*, New York-Paris, 1924, p. 330.

England alone entered World War Ⅰ with a national income tax in Operation; the United States began its Federal income tax during the war. Most of the belligerent nations in 1914 were not equipped for a non-inflationary tax system. Indirect taxation provided a weak and insufficient basis for war finance. Furthermore, customs revenues, then the chief source of income of many governments, declined rapidly in wartime. [①] Progress in tax methods makes a different picture in the present war. Taxes and other revenue were 46 per cent of the total expenditures of the United States government in 1941, 30 per cent in 1942, 38 per cent in 1943 and 46 per cent in 1944. Great Britain has relied much less heavily upon borrowing in this war than has the United States and also less than the British Government did in the last war. Canada raised an even larger amount from taxation than from borrowing. In the United States, total Government expenditures in 1944 were about 10 times those of 1940, and total receipts about 8 times those of 1940. In the four years of defence and war ending December 1944, a net $180 billion have been borrowed to finance the Government expenditures, of which $243 billion were war costs. The financing program may be seen from Table 1 (a comparison with World War Ⅰ made In Table 18 on page 393).

Table 1 Government Financing (Billions of Dollars)

Calendar years	1941	1942	1943	1944
Receipts and expenditures Income & profit taxes	4. 3	11. 1	26. 6	34. 3
Other	4. 5	5. 3	8. 0	10. 1
Net Receipts *	8. 8	16. 4	34. 6	44. 4
War expenditures	13. 9	52. 4	85. 1	91. 2
Other expenditures **	6. 6	5. 2	4. 7	5. 2
Total Expenditures	20. 5	57. 6	89. 8	96. 4

---

① Cf. Horst Mendershausen, *The Economics of War*, New York, 1943, p. 222.

Continued table

Calendar years	1941	1942	1943	1944
Net expenditures	11. 7	41. 2	55. 2	52. 0
Increase in general fund	1. 6	7. 0	1. 8	9. 9
Borrowing(increase in interest-bearing debt)	13. 4	47. 8	57. 1	61. 6

* Exclude net appropriations to Federal old-age and survivors insurance trust fund.

** Includes net expenditures of trust funds and Government agencies except for war and debt retirement.

Source: *Annual Report*. Federal Reserve Bank of New York, for 1944, p. 10.

A comparison of wartime financing in the United States, the United Kingdom and Canada is shown in Table 2. The figures are for fiscal years and therefore are not comparable with those in Table 1.

Table 2　Wartime Finance in the United States, the United Kingdom, and Canada (Millions of Dollars)

Fiscal Years	1940	1941	1942	1943	1944	Total
The United States						
Borrowing($)	2606	6836	21659	63805	61830	156736
Taxation($)	5114	7093	12513	21365	41857	86942
The United Kingdom						
Borrowing(£)	768	2466	2673	2780	2736	11423
Taxation(£)	1017	1359	1962	2483	2948	9769
Canada						
Borrowing($)	308	678	1414	1963	2779	7142
Taxation($)	468	778	1361	2137	2592	7336

Source: Harold L. Seligman, " Patterns of Wartime borrowing in the United States, the United Kingdom, and Canada," *Federal Reserve Bulletin*, November 1944, p. 1057.

The policy of war financing is burdened with many complicated problems, not only in regard to the source of funds, but also in regard to its broader effects upon national production and economic well-being. A drastic tax program has many advantages, provided taxes are not paid out of idle balances. The more money is raised through taxation, the less is available for private outlays. Thus it may prevent inflationary developments during and after the war and relieve future generations of the transfer difficulties associated with servicing a large public debt. It may prevent large war profits in business and narrow the inequality of incomes through progressive tax rates. But a vigorous tax program may affect production adversely. There may also occur injurious effects on the incentive to work and on morale of the people at a time the cooperation and the utmost effort of the people are required. In addition, there is the argument that a high and progressively graduated income tax tends to curtail people's savings, because changes in an individual's expendable income tend to affect his savings more than his expenditures.

In any event, in war on a large scale, a "policy of finance Through taxation alone, however excellent it might be in theory is in practice out of question. "[1] The problem of tax policy at present is, by and large, technical in nature. The types of tax measures that should be adopted will depend upon the extent to which resources are being utilized. In the early stages of war, when the economy is operating far below capacity, an expansionary policy may be desirable to stimulate the necessary increases in production. As resources are used more fully, fiscal policy should become increasingly restrictive. When output approaches its peak, the creation of new money must come to an end.

Experts generally agreed in 1941 that a large rise in taxation should not be imposed until full employment, or at least a high measure of employment, was attained, or until a substantial rise in prices threatened. [2] But there were different opinions in regard to the timing of increases in taxation and the nature of the taxes to be imposed. The level of full employment can be determined only with great difficulty, and prices may rise long before that level is reached. Since the point of maximum output may be attained before resources are fully utilized, because of

---

① A. C. Pigou, *Political Economics of War*, 1941, New York, p. 3.

② E. g. Profs, A. H. Hansen, J. W. Angell, J. K. Galbraith, A. G. Hart, C. Stoup, etc. Cf. Seymour E. Harris, *The Economics of America at War*, New York, 1943, p. 195.

bottlenecks and the technical difficulties encountered in a complete reorganization of the economy, the introduction of restrictive taxation may become necessary even before that time. ①

Although it is outside the scope of this thesis to discuss details of wartime tax policy, we may conclude that consistent with the extent to which borrowings may be employed to finance the war, increases in tax levels should tend to parallel the expansion of production, and that since measures of the level of employment are not always reliable, new taxation should be considered whenever there is a substantial rise in price levels. The policy announced by the President of the United States, that the budget should be balanced whenever the country approaches a condition of full utilization of its economic capacity, is, in effect, an epitome of the generally accepted theory of public finance. ②But Government financing is more a matter of art than of science. Every Secretary of the Treasury is eager to say of his budget that it will be balanced someday. Actual balance, however, is not so easily achieved. The printing press may be started by pushing a button, but the imposition of new taxes involves tremendous difficulties and long delays.

Borrowing Does Not Postpone the Burden of War

Though the practice of Government borrowing has been commonly used in war and peace, its real significance is easily misunderstood. On the one hand, too great a contrast is seen between borrowing and taxation.

They are regarded as opposing alternatives. First, taxation meets the cost of

---

① Of. E. Stein and G. Backman, *War Economics*, New York, 1942. p. 121.

② In his budget speech of January 1941, the President said: "As the national income increases, a larger and larger portion of the defense expenses should be met by tax revenues rather than borrowing. Whatever the point may be at which the budget should be balanced, there cannot be any question that whenever the country approaches a condition of full utilization of its economic capacity, with appropriate consideration of both employment and production, the budget should be balanced. This will be essential if monetary responsibility is to be discharged effectively."

the war immediately while borrowing postpones the burden to the future. Secondly, borrowing is inflationary by nature whereas taxation is essentially deflationary. On the other hand, it is frequently said that we need not worry about the internal national debt, because we "owe it to ourselves," and that public debt may be increased almost indefinitely, because national income will always rise faster than the debt.

It is a commonly recognized but easily neglected fact that we can fight a war only with the services and commodities produced during the war or existing at the outset. Payment of only a very small part of the real cost of war can be deferred. This can be done by diverting resources from maintenance, repair and replacement of public and private capital and by reducing inventories of consumers' goods in relation to sales to a level below the normal ratio. Both of these expedients involve real costs to future consumers because resources will later have to be withheld from them to rehabilitate capital and build-up stocks. Nevertheless, by far the greater portion of the real costs of the war must unavoidably be borne by the present generation. From this point of view, taxation and borrowing are interchangeable. Both mean that there is less money and fewer goods for either the taxpayers or for the lenders to consume. As Professor Pigou said: "When a given sum of money is raised by the government from anybody, and he does not shift the task of shouldering it on to somebody else, the choice that he makes between these various sources is not determined by the form in which the levy is made upon him."[1] Therefore, it makes no difference to the people as a whole whether the Government collects $1000 in taxes from them, or borrows $1000 from them and informs them that the interest on and repayment of their loan will be collected by taxation.

The real cost of the war must be paid when it is being fought. But, as pointed out by Professor John M. Clark, this does not mean that there are not future burdens to be borne as well.[2] This may take the form of direct outlays of goods and

---

[1]   A. C. Pigou, *Political Economics of War*, New York, 1941, pp. 74, 76.

[2]   John M. Clark, *The Cost of the War to the American People*, New Haven, 1931, p. 81.

services as for the care of veterans, or of resources which must be withheld from consumption to rehabilitate capital and replenish stocks, or of a depression of industrial activity, such as may result from destruction or disuse of capital or postwar maladjustment. These involve concrete costs to future consumers, whether the war is financed by taxation or whether it is financed by borrowing. The fact that funds are obtained by restriction of present consumption through taxation or other means is not wholly irrelevant for the future. For, up to a point, personal consumption is investment in individual productive capacity. [1] Moreover, the decline in morale and the deterioration or loss of education because of the overriding demands of war, create costs which are necessarily paid by future generations. [2]

Borrowing and the Redistribution of Incomes

Borrowing, however, postpones the final allocation of the burden of war. Loans and interest thereon must be repaid by funds from taxation. When future generations repay the loan, the burden is gradually shifted from bondholders to taxpayers. This involves a redistribution but not a diminution of the national income. It has been asserted that voluntary loans are generally obtained from the richer classes and taxes are collected mainly from the poor, and that the burden of war borrowing is thereby shifted from the rich to the poor. On the other hand, it has also been argued that public debt promotes a wider diffusion of property because small savers and thrift institutions seek the safest type of security, namely, Government issues. In 1937, however, individuals with net incomes of $5000 and over, including partnerships and trusts, held about 90 per cent of

---

[1] A. C. Pigou, op. cit. , p. 44.

[2] The best expression seems to be the conclusion made by Professor Davenport. War consumption has no future tense. And still there is a sense in which this burden can be shifted. The people who bear the burden now may be indemnified later at the cost of other people. Such is, in fact, the sole significance of bonds. . . the future does not provide for the war; future producers merely indemnify the present providers. H. J. Davenport, "The War Tax Paradox," *American Economic Review*, Vol. IX, March 1919, p. 36.

the aggregate privately held Federal, State and local debts. [1]The observation made by Professor Hansen seems correct: "A limited increase in the public debt tends to promote a wider distribution of property in so far as the new issues are purchased by thrifty institutions. On the other hand, a very rapid increase in this public debt necessarily implies a relatively light tax burden on upper-income groups and on corporation, tending to promote concentration of wealth and income. "[2]

It is a strong practical argument in favor of wartime borrowing against taxation that under a system of loans those who base free money contribute it spontaneously,[3] and it is equitable that a rich man should contribute more to the costs of war than a poor one. [4]During the period May 1941 to February 1942, 90 per cent of the total sales of savings bonds were in denominations of $100 or higher, and roughly 25 per cent of them were in denominations of $10000. Only $440 million out of the total subscription of $4.4 billion consisted of small bonds in denominations of $25 or $50. [5]This indicates that bonds were sold chiefly to members of high income groups and that a large amount was purchased by corporations and savings institutions. The trend, however, has changed since 1942. As may be seen from the following table, the percentage of sales of the large denomination Series E bonds dropped steadily until 1945. Sales of $25 and $50 bonds increased from 13.6 per cent of total sales in 1941 to 49.2 per cent in 1943 and 49 per cent in 1944. The trend apparently was reversed in late 1944 and early 1945, when individual incomes raised to an extremely high level.

---

① Horst Mendershausen, *The Economics of War*, New York, 1943, p. 240.

② Alvin H. Hansen, *Fiscal Policy and Business Cycles*, New York, 1941, pp. 184 – 185.

③ Cf. A. C. Pigou, op. cit., p. 81.

④ The loans obtained from the wealthy class do not, however, cause a significant reduction in consumption; most of the loans arise from savings.

⑤ *Treasury Bulletin*, May 1942, p. 28.

Table 3   Sales of Series E Savings Bonds (Percentage of total sales)

Denominations	$ 25	$ 50	$ 100	$ 500	$ 1000
1941	7. 1	6. 5	20. 4	20. 0	46. 0
1942	17. 5	9. 7	23. 0	18. 1	31. 7
1943	36. 1	13. 1	20. 7	12. 2	17. 9
1944	35. 1	13. 9	21. 9	11. 8	17. 3
1945 *	28. 6	13. 2	20. 6	13. 4	23. 6

* Five months.

Source: *Treasury Bulletin*, August 1945.

Interest payments on public loans represent part of the shift of income from taxpayers to bondholders. During World War I , interest paid by the Federal Government to individuals increased from $ 17 million in 1915 to a peak of $ 785 million in 1919, according to the estimates of Will-ford I. King. [1]The effect on individual income may be seen from the following table.

Table 4   Interest Payments by Government (Amount in millions of dollars)

Years	Total Interest Payments	Paid to individuals by Federal Government		Total realized Incomes($) *	Interests as % of total income
		Millions($)	% of Total		
1914	312	17	0. 05	33227	0. 94
1915	343	17	0. 05	34690	0. 99
1916	356	18	0. 04	40585	0. 88
1917	454	88	0. 18	48314	0. 94
1918	766	285	0. 50	56658	1. 35
1919	1412	780	1. 27	61628	2. 29
1920	1413	771	1. 12	68442	2. 07
1921	1427	741	1. 26	58271	2. 45
1922	1524	758	1. 24	61187	2. 49
1923	1540	702	1. 01	69295	2. 22
1924	1490	594	0. 82	71905	2. 07
1925	1499	560	0. 73	76561	1. 96

* Total individual realized money income in current dollars.

Source: Based on King's data, Will ford I. King, *The National Income and Its Purchasing Power*, New York, 1930, pp. 74, 370.

---

[1]   Will ford I. King. *The National Income and Its Purchasing Power*, National Bureau of Economic Research, New York, 1940, pp. 74, 370.

It may be seen that the relative position of interest payment by Government in total individual incomes rose after 1917, following by one year the huge increase in war loans. At the same time, the relative positions of profit and dividends in individual total income declined. Thus the rentiers (interest receivers) gained at the expense of ownership. In the period, 1923 – 1928, both profit and dividend incomes rose considerably. Interest income from Government became relatively less important, as the total money incomes increased. This period, however, was one of very great prosperity for the well-to-do. It may also be recalled that when all kinds of income (wages, salaries, profit, dividends) declined rapidly during tabs depression of 1929 – 1933, interest income remained fairly stable. Interest payments, in relation to their 1929 level, including those of Corporate funded debt, remained at 99.5 per cent in 1931 and 96.7 per cent in 1932, while the similar indexes of wages and salaries dropped to 59.7 per cent and profits dropped to 55.6 percent in 1932.

The above analysis does not include the repayment of Government debt at maturity, which represents another shift of wealth from taxpayers to bondholders. This amount, however, can be easily ascertained from the magnitude of the public debt, on the assumption that all debts are to be paid out of taxes and that refunding debts are regarded as new deficits of the Government.

Because of the complicated structure of individual income, the regressive nature of war borrowing cannot be precisely analyzed. It may be said that, as a consequence of war borrowing, the shift of national income from taxpayers to bondholders is significant whenever a large portion of the public debt is held by a small part of the population. But in the overwhelming periods of inflation and deflation, which are likely to follow the war, redistribution of national income occurs from a variety of economic factors. [1] It is frequently argued, for instance,

---

[1] One of the most important problems is the effect of price variation. Owners of debt are members of the fixed-income group, and, according to the traditional theory of price changes, they are beneficiaries of falling prices. But even in the face of falling prices, this group may find itself in a disadvantageous position in respect to real income in comparison with other classes which share in the general expansion of the country. For further discussion, cf. Henry George Hendricks, *The Federal Debt, 1919 – 1930*, Washington, D. C., 1933, pp. 318 – 320.

that the immediate effect of the financing of World War Ⅰ was in the direction of greater equality in the distribution of personal incomes. ①

Borrowing and Inflation

The second misconception, that borrowing is necessarily inflationary in nature, has evidently arisen from the Government's practice of borrowing from the banking system.

Broadly speaking, inflation may easily but not inevitably result from wartime borrowing. The fundamental alternative of war finance is diversion of purchasing-power vs. creation of purchasing-power, not borrowing vs. taxation. Tax payments may also be financed by creation of bank credit. To the extent that loans are secured from current income, or from current and future savings, there need be no inflation. The effect of such loans is to divert purchasing power from civilians to the Government, to the extent that loans are made, on the other hand, by banks for their own amount through credit creation, or by individuals through bank loans in the nature of long-term engagements rather than of instalment purchases, inflation may result.

No country, however, can fight a war on the modern scale without the aid of bank credit. The effect of war on the banking system was well summarized by the London Economist, as follows:

> The wartime pressures on a banking system are two-fold and complementary. In the first place, the expanding economy needs more money—both currency end credit—to finance its operation. The increase in monetary requirements can be expected to be at least proportional to the expansion in the flow of national income, and there are strong influences, operating both on currency and on deposits, tending to make the increase still more rapid. A

---

① C f, John M. Clark, *The Cost of World War to the American People*, New Haven, 1931, p. 162, Cf. also W. I. King, op. cit. , pp. 167 – 169.

community at war both has more income than one at peace, and also chooses to hold a larger proportion of it in monetary form. Secondly, the government deficit to be financed. No belligerent government has yet succeeded in covering 100 percent of its expenses from individual income; there is always a substantial margin left that has to be borrowed from the banking system. [1]

The picture will be clear if we recall that in the four years ending in 1944, money in circulation in the United States trebled, bank deposits doubled, and that the banking system held about 42 per cent of Government obligations. The same situation is true in other belligerent countries.

To a certain extent, financing the war by credit creation can be justified. Modern wars may be accompanied by a tremendous expansion of production, and the injection of more money than at peace time will not necessarily lead to price inflation. Furthermore, it is generally accepted that a slight rise in wartime prices has the advantages of stimulating war production, of increasing tax revenue, of discouraging civilian consumption, and of maintaining the level of monetary expenditure on consumption and private capital formation. [2] The effect of bank credit financing is to give the Government more purchasing power every year, and thus to deplete the real value of the purchasing power left to private persons. In this way it enables the Government to get possession of more goods and services, and so constitutes, as against the public, a concealed form of taxation. Whereas the money cost of the war program rises, the real burden is kept down by the rise in prices.

This rise makes the real cost of a given outlay for debt servicing less. It is a wellknown fact that inflation reduces the burden of debtors. This advantage, however, may be viewed from another point of view. Any price inflation would increase war expenditures, and thus add unnecessarily to the volume of public debt. In addition, it might also be followed by a deflation, and thereby increase the

---

[1] "American Monetary Plethora," *The Economist*, London, July 17, 1943, p. 81.

[2] Cf. S. E. Harris, *The Economics of America at War*, New York, 1943, p. 161, and Horst Mendershausen, *The Economics of War*, New York, 1943, p. 15.

burden of the national debt, that is, a huge debt incurred at inflated prices would have to be serviced out of a reduced national income at low prices; in order to do this, tax rates would have to be raised when business is suffering from a depression.

While credit creation is inevitable in war financing, even under the tax system,[1] the problems are how to minimize the volume of bank credit financing and how to moderate the development of its inflationary potentialities. These are, in essence, the essential points in this essay.

The Limits of Public Debt

The most interesting question of Government borrowing is: How large a domestic debt a nation can afford to bear? It has been argued, in some quarters, that since the domestic debt, is owed to ourselves, it may be increased, apparently, to an indefinite degree.[2] Prominent economists have suggested that public debt may be increased until full employment is reached.[3] Some estimated that a public debt as large as $4000000000000 may be carried by the United States Government without collapse of the capitalist system, repudiation of the debt, or a great inflation.[4] Occasionally, high government officials expressed the same philosophy. For instance, President Roosevelt said in a public address in May 1939:

---

[1] If the war funds are raised entirely by taxation, people must resort to bank credit for the tax payment. The taxpayers will probably resort more quickly to bank credit for loan payment, as they did in the last war, because, with the loan system, they do not feel so sharply the impact of the loan and are less keenly driven toward harder work. Moreover, Government securities provide good collateral for bank loans. Cf. A. C. Pigou, op. cit. , p. 80.

[2] E. g. R. Y. Gilbert, G. H. Hildebrand Jr. , A. S. Stuart, M. Y. Sweezy, L. Tarshis an J. D. wilson, *An Economic Program for American Democracy*, New York, 1938. For discussion of the program, cf. David M. Wright, "The Economic Limit and Economic Burden of an Internally Held Debt," *Quarterly Journal of Economics*, Vol. LV, November 1940.

[3] E. g. Alvin H. Hansen. Cf. Hansen, *Fiscal Policy and Business Cycle*, New York, 1941, pp. 170 – 171. Hansen once Said: "A government debt internally held (italics his) is so completely different from an ordinary personal or business debt that it could hardly be called a debt at all. " Cf. A. H. Hansen and Guy Greer, "The Federal Debt and the Future," *Harper's*, April 1942, p. 498.

[4] S. E. Harris, *Postwar Economic Problems.* New York, 1943, p. 184. This attitude, however, is not shared by most other economists who prefer a large domestic public debt.

And when, this week you see all the crocodile tears about the burden of our grandchildren to pay the government debt, remember this: our national debt, after all, is an internal debt, owed not only by the nation but to the nation. If our children have to pay the interest on it, they will pay that interest to themselves. ①

Mr. Eccles, chairman of the Board of Governors of the Federal Reserve System, said on one occasion:

The burden of interest that we speak about is not of itself, a burden if the debt is held within our own economy, because the interest which is paid also goes back to the economy as a whole, increases income, and therefore increases our ability to pay taxes.

The principal points of their arguments, though differing in some respects from each other, may be summarized as follows:

(1) Looking at the whole nation as a going concern, its domestic debts are merely another aspect of its assets. Debt in the broad sense is the obverse of investment. The expansion of debt at a rate sufficient to absorb the nation's savings is both sound and necessary. This rate could be excessive only in the sense that the rate of savings itself was excessive. ②

(2) The process of accumulation of public debt may be accompanied by the acquisition of income-yielding assets, which will provide income against the

---

① Of course, they do not mean that internal debt can be expanded indefinitely. President Roosevelt said, " A reasonable internal debt will not impoverish our children," Mr. Eccles said in his address of January 23, 1939, " I do not believe, and I have never said, that the federal debt should continue to grow indefinitely and no part of it ever be paid," See Monthly Letter, National City Bank of New York, December 1943, p. 140.

② This expression appears in the suggestion made by R. T. Gillbert, G. H. Hildebrand Jr. , etc. Cf. *An Economic Program for American Democracy*, op. cit. , p. 62, et Seq.

increased charged of the public debt. [1]

(3) The process of debt accumulation may contribute to a rise in income. Any ensuing rise in income, given the proper milieu, will result in a rise in savings or investment, and to that extent, the rise of debt will be offset by a rise of private assets. [2]

(4) When there is an increment of aggregate investment, income will increase by an amount which is the increment of investment multiplied by the " investment multiplier ", [3] Thus Government spending has a multiplied and cumulative effect on investment and consumption. The monetary taxable capacity, therefore, will be increased sufficiently to match the increased tax requirements. [4]

These do not, of course, cover all the arguments in favor of a large national debt. It is clear, however, that the problem of an expansion of public debt is being discussed in terms of savings and national income. This is the center of the problem. But first let us view the problem from another angle.

In the first place, what is the real cost of national debt? Public debt, in this sense, represents resources and manpower diverted from private industry. Evidently, if there are unemployed resources and manpower, government spending may take place without drawing any of them from private enterprise. But when the economy approaches its full capacity, as in the case of wartime prosperity, any increase in government spending means a smaller percentage of total output from private production. [5] So long as the capitalistic system is to be maintained, the shift of resources from private to public employment sets the real limit of the public debt.

---

[1] S. E. Harris, *Economics of America at war*, New York, 1941, p. 382.

[2] S. E. Harris, op. cit., p. 382. The impact upon income will be the same regardless of the purpose for which the debt is incurred. Cf. B. F. Haley, "The Federal Budget; Economic Consequences of Deficit Financing," *American Economic Review*, Supplement, Volume XXXI, February 1941, p. 7.

[3] Kynes, John M., *The General Theory of Employment, Interest and Money*, New York, 1936, p. 115.

[4] A. H. Hansen, op. cit., p. 170.

[5] Cf. David M. Wright, *The Creation of Purchasing Power*, Harvard University, 1942, pp. 134 – 145.

Secondly, from the practical point of view, there are many other limits which confine the growth of the national debt. The statutory limit, of course, is unimportant. It can be changed or even eliminated; yet, here must be good reasons to convince the representatives of the people to do so. Next, the limit of bank reserves requires some practical consideration. As has already been pointed out, part of government securities must always be sold to banks, especially when the debt becomes very large. This practice increases bank deposits and diminishes the supply of credit for other purposes. ①Currency in circulation usually increases in times of large government borrowing, thus further depleting bank reserves; this necessarily results in an expansion of central bank credit, with all its far-reaching influences on the national economy. In spite of the huge amount of gold accumulated in this country, it became necessary for Congress to reduce the legal reserve requirements for the Federal Reserve Banks. In countries with small gold holdings and a large foreign trade problem, this might be an embarrassment to the national economy.

Thirdly, a more important limit on the expansion of public debt, from the practical viewpoint, is the willingness of the public to buy government securities. Of course, under nearly all circumstances government issues can be sold at some price. But the government has to consider the costs of debt, which are

---

① One danger of a large public debt, which has occasionally been pointed out, is the progressive absorption of loanable funds which may lead to a scarcity of funds for private borrowers. This danger, however, is not likely to materialize, because there are deflationary uses of income received from the public spending and the funds in such cases come into banks or strengthen someone's credit position. Cf. John M. Clark, "An Appraisal of the Work ability of Compensatory Devices," *American Economic Review*. Supplement, Vol. XXIX, No. 1, March 1939, p. 203. Furthermore, as is pointed out by Robertson, "The money-creating banks are not averse to intervention in one specialized department of the capital market, namely, that concerned with government debt. By relieving holders of their holdings, furnishing them instead with money which can be turned to other uses, the banks are thus able indirectly to propel a stream of long-term loanable funds in the direction of those who wish to use them for the purchase of capital. " Cf. Dennis H. Robertson, *Essays in. Monetary Theory*, London, 1940, p. 136. Hence here we are concerned only with the limiting factor of bank reserves, not with the scarcity of either long-term or short-term loanable funds. Such problems, however, might arise during an unusual government borrowing in a concentrated period or places.

to be met by tax revenue. The ability of a community to lend at a fair interest rate is limited, not only by the physical amount of loanable funds, but also by psychological factors. As will be discussed in Chapter IV, individuals' "liquidity preferences" increase during the war, they prefer to keep their surplus income in currency and in bank deposits. A time could unquestionably come when the public would refuse to buy government bonds, if security issues increased indefinitely. Whether this could happen in the case of banks is determined by the central bank policy. Unless the central bank extends its credit freely, commercial banks may refuse to finance the government under certain conditions. As long as the loans are voluntary the willingness of the public to lend must be reckoned with.

Finally, we arrive at the money burden of public debt. There have always been difficulties in the practical aspect of tax collections, which are the only source of the funds for interest charges. On the one hand, the interest burden is a fixed charge to the Treasury. It is true that the solvency of the government is not subject to the risk of business depression,[1] yet the rigidity imposed by a large annual fixed outlay is a constant menace to a nation's fiscal policy. The national income would have to be maintained, by whatever device, at a high level, and prices must not drop even from an inflated basis. A very large tax bill may prevent the adaptation of the tax structure toward accelerating savings or consumption. In addition, the cost of tax administration and collection must also be reckoned with. On the other hand, people are simply not willing to pay taxes. The individual taxpayer takes little comfort in the fact that the taxes the people pay are paid to the people themselves, in the form of interest. All he cares about is that his taxes are going up, and he does not like it.

Aside from the practical viewpoint, the regressive nature of public debt, as discussed before, must be considered when the debt grows very large. National income would shift from taxpayers to well-to-do bondholders. The proposed plan to collect all the taxes from the bondholders for interest payment on public debt, even

---

[1] Cf. A. H. Hansen, op. cit., p. 159.

if possible, does not seem reasonable. As pointed out by Professor Catchword[1], this means in the case of war debt, concentrating the tax burden on the very people who had supported the war loan drives during the war, and exempting those who were either unable or unwilling to subscribe when the nation needed money badly. Another disadvantage of a program of high taxes is that it penalizes public savings and investments. [2]Taxes are more likely to be paid out of savings than out of consumption. Drastic taxes discourage incentive and risk-taking, which are essential in the present economic system. A progressive tax program, as pointed out by Kuznets,[3] will have the effect of taking funds away from persons who can generate income more efficiently than others. It has also been said that the tax system is based more upon political expediency than upon sound economic considerations, with constantly rising taxes levied upon the corporations and individuals of higher income, who have relatively few votes and are always good political targets. The pushing and pulling of conflicting social philosophies are likely to be related to decisions on tax policies. [4]

The Multiple Effect of Government Spending

A general discussion of the multiplier theory and income acceleration is not relevant to this essay. So far as the financing of government deficit is concerned,

---

[1] B. U. Catchword, "The Burden of a Domestic Debt," *American Economic Review*, Vol. XXX, September 1942, p. 456.

[2] Angell contends that heavy taxation is the most important factor which has reduced the demand for investment funds in recent years. Cf. James W. Angell, *Investment and Business Cycles*, New York, 1941, p. 273, footnote, and p. 2781.

[3] Kuznets refers to it as a "transfer of income from areas in which its power to stimulate production is great to others in which such power is less." Simon Kuznets, "National Income and Taxable Capacity," *American Economic Review*, Supplement, Vol. XXXII, March 1942, p. 59. Cf. also B. U. Ratchford, op. cit., p. 459: "A progressive tax structure which bears heavily upon capital gains and income from property and most large incomes are from property takes funds away from strategic income generating points in the income stream and restores them to the stream at lass strategic points."

[4] Cf. *Monthly Letter*, National City Bank of New York, December 1943, p. 141.

the theory only gives the implication that the national income increases with government spending in, presumably, a multiplied and cumulative way. Thus the problem of a rise in public debt may be discussed in terms of the relationship between the rise in debt charges and the rise in the national income. To such an extent, the multiplier theory may be taken as containing a significant truth. It is important, however, to make the following observations:

(1) Neither Keynes himself nor any other prominent economist says that income necessarily increases in a multiple way. [1] Keynes acknowledges the offsetting factors through decreased investment in other directions, especially the changes in the propensity of the community to consume. [2] It is possible, therefore, that government spending may cause no increase in investment and consumption, but merely offset voluntary savings or hoarding. [3]

(2) While we accept the multiplying effect of deficit financing we must reject the perpetuating effect of government spending. "No expenditure of any kind has a self-perpetuating effect, and the multiplied effect of any expenditure is bound to be limited if there is any leakage at all through saving."[4]

(3) As pointed out by Professor Clark, the multiplier works downward as

---

[1] Some, however, explain the multiplier in a much more rigid fashion. A. Berle is an example. Cf. David M. Wright, *The Creation of Purchasing Power*. Harvard University, 1942, p. 138.

[2] Keynes, *General Theory*, p. 122. However, in another place (p. 118) he says: "Unless the psychological propensities of the public are different from what we are supposing, we have here established the law that increased employment for investment must necessarily stimulate the industries producing for consumption and thus lead to a total increase of employment which is a multiple of the primary employment required by the investment itself."

[3] Cf. Dennis H. Robertson, "Saving and Hoarding," *Economic Journal*. Vol. XLIII, September 1933.

[4] John H. Williams, "Deficit Spending," *American Economic Review*, Vol. XXX, No. 5, February 1941, p. 55. It was the intention of some earlier pump-priming arguments, however, to emphasize the perpetuating nature of the multiplier. When the recovery gave way in 1937 to a new depression, the emphasis shifted from pump-priming to deficit financing as compensation for long-run economic depression, on the theory that deficit financing is not pump-priming in its effects because it is not self-perpetuating. Deficit should be continued so long as underemployment prevailed. Cf. Hansen, Fiscal Policy, op. cit., pp. 261 – 262.

well as upward, and presumably at the same rate. [1]Every failure to spend has a negative multiplier. Hence the shrinkage of income after the tapering off of public spending cannot be avoided unless the multiplier increases in magnitude or some private investment spending comes into being. A flow of private investment remains a prime requisite of successful policy.

(4) When public investment on a large scale is operated, it may have the competitive effect of preventing private investment from rising. "Where this is the ease, one dollar of public capital expenditure can easily scare away several dollars of private outlays. "[2] This means that the total deficit may reach a point at which it is doing more to hold business back than the current spending is doing to stimulate it.

The first remark implies that the increase in income may at times not warrant tax revenue sufficient to pay the interest charges on the debt. Here we see the significance of the difference between public debt and private debt. In the case of private debt there is never any question about who is to pay the interest. While in the case of public debt, the interest is a cost to the Treasury and the income is income to the public; and the Treasury cannot get back all of its outlays in the form of taxes, unless a large multiple increase in income has resulted. If the government spending is offset by an increase in hoarding, or if the increase in public debt is offset by a decrease in private debt, as occurred in 1929 - 1936, the income generated from private business will not increase as expected. Additional taxes for interest charges, however, must be collected. Unless these taxes fall entirely upon hoarding, which seems impossible, the burden must fall elsewhere. Since no one would buy government bonds if his entire income from the bonds would be taxed out of existence, the bondholder will gain at the expense of private industry.

The second and third remarks imply that in order to maintain national income,

---

[1] John M. Clark, "An Appraisal of the Work ability of Compensatory Devices," *American Economic Review*, Vol. XXXIX, March 1939, p. 201.

[2] Ibid. , p. 204.

government deficit must continue permanently, unless private investment increases rapidly and sufficiently to replace public spending. When the national income stands at a very high level, as it does today, it is not likely that private investment can rise to fulfill the gap. ① Professor Williams concludes: "If deficit spending were permanently carried on as compensation for tendencies toward contraction which would otherwise exist in the economy, and especially if we should take as our goal full employment, it would either eventually break down or would entirely transform our democratic, private capitalistic system; for its cost would become a constantly increasing fraction of the national income." ②

The fourth observation implies that, when the public debt has grown to dangerous proportions, current additions will not stimulate further industrial activity and provide increasing income. Such a situation, if it comes about, will call for a general repudiation of public debt.

So far we are talking about deficit financing. War borrowing seems to have no theoretical difference from other government debts in regard to its effects upon income and investment. Any expenditure spent by the government constitutes income of the people. In the practical aspect, however, there are particular characteristics in war debt. This will be discussed in the next chapter.

The growth of wartime public debt in relation to national income may be seen from the following table. ③

---

① The shrinkage of private investment has generally been explained by two theories: the under investment theory and the over saving theory. The former is based on the "mature economy" thesis. As the capitalistic economy progresses, opportunities for investment decline, hence there is little chance for a large increase in private investment to replace government spending in an economy of high-level development. The well-known over saving theory, as expounded by Keynes, is derived from psychological laws. The "propensity to consume," however, cannot he changed by deficit spending. The "liquidity preference" of the public is not likely to be overcome by monetary policy. Thus a large rise in private investment is not easily achieved by government authorities unless the market conditions warrant such a rise.

② John H. Williams, op. cit. , p. 61.

③ Harold L. Seligman, "Patterns of Wartime Borrowing in the United States, the United Kingdom and Canada," *Federal Reserve Bulletin*, November 1944, p. 1056.

Public debt as a percentage of national income

Year	1939	1944
United States	70%	129%
United Kingdom	170%	246%
Canada	100%	125%

Interest payment on public debt as a percentage of national income

Year	1939	1944
United States	1.4%	1.7%
United Kingdom	4.5%	4.8%
Canada	3.1%	2.8%

From 1939 to 1944, public debt in the United States increased almost six-fold, national income doubled and interest payment on debt trebled. As a result the interest burden as a percentage of national income increased only by 0.3 points. Compared with Great Britain and Canada, the postwar outlook in this country appears to be favorable. But there are other things to be considered. Interest rates may not always be kept as low as it has been. National income will rise less rapidly because of the fuller employment of resources and may shrink in the postwar period. The postwar inflation and deflation are still to come. It is a great controversy whether contraction should be allowed or full employment should be maintained. In either case, however, there is no sign that the government debt could be paid off in a substantial degree. It is worthwhile at this time to reread some of the conclusions drawn by Professor Clerk in 1939: [1]

We have not reached the limit of our debt-bearing power, but we do seem to have reached a point at which the piling up of public deficits is a deterrent to private capital outlays, and probably to a larger extent than further public spending can safely undertake to neutralize. Private investment has not vanished, but it has not fully recovered, especially investments involving considerable risk and looking to a long future. Fears of future deficits

---

[1] J. M. Clark, op. cit., p. 206.

and exorbitant taxes awake easily and make revival an unduly sensitive plant. We can stand this for a while longer—preferably with some assurance that the Treasury is not to be treated as a bottomless grab bag for pressure-group interest—and provided we are meanwhile making progress toward more enduring adjustments.

Chapter II   Policies of War Borrowing

The principles of war borrowing have been stated explicitly by the United States Department of the Treasury. In his annual report to Congress, the Secretary of the Treasury enumerates them as follows: [1]

1. The necessary funds should be raised in such a manner as to minimize the risk of inflation.

2. The liquidity of the nation's institutions should be maintained and increased, thereby placing them in a strong position to confront the problems of the postwar period.

3. Small investors in Government securities should be protected against loss.

4. The cost of financing the war should be kept at a reasonable level.

In practical terms, the first principle means to borrow as much as possible from non-bank investors, because in this country commercial banks are the only type of financial institutions which can pay for what they buy by creating their own credit. The second principle explains why the short-term financing policy has been adopted. The third principle explains the adoption by the Treasury of the redeemable savings bonds. The fourth principle is merely another form of expressing the Treasury's cheap money policy.

---

[1] *Annual Report*, Treasury, for 1943, p. 5.

Non-inflationary Borrowing

As pointed out in Chapter Ⅰ, inflation may easily, though not inevitably be a result of wartime borrowing. The essential thing in selling public debt is, therefore, to sell as much as possible to the ultimate investors. The Treasury's report says, "Bonds sold in this manner absorb consumer purchasing power directly at its source and, consequently, have a maximum impact upon consumer spending. "[1] If all the debt were sold to non-banking investors, the effect would be the same as if the fund was raised from taxation. This does not mean, however, that consumer purchasing power would be reduced to the full amount of the bonds sold. The qualifications must be taken into account. First, investors may buy Government bonds with borrowed funds; Second, they may buy Government bonds with their past savings.

Of the funds raised through borrowing during this war, about 59 percent was contributed by non-bank investors, while during World War Ⅰ the percentage was 81%. This does not mean that it was more successful in the last war, because in World War Ⅰ the practice of borrowing from banks in order to purchase Government securities was much more common than in the present war. The National City Bank of New York described the practice in 1918 thus, "During the war the Federal Reserve Bank as fiscal agent of the Government had to encourage a program of 'borrow and buy', among banks in order that they might buy certificates of indebtedness far in excess of their available funds, and among individuals that they might buy bonds far in excess of their current savings. The results was an immense increase in the loan accounts of the member banks, and a proportionately great increase in their rediscounts with the Federal Reserve Bank. "[2] We shall see later that during this war a considerable volume of bank

---

[1]　Ibid. , p. 6.

[2]　*Monthly Letter.* National City Bank of New fork, February 1918, p. 3. Cf. also B. H. Beck hart, *Discount Policy of the Fidel Reserve System*, New York, 1924, p. 292.

loans on Government securities has also been extended by commercial banks to brokers and dealers and to others in times of War Loan Drives. Such loans by the member banks which report weekly amounted to 3. 8 billion dollars at the close of the Seventh War Loan Drive (July 20 , 1945). [1]

Funds used to buy Government securities may come from the nation's past savings in various ways. Individuals may draw upon their savings deposita to buy bonds or they may invest their funds in Government securities indirectly through insurance companies and savings banks. The Government itself invests trust funds in Government obligations. In these cases the funds so invested do not have the effect of curtailing current consumption. If such funds were previously invested in private business, the transfer represents a shift of capital from private business to war effort. If, however, the funds were previously uninvited, such as those hoarded by the public, this practice tends to make idle funds active and hence tends to increase inflationary forces.

The largest part of the funds invested in Government securities by ultimate investors come from their current savings. It does not follow, however, that if current saving were not invested in Government securities, an increase in current consumption by the same amount would occur. A large portion of Government securities is apparently purchased by personal who would have saved part of their income in the ordinary course of events. This group merely substituted the direct ownership of Government bonds for a savings deposit or life insurance policy, which, in turn, would probably have resulted ultimately in an investment in Government bonds. This is especially true for purchases made by the higher-income classes. As a result, non-bank holdings of Government securities have greatly increased with only a relatively very small increase in time and savings deposits. From 1940 to 1944, inclusive, demand deposits increased by about 125 per cent, while time deposits in commercial banks and savings banks increased by

---

[1] For details, see p. 388.

only 47 per cent. [1]

The reduction in new capital formation for private enterprises is an important source of war funds. It is desirable, therefore, that ordinary current savings be diverted from its ordinary investment to war debts. Regulation of new capital issues, therefore, may be viewed as a means of assisting the flotation of war bonds. New security issues were extremely large in 1941, [2] the total amount of new and refunding issues being 5.5 billion dollars, compared with an increase of 12.1 billion dollars in the Government interest-bearing debt during that year. New security issues remind stationary at 2 billion dollars in 1942 and 1943, and increased to 4 billion dollars in 1944.

With the object of raising funds as far as possible from non-bank investors, the Treasury Department on May 1, 1941—more than six months before Pearl Harbor-introduced, and initiated a popular sales campaign for three new issues of savings bonds-Series E, F and G. Immediately after the entrance of the United States into the war, the Treasury began to emphasize the development of the payroll saving plan for the purchase of Series E bonds. In May 1941, the Treasury also initiated a campaign for the sale of other types of Government securities. In the fall of 1942, it decided to supplement continuous sales program by periodic sales campaigns—the War Loan Drives—which will be discussed fully in Chapter Ⅲ.

No matter how persuasive the theory of non-bank borrowing is, historical data reveal that the banks have always been indispensable investors in financing large wars. Banks were first directly used under a plan in which they subscribed all of a given loan; later they were used merely as agents for the Government, but they still held a large amount of the public debt. One or the other of these methods was employed in floating all the loans previous to the war of 1812, with the exception of the 8 per cent loans of 1798 and 1890. Even the first loan of the War of 1812 was taken directly by the banks. Only the unwillingness of Secretary Chase to give

---

①   Cf. E. Stein and G. Backman, *War Economics.* Now York, 1942, p. 135.

②   Gross capital formation in 1941, including consumer durable goods, was around 38 billion dollars. See *Survey of Current Business*, February 1942, p. 7.

up the sub-treasury system and the policy of maintaining payment in coin account for the failure to utilize the banks during the earlier part of the Civil War. [1]During World War I , commercial banks took up 4. 3 billion dollars of Government securities and lent 2. 3 billion dollars on Government obligations. During World War II , in which greater emphasis has been placed on non-bank investors, the banking system owned 37. 7 per cent of the total interest-bearing Government debt.

Short-Term Financing

Although theories and policies with respect to the duration of public loans have been a matter of much controversy, short-term financing has in fact been an American tradition. Mr. Love states in his conclusion: [2]

In each major period (including the 1990's) the practical financiers assumed the roles of debaters on the academic question of funded versus floating debt. In every instance, those who argued for the funded debt, would doubtlessly have been given the decision if they had been judged on the basis of logic—and especially if bankers sat in the judges' sect. However, without exception, short terms were attached to a sufficient proportion of government obligations to enable the resulting notes to make an important contribution to the Treasury in the form of what was, for all practical purposes, a paramount fund.

A glance at our history serves at once to leave a rather definite impression as to the importance which this type of financing has played in Treasury operations.

---

[1]   Cf. Robert A. Love, *Federal Financing*, New York, 1931, pp. 214 – 215. in 1941, 41. 1 percent in 1942, 42. 3 per cent in 1943 and 41. 9 per cent in 1944, Commercial bank holdings of Government securities increased from 20. 9 billion dollars at the end of 1940 to 85. 9 billion dollars by the end of 1944. The details of the distribution of war debt will be described in Ch. III.

[2]   Robert A. Love, *Federal Financing*, New York, 1931, pp. 228 – 230. Cf. also Ch. III , "Short Term Financing and the Resulting Seniority Features," pp. 57 – 73.

Especially during the 1812, the 1837, the Civil War and the 1890 periods, resort to short-time obligations grew out of what was ordinarily thought to be dire necessity...

With the exception of the 1890 period, when the situation was remarkably similar to the 1837 period, the later periods present slightly different situations. During the World War, the resort to short-term obligations could hardly be explained in terms of necessity unless, indeed, one cares to claim that the motive of necessity is back of the attempt to secure low nominal interest rates by means of resorting to an inflation which in turn is attained through supplying currency equivalents...

... Why should government officials invariably have turned to the practice of making their wartime obligations payable within a short time? The answer is undoubtedly to be found in the fact that the promise of early maturity lends an element of currency to the government obligations. Equipped with this feature, the government's promise to pay need no longer depend upon the investment appeal. Instead they could rely upon their liquidity, upon their close resemblance to currency, if you please, to make them attractive to the public. It is apparent for this reason that the Treasury, in its search for a shortcut to financial strength, has so often resorted to the use of notes.

Mr. Love is correct in his conclusion. The principle announced by the Treasury that the liquidity of the nation's institution should be maintained and increased is, in effect, another way of stating the fact that the liquidity of Government obligations induces the nation's institutions to purchase more than they would in the ordinary course of events. The low interest rate on public issues is another factor which leads the Treasury to resort to short-term financing. Especially when short rate is pegged and is fixed lower than the longer term rates, as is true today, the Treasury is induced to borrow at the short end of the interest curve. Short-term financing and cheap money policy have ever been twins.

Another object of the policy of short-term financing which the Treasury stated in its announcement is to place the nation's institutions " in a strong position to confront the problems of the postwar period" . The Secretary of the Treasury said in his report: [1]

> The composition of the public debt will also contribute to economic stability by releasing purchasing power when the stimulus of increased spending is needed... The same circumstances which have made it advisable to concentrate a large proportion of the war-time debt in securities of short maturity will continue in time of peace. The contribution which such a structure of the public debt furnishes to the liquidity of the whole economy will be an important factor in the maintenance of full employment in the postwar period. The funding of a major portion of the short-term debt into long-term securities, on the other hand, would serve merely to increase the interest cost to the Government and to shift the risk of future changes in interest rates (and corresponding movement in the opposite direction of bond prices) from the Government to private investors. Such a policy would increase, rather than reduce, the factors making for instability in the postwar economy, as the Government is in a better position to bear the risk of changes in interest rates then most classes of investors and—unlike class of investors—is in a position to minimize it.

This suggests that the short-term securities held in the hands of the public may serve as a cushion for postwar spending. And for this reason the Treasury opposes the suggestion that such a short-term debt should be refunded into funded debt in due course. What the postwar situation will be is a matter of dispute. Experience, however, has shown that a large volume of floating debt is never desirable after a great war. In the years following world war I , it was found necessary in each

---

[1] *Annual Report*, Treasury, for 1944, p. 8.

country to reduce this kind of public debt. During the war, patriotism and lack of other investment opportunities played a large part in making it easy for nations to borrow, but in the postwar period, it became more and more difficult continually to renew large amounts of floating debt at time when longer-term issues had to be refunded and redemptions of war saving securities were heavy. By 1925, the size of the floating debt in France had become an embarrassing problem to Treasury and urgent efforts were made to refund the debt during the Caillaux Ministry. The problem is complicated by the desire to maintain a low interest rate on short-term debt. Unless the Treasury raises short-term interest rates to induce investors to retain their short-term debt, the practice of short term borrowing must be stopped. In general the short-term debt should be used to meet temporary cash shortages or to provide cash in anticipation of a long-term financing program. It should be discharged (paid off) or refunded into long-term debt in due course. [1]

During the war, short-term borrowing has predominated in all belligerent countries, especially in the United Kingdom, which previously had much the smallest percentage of floating debt. By the end of fiscal year 1944, [2] about 54 per cent of the United States public marketable debt was due or callable within 5 years, as against 45 per cent of the Dominion debt and 44 per cent of the United Kingdom debt. By June 30, 1945, the floating debt of the United States Treasury, consisting of bills and certificates, has amounted to 51.2 billion dollars, about 20 per cent of the total public debt. In addition, 23.5 billion of Treasury notes and about 20.6 billion of Treasury bonds maturing within 5 years were outstanding. This makes a total of about 52 per cent of the total marketable public debt of 181.3 billion dollars. Added to this, there were outstanding on June 30, 1945, 10.1 billion dollars of Treasury tax and savings notes and 45.6

---

[1] See the analysis made by Miss Gail K Sharpe, "The problem of the Floating Debt," *Financing Highlights*, The Chase National Bank, Vol.7. No.1, January 11, 1945 (mimeographed).

[2] Harold L. Seligman, "Patterns of Wartime Borrowing in the United States, the United Kingdom, and Canada," *Federal Reserve Bulletin*, November 1944, p. 1056.

billion of savings bonds. The former are redeemable and are likely to be used as payments for taxes within a short period. The savings bonds, though having a longer maturity of 10 or 12 years, are also redeemable and therefore, are as liquid as saving deposits. The maturity distribution of public debt is shown in Table 5. Table 6 shows the short-term Government obligations outstanding on June 30, 1945.

Table 5　Maturity Distribution of Marketable Public Debt (In Millions of Dollars)

Issues	1941 Dec.	1942 Dec.	1943 Dec.	1944 Dec.	1945 June.
Bills	2002	6627	13072	16428	17041
Certificates	—	10534	22843	30401	34136
Notes	5997	9863	11175	23039	23497
Bonds	33367	49268	67944	91585	106448
Within 5 Years	3460	5830	8524	7824	
In 5 – 10 years	7585	17080	28360	44087	
In 10 – 20 years	17252	16295	14310	14445	
After 20 years	5070	10065	16751	25227	
Total Marketable	41562	76488	115230	161646	181319
Cross direct debt	57938	108170	165877	230630	258682

Source: *Federal Reserve Bulletin*.

Table 6　Maturity Distribution of Marketable Public Debt Outstanding on June 30, 1945 (In Millions of Dollars)

Issues	1 yr.	2 yr.	3 yr.	4 yr.	5 yr.
Bills	17041				
Certificates	34136				
Notes	5238	10. 118	4394	3784	
Bonds	4099	—	6860	2036	7630
Total	60514	10118	11254	5784	7630
Percentage of Total Marketable	33. 3	5. 5	6. 1	3. 1	4. 2

Source: *Federal Reserve Bulletin*.

Table 7　Maturity Distribution of Marketable Public Debt
in World War Ⅰ and World War Ⅱ（Percentage of Total Marketable Debt）

End Years	Total *	Bills	Cert.	Notes	Bonds
World War Ⅰ					
1917	7102	0	8. 1	0. 3	76. 5
1918	19846	0	11. 3	0. 04	79. 0
1919	24696	0	14. 1	18. 9	64. 0
1920	22988	0	11. 3	18. 4	66. 6
Word War Ⅱ					
1941	41562	4. 1	0	14. 4	80. 2
1942	76488	8. 6	13. 7	12. 9	64. 4
1943	115230	11. 3	19. 8	9. 7	58. 9
1944	116648	10. 2	18. 9	14. 3	56. 1

＊ In millions of dollars, including pre-war and postwar savings bonds.

Source: "Banking and Monetary Statistics," 1941, *Federal Reserve Bulletin*.

It is clear from Table 6 that 33. 3 per cent of the total marketable debt maturing within one year and 52. 2 per cent within 5 years. The situation has changed little during the course of the war. In spite of the growing demand by the public for longer-term issues, especially in the second half of 1944, and the first half of 1945, the Treasury appears to have no intention of refunding its floating debt into long-term securities, nor does the treasury expect to do so in the near future. Table 7 gives the date for the various issues as percentages of the total marketable debt, in comparison with those of the last war. The Table shows clearly the shift from long to short-term securities during both wars. In World War Ⅰ treasury bills were not issued. Certificates outstanding increased from 8. 1 per cent in 1917 to 14. 1 per cent in 1919, the year of highest debt level, while bonds declined from 76. 5 per cent to 64. 6 per cent. In World War Ⅱ, bills and certificates increased rapidly from a total of 4. 1 per cent in 1941（certificates were first issued in 1948）to about 30 per cent in 1944. During the same period bonds issues declined from 80. 2 per cent to 56. 1 per cent.

Treasury bills have been made even more liquid by the fixed buying rate of the

Federal Reserve Banks and the repurchase option; thus they are looked upon by commercial banks as tantamount to excess reserves. Banks, however, have gradually reduced their holdings of bills and increased their holdings of bonds and certificates, using the latter to adjust their reserve situation. By the end of 1944, commercial banks held 72 billion dollars of Government securities, out of which 4.1 billion were bills, 15.0 billion were certificates, 15.4 billion were notes and 4.8 billion were bonds maturing within five years. About 54.5 per cent of their holding were securities maturing within five years and about 48.6 per cent were securities maturing within three years. Banks have lengthened their holdings recently; at the end of 1944, about 50 per cent of their holdings were maturing within three years. Since February 1942, the Treasury adopted the policy that no bank should buy Government securities for the investment of their demand deposits with a maturity on original issue of longer than 10 years. Limited amounts of the 2.5 percent long-term bonds were offered to banks for the investment of their time deposits only.

The certificate of indebtedness has assumed a greater and greater importance in the Treasury's short-term financing. This kind of security was an important investment in the financing of world war Ⅰ. But at that time certificates were issued in anticipation of the proceeds of taxes and liberty loans, and were later funded or extinguished by means of such taxes or loans. After the war, they were rapidly refunded or paid off. [1]This kind of short-term negotiable obligation had been used in the war of 1812, the crisis of 1837, the Mexican War, the crisis of 1857, the Civil War and the crisis of 1907. The first four cases arose from the inability to sell long-term bonds; the issues of the Civil war were largely a result of secretary chase's opposition to long-term bonds, heightened by his reluctance to adjust the interest yield of funded loans to the prevailing rate of the money market. [2]Their use in 1907 was limited. In this war, they have been used more

---

[1]   Cf. Gail E. Sharp, op. cit. , p. 3.

[2]   Jacob H. Hollander, *War Borrowing*, New York, 1919, pp. 8, 20.

extensively than in the last war, and the Treasury gives no evidence of an intention to follow the normal course of refunding them. They are hardly used in anticipation of taxes of funded debt. This policy of the Treasury has been a matter of much debate.

Redeemable Savings Bonds

As a third principle of war borrowing announced by the Treasury, the savings bonds are made redeemable to "protect small investors against losses." They are non-negotiable and payable on demand 60 days after the issue date. Their investment yield if held to maturity 2.9 per cent on Series E bonds is the highest obtainable on any United States Government security. This feature undoubtedly affords the investor protection against fluctuations in market value and provides him with a kind of liquid funds which can be converted at any time into cash.

When the savings bonds were issued in large amount in 1941, there was considerable discussion of the redeemable feature. Some held that investors would demand cash on a large scale should there be any adverse changes in the economy or in the political and military situation. The Treasury would have to take them up in large amounts if patriotism faded in certain phases of the war. And whenever large scale redemption took place, there would be the danger of inflation when the public liquidated its holdings and increased its purchasing power.

To these arguments, the Treasury answered as follows: Should there be any adverse changes, the nation suffers in the same way whether redeemable or marketable bonds are used. Marketable bonds may be disposed of by their owners and the proceeds spent for consumers' goods and services. "It does not matter," stated the Secretary of the Treasury. [1] As far as the main issue is concerned, whether the securities so disposed of are presented directly to the Treasury for redemption or are sold in the market. The Treasury department has considered itself the trustee for the inexperienced investor who purchases Government Securities,

---

[1] *Annual Report*, Treasury, 1943, p. 7.

therefore, it will maintain the value of such bonds by redemption. Moreover, the redemption feature is also advantageous to the Government: " (1) Non-negotiable securities with a guaranteed redemption value are not subject to the panicky liquidation which is likely to occur among small holders of marketable securities in the event of a decline in their market value, and so are not likely to be disposed of until the holder feels an actual need for the use of their proceeds. " And " (2) when non-negotiable securities are redeemed, they can be refunded in an orderly manner through the issuance of the types of new securities best fitted to the market at that time. In this respect, nonnegotiable securities are much superior from a technical point of view to marketable securities, which, under similar circumstances, would dribble into the market in small blocks—in part through irregular channels where the original holders may not have received full value. "

The Treasury is probably right in this respect. The savings bonds are designed to appeal to the mass of small investors who are not familiar with the fluctuations of the bond market. They need protection. Moreover, savings bonds were issued against a background of patriotic endeavor. People were urged to do their duty by buying more bonds. They should not be encouraged to speculate on the market. As Secretary Morgenthau says, "The Government must do more than finding billions of dollars. It must find these dollars in a way that will best safeguard the nation against the evils of inflation, and will give all American citizens a sense of taking a direct part in the defense of the country. "[1]

The redeemable feature, however, may be viewed from another angle. It is a device to make the securities more liquid, and, therefore, more attractive. The same motive, it was earlier pointed out, lies behind the philosophy of short-term borrowing. Various devices may be used to make a long-term obligation short. " Making notes receivable in payment of dues to the government, making them payable upon demand, and of course making

[1]   Speech, Spring 1941, Cf. Stein and Backman, *War Economics*, New York, 1942, p. 134.

them legal tender for all debts, simply constitute what is from our present point of view merely a means of minimizing, or eliminating entirely, that factor—the time element involved in maturity—which stands in the way of the acceptance of government obligations as currency. "①

Table 8   Savings Bonds Issues and Redemption (Millions of Dollars)

	Issued *	Redeemed *	Outstanding End of Period	Per cent Redeemed **
Series A-E				
1935 – 40	3573	379	3195	—
1941	1721	166	4750	5. 2
1942	6090	313	10526	6. 6
1943	10508	1461	19574	13. 9
1944	12662	3082	29153	15. 7
1945 Jan-Feb	1533	610	30075	—
Total	36087	6011	97273	
Series F-G				
1941	1393	3	1390	—
1942	3170	37	4523	2. 7
1943	3389	124	7789	2. 7
1944	3678	259	11208	3. 3
1945	469	54	11623	—
Total	12099	477	36533	

∗ Includes accrued discount.

∗∗ Redemption as a percentage of amount outstanding and of previous year.

Source: *Monthly Review*. Federal Reserve Bank of New York, April 1945, p. 27.

The redemption of savings bonds is shown in Table 8. It is noticeable that the rate of redemption has been accelerating. In 1941, the amount of Series E bond redeemed was only 5. 2 per cent of the amount outstanding at the end of previous

① Robot A. Love, *Federal Financing*, New York, 1931, p. 230. Cf. Jens P. Jensen, *Problems of Public Finance*, New York, 1921, p. 474.

year. The percentage increased to 13. 9 in 1943 and to 15. 7 in 1944. The projection of 1945 may be as high as 16. 2 per cent. A similar trend, but to a lesser extent, occurred in the Series F and G bonds.

Monthly redemption figures (not shown in the table) give a better idea of the picture. In March and June of 1945 the savings bonds redemptions of all series represented 1. 11 per cent and 0. 92 per cent respectively of the total outstanding at the end of the previous month. For the same months in 1944 the percentages were 0. 85% and 0. 74% respectively, and in 1943 were 0. 77% and 0. 68% respectively. The National City Bank of New York studied the situation in August 1944, and concluded: "The redemption of savings bonds may fairly be compared with the withdrawal of savings bank deposits, or the surrender of life insurance policies, where experience has shown that a fairly substantial turnover is normally to be expected. There is evidence that withdrawal of savings bank deposits run annually to 20 per cent or more of total balances. Insurance surrenders and lapses combined have run from 4 to 6 per cent of the total even in prosperous years, although currently they are lower. " [1]Thus the National City Bank expected at that time the redemption of savings bonds would rest at something like 9 per cent annually of total balances. The data for 1945, however, show that the rate may run as high as 1 per cent monthly or 12 per cent annually, and the trend is rising.

The more important is the circumstances that the later issues are redeemed more rapid and that the lower denomination of the bonds the higher is the rate of redemption. The 1942 issue was redeemed at a greater rate than any of those preceding issues; and the 1943 issue has returned faster still. Treasury figures show that at the end of the first year, the redemption of the 1942 issue was 16 per cent for the $ 25 denomination bond, but only 4 per cent for the $ 500 and $ 1000 bond. These facts directly affect the policy of the Treasury. The redemption is used, as announced by the Treasury, for the protection of small investors. Therefore, unless the bonds sold " stay sold " to a satisfactory extent, and a large quantity of small

---

[1] *Monthly Letter*, National City Bank of New York, October 1944.

denominations is held by the lower-income classes, the objective of the financing program is not being reached.

Cheap Money Policy

The last principle of wartime borrowing announced by the Treasury is that "the cost of financing the war should be kept at a reasonable level. " In other words, the yields on Government securities should be kept low. Much debate turns about this principle. The actual course of the movement and the structure of interest rates during the war will be discussed in connection with the Federal Reserve policy in Chapter IV. At present, emphasis is put on the desirability of the cheap money policy.

Cheap money policy did not begin with the war. It was the essential part of the economics of the New Deal regime. In fact, it has been the principle of Government borrowing at all times. Mr. Love, in his study of federal financing, draws the following conclusion:

The limitation upon the rate of interest has apparently arisen in the main out of political pressure (or fear of it) aimed toward keeping the rate down to a level which would appeal to the populace as reasonable and economical. In connection with this aim practically every authorizing act has limited the rate which the Treasury could pay. Freedom from such restrictions is indeed to be found, as, for example, in 1813 when the usual limitation was omitted, and during the World War when Mr. McAdoo induced Congress to leave the rate of interest to his discretion. By and large, however, we may consider that Congress has ever considered it a duty either to specify the rate of interest or to limit the maximum to be paid.

A factor which has been far more effective than this legal restriction, however, is to be found in the bias which political pressure has instilled into Treasury officials, which succeeded in restraining them from adopting a nominal rate high enough to encourage the purchase of bonds. Illustrations of such an influence appear repeatedly throughout our history. During the period following the Revolutionary War, objection to high rates led to interesting compensations in the form of premiums, commissions, and discounts in order to keep the nominal rate of interest down. This procedure was repeated in 1812, when such sentiment was also partially responsible for resort to Treasury notes as a means of securing funds at low rates. During the Civil War, the desire to secure loans at low cost was a predominant reason for the legal tenders and the resulting financial chaos. In the modern period, the same reason again accounted for a series of features and for organized efforts to revise the entire financial and monetary structure to contribute to the purpose at hand. [1]

The situation in the 1930's, however, is somewhat different from Mr. Love's observations. Under the New Deal the financing policies which began with the pump-priming and then resulted in the compensatory deficit financing, were based on the theory of over saving. The essence of the New Deal policies was to increase the volume and to alter the distribution of money income in such a way as to raise the total effective demand. It was hoped that the reduction of interest rates, which followed the expansion of monetary supplies that accompanied the huge inflow of gold and the sales of Government securities to banks, would raise the propensity to consume, that is, increase the effective demand. While during to twenties the emphasis was on central bank policy in order to influence the national economy through the control of the interest rate (with more or less an idea of a "natural rate", which would equate saving and investment), the emphasis was shifted during the thirties from central bank policy to Government spending. Professor Williams observed that "deficit spending is the logical sequel to central bank policy, and it was entirely logical that its first phase should be pump-priming, for

---

[1] Robert A, Love, *Federal Financing*, New York, 1931, pp. 208 – 209.

the latter does not differ in purposes or in general analysis of the problem from central bank policy, but seeks to make more effective the methods of attack. The financing of deficits represents a further step toward making an easy money policy effective, for when combined with pressure through reserves, it affords an avenue for expansion of bank assets and deposits accompanied by a declining yield on government securities. "[1]

The achievements or failures of the New Deal financial policy are outside the scope of this discussion. The pertinent fact is that the United States, before the outbreak of the war in Europe, had raised 24. 2 billion dollars of Federal debt in the period of cheap money policy since 1933. In the first period, from 1933 to 1936, 50 per cent of the Federal expenditure was raised by borrowing, of which one half was from commercial banks and the Federal Reserve Banks while less than one half came from savings institutions, trust funds and the public. In the second period, from 1937 to 1939, 30 per cent of the Federal expenditure was raised by borrowing, all of which came from savings. [2] Yield on long-term Government bonds declined from 4 per cent per annul at the beginning of 1932 to 1. 89 per cent at the end of 1940. During the same period yield of high grade corporate bond declined from about 4. 5 per cent to 2. 5 per cent. Short rates fluctuated abruptly in 1932 and 1933, and were maintained at low level thereafter.

During World War I , Government securities were floated at the rates below the market rates. The first Liberty Loan bonds were issued at 3. 5 per cent, subsequent issues were floated at rates varying from 4 per cent to 4. 5 per cent, as compared with English war loans of yields from 4 per cent to 6. 6 per cent and Canadian War loans of yields over 5 per cent. [3] When the first Liberty Loans were floated on June 15, 1917, the interest rate was 5 per cent on sixty to-ninety day

---

[1] John H. Williams, "Deficit Spending," *American Economic Review*, Vol. XXX, No. 5, February 1941, p. 52.

[2] A. H. Hansen, "Defense Financing and Inflation Potentialities," *Review of Economic Statistics*, February 1941, p. 5.

[3] *Federal Reserve Bulletin*, November 1918, p. 1070, the tax-exempt privilege of the Liberty Loans must be taken into account.

commercial paper in New York, and 4. 76 per cent on ten selected American railway bonds, the comparatively low rate Liberty bonds had to rely upon the tax-exempt feature in its flotation. Professor Beckhart describes the Treasury's views as follows:

The Secretary thought that the payment of high rates would enable bondholders to become wealthier, and in some mysterious way he linked high interest rates with inflation, feeling that prices would be forced up by the payment of rates commensurating with the market rates then prevailing. [1]

In his annual report in 1918, the Secretary of the Treasury listed two reasons for his attempt to maintain a low rate of interest. First, higher rates would result in the increasing cost of the war. Secondly, they would result in greater "depreciation in all other forms of investment securities". [2]

The Treasury's low interest rate policy in the Liberty loans aroused much criticism. The first Liberty bonds had to carry tax-exemption and conversion features to be attractive, and in the subsequent issues, higher rates had to be offered. Some /who favored low rates even considered forcing the purchase of bonds by resorting to a method equal to legal tender financing. [3] Another consequence of the Treasury's policy, we shall see later, is that the Federal Reserve Bank lost control over the market through their Bank rate policy. Professor Beckhart describes the alternative policy thus: [4]

What would have been consequences had the Treasury Department floated its obligations at market rates of interest?

(1) It would have been easier to lodge the bonds with the ultimate investor, for it is a truism that the higher the rate of interest the more are

---

[1] Benjamin H. Beck-hart, *Discount Policy of the Federal Reserve System*, New York, 1924, pp. 275 – 276.

[2] *Annual Report*, Treasury, 1917, p. 4.

[3] Cf. Robert A. Love, *Federal Financing*, New York, 1931, p. 153.

[4] Benjamin H. Beckhart, *Discount Policy*, op. cit, p. 278.

people inclined to save. Because the bonds would have been lodged to a greater extent with the ultimate investor and because they would not have been so inclined to dispose of them either from need of funds or from the desire to invest in more attractive ways.

(2) Because people would have been more inclined to save in order to purchase bonds and less inclined to borrow, the Federal Reserve System would not have been compelled to resort to inflationary tactics Prices in the war and post-armistice period which would not have risen to the same extent. Credit could have been controlled through fluctuations to the Bank rate.

(3) Since prices would have been lower, the Government would have had to float fewer bonds and in this manner would have been fully compensated for the increasing interest charges.

(4) Such a policy would have tended to transfer existing capital from non-essential and low rate investment to government bonds thereby absorbing free capital, discouraging non-essential production and reducing consumption.

During this war, the interest rates on public debt have been much lower than those in the last war, even lower than the lowest level during the new Deal regime. On June 30, 1940, at the beginning of the defense program, the average rate of interest on the public debt was 2.51 percent; by June 30, 1945, it had fallen to about 1.51 per cent. In October 1942, the Treasury stabilized the rates of interest on borrowings over a range of 3/8ths of 1 per cent on bills and 7/8ths of 1 per cent on certificates up to 2 per cent on 10 – year bonds and 2.5 per cent for long-term bonds. This was known as the "treasury curve".[1] In recent times, the increasing demand for long-term securities has bid up the prices and hence pulled down their yields. Since 1943 and until July 1945, there has been a slight but persistent tendency to lower the yields on Government securities, especially in the first half of 1945. The trends are shown

---

[1] See p. 414.

in Chart 7 on page 416. The annual average rates on Government obligations are shown below: ①

	7 to 9 years Taxable(%)	15 years Taxable(%)	15 years Partially exempt(%)
1940	—	—	2. 21
1941	—	—	2. 05
1942	1. 93	2. 46	2. 09
1943	1. 96	2. 47	1. 98
1944	1. 94	2. 48	1. 92
1945 *	1. 69	2. 39	1. 71

* First six months.

The average rate of interest on all new borrowing during the five years of defense and war is about 1. 70 per cent per annum, despite the fact that over 97 per cent of the borrowing consisted of taxable securities. The average rate of interest on war borrowings during the last war was 4. 25 per cent and all the securities issued were either wholly or partially tax-exempt. ②It is clear that reduction of interest rates has resulted in tremendous savings in the cost of interest on the Government debt during the present war.

Interest rates of the national debts of England and Canada have also dropped. The largest decline occurred in Canada but the rate there still remains above that in England and considerably above that of the United States. A comparison of the cost of public debt in the three countries based on the total amount of debt and annual interest payments appears below:③

The table reveals that the United States Government has borrowed the most cheaply during this war. Since a public debt of 300 billion dollars after the war

---

① *Federal Reserve Bulletin*, July 1941, 1944, 1945.

② *Annual Report*, Treasury, 1945, p. 8.

③ Harold L. Seligman, "Patterns of Wartime Borrowing in the United States, the United Kingdom and Canada," *Federal Reserve Bulletin*, November.

Cost of Public Debt

Fiscal year	United States(%)	United Kingdom(%)	Canada(%)
1939	2. 53	3. 09	3. 71
1940	2. 51	2. 96	3. 60
1941	2. 44	3. 61	3. 31
1942	2. 26	2. 56	3. 20
1943	1. 98	2. 47	2. 83
1944	1. 92	2. 44	2. 75

appears probable, the government would pay at the present rate, an interest charge of 6 billion dollars annually for many years to come. If the interest rate were as high as it was during the last war, a fixed debt charge of 12. 5 billion dollars, or more than three times the average total receipts of the government in the decade of the twenties, would be necessary. Evidently this is the fundamental motive of the Treasury's cheap money borrowing policy.

Contemporary economists have disagreed among themselves as to whether this policy of borrowing at a low interest rate is justifiable. Interest payments have been reduced, but not without other costs. [1]All the weaknesses of this policy displayed during the last war have reoccurred in the past four years. The most important, of course, is the effect on the incentive to save. The National City Bank makes the following analysis. [2]

While a further lowering of interest rates would enable the Government to borrow more cheaply, the effect upon the incentive to save needs most serious consideration. As well stated by Mr. Beaudry Leman, president of the Banque Canadienne National, at the annual shareholders' meeting of that institution in January, "When the States is the largest borrower, low money rates are

---

[1] Some even go so far as to say that cheap money makes Government borrowing cost more, Cf. W. W. Townsend, "How Cheap is Cheap Money," *Commercial and Financial Chronicle*, August 31, 1944, p. 942.

[2] *Monthly Letter*, National City Bank of New York, March 1945, p. 29.

equivalent to an impost and are tantamount to a levy on the many forms of savings, such as life insurance, legacies, fixed interest-bearing securities. To ransom savings is to discourage thrift and the consequences are not slow to become manifest. " If savings banks and insurance companies are unable to get even the yields heretofore accepted as "wartime lows", they will have to pass on the reductions to the great masses of people who save through them. Already these institutions have had to cut substantially their rates paid on policies and accounts, and today these rates are at their all time lows.

The effects on individual holders of Government obligations are the same. Evidently a large, perhaps larger, portion of the bonds sold to individuals has been disposed of under patriotic pressure instead of a profit inducement. It is true that the interest rate on savings bonds are not affected by market changes, but the l0-year maturity rate of 2. 9 per cent is already very low in comparison with the high rate of wartime profits. Moreover, many investors prefer the straight coupon marketable bonds to the savings bonds, which must be registered and held to maturity in order to receive the maximum interest.

In the second place, while a prolonged period of low interest rates will force savings institutions to cut down rates of interest paid by them to depositors or policyholders, it at the same time will impel commercial banks to enter into risk loans. Criticism had previously been voiced when commercial banks engaged in term loans, personal loans, instalment loans, etc. during the period of low interest in the thirties. Since that time banks have relied to a greater and greater extent upon investment for maintaining their earnings. By the end of 1944, 78 per cent of the earning assets of all banks in the United States consisted of investments, and of this amount 92 per cent more Government securities. Should the yields on Government obligations decline further, or should the yields remain significantly low in comparison with industrial profits for a considerable time, banks would either have to turn to risk loans or switch to corporate securities of high-yield but lower quality. Bank assets would then mature later than the liabilities, thus causing lack of balance in bank statements.

In the third place, the present pattern of the structure of interest rates, with the short rate materially lower than the long rate, would have the effect of inducing business to borrow on short terms. This is an especially important problem in the postwar period. The Treasury's present borrowing policy seems to have continued the advantages of cheap money and short-term borrowing. This indicates that some time in the future, the Treasury will suffer from that same policy when it is obliged to refund its floating debt into long-term obligations. Should private business take advantage of short-term borrowing in the post-war period, they would probably gain at the expense of the Government. And if businesses borrow funds on short-term for long-term purposes, we would face the danger of insolvency as other countries had in the crisis of 1931.

A fourth major disadvantage of the cheap money policy is that of distortion in the relationship of interest rate and profit rate. If current saving earns only a low return, then the capital value of past savings which earn at a higher fixed rate must inevitably rise in proportion. And, if the long rate falls while profit rises, profits of industry would then be capitalism in the stock market in unhealthy boom conditions. [1]This is why a speculative stock market boom is usually a concomitant of a prolonged period of cheap money policy. Sometimes a similar speculation occurs in the real estate market. The housing boom in England and the building boom in Sweden during 1933 – 1939 were caused at least in part[2] by a cheap money policy. The combined result of these developments is the road towards inflation. It has been argued that interest charges are not a major factor in the cost of industry and that businesses are not greatly influenced by low money rate. Nevertheless low interest rates generally induce business activity, or, at the very least, the

---

[1] Cf. F. G. Conolly, "Reflections on the Cheap-Money Policy, Particularly in England," Supplement to Svenska Handels Banken's Index, October 1939.

[2] The housing boom in England was partly due to the fact that food prices declined while money incomes remained stable. Cf. *The Economist*, London, October 1935, p. 795. The building boom in Sweden was partly fostered by the Government's program of public works, Cf. Richard A Lester, *Monetary Experiments*, Princeton University, 1939, pp. 271 – 272.

psychological effect of the buoyancy of the share market offers a strong stimulus. [1]

It was earlier observed that a cheap money policy compels the central bank to resort to inflationary methods to maintain the market for Government securities. Because of the reduced incentive to save, a larger part of the Government's debt must be financed through banking institutions. This, together with the inflationary potentialities just reviewed, puts the national economy in a critical position. So far these inflationary forces have been suppressed by drastic wartime controls—over prices, wages, manpower, raw materials and consumption—which are probably the most essential elements in the success of the American war economy. However, it cannot be expected that these controls will continue indefinitely in the postwar period, unless we decide to substitute totalitarianism—the evil against which the war was fought-for capitalism.

Still a fifth point to be stressed is the social influence of the cheap money policy. A prolonged period of cheap money tends to exploit the rentier class, among which are most of the small savers depositors in savings banks, holders of life insurance policies, etc. , and a large part of the bondholders. The larger savings of the rich classes are generally invested in property and equity shares, which, we have shown before, tend to rise in value during periods of low return on current savings. Even in certain phases of inflation, owners of equities may profit, or at least maintain the value of their holdings. Thus the small savers, the middle class, are the most vulnerable part of the community in times of cheap money and the subsequent inflation. We must emphasize, furthermore, that the middle class is the stabilizing element in the community. When it is destroyed, power will shift either to the extreme left or to the extreme right. That is, either communism or fascism will be the final result.

---

[1] Referring to the cheap money policy in England in the thirties, Connolly says : "Businessmen are relieved from the depressing influence of low and falling share prices. . . This cherry brandy effect of cheap money is, I believe, its most significant influence at the turn of the business cycle. " And this is "the most important single contribution towards overcoming the great depression in England or elsewhere. " F. G. Connolly, op. cit. , p. 10.

Diversification of Securities

Two additional features may be observed among the principles of borrowing announced by the Treasury. These are the diversification of securities offered and the abolition of the tax-exemption feature.

During the last war, successive issues of the Liberty loans were essentially uniform in their characteristics, except that the certificate of indebtedness was used for short-term accommodations. During this war, a deliberate diversification of the various types of instruments has been employed in the borrowing process. The securities offered have been described by the Secretary of Treasury Morgenthau as follows: [1]

> The Treasury has so diversified its offerings of security as to provide a security adapted to the requirements of each major class of investors. Long-term marketable bonds have been sold principally to insurance companies and savings banks; commercial banks have been offered more liquid marketable obligations having terms of 10 years or less; one year certificates of indebtedness and Treasury savings notes having a maturity of 3 years but redeemable at the owner's option after six months, have been especially attractive for the investment of temporary accumulations of business concerns. The principal emphasis in sales of securities to individuals has been upon Series savings bonds, which have a maturity of 10 years but which are redeemable at the owner's demand after 60 days.

In other words, typical securities have been offered to four major groups:

(1) To savings institutions long-term bonds.

---

[1] *Annual Report*, Treasury, 1944, p. 7.

The 2.5 per cent Treasury bonds, callable within 21 years, maturing within 26 years

The 2 per cent Treasury bonds, callable within 8 years, maturing within 10 years

(2) For business concerns: Medium and short term issues.

The 2 per cent Treasury bonds

The Treasury Tax savings notes maturing within 3 years, redeemable after six months

The series F and G savings bonds, offered at discount, maturity 12 years.

(3) For commercial banks: Medium and short-term securities.

The 2 per cent Treasury bonds.

The 0.875 per cent certificates of indebtedness, maturity 1 year

The Treasury bills, offered at discount, maturity 3 months

(4) For individuals: Non-marketable bonds,

The Series E savings bonds, offered at discount, maturity 10 years, redeemable after 60 days.

Of course, the above list does not include all the types of securities issued, nor does it include all the classes of investors. The Series F and G bonds, for instance, are designed for pension funds, associations, and trust funds as well as corporations. Five-year bonds at 1% – 0.75% and 1.5%, three-year notes at 1.25%, and long-term bonds at 2.25% were also used. In the War Loan drives, a variety of issues were offered in order to attract funds from all groups of non-bank investors. Each of these drives has included the three types of savings bonds and the saving notes that are continuously available, as well as three issues of marketable securities of different maturities, consisting of certificates of indebtedness, intermediate-term Treasury bonds and long-term Treasury bonds. [1]

---

[1] See pp. 369 – 370.

The objectives of the diversification of offerings, as explained by Secretary Morgenthau, were to eliminate the motive of open market sales after the war, to promote a smooth transition to peacetime economy and to cushion purchasing power in the postwar period when increase of spending power would be needed. [1]

In offering securities to different classes of investors, the Treasury has always borne in mind the fact that the time which the original purchaser of a security will hold it will depend, principally, upon his own future needs and convenience and to a very minor extent upon the nominal maturity of the security... The adaptation of the securities offered to the particular needs of different classes of investors, taken in conjunction with appropriate open market policy, obviates the possibility of a disorderly liquidation of securities through the market...

Smooth transition to peacetime economy will be promoted by the distribution of public debt securities of different types among various classes of investors. Corporation which have invested their reserves for reconversion and postwar expansion in certificates of indebtedness and Treasury savings notes suffer no impairment in the liquidity of their reserves by such investment. After the War they may sell or allow their holdings of certification to run off and may present their savings notes for redemption without loss of principal.

The composition of the public debt will also contribute to economic stability by releasing purchasing power when the stimulus of increased spending is needed... The distribution of saving bonds among many individuals in the relatively low income groups will enhance the contribution of such spending to the maintenance of economic stability.

While the diversification of securities offered is a creditable policy in the

---

[1]　*Annual Report*, Treasury, for 1944, pp. 7 – 8.

distribution of public debt, the advantages to postwar economy which are claimed for it by Secretary Morgenthau are matters of question. Whether the investors will dispose of or redeem their holdings depends in a large part upon the market conditions. Theoretically, investors purchase securities for investment, that is, with the intention to hold them until maturity. But, in reality, this is seldom the case in the War Loans. War bonds are purchased by individuals and business institutions for two reasons: patriotism and the leak of opportunity for more profitable investment. It is improbable that either of these factors will continue to exist in the postwar period. Furthermore, the use of liquid Government securities as a cushion for postwar spending may be viewed from the opposite perspective. Should inflation be a menace to the postwar administration, the result would be equally bad.

Abolition of the Tax-Exemption Feature

Exemption from tax was a traditional characteristic of Government borrowings prior to this war. Prior to the civil war, legislation authorizing public loans contained no reference to taxation. This omission was doubtlessly caused by the fact that no one foresaw any possibility that the securities might be taxed. During the Civil War, when considerable agitation arisen from taxation by the states, the authorizing acts first specified that the securities were exempt from all taxes including federal taxes. This precedent paved the way to adopting the tax-exemption feature for the First Liberty Loan. The Second Liberty Loan, and the two succeeding loans, provided exemption only for limited holdings. The last loan—the Victory notes—were exempt from tax in unlimited amounts. [1]

During this war, nearly all issues of war bonds are subject to Federal taxes. The abolition of the tax-exemption feature on Government debt marks a significant progress in public financing. The old theory was that the tax-exemption

---

[1] Cf. Robert A. Love, *Federal Financing*, New York, 1931, pp. 218 – 219.

feature would be compensated by additional sales or by a lower rate of interest. The loss in tax collection may be justified, however, only if the investor's ideas of future tax possibilities are sufficiently definite that he is willing to pay more than the Treasury expects to lose by foregoing the revenue from this source. When the tax rate is being changed with the progress of the war, the exemption obviously cannot be justified so far as the distribution of burden is concerned. More evident still is the fact that when progressive taxes are in effect, the loss of tax varies with the income status of the holder. Thus the holders in the high-income group enjoy the maximum benefits of the tax-exemption feature and those in the lowest income group enjoy no benefit at all. Under this condition all of the Government's loss is not effective in producing the desired results.

Chapter Ⅲ War Borrowing and The Banking System

War Loan Drivers

Although the details of the mechanism of war borrowing are beyond the scope of this essay, the effects of the war loan drives upon the banking system are of primary importance in discussing the policies of the federal reserve system. It shall be noticed, however, that, however important these periods of concentrated financing are, they are not the only method of borrowing. War funds have been raised continuously through sales of marketable and savings bonds, through the payroll deduction plans, through the tax saving devices, through the weekly offering of Treasury bills, and, occasionally, through special issues.

The Treasury launched seven War Loans during the war, and an eighth one, a Victory Loan, will probably be inaugurated shortly after peace has been assured. Table 9 gives the dates and the amounts of funds raised in each Drive. It may easily be seen that all the Drives exceeded the goals.

Important features of the War Loan Drives, the Treasury has stressed, have been the offering of a variety of issues in order to attract funds of all groups of non-bank investers, full allotment of subscriptions, and a nation-wide organization of volunteer workers. Each of the drives has included savings bonds of series E. F and G. savings notes, and three or four issues of marketable securities of different maturities, consisting of certificates, and intermediate-term and long-term Treasury bonds. Treasury bills also were used in the first two drives, as offerings to commercial banks. The 2.5 per cent long-term bonds are not available to banks unless sold within 10 years of maturity. In the first two drives, the intermediate-term bonds and certificates were available to banks but the allotments were limited. Since the third War Loan in September 1943, banks have been excluded from the drive. The terms and amounts of the marketable issues during each war Loan are summarized in Table 10.

These bonds were issued in coupon or registered form at the option of the buyer. All subscriptions for all issues, except those for banks in the first drives, were allocated in full. Thus there was no upper limit for the volume of funds raised. During the whole period, investors were advised to buy as many bonds as possible, except for the limit set on annual purchases of savings bonds.

The first War Loan, originally named the Victory Loan, was operated jointly by the Victory Fund Committees, which promoted the sales of securities E bonds, and by the War Saving Staff, which promoted the sales of E bonds. In early March, 1943, the United States Treasury War Finance Committees were organized. The new committees welded the Victory fund Committee and the War Saving Staff into a single and unified organization. The presidents of the 12 Reserve Banks are in charge of district organization and have full authority and responsibility to direct the drive in their respective districts.

Table 9 War Loan Drives (Billions of Dollars)

War Loan Drives	1st	2nd	3rd	4th	5th	6th	7th
Year	1942	1943	1943	1944	1944	1944	1945
Began	11/30	4/12	9/9	1/18	6/15	11/15	5/14
Ended	12/23	5/1	10/2	2/15	7/8	12/20	6/30
Quota: Total	9.0	13.0	15.0	14.0	16.0	14.0	14.0
Individuals		2.5	5.0	5.5	6.0	5.0	7.0
E saving bonds	0.7	1.5	2.5	3.2	3.0	2.9	4.0

Continued table

War Loan Drives	1st	2nd	3rd	4th	5th	6th	7th
F&G saving bonds	0. 3	0. 7	0. 8	1. 0	0. 8	0. 7	1. 0
Saving Notes	1. 3	1. 6	2. 5	2. 2	2. 6	2. 4	2. 7
Treasury Bills	0. 9	0. 8	—	—	—	—	—
Certifications	3. 8	5. 2	4. 1	5. 0	4. 8	4. 4	4. 8
Treasury Notes	—	—	—	—	1. 9	1. 6	—
Medium-term bonds	3. 1	4. 9	5. 3	3. 3	5. 2	6. 9	1. 7
2. 5% Bonds	2. 8	3. 8	3. 8	1. 9	2. 3	2. 7	12. 2 *
Total **	12. 9	18. 5	19. 0	16. 6	20. 6	21. 6	26. 4
Total fund raised ***	12. 9	18. 6	22. 1	17. 6	22. 0	23. 4	28. 7

 * Including $ 5. 1 billion of 2. 25% bonds and $ 7. 1 billion of 2. 5% bonds.

 ** First and second include offerings to banks and Government agencies and trust funds, third includs offerings to Government agencies and trust funds, fourth, fifth, sixth, and seventh exclude purchases by banks and Government agencies and trust funds.

 *** Includes offerings to banks and Government agencies and trust funds, and, in third offerings to banks after the drive.

 Source: *Treasury Bulletin*, various issues.

Table 10   Marketable Securities Offered During War Loan Drives

Date of Issues	Title of the Offering	Mature & Call Date	Term of Issue	Amount Issued ($ Million)
First War Loan				
12/1/42	2. 5% Tres. Bond	12/15/63 – 68	26 yr.	2283
12/1/42	1. 75% Tres. Bond	6/15/48	5 yr. 4m.	3062
12/1/42	0. 875% Certificate	12/1/43	1 yr.	2211
Second War Loan				
4/15/43	2. 5% Tres. Bond	6/15/64 – 69	26 yr. 2 m.	3762
4/15/43	2% Tres. Bond	9/15/50 – 52	9 yr. 5 m.	4939
4/15/43	0. 875% Certificate	4/1/44	1 yr.	5251
Third War Loan				
9/15/43	2. 5% Tres. Bond	12/15/64 – 69	26 yr. 3 m.	3779
9/15/43	2% Tres. Bond	9/15/51 – 53	10 yr.	5257
9/15/43	0. 875% Certificate	9/15/43	1 yr.	4122
Fourth War Loan				
2/1/44	2. 5% Tres. Bond	3/15/65 – 70	26 yr. 1 m.	2212

Date of Issues	Title of the Offering	Mature & Call Date	Term of Issue	Amount Issued $ Million
2/1/44	2.25% Tres. Bond	3/15/56 – 59	15 yr. 7 m.	3728
2/1/44	0.875% Certificate	2/1/45	1 yr.	5048
Fifth War Loan				
2/1/44	2.5% Tres. Bond	3/15/65 – 70	25 yr. 9 m.	2909
6/26/44	2% Tres. Bond	6/15/52 – 54	10 yr.	5825
6/26/44	1.25% Tres. Note	3/15/47	2 yr. 9 m.	1448
6/26/44	0.875% Certificate	6/1/45	11 m.	4770
Sixth War Loan				
12/1/44	2.5% Tres. Bond	3/15/66 – 71	26 yr. 3 m.	3447
12/1/44	2% Tres. Bond	12/15/52 – 54	10 yr.	7992
12/1/44	1.25% Tres. Note	9/15/47	2 yr. 9 m.	1550
12/1/44	0.875% Certificate	12/1/45	1 yr.	4395
Seventh War Loan				
6/1/45	2.5% Tres. Bond	6/15/67 – 72	27 yr.	7699p
6/1/45	2.25% Tres. Bond	6/15/59 – 62	17 yr.	5284p
6/1/45	2.5% Tres. Bond	12/15/50	5 yr. 6 m.	2636p
6/1/45	0.875% Certificate	6/1/46	1 yr.	4799p

Source: *Treasury Bulletin*, various issues.

Several hundred thousand persons, nearly all of whom are unpaid volunteers, have enlisted in the selling campaign. The staff and volunteer workers increased as the volume of loans expended. The campaign represented a joint effort of various institutions and individuals, including the banks, security dealers and brokers, insurance companies, savings banks and numerous business and social organizations.

The war Loan Drives, as a whole, have been uniformly successful in financing the war. Even the smallest amount raised in a drive, the total of 12.3 billion dollars of the first drive, was by far the largest ever raised up to that time in any country during a comparable period, and contrasted with the previous record of $6993000000 for the fourth Liberty loan issue in 1918. The amounts raised have increased successively in each drive, with the exception of the smaller fourth drive. In appraising the results of the War Loan drives, however, one must bear in mind the two-fold objective: first, to raise the money required, and, secondly, to raise as large a share as possible from non-inflationary resources. The latter purpose is of more importance because War Loans are regarded as a means of absorbing the surplus purchasing power in the hands of the public. With this purpose in mind, we shall examine in the following sections the effects of War Loan drives upon the banking system.

Financial and Business Institutions

A prime principle of war borrowing has been to raise money as much as possible from non-bank lenders. Concentrated War Loan drives have been inaugurated as the most effective means of absorbing the growing individual income and savings. Efforts were made, therefore, first, to sell securities to non-bank investors as much as possible, and, secondly, to sell as much as possible to individuals. The percentage of the goals to be taken by individuals increased in each successive drive (see Table 9) . In the first two drives, the grand totals of sales were swelled by commercial bank subscriptions amounting to $ 5 billion in each case. Beginning with the third drive, banks were excluded from the subscription except for a limited amount for their time deposits. Even so they increased their holdings of Government securities indirectly from the market. The amounts and percentages taken by non-bank investors and individuals (including partnerships and personal trust accounts, as classified by the Treasury) are shown in Table 11.

During the first War Loan, of the total of $ 7. 6 billion raised from non-bank sources, $ 5 billion, or 67% were subscribed by insurance companies, savings banks and business corporations. One of the remarkable features in this drive was that subscriptions were received in predominant weight from financial and business organizations and represented " skimming the cream " from such reservoirs of available funds. These institutions may have liquidated holdings of other securities and thereby obtained funds of a non-recurring type in order to augment their subscriptions. Many institutions must have used their accumulated funds, which represented past savings, to purchase war securities. To such an extent, these purchases would have no effect in reducing the current demand for consumer goods. Their subscriptions during the first drive in December 1942 were so large that it was the general opinion that insurance companies and savings banks would have no funds for the second drive in April 1943, [1] but this belief was proved to be an error. In the second drive, they subscribed an even greater amount, $3.6 billion. Subscriptions by corporations were almost double the previous amount. It is believed that these institutions must have sold other securities to build up their cash to a greater extent than we generally realized.

Table 11   Distribution of War Loans (Billions of Dollars)

	1st	2nd	3rd	4th	5th	6th	7th
Individuals, partnerships, personal trust accounts	1.6	3.3	5.4	5.3	6.4	5.9	8.7
Insurance companies	1.7	2.4	2.6	2.1	2.8	3.2	4.2
Mutual savings banks	0.6	1.2	1.5	1.3	1.5	2.3	2.2
Corporations and associations	2.7	5.1	7.0	6.8	8.2	8.6	9.1
Dealers and brokers	0.8	0.5	0.9	0.4	0.5	0.3	0.3
State & local gov'ts	0.2	0.5	0.8	0.8	1.3	1.3	1.8
Total non-bank	7.6	13.0	18.2	16.7	20.7	21.6	26.3
Government agencies & trust funds	0.3	0.4	0.6	0.3 *	0.6 *	0.8 *	1.1 *
Commercial banks	5.1	5.1	3.2 *#	0.6 *	0.8 *	1.0 *	1.3 *
Total funds raised	13.0	18.6	22.1	17.6	22.0	23.4	28.7
Percentages of total Amount in drive:							
Individuals	12.3	17.7	28.4	31.7	30.8	37.2	33.0

---

[1]   Cf. *Monthly Letter*, National City Bank of New York, April 1943, p.41.

Continued table

	1st	2nd	3rd	4th	5th	6th	7th
Corporations and other investors	48. 4	54. 9	71. 6	68. 3	69. 2	72. 8	67. 0
Commercial banks	39. 3	27. 4	—	—	—	—	—

* Not included in the drive.

\# Sold to banks after the drive.

Source: *Treasury Bulletin*, various issues.

Before the third War Loan in September 1943, observations were again made that institutions would not have funds to take a large amount of securities during the drive. ① Once more this has been proved to be a mistake. They subscribed an even larger amount – $4.1 billion by financial institution and $7.0 by business organizations. But the percentage of the total that was taken by institutions began to decline somewhat. In this loan purchases by insurance companies included for the first time orders placed for securities to be delivered and paid for at any time during the month following the drive. Their large subscriptions in excess of their normal accumulation of funds forced them to resell their holdings after the drive. In the case of the insurance companies and saving banks, for example, they didn't increase their holdings from November 30, 1942 (before the first drive) to September 30, 1943 (end of the third drive) amounted to but $6.3 billion, while their total subscription in the three drives was $10 billion. Between drives they rearranged their portfolios by disposing of a considerable amount of holdings, thus paving the way for larger subscriptions to the new issues than would other have been possible. Other groups of investors have done the same thing.

Sales to financial and business institutions fell off, however, in the fourth War Loan. They were held at a lower proportion in the fifth, and showed some increase in the sixth. During the seventh War Loan, restrictions on sales were strengthened. The quota for corporations and investors other than individuals was

---

① Ibid. , August 1943, p. 89.

reduced to 7 billion dollars, compared with 10 billion in the third, 8. 5 billion in the fourth, 10 billion in the fifth and 9 billion in the sixth. Unrestricted securities available for such investors consisted of only one issue, the 0. 875% certificates. The 1. 5% bonds were offered only to individuals because it was on an issue of this type that corporations had entered speculative subscription in previous drives. A letter was sent to all banks requesting their assistance in discouraging speculative subscriptions. However, financial and business institutions purchased 15. 5 billion dollars in the seventh drive, or about 59 per cent of the total, compared with 65 per cent in the sixth and 61 per cent in the fifth.

Besides financial and business institutions, a small amount was subscribed by dealers and brokers in each drive and by state and local governments. These figures are given in Table 11. Government agencies and trust funds also purchased a small amount of the securities offered, but this portion has been excluded from the quota since the forth drive.

From table 11, it may be seen that the portion of securities taken up by corporations and investors other than individuals has been held at a high level despite constant efforts to encourage individual purchases. The highest portion was the 72. 8 per cent of total sales in the sixth War Loan. Only in the third and the seventh drives did it decline somewhat. The low percentage figures in the first two drives were due to the fact that a large portion was allocated to commercial banks. From Table 12, it may be seen that the amounts taken up by corporations and other investors have been far in excess of their quota. In spite of efforts to restrict their purchases and the lowering of their quota in the seventh drive, their subscriptions increased substantially.

Table 12   Quota and Sales in War Loan Drives (Billions of Dollars)

	1st	2nd	3rd	4th	5th	6th	7th
Total quota	9	13	15	14	16	14	14
Total sales	12. 9	18. 6	18. 9	16. 7	20. 6	21. 6	26. 3
Individuals Quota	*	2. 5	5. 0	5. 5	6. 0	5. 0	7. 0

Continued table

	1st	2nd	3rd	4th	5th	6th	7th
Sales	1. 6	3. 3	5. 4	5. 3	6. 4	5. 9	8. 7
Indiv. E Bonds:							
Quota	—	—	3. 0	3. 0	3. 0	2. 5	4. 0
Sales	0. 7	1. 5	2. 5	3. 2	3. 0	2. 9	4. 0
Corp. & Others:							
Quota	*	5. 5	10. 0	8. 5	10. 0	9. 0	7. 0
Sales	6. 3	10. 2	13. 6	11. 4	14. 4	15. 7	17. 6
Commercial Banks:							
Quota	5. 0	5. 0	—	—	—	—	—
Sales	5. 1	5. 1	—	—	—	—	—

* Including the $ 4 billion of non-bank quota.

Source: *Treasury Bulletin*, August 1945.

Appeal to Individuals

In the first war loan, the sales classification " Individuals, partnerships, and personal trust accounts" took only about $ 1. 5 billion, or 12. 3 per cent of the grand total of $ 12. 9 billion, and the restricted character of the distribution was further shown by the fact that the total number of subscribers of all classes was only about 340000 in a nation of over 130000000. The second War Loan did a better job of distributing the securities, but the amount taken up by individuals still stayed at a low level of 17. 7 per cent. At that time it became clear that unless a large portion could be sold to the mass of the population there would be little chance of success in the subsequent drives. The Securities and Exchange Commissions and the Federal Reserve System made studies of the savings income of individuals during the second drive;[1] their figures revealed that liquid savings

---

[1] Cf. *Federal Reserve Bulletin*, March 1943.

in the hands of individuals had increased enormously and should be the real source of funds of government borrowing. The task of appealing to individuals was further emphasized by the supposition that insurance companies and savings banks would no longer have accumulated funds for subscription in the subsequent drives.

Sales to individuals increased in the third War Loan to $5.4 billion or 28.4 per cent of the total. Part of this success was due to the prohibition against commercial banks in the drive. A still larger percentage, 31.7 per cent, was achieved in the fourth drive, when the total sales in the drive were comparatively small. The quota of $5.5 billion for individuals, however, was not reached, since only $5.3 billion was sold. During the first two weeks of the drive, only sales to individuals were reported, thus focusing attention upon this part of the program, and avoiding publication to large institutional purchases which might discourage the small investor. This became the practice in the subsequent drives. One reason given for the larger purchases of individuals in the fourth War Loan was that it was started during a time of increasing activity on many front and when the United Nations' plans for the invasion of Europe were shaping up rapidly.

The fifth War Loan came with the invasion of Europe by Allies, and a high quota was set for individual purchases. This was the result of consideration that individual liquid savings, as revealed by the study of the Security and Exchange Commission, had reached the enormous sum of $37 billion in 1943, compared with $28.9 in 1942, $10.3 in 1941 and only $4.3 in 1940. Spending on non-essentials and luxuries was high in 1944, and there was an increase in gambling and betting with bookmaking rife in many factories and communities. [1]Sales to individuals reached a new high of $6.4 billion in the fifth War Loan, but the percentage was only 30.8% of the total. In the sixth War Loan the amount sold to individuals deadline to 5.9 $ billion; the percentage, however, increased to 37.2%. The first time sales to individuals materially exceeded the quota. In the so-

---

[1] Cf. *Monthly Letter*, National City Bank of New York, June 1944, p. 66.

called "Mighty Seventh", special efforts were made to reach individual investors by restricting speculative purchases and restricting the volume of securities available to corporations and other investors, as we have stated before. In this drive, there was a need for extra effort to offset any possible psychological let-down as a result of the victory in Europe. The very high quota for individuals, $7 billion, was easily attained. Sales amounted to $8.7 billion, or 33 per cent of total.

The Series E bonds, it will be seen in Table 12, have been the principal instrument for sales to individuals. Such sales barely reached the quota in most cases, and in the third War Loan, the sales of Series E bonds were $500 million below the quota. It is believed that the Series E bonds are the best type of securities to be held by individuals for maturity or for a longer period, while holding of other securities by individuals are likely to be resold after the drive. Nevertheless, the redemption of Series E bonds has been increasing in amount and in the percentage of outstanding issues. [1]

In consequence, part of the sales during the drive represents an over-purchase by investors arising out of the desire to reach the quota, the 1.25% Treasury notes were included in the fifth and sixth drives and were purchased by individuals in large amounts. They also purchased the 2% and other medium-term bonds. Such securities, however, were resold to banks after the drive in considerable amounts. The National City Bank of New York comments on this fact, thus: [2]

It is not surprising that during a great nation-wide sales campaign, when everyone is trying to make a record and there is appeal to buy up to the limit, many purchasers will overestimate their ability to carry the full amount of their commitments. So long as the "lightening-up" by such purchasers following the drive does not become excessive, the overall results can still be considered satisfactory.

---

[1] See pp. 350 – 351.

[2] *Monthly Letter*, National City Bank of New York, January 1944, p. 5.

Bank Credit Involved

The War Loan Drives are the biggest financing programs ever accomplished in the history of any nation in the world. Although the loans are borrowed from various classes of investors, only two sources of funds in the final analysis, are big enough to absorb such tremendous issues of securities: either the current and accumulated savings of the great mass of the American people, now enjoying the highest aggregate income in the history of the country; or the banking system which can absorb Government obligations by creating its own credit. All other investors have a limited capacity to purchase the loans. Any amount not absorbed by the public must be taken up by commercial banks, and any amount not kept by commercial banks must be taken up by the Federal Reserve Banks, which, as will be soon later, have practically unlimited power to do this job. This is the final secret of the success of War borrowing.

Throughout the whole period of War Loan Drives, commercial banks have been discouraged to extend their credit. During the first two drives a quota of $5 billion was set for banks, and their allotments of the 2 per cent bonds and the 0.875 per cent certificates were limited to the $2 billion or thereabouts of each issue. The 2.5 per cent long-term bond has not been available for banks, except those with 10 years of maturity. Commercial banks took up $5.1 billion in each drive. In the first one, they purchased substantial quantities of the now certificates and 1 - 0.75 per cent bonds after the allotments had been made. In the second drive, their subscriptions were many times oversubscribed, and they purchased heavily after the drive; their total holdings increased by no less than $8.6 billion.

Beginning with the third War Loan, commercial banks were excluded from the drives. In the third drive, however, $3.2 billion or 2 per cent bonds and 0.875 per cent certificates were sold to banks after the conclusion of the drive. Commercial banks were requested not to buy in the market, and the market was requested not to trade in the securities offered in the drive until the books for bank subscriptions were closed. This innovation was designed for discouraging speculative purchases by institutions in the drive for resale largely to banks. The same request was made to banks in the subsequent drives; they were requested not to buy the securities offered in the drive until the drive was over. Beginning with the fourth War Loan, commercial banks were permitted to make a limited investment of their time and savings deposits under a prescribed formula. These investments were made outside the drive. In the fourth drive, they were permitted to purchase the Series F and G bonds and the 2. 25% and 2. 5% bonds up to 10 per cent of their time deposits or up to $ 200000, whichever was less, of which not more than $ 100000 could consist of savings bonds. In the fifth, they were permitted to purchase the Series F and G bonds and the 2% and 2. 5% bonds up to 20 per cent of the bank's savings and time deposits, but not more than $ 400000 by any bank, of which not more than $ 100000 could consist of savings bonds. Similar limitations were made in the sixth and seventh War Loans.

Since banks were excluded from the War Loan Drives, they have expanded their holdings of Government securities during and after the drive from indirect purchases of outstanding issues in the market. These securities were supplied by non-bank investors who desired to increase their ability to subscribe for new issues, or who desired to switch from short-term to longer-term securities. Since the first drive in 1942, there has been a definite preference on the part of many inventors for the long-term marketable issues over the short-term issues and savings bonds. During the earlier period, insurance companies, savings banks, and corporations used to place their accumulating funds temporarily in short-tern securities, costly certificates and bills, and then sell them to commercial banks in the following drives when longer-term issues were available. They also sold substantial amounts of their partially tax-exempt issues for the purpose of switching funds into the higher-yielding taxable issues; this was due to the fact that they paid little or no taxes on their holdings of federal securities. [1]The prices of Government securities rose rapidly and speculative trading became more active during the latter period, as public confidence in the Treasury's Policy of maintaining interest rate structure was growing, especially when there were rumors in late 1944 and early 1945 that the Treasury would offer no more 2.5 per cent bonds. While some readjustments of investor portfolios are legitimate and not to be criticized, a large turnover induced by competitive bidding for outstanding issues by banks has the effect on padding the figures of sales in the drive.

The expansion of bank investment, on the other hand, was motivated by many considerations. First, commercial banks desired to obtain sales credit or war loan deposits during the drive, because war loan accounts were exempted from reserve requirements, thus a portion of their reserve funds might be released for temporary uses. Secondly, commercial loans have continued to decline and new corporate issues were scarce, thus freeing funds for investment in Government securities. Thirdly, banks over the country have been showing a disposition to invest their excess reserve more fully. This was due partly to a growing acceptance of the present interest rate structure as likely to prevail in the future, and partly to wider understanding of the advantages from an earning standpoint of full investment and reliance upon an adequate portfolio of bills and certificates for adjustment of reserve position. Fuller investment was also encouraged by the Treasury and the Federal Reserve System as part of their educational campaign.

Despite the discouragement made by monetary authorities, commercial banks evidently absorb Government securities willingly. In commenting on this matter, the annual report of the Federal Reserve Bank of New York discloses:

> As a corollary, a definite abuse of the War Loan deposit account mechanism appeared to be developing through the over eagerness of banks to acquire and non-bank investors to sell, Government securities especially prior

---

[1]　See *Monthly Letter*, National City Bank of New York, July 1943, p. 79.

to, during, and immediately following Loan Drives. Banks were soliciting sales of outstanding securities, either directly from customers and others or through the government security market, with the understanding that the sellers would use the proceeds of such sales to pay for subscriptions entered through these banks for subsequently equivalent amounts of new securities offered during the drives. In other cases, the initiative appeared to have come from security holders, who wished to sell the securities to a bank (perhaps at a price above the prevailing market), with the same understanding with respect to a subsequent subscription to be made through the bank. In either case the banks appeared to be encouraging sales of government securities which the banks could purchase with deposits that would be converted into War Loan deposit balances when the sellers subscribed for new securities during the drive, an undesirable practice in itself, and one which aggregated natural adjustment in security portfolios. [1]

In the effort to discourage practices and to minimize speculative subscriptions, the Reserve Banks cooperated with the Treasury, sent a circular letter on November 13, 1944, calling attention to the practices which were considered abuses of War Loan procedure, or otherwise undesirable, and requesting the bank's cooperation in avoiding and discouraging them.

The estimated net changes of all commercial bank portfolios during the seven War Loans are shown in Table 13. The percentages figures of bank credit (including security loans) to total debt increased are important illustrations. It will be seen that 47 per cent of the debt in the fifth drive was financed by commercial bank credit. Although banks were excluded from the drive, they increased their Government security holdings by $8.8 billion, or 40 per cent of the amount of securities sold during the fifth drive.

---

[1] *Annual Report*, Federal Reserve Bank of New York, 1944, p. 26.

Table 13　Bank Credit in War Loan Drives（Billions of Dollars）

Increase in:	1st	2nd	3rd	4th	5th	6th	7th
Gross national debt	11. 9	20. 1	21. 0	17. 2	22. 2	20. 3	23. 0
Commercial banks:							
Gov't securities	4. 6	8. 7	6. 7	5. 1	8. 8	6. 9	6. 8
Loans on securities	0. 5	0. 6	1. 5	1. 1	1. 7	1. 6	2. 5
Total	5. 1	9. 3	8. 2	6. 2	10. 5	8. 7	9. 3
% to debt in crease	43. 0	46. 0	39. 0	36. 0	47. 0	43. 0	41. 0
Federal Reserve Banks:							
Gov't securities	1. 1	0. 3	0. 1	—	0. 6	1. 5	1. 2
Banking system:							
Total credit	6. 3	9. 6	8. 3	6. 2	11. 1	10. 1	10. 5
% to debt increases	53. 0	48. 0	40. 0	36. 0	50. 0	50. 0	46. 0

　　* The net increase in public debt differs from reported War Loan sales because of many factors, including deferred payment sales, redemption of savings bonds, tax notes and other prosecution, the issuance of special securities to Government trust funds, and exclusion from drive quotas of Treasury Bills, sales to government agencies and to commercial banks on time deposits.

　　N. B. periods of estimation do not necessarily coincide with the official dates of War Loans.

　　Sources: First to sixth War Loans, estimated by National City Bank of New York, *Monthly Letter* of the bank, January 1945, p. 4. Seventh War Loan, estimated by the writer, based on estimates made by the Federal Reserve Bank of New York and other sources, *Monthly Review*, Federal Reserve Bank of New York, August 1945.

　　Substantial amounts were also purchased by banks during the sixth War Loan, amounting to $7 billion. During the seventh drive, the increase in bank holdings was comparatively smaller than the two previous drives, but multiparty loans extended by banks during the drive was much larger than before.

　　In the periods between the drives, commercial banks reduced their holdings of Government securities by about $2 billion. They sold their holdings, largely in bills and certificates, to Federal Reserve Banks, as their required reserves increased by the Treasury's actions of transferring funds from war loan accounts to private accounts. During the earlier period, banks had reduced some of their holdings of securities other than Government. The general trend of commercial bank holdings in regard to War Loan drives is shown in Chart 2.

The Federal Reserve Banks used to reduce some of their Government security holdings during the latter weeks in the drives. This was because banks had eased their reserve positions by shifting deposits to war loan accounts which were not subject to reserve requirements. For the entire War Loan period, however, their holdings were, in the main, increased. The increase, as will be seen in Table 13, was particularly large in the sixth and seventh drives (Large also in the first one, when war loan accounts were not yet freed from reserve requirements). In the sixth drive, income taxes were paid toward the end of the drive, a large amount of fund was then transferred from commercial banks to the Reserve banks, thus tightening the cash position of commercial banks. In the seventh drive, the Reserve Banks made net purchases of Treasury bills during the week which included the principal date of payment for corporate subscriptions. It is believed that these bills came from non-bank investors, particularly corporations which had acquired them as temporary investments pending more permanent investment of funds in drive securities, the trend of Federal Reserve holdings is also shown in Chart 2.

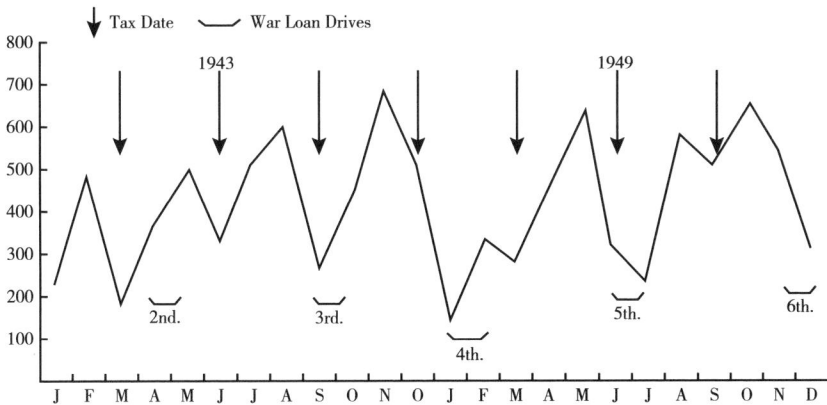

Chart 1   Estimated Month-to-Month Changes in Currency Outstanding *

* Money in circulation outside the Treasury and the Federal Reserve banks, adjusted by Federal Reserve Bank of New York to exclude estimated changes in vault cash held by weekly reporting member banks. *Monthly Review*, Federal Reserve Bank of New York, January 1945.

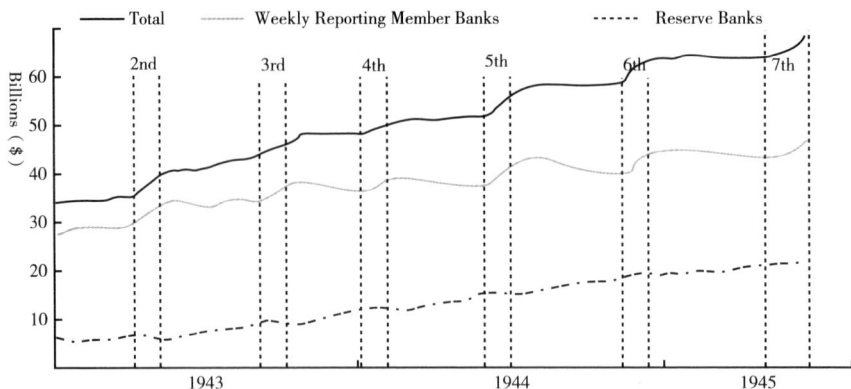

Chart 2　Government Security Holdings

Another aspect of bank credit which has a bearing on War Loans is the increase in bank loans extended to brokers, dealers and to other Government securities. Such loans usually reached their peak near the end of a drive, declined gradually in the inter-drive period as borrowers paid off their borrowings from current income and reached the lowest point at the beginning of the next drive. The picture is shown in Chart 3, and the estimated amounts involved in each drive are given in Table 13.

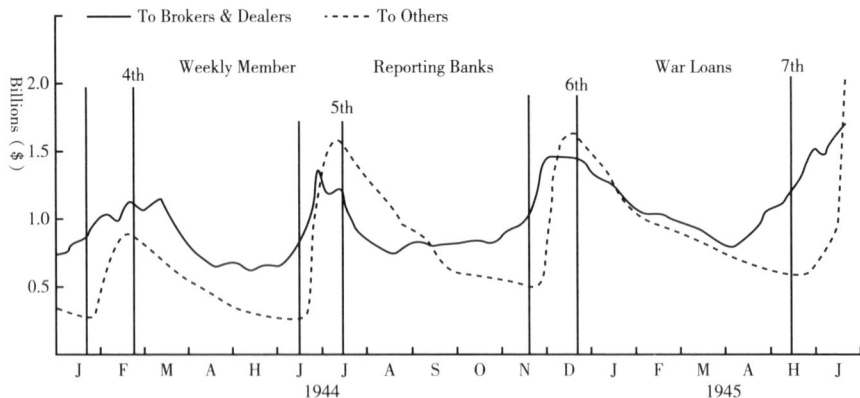

Chart 3　Loans for Purchasing or Carrying Government Securities

In the first two War Loans, bank loans on Government securities were very small, $500 and $650 millions respectively. The volume increased rapidly in the third drive, amounting to $1. 5 billion. Part of these loans was made to investors who would repay them out of future income, and part was speculative in nature, representing purchases of securities to be sold later at a profit. Beginning with the fourth War Loan, the Treasury requested the cooperation of all banking institutions in declining to make security loans for the purchase of Government securities for speculative purposes. This policy, however, was not intended to imply any disapproval of loans to enable investors to purchase securities in anticipation of income, provided that the loans were on a short-term or amortization basis, fully repayable within six months. This was the policy set in the joint announcement on November 22, 1942. [1] In addition, subscriptions of dealers and brokers were limited to amounts that they would be able to sell to non-bank customers for investment end to the amounts required for investment of their own funds. Hence security loans in the fourth drive were smaller, less than $1. 1 billion. This was partly due to the fact that loans made in connection with the third drive had not been completely liquidated by the time the fourth was initiated. Moreover, loans to brokers and dealers continued to rise for weeks after the drive was concluded.

In the fifth and sixth War Loans, bank loans on Government securities reached a peak of $1. 7 billion, this was largely due to the greater volume of total sales in these two drives as well as to the fact that pre-emptive sales of securities in connection with portfolio readjustments by insurance companies and other institutional investors merely lighter than they were in previous drives. Funds realized by non-bank investors from bank loans played an important role in the attainment of the high sales total for the fifth and sixth drives. A still larger amount of bank loans over $2. 5 billion was used in the seventh drive. This unusually large expansion of bank loans was believed to be caused, in part, by a sizable amount of loans for bond fade investment purposes, particularly to institutional investors. [2] Borrowings by institutional investors seemed to have been incurred as a

---

[1] See pp. 454 – 455.

[2] Cf. p. 58. *Monthly Review*, Federal Reserve Bank of New York, August 1945.

precautionary measure against the possibility that the Treasury might modify the terms of its future offerings of long-term bonds, either by elimination bonds caring 2. 5 per cent coupons, or by extending the maturity of bonds offered at that rate. In addition, there appeared to have been an expansion of loans to finance speculative purchases of new issues for resale after the seventh drive since profit seemed realizable because Government bond prices had been rising rapidly since the beginning of 1945. The sales total in the seventh drive increased largely because of bank loans.

It is interesting to notice the combined figures and percentages in Table 13, showing the total bank credit involved in War Loan Drives, including bank holdings and bank loans and Reserve Bank holdings. In general, credit extended by banks accounted for approximately 45 per cent of the total amount of funds raised in the seven War Loan Drives. The highest portion taken by bank credit was in the first drive, and lowest in the fourth drive. In the fifth and sixth drives, half the funds raised reflected bank credit. Relative improvement occurred in the seventh drive, but the absolute amount of bank credit was the largest of all drives, reaching $ 10. 5 billions.

In examining the table, however, it should not be assumed that the figures can be accumulated to show the expansion of credit during the entire period. After the drives, as Government deposits were withdrawn by the Treasury and reconverted into ordinary deposits requiring reserves, the banks became sellers of government securities, a large part of which was taken by the Reserve Bank. This gives to the curve of expansion of bank credit a generally Dig-Nag appearance, but with the trend moving steadily upward, as shown in Chart 2.

When comparison is made between bank purchases of Government securities and increases in the debt on an annual basis, it will be found that a protion taken by the banking system declined in 1943 and declined a little more in 1944. This is demonstrated in the following table. This fact was due largely to the improvement in tax policies and to the timing of War Loans.

Table 14   Increase in Government Debt and Portion Taken by Banks

(Billions of Dollars)

	1941	1942	1943	1944
Interest-bearing debt, Direct and Guaranteed, Net Increase	13. 4	47. 8	57. 1	61. 7
Taken by banks:				
Commercial banks	4. 0	19. 7	18. 7	17. 9
Federal Reserve Banks	0. 1	3. 9	5. 3	7. 3
Total	4. 1	23. 6	24. 0	25. 2
Percentage taken by balances(%)	31. 0	49. 0	42. 0	41. 0

Effects on Money Market

The War Loan Drives usually eased the money market since funds were transferred from ordinary deposit accounts to war loan accounts, which did not need reserved. This is shown in Table 15. Excess reserves of the banking system increased by about 500 million dollars during the drives, and required reserves declined by a larger amount. In the case of the first War Loan, the situation was reversed, because war loan accounts were not yet exempt from reserve requirements at that time. As banks tended to invest their funds more fully through the war and tended to adjust their reserve positions by sale and repurchase of Treasury bills with the Reserve banks, the figures of Treasury bills holdings of the Reserve banks under repurchase option showed the same changes as reserve deposits during the War Loan period. Table 15 shows that their decline is quite comparable with that of excess reserves. In addition, banks paid off some of their indebtedness to the Reserve Banks during the drive periods.

As may be expected, Government deposits increased and other deposits declined during the drive periods. The increase in the former, however, was always exceeded by far the decline in the latter.

Table 15　Effects of War Loan Drives on the Money Market（Billions of Dollars）

	1st	2nd	3rd	4th	5th	6th	7th*
Gov't. Deposits	+3.7	+7.9	+10.1	+7.0	+13.2	+12.5	+3.5
Demand Deposits Adjusted**	-0.5	-3.5	-6.0	-4.4	-6.0	-5.1	-1.5
Money in Circulation	+0.6	+0.3	+0.3	+0.3	+0.3	+0.3	+0.2
Required Reserves	+0.8	-1.3	-0.8	-1.0	-1.1	-0.9	-0.3
Excess Reserves	-0.9	+0.1	+0.4	+0.2	+0.5	+0.5	+0.4
Bills under repurchase Option	+0.3***	-0.1	-0.3	-0.4	-0.6	-0.6	-0.4

Deposits of weekly reporting member banks:

* Seventh War Loan up to July 20, 1945.

** Demand deposits other than inter-bank and Government less cash items in process of collection.

*** Total bill holding of Federal Reserve banks.

Sources: *Federal Reserve Bulletin*, various issues. Some figures are estimated by the writer. Date of changes does not coincide with official dates of War Loans.

This was caused by the fact that funds used in the purchase of securities were also raised from sources other than deposits, some being drawn from the currency in circulation. Currency in circulation increased by about 300 million dollars during drive periods, which was about 100 millions smaller than the normal rate of increase in circulating money during a corresponding period when drives are not taking place. Government deposits and money in circulation were affected to some extent by the fact that some of the drives occurred when the quarterly income tax payments were collected. This accounts for the high figure of Government deposits in the third and the fifth War Loans. The effects of tax payment and War Loan Drives on money in circulation are shown in Chart 1. The influence of the tax date diminished in 1944 and was absent in the sixth drive in December 1944 because the tax date was postponed to January 1945.

Another effect of War Loan Drives on the money market is seen in the movement of funds between various Reserve Districts. We shall see later that there was, especially in the earlier period of the War, a tendency for funds to move away from the financial centers of New York and Chicago. During the first War Loan, the subscription in New York, after deductions to be credited to other districts, amounted to 48 per cent of the total, including 55 per cent of total from non-bank sources. This would not only narrow the distribution of war loans, but also reinforce the tendency of a loss of funds to New York City. During the second drive, districts outside New York had absorbed a larger percentage of loans than in the first, the portion taken by New York being 38 per cent. Beginning in 1943, interior banks purchased a larger and larger amount of Government securities. This gave some relief to the New York money market. Beginning with the fourth drive, the Treasury requested that all subscriptions by corporations and firms be entered and paid for through the banking institutions where funds were located. This suggestion was made to avoid transfer of funds and to prevent disturbances in the money market. In the subsequent drives, the money market in New York was temporarily eased as the Treasury's transactions of funds away from New York were reduced. In the sixth and seventh drives, the relief in Now York money was very slight. For the period as a whole the Treasury has been successful in widening the distribution of war loans over the country.

We have previously referred to the fact that there has been a consistent preference in the market for longer-term Government issues. This tendency to lengthen investments caused the rise in Government bond prices and hence decline in bond yields. A pronounced decline in bond yield occurred during the sixth War Loan and continued through the seventh. The changes in bond prices and interest rates have been discussed in Chapter II and will be discussed more fully in Chapter IV.

Ownership of Public Debt

The distribution of public debt among various classes of investors, according to estimates of the Treasury, is shown in Table 16. It will be noticed that the part taken by commercial banks has declined since June 1943, whereas the portion taken by the Reserve Banks increased considerably through the whole period. Thus the total holdings of the banking system remained above 42 per cent of total debt outstanding in 1943 and above 41 per cent in 1944. To this extent war funds are borrowed from inflationary sources.

Table 16 Estimated Ownership of Interest-Bearing Securities, Direct and Guaranteed (Billions of Dollars)

	1941	1942		1943		1944		1945
	Dec.	June	Dec.	June	Dec.	June	Dec.	Apr.
Total outstanding	63. 8	76. 5	111. 6	139. 5	168. 7	201. 1	230. 4	234. 2
Held by banks								
Commercial banks	21. 4	26. 0	41. 1	52. 2	59. 9	68. 4	77. 8	77. 5
Reserve banks	2. 3	2. 6	6. 2	7. 2	11. 5	14. 9	18. 8	20. 5
Total	23. 7	28. 6	47. 3	59. 4	71. 5	83. 3	96. 6	98. 0
Held by nonbanks								
Individuals	13. 8	18. 2	23. 8	30. 3	37. 1	45. 1	52. 2	53. 8
Insurance Co.	8. 2	9. 2	11. 3	13. 1	15. 1	17. 3	19. 6	20. 5
Mutual savings bk.	3. 7	3. 9	4. 5	5. 3	6. 1	7. 3	8. 3	8. 7
Corp. & Asso.	4. 4	5. 4	11. 6	15. 7	20. 1	25. 7	27. 6	25. 8
State & Local Gov't	0. 5	0. 6	0. 8	1. 3	2. 0	3. 2	4. 2	4. 3
Gov't agencies and trust funds	9. 5	10. 6	12. 2	14. 3	16. 9	19. 1	21. 7	23. 2
Total	40. 1	47. 9	64. 2	80. 0	97. 3	117. 7	133. 6	136. 3
Percentage of total								
Commercial banks	33. 5	33. 9	36. 8	37. 5	35. 5	34. 0	33. 7	33. 1
Reserve Banks	3. 6	3. 4	5. 5	5. 2	6. 8	7. 4	8. 2	8. 7
Banking system	37. 1	37. 3	42. 3	42. 7	42. 3	41. 4	41. 9	41. 8

Source: *Treasury Bulletin*.

Commercial banks held about 78 billion dollars of Government securities by the end of 1944, compared with $21 billion at the end of 1941 and $18 billion at the end of 1940. Federal Reserve holdings increased from $2 billion at the end of 1940 to $2.5 billion in 1941 and to $18.8 billion at the end of 1944.

Table 17 Ownership of Public Debt, Direct and Guaranteed (April 30, 1945)

Total outstanding in billions	percentage of total outstanding				
	7408 Commercial Banks	576 Savings Banks	970 Insurance Co.	Gov't Agencies Trust Funds and Reserve BK.	All other Investors
Bills	$ 17. 0	15. 0	0. 1	76. 5	8. 2
Certificates	34. 5	50. 8	1. 1	15. 8	29. 9
Notes	18. 6	67. 6	1. 9	5. 6	21. 1
Bonds	92. 4	41. 4	8. 8	6. 6	23. 7
Postal Savings and others	0. 2	7. 3	0. 2	18. 0	73. 9
Guaranteed	0. 8	70. 9	0. 6	0. 8	25. 6
Total	163. 5	43. 7	5. 4	12. 0	23. 1

Source: *Treasury Bulletin*, August 1945.

Table 17 shows the distribution of various kinds of Government issues among various classes of investors on April 30, 1945. It will be seen that over half of the Treasury bills was held by the Federal Reserve Banks. Half of the certificates outstanding was held by commercial banks, which also held 67. 7 per cent of notes and 41. 4 per cent of Treasury bonds outstanding. Business corporations held about 23 per cent of the bonds outstanding, and insurance companies and savings banks held about 28 per cent. As investors tended to lengthen their portfolio in recent periods, the Federal Reserve Banks had to absorb more bills and notes and to sell out their bond holdings. Federal Reserve bond holdings declined from $ 2. 7 billion at the end of 1942 to $ 1. 2 billion at the end of 1944, whereas their bill holdings increased from $ 1 billion to $ 4. 9 billion, and note holdings increased from $ 1. 3 billion to $ 1. 6 billion. The figures are given in Table 26.

Comparison with World War I

It is interesting to compare the bank credit participation in the financing of the two wars. An analysis made by the Federal Reserve Bank of New York shows that the patterns of bank credit expansion are quite different in the two cases. [①] During the four years ended Jane 30, 1944, total loans and investments of all commercial banks increased 54. 6 billion dollars, or 133 per cent, compared with an increase in the four years ended June 30, 1919 of $ 14. 2 billion, or 82 per cent. Of these increases, 95 per cent took the form of investments in Government securities, whereas in the First World War 62 per cent of the increase was in loans and only 30 per cent was in Government securities. These differences, the Reserve Bank of New York points out, are accounted for mainly by three factors:

1. The vastly greater magnitude and cost of the present war, and the consequent difficulty of financing as large a part of the cost through taxes and sales of securities to the public;

2. The change in war financing methods, which this time avoid "Borrow and Buy" feature of World War I ;

3. The much larger part of war plant and production coasts financed by the Government this time, instead of by the bank loans to industry, as in the previous war.

In the four-year period, the Government spent 200 billion dollars for this war, or about eleven times the war outlays of the four-year period in the last war. Taxes covered a somewhat larger proportion of total expenditures in this war than in the first. Of the total funds required, however, taxpayers and non-bank investors (including Government agencies and trust funds) have supplied 79 per cent during this war as against 90 per cent during the first. The figures are shown in the Table below.

---

① *Monthly Review*, Federal Reserve Bank of New York, January 1945, p. 3.

Table 18 Government Finance in World War Ⅰ and Ⅱ

World War Ⅰ : June 30, 1915 – 1919

World War Ⅱ : June 30, 1940 – 1944

Items	In Billions Of Dollars		Percentage of Total Expenditures	
	War Ⅰ	War Ⅱ	War Ⅰ	War Ⅱ
Financial Requirements				
Total Expenditures	33. 9	222. 0	100. 0	100. 0
Increase in balance	1. 1	18. 1	3. 2	8. 2
Total funds raised	35. 0	240. 1	103. 2	108. 2
Source of funds				
Taxes & other revenues	10. 8	86. 8	31. 8	39. 1
Borrowing	24. 2	153. 3	71. 4	69. 1
Nonbank investors	19. 7	88. 9	58. 1	40. 1
Commercial banks	4. 3	51. 9	12. 7	23. 4
Reserve Banks	0. 2	12. 5	0. 6	5. 6

Source: *Monthly Review*, Federal Reserve Bank of New York, January 1945, p. 4.

Of the funds raised through borrowing, only 58 per cent was contributed by nonbank investors in the present war compared with 81 per cent in the first one. However, in the first war the practice of borrowing from banks in order to purchase Government securities was much more common than in this war, thus inflating the apparent absorption of securities by nonbank investors in that period. Excluding the increase in bank loans on Government obligations during both wars, the spread between the two periods is narrowed considerably, with purchasers other than banks accounting for 56 per cent of all borrowing in the present war and 72 per cent in the first one. In other words, the comparatively small scale of credit financed purchases of Government securities by nonbank investors has been one factor in the smaller proportion of Government expenditures covered in this war by taxes and the absorption of Treasury securities by nonbank investors combined.

The relatively small amount of security loans extended by banks during the present war is accounted by many factors. The Federal Reserve Bank of New York summarizes these causes as follows: (1) the discouragement of bank loans to finance subscriptions except under restricted conditions, (2) the widespread adoption by individuals of the payroll deduction plan of acquiring Government bonds, (3) the substantial cash assets held by corporations at the outbreak of the war together with their wartime accumulations of funds for tax payments and other purposes, a large part of which has been available for temporary investment in tax notes and other short-term securities, (4) the marked inter-war growth of institutional investors, such as, life insurance companies and mutual savings bank, and (5) the growing importance of Government agencies and trust funds as investors in Government securities.

Another factor, probably more important in restricting the proportion of Treasury security issues absorbed by the public than limitations on the use of security loans, has been predilection of the public to accumulate larger amounts of idle funds, thus marking it necessary for the banks to absorb an increased proportion of the expansion in the public debt. Large hoards of currency have been accumulated as savings to evade taxes and to conceal black market transactions. In addition the public has built up large demand and time deposits.

The increase in loans and investments of commercial banks is shown in Table 19. Loans on Government securities amounted to only 5.5 per cent of the total amount of loans and investments during this war, compared with 16.1 per cent in the first war. The expansion of loans other than security loans during the present war has been small, increasing by only $ 600 million compared with $ 6.5 billion in the first. In contrast to the last war, the high degree of economic mobilization attained during this conflict has brought about a marked contraction in bank loans for non-war purposes. A much larger part of war production has been financed by the Government which has resulted in increased borrowing by the Treasury. Thus the banks have financed war production indirectly and to a reduced extent through loans to industries and purchases of corporate securities.

Another factor in the larger proportion of war borrowing taken up by the banking system in this war may be found in the banking system itself. The existence of a huge volume of excess reserves at the outset of the war led the banks actively to expand their earning assets. The moderate decline, over the war period, in other investments of the banks due to the retirement of debt by States, municipalities, and some corporations, and the decline in bank loans outside the large cities after 1941, created a need for earnings and left Government securities as the only alternative outlet for idle funds.

Table 19 Commercial Bank Credit in World War Ⅰ and Ⅱ

World War Ⅰ : June 23, 1915 – June 30, 1919

World War Ⅱ : June 30, 1940 – June 30, 1944

Items	In Billions of Dollars		Per cent of Total Loans & Investments	
	War Ⅰ	War Ⅱ	War Ⅰ	War Ⅱ
Total Loans	8. 8	3. 6	61. 9	6. 6
On Government Securities*	2. 3	3. 0	16. 1	5. 5
All Other Loans	6. 5	0. 6	45. 8	1. 1
Total Investments	5. 4	51. 0	38. 1	93. 4
Government Securities	4. 3	51. 9	30. 4	95. 0
Other Securities	1. 1	- 0. 9	7. 7	- 1. 6
Total Loans & Investments	14. 2	54. 6	100. 0	100. 0

* Estimated.

Source: *Monthly Review*, Federal Reserve Bank of New York, January 1945, p. 4.

Chapter Ⅳ Federal Reserve Policy (Ⅰ)

Never before has a nation upon entering a war been so strongly equipped with adequate financial and banking mechanisms as was the United States in 1941. The Federal Reserve System, established at the outbreak of the first World War, had experience twenty-seven eventful years of war and peace, great depression and prosperity. At the eve of the war, the United States owned two-thirds of the world's gold stock. As a result member banks had accumulated 14 billion dollars of reserve balances, four times that of 1934. While the potential lending power derived from the unprecedentedly huge reserves created a serious problem of control, it nevertheless strengthened the government financing program for war. Thus, when the United States entered the war in December 1941, the Federal Reserve System confidently issued the following statement:[1]

The financial and banking mechanism of the country is today in a stronger position to meet any emergency than ever before.

The existing supply of funds and of bank reserves is fully adequate to meet all present and prospective needs of the Government and of private activity. The Federal System has power to add to these resources to whatever extent may be required in the future.

The System is prepared to use its powers to assure that an ample supply

---

[1] *Annual Report*, Federal Reserve System Board of Governors, for 1941, p. 1.

of funds is available at all times for financing the war effort and to exert its influence towards maintaining conditions in the United States Government security markets that are satisfactory from the standpoint of the Government's requirements.

Continuing the policy which was announced following the outbreak of war in Europe, the Federal Reserve Banks stand ready to advance funds on United States Government securities at par to all banks.

The statement outlines the two principal functions of the Federal Reserve System in the war financing program, namely, the supply of reserve funds whenever needed and the maintenance of market conditions for Government borrowing. As the war went on, however, new problems arose. In the first year of warfare, industrial production increased by 16 per cent, but over 60 per cent of the national manufacturing capacity had to be shifted to war production. The cost of living rose by 10 to 15 per cent in 1942 in spite of the imposition of price control and the adoption of the Little Steel formula. Thus monetary authorities were facing the problems of financing war production and of curbing inflation.

The objectives of Federal Reserve policy during the war may, therefore, be summarized as follows:

1. Making available to member banks sufficient reserves to enable them at all times to meet the demand of war finance.

2. Maintaining stability in money markets in respect to the prices and yields of Government obligations to facilitate Government borrowing.

3. Controlling the volume and direction of bank credit to facilitate the financing of war production and to prevent inflationary developments.

Maintenance of Bank Reserves

The unprecedented growth in bank reserves, which had resulted from the heavy gold import since early 1934, came to an end at the beginning of

1941. When the United States entered the war in December 1941, member bank reserves stood at 12450 million dollars, a drop of 1. 5 billion from the high level of $ 14 billion in December 1940. The trend then fluctuated rather widely through 1942 and 1943, rose after the second quarter of 1944, reaching 14. 4 billion dollars in December 1944, and then came to the present level of over 15 billion dollars. The amount of excess reserves, however, declined persistently from the high level of about 7 billion dollars in the autumn of 1940 to 3 billions dollars in December 1941, 1. 2 billion in December 1944, and to a low of about 800 million at the present time (May 1945). The trends of reserve balances may be seen from Chart 4 and Table 20.

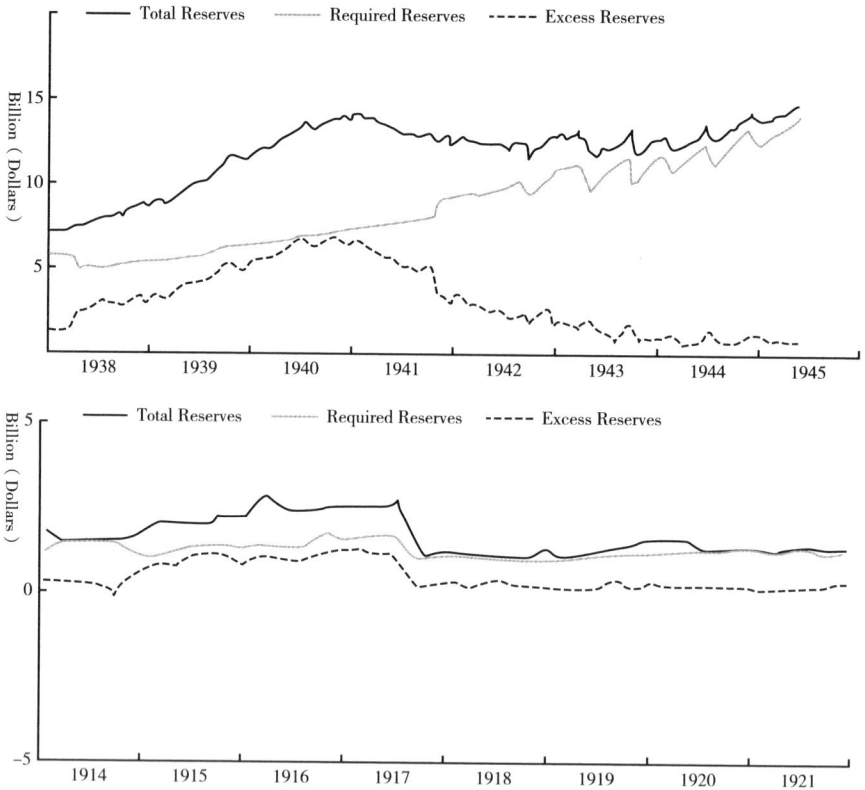

Chart 4 Member Bank Reserves

Source: World War I, *Banking and Monetary Statistics*, 1944; World War II, *Federal Reserve Bulletin*, July 1945.

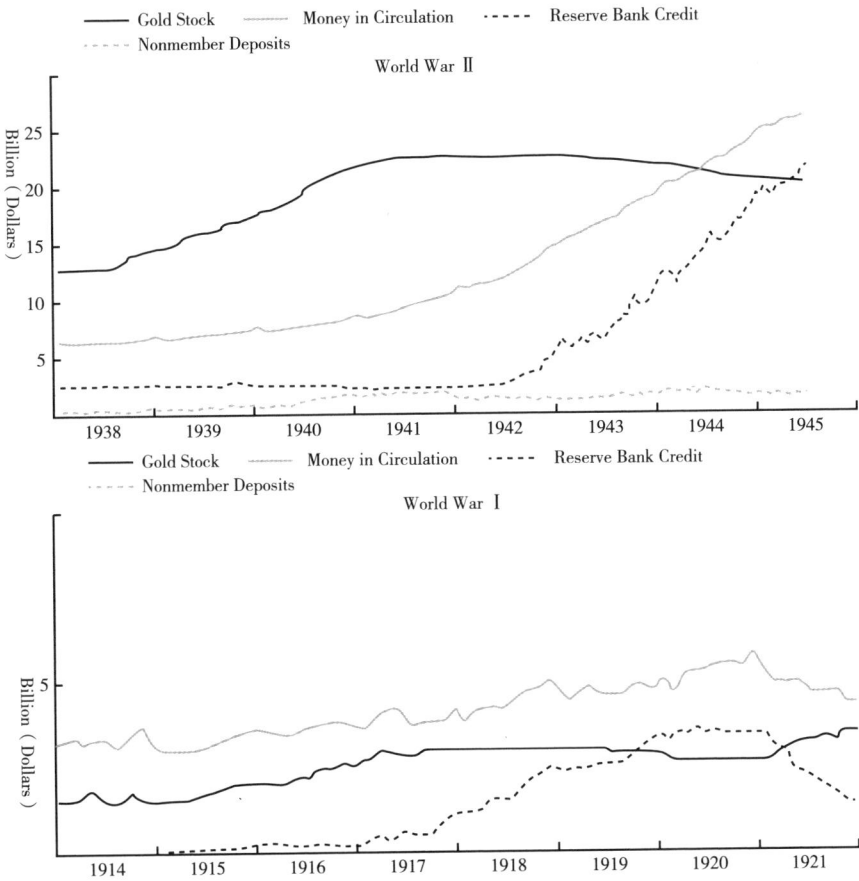

Chart 5   Member Bank Reserves—Related Items

Source: World War I , *Banking and Monetary Statistics*, 1944; World War II , *Federal Reserve Bulletin*, July 1945.

Credit Expansion Does Not Use Up Bank Reserves

The first question to be discussed is: What are the reasons that require the Federal Reserve Banks to take actions to maintain member bank reserves. A common misconception is that banks need more reserve funds when they purchase a large quantity of Government securities. This is definitely untrue. The banking system as a whole does not buy investment or make loans out of its reserve

399

funds. The securities or loans are purchased or made by the creation of the banks' own deposit liabilities, not by conversion of one type of assets, reserves, into another type, Government securities or loans.

This may be illustrated by a simple example. A commercial bank buys $1000000 of Government securities. In making payment, it credits a special deposit account in favor of the United States Treasury, known as war loan deposit accounts. When the Treasury needs these funds to pay, say, for airplanes, the $1000000 of deposits will be transferred to a Reserve Bank, (since the Treasury maintains its checking accounts with the Reserve Banks), and against the latter a check of $1000000 will be drawn and paid to the airplane company. The effects are that the assets of the commercial bank (Government securities) increased by $1000000 and its reserve balances reduced by the same amount. Now, assuming that the airplane company has an account at the commercial bank, it will be given, upon deposit of the Treasury's check, a deposit credit of $1000000; while the commercial bank, upon collection of the check from the Reserve Bank, acquires reserves of the same amount. The net effects on the bank are that both its investment (Government security) and deposit liability (due to airplane company) increased by $1000000, without any change in its reserves. In case the commercial bank buys the securities and makes payment by drawing against its reserve account at the Reserve Bank, the results are the same. At first its reserve balance is reduced by $1000000, and then, after the Treasury's check to the airplane company has been deposited at and collected by the bank, its reserve balance is replenished. [1]

The erroneous idea that the banking system uses up its reserves when it purchases Government securities arises from the mistake of regarding the banking system from the point of view of an individual bank. For individual banks, the making of loans or investments is conditioned by the volume of their reserves. They

---

[1] For a detailed analysis of this fact, see J. Brooke Willis, *The Relation of Bank Deposits to War Finance*, March 15, 1943, The Chase National Bank (mimeographed).

lose reserves in expanding their assets. In practice, however, the reserves which an expanding bank may lose will be acquired by some other banks. For the banking system as a whole, therefore, the purchase of Government securities is not dependent upon the volume of total reserves, but upon the concurrent expansion of all banks at the same rate so that no maldistribution of reserves results. And this is the case during the war.

Table 20   Member Bank Reserves, Reserve Bank Credit and Related Items
(Millions of Dollars)

End of Period	Reserve Total	Bank Credit Gov't Sec.	Gold Stock	Money in Circulation	Member Total	Bank Reserves Excess
1936	2500	2430	11258	6543	6606	1948
1937	2612	2564	12706	6550	7027	1212
1938	2601	2564	14512	6856	8724	3205
1939	2593	2484	17644	7598	11653	5209
1940 June	2531	2466	19963	7848	13781	6857
Dec.	2274	2148	21995	8732	14026	6615
1941 June	2267	2184	22642	9612	13051	5210
Dec.	2361	2254	22737	11160	12405	3085
1942 June	2775	2645	22737	12383	12305	2362
Dec.	6679	6189	22762	15410	13117	1988
1943 June	7576	7202	22388	17421	12085	1212
Dec.	12239	11543	21938	20449	12886	1236
1944 June	15495	14920	21214	22296	13518	1773
Dec.	19745	18846	20619	25307	14373	1773
1945 June	21271	22318	20263	26561	15415	1339

Source: *Federal Reserve Bulletin.*

Bank Reserves Large Enough for Deposit Expansion

A second explanation for the need to supply member bank reserves is usually based on the expansion of bank deposits during the war. Although the purchase of Government securities does not reduce the total amount of bank reserves, it nevertheless requires a larger amount of reserves to satisfy legal requirements. It is clear from the above example that bank deposits increase at the same rate as bank investment in Government securities. So long as member banks are required to maintain reserve funds of a certain percentage of their deposits, their purchases of Government securities inevitably increase the need for reserve funds.

From December 31, 1941 to December 30, 1944, member bank deposits increased from 61.7 billion dollars to 110.9 billion, or almost doubled. In addition, there has been a shift from time deposits to demand deposits. Against the latter, a higher reserve ratio is required by law. The following table shows that demand deposits increased by 106 per cent in the three-year period of war while time deposits increased only 56 per cent. This situation makes it necessary that the required reserves be increased more than merely in proportion to the increase in deposits.

All Member Banks (Millions)

	Dec. 31,1941	Dec. 30,1944	Increases	
Demand Deposits	38846 $	79774 $	40928 $	106%
Time Deposits	12347 $	19259 $	6912 $	56%
Total Deposits	61717 $	110917 $	47200 $	80%

This, however, does not mean that the expansion of bank deposits is a main factor in forcing the Federal Reserve System to take action during the war to supply bank reserve funds. As a matter of fact the total amount of reserves remained unchanged from 1940 through 1944, in spite of the large increase in deposits. The reason is that the banking system had built up a huge amount of excess reserves before the war – up to 7 billion dollars sometime in 1940. Despite the doubling of deposits, reserve requirements increased by only 3.2 billion dollars during the three years ending 1944 (taking in to account the reduction in reserve requirements for banks in New York and Chicago in 1942) . This sum is about equal to the excess reserves possessed by the banking system at the beginning of the period. This means that the total amount of reserves accumulated in the banking system before the war was so large that, if not depleted by other outside factors, they could cover all the need for legal reserve requirements in spite of the expansion of bank deposits, until the end of 1944.

Therefore, theoretically, had there been no outside factors which exhausted bank reserves, the Federal Reserve System would have little need to provide funds for maintaining bank reserves. ①In fact, however, by the end of 1944, the System had extended about 17. 5 billion dollars of Federal Reserve credit to provide funds for commercial banks, mostly for the purpose of replenishing their reserve balances. The question, therefore, is: what are the real causes of this policy?

Currency Expansion Depletes Bank Reserves

The answer may be found in the analysis made in Tables 21 and 22, which show the changes of member bank reserves and related items from December 30, 1940 to December 30, 1944. Since large operations of Federal Reserve open market purchases did not begin until the summer of 1942, member bank reserves declined, reaching their lowest point in September 1942, and then rose again. The analysis in Table 22, therefore, breaks up the whole period into two parts:

During the first period, December 30, 1940 to September 30, 1942, the total amount of member bank reserves declined by $2432 million. The principal factor leading to this reduction was the increase of $4917 million of money in circulation, which was only partly offset by the Federal Reserve purchase of $1383 million of Government securities.

During the second period, September 30, 1942 to December 30, 1944, the total amount of member bank reserves increased by $2781 million. The principal

---

① We shall see in the next section that the demand for currency is the main factor in exhausting bank reserves. If people did not hold their assets in the form of currency to such an extent as they have done, bank deposits would increase by a larger amount, and the required reserves would increase proportionately.

factor leading to the increase was the Federal Reserve purchase of $15299 million of Government securities, which was more than offsetting the factors that used up reserve funds. Again, the most important factor using up bank reserves was the increase in money in circulation ($11604million). This time, however, the reduction in gold stock exerted considerable pressure on bank reserves. Gold has been lost since 1942; this was a result of the fact that most of United States exports has been on the Lend-Lease basis and that imports have been on a cash basis. Countries that have sold commodities to the United States have not been able to buy goods here, on account of war restrictions, and therefore have either withdrawn or earmarked gold. [1]

Table 21　Member Bank Reserves, Reserve Bank Credit and Related Items
(Aanlysis) (Millions of Dollars)

	Dec. 30,1940	Sept. 30,1942	Dec. 30,1944
U. S. Gov't securities	$2184	$3567	$18864
Loans, discounts, and advances	3	8	80
Other Reserve Bk. Credit	87	199	819
Total Reserve Bk. Credit	2274	3774	19763
Gold stock	21995	22754	20619
Treasury currency cut	3087	3353	4131
Treasury deposits with Reserve Banks	368	661	440
Treasury cash holding	2213	2222	2375
Money in circulation	8732	13703	25307
Nonmember bank deposits	1732	1407	1598
Other F. R. accounts	284	296	402
Member bank reserves	14026	11592	14373
Excess reserves	6615	1690	1773

Source: *Federal Reserve Bulletin*, various issues.

---

[1]　Secretary of Treasury Moregnthau stated at the Senate Banking Committee in 1943 that experience had revealed no better means of settling international balances during the war than the shipment of gold. He cited the fact that during the fiscal year 1941 – 1942 the Exchange Stabilization Fund had sold $644 million of gold to foreign countries and bought $162 millions. In 1942 – 1943 (up to April 1943) the Fund had sold $401 million of gold and bought $27 million Cf. *Economist*, London, April 24, 1943, p. 526.

Table 22　Changes in Member Bank Reserves and Related Items

(Millions of Dollars)

	Dec. 30 ,1940 – Sept. 30 ,1942	Sept. 30 ,1942 – Dec. 30 ,1944	Dec. 30 ,1940 – Dec. 30 ,1944
U. S. Gov't securities	+ 1383	+ 15279	+ 16662
Loans , disc't , advance	+ 5	+ 72	+ 77
Other Reserve Bank Credit	+ 112	+ 620	+ 732
Total Reserve Bank credit	+ 1500	+ 15971	+ 17471
Gold stock	+ 759	– 2135	– 1376
Treasury currency out.	+ 266	+ 778	+ 1044
Treasury deposit with Reserve Banks	+ 293	– 221	+ 72
Treasury cash holding	+ 9	+ 153	+ 162
Money in circulation	+ 4791	+ 11604	+ 16575
Nonmember bank deposits	– 325	+ 191	– 134
Other F. R. accounts	+ 12	+ 106	+ 118
Member bank reserves	– 2434	+ 2781	+ 347
Excess reserves	– 4925	+ 83	– 4842

Source : Table 21.

Table 23　Factors Affecting Member Bank Reserves

Member Bank Reserves – 2434 (Dec. 30 ,1940 – Sept. 30 ,1942)

Factors Leading to Increase		Factors Leading to Decrease	
U. S. Gov't securities	+ 1383	Money in circulation	+ 4791
Loans , disc't , advances	+ 5	Treasury cash	+ 9
Other Reserve BK. credit	+ 112	Treasury deposits with Reserve Banks	+ 293
Total Reserve BK credit	+ 1500		
Treasury currency	+ 266	Other F. R. accounts	+ 12
Gold stock	+ 759		5105
Nonmember bank deposits	+ 325	Member bank reserves	– 2434
	2850	total	2671

Member Bank Reserve – 2781 (Sept. 30 ,1942 – Dec. 30 ,1944)

Factors Leading to Increase		Factors Leading to Decrease	
U. S. Gov't securities	+ 15279	Gold stock	+ 2135
Loans, disc't, advances	+ 72	Money in circulation	+ 11604
Other Reserve BK. Credit	+ 620	Treasury cash	+ 153
Total Reserve BK credit	+ 15971	Nonmember bank deposits	+ 191
Treasury currency	+ 778	Other F. R. accounts	+ 106
Treasury deposits with Reserve Banks	+ 221	total	14189
		Member bank reserves	+ 2781
	16970		16970

Member Bank Reserves − 347 (Dec. 30 ,1940 − Dec. 30 ,1944)

Factors Leading to Increase		Factors Leading to Decrease	
U. S. Gov't securities	+ 16662	Gold stock	− 1376
Loans, disc't, advances	+ 77	Money in circulation	+ 16575
Other Reserve BK. Credit	+ 732	Treasury cash	+ 162
Total Reserve BK credit	+ 17471	Treasury deposit with Reserve Banks	+ 72
Treasury currency	+ 1044		
Nonmember bank deposits	+ 134	Other F. R. accounts	+ 118
	18649		18303
		Member bank reserves	+ 347
N. B Adding absolute amounts.			18650

Source: Table 22.

It is clear from the third part of the analysis in Table 22, that, in the four years of warfare ending 1944, the reason why the Federal Reserve System has been so anxious to maintain member bank reserves has been the increase in money in circulation. Interestingly enough, during this period the amount of Government securities purchased by the System—the most important measure in supplying bank reserves—is almost equivalent to the amount of the currency increase.

In the year 1944 member bank needs for reserve funds were greater than in any previous year, increasing by approximately $ 7. 5. billion. The Reserve Banks, accordingly have extended a larger and larger volume of credit throughout the period. The Reserve Bank of New York states that the reasons for this increasing trend: (1) the previous exhaustion of excess reserves (the total of excess reserves declined to below $1 billion by the end of January 1945), (2) the absence of special factors tending to reduce the bank's needs for reserves, such as, the reduction in reserve requirements at central reserve cities in 1942 and the removal of reserve requirements against war loan deposit accounts in 1943, (3) the heavy demand for reserve funds arising out of the continued large demand for currency, the conversion into gold of dollar balances acquired by foreign central banks and governments, and a continued increase in member bank reserve requirements accompanying further growth in deposits. [1]

Table 24 gives a clear picture of the annual changes in reserve needs and other factors. It will be observed that the increase in currency by expansion was accelerated. [2] The increase in required reserves caused by expansion of bank deposits was smaller in 1944 than in 1941 and 1942; it was nearly double that of 1943, chiefly because the 1943 increase was substantially reduced by the removal of the reserve requirements against war loan deposits. Federal Reserve credit in use increased rapidly through the years.

Table 24   Factors Affecting the Reserve Position of Member Banks and the Need for Federal Reserve Credit (Millions of Dollars)

	1941	1942	1943	1944
Factors affecting Member-bank reserves: Increase in currency	− 2428	− 4250	− 5039	− 4853
Net Gov't. Expenditures(+)or receipts(−)	$	+ 1211	− 164	+ 104
Gold and foreign account operation, net	+ 1101	− 30	− 1355	− 1163
All other	− 15	− 537	+ 761	− 159

---

[1]   *Annual Report*, Federal Reserve Bank of New York, 1944, p. 22.

[2]   This increase in circulating currency was nearly large amount of previously accumulated currency to pay for war bonds during the sixth War Loan, the increase during 1944 might have been fully as great.

	1941	1942	1943	1944
Total	− 1683	− 3606	− 5797	− 6076
Increase in required reserves	+ 1927	+ 1771	+ 499	+ 1112
Net increase in need for reserves	+ 3610	+ 5413	+ 6296	+ 7188
changes in excess reserves	− 3523	− 1095	− 736	+ 314
F. R. Credit in use	+ 87	+ 4318	+ 5560	+ 7502

Source: *Annual Report*, Federal Reserve Bank of New York, 1944, p. 23.

Whenever the public demands currency, commercial banks have to provide it by drawing upon their reserve balances at the Reserve Banks, because only the Reserve Bank are authorized to issue bank notes. Thus public election to hold currency uses up bank reserve dollar for dollar, while the public choice to hold bank deposits increase the reserve requirement only by a fraction, 20 per cent in large cities. This suggests that, if the public did not demand currency to such an extent during the war, that is, if they preferred to keep all their increased incomes in the form of bank deposits, savings bonds or other investments rather than in Federal reserve notes, there would have been little need on the part of the Federal Reserve authorities to take action toward replenishing member bank reserves.

Liquidity Preference of the Public and Money Hoarding

During World War I , currency in circulation increased from 3 billion dollars in 1915 to 5 billion in 1918 and reached a peak of 5. 4 billion in 1920. During this war, as may be seen in Table 20, currency increased from 9. 6 billion dollars at the beginning of 1941 to over 25 billion by the end of 1944. The rate of expansion was about 4 billion in 1948, 5 billion in 1943 an 6 billion in 1944.

Just what considerations have motivated the continuous accumulation of currency has been a subject of much speculation. Evidently there has been an increased need for currency to meet additional working cash requirements incident to the extraordinary expansion in production and trade over the war period. The rise in commodity prices and the tremendous expansion of employment necessitated a larger volume of cash transactions. In addition, there has been a larger volume of movement on the part of workers and a shift of industries during the war, an increase in travelling activities, and, moreover, a continuous movement of armed forces. A large amount of money has gone abroad with American service men. Taking all of these factors into account, however, there still is a large volume of currency in circulation to be accounted for by other reasons. It will be seen in the following table, that the volume of currency increased faster than increased in various business activities in each year with only one exception, that of factory payrolls in 1941 – 1943. This means that the growth in circulating money has run far ahead of the need for current transactions. Particularly striking is the fact that, in 1944, currency in circulation has failed to show a tendency to level off in consonance with the relative stabilization of war expenditures, gross national product, employment and prices. [1]Factory payrolls increased by only 1. 2 per cent in 1944 and employment actually declined by 5. 2 per cent, yet currency in circulation continued to rise by 23. 4 per cent.

Table 25   Changes in Money in Circulation and in Business Activities

Per cent increases from previous year	1940	1941	1942	1943	1944
Money in circulation	14. 9	28. 8	37. 5	33. 1	23. 4
Income payments to Individuals	7. 4	21. 6	24. 4	20. 3	8. 5
Department store sales	6. 8	17. 0	12. 6	12. 3	10. 9
Factory employment	7. 5	22. 9	16. 6	14. 1	- 5. 2
Factory payrolls	14. 5	46. 3	46. 4	34. 7	1. 2
Freight car loadings	7. 9	18. 3	6. 1	- 0. 7	2. 2
Wholesale prices	1. 9	11. 1	13. 2	4. 5	0. 9
Cost of living	0. 8	4. 9	10. 7	6. 1	1. 6

Source: *Federal Reserve Bulletin*, various issues.

---

[1]   Cf. *Annual Report*, Federal Reserve Bank of New York, 1944, p. 20.

In explaining this feature, the following reasons have been suggested for the extraordinary expansion of currency:

1. The low interest rates paid on time and savings deposits and the service charge imposed on checking accounts by banks before and during the war discouraged people from keeping money with in banks.

2. Income expansion has been large in the lower and middle income groups who lack experience with bank connections.

3. The shift of population disrupted banking connections. Many new war industry centers did not have sufficient banking services.

4. Currency has been held to evade tax payments.

5. Currency has been used to cover black-market transactions.

Perhaps only 4 and 5 among these reasons could have a considerable influence on the demand for currency over a period of three and a half years of warfare. The amount used in black-market transactions is quite uncertain. Although no estimate has been made, the requirements apparently does not exceed 1 billion dollars. [1] Requirements to offset holdings for the purpose of evading taxes are probably even less because this occurred only among higher income groups.

The major factor in the expansion of currency may be found in the people's liquidity preference, that is, individuals prefer to keep their excess income in the form of hand-to-hand currency. The factors described above may constitute part of the motivation toward increasing liquidity preference during the war. The psychological change on the part of the public, however, may be in part an aftermath of the speculative misadventures of the twenties, and may be an extension and repetition of the great money hoarding of the thirties. The tendency is probably reinforced by consideration of the uncertainties, both personal and national, arising in the war years.

Whatever the motives may be, it seems evident that money has been hoarded by the public in large amounts. The hoarding of money may be further proved by

---

[1] Cf. *Federal Reserve Bulletin*, April 1944, p. 322.

the following facts. First, bank notes of large denominations have increased more rapidly than small denominations especially after 1942. In 1943 and 1944 small note ($ 20 and under) and coins increased by 52 per cent, while large notes ($ 50 and over) increased by 101 per cent. Large notes are believed to be used either in covering black-market purchases or as a form of wealth, that is, hoarding. ① During the War Loans, the reduction in currency expansion occurred particularly in small denomination. This shows that the large notes kept by the public were not intended for use in prospective investment or in any other form of payment, in other words, they are hoarded.

Secondly, a further analysis shows that the close relation between the growth in money and the growth in wage and salary payments since 1935 collapsed by 1942. After 1942 the disparity has increased ; currency increased more rapidly than income payments and far more rapidly than consumer expenditures. The same analysis also shows that currency increased in rough proportion to the increase in demand deposits until 1942, but exceeded the rise in demand deposits thereafter. The recent tendency has indicated that demand deposits are used as "business money" and currency as "personal money" . After 1942, demand deposits grew roughly parallel with the growth in wage and salary payments. All these facts suggest that the increasing volume of currency represents an increasing volume of money hoarded by the public. ②

It is this liquidity preference of the public that has forced the Federal Reserve Authorities to take action to maintain member bank reserves in the banking system. In a sense, Federal Reserve credit has been expanded partly to finance

---

① In May 1943 the British government announce that no more notes of 10 pounds or over would be issued, This announcements was accompanied by publicity and speculation that ownership of large denomination notes might be interpreted as evidence of income tax evasion or black market activities. Immediately after that the over-all increase in circulation was checked for about three months. Large bills returned to banks, and there were unconfirmed reports that large notes actually sold at a discount during this period.

② Cf. G. l. Bach, "Currency in Circulation," *Federal Reserve Bulletin*, April 1944, pp. 318 – 323. Cf. also *Federal Reserve Bulletin*, June 1943, p. 499.

public hoarding. Hoarded money, we may add, is the most dangerous money because nobody knows when it will appear and when it will demand goods and because monetary authorities can do nothing to bring it back into the banking system. It is the most dangerous of the several classes of inflationary potentialities emerging from war borrowing.

Significance of the Maintenance of Bank
Reserves Questionable

Member bank reserves so far have been satisfactorily maintained, and, as will be analyzed later, the Federal Reserve authorities seem to have unlimited power to supply funds for this purpose. One important point, however, must be borne in mind: The maintenance of member bank reserves does not mean the maintenance of banks' liquidity and solvency. From the banker's point of view, the legally required reserve does not have much significance. It is of value only for final settlement when the bank is insolvent. It can be used only in case of emergency, and only under penalty interest charges. [1] It is an iron ration which you must not touch even in the throes of starvation. [2]

The legal reserve and its maintenance are of legal meaning only. It does not provide a cushion for bank risks. Conservative bankers, therefore, usually exclude it from their primary reserves against deposit liabilities. Yet it is not an uncommon impression that bankers heavily involved in Government bond investment today may feel at ease in view of the large amount of reserve funds they hold at the Reserve Banks. Robertson once observed that a legal arrangement of this kind is open to the objection that human nature being what it is, the law is sometimes held to encourage what it does not expressly forbid, and a bank may therefore be tempted to keep its proportion of reserves very near the bed-rock legal minimum. Any

---

[1] On July 7, 1942, The Board of Governors amended Regulation D to facilitate use of reserve funds by member banks in case of need, but remained. For details, see pp. 459 – 460.

[2] Robertson, *Money*, New York, 1989, p. 61.

unexpected demand for common money may then present the bank with the alternatives of infringing the law or declaring itself insolvent while its reserves are still far from exhausted. [1]From this viewpoint, the policy of maintaining member bank reserves is nothing but a legal device, whereas, behind the scenes, inflationary borrowing may go on.

Before leaving the problem of member bank reserves, two points may be mentioned. First, banks throughout the country have more and more fully utilized their funds. This has also been encouraged by the Treasury and the Federal Reserve System. In recent months, many banks in financial centers have maintained no excess reserves, or very low excess reserves, thus lessening to some degree the responsibility of the Reserve Banks to take up Government securities in the market. The total excess reserves of the banking system, however, are being held at the 1 billion dollars level for time being. Secondly, commercial banks have to an unnecessary extent adjusted their reserve position by selling and purchasing short-term securities, especially Treasury bills. The Treasury has encouraged the practice by pegging the buying rate at Reserve Banks and by the practice of a repurchase option on the part of the sellers. This will be discussed in Chapter VI.

Stabilization of Money Market

In wartime borrowing, the maintenance of a stable security market is no less important than the supply of bank reserves. A drop of 10 points in the price of Government securities at their present volume would be enough to wipe out the capital, surplus and undivided profits of many, perhaps even most, of the large banks in this country. [2] A rise in interest rates would not only greatly increase the cost of Government borrowing but also place a burden on the continuous sales of war loans. In the First World War, prices of Government securities tended to

---

[1]   Ibid. , p. 60.

[2]   Cf. "Danger in Declining Federal Reserve Ratio," *Commercial and Financial Chronicle*, March 16, 1944, p. 1121.

decline. The Treasury found it necessary to offer more favorable terms on the successive issues, at first by increasing the coupon rates and subsequently by granting added tax exemption. People thus deferred their purchases and waited for better terms. A stable market, on the other hand, assures investors that their holdings will not decline sharply in price as new issues are offered and that they have nothing to gain by waiting for more attractive terms.

Stabilization of Government Security Market

In September 1939, when the war in Europe had actually begun, prices of United States Government and high-grade corporate bonds declined abruptly. Prices of Government bonds had advanced almost continuously from September 1937 to June 1939, and were at that time at the highest level on record, with the average yield on long-term bonds at 2.25 per cent. On September 1, 1939, the System announced that all the Federal Reserve Banks stood ready to make advances on Government securities to all banks at par and at the discount rate. Together with open-market operations the prices of Government obligations had almost recovered by the end of 1939.

The market in 1940 and 1941 was relatively steady, with a rising trend on both Government and corporate bond prices. There was no occasion until December 1941 for open market operations by the Reserve System. Quotations on long-time Government bonds advances to a peak about the first of November 1941 and then declined slowly to December 6. From the time the United States entered the war until shortly before the end of the year, quotations on long-time bonds declined by about 2.5 points and on short-term securities declined moderately. During this period the Reserve Banks purchased 60 million dollars of bonds and 10 million of bills. The Treasury also supported the market by investing some of its trust funds in Government obligations. In a relatively short time the market for Government became steady on the basis of yields slightly above the low points reached in November (see Chart 7, p. 416).

A stable bond market, however, occurred in 1942. At the end of April 1942, the System established the fixed rate of buying Treasury bills at 0. 375 of one per cent. Thus the shortest end of the interest schedule was pegged. A definite pattern of interest rate structure has already been in existence by that time, with yields rising progressively from short to long-term securities. In October 1942, the Treasury announced that rates on the war financing program would be stabilized on a scale running from 0. 375 per cent for 90-day Treasury bills and 0. 875 per cent for l-year certificate of indebtedness, up through 2 per cent for 10-year bonds and 2. 5per cent for long-term bonds, with new issues eligible for investment of commercial bank deposits to 10-year maximum. This ascending shape of the interest curve has come to be known as the "Treasury curve" (see Chart 6). Short rates, after a sharp rise from the low point reached in 1940, were still low compared with past periods. Long-term rates on Government bonds, after a decline lasting for 23 years, have become stabilized at the lowest levels in American history.

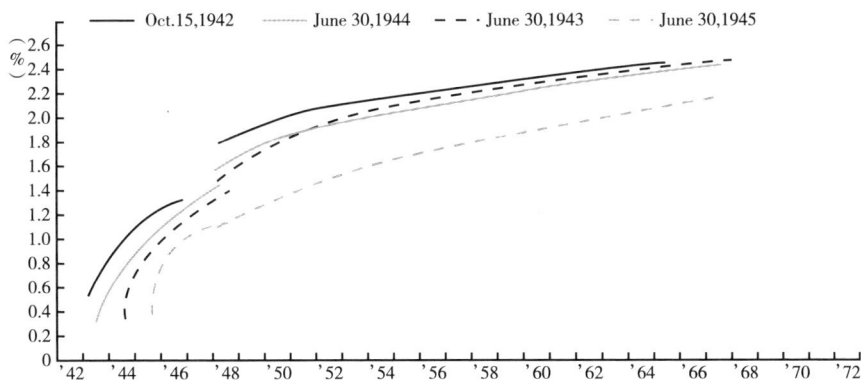

Chart 6   Yields of Treasury Securities (1942 – 1945)

The rate at the lowest end was pegged by the 0. 375 per cent fixed buying rate of bills. Yields on other securities were not frozen, but have been closely controlled by the buying and selling operations of the Federal Reserve Banks. The most prominent examples are the purchases and sales of long-term bonds in 1942 and

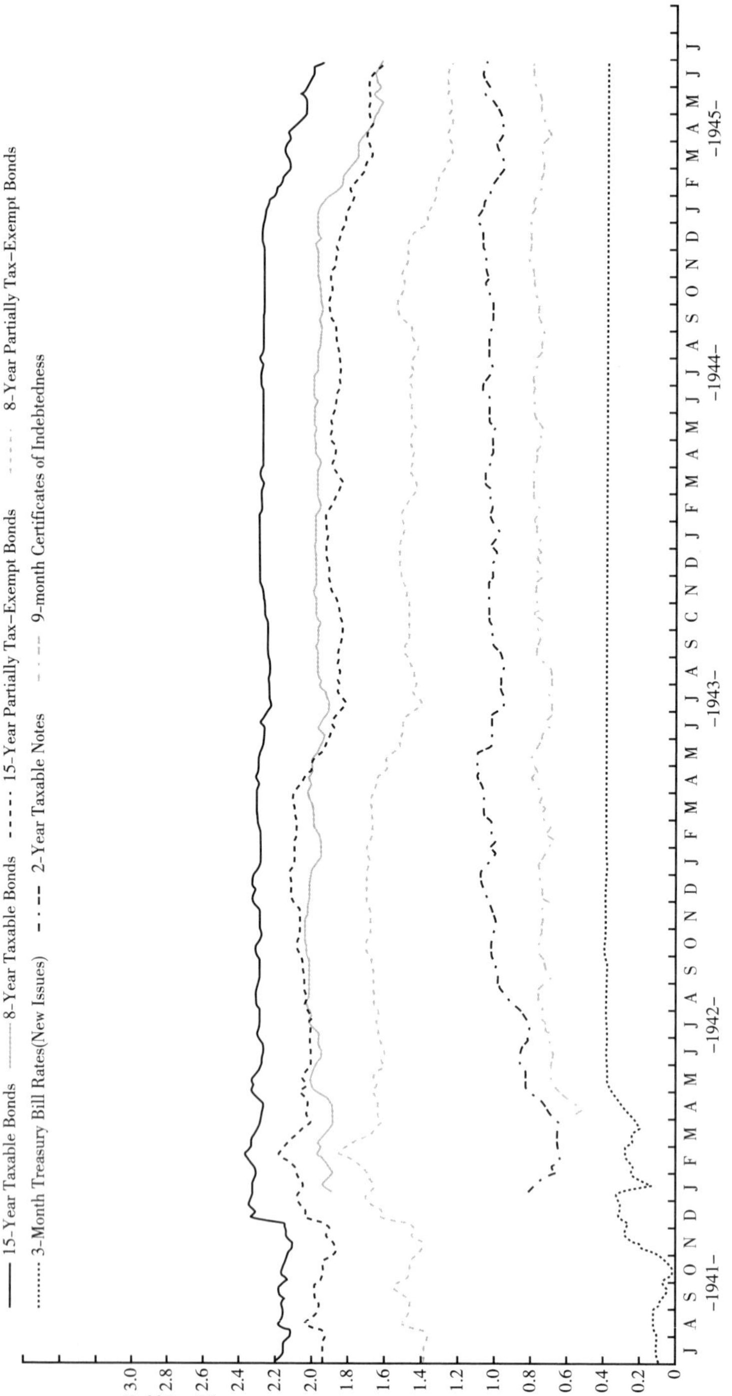

Chart 7 Yields of U. S. Treasury Issues

Source: Courtesy of Federal Reserve Bank of New York Securities Department.

1943. In 1942, when the rates were just established, the System purchased large amounts of newly-issued bonds and notes to maintain their prices. As the public became aware that a pattern of rates would be maintained, banks began to lengthen their holdings. Early signs of developing confidence in the stability of rate structure appeared in the spring of 1943 in a strong demand for medium and long-term Treasury bonds. This demand was diverted chiefly to the tax-exempt issues. Thus during the first half of 1943, despite large offerings of new issues by the Treasury, the System reduced its holdings of bonds and notes by almost as large an amount as the 1942 increase. The sales helped to keep the long-term yield from dropping. [1] At the same time, the System absorbed large quantities of bills offered by banks in adjusting their reserve position. Since then the Federal Reserve bill holding was increasing persistently and its bond holding was declining. In this way the System tended to stabilize the rate structure by restraining the fall of longer yields and the rise of shorter ones. In August 1943, however the lowering pressure appeared at the short end of the curve. The August issue of the 0.875 per cent certificates jumped immediately to a premium which reduced the yield to less than 0.375 per cent, with demand so insistent as to indicate a possible lowering of the rate. Instead of changing the rate, the Treasury made larger amounts of certificates available. [2] Increasing the amount of issues also helped stabilize the yield and rate structure in some other minor cases.

Decline of Government Security Yields

When the Treasury first announced its rate stabilization policy in 1942, few people expected to see the interest rates decline. Yet that is precisely what been happening. This is clearly shown in Charts 6 and 7. A major departure from the

---

[1] Cf. *Federal Reserve Bulletin*, August 1944, p. 752.

[2] Cf. *Monthly Letter*, National city Bank of New York, March 1945, p. 28.

established Treasury pattern, however, first came in the sixth War Loan of December 1994, though the tendency had long been in existence. After the sixth War Loan, as may be seen in Chart 6, rates tended to break away on the down side, bending the curve downward in the middle and longer maturities. Comparing the figures on October 31, 1944 and February 26, 1945 (before and after the sixth War Loan), the advances in prices were 0.29 on 2% 5-year bonds, 1.27 on 2% 10-year bonds, and 2.09 on 2% 15-year bonds; the declines in the yield were 0.21 on 2% 5-year bonds, 0.26 on 2% 10-year bonds and 0.22 on 2.25% 15-year bonds. The factors responsible for this fall in interest, as interpreted by the National City Bank of New York,[1] were:

1. The growing tendency to shift from to long-term investments.

2. In the presidential campaign both the Democratic and Republican parties announced the aim of maintaining low rates for future financing and for the refunding of Government debt.

3. The British Treasury, in November 1944, discontinued the sales of National War Loan 2.5 per cent bonds of 1952 – 1954, and offered in their place 1 – 0.75 per cent Exchange Bonds of 1950, thus lowering the interest on bonds in London.

The decisive factor has been the consistent demand for longer-term securities by banks and other investors. This tended to lower the yields of long-term bonds and to raise the yields of short-term securities. But when the shortest end of the interest curve was pegged, this tendency pulled down the whole interest level. This demand in turn reflected growing confidence among investors in monetary authority's control over the rate interest.

As interest rates fell materially, there were speculative rumors in the market that the Treasury would in the next War Loan either cut down the coupon rate on the 2.5 per cent long-term bonds or increase the maturity date of bonds carrying that coupon rate. Such rumors helped to bid up the prices on the long-

---

[1] *Monthly Letter*, March 1945, p. 28.

term bonds and hence further depressed their yields. The announcement early in March 1945 of the type of issues to be offered in the seventh War Loan stopped the rumors, but it further stimulated the market. The terms in the seventh War Loan greatly restricted the volume of intermediate and long-term securities available to banks, either on subscription or by purchase in the market. Banks seeking an outlet for their funds were forced to turn to outstanding issues in the market, and at the same time the Treasury requested corporations not to sell existing issues except for normal portfolio adjustments. From December 30, 1944 to May 29, 1945, before the seventh War Loan, the yields declined by 0. 36 on 2 per cent 5-year bonds, 0. 28 on 2. 25 per cent 10 – year bonds, and 0. 13 on 2. 5 per cent 15-year bonds. It may be seen that those available for banks declined (See Chart 7). On the other hand, the yields on the short-term securities certificates, notes and the other bond, the yields on the short-term securities, certificates, notes and the 8-year partially tax-exempt bonds have risen slightly since April 1945 after a rapid decline since the sixth War Loan.

The trend continued during the seventh War Loan, but was reversed by July 1945. The figures for the latest movement, however, are not yet available at the present time.

Short-Term Borrowing and the Money Market

It has been said that the job of stabilizing the market has been partly done by the Treasury through the issuance of short-term securities. Certificates of indebtedness, which were used in the last war and reintroduced in 1942, are especially designed for this purpose. The theory is that short-term securities are issued in anticipation of tax revenues or the proceeds of subsequent funded debt; thus they enable the Treasury to receive a regular flow of funds and prevent strain and drain upon the money market during large sales in war loan. This is explicitly set forth in the following statement in the first issue of the certificates during the last war:[①]

> The Secretary (of the Treasury) appreciates the desirability of avoiding any derangement of money market, and in the financial operations in which the Government is about to engage it will be his purpose to adjust receipts and disbursements in such a way that as far as possible money paid in will be promptly returned to the market. The contemplated sale of Treasury certificate is in line with this policy. Should the bank during the next few weeks absorb several hundred million dollars of these certificates, the proceeds being paid in the course of business, the bank will possess ready means with which to meet withdrawals made later by depositors in paying for bind subscription. The result of this method will be gradual anticipation of payment on account of bonds with a steady and continuous return to the banks and the money paid in.

This policy was regarded as an important advantage of war borrowing in the last war. Thirty-one issues of certificates in 1917 and 1918 were all in anticipation of income tax, Liberty Loans or Excess Profits tax. Subscriptions of Liberty bonds, although nominally payable in instalment, were usually overpaid or paid in full at the first instalment date. The practice of short-term borrowing, therefore, prevented the strain in money market on such occasions. [②]

However, as already discussed in Chapter II, the practice of short-term borrowing has many drawbacks. This policy has the advantage of stabilizing the money market only when the funds are borrowed directly from the public. If the borrowing process is accompanied by the creation of bank credit, as it has been during this war, the strain upon the money market will be equal, whether borrowing through long-term bonds or short-term certificates. The following

---

① *Federal Reserve Bulletin*, May 1917, p. 342.
② Jacob H. Hollander, *War Borrowing*, New York, 1919, p. 30.

passage, written by Professor Hollander in connection with the financing of the last war, still holds true today:

> The possibility of avoiding monetary dislocation and of reducing monetary strain in connection with war borrowing will thus be a consequence not of the use of anticipatory certificates of indebtedness in lieu of direct long-term loans, but of an effective credit mechanism developed and utilized by the banks in connection with such certificates just as in the case of loans... Not the particular borrowing device but the accompanying credit apparatus becomes the essential element in the situation. [1]

Professor Hollander has shown that the banking mechanism to avoid strain in the money market is made up of four elements:

1. The redeposit of borrowed funds in deposits banks until required for public expenditures.

2. The exemption of war loan deposits held by depositary banks from reserve requirements.

3. The permissive payment by credit on the part of lending banks for Government securities.

4. The extension of Federal Reserve credit whenever needed—the open market operation, the fixed buying rate on bills, the rediscount facilities of member and non-member banks, etc..

The first element enables commercial banks to enlarge their portfolio without a sudden withdrawal of their reserve funds. The second one enables commercial banks to avoid large transfers of funds to Reserve Banks and to use their surplus funds temporarily in purchasing Treasury bills. The most important elements, however, are the third and the fourth ones. They enable the lending banks to make the necessary advances to the Treasury without a corresponding curtailment of

---

[1] Ibid. , p. 125.

ordinary business accomodations. In fact the banking mechanism has been operating in such a way that the Treasury can practically borrow from the banking system any amount it needs without depleting bank resources for business and the public. Any difficulty met by the banks may be relieved by credit extensions on the part of Federal Reserve Banks.

Chapter V　Federal Reserve Policy（Ⅱ）

Credit Control

A third objective of wartime Federal Reserve policy lies in the principle of credit manipulation that bank credits should be diverted from consumption and other non-essential purposes into the war effort, so as to facilitate war production and to prevent price inflation. This has been done mainly through two kinds of measures: the guarantee of loans to war industries, known as "V loans" and "VT loans," and the restriction on consumer credit, known as the "selective credit control". Both of these practices will be described in the next Chapter. For the present our attention is concentrated upon the effectiveness of such measures, especially in connection with the anti-inflation program.

Credit Policy Plays a Minor Role in
Economic Stabilization

In recent years it has become fashionable to ascribe, often without making important qualifications, far-reaching influence to monetary and credit policy in the regulation and control of economic life. Experience, however, shows little evidence to support the theory.

Though everybody is talking about credit control today, the practice arose very late in American monetary history. Apparently the idea of credit control did not exist in this country before 1914, though European central banks were aware of its use in the 19th century.[1] We are told that the founders of the Federal Reserve System never intended to use it as an agency for credit control, whether for price stabilization or any other ambitious purpose, but as an agency of elastic supply of money for the needs of industry and trade.[2] This seems true. The Federal Reserve Act defines the objectives of the operation of the System only vaguely. The preamble indicates, as the purposes of the Act, "to furnish an elastic currency, to afford a means of rediscounting commercial paper, to establish a more effective supervision of banking in the United States." Important, but very indefinite, is the provision of Section 13 that the rates of discount of the Reserve Banks "should be fixed with a view to accommodating commerce and business." Accommodation, however, is not control, but the "responsiveness of the volume of currency in use to the public's requirements and the promptness with which the net volume of inflow or outflow of currency of all kinds at the Reserve Banks responds to changes in the demand for each."[3] Changes in prices or income are, therefore, not a guide to Federal Reserve credit policy;[4] moreover, domestic monetary stability

---

[1] Cf. Benjamin H. Beckhart, *The Discount Policy of the Federal Reserve System*, New York, 1924, p. 99.

[2] Cf. John H Williams, "Monetary Stability and the Gold Standard," in a volume entitled *Gold and Monetary Stabilization*, University of Chicago, 1942, p. 134.

[3] *Annual Report*, *Board of Governors*, *Federal Reserve System*, for 1924, p. 7. Cf. also: "Administratively, therefore, the solution of the economic problem of keeping the volume of credit issuing from the Federal Reserve Banks from becoming either excessive or deficient is found in maintaining it in due relation to the volume of credit needs as these needs are derived from the operating requirements of agriculture, industry, and trade, and the prevention of the uses of Federal Reserve credit for purposes not warranted by the terms or spirit of the Federal Reserve Act." *Annual Report*, op. cit. , 1923, pp. 34 – 35.

[4] See the interpretation formulated by Governor R. A. Young of the System Board in 1928: "A healthy banking situation must be forever the primary concern of the managers of the Federal Reserve Banks and of the Federal Reserve Board. These responsibilities are sufficient to require our best efforts in the determination of the wise course of action. This is one of the reasons why it would be unfortunate if the Federal Reserve System were to be charged with still further responsibilities which are not directly related to banking, such as, responsibility for the stability of the general price level or for the moderation of ups and downs in business conditions." Address before the Convention of the American

was regarded as incompatible with the then much-praised international gold standard. ①

The passive theory of central banking prevailed until 1922, when the Federal Reserve authorities for the first time found themselves faced with a definite problem of credit control and at the same time possessed sufficient in dependence to make their decisions significant. ②Open-market operations became active under the leadership of Governor Strong of the Reserve Bank in New York. Then came the restrictive policy of 1923, the easy money policy of 1924, a period of neutrality of 1925 and 1926, and the credit relaxation in 1927. The rest test of the ability of the System to stabilize the nation's economy came first in 1928 – 1929 in the attempt to control the stock market speculation and then in 1930 – 1931 in the effort to save the nation from depression and monetary crisis. Unfortunately the results in both cases were far from satisfactory. This business collapse of 1924 was extremely severe. For six months, in spite of a vigorous expansion policy on the part of the Federal Reserve System, credit contracted more rapidly than it did in 1920 – 1921.

In 1927 business activity declined much less, but most of the credit poured into the banks flowed after business had started to pick up. The stock market speculation was not checked in 1928 by the discount rate policy and open market

---

Bankers' Association, October 1, 1928, *Journal of the American Bankers' Association*, October 1928, p. 281. Cf. also the interpretation made by Professor Reed. Harold R. Reed, *Federal Reserve Policy*, 1921 – 1930, p. 60.

① The principle of central banking control is based upon recognition that a banking system must have a surplus of reserves, for protection against both internal and external drains; while the price specie gold-standard principle assumes that banking system is loaned up, so that prices are responsive to gold movement. "There is logical conflict between the gold standard and domestic monetary stability. The former imposes external control; the latter insists upon internal control. " John H. William, op., cit., p. 153. Cf. also R. G. Hawtrey, *Currency and Credit*, London, 1934, p. 115, and J. M. Keynes, *Treatise on Money*, New York, 1935, Vol. 1, p. 349.

② Charles O. Hardy, *Credit Policies of the Federal Reserve System*, Washington, D. C., 1932, p. 34. Federal Reserve Banks, however, did impose or suggest some kind of measures to control credit expansion during World War I and the period of postwar inflation. Cf. Beckhart, op. cit., pp. 301, 351.

operations, nor did the direct control in 1929 achieve greater success as a stock market sedative than did the rate policy. There is no evidence that Reserve System efforts in 1930–1931 were successful in stimulating business activity, though there is little doubt that in the emergency of the autumn of 1929 and again in the autumn of 1931 the System's capacity for quick expansion staved off a currency panic. In short, aside from the handling of the seasonal problem and of acute emergencies the stabilization of business by credit control has certainly not been validated by experience. [1]During the thirties, monetary policy was concentrated upon the manipulation of the prices of gold and silver. With the rapid growth in bank reserves and idle money, the central bank could exercise less and less influence over credit market.

We have no space to discuss the theory of the credit control, but we do want to point out that monetary policy plays only a minor role in the nation's economic stabilization. The following passages of the report of the Federal Reserve System in 1943 give us a clear explanation:[2]

It is believed by many that inflation and deflation can be prevented by monetary action. The fact that the Federal Reserve System has the power, through changes in the discount rate, through open-market operations, and through modifications in reserve requirements, to make money dearer and scarcer in a boom and cheaper and more abundant in a depression has been taken as an indication that monetary authorities are able by their actions alone, to maintain economic stability, this is a general magnified view of the influence of monetary action on the course of economic life.

In the past quarter century it has been demonstrated that policies regulating the quantity and cost of money cannot by themselves produce

---

① Cf. Charles O. Hardy, op. cit., pp. 90, 94, 139. The measures imposed by the System, however, are many. For details of, Seymour E. Harris, *Twenty Years of Federal Reserve Policy*, Harvard University, 1933, Vols. I and II.

② *Annual Report*, Board of Governors, Federal Reserve System, 1942, p. 10.

economic stability, or even exert a powerful influence in that direction. The country has gone through boom conditions at times when monetary restraints were being exerted and interest rates were extremely high, and it has continued in depression at times when an active policy of monetary ease was in effect and money was both abundant and cheap. Economic stability depends on a complex of forces and policies, of which credit policy is only one. In order to be effective in bringing about stability the regulation of the availability and cost of money must be integrated with a flexible fiscal policy and at critical times reinforced by direct controls which are discussed in this report, may also bring fruitful results.

In face of the exigencies of war, the problem of credit control becomes more difficult. Central banks in wartime are more important as fiscal agents of the Government than a banker's bank; its credit policies become subordinated to its fiscal functions. The size of credit expansion is primarily determined by the scale of the government's spending program and by the extent to which this expenditure is covered by taxes and by sales of government securities to nonbank investors. When the government's war financing program has assumed definite form the Federal Reserve authorities are obliged to do their best in carrying it out. [1] All that they can do is to choose the least dangerous means of aiding the banks to finance government deficit. As pointed out by Dr. Youngman, [2] once deposits have been generated by their action, and the funds have been spent, the Federal Reserve authorities have one direct means of influencing the subsequent utilization of deposits except through certain selective controls over lending activity, which we shall see later on, are effective only within very limited areas. Furthermore these

---

[1] In wartime the Government also dominates the money market. The discount market is governed by the Treasury bill rate, for situations in America and in England in World War I, of R. G Hawtrey, Currency and Credit London, 1930, pp. 396 – 397.

[2] Anna Youngman, the Federal reserve System in wartime, National Bureau of Economic Research Occasional paper, 1945, p. 45.

methods of control are obviously ineffective to regulate the utilization of available funds in the hands of the public. The Federal Reserve authorities are powerless to prevent price advances resulting from expansion of currency and deposits nor can they regulate the redemption or liquidation of Government securities held by the public. Under such conditions, credit controls are of only secondary importance. Non-monetary controls—controls over production, consumption and prices—have been the most efficient methods. And next, the fiscal policy should assume a greater responsibility. To the extent that fiscal policy is effective, it can be implemented by credit policy.

Fiscal Policy Not Effective in Preventing
Wartime Inflation

There are two aspects of fiscal policy in connection with the anti-inflation plan. First, the Treasury may minimize the inflationary effects of borrowing by deliberate methods of floating war loans; secondly it may curb the growth of inflationary potentialities by proper taxation. [①]

The first category is a matter of policy as well as technique. It has been pointed out in Chapter I that not all public loans are inflationary. To the extent that loans are made ultimately from current income, from liquidated investments, or from current and future savings, there need be no inflation. Policies and measures to achieve this end were discussed in Chapters II and III. In summary, the principal emphasis has been placed upon the diversification of terms of borrowing to meet the needs of various classes of investors, and the appeal to individuals savings through carefully managed War Loan drives. The results, we have seen, are not very

---

[①] In an address on the National Radio Forum, April 14, 1943, Marriner S. Eccles, chairman of the Board of Governors, stated: "If the Government's expenditures were entirely financed by taxation and borrowing from the general public, there would be no need to turn to the inflationary method of financing through the commercial banks. The Federal Reserve in turn would not then be confronted with the necessity of supplying reserves for what it knows to be a dangerous process of financing the war through the banks." *Federal Reserve Bulletin*, May 1943, p. 393.

satisfactory. Bank credit involved in War Loan drives has been large 50 per cent of the net increase in debt in the fifth and sixth drives. About 42 percent of the total public debt has been held by the banking system since 1943. Despite the constant effort made by the Government and by society, in April 1945, individuals held less than 23 percent of the total public debt.

One of the most important factors concerning the success of the borrowing policy is the level of interest rates on Government obligations. Cheap money policy has been advocated by the Treasury. From the Treasury's point of view this may be indispensable, but it is a policy contrary to the general principle of preventing inflationary developments. First, the lower the interest rate, the less are people inclined to save, and the more money must be borrowed from banks. Secondly, low interest rates compel monetary authorities to resort to inflationary tactics-to take up public loans not absorbed by the public and to extend central bank credit to prevent market rates from rising. Many of the disadvantages of the low rate policy have been discussed in chapter Ⅱ. An alternative policy, however, might be more deleterious from the fiscal point of view. If larger interest charges would have to be borne by the Treasury, a higher tax rate would have to be imposed. Again, substantial loss would be assumed by business institutions, especially commercial banks, when they are heavily involved in Government financing. Price declines on Government bonds would cause disturbances in the market with far-reaching influences. It is hard to maintain a chronic cheap money market and it is even harder to upset such a market.

Taxation assumes a greater role than borrowing techniques in fiscal policy to curtail inflationary potentialities. Heavy taxes, however, do not necessarily keep prices from rising; the economic situation in the country and the methods of raising funds must be taken into consideration. The inflation of the 1920's occurred despite an excess of Government revenues which made possible a substantial reduction in Government debt. The activation of the funds, or the dishoarding of money, may replace the purchasing power diverted by tax methods to the Government and be used to bid for goods. The huge amount of liquid assets held by the public may serve to offset partly the power of taxes to reduce civilian purchase during and after the war. Heavy taxes may lead to the liquidation of past savings, and may exert no effect in curtailing current consumption. A fear of inflation or of future scarcities might lead to a flight from money despite a severe tax program. This limitation of tax policy as a measure of restraining a general price rise is often overlooked; and since enough time has not elapsed to test this device in practice, it must be considered with reservations. [1]Besides, there are many difficulties in the practical application of a drastic tax program, as we have explained in chapter Ⅲ. Another point is the methods of collecting funds. In order to avoid social criticism, a severe tax policy in modern times must rely upon the progressive income tax. However, as Mark C. Mills shows, [2] to increase the tax rate in the higher-income brackets is not an efficient method of avoiding price inflation. First, the higher the income the less a dollar of taxation reduces consumption expenditure because the tax is paid out of savings. Secondly, the major part of total current expenditures for consumption, especially those for necessities, is paid by the lower-income groups.

Besides borrowing and tax measures, the Secretary of the Treasury can, if he so desires, exercise a considerable influence on the credit situation. [3]With the approval of the President of the United States, he can increase the monetary value of the gold stock by raising still further the price of gold. He can increase the volume of Treasury currency by speeding up the purchase of silver under the Silver Purchase Act of 1934. But he can exert perhaps the most important influence of all by varying the volume of "Treasury cash and deposits at the Federal Reserve Banks." By increasing these items he can reduce member-bank reserves and tighten credit. By decreasing them he can release funds to member-bank reserves and ease credit. He can also cause a shift of funds from commercial banks to

---

① E. Stein and G. Backman, *War Economics*, New York, 1942, p. 171.

② Mark C. Mills, "The Federal Reserve Policy," in *Economic Problems of War*, edited by George ASteiner, New York, 1942, pp. 4 – 9.

③ Some one states that the Secretary of the Treasury exercise on the credit situation "an influence fully as great as that of the Federal Reserve authorities." F. F. Luthringer, L. V. Chandler, and D. C. Cline, *Money Credit and Finance*, Bonston, 1938, pp. 123 – 136.

Reserve banks through the management of the Exchange Stabilization Fund and the management of the reserve funds of the social insurance plans. Before the passage of the Act of June 12, 1945, the Treasury also possessed the authority to issue United States Notes under the Thomas Amendment of May 12, 1934.

Neither credit policy nor fiscal policy alone is effective in restraining tendencies of inflation. With respect to this, the System has been looking toward a greater responsibility on the part of the Treasury, as may be seen from the following statements of Mr. Eccles, chairman of board of Governors of the system:

> ... Inflation can not be dealt with solely by monetary and credit measures. As a matter of fact, at this stage of our defence effort such measures are of secondary importance. Fiscal policy, involving both types of Government financing and taxation, and direct control are far more important at present. [1] ... Fiscal policy has assumed the greatest importance as a democratic instrument of economic action, while monetary policy assumes a secondary place; both must be coordinated by deliberate action. [2]

Bank Rate Policy Has Never Been an Effective Instrument

The measures that the monetary authorities can use in controlling credit are many:

1. The issuance of warnings;
2. The use of moral suasion;

---

[1] Address on May 1, 1941. "Financial Problems of Defence," *Federal Reserve Bulletin*, June 1941, p. 50.

[2] M. S. Eccles, "Economic Aspects of Federal, State and local Taxation," *Federal Reserve Bulletin*, November 1941, p. 103.

3. The supervision policy;

4. Direct action to member bank borrowing;

5. Change in reserve requirements;

6. Bank rate policy;

7. Open market operations;

8. Qualitative control;

Warnings may have some influences only when they are used very infrequently; moral pressure is likely to have little effect in dealing with a real problem. Supervision and bank examination policy and direct action in governing member bank borrowing, such as, varying the eligibility of paper discounted, have limited influence. Changing member bank reserve requirements is too rigid to correct market fluctuations. By far the most important instruments of central bank credit control have been the discount rates and the open market operations. Qualitative control, and these-called selective credit control, has assumed an increasing significance in recent years. All such measures which the Federal Reserve System imposed during the war will be discussed in Chapter VI.

It is interesting to notice that the historically well-known bank rate policy is no longer an important feature of wartime central banking. It has become, as Sir Ernest Harvey said in discussing borrowing on Consols before the Macmillan Committee, "a relic of past history."① Interesting enough is the conclusion of the Macmillan Report: "There can be no doubt, in our judgment, that Bank rate policy is an absolute necessity for the sound management of a monetary system, and that it is a most delicate and beautiful instrument for the purpose."②

It will be observed that this "most delicate and beautiful" instrument has

---

① Cf. R. G. Hawtrey, *The Art of Central Banking*, London, 1933, p. 152.

② It was also argued that the open market operations could not replace the function of bank rate policy, See F. C. Conolly, "Reflections on the Cheap-Money Policy Particularly in England," Supplement to Svenska Handelsbanken's Index, October 1939, pp. 14 – 16.

never played an important role in the history of credit regulation of the Federal Reserve System, During World War I , Reserve Banks could not exercise rate control because of the low interest rates on Government securities, though commercial banks at that time were borrowing heavily from the Reserve Banks. ①The treasury had established its policy and the Reserve Banks were forced to follow; ② through the whole war period the Bank rate was below the market. ③In the twenties the rediscount rate was not an efficient instrument for controlling the volume of credit because member bank borrowing did not respond to rate changes. Rediscounts were usually low in times of low rate and high when rediscount rates were high. ④The traditional reluctance of banks to borrow and the well-established principle of the System that a bank ought not to borrow merely in order to re-lend at profit forestalled the expected inverse movement between the level of discount rate and the volume of member bank borrowing. Banks borrow to replenish their reserves, and the higher rates which are exacted at such times have no apparent restrictive effect. ⑤During the thirties , banks were out of debt

---

① Cf. Beckhart, *Discount Policy*, op. cit. , pp. 320 – 321.

② Discount rate increases were postponed because the sales of the Victory Loan were too late and because the Treasury believed it had a substantial commitment to keep money relatively easy for some months after the sales of the Victory notes, Cf. W. Randolph Burgess, *The Reserve Banks and Money Market*, New York, 1936, pp. 270 – 271.

③ Beckhart, *Discount Policy*, op. cit. , pp. 278–279. The rate of the bank of England was maintained above market rates, but its Bank rate also became ineffective because the assets of the bank were swollen by advances to pay-off pre-moratorium bills and other transactions. See R. G. Hawtrey, *The Art of Central Banking*, op. cit. , p. 151

④ A chart prepared by Charles O. Hardy shows the movements. See Hardy, *Credit Policies of the Federal Reserve System*, Washington. D. C. , 1932, p. 229. An interesting question, however, is the efficacy of the discount rate policy of the Federal Reserve Banks in the fall of prices in the summer of 1920. There were two schools of thought with quite opposite opinions. The one holds that the Bank rate was an affective cause of the fall in prices, the other holds that the bank rate had no effect. The latter asserts that it was not the increase in bank rate which brought on the period of deflation, but a downright refusal of banks to extend additional amounts of credit. For a full discussion, cf. Benjamin H. Beckhart, *Discount Policy of the Federal Reserve System*, New York, 1924, pp. 454 – 470.

⑤ Another point emphasized by Burgess is that a loan to member banks is only the first step in a chain of operations. It would be of little value to exercise control over the first use of the money when the succeeding uses are not subject to control. Cf. W. r. Burgess, op. Cit. , pp. 64 – 65.

and built up large excess reserves; the discount rate exerted almost no influence on member bank borrowing. From time to time, the abnormal condition prevented the application of this "delicate and beautiful" instrument. During the critical times of the thirties, the policy had to thread its difficult way between these two opposite necessities—rates high enough to avoid inflation and rates low enough to avoid attracting more gold. [1]Another factor causing the inefficacy of a discount rate policy is that rates do not change equally in foreign financial centers. Funds will be shifted among nations to offset the effect of rate measure in one center. [2]

As between the two chief tools for credit manipulation, primary importance must be ascribed to the open market operations. There has been a positive correlation between open market operations and the size of member bank reserves. This instrument was relatively less important during the last war than in this one. It has been the sole significant measure during this war in maintaining bank reserves and markets stability. Hardy points out[3]that, so long as reliance is placed on quantitative rather than qualitative control of member bank credit, as it has usually been placed in the past, it makes little difference whether the rediscount rate is effective or not. Open market operations serve the same purpose. But open market operations give the system no control whatever over the use made of their reserves by the member banks and hence no opportunity for the use of "direct pressure" upon banks or for discrimination among the various purposes of customer's borrowing. If an attempt is ever to be made along the line of qualitative control, it will be essential that much less use shall be made of open market operations and that rate control shall be substituted for a traditional ban on continuous borrowing as a means of keeping borrowing within limits.

---

[1]　For explanation of the dilemma, cf. Burgess, op. cit. , pp. 275 – 276.

[2]　Cf. R. G. Hawtrey, *Currency and Credit*, London, 1934, pp. 140, 146.

[3]　Charles O. Hardy, op. cit. , p. 232.

Why Banks Should Not Go into Debt

This leads up to the interesting question whether it is desirable on the part of the Federal Reserve System to provide funds for commercial banks through open market purchases and lowering of reserve requirements instead of forcing commercial banks to adjust their reserve balances through borrowing at the Reserve Bank. The London Economist raised and answered the question in this way : [1]

It is legitimate, however, to ask why they (banks) should not go into debt. The Federal Reserve System can fairly be said to have got its start in the last war, when a precisely similar set of circumstances led the member banks to seek rediscounts amounting at one time in 1920 to $ 2. 8 billion dollars (a very large sum in those days) ; and until 1933 it was considered entirely normal for the member banks to be in debt to the Federal Reserve Banks. Fear of rising interest rates can hardly be the explanation for the present reluctance to borrow, since the rediscount rate of the Federal Reserve Bank of New York was reduced to 0. 5% on the security of Government bonds and 1 percent on other securities. It appears to be the case that the banking disturbances of a decade ago coupled with the ensuing period of super-plentiful credit, have left in the member bank mind a strong disinclination to be in debt to the System.

Whether this unwillingness would be so readily respected by the Reserve authorities in time of peace is an open question. In wartime large subscription to Government issues by the New York City member banks is essential, and the authority could not afford a situation in which the member banks preferred to stabilize their holdings rather than rediscount. But if the unwillingness to borrow survives into peacetime, it will constitute an important new element in the structure of American banking.

---

[1] "American Monetary Plethora," *The Economist*, London, July 17, 1943, p. 82.

The Economist's viewpoint is correct. During the period of multiple bank failures between the two wars, the public came to regard borrowing from the Reserve Banks as an evidence of weakness. In addition, banks that discounted heavily during War I were put under severe pressure by a sharp postwar rise in discount rates. In New York, for instance, discount rates advanced from 4 to 7 per cent between October 1919 and June 1920, while bills discounted rose simultaneously from $2.1 billion to $2.5 billion.[①] However, the policies and attitudes of the monetary authorities must also be taken into account. The short-term financing policy of the Treasury aiming at maintaining liquidity of banking system and the deliberate open market purchases of the System have enabled banks to seek securities of every kind of maturity as a means of obtaining reserve funds; the stabilization of the Government security market has further protected them in doing so without risk of loss. Moreover, the Reserve Banks' fixed buying rate and the repurchase option on Treasury bills made the latter as liquid as reserve cash. Banks thus have preferred this mechanism for adjusting their reserve position to rediscounting. The traditional attitude of the Reserve authorities against member bank borrowing has made a deep impression on member banks. As the Board of Governors state,[②] "it is a generally recognized principle that Reserve Bank credit should not be used for profit, and that continuous indebtedness at the Reserve Banks, except under unusual circumstances, is an abuse of Reserve Bank facilities. " Such an opinion is repeated elsewhere in official publications.[③]

There are many arguments on the theory of member bank borrowing.[④] Both the "need theory" and the "profit theory", however, seem more or less to overlook the effects which the policies and attitudes of the monetary authorities have caused. It is true that the spread between the 1 percent discount rate and the coupon

---

① Cf. Anna Youngman, *The Federal Reserve System in Wartime*, National Bureau of Economic Research, Occasional paper, 1945, p. 29.

② *Annual Report*, Board of Governors, Federal Reserve System, 1928, p. 8.

③ Cf. Ibid. , 1925, pp. 15 – 16; Ibid. , 1926, pp. 4 – 5; and W. W. Riefler, *Money Rates and Money Markets in the United States*, New York, 1930, Ch. Ⅱ.

④ Cf. Robert C. Turner, *Member Bank Borrowing*, Columbus, 1938, Chs. Ⅳ, Ⅴ.

rates on Government bonds still make borrowing more profitable than bill sales as a means of obtaining temporary accommodation and that 0. 875 per cent certificates of indebtedness can be discounted at 0. 5 per cent. However, so long as the yields on Government obligations are maintained at the present low level, and are likely to be still lower some time, banks must be ready to dispose of their holdings whenever funds are needed. The lower the interest rates on public debt, the more liberal must be the open market purchase, and the more liberal the open market policy of the Reserve authority, the less willing will commercial banks be to borrow.

Qualitative Controls Have Limited Effects

While restriction of the volume of credit is impossible under the pressure of war finance, emphasis has shifted from the quantity of credit expansion to the quality of credit extended. In general, the so-called qualitative control deals only with central bank discount policy. It holds that the central bank should look back of the collateral offered by the prospective borrower and take cognizance of the purpose for which the borrower proposes to use the funds, discriminating against speculative and unhealthy uses. The theory in a crude form is that as long as the Reserve Banks accepted only business paper arising out of bona fide commercial transactions there could not be excessive expansion of credit. ①This theory has been

---

① Cf. Burgess, op. cit. , pp. 53 – 54. It may be noticed that this was the principal argument of the Bank School in the Bullion Committee of 1810. From another angle of approach, the theory "emphasizes the importance of the exchange ability of goods, and relates the study of credit closely to the study of economic value; for the sound expansion of credit is seen to be limited by the increase in exchange values. . . An adequate study of credit requires that emphasis be given to the kinds of production, and to the conditions under which exchange is to take place, or to relative prices. . . Since the extension of credit always involves the estimate of values in anticipation of the sale of goods, the real problem is that of estimating these values as nearly correctly as possible. " william E. Dunkman, *Qualitative Credit Control*, New York, 1993, pp. 22 – 23. This approach overlooks the fact that the decision of the central bank credit policy must be based on the national economy as a whole. Unless credit is rationed by central authority, it is impossible to control the flow of credit in such a way. The rationing of credit, however, requires a nationalization of all banks and leads to totalitarianism.

the source of many disputes in Federal Reserve policy. [1]In practice, qualitative control had not been used until February 1929, when there was instituted the device called "direct pressure" to curb stock market speculation. This consisted of a refusal of the rediscount privilege to those banks which maintained a volume of speculative security loans in excess of that deemed reasonable by the Reserve Banks. [2]The result, so far as the stock market is concerned, was by no means successful. Dr. Burgess pointed out that the borrowing bank taken only the first step in the use of Federal Reserve credit, the full and final use of the credit is usually quite outside the control of the borrowing banks. [3]In addition, the immediate case of borrowing is often outside the bank's control, as, for example, when the bank's reserves are depleted by a withdrawal of deposits. [4]

During World War I, the monetary authorities tried to ration credit on the New York Stock Exchange and to ration investment credit. Up to August of 1918, control was exercised to insure a sufficiency of funds in the Stock market to prevent interest rates from rising too high; after that time the task became one of preventing the stock market from absorbing too large a share of the funds of the country and from hindering in this way the flotation of Government securities. [5]The rationing of investment credit was directed at preventing, through control over the issuance of securities, non-essential undertakings from securing labor and

---

[1] The dispute goes back to the arguments between Governor Benjamin Strong of the Reserve bank of New York and Adolph C. Miller of the Federal Reserve Board, or, as they were called, the New York theory and the Washington theory. The former holds that the only feasible control of the Reserve authority over the money market is through the volume of credit outstanding, and not through its allocation to particular uses. This continued to be the official standard of Federal Reserve policy down to the end of 1927. Cf. Charles O. Hardy, op. cit. pp. 53 – 54.

[2] In 1928 the System tried futilely to control speculation by curtailing the total amount of Reserve credit in use. When the qualitative control was introduced in 1929, the Reserve Bank of New York, as testified by Governor Harrison, refrained from action on the recommendation of the Board. Cf. Hardy, op. cit., pp 131 – 133.

[3] Burgess, op. cit., p. 64.

[4] Another point made by Dr. Burgess is that the officers of the Reserve Bank can gain only an imperfect knowledge of the operations of any single borrowing bank, no matter how carefully the investigation is made. Ibid., p. 63.

[5] Cf. Beckhart, *Discount Policy*, op. cit., p. 305.

materials sorely needed by the Government. This is an important function in the wartime monetary policy; the curtailment in new capital formation for non-essential business is a part of war funds, especially at the beginning of the war. [1]In addition, the Federal Reserve Board from time to time admonished member banks not to grant loans for non-productive or non-distributive purposes; bankers were advised to curtail non-productive credit at their own discretion. [2]These controls doubtlessly have some effects. But on the whole their efficacy was limited, especially with respect to restraining the production of non-essential consumers' goods. An observation made by Professor Beckhart follows: [3]

Had the Government exercised complete control over labor and industry, had labor and industry been commanded, the Capital Issues Committee (which were responsible for the control of corporate security flotation) would have been unnecessary. This rather than the rationing of investment credit would have been the more effective way of preventing non-essential industries from securing goods.

In regard to the control of commercial credits, Professor Beckhard writes: [4]

(1) The type of banking system existing in America, composed of 30000 independent competitive banks, renders any effective control over commercial credits most difficult. Such control would be much simpler in Canada with seventeen banks or in England with five large institutions. In America bankers would be induced to loan to non-essentials for fear of losing valuable customers to a competing bank.

---

① The condition at the beginning of this war was very unsatisfactory. In 1941 gross capital formation, including consumers' durable goods, was around $ 38 billion. Of this total, $ 10 billion to $ 14 billion may be classified as non-essential. *Federal Reserve Bulletin*, October 1942, p. 1026.

② Beckhart, *Discount Policy*, op. cit. , pp. 310 – 311.

③ Ibid. , pp. 309 – 310.

④ Beckhart, *Discount Policy*, op. cit. , pp. 311 – 312.

（2）This method of controlling the production of non-essentials was predicated upon the belief that all industries must rely upon banks for accommodation. Such was not the case during the war period. There were many non-essential industries whose receipts consisted so largely of cash, owing to prosperity and to the habit of paying cash for goods, that they could handle the financing of their own operations without resorting to banks.

（3）Bankers were uncertain of the meaning of the term " non-essential". Each was inclined to consider the needs of his own community essential.

The rationing of credit is by no means as direct a method of controlling production as is general control over the basic raw materials.

During this war, direct controls over production and labor have been very successful. Credits for war production have been encouraged by the guarantee system. Emphasis, therefore, has been put on the curtailment of consumer credit and on the restriction of security loans. The methods used, known as the "selective credit control" are quite different from those in the last war. The characteristics of these methods are well described by the System in its report:

... Among the several instruments of credit control at the disposal of the Board of Governors, however, there are two which differ in principle and in method from the others. These are the regulation of stock-market credit by fixing minimum margin requirements and the regulation of consumer credit by such methods as prescribing minimum down payments and fixing the maximum maturities. The mechanism of these controls, like that of the others, is such that they can be either stiffened or relaxed from time to time, by administrative action, as circumstances may demand. They differ from the other methods, however, in two respects. （1）They impose a limit on the amount of credit that borrowers and other credit users are in position to demand, rather than on the cost and volume of credit that lenders have available; they may, therefore, limit the use of credit, regardless of the fact that there may be an abundant supply. (2) They influence the volume of credit by affecting the amount used for specified purposes rather than by limiting the amount used for all purposes. Because of this last characteristic, these instruments of credit control are sometimes called "selective" instruments.

The addition of such instruments as these to the formal arsenal of a central banking system is a comparatively recent innovation. They have been used informally by different central banks for a long while, but significant legislation dates back only to 1934, when the Securities Exchange Act directed and empowered the Board to fix margin requirements "for the purpose of preventing the excessive use of credit for purchasing or carrying securities." The analogous power to regulate consumer credit was inaugurated in August 1941, when an Executive Order, effective for the present national emergency, was issued by the President. Up to the present time (1943), therefore, the System's experience with these new instruments has been of short duration, but it has nevertheless been long enough to provide significant materials for the study of the principle which they embody. [1]

Truly the selective principles are quite new in our history of credit policy. Development along this line might make many new contributions to our central banking technique. In their application during the past three years, however, these instruments have evidently played a small part in the national effort to restrain inflationary forces.

---

[1] *Annual Report*, Board of Governors, Federal Reserve System, 1943, p. 22.

Consumer Credit and Consumer Expenditures

A study of the courses of consumer credit and consumer expenditures during the war reveals many important features of the task of credit control. Regulation W, the regulation that restricts consumer credits, was prescribed in September 1941. Consumer credit declined from $ 9. 9 billion at the end of 1941 to $ 6. 5 billion at the end of 1942. In 1943, the decline was less rapid and a slight rise appeared in the second half of the year. The level stood at $ 5. 3 billion at the end of 1943 and rose $ 5. 8 billion in 1943 and 1944. [1]Outstanding consumer credit at the end of 1944 was as large as it was in 1935. In fact, as may be seen from Chart 7, consumer credit was not directly associated with heavy durable goods, at its lowest war point in 1943, was about as high as it was in 1937 and 1938. [2]

The reduction in consumer credit has been primarily due to the large increase in individual income, which enabled consumers to buy on cash, and to the curtailment of the supply of consumer durable goods. Striking is the fact that during the entire period of war the public has been spending more money than before the war though with less use of consumer credit. It may be seen from Chart 8, that consumer expenditures in money values have been increasing persistently from year to year. The Department of Commerce estimates of output of consumer goods and services rose from $ 61. 7 billion in 1939 to $ 74. 6 billion in 1941, $ 90. 5 billion in 1943 and $ 105 billion in 1944. What these figures would be when corrected for the rise in prices is a matter of dispute. On the other hand, it must be recalled that the flow of durable good, such as, automobiles, refrigerators, radios, washing machines, has been drastically reduced. Allowing for expenditures on such goods,

---

① *Federal Reserve Bulletin*, December 1944, p. 1177, "The Revised Statistics of Consumer Credits," which shows the previous estimates for consumer credit in the years following 1942 to have been too low.

② *Annual Report*, Board of Governors, Federal Reserve System, 1943, p. 25.

of which aggregate sales were $6. 5 billion in 1941,[1] the flow of other goods and services to consumers was actually greater than before. Moreover, the official statistics of consumer expenditures do not include Government expenditures on ordinary civilian goods for the armed forces. [2]Taking everything into consideration, the total consumer expenditures on available civilian goods must have been much larger than before the war.

Beyond any doubt, the year 1941 was one of a high level of consumption in the United States. In reviewing the above-mentioned facts, we must conclude that thus far there has been no real contraction of consumption expenditures. Consumption in 1942 and 1943 was in the aggregate about as high as in any previous year and substantially above 1939. [3]Real shortages of civilian goods appeared in 1944. But individual incomes have continued to increase and the dollar value of consumer expenditures, which had slackened to some extent after the strengthening of price control in 1943, has also shown substantial increases since the first half of 1944. Since the second quarter of 1944, consumer buying has again become very active; consumer outlays have further increased by approximately $6 billion. Purchases at food and clothing stores had increased by the fourth quarter of 1944 to a rate which was 12 per cent higher than in the same period of 1943. [4]During the first quarter of 1945, consumer expenditures increased further to an annual rate of 105 billion dollars, compared with about 95 billion a year before. This rate was 10 per cent above the 1944's high level[5] (see Chart 8).

The report of the Federal Reserve System says in 1945:[6]

---

[1] An analysis made by the Office of Price Administration, *New York Times*, July 30, 1945, Editorial.

[2] *Annual Report*, Federal Reserve Bank of New York, for 1942, p. 8.

[3] Ibid. , for 1943, p. 5.

[4] "Civilian Supplies and Prices," *Federal Reserve Bulletin*, March 1945, pp. 211 – 212.

[5] "Economic Effects of Changing War Program," *Federal Reserve Bulletin*, July 1945, p. 642.

[6] *Annual Report*, Board of Governors, Federal Reserve System, for 1944, p. 13.

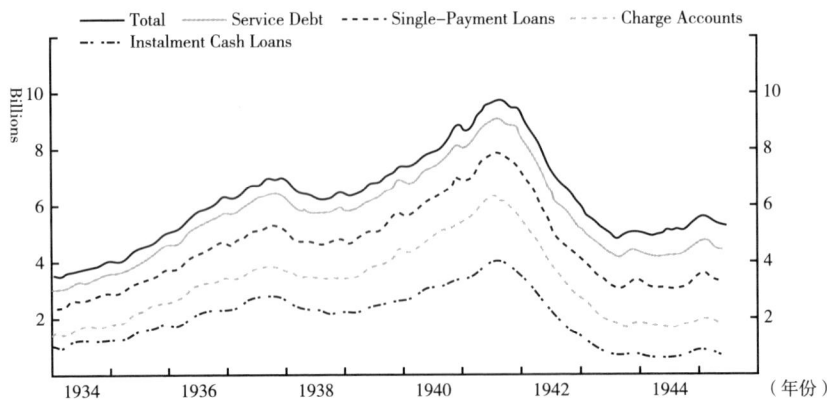

Chart 8   Estimated Consumer Credits

Sources: 1934 – 1942, Department of Commerce; 1943 – 1945, *Federal Reserve Bulletin*.

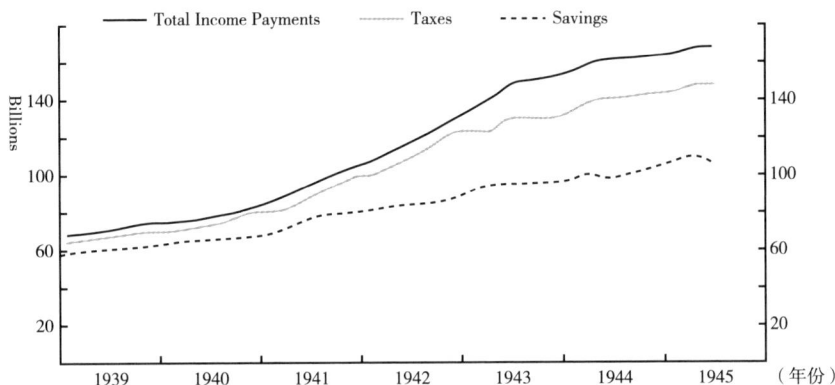

Chart 9   Individual Incomes and Expenditures

Sources: *Federal Reserve Bulletin*, July 1945, p. 642, "Savings" represents excess in individual incomes over consumer expenditures and taxes.

During the entire period that this country has been at war, the consuming public has been spending more money than before the war and doing so with less use of consumer credit. People have bought more goods and services every year than they did before the war, at generally higher prices, but have been paying for them more largely out of current income. They have been able to do this because, even after paying taxes, consumers as a whole have had more current income left for spending and for saving and because the only consumer goods on the market were more largely of nondurable kind. Such goods sell per unit prices that people can pay without going into debt. On the net balance, up to February 1944, people paid off currently more debt than they incurred. The volume of consumer credit outstanding went down by more than 5 billion dollars or about 50 per cent. Since then debt incurred has slightly exceeded debt paid off, but consumer credit outstanding has remained close to the 5 billion dollars level, about what it was at the end of 1935.

It is clear that the decline in consumer credits during the war was not due to the contraction of consumption, but was due to the increase in individual money income and the scarcity of durable goods which were commonly bought on long-term credit. This suggests that consumer credit would have declined even if the selective control. Regulation W, had not been imposed. The trend, however, has changed in 1944. New debt has been incurred more rapidly than debt paid off. Lavish spending spreads over the country. With the reconversion of many consumer durable goods, the volume of consumer credit is not likely to contract from its present level.

Chapter Ⅵ   Measures of
The Federal Reserve System

In pursuing the objective discussed in the last two chapters, the Federal Reserve System has introduced various measures. As our principal interest is the policy of the System and its influences, the measures described in this chapter present only a general picture. Details of the practices are to be found in the System's reports and in the Federal Reserve Bulletins.

Open Market Operations

The Growth of Federal Reserve Portfolio

As mentioned earlier, open market operation has been the principal measure taken by the Federal Reserve authority to maintain member bank reserves and the stability of the Government security market. The operation is directed by the Federal Open Committee and is carried out by the Federal Reserve Bank of New York. Transactions for the System open market account are arranged by an executive committee of five members, usually by telephone.

Before Pearl Harbor, the executive committee was informed that the aggregate amount of securities held in the System account should not be increased or decreased by more than $ 200000000. On September 24, 1941, the System decided to increase reserve requirements of member banks, effective on November

1, 1941. This action caused a considerable liquidation in bank holdings of Government securities ; and the System was called upon to purchase a greater amount of securities. On December 8, 1941, the day after the attack by Japan on Pearl Harbor, the members of the Federal Open Market Committee approved an increase from $ 200000000 to $ 400000000 in the limit on the authority granted to the executive committee to increase or decrease the total amount held by the System account. The increase in the limit was intended to give the executive broader authority to take whatever action was necessary for preventing any adverse development on the security market. After the entrance of the United States into the war, the Open Market Committee decided on December 12, 1941, to increase the limit further to $ 500000000. The securities purchased for the System account during the week following the outbreak of the war included $ 45270000 of the new 1951 – 1955 and 1967 – 1972 bonds, and $ 12370000 of Treasury bills, $ 2000000 of which were resold during the week. [1]

In the first quarter of 1942, open market operations were relatively small in amount. Excess reserve of member banks exceeded 3 billion dollars at the beginning of that year. The total amount of Federal Reserve holdings of Government securities, amounting to 2. 2 billion dollars, had almost no increase until April. On April 30, 1942, the fixed purchase rate of 3/8 per cent for Treasury Bills was established. From April until early October the operations consisted principally of purchase of Treasury bills and certificates of indebtedness, and were primarily for the purpose of supplying additional reserves to banks, which decline from 12. 9 billion dollars at the beginning of the year to 11. 6 billion on September 30, 1942. During October, in connection with Treasury financing operations which were necessary substantial subscriptions by banks to new offerings of notes and medium-term bonds, the System purchased large amounts of notes and bonds. The purchases were for the double purpose of supporting the market and of supplying bank reserves. The total amount of Federal Reserve holdings increased by

---

[1] *Annual Report*, Board of Governors, Federal Reserve System, 1941, p. 65.

more than a billion dollars in October. In the latter part of November and early in December, prior to and during the Victory Bond Drive (the First War Loan), the System again made large purchases from November 18 to December 9, the total amount increased by 850 million dollars. During this period excess reserve were generally maintained at 2. 5 billion dollars.

On March 27, 1942, the Second War Power Act authorized the Federal Reserve Banks to purchase Government securities directly from the Treasury, provided the aggregate amount did not exceed $ 5000000000. In accordance with this change in law, the Federal Open Market Committee issued a directive on May 8, 1942, explicitly providing for purchases "whether in the open market or directly from the Treasure and for purchase whether for the purpose of maintaining the general level of prices and yields of Government securities or for the purpose of maintaining an adequate supply of funds in the market. " The limit for increasing or decreasing the System account was still $ 500000000, but excluded Treasury bills purchased pursuant to the directive issued on April 30, 1942, that is, the directive for the fixed rate of purchase of bills. On July 6, 1942, the limit was increased to $ 850000000, and it was further increased to $ 1000000000 on August 3, to $ 2, 500000000 on October 9, and to $ 3000000000 on December 9, 1942. On December 14, the limit was again set at $ 1000000000; in addition, the executive committee was authorized to arrange for the purchase of special short-term certificates directly from the Treasury providing that the aggregate amount held in the account should not exceed $ 1000000000. At the end of 1942, total securities, including guaranteed, held by the System amounted to $ 6188635000, an increase of $ 3934160000 in this year.

In 1943, large purchases also began in the second quarter of the year. During the year total holdings increased by 5. 4 billion dollars. Bill holdings increased by 5. 8 billion and certificate holding by 1. 4 billion while holdings of bonds and notes declined by 1. 8 billion. Treasury bonds were sold by the System in the first half of the year, when there was a large demand in the market. These sales helped to maintain the structure of interest rates. ①The increase in certificate holdings came toward the close of the year and reflected largely the sales made by commercial banks in order to replenish their reserves drawn down by currency outflow. Purchase of special short-term Treasury certificates directly from the Treasury was made from time to time, principally to avoid temporary declines in member bank reserves around income tax dates. Throughout the year the Reserve Banks purchased and sold large amounts of Treasury bills. By the end of the year, bill holdings amounted to 6. 8 billion dollars, or about 59 per cent of the total Federal Reserve holdings.

At the meeting of the Federal open market committee on March 2, 1943, the limitation of the authority of the executive committee to increase or decrease the amount of securities in the system account and to purchase short-term certificates for the temporary accommodation of the Treasury was increased from $1000000000 to $1500000000 in each case. This action was considered appropriate on the basis of discussion of plans for the second war loan drive. This policy and limitation was continued through 1943 and 1944. The committee reviewed the situation before each subsequent War Loan drive, but no change in policy was made. Only on March 1, 1942, it exempted from the limitation the redemption of maturing Treasury bills held in the system account.

In 1944, total holdings of Government securities in Federal Reserve Banks increased by 7. 3 billion dollars, amounting to 18. 8 billion dollars at the end of the year. Bill holding increased by 4. 3 billion dollars, certificate holding increased by 2. 2 billion dollars, note holdings increased by 901 million dollars, and bond holding declined by 316 million dollars. By the end of the year, over 60 per cent were in certificates. After 1943, open market operations were particularly important between the War Loan drives when the Treasury drew upon their war loan accounts, which have been exempt from reserve requirements since April 1943. The total holdings fluctuates in response to the war loan drives, especially in

---

① See p. 415.

1944. The trend is reflected on the reserve bank credit curve of chart 5.

In 1945 the same trend continued. By the end of May, total holdings of Reserve Banks increased by 2. 1 billion dollars. Bill holdings increased by 1. 8 billion, certificate holdings by 983 million, note holdings reduced by 449 million dollars and bond holdings reduced by 130 million. The figures are given in Table 26.

Table 26　Government Securities Held by Federal Reserve Banks
(Millions of Dollars)

End month	Total	Bills	Certificates	Notes	Bonds	Guaranteed Issues
1940 Dec.	2184			900	1280	5
1941 June	2184			820	1359	5
Dec.	2254	10		777	1462	5
1942 June	2645	243	66	714	1617	5
Dec.	6189	1010	1041	1324	2777	37
1943 June	7202	3815	1092	774	1468	54
Dec.	11543	6768	2467	665	1559	85
1944 June	14901	8872	3382	1180	1464	3
Dec.	18846	11146	4887	1566	1243	3
1945 May.	20954	12954	5870	1017	1113	—
Change						
Dec. 1941 – May 1945	+ 18700	+ 12944	+ 5670	+ 240	– 349	– 5

Source: *Federal Reserve Bulletin.*

Establishment of Bill Buying Rate and Repurchase Option

On April 30, 1942, in connection with the announcement of the May Treasury financing, which included an increase to $ 250000000 in the weekly offering of Treasury bills. [1]The Federal Open Market Committee directed the twelve Reserve Banks to purchase for the System open market account all Treasury bills

---

[1]　The weekly offering of Treasury bills was approximately $ 100000000 in the fiscal year of 1940 – 1941, Increased to $ 300000000 by June 1942, $ 1000000000 by June 1943, and $ 1300000000 by October 1944, with no substantial increase thereafter.

that might be offered to such banks on a discount rate of 3/8 of one per cent per annum. Adoption of this policy, as stated in the Report of the System,[1] was for the purpose of stabilizing the bill market, effecting a broader distribution of bills, and facilitating prompt adjustment of bank reserves to changing conditions. Readiness of the System to buy bills at an established rate assured banks and other holders that, if at any time it was necessary to obtain reserves or each, they could sell their bills at an established price. This offered an encouragement to banks and others to utilize available liquid funds to purchase bills.

On August 3, 1942, the Federal Open Market Committee issued a supplementary direction to the Reserve Banks to give the seller of bills, if he desired so, an option to repurchase at the same rate the same amount of bills of the same maturity. The same privilege extended to banks, both as to selling bills to Reserve banks and as to repurchase options, was accorded to dealers in securities, corporation, and other holders of liquid funds. This practice further increased the liquidity of the bill holdings and it was believed that it would encourage fuller investment of idle short-term funds and thereby bring about a wider distribution of bills.

The purchase of securities under a repurchase agreement is, in effect, a 100 percent loan. The buyer takes the title and enjoys the income from accruing interest, but the risk of a value changing remains with the seller. The practice was begun by the Federal Reserve Banks during World War I and continued thereafter. [2]This time, however, the repurchase price was fixed at the same rate as the selling price. This eliminated the risk of a capital loss to the seller. Treasury bills in the hands of banks thus became practically equivalent to excess reserves. In the even it became necessary for a banker or other holders of bills temporarily to adjust his cash position, he could sell the bills to a Reserve Bank under repurchase option and reacquire them after the need for founds had passed. Banks

---

[1] *Annual Report*, Board of Governors, Federal Reserve System, for 1942, p. 14.

[2] Cf. R. B. Westerfield, *Money, Credit and Banking*, New York, 1938, p. 629.

throughout the country, but more particularly in New York and Chicago, have made increasing use of this advantage to keep their funds more fully employed. Consequently, the balance in total holdings of bills on option account at the Federal Reserve Banks reflected the general market changes, just as call loans had done under different conditions in the past. The amount on such account declined during each War Loan drive when member banks released part of their required reserves and increased after the drive when the Treasury withdrew funds from commercial banks. ①

On September 28, 1942, the Federal Open Market Committee amended the direction regarding the purchase of bills at the posted rate by stipulating that all bills purchased outright were to be purchased for the System open market account and that all bills purchased under repurchase option were to be held by the purchasing Reserve bank in its own account and prompt reports of all such purchase were to be made to the manager of the System open market account. The purpose of this amendment is to increase further the liquidity of the bills sold under repurchase option. It had been the practice of the Reserve Banks in purchasing bills at the posted rate to make such purchase for delivery in the falling full business day, the customary market practice. Repurchase by the original sellers had been on the same basis. Under this amendment, the bills are available at the Reserve Banks for immediate delivery when repurchase is desired. From the accounting and operating standpoint, however, it is helpful to hold all the bills purchased in the Reserve Banks' own account. A directive, therefore, was issued on May 15, 1943, to treat all bills purchased as being subject to the right of repurchase and holding them at the purchasing Reserve Banks in accordance with the policy of having the bills available for immediate delivery if desired in the even of their repurchase.

---

① An analysis showing the changes in the balance of bill holdings under repurchase option in connection with the changes in the general market condition has been made by the System. Cf. *Federal Reserve Bulletin*, May 1943, p. 376. Their relationship, however, has changed since late 1943 due to the change in accounting procedures explained in the next paragraph.

As the Reserve Banks held large amounts of Treasury bills, the amount of maturing bills was substantial each week. On January 26, 1943, the Federal Open Market Committee authorized the executive committee to arrange with the Treasury to permit full allotment to the System of securities issued to refund maturing direct obligations. The problem of direct replacement of Treasury bills, however, was not resolved, until October 1943, when the Committee directed the executive committee to work out with the Treasury an arrangement under which a tender would be made each week for new bills in an amount not exceeding the total amount of maturing bills in the System and option account. By that time the weekly maturities of the Reserve Bank holdings increased from 400 million to 500 million dollars and the System was expected to purchase additional bills in order to supply the market with reserve funds. The Treasury, however, did not like to change the procedure for issuing bills. In lieu thereof, it requested the Federal Reserve Bank of New York as fiscal agent of the United States to use its best efforts to see that sufficient tenders for bills were forthcoming from the market each week. Under this procedure, the volume of the purchases of bills from the dealers by the Reserve Bank of New York in its option account became very large. To make it possible for all of the Reserve Banks to participate in these purchases, an arrangement was worked out under which dealers would offer bills to the Reserve Bank of New York without a repurchase option and the Bank would purchase these bills for the System account.

Direct Purchase of Securities form the Treasury

The second War Powers Act, 1942, approved on March 27, authorized the Federal Reserve Banks to purchase Government securities directly from the Treasury, provided that the aggregate amount of securities so purchased and held at any time did not exceed 5 billion dollars. In accordance with this change in the law, the Open Market Committee authorized purchases of securities for the purpose of granting temporary accommodation to the Treasury. The securities so purchased were the Treasury one-day certificates of indebtedness. They were issued in anticipation of tax revenues or issuance of other securities. The direct purchases helped to avoid temporary declines in member bank reserves around income tax dates. The holdings of these securities have been small—they never exceeded 450 million dollars in 1942, remained below 1 billion dollars through most of 1943, and were still smaller in 1944.

The practice of direct purchase of the short-term certificates of indebtedness had been used before 1935. The collection of income-tax checks by the Treasury was spread over a number of days. The Treasury used to obtain the funds by selling to Federal Reserve Banks, the one day special certificate of indebtedness, which was renewed in reduced amounts for several succeeding days. The Banking Act of 1935 prohibited the Reserve Banks from buying Government securities except in open market, and hence prohibited them from advancing to the Treasury directly. But there is nothing to prevent the sale of special certificates of indebtedness directly to member banks negotiated by the Reserve Banks. Dr. Burgess demonstrated that the only effect of the Act is that the certificates were purchased by the Reserve Banks from the open market as a matter of credit policy rather than as an aid to the Treasury. [1]

Supervisory Policy Regarding Government Securities

Another measure designed to encourage wider distribution of Government securities among banks was the adoption on November 22, 1942, by the bank supervisory agencies, of a joint statement of examination and supervisory policy with special reference to investments in and loans upon Government securities. This statement reads:

The Comptroller of the Currency, the Federal Deposit Insurance

---

[1] W. Randolph Burgess, *The Reserve Banks and the Money Market*, New York, 1936, p. 117.

Corporation, the Board of Governors of the Federal Reserve System, and the Executive Committee of the National Association of Supervisors of State Banks made the following statement of their examination and supervisory policy with special reference to investments in and loans upon Government securities.

1. There will be no deterrents in examination or supervisory policy to investments by banks in Government securities of all types, except those securities made specifically ineligible for bank investment by the terms of their issue.

2. In connection with Government financing, individual subscribers relying upon anticipated income may wish to augment their subscriptions by temporary borrowings from banks. Such loans will not be subject to criticism but should be on a short-term or amortization basis fully repayable within periods not exceeding six months.

3. Banks will not be criticized for utilizing their idle funds as far as possible in making such investments and loans and availing themselves of the privilege of temporarily borrowing from or selling Treasury bills to the Federal Reserve Banks when necessary to restore their required reserve positions.

The supervisory attitudes naturally affected the management policy of commercial banks. Commercial banks' investment in Government securities increased from 21. 8 billion dollars at the end of 1941 to 75. 9 billion at the end of 1944, whereas their loans on securities increased from 1. 3 billion to 4. 5 billion. The practice of purchasing War obligations with borrowed funds has been relatively infrequent in comparison with the last war.

Reserve Requirement Policy

Reduction of Reserve Requirements at Central Reserve Cities

After the outbreak of the war in Europe in 1939, gold imports increased rapidly and member bank excess reserves reached their peak at the end of 1940. Excess reserves declined in 1941, but they were still above 5 billion dollars in September, while bank credit expanded more rapidly than in any previous year. As a part of the Government program to combat inflation, the Federal Reserve System on September 23 increased reserve requirements to the limit of its statutory power, effective on November 1, 1941. About 1. 2 billion dollars of excess reserve were absorbed by this action.

Excess reserves of member banks declined sharply in the three years after 1941 – from 6. 8 billion dollars in January 1941 to about 1 billion dollars by the end of 1943. Most of the decline in 1941 and the first half of 1942 was at banks in New York city and Chicago, which at the peak had owned half of the excess reserves of all banks. By July 1942, they owned only one-seventh of the total. This was the reason for the reduction of reserve requirements at central reserve cities in July 1942. The shift of reserves away from New York, however, continued until the middle of 1945.

The largest factor contributing to this movement has been the transfer of funds on Treasury account—Treasury receipts from security sales and tax collections in the New York area continued to exceed by a wide margin Government disbursements in the area. These funds were expended elsewhere by the Treasury. The flow of funds between New York city and other parts of the country through commercial and financial transfers also resulted in a net loss to New York city in 1941 and 1942, but the course was reversed in 1943. A third factor in the drain on the reserves of New York City was the persistent demand for currency. The demand for currency, however, was relatively even greater in some other districts than in New York, especially in those in which there had been an unusually rapid growth of war industries. Another factor which had its immediate impact on New York City banks was the accumulation of funds in the accounts of foreign central banks and governments. The accumulation involved the transfer of funds from commercial banks and thus resulted in a drain on their reserves.

Under the earlier provisions of the Federal Reserve Act, the Board of

Governors could not change the reserve requirement of member banks in central reserve cities without making the same change with respect to member banks in reserve cities. In anticipation of an uneven distribution of reserves that might hinder the financing of the war, the Board of Governors requested Congress to dissociate the reserve requirements for the two classes of banks so that each could be regulated without reference to the other. This was done on July 7, 1942 by amending section 19 of the Federal Reserve Act. Under the amended Act the Board may make changes in requirements separately for each class of banks or simultaneously for all classes.

Such action was taken on August 6 1942, by amending the supplement to Regulation D, Reserves of Member Banks, to require that member banks in central reserve cities (New York and Chicago) maintain reserves of 24 per cent, instead of 26 per cent of their net demand deposits. This reduction, effective on August 20, increased excess reserves by approximately $ 350000000 in New York city banks and $ 75000000 in Chicago banks. The reserve requirements at central reserve cities were further reduced from 24 per cent to 22 per cent on September 14 and from 22 per cent to 20 per cent on October 3, the same as that for reserve city banks while that for country banks remained at 14 per cent and that for time deposits for all classes of banks remained at 6 per cent. This schedule has remained unchanged until the present. When the last reduction was being made, a motion was made by Mr. Mckee of the Board to reduce the requirement for reserve city banks to 18 per cent and that for country banks to 13 per cent, on the theory that there were individual banks in reserve city and country classes that had utilized their reserves for purchase of Government securities and that a differential requirement schedule should be maintained. The motion was rejected. [1]

It may be observed that the reserve requirements, during the last year, as lowered by the amendment of June 21, 1917, were 13 per cent for central reserve city banks, 10 per cent for reserve city banks, 7 per cent for country banks and 3 per cent for time deposits of all classes of banks. It may also be recalled that the

[1] *Annual Report*, Board of Directors Federal Reserve System, for 1942, p. 99.

separate change in reserve requirements for banks in different districts was also recommended by the Federal Reserve System during the last war, but with the opposite purpose to raise the requirements to check the effect of gold inflow and to curb price inflation. The suggestion was never enacted into a law. [1]But it might be reconsidered by the monetary authorities in their postwar policies as the war program has disturbed to the original balance of monetary transactions and commodity prices in various districts.

Exemption of War Loan Account from Reserve Requirements

Beginning with the first world war, it was the practice of the Treasury to authorize banks to pay for Government securities purchased for their own account or for the account of their customers by giving the Treasury credit in so-called war loan accounts. This practice, as pointed out earlier, avoids large transfers of funds to the Reserve Banks when securities are sold and makes for greater stability in the money market. The Treasury gradually calls on depositary banks for such amounts as it requires, and since these calls correspond closely to current disbursements, the effect of Treasury transactions on the money market is greatly diminished.

Commercial banks had been urged by the Treasury and the Federal Reserve authorities to make full use of their war loan deposit accounts. At the beginning of 1943, however, a great many commercial banks had not been qualified for carrying war loan accounts. To encourage their use the Board of the System recommended, and in April Congress enacted legislation, signed by the President on April 13, 1943 which provided that, until six months after the cessation of hostilities in the present war, (1) banks would not be required to pay Federal Deposit Insurance assessments on deposits held in war loan accounts, and (2) member banks would not be required to maintain reserves against such

---

[1] *Federal Reserve Bulletin*, 1917, pp. 102, 108.

deposits. The second part of the legislation was implemented at a meeting of the Board of Governors of the system by amending Regulation D, Reserve of Member Banks.

As a result of this legislation, the amount of reserves that banks were required to hold declined temporarily in periods of extensive Government financing, as during the War Loan drives, when bank customers drew on their deposits to pay for governments securities. This gave the bank additional temporary reserves funds, a part of which they invested in Treasury bills or other securities. Later, as the Treasury drew upon the war loan accounts and the fund returned to other accounts, thus increasing the amount of required reserves, the banks sold some of the securities in order to obtain the additional reserve needed. The effect on required reserves is clearly seen from Chart 4.

In these transactions the banks made use of the posted buying rate on Treasury bills established in 1942. The fixed discount rate on bills and the repurchase option, as described in an earlier section, together with the exemption of war loan accounts from reserve requirement thus served to stabilize the money market.

Other Measures on Reserve Requirements

The Federal Reserve Act contained a provision permitting subject to regulations and penalties prescribed by the Board of Governors, the reserves of member banks to be withdrawn for the purpose of meeting existing liabilities. This provision however was to some extent nullified by another provision in Section 19, which prohibited banks from making new loans or paying dividends while their reserve were deficient. An Act of July 7, 1942 removed from Section 19 the Latter provision. On July 14 the Board amended Regulation D, Reserve of Member Banks to conform to the Act of July 7, and added a provision authorizing a Federal Reserve Bank at its discretion, to refuse at any time to permit the withdrawal or other use of credit given in a member bank's reserve account for any item for which the Federal Reserve Bank had not received payment in actually and finally collected funds. This amendment enabled member banks to use their reserve funds in case of need and increased the power of the Reserve Banks to control credit on a qualitative basis.

The Board explained this amendment, thus:[1]

In View of the wide fluctuation that may occur from day to day in the reserves of an individual bank, some banks had followed the practice of maintaining at all times a larger volume of excess reserve than they actually needed to meet their average requirements. Under the law as now amended the banks are not restricted in making new loans or paying dividend even though their reserves are below the minimum requirements. The power of Board of Governors to prescribe penalties for deficiencies in reserves remains unaffected by the change in the law, and the first amendment to Regulation D referred to above was for the purpose of eliminating from the regulation references to the making of loans and the payment of dividend during periods of deficient reserves and to personal liability of directors for permitting violations of this kind.

On February 21, 1942, an amendment to Regulation D changed the method of computing deficient reserves. Before this change, regulation D required that deficiencies in reserves of member banks in cities in which Federal Reserve Bank and their branches were located and in a few other reserve cities be computed on the basis of average daily net balances covering semi-weekly periods, while member banks in other reserve cities were required to compute their reserve on a weekly basis. The amendment placed all banks in central reserve and reserve cities (except banks in outlying sections of such cities) on the same basis, that is, on a weekly basis. The Board explained the amendment in the following manner:

---

[1] *Annual Report*, Board of Governors, Federal Reserve System for 1942, p. 96.

Increased activity resulting from the war effort had resulted in wide fluctuations in member bank reserves in financial centers from day to day which caused many banks to maintain unnecessarily large excess reserves in order to avoid deficiencies because of the short period over which their reserves could be averaged. It was anticipated that this condition would be accentuated as war production increased, and the amendment was made for the purpose of providing for the banks affected greater flexibility in adjusting their positions to meet the situation. [1]

Bank Rate Policy

Reduction in Discount Rates

Reduction in discount rates is another measure to ease the money market and to facilitate banks to obtain needed reserves by borrowing from Reserve Banks rather than by selling their holdings in the market. This measure was very important during the last war, when banks borrowed heavily from Reserve Banks. During this war, as stated previously, member bank borrowing was comparatively insignificant.

After September 1939, the Reserve Banks of Atlanta, Chicago, St. Louis, Kansas city and Dallas had in effect a rate of 1 per cent on advances to member banks secured by Government obligations and a rate of 1 per cent on other eligible paper. At the Reserve Banks of Philadelphia Cleveland, Richmond, Minneapolis and San Francisco a rate of 1. 5 per cent had been in effect on both types of paper, while the Reserve Banks of New York Boston had had a 1 per cent rate on both types.

Reduction of rates began on February 28, 1942, when the Board approved for the Reserve Bank of Chicago a rate of 1 per cent on discounts for and advances

---

[1] Ibid. , p. 86.

to banks under sections 13 and 13a of the Federal Reserve Act, that is, advances secured by Government obligations maturing or callable beyond one year, and discounts and advance secured by eligible paper. This followed the rate established previously in New York and Boston. The same reduction was made on March 14, 1942 at the Reserve Banks of Richmond and St, Louis; on March 21, 1942 at Philadelphia Atlanta and Dallas; on April 4, 1942 at San Francisco; and on April 11, 1942 at Cleveland and Kansas City. In explanation of these reductions, the Board said:[①]

> While, in the aggregate, sufficient reserves for this purpose (purchasing Government securities) would be available, individual banks might at time be subject to temporary deficiencies in their reserves. It would be better in such cases if banks could obtain the needed reserves by borrowing from the Reserve Banks, rather than by selling their Government securities in the market. Reductions in the discount rates of the Reserve Banks therefore might have some influence in causing member banks to make fuller use of their existing reserves for war financing, as they would have the assurance that, if necessary, they could replenish their reserve by borrowing from the Federal Reserve Bank at low rates.

Following this action the Board also approved reductions in rates at the Reserve Banks of Philadelphia, Cleveland, Richmond, Minneapolis, and San Francisco on advances to non-member banks secured by direct obligations of the United States to 1 per cent effective March 21, April 11, March14, March 28 and April 4, 1942, respectively. These reductions were in accordance with the announcement made by Board on September 1, 1939 that the Reserves Banks were prepared to make advance to member and nonmember banks on Government obligations at par at the rates prevailing for member banks. The other seven

---

① Ibid. , p. 88.

Reserve Banks had established 1 per cent rate on such advances in 1939.

Another reduction was made in the rate on advances to member banks under Section 10 (b) of the Federal Reserve Act, that is, advance secured by types of acceptable assets other than eligible paper. This rate is required to be at least 0. 5 per cent higher than the highest discount rate in effect on loans and advances under Section 13 and 15a. In view of the underlying reasons for the approval of the basic discount rate of 1 per cent, the Board approved reductions to 1. 5 per cent effective in 1942 on March 14 at st. Louis, August 29 at Chicago, September 12 at Cleveland, October 15 at Atlanta, October 17 at Philadelphia and Dallas, October 27 at Boston and Kansas City, October 26 at Richmond and San Francisco and October 30 at New York and Minneapolis.

Thus by October 1942 the United States had in effect a uniform rate of 1 per cent on discounts and advances under Section 13 and 13a, a uniform rate of 1. 5 per cent on advances under Section 10 (b) and a uniform rate of 1 per cent on advances to nonmember banks under Section 1% .

Establishment of Preferential Rate

Preferential rates had been used during World War I , though with different types of loans. Criticism has been heard from time to time against them. [1]

Effective October 15, 1942 the Reserve Bank of Atlanta, approved by the Board, established a rate of 0. 5per cent on advances to member banks secured by direct and fully guaranteed Government obligations which had one year or less in maturity or call date. The same rate was established in the other eleven Reserve Banks, effective October 17 at Philadelphia, Chicago and Dallas, October 27 at Boston, Cleveland, Louis and Kansas City, October 28 at Richmond and San Francisco, October 30 at New York and Minneapolis.

---

[1] Backhart, *Discount policy*, op. cit. , pp. 283 – 284.

In explanation of these actions the Board said: [1]

The Board of Governors had considered informally and had discussed with the Presidents of the Federal Reserve Banks about the question of reduced discount rates at the Reserve Banks as means of encouraging banks to utilize their excess reserves for the purchase of Government securities. The Board reviewed the arguments that had been advanced against preferential rates of discount and felt that in ordinary circumstances such rates should not be established. It was recognized, however, that the war financing program would require substantial purchase of Government securities by the banks and it was the belief of the Board that if there were a preferential rate for advance secured by Government obligations that fact would encourage member banks, particularly outside the financial centers, to invest more of their excess reserves in short-term Government securities, and that the preferential rate could be eliminated with less misunderstanding when the need had passed than might arise if there were corresponding changes in the general discount rate.

Other Reductions in Bank Rates

At the same time as the preferential rate was established at Atlanta, the Reserve Bank also reduced its rate to 2 per cent on advances to individuals, partnerships, and corporations secured by direct obligations of the United States under the last paragraph of Section 13 of the Federal Reserve Act. The Board approved the reduction "for the reason that the System had strongly advocated a policy of selling as many Government securities outside the banking system as possible and it was felt that, although there was little or no occasion for such advances at the present time, it would be more consistent with this policy if

---

[1] *Annual Report*, op. cit., 1942. p. 101.

Federal Reserve Bank rates on loans to such borrowers on the security of Government obligations were at a lower level. "[1] Following the example of Atlanta, the Reserve Banks of Boston, Philadelphia, Cleveland, Chicago, ST. Louis, Kansas City and Dallas also lowered their rate to 2 per cent in October, while the Reserve Banks of New York, Richmond, Minneapolis and San Francisco established, a rate of 2. 5 per cent on such advances in the same month.

On April 30, 1942, the Board made an amendment to Regulations, Industrial Loans by Federal Reserve Banks, so as to rate the procedure of borrowing by industry and commercial business from Reserve Banks.

On May 8, 1942, the Board approved the schedule of rates on industrial Loans and commitment made by the Reserve Bank of Cleveland under section 13b of the Federal Reserve Act. This schedule was also used subsequently at the other Reserve Banks in May and June. The rates are listed in 6 to 10 in the following schedule.

Thus, since October 30, 1942, these have been the rates of Reserve Banks:

1. Advances secured by Government obligations maturing or callable in one year or less (Sec. 13),

   0. 5 per cent in districts.

2. Advances secured by Government obligations maturing or callable beyond one year and discounts of and advances secured by eligible paper (Sec. 13 and 13a),

   1 per cent in all districts.

3. Advances secured by types of acceptable assets other than (Sec. 10b),

   1. 5 per cent in all districts.

4. Advances to nonmember banks secured by Government direct obligations (last paragraph of Sec. 13),

---

[1] *Annual Report*, Ibid., 1942, p. 101.

1 per cent in all districts.

5. Advances to individuals, partnerships or corporations other than banks secured by direct Government obligations (last paragraph of Sec. 13),

2.5 per cent in New York, Richmond, Minneapolis and San Francisco,

2 per cent in the other eight districts.

6. Advances to industrial or commercial business (Sec. 13b),

2.5 – 5per cent in all other districts.

7. Commitment to industrial or commercial business (Sec. 13b),

0.5 – 1 per cent in Boston, 1.25 – 2 per cent in all other districts.

8. Discount or purchase to financing institution (Sec. 13b)

a. Portion for which institution is obligated,

2 per cent in Philadelphia,

2.5 – 5 per cent in Chicago,

1 – 1.5per cent in St. Louis,

Rate charged borrower less commitment rate in all other districts.

b. Remaining portion,

2.5 – 5 per cent in Chicago,

Rate charged borrower in all other districts.

9. Commitment to financial institution (Sec. 13b),

0.5 – 1 Per cent in Boston,

0.25 – 1.24 per cent in Chicago and St. Louis,

0.5 – 1.25 per cent in all other districts.

Credit Policy

Guaranteed Loans to War Industry

The financing of war industry was a new responsibility conferred upon the

Federal Reserve System. The Regulation V and its many amendments provided a complicated system of the government. As our major interest is the policy of the system, no details of the regulated procedures will be discussed here.

Guaranteed loans to industry for war production were first provided by the President's Executive Order 9122, issued on March 26, 1942. The war and Navy Departments and the United States time Commission were authorized to guarantee and to make loans for the purpose of financing contractors, subcontractors, or others engaged in any business or operation deemed by those agencies to be necessary, appropriate, or convenient for the prosecution of the war. The Federal Reserve Banks were authorized to act as agents in carrying out the provisions of the order, subject to the upper vision of the Board of Governors.

After consultation with the guaranteeing agencies, the Board issued its Regulation V, effective April 6, 1942, prescribing general rules and policies for the guidance of Reserve bank in handling guaranteed loans under the war financing program. The functions of the Reserve bank with respect to negotiation of these loans included analysis of the financial integrity of the applicant, determination of the type of financial best suited to meet different situations, and preparation of the necessary documents. Most of these loans were made by commercial banks, but other financing institutions have also participated. In a few cases the reserve banks have agreed to make advance and the reconstruction finance corporation has a number of guaranteed commitment. The utilization of the facilities of the twelve Federal Reserve Banks and their twenty four branches throughout the country also make it possible to decentralize the war financing program to a large extent.

On April 6, 1943, a new standard form of guarantee agreement was adopted by the guaranteeing agencies, but no change was made in policy with respect to loans. The scope of operations under the guarantee program was enlarged by Executive order 9336, issued by the President on April 24, 1943. The order authorized the office of Lend-Lease Administration and the War Shipping Administration to indemnify any guarantees made on their behalf or for their benefit

467

by the War and Navy Department and the Maritime Commission.

During the summer of 1943, it became increasingly evident that many businesses engaged in war production were reluctant to assume additional war contracts because of the fear that their working capital would be tied up in such contracts at the termination of the war. They felt this might delay their return to peacetime operation and thus put them in to an unfavorable competitive position. In order that war production schedules might not be interfered with because of such fears, the guaranteeing agencies and the Board announced on September 1 a broadcast basis for the guaranteeing of loans under Regulation V which enables contractors who make arrangement in advance to obtain the use of most of their own working capital promptly upon termination of their contracts.

Loans guaranteed upon this broadened basis are known as VT loans to distinguish them from loans made without special reference to release of working capital. The maximum amount of credit which a contractor may obtain under a VT loan is based on his receivables, inventories, work in process, and, without duplication, amounts paid or to be paid by him to subcontractors or suppliers because of contract cancellations. Guarantee agreements for VT loans provide that the percentage of the loan guaranteed is not subject to increase upon cancellation of war production contracts as is the case with V loans. Also, provision is made for the guaranteeing agency to share in any commitment fee charged the borrower on the undisbursed portion of the loan.

The Board prescribed on April 6, 1942 a maximum interest rate of 5 per cent on loans guaranteed and a flexible guarantee charge on the portion of loans guaranteed; the latter has been revised subsequently. On May 12, 1943, the Board prescribed a maximum commitment fee of 0.5 per cent on the undisbursed portion of the guaranteed loans. On August 30, 1943 the Board decided that in case special provision was made for freeing working capital upon cancellation of contracts, that is, the VT loan, the amount of any commitment fee charged the borrower by the financing institution should not exceed 1/2 per cent on the undisbursed portion of the loan.

On August 18, 1944, following the passage of the Contract Settlement Act of 1944, the Director of Contract Settlement issued his general Regulation No. 1 prescribing procedures and policies to be followed by the guaranteeing agencies in guaranteeing termination loans, are for the Reserve Banks. Such termination loans, known as T loans, are for the purpose of enabling war contractors to obtain the use of funds tied up in war production pending final settlement of claims arising from terminated contracts. The T loan program is a logical extension of the V and VT loan programs, and the Board's Regulation V was revised on September 11, 1944, to cover loans made under the Contract Settlement Act as well as loans for war production made under the President's Executive Order 9112 of March 26, 1942.

The T loan program has been simplified and liberalized as compared with the preceding V loan program. The War Department and Maritime Commission have delegated to the Federal Reserve Banks authority to execute guarantees of loans totaling (a) $500000 or less to any borrower when the requested percentage of guarantee is not in excess of 90 per cent and (b) $100000 or less to any borrower when the requested percentage of guarantee is not in excess of 95 per cent.

Since the beginning of the T loan program, only two types of guarantee loans have been authorized—T loans and 1944-V loans. The 1944-V loans, made under the Executive Order 9112, are loans to provide working capital for war production or to provide for both production and termination financing. These new V loans are similar to the VT loans made prior to September 1944, except that the form of guarantee agreement has been simplified and shortened. The War Department has delegated to the Reserve Banks authority to execute guarantees of V loans totaling $250000 or less to any borrower when the requested percentage of guarantee is not in excess of 90 per cent. Similar authority has been delegated by the Maritime Commission totaling $100000 with the same provision. In connection with the revised Regulation V, the Board prescribed a maximum rate of interest of 4.5 per cent on guaranteed loans and a flexible schedule of guarantee fess, all effective September 11, 1944.

The number and amounts of the guaranteed loans are shown in Table 27. A majority of the borrowers have been relatively small business concerns. Over one-half of the loans so guaranteed were for $ 100000 or less. One half, however, of the amount of the loans of 25 million dollars or more. Most of these loans and agreements to make loans were made by commercial banks.

Table 27 Guaranteed Loans (Amount in Millions of Dollars)

End of Month	Authorized		Outstanding		Additional
	Number	Amount	Total	Guaranteed	Available *
1942					
June	565	311	81	69	138
Sept.	1658	944	427	356	231
Dec.	2665	2688	803	632	1431
1943					
Mar.	3534	3725	1246	999	1866
June	4217	4719	1428	1534	2216
Sept.	4787	5452	1708	1414	2495
Dec.	5347	6563	1914	1602	3146
1944					
Mar.	5904	7476	2009	1680	3616
June	6433	8047	2064	1736	3811
Sept.	6882	8686	1960	1663	4301
Dec.	7434	9311	1735	1482	4454
1945					
Mar.	7885	9645	1599	1366	3964
June	8421	10149	1386	1191	3694

* Available for borrowers under guarantee agreements outstanding.

Note: The difference between guaranteed loans authorized and sum of loans outstanding and amounts available represents amounts repaid, guarantees available but not completed, and authorization expired or withdrawn.

Source: *Federal Reserve Bulletin.*

Regulation of Consumer Credit

The principles and results of the restriction on consumer credit have been discussed in Chapter V; a brief description of the procedures used is given in this section.

The Federal Reserve System was authorized and directed by the President's Executive Order 8843, issued on August 9, 1941, to exercise a measure of control over consumer credit during the period of national emergency arising out of the war. Pursuant to this Order, on August 21, the Board issued Regulation W which, with the exception of certain provision, became effective September 1, 1941. The Regulation applied moderate restrictions on consumer credit at the beginning and has been amended from time to time. All persons subject to Regulation W were required to register before the end of 1941 with the Reserve Banks of their district and licenses were issued to the registrants.

Regulation W prescribed minimum down payments and maximum maturities for consumer credit extended through instalment sales of certain listed articles and instalment loans for the purchase of these articles. In addition, it limited the maximum maturity of miscellaneous cash loans of $1000 or less repayable in instalments, which include many instalment loans made to finance consumer purchases.

Effective September 20, 1941, the Board amended the part of the Supplement to Regulation W pertaining to the method of determining the maximum credit value of new automobiles; and effective December 1, 1941, the regulation was amended in a number of respects, the more important of which were to exempt business loans, require a statement from the borrower as to the purpose of the loan, provide more flexibility for the schedule of payments by farmers and in connection with consolidating obligations, prohibit instalment loans for the purpose of making down payments on listed articles, and make the regulation applicable to instalment loans of $1500 or less instead of $1000 or less as previously.

From September 1, 1941, until the spring of 1942, Regulation W had applied only to instalment sales and to loans repayable in instalments, but effective May 6, 1942, the scope of the regulation was extended to include sales made on charge accounts and loans repayable in single payments. This was in compliance with point 7 of the President's anti-inflation message of April 27 to Congress, which said in part that in order to keep the cost of living from spiraling upward we must "discourage credit and instalment buying and encourage the paying off of debts. . . ".

Prior to this time the Board had already taken action, effective March 23, to reduce the maximum maturity from 18 months to 15, and to increase the minimum down payments on most articles to 33 – 1/3 per cent and 20 per cent. The action, effective May 6, 1942, reduced the maximum maturity of instalment sales still further to 12 months (with exceptions for automobiles) and increased the required down payment on all articles except furniture to 33 – 1/3 per cent, and expended the list of articles covered to include almost all consumer durable and semi-durable goods. The rule laid down for charge accounts prohibited the sale of any listed article on credit to any customer whose charge account was in default, and set the tenth day of the second calendar month after a charge sale as the date on which the account went into default unless payment (or specified arrangement to pay) had been made. Instalment loans were also limited to 12 months, and single-payment loans to 90 days with renewals totaling not more than 12 months from the date of original loan. Since then, there have been no material changes in regard to maturity, down payment, charge accounts and cash loans.

In a few respects, however, Regulation W was relaxed during 1942, generally for the purpose of improving its practical working or of supporting some phase of the war program sponsored by other branches of the Government. For example, an amendment was made to relieve from restriction extensions of consumer credit for converting oil-burning furnaces to coal and for insulating homes. This was of concern primarily to the War Production Board and other war supply agencies to save the consumption of oil.

During 1943, 1944 and the first half of 1945, the typical requirements of Regulation W, effective May 6, 1942, continued. Many amendments, however, have been made in various administrative respects.

Increase in Margin Requirements

Margin requirements on loans by banks for the purpose of purchasing or carrying stocks are another example of the so-called selective credit controls. The requirements are prescribed by the Board in accordance with the Securities Exchange Act of 1934, in Regulation T and U. These regulations limit the amount of credit that may be extended on a security by prescribing a maximum loan value, which is a specified percentage of its market value at the time of the extension; the margin requirements are the difference between the market value (100%) and the maximum loan value. From November 1, 1937 until February 5, 1945, the margin requirements had been 40 per cent on security loans and 50 per cent for short sales.

During the seven-year period after 1937, the stock market operated within a relatively narrow range and the volume of trading was relatively low. Advance in stock prices, however, became apparent in the second half of 1942 and the rise was rapid in 1943 and especially persistent in 1944 and the first quarter of 1945. The amount of credit employed in trading in corporate securities, while still far below the level of earlier years, increased fairly substantially in 1943 and 1944. [1]The Board therefore amended the Supplements to Regulation T and U on February 5, 1945, to increase the margin requirements from 40 to 50 per cent as shown in the following Table. At the same time, on March 5, 1945, the New York Exchange raised from $ 5 to $ 10 the minimum price of stocks for which immediate payment in full was required, established an initial margin requirement of 10 points on stocks selling over $ 10 a share, and required a minimum equity of $ 1000 on all margin accounts. Effective July 5, 1945 the margin requirements were further increased from 50 to 75 per cent.

---

[1]　For a detailed analysis, cf. "Security Market During the War," *Monthly Review*, Federal Reserve Bank of New York, May 1945, p. 35.

Percentage of Market Value

	Nov. 1 ,1937 – Feb. 4 , 1945	Effective Feb. 5 ,1945	Effective July 5 ,1945
For extension of credit by brokers and dealers on listed securities(T)	40	50	75
For short sales(T)	50	50	75
For loans by banks on stocks(U)	40	50	75

In addition, the latest regulation prescribes a new provision that the proceeds of sales of securities in accounts that are under marginal under the new requirements shall be used to the extent necessary to increase the margin on the remaining securities in the account until they are on a 75 per cent basis.

Other Measures Restricting Consumer Credit

In accordance with that part of the President's special Message to congress of April 27, 1942, which urged the paying off of debts as a restraint upon rising living cost, the three Federal Bank supervisory agencies issued a joint statement on May 7, 1942, urging banks to adopt even more generally the principle of amortization for their loans:

> One of the greatest advances in banking practices during recent years has been the wide acceptance of the principle of amortization of debts. This principle is incorporated in Regulation W, issued by the Board of Governors of the Federal Reserve System, which relates to consumer credit and applies to certain types of bank loans.
>
> In the exercise of their supervisory responsibilities, the Comptroller of the Currency, the Board of Directors of the Federal Deposit Insurance Corporation, and the Board of Governors of the Federal Reserve. System urge that the principle of amortization be extended to other loans which are not subject to the provisions of Regulation W, particularly to the volume of

single-payment loans to individuals for non-productive purposes presently outstanding.

The examiners for the respective agencies are being instructed to pay particular attention in the course of their examinations to individual debt to determine whether it is being reduced and to the circumstances which may be preventing its reduction or preventing it from being put on an amortization basis. The examiners are likewise being instructed to include in their reports of examination comments as to the extent to which the bank has so operated in the program for reduction of personal indebtedness incurred for non-productive purposes, and as to the results achieved.

In order to provide a measure of the volume of personal loans, banks will be asked from time to time to report information as to the amounts of single-payment personal loans on their books in addition to information now being reported as to instalment paper.

On June 17, 1942, following a meeting of Government officials concerned with the possible consequences of use of credit for accumulation of inventories, the Board of Governors addressed a letter to all banks and other financing institutions urging the voluntary curtailment of credits for the accumulation of inventories of consumer goods. This did not apply to special situations, such as, the accumulation of fuel stocks and stocks of goods held because of freezing or rationing orders. The Federal bank supervisory agencies requested that their examiners inquire especially during the course of each examination as to the consideration given by banks to this letter. In part, the letter reads:

There was complete agreement that in the present situation, when all possible production must be diverted to military purposes, accumulation of inventories of civilian consumer goods should be discouraged. We are sure that it is clear to you why this is desirable from the standpoint of avoiding inflationary developments as well as of endeavoring to assure fair treatment of the needs of all dealers and all consumers.

Various ways by which this purpose might be accomplished were canvassed. It was agreed that, whether or not other steps may be necessary under the authority of legislation or executive orders, it is of the utmost importance to enlist your voluntary cooperation and that of your customers on helping to achieve this objective. To this end, it is hoped that you will use your influence in your community to discourage all unnecessary purchases of civilian goods and that you will scrutinize carefully every application which might enable a borrower to carry a greater supply of goods than his minimum requirements.

In the field of agricultural credit steps were also taken to discourage unnecessary credit expansion. Special efforts were made, however, by authorities responsible for formulating agricultural policies, as well as by farm borrowers and by lenders, to achieve war expansion of farm output without stimulating a speculative rise in farm values or involving producers in heavy indebtedness. Credit problems confronting farmers have been under constant consideration by a National Agricultural Credit Committee, organized under the auspices of the Farm Credit Administration and composed of representatives of farm organizations, banks, life insurance companies, and Government agencies, including the Federal Reserve.

Reserve Ration and Powers of Reserve Banks

Reduction in Reserve Ratio

The Federal Reserve Bank requirements in effect until the recent reduction on June 12, 1945 had stood, with only minor technical changes, since the establishment of the System more than thirty years ago. These requirements were that each Reserve Bank must maintain reserves in gold certificates or lawful money of not less than 35 per cent against its deposits, and of not less than 40 per cent against its Federal Reserve notes in actual circulation. Only twice in Federal Reserve history have the reserves of the System fallen close to the legal minimum— at the peak of the inflationary boom of 1920 and at the time of large currency expansion and gold outflow preceding the banking holiday in March 1933. It again approached a critical position at the end of 1944 during this war. The aggregate reserve ratio had fallen steadily from 91 per cent at the end of 1941, soon after Pearl Harbor, to less than 50 per cent at the end of 1944. This may be seen from the following Table:

Federal Reserve System (In Billions of Dollars)

	Dec. 31 ,1941	Dec. 30 ,1944	Projection* Dec. 1945
Reserves	20. 8	18. 7	17. 7
Deposits	14. 7	16. 4	18. 4
Federal Reserve notes outst	8. 2	21. 7	26. 7
Liabilities requiring reserves	22. 9	38. 1	45. 1
Required reserves	8. 4	14. 4	17. 1
Reserve Ratio(%)	90. 8	49. 0	39. 2

* If the requirements were not changed. *Federal Reserve Bulletin*, March 1945, p. 215.

The factors responsible for the heavy demand for Federal Reserve credit during the war years were also responsible for the decline in the reserve ratio. The major cause was, therefore, the demand for currency in circulation. Second in importance has been the loss of gold stock. And the third in importance has been the increase in deposits of Reserve Banks, which has reflected mainly the growth in member bank reserves arising out of the rapid growth of bank deposits. Deposits of foreign central banks and governments in the Reserve Banks also increased during the war. Most of the currency in circulation is issued by the Reserve Banks and results in a direct, though fractional, increase in reserve requirements of the Reserve Banks. Bank deposits, on the other hand, require only fractional amounts of reserves in the form of member bank reserves in the Reserve Banks, and these in turn are subject to fractional requirements of reserve at the Reserve Banks. Currency expansion, therefore, puts six or seven times as much strain on

Reserve Banks reserve as does an increase in deposits at member banks. [1]The tendency of liquidity preference which we discussed in connection with the decline in member bank excess reserves thus has the same effect on the reserve ratio of the Reserve Banks. [2]

The problem of falling reserve ratio is by no means peculiar to this country; in fact it appeared much later in the United States than in most other belligerent countries. Most of the other belligerents had taken action to reduce their reserve requirements or release the restriction before 1944. [3]In general, the Federal Reserve Banks may be released from their embarrassment by one or more of the following measures:

1. To reduce member bank reserve requirements to statutory minima;

2. To use the $1.8 billion of gold held in the Stabilization Fund as reserve;

3. To issue 3 billion dollars of United States notes under the Thomas Amendment of 1943;

4. To issue Federal Reserve Bank notes, as authorized by the Emergency Banking Act of 1933, for which no reserve is required;

5. To suspend Reserve Bank reserve requirements by the Board of Governors under Section 11 (c) of the Federal Reserve Act;

6. To reduce reserve requirements of Reserve Banks by Congress.

The last method was finally adopted. By Act of Congress, approved June 12, 1945, the reserve requirements of Federal Reserve Banks were reduced to a uniform minimum of 25 per cent in gold certificates against Federal Reserve notes in

---

[1] Roland I. Robinson, "The Reserve Position of the Federal Reserve Banks," *Federal Reserve Bulletin*, March 1945, p. 215.

[2] See p. 410.

[3] Cf. "wartime Changes in Foreign Central Bank Reserve Requirements," *Monthly Review*, Federal Reserve Bank of New York, September 1944, p. 67.

circulation and deposits liabilities. In addition, the Act extended the authority for the use of direct obligations of the United States as collateral security for Federal Reserve notes, while before the Act such use was authorized by the Glass-Steegall Bill renewed annually. On the other hand, the Act terminated the authority to issue United States notes under the Thomas Amendment of May 12, 1943 and the authority to issue Federal Reserve Bank notes under the Emergency Banking Act of 1933.

Powers of the Federal Reserve System

We have discussed the objectives of wartime Federal Reserve policy in chapters IV and V and have reviewed all the important measures taken by the System during the four years of defense and war. It is logical to ask how great is the power of the System to supply member bank reserves and to stabilize the money market, or, in other words, how great is the power of the System to expand its credit.

From the problem of reserve ratios discussed above, it seems that the amount of gold stock is the only limit of the power of the Reserve Banks to expend their credit. Gold, however, is at the present time not used as money in circulation. Deposits and currency are convertible into gold only for international transactions and then only with a license from the Secretary of the Treasury. The present gold reserves in this country are evidently adequate for any conceivable foreign demand. The United States holds about half of the world's gold stock, and there are no grounds for expecting a loss of gold reserves through an adverse trade balance in the post war period. So long as gold is used only for international transactions and is barred from domestic monetary use, the amount of gold reserve possesses practically no significance in regulating the volume of money and credit in the community.

The important thing is to notice that the Federal Reserve Banks derive their lending power from the nature of their organization and functions, as determined by Congress in the Federal Reserve Act, unlike other banks which derive their lending power from their capital, deposits and undistributed earnings. [①]The Reserve Banks are the legal holders of member bank reserves. Hence transfer of funds between member banks results only in a transfer of credit on the books of Reserve Banks. When a Reserve Bank makes loans or purchases securities by deposit credits, the proceeds are generally not withdrawn, but left in the Reserve Bank as reserve of the borrowing bank, unless currency is demanded by the public. When currency is demanded by the public, the Reserve Banks may issue Federal Reserve notes; this is one of the Reserve Banks' special powers authorized by the Act. Notes and deposits, two types of liability, are interchangeable in the Reserve Banks at the option of the member banks, or, more correctly, at the option of the public. The only effect of such an exchange is that, before June 20, 1945, a larger amount of gold reserves was required against notes than against deposits. This amount, however, may be lowered or even eliminated by Congressional action, and the Board of Governors, under Section 11 (c) of the Federal Reserve Act, has the authority to suspend the reserve requirement against note issues as well as against deposits in time of emergency.

In extending their credit, the Reserve Banks may either purchase securities in the open market or make loans to member banks. So far as the resources of the Reserve Banks are concerned, there is no difference between these two. The loans made, as pointed out before, are generally left in the Reserve Bank as deposits of the borrowing bank, and the checks drawn for the purchase of securities will also be deposited at a Reserve Bank by a member bank as deposits.

Thus we see that the lending power of the Reserve Banks does not depend upon their capital or surplus, nor on the amount of funds that the member banks choose to hold against their deposits. Only the withdrawal of gold can lower their lending power, but the effect of gold withdrawal can be offset by action of Congress or, under certain circumstances, of the Board of Governors itself.

[①]　For a fuller discussion, cf. "Sources of Bank's Lending Power," *Federal Reserve Bulletin*, February 1940, and "Sources of Lending Power of Federal Reserve Banks," *Federal Reserve Bulletin*, March 1940.

Chapter VII Summary and Conclusion

Theory of War Borrowing

Modern Wars have always been partly financed by borrowing. As the national income increases, however, a larger and larger portion of war expenditures should be met by tax revenues rather than by public loans. New taxes ought to be imposed in accordance with the expansion of production and employment. Since the maximum output may be attained before the time when resources are fully utilized, and since prices may rise long before that point is reached, restrictive taxation may become necessary at any time before the level of full employment is attained.

Borrowing does not postpone the burden of the war to future generations; the real cost of the war must largely be met when it is being fought. Both taxation and borrowing are means of diverting resources from private to public employment, that is, civilians will have less money and also fewer goods and services to consume. On the other hand, both taxation and borrowing to some extent also involve real costs to future generations. Capital must be rehabilitated, the stock of goods has to be rebuilt, and, up to a point, the curtailment of personal consumption during the war results in a curtailment of personal productive capacity.

Borrowing, however, postpones the final allocation of the burden of the war. As future generations service and repay the loan, the burden is gradually shifted from bondholders to taxpayers. This involves a redistribution of national income. Whether government borrowing will have the effect of concentrating or diffusing the national wealth among the people depends upon the distribution of ownership of the debt and its magnitude. Generally speaking, the regressive nature of government borrowing, that is, the shift of national income from universal taxpayers to the well-to-do bondholders, is significant when government borrowing is carried on a very large scale.

Inflation may easily but not inevitably result from wartime borrowing. To the extent that loans are derived ultimately from current income, from liquidated investments, or from current and future savings, there need be no inflation. However, no capitalistic country can fight a war on the present-day scale without the help of bank credit. The pressure of war on the banking system is two-fold and complementary. In the first place, the expanding economy needs more money to finance its operation. A community at war not only has more income than one at peace, but also chooses to hold a larger proportion of it in monetary form. Secondly, the government deficit has to be financed. No belligerent government has yet succeeded in covering all its expenditures from individual income.

To a certain extent, financing the war by credit creation can be justified. Since modern wars are accompanied by tremendous expansion of production, the injection of more money will not necessarily lead to price inflation. In addition, a slight rise in wartime prices has many advantages. Most of them, however, will have their counterpart in disadvantages in the postwar period.

The philosophy of "we owe it to ourselves" results in a fallacious conception of the nature of internally held public debt. The extent of government borrowing is limited by many considerations, both theoretical and practical. Firstly, national debt represents the shift of resources from private production to the government, and private industry may be affected by government borrowing even when employment is far below its full capacity. Secondly, bank resources limit the expansion of public loans, as part of the government debt always has to be sold to banks when borrowing reaches a large volume. In countries with a small gold stock and large foreign trade, the depletion of bank reserves might cause embarrassment to the national economy. In addition, consideration must be given to the expansion of bank credit and central bank accommodations, with all their far-reaching consequences on the economy. Thirdly, the ability of the community to lend voluntarily at a fair interest rate is limited not only by the amount of loanable funds, but also by psychological factors. Liquidity preference usually increases during the war. Fourthly, unlike private debt, there is the problem of taxation in connection with the servicing and repayment of public debt. The Treasury can not recover all of its outlay in the form of taxes. Various problems arise when the tax bill becomes very large. Fifthly, the regressive effect of government borrowing, the redistribution of national income, and the social influences of a large debt and large tax program must be considered.

In applying the "multiplier theory" to government borrowing, certain reservations must be made. First, income might not increase with government spending in a multiple way, because of certain offsetting developments, such as, changes in the propensity of the community to consume. If this occurred, increase in income might not warrant a tax revenue sufficient to service the debt. Secondly, the multiplier works downward as well as upward; every failure to spend has a negative multiplier. The shrinkage of income after the tapering off of public spending cannot be avoided unless private investment rises high enough to replace it. Thirdly, no expenditure of any kind has a self perpetuating effect. A flow of private investment remains a prime requisite of a successful policy, otherwise government deficit must continue until final collapse. However, when the national income stands at a very high level, it is not likely that private investment can rise to fill the gap. Fourthly, when public investments are carried on a large scale, it will have the competitive effect of preventing private investment. The total deficit may reach a point at which it is doing more to hold business back than the spending is doing to stimulate it.

Policies of War Borrowing

The essential principle of war borrowing is that the necessary funds should be raised as much as possible from nonbank sources. Historical facts reveal, however, that banks have always been important investors in large scale wartime financing. Of the funds borrowed during this war, about 42 per cent was contributed by the banking system, compared with 19 per cent during World War Ⅰ. But this does not mean that financing by taxation was more successful in the last war, because then the practice of borrowing from banks to purchase Government securities was much more common than in the present war.

Not all the debt sold to ultimate investors represents curtailment in consumers' purchasing power. Besides the portion which is financed by bank security loans, a part may be paid for out of past savings. Without reducing current consumption, this procedure may even make idle funds active. A large portion of the purchase of Government securities appears to have been made by persons who would have saved part of their income in the ordinary course of events. This group merely substituted the direct ownership of Government bonds for a saving deposit or insurance policy, which would probably also have been invested in Government bonds.

The policy of short-term financing has been an American tradition. Its principal motive has been the desire to make Government securities more attractive by increasing their liquidity. Another major consideration comes from the cheap money policy, especially when short-term rates are maintained substantially below long-term rates. The announced objective of maintaining the liquidity of financial institutions is necessary only when banks are heavily involved in Government financing. Even in such cases, shortening the maturity of bank holdings does not present a real remedy. The announced objective of regarding short-term financing as a factor in maintaining postwar full employment seems illusory. On the contrary, this policy will produce the serious problem of floating debt in the postwar periods.

The polity of offering redeemable savings bonds rather than marketable securities to individuals is a sound one. However, the accelerating rate of savings bond redemptions and the fact that the later issues are the most rapidly redeemed and that the lower the denomination of the bonds the higher is the rate of redemption, creates serious problems for the postwar period, especially if inflation threatens. Unless the bonds which are sold to a satisfactory extent the objective of the financing is not reached.

The low interest rate policy on Government obligations is a subject of much controversy. The United States Government has been the cheapest borrower in the world during the war, but not the one which derives most advantage from it because the low yields on war bonds are but an extension of the pre-war cheap policy, whereas in other countries interest rates have declined more rapidly from their peace-time levels. While low interest rates are desirable when the Government is engaged in a costly war, a prolonged period of cheap money is questionable so far as the national economy is concerned, especially when the structure of interest rates takes the pattern of an ascending shape with long-term rates substantially above short-term rates. The major disadvantages of a prolonged low rate polity are: (1) it has adverse effects on the incentive to save; (2) the central bank tends to lose control over interest rate market; (3) monetary authorities are compelled to resort to inflationary methods to maintain the Government security market; (4) banks are forced to resort to risk loans and other higher-yield investments; (5) business is induced to borrow on short-term for long term employment; (6) the distortion in the relationship of interest rate and profit rate may lead to a speculative stock market boom and real estate boom; (7) a prolonged period of cheap money tends to exploit the rentier class which includes most of the small savers; (8) the above effects together might lead to an inflation, and totalitarian control might become indispensable.

The diversification of securities offered during the war and the abolition of tax-exemption on Government obligations are both wise measures and mark the progress of Government borrowing in principle and in technique.

The War Loan drives as a whole have been successful in raising the largest amount of funds in the history of the world. The program also reflects the utmost cooperation between Government and public, including banks and other financial and business institutions and various social organizations. Bank credit involved in the drives, however, has been large. The appeal to individuals has not been so satisfactory. Not infrequently the amount sold was swollen by institutional purchases. The constant demand for longer-term bonds by banks created an active bond market transaction; and the switching and speculative purchases of Government securities have been remarkably large in volume.

Maintenance of Member Bank Reserves and the Government Security Market

Credit expansion of commercial banks for financing the war does not use up bank reserves. For the banking system as a whole, Government securities are purchased by the creation of the banks' own deposit liabilities, not by conversion of their reserve funds to security assets.

The financing of the War by bank credit, however, results in an expansion of bank deposits, and thereby increases the required reserves. But this is not the major factor which requires the Federal Reserve System to take action during the war so as to supply bank reserves. The banking system had built up, before the war, a huge amount of excess reserves. The total amount of reserve funds before the war was so large that, if not depleted by other outside factors, it could have covered all the need for legal reserve requirements in spite of the expansion of bank deposits until the end of 1944.

The principal factor which caused the Federal Reserve System deliberately to maintain member bank reserves was the rapid and accelerating increase in currency. Whenever the public demands currency, commercial banks have to provide it by drawing upon their reserve balances at the Reserve Banks. The public's choice to hold currency uses up bank reserves dollar for dollar, while its choice to hold bank deposits increases the reserve requirement only by a fraction.

Currency expansion is also responsible for the decline in the reserve ratio of the System. Most of the currency in circulation is issued by the Reserve Banks; and its expansion results in a direct, though fractional, increase in reserve requirement of the Reserve Banks. Bank deposits, on the other hand, require only fractional amounts of reserves in the form of member bank balances at the Reserve Banks, and these in turn are subject to a fractional requirement of reserves in the Reserve Banks.

Many reasons account for the tremendous expansion of currency during the war. The most important and influential one, however, is the increase in liquidity preference, that is, people preferred to keep their excess income in the form of hand-to-hand currency. The growth in circulating money has run far ahead of the need for current transactions. Bank notes of large denominations have increased more rapidly than small denominations. After 1942, currency increased more rapidly than income payments and far more rapidly than customer expenditures. All these indicate that people have kept money as a storehouse of value rather than as an exchange medium, in other words, money has been hoarded. Hoarded money is the most dangerous money because nobody knows when it will appear and increase the demand for goods, and because monetary authorities have no power to bring it back to the banking system.

It is the preference of the public for liquidity that requires the Federal Reserve System to take action to supply bank reserves. In other words, if the public preferred to keep all its increased income in the form of savings bonds, bank deposits or other investments, there would be much less need on the part of the System to maintain member bank reserves.

Member bank reserves have been satisfactorily maintained. But this does not mean that the liquidity and solvency of member banks have been satisfactorily maintained. The legally required reserves have only legal meaning. From the banker's viewpoint, it is of value only for final settlement when the bank goes into bankruptcy. It can be used only in the case of emergency and only under penalty interest charges.

The structure of interest rates set up by the Treasury and elaborately managed by the Federal Reserve System during the war is by no means representative of normal conditions. From a long-run point of view, such an ascending shape of the interest rate structure has its advantages as well as many drawbacks.

The desire of financial institutions and other large investors to lengthen the maturity of their investments is a result of maintenance of such a pattern of interest rates, and it reflects the public confidence that this pattern will be maintained by monetary authorities. This desire, however, has the double effect of bringing about an undue absorption of Government securities by the banks, and of pushing up prices and depressing yields of the medium and long-term issues. The decline of interest rates in early 1945 aroused in the market much speculation in regard to the future policy of the Treasury. A further lowering of the rate level may have far-reaching influences upon the national economy and most of them will be deterrent to saving, investment and individual incentive.

There is no doubt that the monetary authorities can maintain a high degree of control over interest rates, even in the face of strong opposing forces, if they are willing to pay the price. The price is an inflating of bank credit brought about by use of the banking system as the instrumentality for supporting the bond market and keeping up the supply of bank reserves. Government borrowing receives its final support from the Reserve Banks. Any amount of the loans not absorbed by the public is taken by commercial banks, and any amount not kept by commercial banks must be taken up by the Federal Reserve Banks. This is the real secret of the success of war borrowing.

Credit Control

Monetary policy plays a minor role in the stabilization of the national economy. The Federal Reserve System has the power, through changes in discount rates, through open-market operations, and through other devices, to make money dearer and scarcer or cheaper and more abundant; but it has no power to counteract a real inflation or depression. In the past quarter century it has been demonstrated that policies regulating the quantity and cost of money cannot by themselves produce economic stability, or even exert a powerful influence in that direction. In the face of the exigencies of war, the problem of credit control becomes more difficult. The central bank in wartime is more important as a fiscal agent of the Government than as a banker's bank; its credit policy becomes subordinated to its fiscal function.

Fiscal policy is not effective in preventing wartime inflation either. Heavy taxes do not necessarily keep prices from rising. The activation of idle funds, or the dishoarding of money, may replace the purchasing power removed by taxes. Liquidation of current assets and past savings has the same effect. A fear of inflation or of future scarcities might lead to a flight from money despite a severe tax program. In addition, to increase the tax rate in higher-income groups, which is likely to occur in times of heavy taxes, is not an efficient method of curtailing current consumption. Nor has the Treasury been able to borrow all or a satisfactory portion of its needed funds from individual incomes. Bank credit has been used to a large extent. One of the important factors contributing to this fact is the low interest rate on Government securities, which was considered necessary for many other reasons.

Bank rate policy has never been an effective instrument in regulating bank credit in this country. Bank rate manipulation met difficulties both under an international gold standard and under a system of managed currency. Discount rate policy is no longer an important feature of central banking during this war. Wartime interest rates are controlled by Treasury issues. However, so long as reliance is placed on quantitative rather than qualitative control of member bank credit, it makes little difference whether the rediscount rate is effective or not; open market operations serve the same purpose.

One interesting question in the wartime banking policy is why banks should not go into debt with the Reserve Banks, as they did in the last war. Fear of rising interest rates can hardly be the explanation for the present reluctance of banks to borrow. It appears to be the case that the banking disturbances of a decade ago, coupled with the ensuing period of super-plentiful credit, have left in the member banks minds a strong disinclination to be in debt to the System. Thus the System during the war was compelled to resort to open market purchases to provide reserve funds for member banks. But if the unwillingness to borrow survives into postwar peacetime, it will constitute an important new element in the structure of American banking. This is a problem to be considered seriously. On the part of the System, the policy of liberal open market purchase and the traditional attitude against member bank borrowing must also be responsible for such a development.

Qualitative credit controls have only limited effects. The old-fashioned methods, which in effect deal only with central bank discount policy, are obsolete today. They never produced satisfactory results even in the old days. During this war, emphasis has been put on the curtailment of consumer credit and the restriction of security loans, or "selective credit controls." They differ from the ordinary methods in that, first, they impose a limit on the borrower's side rather than on the cost and amount of credit that is available to lenders, and, secondly, they limit the credit used in specified purposes without affecting that used for other purpose.

The selective principle is quite new in American credit policy; development along this line may make many new contributions. In their application during this war, however, the instruments of this policy have played a very small part in the national effort to combat inflation. Consumer credit declined substantially, but primarily due to the expansion of individual money income and the curtailment of consumer durable goods; and the declining trend seemed to be reversed in 1944. The striking fact is that during the entire period of the war the public has been spending more money than before the war though with less use of consumer credit. Allowing for the rise in prices and all other related factors, the conclusion must be that there has been no real contraction of consumption expenditures. There is good reason to believe that the American citizen has consumed a larger volume of goods and services during the war than before.

Final Conclusion

Despite the greater and greater scale of the war effort, the United States has thus far progressed toward its goal with no major inflationary development. Broadly regarded, the behavior of prices has been good – much better than in the last war. Though diverse tendencies were apparent in 1944 in the commodity market and there has been lately discussion of rising security and real estate prices, the official Bureau of Labor Statistics indexes show that the total rise of wholesale prices from 1940 to June 1945 has been only about 35 per cent and the rise in the cost of living has been about 28 per cent. However, for the comparative success thus far in avoiding a severe wartime inflation, chief credit must not be ascribed to the monetary controls. The most important factor in offsetting inflationary developments has been the overwhelming expansion of American production. In 1944 the nation produced goods and services having a value of nearly 200 billion dollars at current prices, compared with about 90 billion dollars in 1939. Output at factories and mines in 1994 was 235 per cent of the 1935 – 1939 average. Even allowing for the rise in prices, this undoubtedly represents a rate of expansion of physical production that is without any parallel in economic history. This explains why civilian consumption has not contracted greatly in the face of the unprecedented war demand. The second major reason for the comparative success in avoiding inflation has been the use of direct controls. The control of both raw materials and labor, and the control of prices have been much more effective than ever before in American history.

Monetary policy plays a minor role in the effort to stabilize the national economy. The traditional instruments which a central bank uses in regulating the volume and the cost of bank credit, namely discount rate policy and open market operations, are inapplicable in the attempt to curb inflationary developments in time of war. Qualitative control in its ordinary sense has only very limited effects in this effort. The so-called selective principle, as used in margin requirements and

Regulation W, may have some effect in the field to which it applies. Its importance, however, is still to be proved. Fiscal policy assumes a greater responsibility in the attempt to restrain wartime inflation than does the credit policy. Its application, however, is conditioned by the scale of the war and the structure of the nation's economy. Inflationary borrowing is certainly inevitable in any capitalistic economy, waging a global war.

In time of war, the monetary authorities assume double responsibilities: to facilitate Treasury operations and to stabilize the national economy. These two, unfortunately, are by nature inconsistent. As a matter of fact, price levels have not infrequently been enhanced as a result of the attempt to facilitate government borrowing. In both the 1812 and 1837 periods, tampering with the currency resulted from the attempt to facilitate the sales of Treasury notes by giving them the qualities of money. During the Civil War, direct issues of paper money precipitated an era of inflation. In the Spanish-American war, the circulation privilege was given to Government securities. In World War I financing, as pointed out earlier, credit expansion and the maintenance of an artificially low rate of interest were used as the chief means of disposing of securities. The result was a 50 per cent rise in commodity prices. No matter how elaborate the technique of Treasury borrowing may be, credit and currency inflation have been one of the most important means of insuring the success of war borrowing.

Bibliography

I. **Books**

Angell, James W. , *Investment and Business Cycles*, New York, 1941.

Beckhart, Benjamin H. , *Discount Policy of the Federal Reserve System*, New York, 1924.

Beckhart, Benjamin H. and others, *The New York Money Market*, 4 vols. , New York, 1932.

Burgess, W. Randolph, *The Reserve Banks and Money Market*, New York, 1936.

Clark, John M. , *The Cost of the World War to the American People* , New Haven, 1931.

Dunkman, Williams E. , *Qualitative Credit Control*, New York, 1933.

Fisk, H. B. , *The Inter-Ally Debts*, New York-Paris, 1924.

Gilbert, R. Y. and others, *An Economic Program for American Democracy*, New York, 1938.

Hansen, Alvin H. , *Fiscal Policy and Business Cycles*, New York, 1941.

Hardy, Charles O. , *Credit Policies of the Federal Reserve System*, Washington, D. C. , 1932.

Harris Foundation, *Gold and Monetary Stabilization*, University of Chicago, 1932.

Harris Seymour E., *The Economics of American at War*, New York, 1943.

Harris Seymour E., *Postwar Economic Problems*. New York, 1943.

Harris Seymour E., *Twenty Years of Federal Reserve Policy*, Harvard University, 1933, 2 vols.

Hawtrey R. G. , *Currency and Credit*, London, 1934.

Hawtrey R. G. , *The Art of Central Banking*, London, 1933.

Hendrioks Henry G. , *The Federal Debt*, Washington D. C. , 1933.

Hollander, Jacob H. , *War Borrowing*, New York, 1919.

Jensen, Jens P. , *Problems of Public Finance*, New York, 1921.

Keynes, John M. , *A Treatise on Money*, Vol. I , New York, 1935.

Keynes, John M. , *The General Theory of Employment, Interest and Money*, New York, 1936.

King, willford I. , *The National Income and Its Purchasing Power*, New York, 1930.

Lester, Robert, A. , *Monetary Experiments*, Princeton University, 1939.

Love Roert A. , *Federal Financing*, New York, 1931.

Luthringer, G. F. , Chandler L. V. , Cline, D. C. *Money, Credit and Finance*, Boston, 1938.

Menderahausen, Horst, *The Economics of War*, New York, 1943.

Pigou A, C *Political Economics of War*, New York, 1941.

Reed, Harold L. , *Federal Reserve Policy*, 1921 – 1930, New York, 1930.

Riefler, W, W. , *Money Rates and Money Markets in the United States*, New York, 1930.

Robertson, Dennis H. , *Essays in Monetary Theory*. London, 1940.

Roberston, Dennis H. , *Money*, New York, 1929.

Stamp, Josish. , *The Aftermath of War*, London, 1932.

Stein E, and Backman G. , *War Economics*, New York, 1942 .

Steiner, George A. , *Economic Problems of War*, New York, 1942.

Turner, Robert C. , *Member Bank Borrowing*, Columbus, 1938.

Westerfield, R. B. , *Money Credit and Banking*, New York, 1938.

Wright David W. , *The Creation of Purchasing Power*, Harvard University, 1942.

Youngman, Anna, *The Federal Reserve System in Wartime*, National Bureau of Economic Research, Occasional paper, 1945.

II. Articles

"American Monetary Plethora," *The Economist*, London. July 17, 1943, p. 81.

Bach, G, L. , "Currency in Circulation," *Federal Reserve Bulletin*, April 1944, p, 318.

Bell, Daniel W. , "Financing the War and the Postwar Adjustment," *Federal Reserve Bulletin*, January 1944.

Clark John, M. , "A Appraisal of the Workability of Compensatory Devices," *American Economic Review*, Supplement Vol. XXIX, No. 1. March 1939, p. 203.

Conolly, F. C. , "Reflections on the Cheap Money Policy. Particularity in England," *Supplement to Svenska Handelbanken's Index*, October 1939.

Davenport, H. J. , "The War Tax Paradox," *American Economic Review*, Vol. IX, March 1919, p. 36.

Eccles, Mariner s. , "War Bonds Taxes and Economic Stability," *Federal Reserve Bulletin*, May 1943, p. 393.

Eccles, M. S. , "Financial Problem of Defence," *Federal Reserve Bulletin*, June 1941, p. 50.

Eccles, M. S. , "Economic Aspect of Federal, State and Local Taxation," *Federal Reserve Bulletin*, June 1941, p. 103.

Eccles, M. S. , "The Postwar Price Problem-Inflation or Deflation," *Federal Reserve Bulletin*, December 1944, p, 1156.

Goldenweiser, E. A. , "Commercial Banking After the War," *Federal Reserve Bulletin*, September 1944, p. 871.

Haley, B. F. , "The Federal Budget; Economic Consequence of Deficit Financing," *American Economic Review*, Supplement, Vol. XXXI, February

1941, p. 7.

Hansen, Alvin H., Greer, Guy, "The Federal Debt and the Future," *Harper's*, April 1942, p. 498.

Hansen, Alvin H., "Defence Financing and Inflation Potentialities," *Review of Economic Statistics*, February 1941, p. 5.

Howe, James A., "Some Limitations of Easy Money and Collateral Theories," *Commercial and Financial Chronicle*, August 31, 1944, p. 882.

Kuznets, Simon, "National Income and Taxable Capacity," *American Economic Review*, Supplement, Vol. XXXII, March 1942, p. 59.

Mills, Mark C., "The Federal Reserve Policy," in *The Economic Problems of War*, edited by Steiner, George A, New York, 1942.

Palyi, Melchoir, "Postwar Interest Rates," *Commercial and Financial Chronicle*, October 19, 1944, p. 1689.

Ratchford, B. U., "The Burden of A Domestic Debt," *American Economic Review*, Vol. XXXII, No. 3, September 1942, p. 451.

Robertson, Dennis H., "Saving and Hoarding," *Economic Journal*, Vol. XXXIII, September 1933.

Robertson, Roland I., "The Reserve Position of the Federal Reserve Banks," *Federal Reserve Bulletin*, March 1945, p. 215.

Seligman, Harold L., "Patterns of Wartime Borrowing in the United States, the United Kingdom, and Canada," *Federal Reserve Bulletin*, November 1944, p. 1056.

Spasr, Walter E., "Danger in Declining Federal Reserve Ratio," *Commercial and Financial Chronicle*, March 16, 1944, p. 1121.

Sharpe, Gail E., "The Problem of the Floating Debt," *Financial Highlights*, The Chase National Bank, Vol. 7, No. 1 (mimeographed).

Smith, Dan Throop, "Economic Consequences of Deficit Financing: A Review," *American Economic Review*, Supplement, Vol. XXXI, February 1944, p. 95.

Townsend, W. W., "How Cheap is Cheap Money," *Commercial and*

Financial Chronicle, August 31, 1944, p. 942.

Wills, J. Brooke, "The Relation of Bank Deposits to War Finance," The Chase National Bank, March 15, 1943 (mimeographed).

Williams, John H., "Deficit Spending," *American Economic Review*, Vol. XXX, No. 5, February 1941, p. 65.

Williams, John H., "Monetary Stability and Gold Standard," in a volume entitled: *Gold and Monetary Stability*, University of Chicago, 1932, p. 134.

Wright, David M., "The Economic Limits and Economic Burden of An Internally Held National Debt," *Quarterly Journal of Economics*, Vol. LV, November 1940.

Young, Boy A., "The Banker's Responsibility," *American Bankers Association Journal*, October 1928, p. 281.

Ⅲ. Reports, Statistics, and References

Annual Report, Board of Governors, Federal Reserve System, various issues.

Annual Report, Treasury Department, various issues.

Annual Report, Federal Deposit Insurance Corporation, various issues.

Annual Report, Federal Reserve Bank of New York, various issues.

Supplementary Report, Treasury Department, July 1945.

Federal Reserve Bulletin, Federal Reserve System, various issues.

Bulletin, Treasury Department, various issues.

Monthly Review of Credit and Business Conditions, Federal Reserve Bank of New York, various issues.

Monthly Letter, National City Bank of New York, various issues.

Banking and Monetary Statistics, Federal Reserve System, 1943.

Commercial and Financial Chronicle, various issues.

New York Times, various issues.

Manufacturing Industries in China: A Preliminary Report[*]

I Method Used

This report attempts to approximate the magnitude of manufacturing industries in China before and after the Sino-Japanese war concerning number of establishments, capitalization, labor force, motive power employed, and value of products. The classification of industries of the International Labor Office is followed.

Owing to lack of reliable data for recent years, we have to take many steps before reaching the final picture. Characteristics of the Shanghai industry in 1933 are first studied, because here we have comparatively most complete information. Next the magnitude of Chinese-owned industries in China proper is approximated from the only comprehensive survey in 1933. These figures are extended to include some smaller factories not covered by the survey; and are carried back to 1931 and forward to 1936 by applying 17 industrial indices; and are supplemented by a revised study of capital investment. To the 1936 estimates we then add estimated figures of foreign-owned industries in China and of industries in Manchuria. This

---

[*] This report was accomplished as a research report for Nobel Laureate Simon Kuznets when the author was working for the research as an assistant, in 1946 on New York.

498

picture is then adjusted to allow for wartime evacuation of industries to Free China during the war and wartime development in Free China. The final estimates are compared with the revised N. R. C. five-year industrial program and the Two Billion Dollars Loan Plan. War damages and the industrial development under the Japanese regime, however, are not covered in our estimates. Industries in Taiwan are also left out.

All dollar figures in this report, unless otherwise specified, are Chinese national currency (Yuan).

II Development of Chinese Industry

Although it might be impossible to draw a picture of future "autonomous development" of China's industry, a general trend of its recent development may be helpful to members of our group.

Unfortunately little reliable information is at hand. Some crude data from 1927 to 1936 as presented by the ex-Ministry of Industry are used in drawing the following 10-year charts. On the basis of these and other data, 18 industrial indices are compiled in Table I. The five industries in Table I represented in 1933 84.3% of the total value of industrial production and 76.4% of total industrial investment. For the largest industry, cotton textile, a table in Appendix A shows the growth of spindles of both Chinese and foreign cotton mills in China. These tables indicate that principal industries were developing even in the period of depression since 1933, when newspapers reported shut-downs of factories and capitalists complained of heavy losses.

The 1931 and 1933 surveys of Shanghai industries conducted by Dr. D. K. Lieu (these are the only extensive surveys ever made) show that factories qualified under the Chinese Factory Law increased in number by 60% during the two-year interval, their capitalization by 20%, labor force by 11%, motive power by 18% and the value of products by 37%. This was a period of industrial depression in China, with a 15% decline of prices in Shanghai. Industrial

499

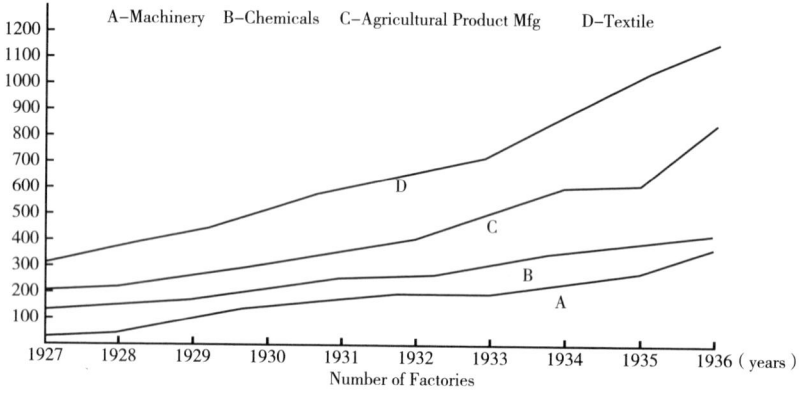

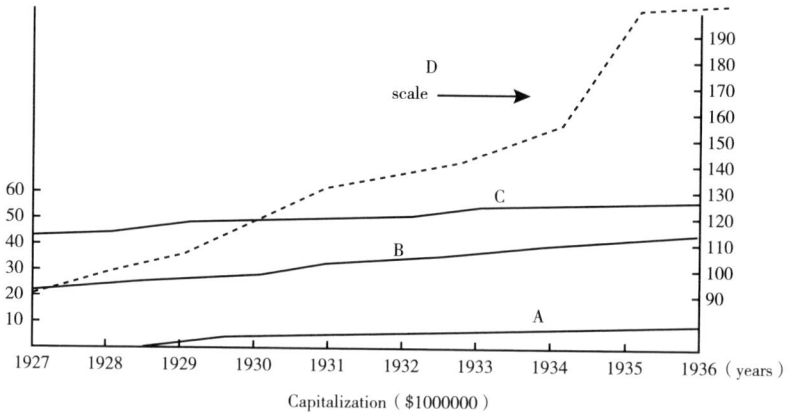

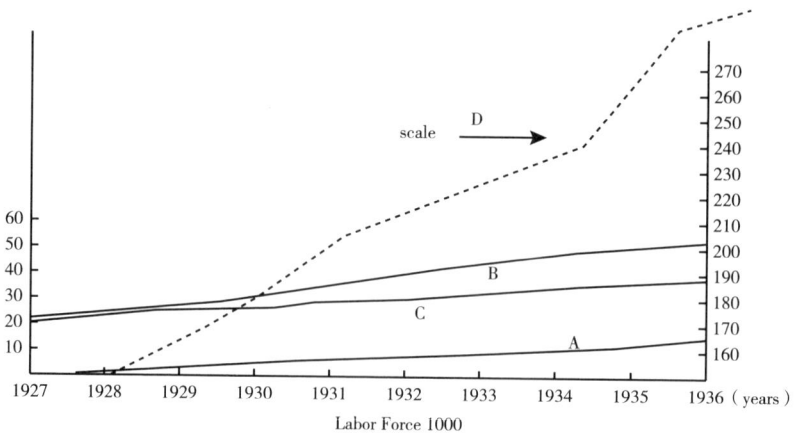

development in this period was largely credited to the protective tariff started in 1931. ①

Table I   Industry Indices, 1933 – 1936

	1931	1932	1933	1934	1935	1936
Textile Industry						
No. of factories	78. 5	87. 4	100	114. 8	138. 4	150. 3
Capitalization	91. 1	96. 1	100	107. 3	136. 9	138. 9
Laborers	89. 6	93. 7	100	105. 6	123. 7	128. 3
Agricultural Product Industry						
No. of factories	70. 8	80. 3	100	118. 3	119. 7	166. 7
Capitalization	93. 1	94. 2	100	101. 7	103. 5	106. 0
Laborers	86. 5	89. 1	100	105. 8	112. 2	119. 9
Machinery Industry						
No. of factories	97. 9	74. 4	100	116. 9	141. 0	193. 3
Capitalization	71. 8	87. 7	100	110. 9	119. 8	129. 5
Laborers	66. 2	83. 3	100	109. 1	123. 2	159. 1
Chemical Industry						
No. of factories	81. 4	87. 4	100	114. 2	125. 6	136. 9
Capitalization	87. 6	91. 6	100	109. 9	114. 7	111. 7
Laborers	81. 6	93. 2	100	110. 0	115. 9	122. 4
Electric Plants						
No. of plants	101. 1	101. 1	100	100. 4	99. 6	100. 4

---

① The comments by Dr. Lieu (*An Analysis of Shanghai Industrialization*, 1937, in Chinese), industrial development in 1929 – 1931 was largely credited to the World depression, Chinese industries benefited because China maintained silver standard at that time. Great Britain and Japan abandoned the gold standard in the autumn of 1931 and prices in China began to decline. But China applied a gradually increasing protective tariff since February 1929. The import duties were raised from an average of 7. 5% to an average of 10. 37% in 1930, 14. 09% in 1931, 14. 45% in 1932 and 19. 74% in 1933. As a result, the import price index in 1933 was 30 points higher than the wholesale price index and the export price index was 40 points lower than the wholesale price index. This gave Chinese industry higher product prices and lower material cost, since exports were mostly raw materials. The decline in agricultural prices during the depression was greater than the decline in industrial prices; this was also favorable to Chinese industry, which had larger material costs and smaller labor costs. Another reason was that most of the Chinese industries were producing consumers' goods, which were in competition with imported goods. During the depression, people with less income purchased domestic goods as substitutes of imported consumers' goods. This does not apply to Japanese goods whose costs were as low as those of Chinese. Japanese goods, however, were boycotted by Chinese people after the Mukden incident in 1931.

Continued table

	1931	1932	1933	1934	1935	1936
Generating Capacity						
Chinese-owned		96	100	107	120	142
Foreign-owned		98. 7	100	111. 4	112. 3	112. 3
Electricity generated		84. 6	100	109. 1	111. 1	122. 1
Industrial Employment						
Four industries	87	90	100	104	118	125
Wholesale price						
General price	121	110	100	92	93	107

Note: Indices of textile, machinery, agricultural product and chemical industries are computed from actual figures given in the *Statistical Abstract of the Republic of China*, 1940, compiled by the Ministry of Industry.

Indices for electric plants are computed from the actual figures reported by the National Committee of Reconstruction, as cited in the N. R. C. Five-Year Program and the *Statistical Abstract*.

Industrial employment index is computed from the employment figures of the four industries in the *Statistical Abstract*.

Price index is an average of price indices of North China and Shanghai, in the *Statistical Abstract*.

"Agricultural product industry" includes food industries and excludes textile industry.

"Electricity generated" index is based on figures in KWH.

The development, however, differed among various industries. Silk and cotton textile were adversely affected by the depression, where chemical and machinery industries showed greatest progress. Among food industries, cigarettes led the development with flour second. While many silk reeling factories were shut down, silk weavers were still working at a profit; while cotton spinning industry claimed losses in this period, cotton weavers were still working at a profit. Some of these figures together with data of other three surveys are given in Appendix B.

Protective tariff was discontinued in July 1933, and the U. S. Government started its silver purchases in 1934, with a resulting collapse in China's prices. It has been contended that real decline in Chinese production began at that time, though we do not see confirmation in our chart and Table I. The Chinese Government abandoned silver standard in 1935, prices began to rise and business recovered quickly in Shanghai. But industries and their markets were handicapped by Japanese pressure in North China, the communist movement in central Yangtze River, floods and famines in Central and South China and various aftermaths of the Mukden and Shanghai incidents of 1931 – 1932. On the other hand, the Government reconstruction program began in 1936, though very few of the works were completed at the outbreak of the war in 1937. For this period, we have no statistical data except those included in Table I and some capital stock estimates to be discussed in Section VI. The N. R. C. has conducted a series of surveys in 1936 and 1937, but none of their results are accesible at our New York office.

Generally speaking, the industrial development in China was slow but tangible during the so-called depression period 1933 – 1936; and we definitely know that there was progress in the deprssion years of 1931 – 1933. The development may have been much slower than in 1914 – 1925, but the upward course had been kept to since 1926.

The growth of China's modern industrial capital may also be judged from the value of capital goods imported. Since China did not herself produce important machines or even important tools and spare parts, the trend of machinery imports is a good gauge of China's industrial progress. Also, as capital goods, especially machines, are usually not used up in a short period, their import value may be cumulated to show total of capital goods invested in China's industry. Such an estimate is given in Appendix C, the table being reproduced from Mr. Tso-Fan Koh's study. The figures in Appendix C are expressed in pound sterling, thus removing any effects of changes in value of the Chinese money unit during this period.

Mr. Tso-Fan Koh comments on the figures as follows:

Although they have been converted into pounds sterling, their accuracy has been modified, as already explained, both by the fluctuations in the value of pounds sterling and in the prices of machines and by the fact that before 1932, they included imports for Manchuria, while after 1932 did not. They grew from £642911 in 1912 to £130611654 in 1938, roughly about 203 times in 27 years. The rate of annual growth, if estimated from a straight secular trend, was £5518698 (The equation used is $Y = 69001547.1 - 5518969.3 X$).

The above calculation include capital goods imported for total investments in China, that is, by both foreigners and Chinese. If, as pointed out above, Chinese native capital counts for only one fourth of the total, the rate of growth for native capital alone would be reduced to £1379742 a year. This means that, with a total population of 450 millions, including Manchuria, each Chinese shared an annual increase of capital goods of a little more than one-hundredth of a pound, including capital goods invested by foreigners, but could by themselves alone—accumulate $\dfrac{1.4}{450}$ of a pound, per annum. [1]

In the past, great international wars always brought favorable circumstances to Chinese industry. The following is a paragraph from Dr. H. D. Fong's conclusion in his study of "Industrial Capital in China". [2]

Since then (early 1860's) industry has grown more rapidly in China, especially after the Sino-Japanese War of 1894 – 1895, with the impetus given by the Treaty of Shimonoseki, which gave foreigners the right of engaging in industrial enterprise in China. When the Great War (1914 – 1918) came, Chinese industries again took a new vigorous turn... The three wars, the Opium War of 1842, the Sino-Japanese War of 1895 and the World War of 1914, have thus each in its turn brought about a new phase in China's industrial development.

III   Shanghai Industry

Various surveys of Shanghai industry 1928 – 1934 are summarized in Appendix B, and their totals are given in Table II. Among these surveys only the 1933 and 1931 (b) and 1931 (bb) are comparatively reliable. The 1928, 1929 and probably 1934 and 1931 (a) surveys are incomplete with respect to foreign-owned

---

[1]   "Problems of Economic Reconstruction in China," Part II, Capital Stock in China, by Tso-Fan Koh, The Eighth Conference of the Institute of Pacific Relations, Dec. 1942, China Council.

[2]   Nankai Institute of Economics, 1936, Bulletin No. 9, Industry Series.

factories in Shanghai. All of them, except the 1928, follow the International Labor Office classification. Other features of these surveys are cited in the explanatory notes to Table II.

It is apparent that we cannot measure the rate of development from these figures, except for years 1931 and 1933. The data, however, help us to form a general idea of the composition of Shanghai industries. Without going into detail we may summarize some of their characteristics as follows:

1. Shanghai industries had been growing even in the depression years after 1931, despite many newspaper reports to the contrary.

2. The growth of consumer-goods industries was much faster than that of producers' goods (including cotton spinning and silk reeling) except machinery manufacturing.

3. Shanghai industries were highly concentrated in textiles and food-stuffs, the percentages of total (1933) of these two groups being as follows:

	No. of factories	Capital	Laborers	Value of Products
Textile	33	39	56	36
Foodstuff	12	19	12	37
Total	45	58	68	73

Next in importance came clothing and attire, leather and rubber and paper and printing. It will be noted below that the distribution is different from that of industry for all China.

Table II   Shanghai Industry, 1928 – 1934

Survey of	Number of factories	Capitalization ($ 1000)	Laborers	Motive Powers H. P.	Value of products ($ 1000)
1928	1500″	103622 *	223691 * ″	—	—
1929	1593″	—	275027″	—	—
1931(a)	1883	155913	212000	116863	—
1931(bb)	1672	142329 *	214152	158429	439329
1931(b)	710	135352 *	192943	152451	407084

Survey of	Number of factories	Capitalization ($ 1000)	Laborers	Motive Powers H. P.	Value of products ($ 1000)
1933	1186	162686	214736	179077	557691
1934	5418″	478293″(1)	299585″(2)	—	—

∗ Incomplete original data.

″ Including foreign-owned factories.

(1) Including 2540 factories.

(2) Including 3893 factories.

Motive power—including power engines and motors using electric power supplied by electric plants.

Value of products—value of previous year.

Survey of:

1928 – Conducted by the Bureau of Social Affairs, Shanghai Municipal Government, appeared in "Industries in Shanghai" (in Chinese). Definition of factory not given. The capitalization figures of foreign-owned factories are deducted from the table, but we are unable to do so for other items. Classification method is entirely different from all other surveys, items in Table B are rearranged. Figures in this survey are generally too low.

1929 – Conducted by the same Bureau, definition of factory unknown, appeared in "Wages and Working Time" (in Chinese).

1931(a) – Conducted by the same Bureau, definition of factory unknown, presumably are those qualified by the Chinese Factory Law and includes foreign-owned factories, appeared in "Machine Manufacture Industries in Shanghai" (in Chinese).

1931(b) – Conducted by Dr. D. K. Lieu, Institute of Economic and Statistical Research, appeared in "Analysis of Shanghai Industrialization" (in Chinese), including all factories qualified by the Chinese Factory Law (uses motive power and employs 30 or more workers).

1931(bb) – The Same as 1931 (b), including all factories that use motive power or employ 10 or more workers.

1933 – The Same as 1931 (b), including all factories qualified by the Chinese Factory Law.

1934 – Conducted by the Bureau of Social Affairs, Shanghai Municipal Government, appeared in "Directory of Shanghai Factories" (in Chinese), including all factories which use motive power or employ 5 or more workers.

4. Generally small volume of capital funds—for qualified factories (by the Chinese Factory Law) the average capitalization in 1933 was only $ 140000 per factory. Including smaller factories, the figure is as small as $ 80000 (1931). Industry was obviously working on borrowed funds.

1933	Average capital per factory in dollars	Value of material purchased as a % of the capital	Value of product as a % of the capital
Cotton spinning	1693706	185	247
Cotton weaving	61984	447	543
Steam filature	23811	637	941

Continued table

1933	Average capital per factory in dollars	Value of material purchased as a % of the capital	Value of product as a % of the capital
Silk weaving	35016	325	517
Flour	416643	966	1163
Cigarette	422281	219	540
Chemical	194873	112	187
Machinery	47681	129	298
Rubber	98144	239	590

Source : D. K. Lieu , *Analysis of Shanghai Industrialization* , p. 294.

The shortage of capital funds may be seen from the above table which shows conditions in principal industries. Some factories had capital funds only enough to buy one week's raw materials.

5. The Size of the factory was generally very—small only about 50% of the factories were qualified under the Chinese Factory Law , which required a factory to use motive power and to employ 30 or more workers. For qualified factories , the average size per factory in 1933 was : Capital , $ 137000 ; Laborers , 181 ; Motive power , 151 H. P. ; Value of product , $ 470000. Industrial combinations were very rare. 60% of the motive power was electric power supplied by outside electric plants. The average H. P. per worker was only 0. 55 , and per factory only 151 , as may be seen from the following table.

1933	Value of product per factory	Material cost as % of value produced	Average H. P. per factory	Average H. P. per worker
Cotton spinning	$ 4189087	75	2133	1. 02
Cotton weaving	368388	88	62	0. 48
Steam filature	146190	82	23	0. 04
Silk weaving	195428	63	24	0. 28
Flour	4845550	83	816	4. 86
Cigarette	2546669	40	64	0. 17
Chemical	374895	55	62	0. 52
Machinery	142199	44	26	0. 38
Rubber	586345	38	169	0. 67
Average of 12 industries		60	151	0. 55

Source : D. K. Lieu , Ibid.

6. Material and material cost—imported raw materials were increasing to replace domestic products. 40% of raw cotton used by textile factories were imported from America. Importation of Canadian and Australian wheat had been increasing. Steel was mostly imported.

7. Labor and labor cost—35.3% of the industrial labor force was male, 53.7% female and 8.5% children, the last mostly female. All female workers were about 61% of the total (1933).

1933	Average laborers per factory	Value produced per worker	labor cost as % of value produced
Cotton spinning	2083	$ 2011	9.3
Cotton weaving	129	2652	5.7
Steam filature	607	241	19.9 *
Silk weaving	85	2131	14.2
Flour	168	28888	0.9
Cigarette	388	6282	3.0
Chemical	118	2894	6.4
Machinery	68	2007	8.5
Rubber	269	2119	8.6

* This industry sustained losses in 1933.

Source: D. K. Lieu, Ibid.

To make the study comparable with our further study on the whole China industry, the Shanghai 1933 survey is summarized in Table Ⅲ. The position of Shanghai industry may be inferred from the following:

	Shanghai industry as a % of all China excluding Manchuria
Number of factories	49
Capitalization	40
Labor force	43
Value of products	50

IV   Chinese Industry 1933

The only extensive survey on industry of all China was conducted by Dr. D. K. Lieu in 1933 on behalf of the N. R. C.. A summary of this survey is given in Table IV. Although similar surveys have been made by Dr. Lieu for the same office in later years, they were not so extensive and, as stated by Dr. Lieu, cannot represent conditions in the whole country.

The 1933 survey, however, is incomplete in many respects:

(1) Manchuria was not covered.

(2) Sinkiang, Yunnan and Kweichow provinces were also left out.

(3) It was confined to Chinese-owned factories.

(4) It was confined to factories qualified under the Chinese Factory Law, which defines a factory as one using motive power and employing 30 or more workers.

(5) It does not include arsenals, mints and moving picture companies.

(6) On account of difficulties of communication, some factories that were not easily accessible to field workers were left out.

The omissions under (5) and (6) are not large, and we have no means to adjust for them. Lack of data on foreign-owned factories, which had a capitalization much larger than the Chinese, is to be deplored. Since foreign owners refused to supply data in both this and the Shanghai surveys, we can only approximate their investment figures in rough totals. Such estimates will be made after our study of the characteristics of Chinese industry. The lack of data for Manchuria is also of importance. Since we have no information about Manchuria until 1940 and such dovelopment in that area differed from Chinese industry, the estimates for Manchuria will be made below. The figures for Sinkiang, Yunnan, Kweichow are also not accessible, except that some of the capitalization estimates for these areas will be added in section VI.

Table Ⅲ Shanghai Industry, 1933

Industries	Number of factories	Capitalization ($1000)	Laborers	Motive Power		Value of products ($1000)
				Motor *	Power Engines H. P.	
Woodworking	10	612	789	538	205	2141
Furniture	7	379	994	211	—	865
Metallurgical	22	361	787	334	—	986
Machinery&metallic ware	167	7724	11379	4210	128	21899
Communication instruments	16	523	3653	1561	1514	8283
Stone, cement, brick, etc.	44	4268	3907	1043	2552	8026
Construction materials	7	165	438	58	—	1112
Water&electric supply	3	11290	1020	1513	48667	7931
Chemicals	78	15200	9246	3876	862	25868
Textiles	391	63624	120165	63406	12056	198220
Clothing&attire	89	4974	10605	1711	2	19469
Leather&rubber	55	5064	11832	6875	604	20989
Foodstuffs	143	31093	27375	17564	1006	205415
Paper&printing	114	16075	9786	5362	2677	32137
Apparatuses, ornaments	18	625	1062	156	—	1719
Miscellaneous	22	710	1698	367	24	2632
Total	1186	162686	214736	108783	70295	557691

* Elect power supplied by electric plants.

Source: Compiled from figures given by Dr. D. K. Lieu, in *Analysis of Shanghai Industrialization*, in Chinese, 1937.

Table Ⅳ Chinese Industry, 1933 (Excluding Manchuria)

Industries	Number of factories	Capitalization ($1000)	Laborers	Motive Power		Value of products ($1000)
				Motor *	Power Engines H. P.	
Woodworking	18	1115	1251	558	490	3269
Furniture	12	420	1903	276	54	1520
Metallurgical	33	2691	2220	372	1752	4755
Machinery&metallic ware	306	16550	21745	5529	8901	32876
Communication instruments	55	19004	16052	2628	14680	22352
Stone, cement, brick, etc.	112	29184	16360	1967	58629	29996
Construction materials	14	298	953	120	69	1746
Water&electric supply	14	32614	1420	5311	62367	13167
Chemicals	148	26327	27719	4931	6724	49694

Continued table

Industries	Number of factories	Capitalization ($ 1000)	Laborers	Motive Power		Value of products ($ 1000)
				Motor*	Power Engines	
				H. P.		
Textiles	821	166828	302472	75877	171053	483583
Clothing & attire	141	6006	15231	2329	207	27425
Leather&rubber	84	6340	14515	7377	2069	30531
Foodstuffs	390	68380	48718	24645	29077	361587
Paper&printing	234	27877	18259	6709	11323	45450
Apparatuses, ornaments	26	812	2291	223	73	2684
Miscellaneous	27	2426	2148	807	445	3336
Total	2435	406873	493257	139407	367893	1113974

* Electric power supplied by electric plants.

Source: Compiled from figures given by Dr. D. K. Lieu in "Notes on China's Foreign Trade and Trade Policy," mimeographed, Institute of Pacific Relations, January 1945. The figures are a summary of an industrial survey conducted by Dr. Lieu on behalf of the N. R. C.

The omission under (4), i. e. , the factories not qualified by the Factory Law, is adjusted for in Table V on the basis of proportions for Shanghai industry. The standard of the Factory Law is not high, but, as Chinese industry was still in its early development, the omission is considerable. Owing to lack of other definitions of factory, we accept the standard used in the 1931 Shanghai survey, i. e. , all factories that used motive power or employed 10 or more workers, but not handicrafts. [1]

---

[1] This is the standard suggested by Prof. T, F. Chen. When the writer started his work on this report, he was influenced by the fact that registration of factories under the Chinese Factory Law had never been complete during this period and also by the consideration that we would be unable to get any acceptable estimates on handicrafts. After all the calculations for Appendix E had been completed, however, the writer began to think that the more restricted Factory Law definition may be better for all further studies. To revise all the calculations will take too much time. Thus Table V remains as basic of this study. It may be noted that, so far as capitalization, motive power, and value of products are concerned, Table V differs from Table IV only slightly, and users can easily reconvert the results in Table V and other tables into the Factory Law definition by applying the following ratios. These ratios are based on the 1931 Shanghai survey and do not include handicrafts. These are the factors by which Table IV is multiplied in arriving at Table V.

No. of factories 2. 35　　Motive power-engines　1. 02

Capitalization 1. 08　　Laborers　　　　　　1. 11

Motive power-motors 1. 06　Value of products　　1. 08

Ratios for every specific industry are also available, but here we used only the average for all industries, except electric and water supply, including both large and small factories. The total figures in Table V, however, are more accurate than those of individual industries.

Table V   Chinese Industry, 1933 (Excluding Manchuria)

Industries	Number of factories	Capitalization $ 1000	Laborers	Motive Power		Value of products $ 1000
				Motors* Engines H. P.	Power	
Woodworking	42	1171	1389	591	500	3531
Furniture	28	441	2112	293	35	1642
Metallurgical	78	2826	2464	394	1787	5135
Machinery&metallic ware	719	17378	24137	5861	9079	35506
Communication instruments	129	19954	17818	2786	14974	24140
Stone, cement, brick, etc.	263	30643	18160	2085	59802	32396
Construction materials	33	313	1058	127	70	1886
Water&electric supply	33	34245	1576	5630	63614	14220
Chemicals	348	27643	30768	5227	6858	53670
Textiles	1929	175169	335744	80430	174474	522270
Clothing & attire	331	6306	16906	2469	211	29619
Leather&rubber	197	6657	16112	7820	2110	32972
Foodstuffs	917	71799	54077	26124	29659	390514
Paper&printing	550	29271	20267	7112	11549	49086
Apparatuses, ornaments	61	853	2543	236	74	2899
Miscellaneous	63	2547	2384	855	454	3603
Total	5721	427216	547515	147771**	375250	1203092

Note: This tabel is derived from Tabel IV, see text.

Inclusive of Chinese-owned factories that use motive power or employ 10 or more workers.

* Electric power supplied by electric plants.

** Not the sum of this column, because some figures are evened out in Table IV.

The characteristics of Chinese industry can be summarized as follows :

1. Modern industry plays a very limited role in the entire field of productive activity. The national wealth of China is small, but it cannot be less than 100 billion dollars. The highest estimate put it at U. S. $ 84 billion in 1929, or roughly $ 200 billion Chinese dollar. A later estimate given in 1932 was $ 106351987466. Investment in modern industry is in any case less than 4% of the total national wealth. [1] The total industrial capital accumulated by Chinese themselves was $ 589 million in 1936 (Table VI), with a population of 450 million, or an average per capita value of only $ 1.31. The total capital of manufacturing industry alone in the U. S. was U. S. $ 52695 million in 1930, a year of severe depression. With population of

---

[1]   T. F. Koh, ibid.

122775000, the per capita value was about U. S. $ 430 or Chinese $ 1433, i. e. , more than 1000 times the average Chinese share.

2. Concentration of factories in coastal cities As pointed out in the last section, Shanghai accounted for about half of the nation's industry. Other industrial centers, Tientsin, Tsingtao, Canton, Fuchow, are also coastal ports. If Liaoning (Manchuria) were included, the coastal areas would claim some 90% of China's industries. Since foreign factories were mostly located in Shanghai and along the seacoast, the percentage would have been much higher were the missing data of foreign industry included.

3. Light industry was in advance of heavy industry One third of all factories was in textile and 16% in foodstuff. Some heavy industries were non-existent. Although there were eight large iron and steel mills in 1933, only five were then in operation. Of acid and soda, there were only two in operation. There was not a single copper refinery, nor any for refining of oil. [1] The percentage distribution was as follows :

1933	No. of factory	Capitalization	Labor force	Motive power	Value of products
Textile	33. 7	41. 0	61. 3	48. 8	43. 4
Foodstuff	16. 0	16. 8	9. 1	10. 7	32. 3
Chemicals	6. 1	6. 5	5. 6	2. 3	4. 5
Machine & metal	12. 6	4. 1	4. 4	2. 9	2. 9
Water & elect.	0. 6 / 69. 0	8. 0 / 76. 4	0. 3 / 80. 7	13. 0 / 77. 7	1. 2 / 84. 3
Paper & printing	9. 6	6. 8	3. 7	3. 6	4. 1
Stone, cement, etc.	4. 6	7. 1	3. 3	11. 8	2. 7
Others	16. 8 / 100. 0	9. 7 / 100. 0	12. 3 / 100. 0	6. 9 / 100. 0	8. 9 / 100. 0

4. Very low share capital goods—The 1933 survey shows that only $ 33813000 or 8. 3% of total industrial capital, was invested in producing capital goods; and 50% of that was in railroad repairing. The product value of capital goods was only $ 43819621 or 3. 9% of the total. The details on capital goods manufacturing are given in Appendix D.

[1] D. K. Lieu, *Notes on China's Foreign Trade and Trade Policy.*

5. The Size of the factory was very small Average capitalization per qualified factory was only $ 167000 which, converted into U. S. dollar at 1933 rate, amounted to some U. S. $ 50000. 612 of the 2435 qualified factories were operated by joint stock companies, with the remainder operated mainly by single proprietorships or partnerships. 27% of total motive power were motors using electricity supplied by outside plants. On account of their small capital, most factories were unable to build their own plants, but had to rent them. Of the 2435 qualified factories, 1368 rented all of their plants, and 44 rented part of them. Some 220 factories rented also their sites, of which the average size was only 4.6 acres. The average size of plant itself was only 1.5 acres. Other information is summarized below:

Average size of factory:

Capitalization	Qualified factories	All factories
Capitalization	$ 167000	$ 74700
Labor force	203	96
Motive power	208 H. P.	91 H. P.
Value of product	$ 457500	$ 210300

The total value of product, when divided by the population of 450 million, shows that per capita consumption of home industry products did not exceed $ 2.70.

6. Female workers dominate—There were 202762 male workers, 243435 female and 47060 child workers in qualified factories in 1933. Female workers, including female children, were 55% of the total. The percentage of male workers is slightly higher when all factory figures are used. For qualified factories, each worker used 1.03 H. P. and produced a value of $ 2258. For all factories, each worker used 0.96 H. P. and produced a value of $ 2197.

V   Development of Chinese Industry, 1933 – 1936

As mentioned before, the only statistical record available for showing industrial development in recent years is that appearing in the 1940 Statistical Abstract and covered in our industrial indices of Table Ⅰ. The five industries in

Table I cover 69% of the total number of factories, 76.4% of total industrial investment, 80.7% of total labor force and 84.3% of total value of product.

By applying these indices, we can estimate changes in these five industries for 1931 – 1936. The results are given in Appendix E. [1] The other 11 kinds of industries, producing about 16% of the total value of output, are derived in total from 1933 by applying the general employment index in Table I , which is merely a combination of the four employment indices in the first four industries. [2] Among these 11 were larger industries like paper and printing and stone, cement, bricks, glass, etc.. Unfortunately we are unable to get their respective indices.

The last year of our calculation, 1936, is summarized in Table VI. Comparing it with Table V , the changes are clearly shown. The 1936 figures are supposed to represent the condition of Chinese-owned industry before the outbreak of the war.

VI A Revised Study on Capital Stock

The foregoing study shows that capital investment in Chinese-owned industries

---

[1] The indices of numbers of factories, capitalization, and numbers of workers are applied directly to respective industries. The figures of capital and value produced are all expressed in 1936 Chinese dollars (The 1933 amounts are, therefore, different from those of Table V) . The price index of Table I is used in the conversion.

   The reason why we used the indices instead of the absolute figures, which are obtainable, is that they, being of different origin and classification, differ much from those in Table V . For instance, we have 148 chemical factories in Table IV where the *Statistical Abstract* shows 317 for the same year. The indices of machinery manufacturing are used for our "machinery and metallic wares"; and the indices for factories of agricultural products are used for our "foodstuff."

   No index of motive power is available, and the relevant employment index is used instead. No index of value of product is available, the respective employment index is used instead and the value is converted into 1936 dollars. For electric and water supply, the index of generating capacity of Chinese-owned "electric plants" are used in calculating all figures except the number of factories (the latter is unchanged because the number of factories index shows changes within 1.5%). But we definitely know that new plants were established in 1936 and 1937. We also have an index of "electricity generated," but since it includes foreign plants, it is not used in calculating the value of product.

[2] Dr. T. C. Lieu used this index for all of the industries in his study of national income, 1931 – 1936. He seems to have overlooked the fact that some of the industries command very high percentage shares in the total and their influence cannot be generalized.

was $ 406873000 in 1933 for qualified factories, $ 427216000 if we include smaller factories, and estimated at $ 587763000 in 1936 for all factories. The estimates are based on the 1933 survey, which, as pointed out before, did not cover Sinkiang, Yunnan and Kweichow provinces. A later study made by Mr. Tso-Fan Koh expanded the original total from $ 406872634 to $ 627812964, by adding some figures revealed by recent reports on localities originally omitted and on factories newly established. The adjustments are given in Table VII. [①]

Mr. Koh's data, except for electricity and metallurgical are based mostly on the 1937 *Chinese Year Book* and the 1936 *Shun Pao Year Book*. The figures so obtained are not as accurate as the 1933 survey.

Table VI   Chinese Industry, 1936 (Excluding Manchuria)

Industries	Number of factories	Capitalization ($ 1000)	Laborers	Motive Power		Value of products ($ 1000)
				Motor*	Power Engines	
				H. P.		
Textile	2899	260340	430760	103192	223850	716978
Foodstuffs	1529	81435	64754	31323	35561	501002
Machinery&metallic ware	1390	24079	38402	9324	14445	60444
Chemicals	476	34813	37660	6398	8394	70291
Electric&water supply	33	52032	2338	7995	90332	21605
Other industries	2219	135064	126516	30624	114456	249995
Total	8546	587763	700330	188856	487038	1620315

Note: Derived from Table V.

Inclusive of Chinese-owned factories that use motive power or employ 10 or more workers.

* Electric power supplied by electric plants.

Table VII   The Revised Chinese Industrial Capitalization

Industries	1933 Survey ($ 1000)	Adjustment ($ 1000)	Revised Estimate ($ 1000)
Woodworking	1115175	—	1115175
Furniture	419500	− 38000	381500
Metallurgical	2690750	+ 7110000	9800750
Machinery and metallic wares	16549708	+ 1143000	17692708
Communication instruments	19004410	− 16665304	2339107
Stone, cement, brick, glass, etc.	29184299	+ 8622861	37807160
Construction materials	298120	—	298120

① For details, see Mr. Koh, ibid.

Continued table

Industries	1933 Survey($ 1000)	Adjustment($ 1000)	Revised Estimate ($ 1000)
Electric and water supply	32613625	+ 102040000	134203625
Chemicals	26326882	+ 22820083	49146965
Textile	166882298 *	+ 28744250	195626548
Clothing & attire	6006076	—	6006076
Leather & rubber	6339839	+ 4372453	10712292
Foodstuff	68380190	+ 57711376	126091566
Paper & printing	27877461	+ 5475611	33353072
Apparatuses, ornaments	812300	—	812300
Miscellaneous	2426000	—	2426000
Total	409926624	+ 217886340	627812964

* The figures differ from our previous tables by $ 54000. This is due to a misprint in the textile figure (28 in other tables and 82 in this table) but we do not know whether the error is in this table or in the other.

Source: Adjustment figures are made by Mr. Tso-Fan Koh, see "Problems of Economic Reconstruction in China", Part Ⅱ, Appendix A, China Council, Institute of Pacific Relations, Eighth Conference, December 1942.

But the $ 102, 040, 000 adjustment in the electric supply branch based on figures released by the ex-Reconstruction Commission and a book published by the Yunnan Provincial government, is reliable. The revised estimates include some newly established large undertakings such as the Central Iron Works, Yung Li Chemical Industries Ltd. , and some Shensi provincial government's companies. It does not, however, include Sinkiang, Kweichow and such industries as mint, arsenals and moving pictures.

The revised capitalization figures are not used in our Tables Ⅴ-Ⅶ, because the adjustments are for the whole period and cannot be broken down by years; because the revised figures do not seem reliable enough for comparison with the basic year 1933; and also because we cannot get any information about the labor force, motive power and value of product to match the revised capital data. But we can definitely say that our capital figures of $ 427 million in 1933 or of $ 588 million in 1936 are too small. The amount in 1936 was probably above $ 700 million. We may keep in mind that figures in Tables Ⅳ-Ⅵ are generally underestimated by 10 to 15%, especially for electric plants and foodstuff industries.

VII Foreign-Owned Industry in China

No statistics are available for foreign-owned manufacturing industries in China; foreign owners refused to supply data in both the 1931 and 1933 surveys.

Mr. Tso-Fan Koh estimated total foreign investment in modern industries, excluding Manchuria, in the years before the war at $ 1076700000, excluding $ 277700000 in public utilities. [1] The Chinese investment in 1936, according to our Table VI, less electric and water supply, was $ 535731000. The ratio of foreign investment to Chinese is thus 2.01. [2] Using the revised capital figure of $ 627812964 and less $ 134203625 of electric and water supply, the foreign-Chinese ratio is 2.18. The 1928 Shanghai survey shows foreign investment at $ 190.0 million and Chinese at 103.6 million, the ratio being 1.83. The Shanghai survey is believed to have included only incomplete foreign data.

This ratio cannot be applied to each industry because foreign investment is highly concentrated in a few industries. Fortunately, some statistical data are available for the largest industry involved, the cotton textile. The figures in 1930, as presented by the Chinese Cotton Mills Association, are summarized in Appendix F. Figures for later years have also been issued by the same Association, but they are not accessible here. The number of spindles, both Chinese and foreign, up to 1935, has been given in Appendix A. Mr. Nai-Yung Kiang mentioned [3] in his book on the textile industry as figures presented by the Association, that there were 132 cotton mills in 1933, with a capitalization of $ 363359298, a labor force of 257568, producing 2332684 bales of yarn and 20121900 pieces of cloth. The "capitalization" figure is too large, since he evidently included reserves in it .

---

[1] T. F. Koh, ibid. , Mr. Koh's estimate is based on Prof. Remer's estimates less investment in Manchuria and other leased territories.

[2] The ratio used by Dr. T. C. Liu in his study of national income is 2.9, this seems too large.

[3] Nai-Yung Kiang, *Chinese Textile Industry* (in Chinese), 1940, Chungking.

From these scattered sources, the condition of foreign textile industry is estimated as follows:

Foreign-Owned Cotton Textile

Years	No. of factories(1)	Capitalization(2)	Laborers(3)	Motive power(4)	Value of products 1936(5)
1931	46	$ 161419917	90028	114075	$ 295803164
1933		203481207	116678	129478	383136715
1936		222321527	138424	146931	454544273

(1) Using 1930 figure for 1931, no information available for other years.

(2) Using 1930 figure for 1931, rates of exchange are 1 Japanese Yen equals 1 Chinese dollar and 1 Shanghai Tael equals 1.39 Chinese dollar.

1933 figure is derived by applying the 1930 ratio of foreign capital to total capital (56%) to the total 1933 capital.

1936 figure is derived by multiplying the number of spindles in 1935 by the 1930 foreign average of $ 88.28 per spindle.

(3) Using 1930 figure for 1931.

1933 figure—in 1931, workers in foreign mills were 45.3% of the total workers; applying the same ratio to the total of 257568 in 1933, the number in foreign mills is therefore 116678.

1936 figure—in 1930 each worker in foreign mills operated 24.14 spindles or 1.1 looms (according to Dr. H. D. Fong's study). Foreign mills had 2518000 spindles in 1935 (Appendix A) and 37528 looms in 1937 (a Reuter report in the Shanghai Daily News, May 1,1939). Using the 1935 and 1937 data for 1936 and applying Dr. Fong's ratio, we calculate the number of workers in 1936 foreign mills at 104,308 spinners plus 34116 weavers or 138424.

(4) According to Dr. Fong's study, the motive power in foreign mills was, in 1930, 0.0484 H. P. per spindle and 0.6673 per loom. We apply this ratio to the number of spindles and looms in 1931 and 1935 – 1937. The 1935, 1937 figure is used for 1936.

1931: 2173998 × 0.0484 plus 13267 × 0.6673 = 114075 H. P.

1936: 2518368 × 0.0484 plus 37528 × 0.6673 = 146931 H. P.

1933: NO loom number is available, the H. P. is derived on the basis of each worker in foreign mills using 1.1097 H. P. (Dr. Fong's study)

116678 × 1.1097 = 129478.

(5) According to Dr. D. K. Lieu's study, each Shanghai worker produced $ 2147.73 in 1933 in Chinese cotton mills (converted into 1936 dollar, $ 2298.07).

Aoording to Dr. Fong's study, each worker produced 9.85 bales of yarn in Chinese mills and 11.95 bales in foreign mills; each weaver produced 261.73 pieces of cloth in Chinese mills and 786.38 in foreign (1930). The ratios Chinese to foreign are 1: 1.214 for spinners and 1: 3.005 for weavers. 88% of all workers were spinners. Hence the efficiency ratio of Chinese to foreign is (1.214 × 88 plus 3.005 × 12) ÷100 = 1.4289

Therefore the value of products is:

1931: 2298.07 × 1.4289 × 90082 = $ 295803146

1933: 2298.07 × 1.4289 × 116678 = $ 383136715

1936: 2298.07 × 1.4289 × 138424 = $ 454544273

The above table includes 4 Japanese mills in Manchuria. For comparison with other tables, the latter are subtracted and the result is as follows:

Foreign-Owned Cotton Textile

Years	No. of factories	Capitalization ($)	Laborers	Motive power	Value of products 1936($)
1931	42	150919917	85470	109012	280658693
1933		192981207	112066	124415	367992244
1936		211821527	133812	141869	439399802

Since no data on Manchurian mills after 1930 is available, the above table is simply the result of subtracting the 1930 Manchurian figures (value of products derived from number of laborers as before) for all the years. Thus the 1936 and 1933 figures may be too large. These figures may also be too large because we used number of spindles as basis, whereas a part of these spindles were idle through the years and especially in 1933 – 1936.

The above estimates are generally very rough. It may be noted that more accurate figures should be obtainable from statistics available now in China.

We assume that there was little or no other foreign textile industry in China, except cotton spinning and weaving.

The next important foreign investment, public utilities, is estimated by Mr. Koh (based on Prof. Remer's figures), at $ 277700000 in 1937. If we assume the same operating picture as for the Chinese electric and water plants, which may be invalid, foreign plants would maintain a labor force of some 12091, have motive power of 576261 H. P. and produce a value of $ 112114000. If this represented the 1936 condition, conditions for 1931 and 1933 would not be much different. The capacity of foreign electric plants, as revealed in Table I , had changed only slightly during that period. The comparison is too tentative, however, because we do not know what kind of plants are included in Mr. Koh's estimates and we know that the Chinese "electric and water supply" figures fail to include telecommunications and some other public utilities included in Prof. Remer's estimates.

For other industries, no figures are available at all. The following table, showing foreign investment ratios in 1928 Shanghai, is very incomplete and is not to be used as basis for further estimates. However, it helps us to get some general idea. As may be seen, considerable amount had been invested in food and chemical industries.

Industrial Investment in Shanghai, 1928

	Chinese		Foreign		
	Amount($)	Per cent	Amount($)	Per cent	Total($)
Textile	45087250	22. 8	152676800	77. 2	197764050
Food	25892760	52. 1	23822200	47. 9	49714960
Chemicals	5418960	73. 3	1976900	26. 7	7395880
Machinery & metal	3058000	96. 1	125000	3. 9	3183000
Printing & paper	12432800	95. 3	615791	4. 7	13048591
Water & electric	8930000	47. 2	10000000	52. 8	18930000
Others	2803010	78. 7	763000	21. 3	3566010
Total	103622800	35. 3	189979691	64. 7	293602491

The condition of foreign-owned industries in China in 1937 is estimated as follows. "Other manufacturing" is based on the investment figures arrived by deducting the estimate in textile from Mr. Koh's estimate and assuming the same operation picture as in the Chinese industry, excluding textile and public utilities. This estimate, however, is very crude and must be taken with caution.

Foreign – Owned Industry in China, 1936

	Capitalization($)	Laborers	Value of products($)
Textile	211821527	133812	439399802
Other Mfg.	864878473	787758	2563491840
Public Util.	277700000	12091	112114000
Total	1354400000	933661	3115005642

VIII   Industry in Manchuria

No statistical information is accessible for industries in Manchuria after 1940.

The pre-1931 data are incomplete except those for the Kwangtung Leased Territory and along the South Manchuria Railway. The writer has been reviewing sources of these Japanese-owned industries as reported by the S. M. Railway in its year books and found results of little help in our present study. A separate report on Manchurian industry 1925 – 1940 will be made, if there is enough time to do it.

Figures for 1940 Manchurian industry in the Kwangtung Leased Territory are shown in Table Ⅷ. This area contained 80% of total industrial investment in Manchuria, 70% of total production value, but only 23% of total industrial employment.

Table Ⅷ　Manchurian Industry, 1940—Kwangtung Leased Area and South Manchurian Railway

Industries	Number of factories	Capitalization 1000 Yens	Staff and laborers	Value of products 1000 Yen
Woodworking	89	3961	795	10668
Metallurgical	154	82689	9049	43667
Machinery	142	20059	6310	34416
Earthware	132	18412	2412	14765
Gas, Electricity, etc.	11	35078	323	16009
Chemicals	177	68376	2829	116738
Textile	98	19511	4090	31867
Printing	101	4526	1168	6246
Foodstuff	353	23030	1625	37070
Others	141	8418	3671	23510
Total	1398	284060	32273	334956

Source: Manchuria, Department of Foreign Information, Manchurian government, 1941.

The small number of "staff and labor" in Table Ⅷ suggests that the Japanese industries were highly modern. Unfortunately we do not have the data on motive power used. Staff, including foremen, of the 1933 Shanghai industry is 7.67% of the total number of employees. By using the same proportion, we find that the

Japanese industries employed only 29798 workers; and each worker produced 11576 yen, while the Shanghai worker produced only 2590 Chinese dollars. On the other hand, the Japanese industries had a larger volume of capital investment, the ratio of value of product to investment being 1. 18; while the ratio was 3. 42 in the 1933 Shanghai industry and 2. 76 in the 1936 Chinese industry.

Industry elsewhere in Manchuria in 1939 is recorded in Table IX. The accuracy of this table is doubtful. They were, according to the table, less developed than Chinese industry. Labor force was comparatively large, 99714 workers and each producing a value of only 1607 yen. The ratio of product value to capital investment is 2. 22.

One Chinese dollar was equal to 1 Japanese yen in 1928, 1. 25903 yen in 1935, 1. 02342 yen in 1936 and 1. 02002 yen in 1937. It is impossible to convert the capital values in Tables VIII and IX into Chinese dollars, because we do not know the new investment made every year. For our purposes, yen in these tables may be assumed as having the same value as a 1936 Chinese dollar.

Table IX Manchuria Industry, 1940

Industries	Number of factories	Capitalization (1000 Yen)	Staff and laborers	Value of products (1000 Yen)
Woodworking and Furnitures	526	1630	6387	5862
Metallurgical	647	2978	7635	15260
Machinery	328	3563	4617	6727
Earthware	405	3833	15522	5560
Chemicals	601	10347	18339	29836
Textile	1139	17387	33389	39232
Printing	275	2706	4859	4799
Foodstuff	711	23913	6708	38137
Others	1773	5561	10541	14781
Total	6497	71918	107997	160194

Source: Manchuria, Department of Foreign Information, Manchurian Government, 1941.

IX Industry in China—Before and After the War

From the foregoing discussions we may estimate total manufacturing industrial forces before the outbreak of Sino-Japanese war in 1937. It must be noted, however, that such an estimate is based on very incomplete data and tentative assumptions.

Industry in China, excluding Manchuria, before the war:

	Capitalization($ 1000)	Labor force	Value of products($ 1000)
Chinese	587763	700300	1620315
Foreign	1354400	933611	3115006
Total	1942163	1633941	4735321

The number of factories was probably in excess of 10000 and motive power in excess of 2000000 H. P.

No reliable estimate is available for the extent of evacuation of industry into interior China after the outbreak of the war. The following table, issued by the Ministry of Economic Affairs, shows factories removed with the help of the Ministry before 1939.

Evacuation of Factories, 1937 – 1939

	No. of Factories	Skilled Workers	Tonnage of raw material and machinery removed
Iron and steel	1	360	1152
Machinery	168	5588	13255
Electric	28	684	5300
Chemicals	54	1376	8093
Textile	92	1603	30822
Food	22	549	3213
Education	31	606	1374
Others	14	270	560
Total	410	11036	63769

According to the table, factories removed were about 17% of the total qualified Chinese factories. Skilled workers evacuated were only 2.2% of the total. Many more workers may have moved without Government help; and many factories also evacuated from Hunan and Kiangsi after 1940. Many of the migrating factories, however, left part of their plants in occupied areas. The total industrial force evacuated, judging from the writer's own impressions, could not be more than 15% of the Chinese-owned industry in 1936.

War damages to industry in occupied areas and its development under the Japanese regime are entirely unknown. At first the writer was inclined to think that the two might counterbalance each other. Latest newspaper reports from Shanghai, however, show that wartime development of industry in occupied China was far from the Japanese propaganda.

Under assumptions stated below, industries in whole China on V-J day may be approximated by the following table.

China's Industries on V-J Day

	No. of factories	Capitalization Million dollars	Labor force	Value of Million dollars
Occupied Area				
Chinese	7100	500	495400	1377
Foreign	2000	1354	933600	3115
Free China	3000	150	200000	350
Manchuria				
Kwangtung & S. M. R.	1400	284	30000	335
Other places	6500	72	100000	160
Total	20000	2360	1759000	5337

Assumptions:

(1) 15% of Chinese-owned industry migrated to interior China, while foreign-owned industry remained unaffected.

(2) War damages to industry in occupied area compensated by the wartime development under the Japanese regime.

(3) Free China figures are based on tentative estimates made by the writer in a previous report.

(4) No growth of Manchurian industries assumed since 1940.

The above estimate represents the available industrial force, or industrial capacity, of China at the end of the war. Not all of it, however, was fully employed at that time. So far as the impact of the Government program, as will be discussed in the next section, is concerned, the writer would suggest the following allowances:

(1) An over-all allowance of 30% obsolescence on the industrial installation in Free China, suggested in the writer's previous report.

(2) A 15% deduction for both Chinese and foreign industries in occupied area, due to obsolescence, depreciation and irreparable war damages.

(3) Exclude industries in the Kwangtung Leased Territory and along the South Manchuria Railway, whose Control in the near future is subject to question.

Making these adjustments in the above table, we derive the following results:

Industry in China Before Launching of Government Industrial Program

	No. of factories	Capitalization Million dollars	Labor force	Value of product Million dollars
Chinese	7035	530	563600	1426
Foreign	1700	1141	793600	2647
Manchuria	6500	72	100000	160
Total	15235	1743	1457200	4233

"Chinese" includes Free China. Notice that the Manchuria figures do not reflect any growth after 1940, nor allow for industrial installations removed by U. S. S. R.

X   Government Reconstruction Program and Chinese Industry

Some details of the revised N. R. C. program are summarized in Appendix G. This summary was prepared by Mrs. Sze. This program, if fully carried out, would establish a new industrial force at the end of five years as follows:

N. R. C. Program at the End of Five Years

	No. of units	Capital invest. ($ 1000)	Operating capital ($ 1000)	Laborers ($ 1000)	Value of products ($ 1000)
Chemicals	96	1050920	152618	44900	918560
Consumer's goods	?	3913197	2390744	974518	5614716
Communication equip.	20	650200	1069800	44000 *	732100
Electric equip.	50	512686	189488	90054	614400 **
Machinery Mfg.	37	620068	296520	44532	658150
Electric supply	59	2246000	106600	16500	500000 ***
Total mfg.	262	8993071	4205770	1214504	9037926
Mining&metallurgical		2886751	706916	556772	1607001
Grand total		11879828	4912686	1771276	10644927

Compiled from the revised summary of the program. The totals are not all in agreement with the sum of separate plans.

* Not including workers in airplane plants.

** No value given in the revised program. This figure is the value given in the first program, which would produce almost the same quantity as would the revised program.

*** No value given in the revised program. This figure is derived from the first program, where 2344000 KW is to be generated and the value given is $ 640000000. The revised program would generate 1988000 KW.

As will be seen, the new proposed investment is more than 5 times as large as the total industrial capital before the launching of the program (excluding metallurgical and mining); while new value produced would be only more than twice the original level. New employment would be as large as in the old industry. In other words, the N. R. C. program would more than double the size of industry in China in five years.

Less than half of the new proposed investment would be in industries producing "consumer's goods". The amount, $ 3913 million, is three times the old investment in consumer's goods industry, if the latter is estimated at $ 1315 million (This is arrived by deducting Chinese and foreign investment in public utilities, less percentages evacuated and obsoleted, from the total of $ 1743 million, and less 8. 2% invested in industries producing capital goods.) The new investment of $ 3913 million is not necessarily to be all Government investment.

Where the revised N. R. C. plan is not the final blueprint, another plan, known as the Two Billion Dollar Loan Plan, is more likely to be the practicable program. Items of this recent plan are summarized in Appendix H. This plan gives only the amount of "cost of imported equipments" in U. S. dollars, no domestic capital figures are included.

The whole program of the Two Billion Dollars Plan runs as follows:

Cost of imported equipment	
Transportation & communication	U. S. $ 781434000
Industry	
Mining & metallurgy	314000000
Chemicals & basic processing	105255000
Electrical goods mfg.	77500000
Mechanical & transportation equip.	117850000
Mfg. of consumer goods	91870000
Electric Power	98300000
Materials & supplies	45076000
Total industry	849851000
Modernization of transportation & industry in Manchuria	160000000
Modernization of transportation & industry in Taiwan	40000000
Planning & engineering service in U. S. A.	35000000
Training in U. S. A.	12000000
Freight cost	130000000
Total program	2008335000

For comparison with our study, the 53 items of industrial program in Appendix H are regrouped in Table X (first column). [1] Since the program does not show the amount of domestic capital required to go with the imported equipment, domestic investment is estimated by applying the ratios for each

---

[1] Tel. & Tel. equip. , Radio & Broadcasting, Wire&Cables, are taken out of "machinery" and put into "communication instrument." Vegetable oil is put in "foodstuff", though the oil is not all for food. Soap and the difference of $ 5000000 in consumer goods (see note of Appendix H) are put in "miscellaneous." "Metallurgical" does not include coal, petroleum, iron ore, and non-ferrous mining and refining.

industry of domestic and foreign capital requirements in the revised N. R. C. plan. The amounts for each industry are shown in the third column of Table X. Together with the equivalent of Chinese dollars of the "import cost", the total amount of investment is shown in the last column of Table X. The total amount of the whole industrial program is, therefore, 3607790000 Chinese dollars of 1936 value.

Table X   The Two Billion Dollars Loan Plan
(1000 US$ or 1936 CH$)

Industries	Import cost (US$)	Equivalent of (CH$ *)	Domestic capital (CH$)	Total Capital (CH$)
Woodworking	670	2144	3477	5621
Furniture	—	—	—	—
Metallurgical	124000	396800	195920	592720
Machinery&metallic ware	86350	276320	239080(1)	515400
Communication instrument	109000	348800	128620(2)	477420
Stone, cement, brick, etc.	8200	26240	176300	202540
Water & elect. supply	98300	314560	191685(3)	506245
Construction material	—	—	—	—
Chemical.	79655	254896	166478	421374
Textile	62900	201280	383690	584970
Clothing & attire	—	—	—	—
Leather & rubber	3500	11200	10500(4)	21700
Foodstuff	16900	54080	49010(5)	103090
Paper & printing	18300	58560	46750(6)	105310
Apparatuses, ornaments	—	—	—	—
Miscellaneous	7000	22400	49000(7)	71400
Total	614775 **	1967280	1640510	3607790

* At 1 US$ equal to 3.2 CH$.

** This figure is $5000000 less than the original plan, due to an error in the items of consumer goods, see Appendix H, note. (1) Using ratio of elect. mfg. plus machinery. (2) Omit aeroplanes, as the plan does not contain. (3) Elect. plants only, as the plan includes no water supply. (4) Rubber only, as the plan includes no leather. (5) Omit rice finishing, as not included in the plan. (6) Using ratio of total paper and rayon, as no separate data are available. (7) Using ratio of total consumer goods.

US$ 45076000 of "materials and supplies" are omitted in the total figures.

This amount is about 9 times as large as total of Chinese-owned industrial investment in the 1933 survey, about 5.5 times as large as the revised Chinese-owned capitalization figure in 1937, and almost double the amount of total Chinese and foreign industrial capitalization (excluding Manchuria) before the launching of the program, as estimated in the last section. Some figures are listed for comparison as follows:

Industrial capital, Excluding Manchuria

New investment, as per N. R. C. revised plan	CH $ 8993071000 (excl. metallurgy)
New investment, as per 2 – Billion dollars plan	3607790000
Chinese-owned, 1933 survey	406873000 (1933 $)
Chinese-owned, 1933, incl. small factory, est.	427216000 (1933 $)
Chinese-owned, 1936, incl. small factory, est.	587763000 (1936 $)
Chinese-owned, revised est. , 1937	627813000 (1933 – 1936 $)
Foreign-owned, est. , 1936	1354400000
Foreign & Chinese, est. on V-J day	2004000000 (1936 $)
Foreign & Chinese est. , before the launching of the program, after obsolescence, depreciation, irreparable war damages	1671000000 (1936 $)

Comparison for individual industries is given in Table XI. The table shows that heavy industries, according to the program, would be increased more greatly than light industries. New investment in metallurgical industry would be more than 200 times as large as the amount (Chinese) in 1933, and in textile industry only 5 times, and in foodstuff only 1.5 times.

The value produced by these new establishments can hardly be estimated. These new plants, with only 11% of their total investment in producing consumer goods, certainly would operate at a less profitable level than the existing industries. The production value estimated in the revised N. R. C. plan is $ 9037926000 for an investment of $ 8993071000 at the end of five years. The value produced in the Two Billion Dollars Loan Plan, judging by the same estimate, would be around $ 3626000000.

Table XI   Chinese Industrial Capital

Industries	New investment 1000 1936 CH$ Table X	1933 Survey 1000 1933 CH$ Table Ⅳ	1933 Estimates 1000 1933 CH$ Table V	Revised 1937 estimate 1000 CH$ (current) Table Ⅶ
Woodworking	5621	1115	1171	1115
Furniture	—	420	441	382
Metallurgical	592720	2691	2826	9801
Machinery&metallic ware	515400	16550	17378	17693
Communication instrument	477420	19004	19954	2339
Stone, cement, brick, etc.	202540	29184	30643	37807
Construction material	—	298	313	298
Water&electric supply	506245	32614	34245	134203
Chemicals	421374	26327	27643	49146
Textile	584970	116828	175169	195627
Clothing&attire	—	6006	6306	6006
Leather&rubber	21700	6340	6657	10712
Foodstuff	103090	68380	71799	126092
Paper&printing	105310	27877	29271	33353
Apparatuses, ornaments	—	812	853	812
Miscellaneous	71400	2426	2547	2426
Total	3607790	406873	427216	627813

Estimated 1936 figure: 587763 (1936 CH$ Table Ⅶ).

Estimated foreign-owned: 1354400 (1936 CH$).

Estimated V-J day total: 2004000 Total Chinese & foreign (1936 CH$).

Estimated 1946: 1671000 (Chinese & foreign, after obsolescence, depreciation, irreparable war damage, etc.).

The 1967280000 CH$ of the "import cost" would be Government-owned investment, but we do not know whether the $1640510000 domestic capital required in the program would come from Government or private sources. Chinese Government owned about $120000000 industrial capital, as part of the estimated $2004000000 as of V-J day.[①] The percentage of total was about only 6% and excluding foreign-owned, about 20%. If private industrial investment (Chinese)

---

① The figure of Government-owned industry is inferred from the tables given in the writer's previous report on Free China industry.

would increase 50% for the five years after the war (the percentage is assumed from their rate of increase for the five years before the war), if half of the $ 1640510000 domestic capital required in the program would have to be met by Government sources, and if the program would be completed in five years, then at the end of the program Government would own about 60% of total Chinese-owned industrial investment.

Appendix:

Appendix A   Number of Cotton Textile Spindles in China

Year	Chinese		Japanese		British		Total	
	Amount	Index	Amount	Index	Amount	Index	Amount	Index
1913	651676	100. 00	233448	100. 00	97688	100. 00	982912	100. 00
1915	687964	105. 57	307048	131. 53	153320	156. 95	1148332	116. 84
1920	1358552	208. 47	540752	231. 64	153320	156. 95	2052624	208. 85
1925	2256624	346. 28	1636156	700. 87	153320	156. 95	4046100	411. 69
1930	2395792	367. 64	1674844	717. 44	153320	156. 95	4233956	429. 78
1931	2730790	419. 04	2033388	858. 17	170610	174. 65	4904788	499. 06
1932	2773273	425. 56	2063448	883. 90	183196	187. 53	5019917	510. 77
1933	2885796	442. 83	2098176	898. 78	187628	192. 07	5171600	526. 20
1934	2951436	452. 00	2242624	960. 65	197628	192. 07	5381688	547. 58
1935	3008479	461. 65	2284860	978. 74	233508	239. 03	5526847	562. 35

Source: Reproduced from Dr. D. K. Lieu, *Analysis of Shanghai Industrialization*, based on data from H. D. Fong, *Chinese Cotton Textile Industry*, 1931 – 1935 figures are calculated by the Bureau of National Economic Research.

Appendix B   Shanghai Industry, 1928 – 1934

Industries	Survey of	No. of Factories	Capitalization ($ 1000)	Laborers
1. Woodworking				
	1928	?	?	?
	1929	23	?	1886
	1931(a)	16	102	503
	1931(b)	22	407 *	985
	1933	10	612	789
	1934	68	9150(39)	4011(52)
2. Furniture				
	1928	?	?	?
	1929	?	?	?
	1931(a)	16	575	1273
	1931(b)	17	836	1588

Industries	Survey of	No. of Factories	Capitalization ($ 1000)	Laborers
	1933	7	379	994
	1934	?	?	?
3. Metallurgical				
	1928	47	121	930
	1929	100	?	1449
	1931 (a)	41	209	824
	1931 (b)	36	375	803
	1933	22	361	787
	1934	489	1089	5498 (355)
4. Machine Manufacture & Metallic Wares				
	1928	241	2899	8085
	1929	418	?	8812
	1931 (a)	342	4447	10729
	1931 (b)	288	3637 *	10171
	1933	173	7,780	11722
	1934	1519	9379 *	23690 (946)
5. Communication Instrument				
	1928	2	38	137
	1929	13	?	6248
	1931 (a)	20	366	2382
	1931 (b)	21	459 *	3495
	1933	17	533 *	3704
	1934	88	8978 (26)	8036 (47)
6. Glass , Cement , Bricks , Earthware , Etc.				
	1928	37	2044	1411
	1929	30	?	3043
	1931 (a)	38	3,207	2620
	1931 (b)	44	3406 *	2910
	1933	41	4038 *	3691
7. Construction-material				
	1928	?	?	?
	1929	?	?	?
	1931 (a)	?	?	?
	1931 (b)	5	70 *	195
	1933	7	165 *	438
	1934	?	?	?

Continued table

Industries	Survey of	No. of Factories	Capitalization ($ 1000)	Laborers
8. Electric&Water Supply				
	1928	8	8930	1781
	1929	?	?	?
	1931 (a)	5	11260	1079
	1931 (b)	5	11260	1079
	1933	3	11290	1020
	1934	13	88010 (10)	5258 (9)
9. Chemicals				
	1928	77	2986	5564
	1929	59	?	6101
	1931 (a)	92	9581	6885
	1931 (b)	60	9394	7564 *
	1933	78	15200 *	9246
	1934	209	15891 (144)	10097 (175)
10. Textile				
	1928	406	44169	167561
	1929	471	?	201933
	1931 (a)	540	55816	130647
	1931 (b)	546	54743 *	129252 *
	1933	391	63624 *	120165
	1934	1006	269271 (542)	147093 (823)
11. Clothing&Attire				
	1928	130	1585	8026
	1929	102	?	8625
	1931 (a)	253	6886	20467
	1931 (b)	170	4455 *	11177
	1933	89	4974	10605
	1934	473	6670 (275)	17264 (369)
12. Leather&Rubber				
	1928	18	1132	554
	1929	150	?	1850
	1931 (a)	36	838	1743
	1931 (b)	57	3227 *	8556
	1933	55	5064 *	11832
	1934	132	351 (83)	13345 (117)

Industries	Survey of	No. of Factories	Capitalization ($ 1000)	Laborers
13. Foodstuff				
	1928	198	15867	15009
	1929	103	?	31815
	1931 (a)	178	28552	21055
	1931 (b)	175	32001 *	23336 *
	1933	143	31093 *	27375
	1934	323	39248 (221)	35872 (255)
14. Paper&Printing				
	1928	238	12510	11042
	1929	226	?	11890
	1931 (a)	154	32186	7541
	1931 (b)	155	16889 *	10692
	1933	114	16073 *	9786
	1934	577	22509 (293)	15839 (385)
15. Apparatuses , ornament				
	1928	18	253	308
	1929	?	?	?
	1931 (a)	37	483	861
	1931 (b)	39	453	1071
	1933	18	625	1062
	1934	124	2233	2354 (104)
16. Miscellaneous				
	1928	?	?	?
	1929	?	?	?
	1931 (a)	115	1404	3439
	1931 (b)	32	707 *	1278
	1933	18	874 *	1520
	1934	262	2100 (117)	5067 (148)

Figures in parentheses are the number of factories included in the figure of capitalization or laborers.

＊Incomplete original data.

For the various surveys and other remarks, see the notes to Table XI.

Appendix C Value of Imported Machines, Tools, Parts and
Railway Materials, 1912 – 1938

Year		Total of Machines, tools, parts, rails.	Grand total in pound sterling	Cumulative totals pound sterling
1912	Tls.	9319247	642911	
1913	"	15530757	2319629	
1914	"	20790804	1071735	
1915	"	10401319	1041440	5075715
1916	"	26243616	3913959	8989676
1917	"	13718006	2743783	11733459
1918	"	15629918	3907733	15641193
1919	"	40428298	12129223	27770416
1920	"	40039310	12013377	39783794
1921	"	93072857	13965361	53749156
1922	"	77814209	11675341	65424497
1923	"	38153846	5723991	71148488
1924	"	36515494	5478531	76627019
1925	"	27922196	4189027	80816047
1926	"	31680385	4752239	85568286
1927	"	35176703	3519108	89087395
1928	"	38784109	3880172	92967567
1929	"	49470519	4948662	97916230
1930	"	66590873	3332509	101248739
1931	"	68066525	3405152	104653891
1932	"	41415591	2071168	106725059
1933	$	14199957	2210633	108935692
1934	"	81858053	4094309	113030001
1935	"	89821933	4493249	117523251
1936	"	106464922	5324299	122847550
1937	"	93576134	4679708	127527268
1938	"	61675052	3084395	130611657

Tls. – Haikwan taels $ – Chinese yuan

Source: "Problems of Economic Reconstruction in China," Part V; Capital Stock in China, by Tso-Fan Koh, Eighth Conference of The Institute of Pacific Relations, Dec. 1942, China Council.

**Appendix D   Chinese Industrial Capital Invested
in the Production of Capital Goods in 1933
(Factories qualified by the Chinese Factory Law)**

Category	Number of factories	Capital invested	Value of products (Principal products)
Metal Industries			
Founding: machines and parts	24	132750	655937. 89
Boilers and pipes	5	5800	325110. 00
Steel refining	3	2400000	2508640. 00
	32	2590750	3489687. 98
Machines and tools			
Printing machines	9	108000	424414. 74
Knitting machines	10	67500	199799. 57
Spinning and weaving machines	21	424500	1678200. 29
Prime movers	22	467600	1688173. 38
Various machines	41	5585276	9382638. 20
Axes, etc.	1	95000	72000. 00
Knitting needles	11	29600	154653. 61
Faucets, valves, etc.	4	56500	635282. 20
Various spare parts and repairs	25	224745	1135334. 33
	144	7058721	15370496. 32
Electric machinery			
Electric machines and apparatuses	5	144790	497400. 00
Electric machines and batteries	1	500000	170000. 00
	6	644790	667400. 00
Foundry Works			
Spinning and weaving machines	5	175000	519005. 00
Prime movers and various kind of machines	11	232240	1306072. 05
Various kinds of machines	22	471120	1474376. 11
Spare parts and repairs	9	2635867	265445. 51
	47	3514227	3564898. 67
Transport			

Continued table

Category	Number of factories	Capital invested	Value of products (Principal products)
Shipbuildings	5	1331314	4976283. 02
Shipbuilding and other		1380000	2440000. 00
Ship repairs	9	115486	748822. 40
Railroad repairs	22	16665304	10865592. 66
Other vehicles:			
Tramcars	1	300000	65178. 05
Motor vehicle spare parts	3	53000	199313. 52
Motor vehicle repairs	2	63857	253075. 90
Bicycles	4	71000	976339. 70
Charcoal gas trucks	1	20000	144000. 00
Bicycle parts	3	4450	58533. 30
	50	20004411	20727138. 55
Grand Total	279	33812899	43819621. 45

Source: the National Survey of Industries in 1933 Appeared in "Problems of Economic Reconstruction in China," China Council, Institute of Pacific Relations, Eighth conference, December 1942.

Appendix E　Chinese Industry, 1931 – 1936

Years	Number of factories	Capitalization ($ 1000 1936 Yuan)	Laborers	Motive Powers [*]	Value of products ($ 1000 1936 Yuan)
Textile Industry					
1931	1514	172248	300827	228394	500711
1932	1686	180120	314592	238845	523623
1933	1929	187430	335744	254904	558829
1934	2214	201112	354546	269179	590123
1935	2670	256592	415315	315316	691271
1936	2899	260340	430760	327042	716978
Foodstuffs Industry					
1931	649	71524	46777	48252	361440
1932	736	72369	48183	49703	372304
1933	917	76825	54077	55783	417850
1934	1085	78131	57213	59018	442085

Continued table

Years	Number of factories	Capitalization ($ 1000 1936 Yuan)	Laborers	Motive Powers [*]	Value of products ($ 1000 1936 Yuan)
Foodstuffs Industry					
1935	1098	79514	60674	62589	468828
1936	1529	81435	64754	66884	501002
Machinery&metallic ware industry					
1931	704	13350	15979	9890	25150
1932	535	16307	20106	12445	31647
1933	719	18594	24137	14940	37991
1934	841	20621	26333	16300	41448
1935	1013	22276	29737	18406	46805
1936	1390	24079	38402	23770	60444
Chemical Industry					
1931	283	25910	25107	9861	46860
1932	304	27093	28676	11263	53522
1933	348	29578	30768	12085	57427
1934	397	32506	33845	13294	63170
1935	437	33926	35660	14007	66558
1936	476	34813	37660	14792	70291
E1ectric & water supply					
1931	33	35176	1513	66474	14606
1932	33	35176	1513	66474	14606
1933	33	36642	1576	69244	15215
1934	33	39207	1686	74091	16280
1935	33	43970	1891	83093	18258
1936	33	52032	2238	98326	21605
Other Industries					
1931	1544	94004	88055	100977	173997
1932	1598	97246	91092	104459	179996
1933	1775	108051	101213	116065	199996
1934	1846	112373	105261	120708	207996
1935	2095	127500	119431	136957	235995
1936	2219	135064	126516	145081	249995
TOTAL					
1931	4727	412212	478258	463848	1122764
1932	4892	428311	504162	483189	1175698

Continued table

Years	Number of factories	Capitalization ($ 1000 1936 Yuan)	Laborers	Motive Powers*	Value of products ($ 1000 1936 Yuan)
TOTAL					
1933	5721	457120	547515	523021	1287308
1934	6416	483950	578884	552518	1361102
1935	7346	563715	662708	630008	1527715
1936	8546	587763	700330	675895	1620315

Note: Based on Table V, see text. Inclusive of Chinese-owned factories which use motive power or employ 10 or more workers. Excluding Manchuria.

* Including motive engines and motors using electric power supplied by electric plants.

Appendix F   Foreign Cotton Textile Industry 1930

	Chinese	Japanese	British	Total
Number of factories	81	43	3	127
	63.8%	33.9%	2.36%	100%
Capital and reserves	$ 126908222	$ 148919916	$ 12500000	$ 288328138
	44.0%	51.6%	4.4%	100%
Spindles	2395792	1674844	153320	4233956
	56.7%	39.7%	3.6%	100%
Looms	16005	11367	1900	29272
	54.7%	38.8%	6.5%	100%
Motive power H. P.				
Motors	91606	78003		169,609
	54.0%	46.0%	?	100%
Motive engines	31021	7490	?	38511
	80.6%	19.4%		100%
Laborers	161949	77082	13000	202031
	64.3%	30.6%	5.2%	100%
Yarn produced(Bales)	1500248	825407	129522	2455177
	61.1%	33.6%	5.3%	100%
Cloth produced(Pieces)	6625544	8153944	?	14779538
	44.8%	55.2%		100%

Source: Chinese Cotton Mills Association, as quoted in Dr. H. D. Fong, *Chinese Cotton Textile Industry*, in Chinese.

Appendix G Summary of Revised N. R. C. Five – Year Plan

Industry	Construction							Operation					
	Capital Requirement		Personnel Requirement – Yr with Greatest Demand					Production Capacity – 5th Year		Personnel Requirement – 5th Year			
	Domestic(CH$)	US(US$)	Managerial	Technical	Skilled	Unskilled		Quantity(Unit)	Value(CH$)	Managerial	Technical	Skilled	Unskilled
Coal	232000000	23290000	930	1395	7854	11773		100000000 Ton	450753000	11695	7940	87470	131000
Iron & Steel	444760000	278600000	950	1450	7500	5850		3328000 Ton	396193200	1775	2725	10900	18800
Non-ferrous Metals	79412000	97090000	808	650	3650	12250		137500 Ton	108628000	938	950	2360	20372
Special Metals	113705800	36593000	1095	693	18438	19842		44500 Ton	73979000	4845	2199	45390	63510
Precious Metals	150000000	4400000	15000	12000	15000	150000		1000000 Tael	120000000	15000	12000	15000	150000
Liquid Fuels	99135000	112445000	930	2976	923	6736		2184437 Ton	457448205	2899	1471	3710	8260
Mining Metallurey, Refining: Total	1119012800	552418000	19713	19164	53365	206451			1607001405	37152	27285	164830	391942
Sulfur and Products	40800000	27000000	48	136	120	600		550000 Ton	91540000	240	680	600	3000
Phosphorus and Products	15000000	5200000	16	55	18	80		216000 Ton	42777000	80	300	100	500
Salts and Products	28600000	20000000	42	88	71	420		415000 Ton	63600000	220	500	380	2200
Electric Furnace products	35100000	20000000	34	72	42	167		107000 Ton	62280000	200	400	250	1000
Pigments	42600000	14200000	56	116	60	200		100000 Ton	66450000	280	580	300	1000
Coal Tar	14200000	5800000	34	47	36	240		86000 Ton	36642000	170	240	180	1200
Wood Distillation Products	8100000	3000000	12	24	24	115		26800 Ton	42723150	80	160	160	800
Fermentation Products	3900000	3000000	19	50	23	217		41000 Ton	13545000	120	300	140	1300
Synthetic products	4500000	6000000	50	127	63	475		23000 Ton	27786000	400	1000	500	3800
Synthetic oil From Coal	24000000	8000000	82	118	270	730		300000 Ton	37500000	328	472	1080	2920
Cement	14420000	6000000	60	180	60	534		12770000 Barrel	19155000	440	1320	440	4000
Glass	4500000	1800000	12	24	15	54		150000 Ton	9900000	60	120	90	300
Rubber products	64500000	21500000	50	131	50	550		3400000 Piece	127500000	400	1000	400	4400
Natural Colloids	25500000	9000000	75	151	85	450		42000 Ton	58362000	300	600	340	1800
Synthetic Colloids	30000000	12000000	35	73	100	375		22000 Ton	66000000	280	560	800	3000
Explosives	30000000	24000000	55	138	88	190		50000 Ton	108000000	440	1058	700	1520
Dyestuffs	30000000	12000000	84	171	117	834		9000 Ton	44800000	500	1002	700	5000
Chemical Industries: Total	415720000	198500000	764	1701	1242	6241			918560150	4538	10292	7160	37740

Industry	Construction							Operation					
	Capital Requirement		Personnel Requirement – Yr with Greatest Demand					Production Capacity – 5th Year		Personnel Requirement – 5th Year			
	Domestic(CH$)	US(US$)	Managerial	Technical	Skilled	Unskilled		Quantity(Unit)	Value(CH$)	Managerial	Technical	Skilled	Unskilled
Textile	1110000000	131751000	903	1310	1210	11841		—	2133026000	4701	2358	53470	96684
Leather & Fur	32000000	5000000	800	120	1200	24000		—	211000000	939	193	2200	15000
Sugar	82000000	30000000	10000	3400	19400	76600		950000 Ton	108500000	5000	4004	20000	70000
Fats & oils	44750000	6250000	810	1550	2700	8100		5000000 Ton	1000000000	500	800	3550	10000
Ceramics	1041487000	41937000	10400	3614	41524	128088		3124250 Ton	577370000	10400	3614	41524	128088
Lumber	28415000	5472830	643	705	542	4955		2201000000 Cubic Meter	39878000	1688	632	46288	117914
Paper & Rayon	180000000	72000000	15000	11000	41000	100000		1342000 Ton	428900000	15000	11000	31000	100000
Flour	56000000	25880000	1640	1040	8400	23600		200000000 Bag	600000000	4880	1280	6600	18600
Rice	8000000		900	100	5500	12500		30000000 Shin Picul	194400000	900	100	5500	12500
Printing	68000000	23000000	1501	702	25000	50000		800000 Ton	174000000	2501	1404	50000	100000
Cold Storage & Canning	9500000	480000	1130	1446	2342	4300		—	146640000	2490	2220	8000	12000
Light Industries ; Total	2660152000	381770830	43527	24987	148818	443984			5614714000	48999	27605	268132	680786
Locomotives & Cars	26600000	17000000	1305	995	15000	5300		6500 Piece	141820000	195	255	3800	2000
Automobiles	62000000	62000000	360	360	2000	400		37500 Piece	225000000	1200	1200	21000	1600
Ships	7040000	2200000	850	770	11000	5600		90000 Ton	36000000	850	770	11000	5600
Aeroplanes		92100000	209	237	6989	719		3700 * Piece	329280000	147	198	4084	416
Transportation Equipment Ind. ; Total	95640000	173300000	2724	2362	34989	12019			762100000	2392	2423	39884	9616
Electric Power	854000000	435000000	2138	2495	8250	8250		1988000 K. W.	350019208 **	7017	3760	4290	17160
Electrical Equipment	173956000	105788000	818	2406	11149	10747		—	600000000 ***	5511	7521	52148	37906
Elec. Power & Equip. Ind. ; Total	1027956000	540788000	3056	4901	19399	18997			850019208	12528	11281	56438	55066
machinery	204348000	129912500	2073	4595	28522	16010		—	658150000	3353	7532	68400	35300
Grand Total	5522828800	1986687330	71857	57710	286335	703702			10510544763	108962	86418	604844	1210450

∗ Complete Planes – 700 ; Motors – 3000.

∗∗ Estimated from rate given in original plan.

∗∗∗ Rough approximation derived from original plan.

Appendix H   The Two Billion Dollars Loan Plan

Industries	No. of establish.	Cost of Imported equipment(US$)	Capacity in Units Expected Or Dollar Values
Mining&metallurgy			
1. Petroleum	5	100000000	407000 tons
2. Coal	20	46000000	30000000 tons
3. Iron ore	4	5000000	1500000 tons
4. Iron&steel(Tayeh)	1	88000000	550000 tons
5. Non-ferrous mining&refining	4	39000000	
6. Refractories	1	1000000	5000 tons
7. Aluminum	1	35000000	20000 tons
Sub-total	36	314000000	
Chemicals & basic processing			
8. Fertilizers&related products	4	44400000	
9. Chlorine products&inorganic chemicals	1	6250000	
10. Organic chemicals&carbide	1	19600000	
11. Alcohol	1	1500000	
12. Rayon	1	8400000	
13. Paper	9	18300000	
14. Rubber	2	3000000	
15. Cement	2	3800000	
Sub-total	21	105255000	
Manufacture-Electrical goods & equipment			
16. Electrical equipment	1	35000000	US $ 35000000
17. Tel. &Tel. equipment	1	7000000	8000000
18. Radio&broadcast equip.	1	14000000	12000000
19. Wire&cables	1	12000000	12000000
20. Insulating material	1	4000000	5000000
21. Batteries	1	2500000	4500000
22. Lamp bulbs	2	3000000	80000000
Sub-total	8	77500000	156500000
Manufacture-Mechanical&transportation equip.			
23. Medium & light machine tools	1	8000000	US $ 10000000
24. Machine tools&industrial equip.	1	6000000	6000000
25. Small tool&band tool	1	3500000	5000000
26. Automotive equipment	1	24000000	20000 trucks
27. Diesel&steam engines and compressors	1	6000000	8000000

Continued table

Industries	No. of establish.	Cost of Imported equipment (US$)	Capacity in Units Expected Or Dollar Values
28. Turbines. pumps and heavy machinery	1	6000000	8000000
29. Boiler works	1	4500000	6000000
30. Textile machinery	1	6000000	7000000
31. Agricultural equipment	3	1500000	2500 tons
32. Well-drilling equipment	1	350000	
33. Locomotive works	1	23500000	800 Locomo.
34. Railroad car works	2	16500000	9000 freight cars 1000 passenger cars
35. Shipbuilding workers	1	12000000	80000 D/W ton
Sub-total	14	117850000	
Manufacture-consumer goods			
36. Soap	4	2000000	4000 tons
37. Cane sugar	3	3700000	90000 tons
38. Flour mills	17	9200000	600000 tons
39. Cotton textile	40	50000000	1000000 spindles
40. Wool textile	10	6000000	50000 spindles
41. Basic spinning and weaving	10	6000000	20000 spindles
42. Cordage&twine	3	900000	2400 tons
43. Glass	3	2400000	15000 tons
44. Wood planing&saw mill	3	370000	100000 board ft/day
45. Wood pressing plants	2	300000	3000 Cu. ft/day
46. Brick plants	4	1000000	100000 bricks/day
47. Earthware	2	600000	4000000 pieces
48. Porcelain ware	2	400000	
49. Salt	1	1500000	60000 tons
50. Vegetable oil	6	2500000	60000 tons
Sub-total	110	91870000 *	
Electric power			
Generating plants		54000000	605000 KW
Transmission system		22800000	
Distribution system		21500000	
Sub-total		98300000	
Materials & supplies			
Chemical		3000000	
Iron, steel		13640000	

Continued table

Industries	No. of establish.	Cost of Imported equipment(US$)	Capacity in Units Expected Or Dollar Values
Copper & aluminum		14136000	
Building		5400000	
Factory stock room supplies		4400000	
Factory-truck, pump, etc.		4500000	
Sub-total		45076000	
TOTAL MINING & INDUSTRY		849851000 *	
Manchuria			
Steel		26000000	
Coal		9000000	
Heavy industrial equipment		9000000	
Shipyard		10000000	
Aluminum and magnesium		8000000	
Paper and pulp		9000000	
Agricultural processing		6000000	
Textile		7000000	
Vegetable oil		6000000	
Chemicals		24000000	
Transportation		40000000	
Power plants		6000000 160000000	
Taiwan			
Sugar		18000000	
Aluminum		4000000	
Food processing		4000000	
Transportation and communication		10000000	
Power plants		4000000 40000000	
TOTAL MANCHURIA AND TAIWAN		200000000	

* There is a difference of 5000000 in the items of consumer goods and their sub-total in the original data, as the sub-total agrees with the grand total, we have no means to correct it. Based on a program titled "Initial Reconstruction Program for China," August 1945.

A Preliminary Report
on Industries in Free China [*]

I Statistical Tables on Principal Industries in Free China

The following tables on the wartime industry in Free China, are compiled from official statistics, and are limited to 11 kinds of industries in the principal industrial districts of Szechwan, Yunnan, Kweichow, Shensi, Kansu and Chungking municipality. The total size and output of Free China industry is estimated in section Ⅲ.

All dollar figures used in this report, unless otherwise specified, are Chinese national currency (Yuan).

Table Ⅰ   Principal Industries in Free China: A Summary, October 1944

	Units	Total	State-Operated		Private-Operated	
			Amount	%	Amount	%
No. of Factories	Million	1106	146	13. 2	960	86. 8
Capital	CH$	2313	1168	50. 5	1144	49. 5
Laborers	Persons	112787	53417	47. 4	59370	52. 6
Prime Movers [*]	H. P.	53046	21095	39. 8	31951	60. 2

---

[*] This report was accomplished as a research report for Nobel Laureate Simon Kuznets when the author was working for the research as an assistant, in 1946 on New York.

546

Continued table

	Units	Total	State-Operated		Private-Operated	
			Amount	%	Amount	%
Max. Capacity (Annual)						
Iron & Steel	M. T.	158523	123690	77. 9	34 833	22. 1
Cotton Yarn	Bales **	195092	91953	47. 1	103139	52. 9
Flour	1000 Bags	4568	153	3. 4	4416	96. 6
Alcohol & Gasoline Sub-stitutes	1000 Gallons	25751	8134	31. 5	17618	68. 5
Chemicals ***	Boxes	362548	1062	0. 3	361486	99. 7
Power Engines	H. P.	15448	7765	50. 9	7483	48. 2
Machine Tools	Pieces	6301	703	11. 1	5598	88. 9
Mining						
Concessions	No.	473	19	4. 0	454	96. 0
Area	1000 Acres	7429	3389	45. 6	4040	54. 4
Annual Production Coal	1000 M. T.	6253	775	12. 4	5478	81. 6
Electric Power generated in 1943	KWH	828122	32370	14. 2	195742	85. 8

* Including steam engines, Diesel engines, gas engines, water wheel engines and other power engines.

** One bale is equal to 400 pounds.

*** Acids and alkali.

Source: Computed from *Statistical Abstract of the Republic of China*, 1945, Chinese Government. Compiled by the Ministry of Economic Affairs from data of registration of factories and mines.

Table Ⅱ   Principal Industries in Free China, October 1944

Industries	Total	State-Operated Amount		Private-Operated Amount	
		Amount	(%)	Amount	(%)
Metallurgical					
Capital (1000 $)	662090	555240	84. 0	106850	16. 0
Personnel *	33235	23329	70. 2	9906	29. 8
Prime Movers ** H. P.	13311	9043	67. 6	4268	32. 4
Capacity [1] M. T.	158523	123690	77. 9	34833	22. 1

Continued table

Industries	Total	State-Operated Amount		Private-Operated Amount	
		Amount	(%)	Amount	(%)
Machinery Mfg.					
Capital (1000 $)	492320	205960	41. 9	286360	58. 1
Personnel *	27796	7611	28. 5	20185	71. 5
Prime Movers ** H. P.	8779	1928	23. 1	6851	76. 9
Capacity (2) H. P.	15448	7965	50. 8	7483	48. 2
(3) Piece	6301	703	11. 1	5598	88. 9
Electric Appliances					
Capital (1000 $)	132770	51240	38. 4	81530	61. 6
Personnel *	6666	3769	56. 7	2897	43. 3
Prime Movers ** H. P.	2019	659	30. 0	1360	70. 0
Capacity (4) KVA	4695	1600	34. 1	3095	65. 9
(5) H. P.	9713	5000	51. 5	4713	48. 5
Acid & Alkali					
Capital (1000 $)	107190	14710	14. 0	92480	86. 0
Personnel *	3523	421	1. 1	3102	98. 9
Prime Movers ** H. P.	379	30	0. 8	349	99. 2
Capacity (6) Boxes	362548	1062	0. 3	361486	99. 7
Alcohol					
Capital (1000 $)	254210	83620	33. 1	170590	66. 9
Personnel *	10783	4006	36. 4	6777	63. 7
Prime Movers ** H. P.	4104	1015	25. 0	3089	75. 0
Capacity Gallons	19013	5462	28. 7	13551	71. 3
Vegetable Oil					
Capital (1000 $)	186590	99320	53. 0	87270	47. 0
Personnel *	6808	2753	39. 7	4055	60. 3
Prime Movers ** H. P.	677	572	84. 5	105	15. 5
Capacity (7) (1000 Gallons)	6738	2672	39. 6	4006	60. 4
Paper Mfg.					
Capital (1000 $)	60030	25080	41. 7	34950	58. 3
Personnel *	2606	974	37. 3	1632	62. 7
Prime Movers ** H. P.	3237	2181	67. 4	1056	32. 6
Capacity (8) Lings	395284	95000	24. 1	300284	75. 9

Continued table

Industries	Total	State-Operated Amount		Private-Operated Amount	
		(1000 $)	(%)	(1000 $)	(%)
Leather					
Capital (1000 $)	51040	3520	6. 9	47520	93. 1
Personnel *	3493	389	11. 1	3104	88. 9
Prime Movers ** HP	372	63	16. 9	309	83. 1
Capacity[9] sq. ft. (1000)	3737	212	5. 4	3525	94. 6
Cement					
Capital (1000 $)	47300	13000	27. 7	34300	72. 3
Personnel *	3795	702	18. 5	3093	81. 5
Prime Movers ** HP	3636	1140	31. 8	2496	68. 2
Capacity Barrels	377600	78000	20. 5	299600	79. 5
Flour					
Capital (1000 $)	146340	21400	14. 4	124940	85. 6
Personnel *	2624	92	3. 5	2532	96. 5
Prime Movers ** HP	4171	160	3. 8	4011	96. 2
Capacity Bags (1000)	4569	153	3. 4	4416	96. 6
Cotton Textile					
Capital (1000 $)	172750	95300	55. 1	77450	44. 9
Personnel *	28109	15117	53. 8	12992	46. 2
Prime Movers ** HP	12361	4304	34. 7	8057	65. 3
Spindles	243720	115720	47. 5	128000	52. 5
Capacity[10] Bags (1000)	195092	91653	47. 1	103139	52. 9

* Number of persons including staff and employees.

** Include steam engines, diesel engines, gas engines, motors, water wheel engines and other power engines in Horse Powers.

(1) Total of grey iron, white iron, steel and steel products.

(2) Power engines and motors in horse powers.

(3) Machine tools (lathes, shapers, milling machines, etc.).

(4) Generators in KVA.

(5) Motors in H. P.

(6) Acids and caustic soda in boxes.

(7) Gasoline Substitutes and Diesel Substitutes in 1000 Gallons.

(8) One Ling is equal to 500 sheets.

(9) Sole leather in 1000 square feet.

(10) Cotton yarn in bags, one bag is equal to 400 pounds.

Capacities are annual maximum

Source: Computed from *Statistical Abstract of the Republic of China*, 1945, Chinese Government. Compiled by the Ministry of Economic Affairs from data of registration of factories. Limited to 11 kinds of industries in the principal industrial districts of Szechwan, Yunnan, Kweichow, Shensi, Kansu and Chungking municipality.

Table Ⅲ　Distribution of Industrial Capital In Free China, 1944

Industries	State-Operated		Private-Operated	
	Million $	Percent	Million $	Percent
Metallurgical	555	47. 5	107	9. 4
Machinery Mfg.	206	17. 6	286	25. 0
Electric Mfg.	51	4. 4	82	7. 2
Acid and Alkali	15	1. 3	92	8. 0
Alcohol	84	7. 3	171	14. 9
Vegetable oil	99	8. 5	87	7. 6
Paper	25	2. 1	35	3. 1
Leather	4	0. 3	48	4. 2
Cement	13	1. 1	34	3. 0
Flour	21	1. 8	125	10. 9
Cotton Textile	95	8. 1	77	6. 7
Total	1168	100. 0	1144	100. 0

Source: Table Ⅱ.

Table Ⅳ　Output of Principal Products in Free China, in 1943

Products	Units	Total	State-Operated Amount		Private-Operated Amount	
			1000 $	%	1000 $	%
Coal	1000 M. T.	6253	775	12. 4	5478	81. 6
Petroleum[1]	1000 Gall.	3653	3653			
Iron Ore	1000 M. T.	50931	50931			
Pig Iron	1000 M. T.	32633	24433	74. 6	8200	25. 4
Steel	1000 M. T.	8948	4400	49. 2	4548	50. 8
Metals[2]	1000 M. T.	1482	1482			
Tungsten	1000 M. T.	8701	8701			
Antimony	1000 M. T.	428	428			
Tin	1000 M. T.	3767	3767			
Power engines	K. W.	8856	2928	33. 0	5928	67. 0
Machine tools	1000 Pieces	1731	258	14. 9	1473	85. 1
Generators & Motors	1000 H. P.	14101	6651	47. 2	7450	52. 8
Transformers	KVA	12486	4268	34. 3	8200	65. 7
Gasoline Substitutes	1000 Gall.	366600	111200	30. 3	255400	69. 7
Motor Alcohol	1000 Gall.	7718	2850	37. 9	4868	63. 1
Soda	1000 M. T.	3251	173	5. 3	3078	94. 7
Sulfuric Acids	1000 M. T.	622	42	6. 7	580	93. 3

Continued table

Products	Units	Total	State-Operated Amount 1000 $	%	Private-Operated Amount 1000 $	%
Cement	Barrels	207126	8900	4. 3	198226	95. 7
Paper	M. T.	3580			3580	
Leather	Pieces	132000			132000	
Flour	1000 Bags	4120			4120	
Cotton Yarn [3]	1000 Bales	117			117	
Electric Power	KWHR.	228122	32370	14. 2	195742	85. 8

(1) Total of gasoline, kerosine, and Diesel oil.

(2) Mainly pure copper, electrolytic copper, pure zinc, etc.

(3) One bale is equal to 4000 pounds.

Source: *Statistical Abstract of the Republic of China.*

Table V   Industrial Producton Indices in Free China

(Monthly average of Jan. -Dec. 1938 = 100)

	1939	1940	1941	1942	1943	Jan-June 1944
General Index [1]	130. 57	185. 85	242. 96	302. 71	375. 64	376. 75
General Index [2]	133. 46	214. 45	275. 56	372. 93	520. 41	528. 13
Production goods [3]	129. 66	181. 13	230. 61	272. 12	316. 07	342. 62
Consumption goods [4]	145. 63	306. 27	404. 07	658. 88	1010. 61	995. 65
Coal	109. 15	119. 50	169. 87	207. 10	213. 96	210. 52
White Iron	116. 67	150. 00	106. 50	82. 00	56. 84	123. 40
Grey Iron	118. 75	648. 63	1299. 75	3134. 25	4050. 21	1744. 78
Gasoline	103. 96	1669. 23	4029. 46	37679. 17	65496. 54	79937. 64
Alcohol	264. 31	1489. 77	1767. 37	2566. 43	2427. 22	2099. 39
Cotton Yarn	142. 37	277. 25	387. 52	718. 97	734. 92	780. 05
Flour	127. 29	214. 09	298. 08	322. 54	272. 97	227. 92
Electric Power	138. 88	205. 01	261. 04	291. 65	340. 77	376. 22

(1) Inclusive of production goods, consumption goods and goods for export (tungsten, antimony, tin and mercury).

(2) Exclusive of goods for export.

(3) Production goods include electric power, coal, iron, steel, working machines, power machines, generators, motors, transformers, cement, soda, alkali, acids (18 kinds of goods).

(4) Consumption goods include gasoline, alcohol, cotton yarn, flour, soap, mache, paper, leather, lamp bulb, ink, pencil, cigarettes (12 kinds of goods).

Source: A summary of indices compiled by the Statistical Department of the Ministry of Economic Affairs, including 108 state-operated factories under the direction of N. R. C. , 38 province-operated mines and factories and 2146 private-operated factories.

II Some Comments on the Statistical Tables

A. On Capitalization

1. Capitalization figures in the tables are misleading. The total of $ 2313000000, if converted into pre-war dollars has a value of only $ 4500000. This is an impossibly small amount for an industry employing 112787 laborers and 53046 H. P.

Some of the large undertakings still carry their capitalization figures in pre-war dollars or in values not adequately adjusted. New firms were established mostly in the earlier years of the war and some of them are still capitalized in their original value.

2. Table I shows that industrial investment distributed almost equally between state-and private-operated industries; but that the former had only 39.8% of the total motive power employed. This is contrary to our expectation. However, capital funds might be larger in Government establishments, though they were in a better position to secure loans from Government banks; while private industries, motivated by quick profit, might have been established in such a hurry that their own capital stock was quite meager. In general, all these industries were short of capital funds, especially those established in the later period.

3. Large private industries have been financed by Government banks in the form of term loans; at least a part of which cannot be regarded as purely commercial loans. During the period of evacuation, the Ministry of Economic Affairs extended $ 112598572 loans to private industry. [①]From September 1937 to December 1941 the four Government banks advanced $ 302718000 industrial loans. In the last period of the war the War Production Board came into the financial picture, for which we have no information at hand. At least part of all

---

① For the period 1937 – 1941, the amount includes $ 22359302 of investment in shares and excludes $ 6416900 of small industrial loans.

these loans, and some others, were used by the industry as capital funds particularly in the later stages of the inflation.

4. Some of the large undertakings are participated in by both private and public funds. We do not know how they are treated in the statistics.

5. Table Ⅲ shows that about 59% of the private investment were concentrated in machine manufacturing (25.0%), alcohol and gasoline substitutes (22.5%) and flour (10.9%) industries; while only 6.7% were invested in cotton textile, and the amount was less than Government investment in this field. The concentration of private investment in the first two groups results in a vulnerable position during the post-war period (see Section Ⅶ).

B. On Production

1. None of these industries has been operating at full capacity. The writer is of the impression that in 1943 and 1944 most of them were operating under 60% of their maximum capacity except in fields such as flour, and cotton textiles. ①

2. Generally speaking, capacity figures (as reported by the management at their registration) are likely to be over-estimated. They overlook the inefficiency of their old machines; and were usually made under the assumption that certain parts of imported materials would be available. Desire of securing Government

---

① For instance, in October 1943, only two of the 18 iron mills in Szechwan were reported in operation, only one of the four steel mills was working. A June report said that 80% of the 25 iron and steel mills were closed. Ta Kung News reported on March 16, 1944 that only three of the latter were working. In machine manufacturing industry, 55 of the 430 shops were closed in 1943 and 15 more stopped working, as reported by the Ministry of Economic Affairs. Another report said 75 of the 320 Chungking shops stopped working in 1943. According to a report by the union in October 1944, only 40% of the machine factories were operating; while the Central News reported only 10% operating. In textiles, the Ta Kung News reported on March 5, 1944 that among the 250000 spindles in Free China only 170000 – 180000 (or 2/3) were in operation. In Jan. 1945, Mr. Ke-Chao Kan reported that 62976 spindles of the total 297409 were not operated. In alcohol, an investigation made by Mr. Cheng-Ching Wang shows that in October 1944 large plants were working at from 16% to 50% of their capacity. In the vegetable oil industry, the Commercial Daily reported that in March 1934 only 10 of the 35 Chungking oil plants were in operation, and in May, only 4. The largest plant, the China Vegetable Oil Co., produced in 1943 only 40% of its 1942 production. The total production in Szechwan was estimated at 280000 gal. in 1943 compared with 1155800 in 1942. These reports, however, may exaggerate the low rate of operations.

financial help and of gaining prestige must also be considered. ①

3. Many of the industries have been making profit from inventory instead of from production. Price inflation made hoarding of materials and products a most profitable business.

4. Serious "bottlenecks" appeared among the industries in Free China, especially during the later part of the war. How the W. P. B. managed the problem we do not know. There was contention in 1943 asserting that Free China industry had reached its point of full employment and reduction in total investment was supplied. The important "bottlenecks" were as follows:

a. Shortage of raw materials—particularly in cotton textile, chemical and paper industries.

b. Shortage of essential parts—spare parts in machinery and electric and textile industries, high-grade steel, imported chemicals, etc. .

c. Shortage of electric power—true generally, but especially in cement and machinery industries.

d. Shortage of skilled labor—true generally, but especially in textile and machinery industries.

e. Shortage of transportation facilities—true generally, but especially for bulky materials and products.

f. Shortage of markets—in iron and steel industry in 1943 and in machinery and oil industries. They were, of course, due to lack of coordination. Owing to the lack of rolling machines, iron and steel ingots could not find their markets at a profit, and the producers claimed "over production." Machine manufacturing industry was "overexpanded" in the earlier period when industry in Free China began to flourish. Unable to produce high quality machines, the hastily-established small machine shops lost their customers. The growth of small machine shops were also stimulated by the truck repairing business in the earlier period, but the latter

① Note, however, that the figures in the table cover only the principal undertakings. For instance, in cotton textile, for which the statistics are likely to be complete, the table shows 243720 spindles in 1944, whereas, a rather extensive survey made by Mr. Ke-Chao Kan shows 307409.

could not continue at high level with the closing of the Burma Road and the absence of imported auto parts.

g. Financial problems Management claimed this to be number one handicap in Free China industry. Capital funds, being insufficient at the beginning of the business, were tied up in inventory. Quick profit in speculative trade and the 10-percent interest rate prevented bank funds from flowing into industry

h. Cost problems Managements also claimed that rises in material and labor costs wore much higher than rises in the price of their products. This was true in certain industries in 1943 – 1944.

5. The production figures in Table IV yield little knowledge as to what extent private industry has been working. We do not know the methods of industrial classification, and for instance, production of cotton yarn of state-operated mills is not given, though Government investment in this field is larger than private investment. This also is true of the figures for the paper and flour industries. On the other hand, in iron ore, metals and special minerals for export, no private production figures are given. These mines are controlled by the Government, but are mostly operated by private firms.

6. The production indices in Table V should not be taken too seriously. The general index is inflated by many products which started at zero, the base year 1938 being one when new industry in Free China just started its establishments. The three or five-fold increase during the five years is an arithmatic necessity, but does not much. As will be seen, real expansion was in 1940-1942, the index rises very little in 1943 and shows almost no change in 1944. In fact many industries reduced their production in 1943 and 1944, with the general index in these years bolstered by the rise in gasoline and some other producer's goods. There is an estimate that Szechwan industrial production in 1944 had declined to 50% of its 1942 level, with some industries declining to 30%. [1] This may be too exaggerated.

---

[1] Based on the report of Visiting Group (Szechwan Area) of the Kweichow Development Co. *Szechwan Economic Quarterly*, Vol. 2, No, 2. The report also gives some production figures as a percentage of capacity for some large firms: Yu Hwa Spinning Mill, 66% ; Shen Sin Cotton Mill,

III　Size of Industry and Output

The average size of each factory in Free China is calculated from Table I as follows:

	Whole	State-Operated	Private-Operated
Capitalization	$ 2091000	$ 8003000	$ 1109000
Laborers	102	366	62
Prime mover	48 H. P.	144 H. P.	33 H. P.

To get an idea of the size of Free China industry, the figures are compared with the Shanghai figures in 1931 and in 1933.

	Shanghai 1931	Free China 1944	Free China as a % of Shanghai
No. of factories	1666	1044	62. 7%
Capitalization	$ 139447714	3300000 *	
Laborers	212723	79787	37. 5
Prime mover	167690 H. P.	39357 H. P.	23. 4

Average Size of each factory:

	Shanghai 1931	Free China 1944	Free China as a % of Shanghai
Capitalization	83702	3160 *	
Laborers	128	76	59. 4
Prime mover	101 H. P.	38 H. P.	37. 6

* Converted into 1932 dollars, this figure is meaningless, see Section II, A – 1.

433%; Szechwan Silk Co. , 142%; Szechwan Cement Co. , 50%; Szechwan Alcohol Go. , 30%; Chien Chun Electrolysis, 15%; Chien Wei Oil Co. , 20%; China Development Co. (steel), 57%; Nanyang Tobacco Co. , 36%. Most of the state-operated factories maintained their production in 1943 – 1944, the decline occured mainly in private plants.

The 1931 figures are based on Dr. D. K. Lieu's survey[1] including Chinese-owned factories and excluding metallurgical industry. The Free China figures therefore also exclude metallurgical industry. The 1931 survey covers factories that were using motive power or employing 10 or more workers. Nevertheless, the average size of 1932 Shanghai factories is more than double that of the 1944 Free China factories. The comparison of the total size is of less importance, because Dr. Lieu's survey covers many industries not included in our Table I.

We cannot calculate directly the value of output in 1944 Free China industry, because the statistics include only 11 kinds of industry in 6 principal industrial districts and because both the capacity figures in Table II and the output figures in Table IV are not available for this purpose. The 1931 Shanghai industry produced a value of 513114000 silver dollars. Assuming the 1944 Free China industry in our table were about 40% of the 1931 Shanghai, then its value of output (excluding metallurgy) would be only around $205000000. Dr. Lieu estimates the value of output per 1931 Shanghai factory at $308000. The estimate is based on 1334 large and small factories. If we assume 3000 large and small factories in Free China, [2] and assume that their per factory production value were less than half the amount of Shanghai factory, then the total value produced by Free China industry (including metallurgy) would be less than $460000000 or $407000000 in 1936 value. These figures, however, are too large, because the Free China factories, except the 1106 covered in our table, are mostly small factories.

---

[1] A Preliminary Report of Shanghai Industrialization, 1933, Institute of Pacific Relations.

[2] The registration number up to 1944 is 3743. However, we do not know how many of them were operating. This figure is apparently too large. An arbitrary estimate was made in the China Handbook, 1943, is 3000. This figure, of course, includes many small factories which have laborers and motive power much below the average level shown above. But Dr. Lieu's survey included all factories that were employing 10 or more workers or that were using motive power. His standard is much lower than the current factory law, which requires an employment of 30 laborers and over for registration. Therefore, the figure "3000" seems reasonable so far as the comparison with Dr. Lieu's figures is concerned.

Comparison with the 1933 Shanghai Survey

	Shanghai 1933	Free China 1944	Free China as a % of Shanghai
No. of factories	1186	1106	
capitalization	162686000	4500000 *	
Laborers	214736	112787	52. 5
Prime mover	169078 H. P.	55046 H. P.	32. 6
Average Size of each factory			
Capitalization	137000	4068 *	
Laborers	181	102	56. 2
Prime mover	151 H. P.	48 H. P.	32. 5

* Converted in to 1936 value, this figures is meaningless, see Sec. II, A – 1.

The 1933 figures are based on Dr. Lieu's survey[1] and cover all chinese-owned factories qualified by the Chinese Factory Law, (larger factories), including metallurgical industry. Thus the figures are more comparable with the Free China data than the 1931's. As may be seen, the average size of Free China industry is about 45% of that of 1933 Shanghai and the total industry is more than 40% of that of 1933 Shanghai. The 1933 Shanghai industry produced a value of $ 557691000. Thus the production value of Free China in our table would be somewhere around $ 240000000. The 1931 Shanghai survey shows that when the number of factories increased by 2. 35 times to include smaller factories not qualified by the Factory Law, the value of product increased by only 1. 08 times. If we expand the number of factories of Free China from 1106 in our table to 3000, the value of product would be increased from $ 240000000 to about $ 294000000 or $ 315000000 in 1936 value.

The figures may also be compared with the 1933 survey of all China industry :

---

[1] D. K. Lieu, *Analysis of Shanghai Industrialization*, in Chinese, 1936.

	China 1933	Free China 1944	Free China as a % of All China
No. of factories	2435	1106	45.3
Capitalization	$ 406873000	4500000 *	
Laborers	493257	112787	22.9
Prime mover	507300	55046	10.9
Average size of each factory			
Capitalization	$ 167000	4068 *	
Laborers	203	102	50.2
Prime mover	208	48	23.5

* Converted into 1936 values, this figure is meaningless, see Sec. II, A – 1.

The 1933 all China figures are also based on Dr. Lieu's survey,[1] and cover Chinese-owned factories qualified by the Factory Law. Its average size was larger than that of 1933 Shanghai, probably because the all China survey covers less smaller factories which were not as easily accessible for the field workers as those in Shanghai. The 1933 China industry produced a value of $ 1113974000. Assuming the Free China industry in our table were about one-fifth of the 1933 China, its value of output would be around $ 227000000. Using the same method to include smaller factories, the total production value of Free China industry would be around $ 280000000 or $ 300000000 in 1936 value.

The last two estimates, i. e. $ 315000000 and $ 300000000 in 1936 value, may be too small for the total value produced by Free China industry in 1944, because the 1900 factories not included in our table of Free China statistics were not all small ones (the statistics cover only 11 kinds of industry in 6 principal industrial districts). Whereas the first estimate of $ 407000000, as pointed out before, is too large. Considering all these factors, the value of output of Free China industry is arbitrarily estimated at $ 350000000 in 1936 value.

---

[1] D. K. Lieu, Notes on China's Foreign Trade and Trade Policy, Institute of Pacific Relations, 1942.

The total value of product of both Chinese-and foreign-owned industries in all China except Manchuria is estimated by the writer in another report at $ 4735321000 in 1936. Thus the value produced by the Free China industry in 1944 was less than 8% of the value of industrial output of all China before the war. This shows how small the size of Free China industry has been.

IV Expansion of State-Operated Industries

During the war, state-operated industries expanded about three folds. The N. R. C. started its work in 1936, but its full-fledged expansion did not come until after the war. The expansion is large in heavy industries, which were as yet undeveloped in 1935. The condition of state-operated industry in 1935 is shown in the following table.

Table VI State-Operated Industry in 1935

Industry	No. of Factories	Capital ($ 1000)	Employees	Prime Movers (HP)	Value of Output ($ 1000)
Metallurgical	4	860	4876	465	1548
Metal	1	4961	706	—	49181
Machinery Mfg.	4	340	765	192	470
Railway Equipment	27	...	14430	9202	4797
Communication Equip.	7	5755	2904	593	3708
Brick, Stone, etc.	2	107	156	45	88
Power	8	6160	1087	22721	2167
Chemicals	1	...	38	—	291
Textile	6	5194	4320	4681	9993
Leather	2	265	697	109	515
Food	2	1433	388	212	273
Printing	2	5151	1795	357	201
Others	6	72	5382	203	1597
Total	72	30298	37544	38779	74829

Source: Statistical Abstract of the Republic of China, 1940. Based on report of Ministry of Industry.

Excluding railway equipment, power, and printing industries (as they are not covered by Table II), and comparing with Table II, the labor force of state-operated industry expanded 2.6 times during 1936 – 1944, motive power expanded 3.2 times, while the number of factories expanded 4.2 times. However, Table II includes some industries operated by Provincial Governments that are not covered in the 1935 table.

Only part of the industries in Table VI have been moved to Free China. Investment figure of the 27 railway equipment factories is not given. In Dr. Lieu's 1933 survey, capital invested in "railroad repairs" is \$16665304[1], almost all of them may be regarded as Government capital. Government also invested large amount in power plants, chemical plants and machinery industry in 1936. Thus the total investment in state-operated industries was far above the \$30298000 in Table VI, perhaps some \$50000000 may be counted. The investment in Free China in 1944, judged from the above comparison, may be somewhere around \$80000000 in 1936 dollars.

V Prospects of Free China Industry—General Assumptions

No one can foretell the future of the industries in Free China. The following remarks are merely assumptions selected as reasonable:

1. The machinery and industrial equipment evacuated from occupied China during the war is likely to stay in Free China where it is.

2. A part of management personnel, engineers and a small part of skilled laborers originally evacuated from occupied areas would probably move back to their hometowns. A 15% removal from the total industrial staff and a 5% removal from the total labor force do not seem excessive. This would remove only 7000 persons from Table II. Part of the reduction may be replaced from native, labor

---

[1] See Appendix D in the writer's report on China's industry.

supply if necessary. However, shortage of skilled labor would be quite a problem if the industry continued to develop. Experienced management reported that training of native labor in the interior is beset with difficulties.

3. Transportation facilities between interior China and coastal areas are believed to have been improved during the war. Thus in time competition of goods from coast ports and from abroad would be more serious than before the war. The flow of outside goods into interior China may be delayed as rehabilitation takes time; but the movement can also be accelerated by the fact that prices in interior China were higher than those in occupied areas[1]. Boats and trucks which move people from Chungking would bring back rice, gasoline and luxury goods from Hankow and Shanghai. The Yunnan-India China railway is likely to be opened before the restoration of the mainland railroad system.

4. Most of the industrial installations in Free China are old-fashioned machines and equipment, some dating back to 1900 (especially in steel mills and power plants). If not for the blocade during the war, they would have been abandoned and replaced long ago. Another part of industrial equipment consists of hastily—made machines and tools, with low efficiency and precision; or are crude improvements of handicraft tools, especially in vegetable oil and alcohol industries (also the 20000 Gohsh type spindles and 800 sets of hand looms). It is difficult to estimate what rate of depreciation and obsolescence should be allowed for their translation into post-war capacity. In comparison with the standard expected in Shanghai, an over-all allowance of 30% obsolescence of the industrial installation in Free China does not seem excessive.

5. Another major factor is the demobilization of war industries. Practically all munition factories are operated by the Government and are not included in our study. It is important to note, however, that demobilization of war production would have much less effect upon the iron and steel industry in China than in most other countries. The vulnerable industries would be alcohol and vegetable oil; and

---

[1] Newspaper already reported the inflow of luxury goods from Shanghai to Chungking.

possibly, machinery manufacturing. In general, the direct effect of the demobilization of war production (in its narrower sense) on industries would be much less than what happened in the U. S. and Great Britain.

6. The most uncertain factor will be the price movement. During the war a large part of the interior industry was built on price speculation. Assuming a stop of price inflation in our reconstruction period, many of the present undertakings would be eliminated. However, much will depend on the Government monetary and economic policies. The writer is under the impression that inflation may continue in the reconstruction period; and that eventually prices in interior China would stand lower than in coast ports.

7. Another consideration is future market capacity of interior China. The following factors may be noted.

a. Interior people in general might have higher income in real terms than before the war. Agricultural products in this area were reported to have increased during the eight years of war, and agricultural prices are not likely to drop drastically in the near future. There will be larger industrial employment than before the war.

b. Farmers and labors in Free China are believed to have improved their economic position during the war and may have accumulated some purchasing power in comparison with the people in the occupied area.

c. Interior China has enjoyed industrialization and economic development throughout the war. The people are more business-minded than before and may be inclined to raise their living standard. Their propensity to consume may have been increased through the eight years of inflationary experience.

d. On the other hand, the interior cities will lose some of their immigration; the return of demobilized soldiers would not be large. Many wealthy people will move out with their fortunes. Government disbursements in this area will be substantially reduced.

VI Government Program in Interior China

In studying the future of private industries in Free China, the program of state-operated industry in these areas should be noted. Table VII, compiled from the data given in the "Rehabilitation Program of State-Operated Mines and Industry", N. R. C., May 1945, shows the expected production capacity in Free China of undertakings that are included in the program. The figures can not be compared with Tables II or III. The program would reduce the number of principal state-operated units from 89 to 56, among the latter 28 would be owned by N. R. C. and 28 state-participated.

Table VII   Expected Production in State-Operated Industries in Free China

	Units	Present Capacity	Expected Capacity	Change
Coal	tons	590000	1290000	+700000
Petroleum	tons	121800	150000	+29000
Pig Iron	tons	23000	21000	−2000
Steel	tons	12000	12000	unchanged
Non-metals	tons	1090	1690	+600
Power engines	H. P.	2260	12000	+9740
Machine	pieces	a 200	3500	+3100
Machine tools	Pieces	325	800	+475
Generators	KWA	2000	50000	+48000
Cement	tons		1115000	
Alkali(soda)	tons	184	800	+616
Phosphorous Fertilizer	tons	0	1500	+1500
Alcohol	Gallons	6715000	10600000	+3385000
Gasoline Substitute	Gallons	96000	360000	+264000
Electric Power	KW	26023	37333	+37333

Note: The Government program requires a new investment 44478000 CH pre-war dollars and 31554000 U. S. dollars, a total of 145450000 CH pre-war dollars.

This program intends to make Free China an industrial base for the rehabilitation of occupied China (the program was written in the spring of 1945). The size of the rehabilitated Free China industry may be seen from the following table which shows Free China expected production capacity as a percentage of the expected whole China production capacity (including Manchuria) after rehabilitation.

Coal	3. 8%
Petroleum	9. 4%
Pig Iron	?
Steel	1. 9%
Power engines	32. 4%
Machine tools	8. 0%
Working Machines	43. 8%
Generators	?
Cement	44. 2%
Soda	1. 1%
Gasoline Substitute	100. 0%
Alcohol	40. 1%
Electric Power	0. 8%

VII Prospects of Free China Industries-Comments on Specific Industries

(1) Alcohol

22. 5% of private industrial capital in Free China were invested in alcohol and vegetable oil industries, which have an annual capacity of 19013000 gallons of alcohol and 6738000 gallons of gasoline substitute and Diesel substitute. Both industries flourished during the war, especially after the closing of the Burma Road.

Before the war, China produced about 2780000 gallons of alcohol and no vegetable oil. The largest import of alcohol was 5080037 gallons in 1929. Imports declined to around 1000000 gallons in 1935 – 1936. In addition about 552000 gallons were imported for military and medical uses. Thus before the war China consumed about 4500000 gallons alcohol, of which at most 4000000 gallons were for industrial and transportation uses. Free China consumption before the war could not have been larger than 500000 gallons. The medical and military demand would not increase very much in the post-war period. Unless alcohol is still largely used in operating motor trucks, 8000000 gallons seem to be enough for post-war years. The production capacity of Free China, however, is 19013000 gallons, and the N. R. C. post-war program would expand the state-operated plants to a capacity of 10100000 gallons in Free China and 26400000 gallons in whole China. This would increase Free China capacity to 22398000 gallons, assuming no expansion in private plants; while the consumption of this area was around 500000 gallons before the war and about 8000000 gallons in 1944 (production figure).

Another thing to be considered is the actual operating picture of the alcohol industry during the war. The factories were operating at less than half of their capacity in 1943 and 1944. 80% of the product was produced in Szechwan from sugar cane and wine, which raise the cost of alcohol much above that produced from wood in other countries. Experienced men told the writer that at least half of the industry would be eliminated after the war. After visiting some of the Szechwan factories the writer believes the statement. Most of these were handicapped by high cost of material and labor; many of them were entirely closed. Their equipment was bad and low efficient. Alcohol can never compete with gasoline (imported) both in efficiency and in cost. Gasoline is free from import duty at present time, and it is likely that the duty will not be high in the future.

The N. R. C. program of expanding alcohol industry is undoubtedly motivated by the "self-sufficient" policy. While Government plants may be operated under steel policy, private plants would have to be sacrificed. Private plants held 71% of the total capacity and produced 63% of total output in 1944. A reduction of their plants to one-half would mean a loss of 7. 5% of the total private industrial investment in Free China.

The three large Government plants (Tze Chung, Lu Hsien, and Kwang Yang) would be able to produce according to the N. R. C. rehabilitation program, an amount almost as large as the total production figure in 1944 (7300000 gallons). One may ask whether the other 12 Free China plants included in the N. R. C. program are necessary for rehabilitation (Government maintained 40 plants in 1944). The N. R. C. call for an investment of 1610000 CH pre-war dollars in Free China alcohol industry.

(2) Vegetable Oil

This is the most vulnerable industry in the post-war period. Its principal product, gasoline substitute oil, is far less efficient than even alcohol for motor trucks. Half of the wartime investment in this industry was private. It has a capacity of 4000000 gallons and produced only 255400 gallons in 1944. The equipment was very simple and many processes were by hand. Costs were high. The industry has never enjoyed a pleasant experience even in the hopeful years of 1942 – 1943. The N. R. C. rehabilitation program would spend 200000 pre-war dollars to expand two vegetable factories to a total capacity of 360000 gallons. The writer would question whether from a longer-run point of view, the whole industry, except few Government-sponsored factories, should not be eliminated in the post-war period. There might be some demand for Diesel substitute in the earlier period, due to the existence of such engines (1720 H. P. used by large industry); but the demand for gasoline substitute would be negligible. This suggests another loss of 7. 5% of the total private industrial investment (or together with the alcohol, 15%).

(3) Machine Manufacturing

This is the largest private industry in Free China, in which 25% of private industrial investment concentrated. It flourished during the first half of the war. Most of the small factories were merely auto repairing shops; and about one-third were shut down after the closing of the Burma Road, whereas many others were maintained by speculative inventory trading. Their efficiency and quality of the product were generally very low. Very few of them can compete with manufacturers in coast ports. Their future depends upon further development of interior industry and highway transportation. Almost all of the management personnel and skilled laborers are evacuees from occupied areas.

The 1931 Shanghai industry had only 297 machine manufacturing factories employing 10663 workers, while in Free China we have at least 422 factories employing 26000 workers. This was partly because Shanghai imported most of needed machinery. The Shanghai industry invested only 2.8% of total industrial capital in machine manufacturing, while in Free china 30% of the total were invested in this field. [①] Assuming that Free China industry is about half the size of Shanghai 1932, as we estimated before, the number of machine shops seems too large in Free China.

Large factories have definitely advantages over small ones in this field. The average private factory in Free China has only 18 H. P. of motive power, the Shanghai factory had 30 H. P. , and the state-operated factory in Free China has 87 H. P.. The N. R. C. rehabilitation program expects a 6-fold expansion of its machine factories, especially in the manufacture of working machines and power engines. The program requires 2800000 pre-war CH dollars and 8960000 U. S. dollars. Among the factories is the Central Machine Works, one of the principal establishment of N. R. C. . While the expansion is necessary for the industrialization of interior China, part of the small private shops would undoubtedly be sacrificed.

Considering all these factors, we may expect that 30% of the private machine shops would become obsolete in the post-war period. This will mean a loss of another 7.5% of private industrial investment in Free China. New factories of larger capital and modern equipments, might be established if the industrialization of interior China would get underway and if iron and steel industry in this area develops. The prospects of this are questionable at the present time.

(4) Cotton Textile

The future of this industry is debatable. The principal problems are supply of raw cotton and competition of yarn from central and eastern China in the post-

---

① As in case of Shanghai, excluding metallurgical industry.

war period. The following describes only one general outlook for Free China mills.

The industry produced about 117000 bags (one bag is equal to 400 pounds) of cotton yarn in 1944, while native hand spindles produced about 260000 bags. It has been estimated that hand spindles supplied about 61% of the total yarn consumption. ①It is expected that in the future machine yarn will eventually replace hand products, and that the total consumption will increase with the industrialization of Free China.

According to Mr. Ke-Chao Kan (see Table Ⅷ), there were 18 large cotton mills and 39 Gohsh type mills in Free China. The large mills had 297409 spindles, of which 234563 were operating in 1944. The Gohsh type mills use Indian or Japanese type machines, and one machine operates only about 150 spindles. The efficiency of these machines is lower than the regular type. Most of these machines were made in Free China. In total, there were about 250000 spindles operating in interior China (excluding Kwangtung, Chekiang, etc. in table Ⅷ).

Table Ⅷ　Cotton Textile Industry in Free China

Provinces	No. of factories	Spindles in Operation	Spindles Idle	Machine Looms
Large mills				
Szechwan	9	134132	33300	1284
Shensi	5	60000	9176	960
Yunnan	2	22600	13200	60
Hunan	1	15000	5000	
Kwangsi	1	2831	2300	
Total	18	234563	62976	2304
Gohsh mills				
Szechwan	12	9012	2454	
Shensi	5	1808		

① Shao-Fu Li, "Textile Industry," *Times Daily*, Chungking, February 2, 1944. The total consumption of cotton cloth was about 9000000 pieces in Free China, 4000000 were produced by faotories and 5000000 by rural families. See Ta Kung News, March 3, 1944.

Continued table

Provinces	No. of factories	Spindles in Operation	Spindles Idle	Machine Looms
Yunnan	3	1008		
Hunan	10	2722		
Kwangsi	2	432		
Kwangtung	1	480		
Kiangsi	4	1008		
Chekiang	1	1024		
Total	38	17494	2454	
Grand Total	56	252057	65430	2304

Source: Compiled from data on 38 cotton mills given by Mr. Ke-Chao Kan in "Textile, paper, Flour and Tobacco Industries," *Szechwan Economic Quarterly*, Vol. Ⅱ No. 1, April 1945.

The 250000 spindles require about 600000 piculs of raw cotton yearly. The mills in Shensi, Hunan and Kwangsi may use local cotton easily. The Yunnan mills must import cotton from Hunan and Hupei during the war, and probably from Indio-China or Burma after the war. The Szechwan mills must ship cotton from Shensi and Honan. During the war the shipping of cotton was controlled and rationed by the Board of Cotton, Yarn, and Cloth Control. Many of the Szechwan and Yunnan mills experienced difficulty in getting their rations.

Table Ⅸ   Cotton Production in Free China

Years	Szechwan	Shensi	Kansu	Kwangsi	Yunnan	Kweichow
Cotton Fields (1000 Mu)						
1936	2792	4883	110	?	153	261
1937	2408	4646	161	293	133	216
1938	2945	3895	123	302	217	263
1939	3650	3187	141	554	274	338
1940	4718	3671	167	609	230	448
1941	4052	3590	202	648	232	465
1942	4018	3229	190	672	243	445
Cotton production (1000 piculs)						
1936	755	1063	24	?	40	78
1937	458	832	47	87	33	66

Continued table

Years	Szechwan	Shensi	Kansu	Kwangsi	Yunnan	Kweichow
1938	763	997	37	82	62	64
1939	1280	862	41	108	81	97
1940	1129	670	50	127	60	134
1941	?	945	57	132	62	115
1942	1190	769	54	136	62	141

Source: Estimated by the Central Agriculture Board.

The cotton production figures are given in table IX. Assuming that a regular spindle consumes 2.5 piculs raw cotton yearly and a Gohsh spindle consumes 3 piculs, the consumption and supply picture of the three principal cotton textile provinces is as follows: [1]

Raw Cotton in Piculs

	Consumption (Full capacity)	Production (1940 – 1942 average)
Szechwan		
Large mills	418580	
Gohsh mills	34398	
Total	452978	1159000
Yunnan		
Large mills	89500	
Gohsh mills	3024	
Total	92524	61000
Shensi		
Large mills	172940	
Gohsh mills	5424	
Total	178364	795000

This does not count the consumption of hand spindles. The Gohsh spindles may be eliminated after the war. Hand spinning, however, as a rural industry, cannot be eliminated promptly and is in a better position to secure local cotton.

---

[1] Wartime efficiency is still lower. Mr. Min Liu estimates a spindle consumes 30642 piculs. *Szechwan Economic Quarterly*, Vol. 2, No. 2.

Assuming that hand spinning consumes 40% of total cotton supply in Szechwan, 60% in Shensi and 50% in Yunnan, total requirement for raw cotton will be: Szechwan: 750000; Shensi: 445000; Yunnan: 186000 piculs. In addition, cotton is also needed for padding winter suits and for industrial and household uses. This consumption must be met before mill requirements.

The native cotton in Szechwan, Yunnan and Kweichow is not suitable for modern spindles (its fiber is below 3/4 inch). The Ministry of Agriculture has tried to plant improved cotton in these areas. Production, however, has been small. The production in Szechwan of improved cotton was:

Years	Piculs
1938	23626
1940	191011
1941	174592
1942	61714
1943	172352

They supplied less than one-third of the mill's needs. Most of the modern mills depended upon imported cotton from Shensi and Honan. Shensi raises some better cotton known as "Si-Jung" (American origin), with fiber between 3/4 and 1 inch.

Thus, cotton supply in Yunnan is definitely insufficient; Szechwan also requires large imports. Mr. Hung-Chin Chen estimated the shortage of cotton in Szechwan at 617000 piculs in 1941 and 524000 in 1942.[1] Shensi is expected to produce more cotton than the 795000 piculs, since it produced 1063000 in 1936. But it cannot help Szechwan very much, since transportation must be by motor trucks.

The present cotton industry in Free China was not developed on an economic basis. Readjustment is expected in the post-war period. Part of the Szechwan spindles will move out, probably to somewhere along the Yangtze River, while Shensi mills may expand afterwards. The Yunnan mills will also be partly sacrificed.

---

[1] "An analysis of wartime cotton production," *Szechwan Economic Quarterly*, Vol. I, No. 1. The supply and consumption data he used, however, are quite different from our table.

We cannot estimate the future competitive picture between domestic production and the interior imported yarn from coastal China. Generally speaking, the former will be unable to compete with the Shanghai, Tiensin or Honan cotton mills where the best cotton are used.

(5) Flour

This is the only large industry that experienced no material handicap during the war, and that may have a rosy future in the post-war period. Only rationing of wheat and shortage of electric power handicapped some of the wartime flour mills.

No flour statistics are available for pre-war years in Free China. The writer knows only that there were one modern mill in Kansu, one in Sinking and one in Szechwan, one or two in Shensi. Their production probably did not exceed 1000000 bags (one bag contains 49 pounds). The consumption of flour in the wheat-eating provinces of Free China was estimated in 1933 as follows:[1]

	Population	Daily consumption(bags)	Yearly consumption(bags)
Shensi	11684564	233691	85197288
Kansu	5762109	115242	41963402
Ningsia	704844	14097	5145624
Sinkiang	2657289	53506	19529617
Total	20826846	416536	151835931

To this total we may add some 3000000 bags for the rice-eating population in Szechwan, Yunnan, Kweichow and Kwangsi. Total consumption will be thus about 155000000 bags. In 1944 Free China had 47 flour mills with a capacity of 4569000 bags. This amounts to only 2.9% of the total consumption; the rest supplied by native flour made on stone mills. [2]

In 1934, 89 modern mills were reported to the Ministry of Industry, 15 of them in Shanghai. They had a capacipy of 142000000 bags and produced

---

[1] Estimated by the Shanghai Commercial and Savings Bank. See *China Economic Year Book*, 1934.

[2] Notice, however, that most of the mills were concentrated in Szechwan and Shensi. The percentage there, of course, is much higher.

75000000 bags. [1] In addition, 15000000 bags were imported from abroad. For a total consumption estimated at 1220000000 bags, native flour would supply 1130000000 bags. In other words, 7.4% of total consumption was supplied by modern mills. Excluding interior areas in the above table, the percentage would be 8.4%. And there had been much progress in flour industry since 1933. Thus before the war, modern mills may have supplied 10% of the consumption in coastal and central China.

With the industrialization and modernization of interior China, more and more people will eat machine-made flour. If 10% of the total consumption would be met by modern mills, it will require a capacity of 15500000 bags, more than three times the present capacity.

The following table shows that flour industry, unlike the cotton textile, has been well distributed in Free China, concentrating in wheat-producing areas of Shensi and Szechwan. Most of the Shensi mills were those evacuated from occupied areas. This table, being compiled from different source, is not comparable with Table Ⅱ.

Table Ⅹ   Flour Mills in Free China

Provinces	No. of Factories	No. of Mills	Daily Capacity (bags)	Wheat Requirement Yearly (1000 piculs)	Wheat Production 1942 (1000 piculs)
Szechwan	10	42	6030	1260	79412
Shensi	13	77	21120	2974	30623
Kansu	3	7	1100	216	11710
Hunan	3	13	1150 *	209	14033
Kiangsi	1	2	400	72	11176
Yunnan	1	4	500	72	12779
Kwangsi	1	6	1200	216	10331

---

[1] Estimated by *China Economic Yearbook*, 1934.

Continued table

Provinces	No. of Factories	No. of Mills	Daily Capacity (bags)	Wheat Requirement Yearly (1000 piculs)	Wheat Production 1942 (1000 piculs)
Kweichow	1	2	400	72	15356
Kwangtung	1	?	?	?	6607
Fukien	1	2	200	36	13120

* Estimated by the writer.

Source: Mills and requirement: Mr. Ke-Chao Kan, ibid. Wheat production: Central Agricultural Board.

A Preliminary Report on Savings in Modern Savings Institutions[*]

First Period: 1914 – 1933

I   Modern Savings Institutions

	No. Established	No. in 1933
Savings Banks	68 ⎤	
Banks having savings department	a60 ⎬	87
Banks receiving sav'g deposits	11 ⎦	
Postal Remittances & Sav'g Bank	1	1
Savings Societies		
In Manchuria	a70	a10
In China Proper	10	1
Organized by banks	2	2
Prize savings societies	8	2
Savings Department of trust co.	?	5
Total	a230	108

Approximate

About 230 savings institutions had been established before 1933, of which about 108 remained by that year. 52 (37%) of the banks having savings departments

---

* This report was accomplished as a research report for Nobel Laureate Simon Kuznets when the author was working for the research as an assistant, in 1946 on New York.

closed by 1933.

This figure does not include native banks, local savings societies, family societies, fraternities, insurance companies, life insurance societies, credit unions, savings in trading companies and in local shops, etc. .

II Distribution of Savings Institutions by Provinces

	Head Office(1933)		Sub-offices(1933)		
	Banks	Others	Banks	%	Postal *
Kiangsu	58	10	87	34	60
(Shanghai)	(54)	(10)	(19)		56
Hopei	5	1	35	14	23
Chekiang	4	—	19	7	60
Fujian	2	—	2	1	15
Kwangtung	4	—	6	2	19
Hunan	—	—	6	2	12
Hupei	1	—	25	10	55
Szechuan	5	—	7	3	2
Shansi	?	?	?	?	31
Shensi	1	—	?	?	2
(Peiping) *					60
Shantung	1	—	21	8	36
Anhwei	—	—	9	4	31
Honan	?	—	6	2	65
Kiangsi	1	—	6	2	7
Manchuria	2	a10	21	8	52
Hongkong	3	?	3	1	—
Total	87	21	260#	100#	586

　* Postal regions, not comparable with provinces. An institution having more than one sub-office in the same place (city or hsien) is regarded as one office.

　# Including 7 in other places.

There were about 950 savings offices opened in 1933. They were concentrated in Kiangsu (esp. Shanghai), Hopei, Chekiang and Hupei.

III   Capital and Reserves

		1933			
		Capital for savings dept. (1000 CH$)		Reserves for savings dept. (1000 CH$)	
		Paid-up	% *	Amount	% **
58	Savings Banks	1400	12	3029#	10
	Banks-sav. dept.	12425			
4	Trust Co. -sav. dept.	250	5	2##	2
2	Sav. Society	1500	100	1090	100
2	Prize Society	3247	100	59###	100
	Total	18822	15	4180	12

* % of paid-up capital for savings department to total paid-up capital of the whole institution.

** % of reserves for savings department to total reserves of the whole institution.

Five out of the 34 banks that had reserves for savings departments did not report, and figures exclude them.

Only one of the four trust companies reported on reserves for savings department.

Only two prize societies included. The most important one, the International Savings Society, which has a capital of $ 2797000, did not report on reserves, and is not included.

Amount of Capital ($)	No. of banks	Amount of reserve ($)	No. of banks
2000000	1	Over 500000	1
1000000	2	200000 – 499999	4
500000 – 999999	6	100000 – 199999	4
200000 – 499999	19	50000 – 99000	2
100000-199999	18	20000 – 49999	9
50000	8	10000 – 19999	5
Unknown	1	Below 10000	9
Total	55		34

IV Savings Deposits

Year	No.	Banks Amount (CH $ 1000)	Postal Savings (CH $ 1000)	Trust Co. (CH $ 1000)	Savings Societies* (CH $ 1000)	Prize Society (CH $ 1000)	Total (CH $ 1000)
1914	2	940					940
1915	3	1821					1821
1916	3	1022					1022
1917	5	4804					4804
1918	5	4715					4715
1919	5	10188	109				10297
1920	6	5920	754				6674
1921	14	11390	2132	11			13533
1922	15	13533	3445	86			17064
1923	16	16745	4649	269	1436		23099
1924	18	21655	5815	432	3032		30935
1925	22	29268	7747	670	7400	13140	58225
1926	21	34367	9516	922	13159	18097	76121
1927	22	40131	8269	1916	17147	25294	92757
1928	27	49026	8747	2025	23465	30250	113513
1929	30	60062	11437	2242	32105	36430	142276
1930	37	81202	17899	2529	41336	44660	187626
1931	46	127325	27822	2913	51828	48510	258398
1932	58	171271	25809	3137	58666	57300	316183
1933	61	242143	25397	5214	80882	65800	419436

* Only one bank society included, except for 1933.

Total savings deposits for 1928 – 1933, a few that include years of revolutionary aftermath, prosperity and depression in rural society, averaged about $ 240000000. The trend, however, is rising. The deposits of $ 420000000 in 1933 amounts to about $ 0. 93 per capita, in silver dollars.

The actual amount of savings deposits in modern institutions in 1933 was larger than that appears in the table, due to the facts;

(1) Only 61 of the 87 existing banks were included in the table.

(2) Only the two savings societies organized by banks were included.

(3) The figures were year-end reports (except for postal savings, a June 30 report) and some of the banks reported 1932 data. The withdrawal of deposits (almost half of the savings deposits were current, see below) at the end of the year could not be very large, because most of Chinese business firms were using the lunar calendar at that time.

(4) Interest accrued is excluded.

Note also that the rapid increase in savings deposits was largely due to the increase in the number of banks included in the statistics. Not all of them were newly established banks, they just did not report for earlier years. Banks closed before 1933 are also excluded from the table. Thus the actual increase may not have been so rapid as is shown in the table.

Percentage Distribution of Deposits by Kinds of Institutes

Year	Banks	Postal Sav'g	Trust Co.	Sav'g Societies	Prize Societies
1925	50	13	1	13	23
1926	45	13	1	17	24
1927	43	9	2	19	27
1928	43	8	2	21	26
1929	42	8	2	22	26
1930	43	10	1	22	24
1931	49	11	1	20	19
1932	54	8	1	19	18
1933	58	6	1	19	16

The decline in the percentage of Postal Savings and the rapid increase in the percentage of bank deposits in 1931 − 1933 indicates the movement of savings from rural communities to large cities. During the great agricultural depression in this period, funds were concentrated in large cities.

V   The Nature of Deposits

Current Savings Deposits-subject to withdrawal at any time by checks or by passbook. Various kinds were used; in reality, they are not savings deposits, though they are so classified.

Average Amount of each:	$ 1000							
	1932				1933			
	Current	%	Time	%	Current	%	Time	%
Bank *	3226	45	4000	55	3431	41	4886	59
Postal Sav'g **	21670	84	4139	16	21412	84 **	3985	16
Trust Co. ***	458	28	1152	72	482	19	2027	81
Sav'g Society ***	8381	14	50284	86	10253	14	67529	86
Prize Society	—	—	28505	100	—	—	62000 ***	100

   * 18 banks in 1932, 22 banks in 1933.

   ** June 30, 1933 for postal savings.

   *** One trust co. included, one society included, one prize society included in 1933 (two in 1932).

The above table includes only 25 savings institutions in 1933. Based on their ratios, the total amount of $ 420000000 savings deposits is distributed in the following table, which shows that 32% of the total were current deposits and 68% time deposits.

1933	Current		Time		
	Amount($ 1000)	%	Amount($ 1000)	%	Total($ 1000)
61 Banks	99278	41	142865	51	242143
Postal savings	21412	84	3985	16	25397
4 Trust Co.	991	19	4223	81	5214
2 Societies by Bk.	11323	14	69559	86	80882
2 Prize societies	—	—	65800	100	65800
Total	133004	32	286432	68	419436

It is likely that small savings were mostly current deposits. This is supplied by the following table of postal savings. We should remember, however, that there was no time deposit in postal savings before 1930.

Postal Savings: $ 1000

Year	Current	%	Time	%	Total
1930	16979	94. 4	921	5. 6	17899
1931	23704	85. 2	4118	14. 8	27822
1932	21670	84. 1	4139	15. 9	25809
1933 *	21413	84. 3	3985	15. 7	25397

∗June 30, 1933.

VI Use of Savings Funds

1932									
	Secured Loans ($ 1000)	%	Securities ($ 1000)	%	Real Estate ($ 1000)	%	Cash& balance with Bk. ($ 1000)	%	Total ($ 1000)
34 Banks	48068	27	34431	20	6669	4	86586	49	175756
1 Trust Co.	139	8	250	14	579	32	842	46	1810
2 Societies	26770	38	25703	36	7143	12	10147	14	69763
1 Prize society	22647	43	22740	43	7682	14	200	—	53269
Total	97624	33	83124	28	22073	7	97775	33	300598
1933									
34 Banks	59584	24	53522	22	10419	4	122802	50	246326
1 Trust Co.	716	26	593	21	588	21	904	32	2802
2 Societies	24334	27	35042	40	8668	10	20566	23	88610
1 Prize society	28286	44	27919	44	7681	12	?		63886
Total	112920	28	117076	29	27356	6	144272	36	401624

As may be seen from the above table, in 1933, 28% of the funds were put in secured loans, 29% in purchasing securities, 6% invested in real estate and 36% were kept in vaults or deposited with banks. The last item was especially large in banks, 50% in 1933 and 49% in 1932. Banks usually carry this item under "Balance with Ourselves", i. e. balance with the banking department of the same institution. The saving deposits were thus transferred to the banking department and employed by it as ordinary deposits. In small banks the saving department was operated by the staff of the banking department and the deposits were treated as their own deposits, only with different title given to the depositors. The accumulation of funds in this item was partly due to the lack of investment opportunities.

A study of 19 large banks shows that the average amount of "Balance with ourselves" was about 46% of the total amount of funds employed by the savings department in 1932; the percentage increased to 49% in 1933.

"Securities" include principally Government securities and foreign securities (securities issued by foreigner-owned firms). Both bonds and stocks were included. Performance of Chinese securities increased in the later years.

Assuming that 36% of the funds in modern savings institutes were employed in investment, the total amount of investment in 1933 would be as follows:

Estimates: Funds available

	Total of 87 banks, 2 societies, 2 prize societies, 4 trust co. and postal savings($)	Funds Invested($)
Capital	26834000	9660240
Reserves	5637000	2029320
Saving Deposit	522689000	188168040
Total	555160000	199857600

The amounts of "Funds Available" are derived by ratios, allowing for all kinds of incomplete reporting. The total saving deposits of $ 522689000 might be too large, because the banks which were not included in the statistics were mostly small banks. A total savings deposits figure of $ 500000000 would be reasonable. By proportion, $ 340000000 would be time deposits, or true savings.

VII Reference Figures

The following figures are cited for reference:

1. Gross national income in 1933 $ 25370000000

2. Savings deposits in 1933 (modern institutions)   500000000

3. Savings deposit less current in 1933   340000000

4. Funds available for investment in 1933 (modern institutions)   372000000

5. Funds invested (modern institutions) in 1933   190000000

6. Capital investment of Chinese owned industry in 1933.

   (Excluding Manchuria)   407000000

Ratio: Savings deposits to total deposit (average)   15%   1932

                                                              18%   1933

Ratio: Savings deposits to capital and reserves   15. 55   1932

       for savings department (average)   20. 31   1933

1. Dr. T. C. Liu's estimate.

4, 5. Less current deposits.

6. Dr. D. K. Lieu's report.

Spatial and Temporal Study
Foreword to *Agricultural Development in Jiangnan, 1620 – 1850*

Dr Bozhong Li's *Agricultural Development in Jiangnan, 1620 – 1850* is the product of his many years of research on Jiangnan economic history. It is also his most recent example of the economic history of productive forces. Dr Li began in the 1970s to study the Jiangnan economy during the Tang Dynasty which led to the publication in 1990 of Tangdai Jiangnan nongye de fazhan (*Agricultural development in Tang Jiangnan*). He continued with his studies of this area through the Song and Yuan periods. Later he devoted his attention to researching the Jiangnan economy during the Ming and Qing dynasties. His research has already resulted in a sequence of articles collected in his doctoral dissertation *Six Studies of Agriculture and Industry of Jiangnan in the Ming and Qing Dynasties* (Xiamen University, 1985). With additional research, these studies have been published in a series of articles and a book. In the present volume Dr Li sets before us an analysis of Jiangnan agricultural development; he covers the late imperial period and includes his assessment of other viewpoints regarding Chinese economic history.

In this book, Li gives high marks to the development path and results of early and mid-Qing Jiangnan agricultural development, as well as its historical significance. The formation of a particularly Chinese model of intensified agricultural production during this period has had a role to play in the economic modernization that has come one hundred years later to China. He criticizes the trend of taking Western Europe as the norm in studies of late imperial China from the 1930s through the 1980s. He also puts forward a challenge to more recent theories about a late imperial population explosion, agricultural "involution" "feudal stagnation" and "capitalist sprouts". I need not enumerate Dr Li's many contributions to the study of Qing agriculture or elaborate upon his views of economic development theory since these are very clearly brought out in this book. Instead, I'll offer my own understanding of the methods of researching productive forces and regional economies that Dr Li employs.

Economic history studies the social production, exchange, distribution and consumption of different historical periods; for which studies of labour productivity forms the basis. But for many years, the study of China's pre-modern economy has focused on economic institutions and production relations; very little research has been done on the development of productive forces. There are probably two reasons for this. First, traditional Chinese historical scholarship has stressed more heavily ideal institutions and rarely looked at records of actual production practices. The measures in old sources are really taxation measures; we also lack systematic price records to establish relative prices in the way that A. P. Usher and W. Abel have for medieval Europe to show agricultural prosperity and decline. Second, economic history became an independent field of study in the 1930s. At this time Marxism was already spreading in China to create a new historiography. Marxism considers productive forces to be the most important element of a mode of production, determining social relations of production and economic institutions. Karl Marx also especially paid attention to the role of labour productivity. But China at the time was in the midst of a democratic revolution and land revolution leading to civil war and socialist revolution. Since changing the old relations of production became a demand of the revolution, economic history research also took relations of production as central. This situation continued until 1965. During this period there was a debate concerning the subject of economic history research. The main position was that economic history should study the process of changing relations of production with productive forces forming simply one of the "conditions" for such changes. These views were influenced, of course, by Soviet scholars' views. After a decade of great chaos (1966 – 1976) there was a movement to critique the "theory of productive forces" which made the study of productive forces a forbidden territory—indeed economic history research in general was stifled.

In 1979 I stated several times at different academic conferences that economic history must research productive forces. I also suggested that the development of productive forces has its own rules; it isn't simply restrained by relations of production. But the term the economic history of productive forces is not mine; it was raised by Dr Li later when he was studying Tang Jiangnan agriculture. Thus, productive forces became a new research topic, an important problem to resolve. If the macroeconomic concepts of GNP, national income, consumption and savings are not appropriate for early and mid-Qing society, then studies of productive forces must be combined with regional studies because most sources on productive forces are local histories (or gazetteers), popular writings, private writings, biographies and literary sources. These require great effort to uncover, organize and evaluate. In this regard, Dr Li has made a great contribution. On virtually every page of his book one finds seldom used sources, the product of his great labour.

When we study earlier conditions of production (even if production conditions of a relatively small area), I believe we first should look at how things were done. Thus, I do not approve of models, that is the use of methods that analyse production elements. Definite economic activities under specific conditions always conform to a certain model, but this should be the result of our researches to appear on the last page, not on the first page. Moreover, the development or decline of productive forces in the final analysis is determined by the quality of the natural resources and the efficiency with which people use these essential factors of production. In this kind of analysis, we cannot make a general determination or a determination of value for productive forces, but we can look at its growth, its level and speed of change to make a quantitative evaluation. In this book Dr Li studies the inputs of population, resources, energy and capital (especially fertilizer) as well as technologies and environment. He sees the development of Jiangnan, agricultural productive forces in the early and mid-Qing dynasty as coming from the more rational use of resources and intensification of many different kinds of agriculture. Perhaps there will be people who do not agree with Dr Li's conclusions since there are pros and cons to the economic results of the Qing dynasty, but with respect to methods, he cannot be attacked.

In China's vast territory, each region's development has been uneven, so that regional economic history has special importance. This also makes me remember an odd phenomenon from roughly ten years ago when most young scholars and students were interested in macroeconomics and ignored microeconomics; they enjoyed studying "national economic history" and did not much like regional economic history. I don't really know why. But I think they were partial to "big" research for economic reasons. Perhaps as China has turned to a market economy, microeconomics has become more popular and as economic history research has grown more sophisticated, regional economic history has developed to the point that even the economic histories of border regions and minorities have new research results which show that these areas have their own concrete models of economic construction.

As I see it, regional economic history research has the two strengths of length and breadth. In terms of length, the focus on a region allows one to extend the time period of study to explore the long-term trends of economic development and its stages and cycles. The research method of spatial and temporal study is best suited to regional research. From the point of view of dialectics, nothing develops in a straight line: social phenomena are especially thus. This can only be seen in a long-term perspective. The rise of an industry or some towns is often accompanied by the decline of some other industries or towns; this is easiest to see in a regional study. In this book, Dr Li examines Qing Jiangnan agriculture, but his earlier work on Tang Jiangnan agriculture means he has studied 1000 years of history. For this reason his work on Qing Jiangnan agriculture can be believed. He has connected his studies of Qing Jiangnan agriculture with the decline of Jiangnan agriculture after 1850 and the current modernization efforts. "Looking ahead and behind" has long been a positive tradition of Chinese history; Dr Li's research well represents this tradition.

From the perspective of breadth, one can never study a region in isolation since other areas form the context for analysis. This includes labour force, capital, movement of products, the spread of technologies and the various relations of diffusion, mutual support and competition. Some foreign scholars have suggested that the development of Chinese economic regions was fundamentally autarkic; some Chinese scholars stress the closed nature of economic regions in Chinese feudal society. In recent years these views have been criticized. I consider this a theoretical problem, not a problem of investigation and research method. Marx used *Verkehr* (social contact) to replace *Austausch* (social exchange); when speaking of the development of productive forces, he spoke of wanting a word with even broader meaning. In sum, when studying the relations among regions one must use many methods of observation. Completely independent economic regions probably don't exist; on the contrary, the development of relations among any regions is always a step forward.

As for Jiangnan, well before the Qing it had had economic links with other regions of China (from the northeast to the southwest) as well as close overseas connections. Li's thesis is that Jiangnan's economic existence and development depended on its external connections and that it sent out more than it received. Li's concept in this book of the "formation of an externally oriented agriculture" offers a new and highly favourable evaluation of the development of early and mid-Qing Jiangnan agriculture. Whether viewed from the perspective of several thousand years of historical accumulation or from the vantage point of Jiangnan's economic position within the entire country, this is a turning point.

Beijing

January 1995

Bozhong Li, *Agricultural Development in Jiangnan, 1620 – 1850*, Macmillan Press Ltd. , 1998.

中国の社会主義
改造と現代化

　今日は中国研究所に参りまして諸先生方とお会いでき，大変光栄に存じ
ております。中研の先生方の中国に関する研究は，日中両国の理解を深め
る上で，大きな役割を果してこられました。この事に関して，私は敬服の
気持を抱いております。

　今日私がお話ししますのは，中国の社会主義改造と現代化の問題につい
てです。今日は私が話す方は簡単にさせていただいて，皆様と一緒に研
究，討論する方に多くの時間を割きたいと存じております。私が知ってお
りますところはそう多くはございませんけれども，皆様方が出された問題
に関しては知る限りのことはお答えしたいと思っております。先生方は中
国を研究していらっしゃるわけですから材料が必要だと思います。私はそ
の一つの生きた材料として今日お話しできればと思っております。私とい
うこの生きた材料は，あまりいいものではないかもしれません。私の知識
には限られたところがありますから。

1

　ご承知のとおり，78 年の全国人民代表大会は，新しい時期における総
任務というものを採択いたしました。すなわち今世紀内に四つの現代化を

実現するという目標であります。目下わが国は，上から下まで全国一致して，四つの現代化のために努力しております。日本の友人の皆様方も，この四つの現代化ということに関し，大きな関心を寄せておられます。

　しかしながら，昨年，全国人民代表大会は三年間にわたって国民経済の調整を行なうという方針をうち出しました。すなわち，「調整，改革，整頓，向上」であります。中国ではこれを八字方針と言っております。こういう方針をうち出したということは，何か，外から見ますと，急いで四つの現代化を実現するという事柄と相反する状況が出て来たのではないかと思われます。したがって，国内国外において，これに関する議論が巻き起ったような次第です。例えば，四つの現代化の速度を落したのではないか，あるいはさらに，ひいては後退したのではないか，後退させたのではないかというような心配さえ生まれております。あるいは中国経済に何か新しい異常な状況が生まれているのではないかというような憶測さえ生んでおります。

　私は経済史を勉強しておりまして，当面の経済状況に関しては，専門的な知識を持っておりませんし，必要な，材料も持合せておりません。従いまして私は，歴史的な角度からこの問題についてお話ししたいと考えます。

　解放前，中国は半封建，半植民地の社会でありまして，経済は大変おくれておりました。解放直前における中国の生産形態は，国民総生産のうちわずか17％が現代化された大企業である他，83％は遅れた小農経済，手工業経済でありました。1949 年，全国の現代化された生産設備——工鉱業鉄道，船舶運輸などを含めまして，その設備の価値は人民幣に換算して128 億元でありました。この128 億というのは大変少ない数字でありまして，現在解放後中国は，毎年新たに生産を始めている設備というのが，300 億元余であります。ということは解放当初，旧中国から残されました経済的な基礎というものが，いかに薄弱，いかに資本が少ない状態であったかということを表わしております。しかしながら中国の現代化は，このような薄弱な基礎から歩みを起こさなければならなかったのです。これは歴史的な制約であります。

　新中国の経済建設は社会主義の経済建設でありまして，資本主義の建設ではありません。政治経済学の原理からしますと，社会主義の経済というのは，社会化された大生産を基礎とするものであります。言い換えますと，相当レベルの高い生産力の上に築かれるものであります。しかしながら中国の革命の勝利はこの生産力があまり発展していない段階において達成されたものであります。ここに一つの大きな矛盾が存在します。この矛盾は，社会主義改造の過程において，適切に解決していくべきものであろうと私達は考えました。

　中国の社会主義改造には二つの方面があります。一つは農業方面でありまして，すなわち分散した単独経営を，集団経営にもっていくことであります。つまり一戸一戸の小農生産を，集団化された大農場にもっていくということです。このような改造は困難なものでした。と言いますのは，中国の農業生産は，工業に比べても更に劣っておるからです。旧中国の農業生産は，ほとんど人力に頼るものでした。すなわち，人にせいぜい手を加えたぐらいの伝統的な農業の生産方式が長く続いておりました。但し，有利な側面もありました。と言いますのは，中国の革命は，農民を主力軍とするものでありまして，農民には社会主義的な積極性がありました。同時に，解放まで十数年にわたる，土地革命のなかで，互助，合作の伝統が生れていたからです。

　もう一つの方面は，資本主義経済の改造であります。この方面での困難は，先程申しましたように，我々に残された財産が128億元しかなかった，そういうような状態から出発しなければならないということでした。しかしながら，確かに資本主義経済の基礎は薄弱で貧しいものではありましたけれども，同時に大変それが集中していたという特徴もあります。すなわち資本主義経済のうち80%は，官僚資本として集中されていました。国民党の官僚資本というのは，一種の国家独占資本でした。国家独占資本というのは，その性格から言いますと，既に社会化された大生産であります。従いまして，そこには直接に社会主義経済に転化する可能性がございます。解放後人民政府は，官僚資本のすべてを没収し，それを社会主義の国営経済に転化させました。このようにして改造された社会主義工業は，三年の間にその生産量を三倍ふやしました。ということは，このような改造が正しかった，やり方が正しかったということ，その，生産力が解放されたということを証明していると思います。

　資本主義経済のうち官僚資本を除いた20％は民族資本であります。民族資本はそのほとんどが中小企業でありまして，その性格から言いますと，自由資本主義に属すると思います。民族資本というのは大変分散しておりまして，49年当時，民族資本に属する工場の数は12万3000余，商店が400万余ありました。このような分散した小企業というのは，直接社会主義経済に移ってゆくことは不可能であります。人民政府のこのような企業に対する政策は，まずある程度これを発展させる，次にこれを国家資本主義の段階に進ませる，その段階を経て社会主義経済に改造してゆくという政策でした。49年から52年にかけて，私営工業は毎年1万ほどずつ増えていきました。新たに開かれた工場というのは1万位ずつ増えていき，生産額は54％増加いたしました。53年より，これらの企業に対して，計画的に社会主義改造を行なうようになりました。

　当時の計画では三つの五ケ年計画，すなわち15年をかけて社会主義改造を完了する予定でありました。この15年間，三つの五ケ年計画の間に，大いに生産力を発展させ，基本的に国家の工業化を完了するという方針でありました。同時にこの15年間の間に，農業の協同化を実現し，民族資本の社会主義改造を実現するという計画でした。

　このようにして，一方では生産力を発展させ一方では生産関係を改造してゆくというやり方は，経済発展の法則にかなうやり方であります。しかしながら55年の後半の半年は，農村に社会主義改造の高まりがおとずれまして，大変短かい期間の間に農業の集団化を完了してしまうことになりました。このような農村における社会主義改造の高まりは，都市の改造をも推し進めまして，最初の15年という計画よりはるかに早く，56年のうちに基本的に工業方面の改造をも完了するという事態になりました。

　社会主義改造の目的は，生産力を解放することにあります。そのような目的はこの改造によって実際に達成されたと思われます。56年に改造された工業の生産額は，55年に比べ2％増加しております。農業の方では，

56年合作化，集団化された後，その生産額は55年に比べ5％増加しました。従いまして社会主義改造を繰り上げて実現し，完了したということはよいことでありまして，その後の社会主義建設に対し，一つの良い条件を提供したと言えると思います。

しかしながら次のようなことも見ておかねばなりません。すなわち56年のこの改造と言いますのは，国家の生産力が比較的まだ低いという状況のもとに達成されたものであります。ということは，この改造自体に，いささかまだ熟さない面を残したまま行なわれたということであります。

社会主義改造が基本的に完了した後，全国の建設の重点は経済建設に移されました。当時毛主席は次のように述べておられました。「われわれの目下の根本的な任務は，生産力を解放することから，生産力を発展することに移った」。私たちは事実このように行ないました。しかしながら我々のやり方は十分良かったとは申せません。そこに妨害があったのも事実です。1964年周恩来総理は毛主席の指示にもとづき，全国人民代表大会において四つの現代化を実現しようという構想を述べられました。これは先程申しました妨害を排除し，我々の戦線を整頓する意味がありました。

しかしながらその後10年にわたり，林彪・四人組のより大きな妨害，破壊を受けたのであります。75年周総理は，毛主席の意見にもとずき，全国人民代表大会であらためて，新たに四つの現代化を行なおうという提案を述べられました。しかしながらこの目標は，77年にいたって四人組が打倒された後，初めて実行に移された次第です。

総じて見ますに，中国の経済建設というのは確かに撹乱，妨害を受けてきました。しかしながらその成果というものは，きわめてはっきりしたものがあると思います。たとえば食糧の生産量は，78年と49年を比較しますと，1.7倍に増えておりまして，これはわずかではありますが，人口の増加率を上回るものがあります。工芸作物の方は更に大きく人口の増加率を越えております。工業生産の方は，第一次五ケ年計画が始まった53年から，1978年までを見ますと，平均して成長率は11.2％です。この53年から78年というような長い時期において，毎年平均11.2％の成長をとげて来たということ，これは大変な成果であろうと思います。

2

79 年すなわち昨年の工農業の生産の発展は歴史上これまでにないほど大きなものがありました。ではなぜこのように大きく中国経済が前進している時に当たり，三年の時間をかけ，調整，改革，整頓，向上という八字の方針をうち出したかということであります。その理由は，中国の経済は，経済構造上なおいろいろ問題があります。例えば企業管理体制が良くないなどの問題がありまして，これが四つの現代化のための前進をはばんでいるという現実があります。

先程申しました八つの方針のうち，最も重要なのは，第一番目の調整ということであります。調整といいますのは，各経済部門のバランスを調整するということです。同時に，消費と蓄積の間のバランスを調整することでもあります。我国の国民経済の中には，いろいろなアンバランスな面があります。最もはっきりした問題となるバランス失調は，農業生産が遅れているということです。農業の生産が工業の発展の必要に追いつかない，工業人口の必要に追いつかないという面であります。また農業部門自体の中にも，バランスを欠いている面があります。それは主として林業及び牧畜業の発展が遅れており，生態的均衡を破壊しているという状況が，農業自身の中にあります。また工業部門自体の中にもバランスを欠いている面があります。それは主として日用品及び衣服類等の供給が，市場の需要に追いつかないという問題です。それからかなり問題なのは，燃料，電力，交通運輸部門が遅れており，必要に追いつかないという点です。その結果，例えば新しく工場ができながら，電力の供給が十分でないために生産が始められないというような問題が起こっております。それから炭鉱では，たくさん石炭を掘り出しながら，それを運搬していくことができないというような状況もあります。

次の方針の一つであります改革ですが，これは主として指している対象は，経済管理体制を改革するということです。われわれの計画体制，管理体制の中には，客観的な経済法則に合わない面が多々あります。例えば，中国の企業にはこういう考え方があります。規模大にして全部を備えており，規模小にしても全部を備えている（「大而全，小而全」）という考え方です。すなわち一つの工場が生産の全過程をかかえ込んでいなければいけないという考え方です。例えば一つの工場が，工場で必要なあらゆる部品，ねじくぎに致るまで全部自分たちで作るというような形です。それからまたわが国の工場は，工場の中に修理部門を設けている所が多いのですが，しかし修理の仕事が毎日あるとは限りません。従ってそこが遊んでいるというような状況が出てきてしまいます。あるいは工場が自分で製品を輸送しようとする。したがって自動車隊であるとか倉庫であるとかいうものをかかえ込むことになるという現象もあります。従いまして商品経済，市場の役割を無視し，軽視する傾向がございました。それぞれの生産単位が，例えば物資ですと国家からもらうということだけを考え，市場から調達するということを考えませんでした。そこで市場には商品が不足する，供給が不足するという状況がありました。

分配に関しても欠陥がありました。その欠陥は主として平均主義の考えによるものです。労働者が立派に働こうが，いい加減に働こうが，労働時間が長かろうが短かろうが，その収入は同じだという形です。このようなことも改革の対象でありまして，改めなければならないことです。

次の方針の一つであります整頓ですが，これは工場の経営管理を整頓するということです。それから合理的な管理制度をうち建てるということです。

最後の向上ということですが，これは技術水準，管理水準を高めるということです。そして労働生産性を高め，投資効果を高めるということをねらっております。以上が八字方針の主要な内容です。

3

中国経済において，どうして先程述べたような各方面の経済のバランスを欠くというような状態が生まれてきたかについて，すこし考えてみたいと思います。私が思いますに，これにはいろいろな原因がありまして，一つ二つから来たものではないと思います。例えば四人組の撹乱というのも一つの重要な原因です。四人組は計画経済に反対しました。総合的な均衡をとることに反対いたしました。我々の計画体制は，本来ソ連にならったものでありまして，これは生産品の平衡表をもとに立てるものであります。例えば銑鉄をどれだけ作るということを立てますと，それに燃料，鉄鉱石，労働力がどれだけ必要かというようなことを表に書きます。このようにしますと，一つの製品を作る時の製品の実際にできる量というのは，必要な燃料とか鉄鉱石とか労働力とかといういくつかの項目のうちの，最も少ないものによってその量が決定されるということになります。四人組はこういう計画の立て方を反対し，批判いたしました。これは消極的な平衡だ，消極的なバランスのとり方だというふうに言って批判しました。彼らは積極的な平衡をとるというやり方を提唱いたしました。

この積極均衡というやり方は，少し具体的に言いますと，一頭の馬がとにかく飛び出す，そうすれば万馬はこれに続くという考え方です。つまり，一つの産品をある所がたくさん作れるというのなら，そこでどんどん作ってもらう。そうすると他の所でもそれに学んで，自然にそれに追いつくように努力して追いかけていくであろうという考え方です。このような理論は，見たところ大変「左」でありますが，実際には経済を乱し，害を与える点が非常に多く，そして総合的な均衡をとるというやり方を破壊してしまいました。

管理の方面でも非常に大きな破壊を受けました。というのは，十年にわたって彼らは造反を奨励して来ましたから，工場のさまざまな合理的な規則，経営管理における規則などというのは大きく破壊され，影響を受けました。平均主義の思想，考え方も四人組が特に力を入れて提唱したものです。彼らは労働に応じた分配ということに反対しました。労働に応じた分配というのは，ブルジョア的権利であるという言い方をしました。商品生産を軽視する，無視するというのも四人組の経済原則の一つでありました。四人組時代に出版されました経済学方面の書籍には，このような理論が書かれていたものです。すなわち商品生産及び市場経済は資本主義のものであって，社会主義建設の中で次第にその存在範囲を小さくし，やがては消滅していくものであるという理論です。

　しかしながら，これらいろいろなことを全て四人組に押しつけるということもできないことだと思います。例えば経済の各方面のバランスが失なわれたということは，決して四人組時代になって初めて現われた現象ではありません。ただ，四人組時代を経て，これらの問題が突出してきた，表に大きく出てきたというのは事実だと思います。我々は社会主義建設の経験が足りず，客観的な経済法則に対する認識が足りず，また，政策の面でも間違いがあり，計画の面でも不十分な点があつた，これらがいろいろマイナスをもたらした原因であります。しかしながらこれら中国経済上の問題について，今日私は歴史的に問題を見てお話したいと思います。と言いますのは，これらの経済上の問題を，歴史上にその原因をたずねますと，いずれもそこに原因を見出すことができるからであります。

　例えば経済のバランスが失なわれているということ，その最も突出した例である農業が工業の発展の必要を満足させることができないという面についてですが，このようなアンバランスの根本的な原因は，やはり中国の農業が先程申しましたように，伝統的なやり方に長く従い遅れていた，工業に比べても中国の農業はずっと遅れていたということに原因を求めることができます。農業の社会主義改造の過程におきまして，この問題は適切に解決しなければならないものでありました。このような矛盾に関して毛主席は当時，「農業の根本的な出路は機械化にある」とおっしゃっております。しかしながら農業の集団化，これは大変速いスピードで完成させましたが，現在にいたるまで機械化の程度は，なお，あまり高くはありません。

　農業内部におけるアンバランス，すなわち林業牧畜業が遅れているという点ですが，これもやはり原因は伝統的な中国の農業生産方式に求めることができると思います。すなわち過去の中国の伝統的な農業といいますのは，食糧の生産を第一に置きまして，生態的な均衡というものを顧みるということはなかったからです。

　工業内部に於けるアンバランス，すなわち日用品，紡績品が足りないということ，これも社会主義改造の過程，歴史のなかに原因を求めることができます。解放時，49年における日用品と紡績品の供給は，その半分は手工業生産によっておりました。56年の社会主義改造の高まりが生じたときに，手工業の改造に関しては十分注意を払うことがありませんでした。当時すでに小商品の供給不足という現象が現われておりました。その当時毛主席はこの問題に関して，改造後ではありますが，一部は以前の手工業的な単独経済を回復してもいいということをおっしゃっておられましたが，しかし，そのやり方，その面が十分に実施されなかったという問題があります。去年の調整の方針が出るにいたりまして，やっとこういう問題を徹底的に解決することに取り組んだと言えると思います。その方法は，都市の集団所有制の経済を発展させる，組織するというやり方です。しかしながら現在の都市の集団所有制は，既に手工業にたよるものではなく，半機械化，あるいは全面的に機械化されたものであります。

　先程改造の問題の中で触れました一つの工場が大規模であれ小規模であれ全面的な生産過程を全部備えている「大にして全，小にして全」というようなやり方，それから商品経済，市場の役割，作用を無視する，軽視するというようなやり方，これらはいずれも自然経済の観念のもたらしたものだと思います。わが国ではこれに対して一つの名前を与えております。すなわち小生産の習慣的な力，という言い方をしております。この小生産の習慣的な力，言い換えれば小農経済思想と言ってもいいと思いますが，これは合作化協同化の過程の中で，過去これを批判したことがあります。しかしながらこれは批判にだけ頼っても効果のないものでありまして，大規模生産が実現される中で解決されていくものであろうと思います。小生産の習慣的な力，小農経済思想，こういうものは自給自足ということを中心に置いております。この考え方が拡大されますと，保守主義，鎖国主義，自ら閉じこもって他の世界と交流しないというところに行きつくと思います。

　さらに先程申しました平均主義の思想も小農経済の考え方から来ていると思います。革命史の上には，いわゆる農業社会主義の思潮が存在しておりますが，これは平均主義をその中心思想とするものです。中国革命と，農業合作化運動の中でも，かつて，平均主義に対しましては批判を加えてきました。しかしながらこのように歴史的な原因を持って残されているものは，しばしば大変その根が深く固いものであります。

　それからもう一つ例を挙げたいと思いますが，工業，農業生産品の鋏状格差の問題です。これも歴史的な原因があって生まれてきているものだと思います。その一番の源は，阿片戦争後，外国資本が中国に侵略的に入って来たということと関係があります。この鋏状格差が非常に厳しい問題となりましたのは，1929年の経済恐慌の時でありました。解放後この格差に対して絶えず私どもは調整を行なってまいりました。しかしながら現在に至るまでこの問題は存在しますし，時には拡大されたことさえあります。この問題もやはり昨年の調整政策にいたって初めて根本的に解決しようという決意を持って取り組むことになった次第です。昨年主要農産品の買入れ価格を改めまして平均24.8％上げました。このために政府が必要とし，支出した金は70億元にのぼります。

4

　総じてみますと，現在の四つの現代化は，中国の歴史的は発展というものと切り離せないものであります。旧中国において経済が遅れていたこと，資本主義が発達しなかったということ，これは現在の四つの現代化にとって大きなマイナスの要素を残しました。これらの困難は解放時われわれが手に入れた経済の基礎が非常に薄弱なものであったということだけに限られません。半植民地，半封建の中国における経済構造や，小生産の習慣的力の問題など，やはり大きなマイナスとして残されたわけです。われわれの経済的な基礎が薄弱であった，資本が少なかったということは，これははっきり見てとれることでありまして，これに対しては，われわれは節約するなどして努力し，解決することは，比較的たやすいと思われます。そしてこれは現在のわれわれの資産，つまり国営企業の国定資産で考えてみますと，既にそれは3500億元になっておりまして，解放時の128億元に比べますと27倍に増えております。もちろんこの3500億という数字は決して十分に大きいと言えるものではなく，今後も発展させなければならず，また外国からの資金も導入しなければならないと思います。

しかしながらもう一つの問題である経済構造，それから古い伝統的習慣的な力，こういうものはなかなかめんどうなものでありまして，経済があまり発展していなかった時，たとえば50年代などにおいては，あまりはっきりとした形でマイナス面として現われて来ない，暴露されてはいないという状況がありました。それから四人組の時代は，多くの工場が生産ストップというような状態にありましたために，経済面各部門におけるアンバランスという状況も，そう大きくは目立たなかった，問題にならなかったという状況がありました。しかしながらここ2年余りの間は，生産は大いに発展し，各業種ともそれぞれ生産に力を入れております。こうなりますといろいろな経済構造上の矛盾，バランス失調の面などが大きく前面に出て来たわけです。したがって，先程申しました，調整，改革，整頓，向上の八字の方針の目的とするところは，一つには四人組が乱した経済秩序を整えなおすことであり，同時に歴史的に残されてきました不適応なものを改めるということでもあります。

同時にまた，このような調整政策は，生産力を新たに組織しなおす，日本の言葉で言いますと生産力の再編成だということであります。つまり生産力自体，新たな生産力を作っていくということであります。一つの例を挙げてみます。目下わが国は35万の国営工業がございますが，その中の一部のものは設備が老朽化したり，経営方法がだめになってしまっているというようなことがあります。改革を行なう際に，このような一部の非常に落後した，遅れたものは，切り捨ててしまうということもやります。そうすることによって，かえって全体の生産を高める方向に進むことができます。従いまして八字の方針というのは積極的な方針でありまして，決して消極的なものではありません。昨年八字の方針を実行に移しましてから，非常に新しい気分，新しい意気込み，新しい雰囲気が生まれておりまして，これは，この政策が積極的なものであるということの証明になろうかと思います。

　中国が四つの現代化を実現するためには，正しい政治路線，しっかりした指導者，人民大衆の熱意，これらが必要です。これらは，我々は既にそなえております。華主席を中心とする党中央及び全国人民は，大きな熱意に燃えて四つの現代化のために邁進しております。四つの現代化実現のためには，安定団結の政治的な状況が必要です。これも既にわれわれはそなえております。昔ありました誤審であるとか事実無根の冤罪であるとかは，全て正しい判決を受け，故なく落しめられた人々は，既に名誉を回復されております。劉少奇も最近名誉を回復されました。現在中国国内は，団結一致，固くまとまっているといえます。と同時に社会主義社会の民主を大いに伸ばし発展させ，法秩序を固めるよう努力しております。

　同時に四つの現代化のためには，中国は平和的な国際環境を必要としており，友好国の支持を必要としております。日本は友好的な隣邦であります，日本はこの20年来，経済上飛躍的は発展をなしとげました。工業技術の面におきましては，欧米の先進的な技術に追いつき，一部においては追越しさえしています。従いまして，技術，資金の面だけではなく，経済を発展させた経験と経営管理の方式というものも，中国にとっては非常に大きな学ぶべき点になります。私どもは中国と日本が交流を深め，経験を交流し，お互いに学び合うことを望んでおります。中国研究所の諸先生方は既にその方面で大きなお仕事をなされて来ております。同時に私は，今後更に文化方面における交流が盛んになることを願うものです。先ず私の話はここまでにさせていただきます。どうも御静聴有難うございました。

〈質疑討論〉───────────────────────（司会　阪本楠彦）

──〔江副敏生〕1956年頃農業の社会主義改造をした時に，手工業の改造が遅れて矛盾が出て来た，それが昨年になって都市の集団企業という形で重要視するようになったという話が私にとっては大変面白く思いました。と言いますのは，日本のソ連研究者が1930年頃のソ連で手工業を軽視したことから来る矛盾が大変大きかったという研究を近頃発表しています。その研究で指摘されているのは，中国語で言うならば鎮に相当するようなところの手工業を軽視したということが指摘されておりますが，何かその1956年頃の手工業の改造を軽視したことから，どんな矛盾が出て来たかについて，歴史的な研究成果が出ておりましたらお話していただきたいと思います。

呉承明：56年の手工業の改造に際して現われた矛盾というのは，二つあります。一つは集中しすぎたということ，もう一つは昇級―単位の位を上げすぎたということです。つまり集中ということは単独経営を集中して合作社とか一つの工場にまとめたということ，これにやりすぎがあったということです。それから昇級という方は，例えばこれを国営にすぐもっていってしまったということ，その結果手工業者の人達の仕事，身分というものを上の位にもっていきすぎたということです。手工業といいますのは，本来消費者の好み，必要に合わせて生産を行なうというところに特徴があります。中国の言い方ですと「前には店を置き，後では生産を行なう」という形，これが需要にすぐ応えるという臨機応変性をそなえているということになります。ところがこれを集中して大工場にしてしまいますと，こういう消費者の需要に適切に応える，巧みに呼応していくということができなくなってしまいました。手工業に従事する人々は勤労者であります。しかし彼らは一部の生産手段，小さな機械などを所有しております。しかし，これを集中して国営にまでもっていくというところに，所有制の上において一つの問題が生じてきます。すなわち所有制では，これは個人の所有を廃止することになりますから。我々がそれに対して調整を加えた時，解決の方法として所有権を保留するという方法をとりました。調整を加えたと言いますのは58，9年の頃のことであります。その方法をもう少し詳しく言いますと，従事する勤労者は大きな工場，場合によっては国営ということもあります，そういうものに人は集中させる，そこに属することになる，しかし本人がそれまで持っていた設備の所有権を認める。更にはそれを息子に譲り渡すというようなことさえ認める。人は統一するが所有権を保留するというのはこういうことであります。ただ残念なことにそのようなやり方を徹底することはできませんでした。またちょうどその時大躍進にぶつかったために，その時の気分，いわゆる共産主義の風というものが吹きまわりまして，その結果こういう調整政策を押し流してしまったということになつてしまったのです。更に惜しいことは，そのような調整について十分に調査し研究し，そして本を著わし，文章にしたという人がおりませんでした。それぞれの工作部門の中においては調査，研究は行なわれましたけれども，それをまとめて一冊の本にするということは，終に行なわれませんでした。

——〔江副〕それに関連して，呉承明先生は《中国国民経済の社会主義改造》の編さんのお仕事に参加されました。この本の改訂版が最近出ましたけれど，私は完全に読んではいませんけれども，先生が今おっしゃったことが改訂版には少しは出ているでしょうか。

呉：たぶん書かれていないと思います。私どもの経済研究所の副所長の巫宝三—《中国国民所得》という本を書かれた方ですが，当時この方が手工業の研究をなされておりました。しかしその方の研究成果は発表されませんでした。なぜ発表されなかったかという原因ですが，私が思いますに，その後の反右派闘争と関係あるのではないかと思います。しかし巫宝三先生は既に名誉を回復されております。

——〔山下龍三〕非常に今日は興味のあるお話をうかがわせていただきましたが，特に社会主義改造は当初三つの五ケ年計画を通して発展させる方針をもっていた，ところが農業の協同化が非常に進んだ中で，工商業の社会主義改造も非常に急速に進んだが，その中にはいろいろ行き過ぎなどがあったとおっしゃいました。つまりいささか熟さない中で協同化が進んだということをおっしゃったのですが，農業の協同化を非常に短期間に促進させたのは，その熟していないということと関連して，農民の小生産的な，小ブルジョア的な，急進的な力がそのように短期間にやらせたのか，それとも農民のいわゆる革命的なエネルギーがそうさせたのか，その点をどうみるかうかがいたい。

呉：私のそれに対する見方は山下先生と大体一致すると思います。農業の協同化の計画は，本来一歩一歩進めるというものでした。53 年，中国には1 万5 千の農業合作社がありました。計画では54 年にこれを倍にするということでした。しかしながら実際には，54 年の夏には10 万の合作社ができておりました。いずれもこれは夏に計算を出したもので，これは季節の関係でそうなっております。55年の計画は更に10万増やす，つまり合計20万の合作社を成立させるということでした。しかし実際には，55年の夏65万の合作社ができておりました。従いましてこの時農民には急進的な気分というものがあり，幹部には楽観的すぎる見通しというものがありました。55年の下半期には合作化に全面的に進むという高まりが生まれました。農業合作社の発展は本来，初級形態を経て高級合作社へと進むべきものでありました。しかしながら55年段階では，一気に高級合作社を形成するということが生まれていました。これは生産力の発展にとってはよくない面がありました。その結果56年には全面的に協同化がなしとげられたわけです。速度は速かったわけですが，私個人の見方では，その時出現した問題はそう大きいものではなかったと思います。ひとつにはこの時期にはまだ，共産風が吹くというような現象がなかったということです。合作社は組織されましたが，土地それから生産手段，これは農民のものであるという考え方がまだありまして，共産風が吹いた時の状況とは大分違っておりました。問題が生じたのは人民公社化の後であります。人民公社化と同時に吹き始めました共産風，これを「一平二調」といっています。その内実は，平均主義とさらに物を徴発して移動させてしまう，例えば食糧を生産したらそれを必要だからといって持っていかれてしまう，生産手段も勝手に本人達の承認も得ずに必要な所に動かしてしまう，ということです。この事が非常に大きな問題を生じさせました。その後共産党は共産風を押えにかかりまして，隊を基礎とするという方針にしたわけです。つまり当時の生産力に呼応するのは隊を基礎とすることになるということです。私の考えでは隊を基礎とするというのを超えてしまうと，これは熟さないという面が生まれてくると思います。

——〔山下〕そうしますと当然ながら高級生産合作社から人民公社化に移ったのは，少しあせりすぎたということになりませんでしょうか。もちろん今おっしゃったように，その後生産隊を基礎とするというように整頓して来たわけですが，こうした問題について，つっこんだ著作はあるでしょうか。また，このような協同化の過程での行き過ぎの問題などは，どのように指摘されているでしょうか。

呉：当時それらの問題について討論を起こした文章はありましたけれど
も，発展速度が速過ぎたなどということを明確に指摘し，原因がどこにあ
るかなどということを究明しようとした文章はなかったように思います。
これらの問題に関しては現在，当時をふり返って研究が進められていると
いう状況です。現在こういう方面の研究は，生産力の発展と生産関係の関
係，これが一歩一歩変革されていく，その相互関係についての研究が重点
になっています。なぜそういう研究がなされるようになったかと言います
と，四人組の時代に一つの理論が出されました。貧しいままで新しい段階
に移っていくというものです。その四人組の理論は，具体的には隊を基礎
とするという所有制を，人民公社基模の所有制に変えるということです。
理論面では生産力の発展ということは変革において必要ない，生産力の発
展を必ずしも必要としないという理論でした。彼らは上海でこのための実
験地域を設けました。しかしそういう一つの公社を実験場にして行なうと
いうことは，問題の説明にはなりません。例えばそういう場合，そういう
人民公社には大きな資金の援助があるとか，軍隊を投入して労働力の面で
も援助するとかいうようなことが行なわれましたから，実際問題としては
役に立たない実験ではないかと思います。現在の研究の重点は，生産力が
どこまで発展したら，公有を拡大しうるかという点にありますが，しかし
その成果を発表したものはまだほとんどありません。

──〔江副〕今のお話によると，58年の共産風が問題になっていると思
います。これは当時の経過を見てみますと，第一次五ケ年計画の総括と56
年の中ソ論争，特にスターリン批判の問題を契機としてこれが展開された
と思いますが，この点についてどう見ておられるのか，さらにもう一点こ
れと関連しまして，この共産風の批判が今出ているということは，つまり
結論として八全大会の路線への復帰というように考えられますけれども，
その点はどう理解していいかというこの2点について教えていただきた
い。

──〔阪本〕付け加えて言いますと，ソ連に反対するためにソ連とは違
ったことをやろう，違ったことをやろうとし過ぎたんではないかという疑
問が日本にはあるのです。

呉：まず共産風につきましては，共産風という言い方はもっぱら58年の大躍進の時のあの熱狂的なやり方を指すものでありまして，それ以後にはこういう言葉は使いません。第一次五ケ年計画の総括あるいは56年のスターリン批判，中ソ論争ということ，いずれも私が思いますのに関係はないのではないか，あるいはソ連と違ったことをやろうとしたこととともまあ関係はないのではないかと私は考えます。八大路線への復帰ということは，共産風の批判の結論としてではなく，その後の極左路線への批判の結果としてあると思います。それから八大路線そのものについては，既にこの内容は肯定されております。肯定すべきだと思います。と言いますのは八全大会では社会主義建設の道，これをはっきり確立，決定いたしました。従って当然これは擁護されるべき，堅持されるべきものだと思います。八大路線の基本的な内容，すなわち社会主義建設の道および当時決定されました建設の総路線―多く，速く，立派に，節約して社会主義建設を行なうというような内容は今日全面的に肯定されております。これは日本に来た後のことなので私は新聞で見ただけのことを申し上げますが，鄧小平氏の政治路線の中から見られますことは，先程言いましたような総路線です。「大いに力を入れて高い目標をめざす」それから「多く，速く，立派に，節約してやる」ということすべてその中に含まれていると思います。しかしながら八全大会の文献の中に一つの理論的な問題が含まれておりまして，これは現在もまだ全面的に中国において見方が一致しているとは言えません。つまり中国社会の主要な矛盾は何かという問題です。といいますのは八全大会での文献の中に見られます主要な矛盾の規定のし方は「進んだ生産関係と遅れた生産力の間の矛盾である」という言い方をしております。この問題に関しましては国内経済学界でちょうど論争されているところです。

―〔江副〕私は過渡期論を研究しているのですが，今のお話と関連して，八大路線の復帰といいますと，資本主義から社会主義への過渡期が56年に終わって社会主義社会がそれから成立するという過渡期論になるわけでして，この過渡期論は現にソ連がとっている過渡期論あるいは社会主義社会の認識と共通のものになるのではないでしょうか。それに対しまして中国では56年以後毛沢東のもとで新しい過渡期論が提起され，そして新しい継続革命の路線がつくられていますから，その過渡期論，その上に立った路線が否定されていることになると思うのですけれど，この点についてはどうお考えでしょうか。主要な矛盾の問題になると思いますが。

呉：この問題については，中国でもまだ結論が出されておりません。過渡期とは何か，これについては目下中国の経済界で大きな問題となっております。私の見るところ，最初に江副先生がおっしゃったように，56年以後は社会主義という学派の方が優勢を占めるように思われます。しかしながら年齢の高い経済学者の中には，社会主義社会こそその社会がすべて過渡期であるという見方をお持ちの方もいらっしゃいます。中国においては，これは実は今，一番激しく熱を込めて議論されている問題でありますが，結論はまだ出ていないと見ていいでしょう。と同時に新聞などにもそれについて触れた文章は少ないと思います。中国はしばしばこういうことがありまして，最も今熱っぽく論じられている問題はかえって新聞などには載らない，つまり結論が出るのを待った後それが出てくるというのが普通であります。

——〔吉田実〕日本の一般的な受け止め方として，劉少奇時代には劉少奇が全部悪い，四人組が悪くなると全部四人組が悪いと，中国の論調はそういうふうに日本人一般には聞こえて来るわけです。今の先生のお話の中で，やはり四人組の時に非常に矛盾が出て来たんだと，しかしそれはもともと歴史が残してきた，中国の長い歴史が残して来た問題だとそういうふうな姿勢で問題を問い直されていく姿勢というものを私はこれからの中国に本当に望みたいところだと思うんですが，そういうお話があったのは非常にうれしかったと思います。例えば大寨が悪いというと全部大寨が悪くなってしまうというような，そういう状況ではなくなって来ている。私は昨年の秋に中国を訪問した時に，農業部の第一副部長の張根生さんが大寨の評価についてやはり肯定面と否定面を出されていましたが，そういう点で今日のお話も非常に嬉しかったと思います。私がご質問したいのは，八全大会についての理論問題として一つ残されているのは，中国社会の主要な矛盾というのは「進んだ生産関係とおくれた生産力の間の矛盾である」

というふうな規定についてまだ結論が出ていないのだ，これ一つだとおっしゃいましたが，今の中国にとっては一面では生産関係を追求した結果出て来た一つの極左路線の問題がひとつあるのと，もうひとつは，中国の社会にひじょうに根強く残っておるフューダル・ビューロクラシー（封建官僚主義）という問題がある。こと両面の問題を中国がやはり抱えておって，この問題の処理をうまくやらないと非常にいけないと思うんですが，いかがでしょうか。

呉：吉田先生の見方に私は全く同感でございます。先程吉田先生がおっしゃられましたように，生産関係を追求した結果極左にいたったということ，このことを認めると同時に，それは同時に提出されました第二の問題，封建官僚主義というものとも強くつながるものだと思います。と言いますのは，先程私が触れました「大にして全，小にして全」すべてを備えているということ，あるいは自給自足という考え方，これらを完全な社会主義だとみなす，これが四人組の考え方です。その証拠は彼らの系統の人が書いたもの，政治，経済学などにそういう考え方があります。それら先程述べましたことが封建主義とつながるものであるとすれば，同時に法家と儒家，儒法闘争—法家をもちあげたということ—これも封建的なものの残りであると思います。例えば江青は女の皇帝になろうとしたなどというところにも見られると思います。四人組は政治上では資本主義の民主にも反対し，同時に社会主義の民主にも反対しました。そして彼らが提唱したのは秦の始皇帝です。中国の学術界では去年の五四60周年あたりを契機としまして民主の問題，封建残余の問題などがいろいろ討議されるようになってきました。それらの討論の中から新たに反封建という任務を提起するに至りました。と言いますのは，五四から既に60年たちました。五四の時のスローガンは「民主と科学」です。しかしながら60年後の現在を見ますに科学はおくれ民主もまだ達成されていない，不足な面がある。発表された何篇かの文章は，四人組の封建的な本質を分析しております。ある論文ではもっぱら彼らの封建的な経済思想，これを批判しておりました。その文章は私が書いたものではありませんけれども，非常に力を入れてこれを書きあげるようバックアップしたものです。そこで私は吉田先生が先程お出しになりました封建官僚主義などという問題に，大変私自身興味を感じているというわけです。

——〔松本与市〕今の問題に関連すると思いますが，先程「大にして全，小にして全」そういう考え方は経済法則に合わない，従ってそれは改革されなければならないというお話がありましたが，その「大にして全，小にして全」のその「全」の中には，実は行政権力も入っている，含まれているというふうに私は理解しておりますけれども，それが改革のテーマにはならないのか，あるいはそういう問題も既に提起されておりますのか，そのへんのことをうかがえたら大変幸いです。

呉：現在改革の内容として企業の自主権を拡げるということが含まれております。昔は上級の行政機関および上級の経済機関の企業に対する管理が厳しすぎたという問題があります。ひとつ例を挙げますと，それぞれの企業は減価償却のための資金を用意することができます。それは本来は設備を更新するものではありますが，しかし自分で企業自らそれを使うことができなかった。それはまず財政部にそれを渡さなければいけない性質のものでした。それからもっと重要なことは，企業，工場が市場の必要，それから供給対象の必要に応じて生産を行なうことができず，規定の，上から降りて来た生産計画だけに従って生産しなければならなかったということです。そういうわけで現在は，企業の自主権を拡げるということを改革の原則のひとつに組入れております。「大にして全，小にして全」ということは，それが経済法則に合わないとしておりますのは，主として分業，ひいては専門化を妨げているからです。社会の分業ということは，アダム＝スミスからマルクスに至るまで非常に重視しております。しかし中国では一貫してこれを重視してきませんでした。中国の昔の考え方ですと，「万事人に求めず」という形を一つの理想としておりました。そういう考え方は，分業を進め，専門的な技術をたくわえ，労働生産性を高めるということの大きな妨げになってきたのです。

（記録整理，文責・古島和雄）

　以上，本年1月から東京大学社会科学研究所の外国人研究員として3ヵ月滞在された呉承明氏〔中国社会科学院経済研究所研究員〕を中国研究所に迎えて行なった研究会（3月15日）での報告と質疑を，『アジア経済旬報』（1150～1号）から再録して掲載しました。文中の1，2…は編集部による。

呉承明氏のプロフィール

　呉承明氏は1969年から3年余，遼寧省営口の五七幹部学校にいた。人民公社の土地を開墾して耕やす生活だった。水稲をムー当り900斤以上とったことがある。日本流に言って10アール当り9俵余。シロウトにしては御見事というほかないが，「いやぁ，化学肥料をどんとぶちこんでるし，労働を計算すると，コストは高い」と御本人は謙遜する。いかにも，高い幹部の給料でコスト計算したら，高い米だったにちがいない。

　酒に関してはもともと海量（ハイリャン）で，胃潰瘍の今でも日本酒の呑みっぷりは鮮やかな人である。車を曳いて町へゆく仕事があれば買ってくるとか，家へ一時帰った人が持ってきてくれるとかする酒をこっそり飲むという"普遍現象"の仲間入りをしていた。

　肉体労働を1日8時間も要求されたわけではない。しかし，3年間経済学の勉強は何もやれなかったから，ふだんは作らぬ詩を作ってみたり，哲学書を読んで思索にふけったりした。そして，つくづく，まったく前の通りだと思った言葉が「我思う，故に我在り」（デカルト）だったという。有名な観念論哲学者の言葉も，状況によっては，力につきおとされて生きる知識人の意地の言葉にもなりうるわけである。

　　〔原載（日本）中国研究所《中国研究日報》1980年6月号（総
　　388号）〕

中国近代経済史の
史料工作の近況について

　中国では，"四人組"が粉砕された後，「実践は理論を験証する唯一の基準である」の討論が提起され，全国に巨大な反応が引きおこされた。経済史学界についていうと，まずいくつかの形而上学的な観点が打破され，実事求是が強調され，中国社会の歴史実践によって歴史を叙述すること，客観的経済法則によって歴史上の経済現象を説明することが強調されている。同時に，生産力の研究を強化するという傾向，および，数量概念に注意し，可能なかぎり数学の方法を用いて歴史上の経済現象について定量分析をするという傾向がある。これらの原因により，史料工作が重視されるようになった。

　北京の故宮博物院所蔵の明清檔案は，九百万件あまりあり，一つの資料宝庫である。経済史の方面では，中国社会科学院歴史研究所が，檔案の中の刑科題本を利用して，清代乾隆期の農村租佃関係の詳細な史料を編輯した（代表は劉永成先生）。中国社会科学院経済研究所が，その項の檔案を利用して，農村雇傭関係の史料を編集した（代表は魏金玉先生）。

　明清の碑刻は，中国近代史を研究する実物資料であり，以前にすでに出版されたことがある。文化大革命の間に，蘇州で258件の明清碑刻が出土した（経済方面のものは51件）。南京大学が，江南数県の出土碑刻の全面的調査を組織している（代表は洪煥春教授）。

　文化大革命の間に，盛宣懐の私人檔案が発見された。その分量は非常に多い。この檔案は，現在上海図書館に保存され，復旦大学によって整理が進められている（代表は汪熙教授）。

中国人民銀行の金融研究所では，数十人の力を組織して，旧中国各銀行の檔案材料を整理している。その中には，外商銀行，官僚資本銀行，民族資本銀行を含んでおり，各銀行ごとに編集して書物にする（代表は楊培新先生）。

企業檔案を利用して進めている研究は，そのほか，上海社会科学院経済研究所編集の英米煙草公司，江南造船廠の資料，天津南開大学編集の開灤炭坑の資料，武漢大学編集の漢冶萍公司の資料，江蘇南通方面編集の大生資本集団〔張謇〕の資料等がある。

中国社会科学院経済研究所，財政部，人民銀行等の単位では，江西中央革命根拠地の檔案・文献に対して整理を行い，また大量の調査と大衆訪問工作をした。これは，文献材料と，調査，訪問工作とを結合する方法によって経済史料を研究した模範例である。かれらはまた，同様の方法を用いてその他の革命根拠地の経済史料を研究する準備をしている。

中国社会科学院経済研究所と上海社会科学院経済研究所が中心となって，『中国資本主義工商業資料叢刊』を編集した（代表は呉承明と徐新吾先生）。すでに八種を出版し，編集中のものが十一種ある（綿紡織工業，製糸工業，絹織物工業，製紙工業，製粉工業，土布業，五金商業，西薬商業，百貨店商業，輸出入商業，武漢の"裕大華"綿紡集団）。編集執筆に参加している者の中に，以前のその業種の経営者が多数おり，また以前のその業種の老職工を大量に訪問した。文献材料と「生きた材料」とを結合した方法だということができる。以前の当事者の多数はすでに死亡しており，「生きた材料」を急いで拾いあげることが，当面の重要な仕事の一つである。以上の各資料は，大部分は今年出版されるであろう。

　　　（近藤邦康訳。原載『東京大学東洋文化研究所・東洋学文献センター報』，1980 年 5 月）

附　录

吴承明年表

吴　洪

1917 年 1 月 3 日　出生于律师家庭，祖籍河北滦县，汉族。

1920 年　随父母来北平，在四世同堂的大家庭中生活。

1923 年　入北京公立第三十七小学（新中国成立后为西直门小学）。

1926 年　退学改为在家念私塾。

1928 年　入北平市立第三中学。曾与人办油印小报，自编自导并参演独幕剧。

1931 年　考入北京四中高中，时值"九一八"事变，作为积极分子和新四军革命烈士黄诚的助手，开始投入反日救国运动。

1932 年　因组织校内学生反日运动被四中校长齐树芸要求转学，投考天津北洋工学院高中部并被录取。

1932 年　进入北洋大学（预科），开始树立"工业救国"思想。作为预科学生代表参加校内进步学生组织"河滨社""荒火社"活动。在抗日宣传基地"工友补习学校"中任教务长。又倡导组织世界语学会，开世界语班。

1934 年　考入清华大学理学院化学系，从"工业救国"转为"科学救国"。二年级时又觉"科学救国"不如"经济救国"更为现实，随从化学系转入经济系。

1935 年　参加中共的外围组织"中华民族武装自卫会"并接受工作任务。

1935 年夏　在学生自治会主办的工友补习学校当教员；任《清华周刊》总发行，利用所掌握的发行网向边远地区左派组织邮寄抗日救亡出版物；在《东方既白》杂志创刊号上撰写论中国土地问题的文章。

1935 年 8 月　在清华党支部内由蒋南翔、何凤元介绍宣誓入党。

1935 年 12 月　作为清华领队参加"一二·九""一二·一六"两次大游行。

1936 年 2 月　被选为清华中共重要的外围团体、青年抗战救亡运动中坚力量的中华民族解放先锋队（简称"民先"）大队长。

1936 年 6 月　因学生运动被清华开除后考入北京大学史学系，仍持"经济救国"思想，故把目标放在近代史上，并听经济系课程及业余时间自学马克思主义经济学。在北大期间参加了"援绥""一二·一二大游行"等抗战活动。

1937 年 8 月　参加学生抗战组织"平津流亡同学会"并被补选进执委，此时发现已在乱世中失掉组织关系为非中共党员了。

1937 年 11 月　参加"民先"号召组成的战地服务团。

1938 年　在西南联大选修了陈寅恪的隋唐史和佛典文学；葛邦福（John J. Gapanovich）的希腊罗马史和赵迺抟的经济思想史等课程。出于兴趣参加西南联大话剧团。

1940 年夏　完成《古代云南与中土关系之研究》一文。从西南联大毕业开始步入社会，到歌乐山的中央银行经济研究处研究战时经济。

1941 年 2 月　到经济会议秘书处和金融组工作，后任金融组秘书，被迫加入国民党，此后具有了"历史问题"。

1943 年　到"中国战时生产促进会"任研究部主任。在重庆的三年被《新蜀报》聘为"主笔"；又主编半月刊《银行界》。在《时事新报》发表《论当前生产政策》《论大小生产——再论当前生产政策》两文；撰写《产业资金问题之检讨》《理想利率》等文。

1943 年冬　怀揣"实业救国"梦想，船行 43 天赴美留学，入哥伦比亚商学院研究生部主修"货币与金融"，辅修"工业管理"。学习了查普曼的银行学、多德的金融市场、莫里斯·克拉克的经济学等课程。

1945 年　以五门并列 A 的课业成绩和一篇题为《认股权、股票股利及股票分裂与扩充公司之投资理论》的论文获金钥匙奖（注：这是美国大学生的最高奖）。

1946 年 3 月 与钢琴家洪达琳女士在美国纽约结婚，洪达琳于 1994 年 1 月在北京病逝。《美国的战时公债与金融政策》一文通过硕士学位答辩。

1946 年 6 月 受雇资源委员会，在纽约办事处工作；作为资源委员会顾问、美国经济学家库兹涅茨（1971 年诺贝尔经济学奖金获得者）的助手由美回国工作。9 月，调日本赔偿拆迁委员会工作。

1947 年初 辞职到上海，任中央信托局信托处襄理，分工管外汇，曾设法给中共地下贸易组织"广大华行"做成小额贷款。

1947 年夏 兼任上海交通大学教授，讲授"货币银行"和"国际汇兑"，后教"工业管理"和"财务报告分析"两课，所讲内容多为当时国内大学首创。

1948 年 开始研究中国工业资本问题，后写成《中国工业资本的估计和分析》一文发表。

1949 年 11 月 到北京中央外资企业局，任业务处副处长。

1950 年 开始研究外国在华投资，1951 年用"魏子初"（"外资处"谐音）笔名发表了三篇论文和三种小册子。其中《帝国主义在华投资》连印三版，并有俄文版。

1952 年 兼任工商行政处副处长，主持私营企业重估财产、调整资本工作。开始注意商业和市场问题，为后来研究市场史做准备。

1954 年 在北京开始经济史研究工作，首先从资料工作做起；编著《帝国主义与开滦煤矿》，署名"魏子初"，1954 年由神州国光社出版。

1955 年 《帝国主义在旧中国的投资》，人民出版社出版。

1956 年夏 任调查研究处处长。

1958 年 任由中央工商行政管理局与科学院经济研究所合设的"资本主义经济改造研究室"主任。

1962 年 负责通稿的《中国资本主义工商业的社会主义改造》，由人民出版社出版。

1969 年 8 月 下放到辽宁盘锦的商业部"五七干校"。

1971 年 11 月 迁到河北固安县粮食部"五七干校"。

1974 年 1 月　借调人民出版社主编《旧中国的资本主义生产关系》。

1975 年 8 月　调到商业部，酝酿、准备编写《中国资本主义发展史》。

1978 年 5 月　到中国社会科学院经济研究所工作，开始主编《中国资本主义发展史》，并在后来通稿时实际上将三卷重写一遍。

1978 年　开始招收经济史硕士研究生。

1979 年 12 月　受日本"国际交流基金"资助在东京大学社会科学研究所作外国研究员。

1984 年 8 月　受洛克菲勒基金会资助赴意大利参加中国经济史讨论会，在发言中提出"史无定法"。

1985 年　开始招收经济史博士研究生。

1985 年　出版论文集《中国资本主义与国内市场》，中国社会科学出版社。

1986 年 3 月　被聘为美国加州理工学院客座教授。

1987 年 2 月　在中国社会科学院经济研究所加入中国共产党。

1987 年 12 月　被聘为南开大学经济研究所教授。

1991 年 6 月　当选为中国经济史学会会长。

1991 年 10 月　获国务院政府特殊津贴。

1992 年　作《濯足偶谈》。

1995 年 4 月　与文铭女士在北京结婚，文铭于 2010 年 8 月在上海病逝。

1995 年 4 月　发表《经济学理论与经济史研究》，提出"在经济史研究中，一切经济学理论都应视为方法论"；"经济史应当成为经济学的源，而不是它的流"。

1996 年　出版论文集《市场·近代化·经济史论》，云南大学出版社。

2001 年 9 月　出版论文集《中国的现代化：市场与社会》，三联出版社。

2002 年　修订再版《濯足偶谈》。

2002 年 12 月　出版《吴承明集》，中国社会科学出版社。

2006 年　出版《经济史：历史观与方法论》，上海财经大学出版社。开始作《濯足四谈》。

2006 年 8 月　获中国社会科学院首批"荣誉学部委员"称号。

2006 年 12 月 《中国社会经济史论丛——吴承明教授九十华诞纪念文集》由中国社会科学出版社出版。

2007 年 4 月 中国社会科学院举办"吴承明、汪敬虞先生九十华诞学术讨论会"。

2008 年 9 月 当选"中国社会科学院健康老人"。

2011 年 发表了最后一篇学术论文《全要素分析方法与中国经济史研究》。

2011 年 7 月 8 日 因病在北京逝世,享年 94 岁。

吴承明先生学术小传

李伯重

    吴承明先生（1917～2011），1917年1月3日生于河北省滦县一个书香门第。他的曾祖父官至清朝内阁中书，博学多才，"研讨经世之学"，曾联名奏请修建芦汉铁路，得李鸿章力赞却终未果。后外放浙江，出任多处地方官，政绩卓著，又任全浙海塘工程总局事及监酒税等职，为官刚正清廉，"处脂膏而不以自润"，受命反贪腐"守正不阿"。辛亥革命中，他敦促浙军起义，为民国建立立下了一份功劳。后北归隐居，"然忧国之心，老而弥笃"，以"思寡过"名其书斋，"以清白遗子孙"，享米寿（八十八岁）而终。祖父曾在杭州为书吏，1920年后定居北京。父亲吴大业先生，1911年毕业于北洋大学堂法科，是一位著名律师。他曾协助民国外交总长王正廷督办"鲁案"善后事宜，为欧战后中国政府从德国收回青岛相关主权和胶济铁路的权益尽了一份力，后为专业民法律师，在当时律师界颇具名望，两度任北平律师公会会长，先后任北平国货陈列馆馆长、财政部北平印刷局局长等职。吴先生之母李翔青女士毕业于我国最早的女子师范学校之一的北洋女子师范学堂，一生相夫教子，贤妻良母。

    吴先生为家中长男，幼年在私塾接受传统教育，熟读古文诗书，但父亲开明，也让他学习算术和英语。他入中学后各科成绩优异，并积极参加学生活动。因立志科学救国，于1932年考入北洋工学院预科，两年后进入清华大学理学院，但后有感于研究中经济问题的重要，又转至经济系。时任系主任的陈岱孙教授的西方经济学说、萧蘧教授的货币银行学和余肇池教授的会计学等课程，杨树达教授、雷海宗教授的文史课程，都使吴先生受到很大的教益。吴先生在读书期间很活跃，参加了世界语和新文字运动，1935 年在《东方既白》杂志创刊号上发表论中国土地问题的文章。其时日寇侵华凶焰日长，国难当头，作为一个爱国热血青年，他奋起投入救亡工作，参加了中华民族武装自卫会等进步团体，是北平爱国学生运动的领袖之一。因从事救亡运动，被迫离开清华。后于 1936 年秋考入北京大学历史系，在此受教于孟森、郑天挺、钱穆等史学名师。"七七事变"之后，他参加由平津学生和医生、护士组成的战地服务团，随军服务。这年冬天他在试马时写下"策马登峰极，边城看雪消；含悲辞燕阙，饮恨建康桥"的诗句，以明抗战决心。1938 年冬服务团解散，吴先生到昆明西南联合大学复学。其时的西南联大，由北大、清华和南开三校组成，名流云集，他亦得聆教于陈寅恪、钱穆、姚从吾、刘文典、赵廼抟诸先生。他还加入西南联大话剧团，参演闻一多为舞美、曹禺任导演的剧目，并到工厂农村演出宣传抗战。以其深厚的文史功底为基础，他完成了论文《古代云南与中土关系之研究》，这是他中国经济史研究生涯的开始。1940 年夏，吴先生从西南联大毕业，步入社会，供职于重庆中央银行经济研究处，并兼任当时国家总动员会议专员以及《新蜀日报》编辑。工作之余，他发表了一些研究战时生产政策和金融的文章，文章产生一定的影响。

为进一步加深经济学修养，吴先生于 1943 年冬赴美，考入哥伦比亚大学商学院攻读研究生，主修货币与金融学。吴先生的导师贝克哈特（B. H. Beckhart）是著名经济学家，在关于美联储的研究方面非常有名，也是大通银行首席经济学家，他明确反对凯恩斯主义。其时凯恩斯经济学盛行，而在治学方面，哥伦比亚大学仍有边际效用学派大师克拉克（J. B. Clark）之遗风。克拉克之子小克拉克（J. M. Clark）主持哥大讲坛，吴先生选修了他开的经济学课程，此外还选了查普曼（T. Chapman）的银行学、多德（D. L. Dodd）的金融市场等课程。吴先生成绩优异，于 1945 年荣获贝塔–西格玛–伽玛（BΣΓ）荣誉学会的"金钥匙奖"（这一奖项要求获奖人课业优秀必须五门成绩并列"A"）。先生共用两年时间修满学分，在贝克哈特指导下完成《美国的战时公债与金融政策》学位论文，顺利通过颇得好评，1946 年获得硕士学位。

吴先生先后就学于北洋大学、清华大学、北京大学、西南联大和哥伦比亚大学，主修过工科、理科、历史和经济学。这些名校中不同学派并存的环境，使得他获得了贯通古今、学兼中文的广阔视野和海纳百川的学术胸襟。这种开放宽容的学术风格和思维逻辑贯穿他一生。

1946 年 3 月 9 日，吴先生在纽约与钢琴家洪达琳女士喜结伉俪，两校师生前来祝贺热闹非凡。婚后，吴先生打消继续攻读博士学位或留在美国就业的念头，选择回国报效祖国之路。此时抗战已胜利，国内百废待兴，国民政府资源委员会聘请被称为"GNP 之父"（后改用 GDP）的著名经济学家库兹涅茨（S. S. Kuznets，1971 年诺贝尔经济学奖获得者）担任该委员会顾问，请他帮助设计资源和工矿产业的调查统计制度，并聘吴先生为该委员会经济研究处专门委员，作为库氏助手，为他准备有关中国的经济资料。吴先生于是于 6 月陪同库氏到南京资源委员会工作。1947 年初，吴先生辞去南京的工作来到上海，任中央信托局信托处襄理。因为他本意还是希望教书和做研究，故兼任上海交通大学、东吴大学等校教授，讲授货币银行、国际汇兑、工业管理和财务报告分析等课程，很受欢迎，还发表了一些相关论文。

吴先生在上海工作和生活直至解放。1949 年冬，他的清华、哥大老学长也是中央银行经济研究处的顶头上司冀朝鼎出任新中国中央财经委委员兼中央外资企业局局长，邀吴先生到北京工作。1949 年底，吴先生举家北迁北京，先后任职于中央外资企业局与中央工商行政管理局，任该局外资处副处长，并参加了在华外资普查等工作。此时，他开始研究外国在华投资问题。1951 年，他以笔名"魏子初"（"外资处"谐音）发表了一些成果，其中最主要的是《帝国主义在华投资》。在此基础上，他将外国直接投资的研究，从前人一般止于的 1936 年延伸至 1948 年，并证实了外国在华投资中来自本国的资本输出很少，而主要是来自外资在华的积累。其成果就是 1955 年出版的《帝国主义在旧中国的投资》一书。

1952 年，吴先生出任中央工商行政管理局工商行政处副处长。1958 年，改任调查研究处处长，此时研究处调来方行、汪士信、梁思达、黄如桐等学者，一时人才济济。尔后在孙冶方、许涤新的积极支持下，由工商局与经济所合设资本主义经济改造研究室，吴先生任主任，研究室的主要任务是编写

《中国资本主义工商业史料丛刊》和撰写《中国资本主义工商业的社会主义改造》。

1966年"文化大革命"爆发后，研究室被解散，吴先生也受到迫害，并于1970年春被下放到辽宁盘锦、河北固安等地的"五七干校"。直到1974年初，许涤新先生联系人民出版社"借调"吴先生等人去编写《旧中国的资本主义生产关系》（1977年出版），才得以离开干校返京。1975年8月，他们又被调到商业部，由许涤新直接领导，酝酿写《中国资本主义发展史》。

"文革"结束后，吴先生和千千万万知识分子一样，迎来了"科学的春天"。1977年7月许涤新先生出任中国社会科学院经济研究所所长，1978年5月，吴先生等人也转到了经济所，任专职研究员，一直到2011年7月8日辞世。他在经济研究所任学术委员会委员，兼任中国社会科学院研究生院和南开大学经济研究所教授、博士生导师，以及日本东京大学客员研究员、美国加州理工学院客座教授，并被选为中国经济史学会首任会长、中国投资史研究会名誉理事长、中国国史会理事、中华全国工商业联合会特约顾问等，2006年被授予中国社会科学院首批"荣誉学部委员"。

1949年冬移居北京之后，在承担政府经济管理工作的同时，吴先生仍然结合工作实践，继续进行经济理论和经济史的研究。在中央外资企业局和中央工商行政管理局工作期间，他着力于研究西方在华投资和中国民族资本两大课题。他先发表了一系列专论和小册子，在此基础上，于1955年出版的《帝国主义在旧中国的投资》一书被广泛引用于教学和研究。其节本《帝国主义在华投资》旋即为苏联科学院译为俄文出版。1956年他的长篇论文《中国民族资本的特点》刊出。此文无论在观点见解方面，还是资料使用方面，均堪开创风气之作。他领导资本主义经济改造研究室之后，组织各方面力量，广泛收集资料，主持编写为《中国资本主义工商业的社会主义改造》一书，于1962年出版，引起海内外重视，其日译本亦于1971年出版。

1960年以后，吴先生主要精力集中于中国资本主义发展史主编写工作。他首先组织人员，搜集、编写史料，主编出版《中国资本主义工商业史料丛刊》(已先后刊出八种),并组织了一系列专题调查。这些工作为"文革"所打断,恢复工作后,他将部分调查成果整理出来,主编为《旧中国资本主义生产关系》,于 1977 年出版。

1977 年吴先生转职中国社会科学院经济研究所后,在以前所做的准备工作的基础之上,和许涤新先生共同主持了三卷本《中国资本主义发展史》的编写工作。这部中国经济史研究中具有里程碑意义的巨著,由北京、上海、天津等地的二十余位专家分章撰写,最终由吴先生统稿,并执笔写了"导论"等重要部分,及承担了全部计量分析工作。此书的编写,前后经历了十五个寒暑,方得大功告成(第一、二、三卷分别于 1985、1990 和 1993 年先后出版)。

吴先生的学术活动开始于青年时代。早在 20 世纪 30 年代,当他还是一个年轻学生时,就已经发表了关于中国土地问题的论文。到了 20 世纪 40 年代,又发表了若干历史考证的论文和一系列关于战时经济的文章。他在哥伦比亚大学的硕士学位论文《评美国战时公债政策》,以非凯恩斯的观点提出新见,受到重视和好评。1946 年归国后,他逐渐转入中国近代经济史的研究,代表作是 1947 年发表的《中国国民所得和资本形成》和 1949 年发表的《中国工业资本的估计和分析》二文。在后一文中,他运用马克思主义的经济理论,来对中国工业资本进行计量分析,这在当时的中国经济史学中,尚属首创之举。20 世纪 50 年代,吴先生在研究资本主义工商业的社会主义改造(即公私合营)时,发现在此运动中问题甚多,因此后来建议《中国资本主义发展史》写到解放为止,不再继续写第四卷"资本主义工商业的社会主义改造"。这一点,在当时是需要大智大勇的。20 世纪 80 年代初,吴先生任《中国大百科全书》经济学卷"前资本主义"部分的中国经济史部分主编,并撰写长条"中国经济史",提出了他对三千年来整个中国经济发展的看法。1984 年以来,他主要精力集中于经济学理论、经济史研究的方法论、中国经济的近代化以及市场等问题的研究,其探讨范围从西方现代经济学理论的最新进展到明清中国的国内市场,从历史主义到近代中国的工业化道路,力图以史为鉴,对今天有中国特色的社会主义建设做出贡献。

吴先生一生著作等身,除了以上谈到的著作外,他还发表多篇专题论文,大多已收入他的几部论文集。这些论文对中国经济史上的问题和经济史研究中的若干重大问题，提出了极为精辟的独到见解，引起中外学者的关注。其中《中国资本主义发展述略》一文，以系统论述和分析见长，发表即有几家书刊转载，并有英、日译本。此书关于明清及近代中国市场与流通的论文，当时属开拓性研究，发表后，很快有了日译本，而在西方最具影响的人文社会科学杂志——法国的《年鉴》——杂志上，也有专文详加评介。他以多年心血主编的《中国资本主义发展史》，刊出后受到国际学界的高度重视，1987 年台北谷风出版社出了繁体字版，稍后，由伦敦大学柯文南（C. A. Curwen）译编的英文本，也与 2000 年由麦克米伦出版社（The MacMillan Press Ltd.）出版。尽管此书与任何著作一样不可避免地带有那个时代的痕迹，但确是中国经济史学的里程碑，被认为是权威性"填补空白"之作和"国内外引用率最高的中国经济史著作之一"等。此书不仅先后获得"中国社会科学院优秀学术成果奖"、"孙冶方经济科学奖"、"郭沫若中国历史学奖"等多种奖项，而且多次再版，成为我国经济史研究的经典著作。

吴先生以学术为终生志业，笃信学术为天下公器，因此在研究中表现出了真正的大家风范。有两个例子，足以充分表现他的这种风范。其一，他主编的《中国资本主义工商业的社会主义改造》一书于 1962 年出版后，饮誉中外，但到了"文革"结束以后，他对这一改造重新作了探讨，于 1981 年发表了《资本主义工商业的社会主义改造是马克思主义在中国的胜利》一文，除了做出更系统的理论阐述而外，也提出了改造中的种种缺失。其二，他关于中国资本主义萌芽的研究著述，把以往的研究推到了一个新的高度，达到了资本主义萌芽研究的最高水平。但是在进行了更深入、更周密的思考之后，他在学术会议上，提出了与自己过去观点不同的新见。这两个例子，表现了他以学术为天下公器的大智大勇，如果"觉今是而昨非"，那么做公开自我批评，甚至放弃以前的观点。这是何等令人崇敬的学者本色啊！

吴先生是一位杰出学者，也是一位性情中人。他以学术为终生志业，但并非一位不食人间烟火的学者。他一生经历丰富，多历磨难，但是始终保持着一颗赤子之心，对生活充满热情，对所有和他相处的人都予以关爱。在他近一个世纪的生涯中，虽然风云变幻无常，但他一以贯之，以高贵的人品赢得世人的敬重。

吴先生有一个幸福美满的家庭。夫人洪达琳是著名钢琴家，毕业于国际著名的朱丽叶音乐学院（The Juilliard School），20世纪50年代随吴先生回国后，任中央音乐学院教授。吴先生和夫人琴瑟和谐、鸾凤和鸣，成为世人所羡慕的幸福姻缘。他们育有一子二女，也都深受家风熏陶，成为科学家和教师。但是天有不测风云，早在60年代初期，吴夫人不幸脑溢血，卧床数十年。她的生活起居，吴先生不放心保姆，均是亲自料理，几十年如一日，毫无懈怠，甘之如饴。吴夫人于1994年病逝，后来吴先生和青年时代就相识的文女士再缔良缘。文女士身体不佳，吴先生虽然年高，但是依然尽力照顾，一起共同度过了相濡以沫的十余年。吴先生的爱子在中国社会科学院欧洲研究所工作，因病于1989年去世，年仅39岁。再到了2006年，时任清华大学经济管理学院党委书记的次女婿也不幸辞世。这一连串的人生不幸，在一般人是难以承受的，但是吴先生坚强地顶住了。当吴先生在工作中从医院的电话得知儿子无救时，眼里满是泪水，欲哭无声，但他却一头埋进写作，一口气写了好几个小时，以工作来抵抗心中无限的悲痛。家人预感他会倒在书桌上，而这种预感绝非空穴来风：一天晚上，吴先生从书桌上起身，一抬脚就直直地栽倒在地，下巴磕裂，鲜血满面，到医院急诊缝针。吴先生的子女，也对父亲予以无微不至的照顾。"文革"结束后的一段时期，为照顾父母生活同时保证父亲工作进展，次女就把自己在清华仅一室一厅的宿舍挤出一块地方，让父母过来同住，以便有个安放病床的地方和同时有个可以安放书桌的地方。

吴先生对于学生和后辈，总是充满关怀，尽力予以指导和帮助。吴先生八旬、九旬大寿时和仙逝后，他们都写了文章，深情地回忆吴先生给自己的指教和帮助。我也是吴先生的私淑弟子，在治学道路上受惠于吴先生至多。

总之，吴先生用他的爱创造出了一个温馨的世界，这个世界也使他度过了一个温馨的人生。

吴先生一生追求学术真谛，对于物质生活一向颇不在意。1979年暑假，我去北京拜见这位蜚声国际学坛的大学者。到了位于东大桥路的吴先生寓所，只见房间狭窄，光线晦暗，家具简陋。由于空间太小，家中仅有一张书桌，堆满书刊和文稿。吴先生的许多著作，就是在这张书桌上，在昏暗的光线下写成的。那时吴师母已瘫痪许多年，生活不能自理，日常起居，都是吴先生亲手料理。尽管工作、生活条件如此恶劣，却不见吴先生有何不悦之色，谈起学问，依然侃侃而言，丝毫没有怨言。我心里不禁深深感叹：像吴先生这样的国际著名学者，真是像孔子赞颜回所说的那样："一箪食，一瓢饮，在陋巷，人不堪其忧，回也不改其乐。"刘禹锡《陋室铭》中的"斯是陋室，惟吾德馨"之语，其吴先生之谓欤？

当然，吴先生是性情中人，虽然淡泊简朴，不慕荣利，但也尽量享受生活的美好。他好酒，自称"酒家"；喜美食，且中西南北菜系不拘，每每笑称："我吃菜和做学问都主张兼容并蓄。"叶坦曾总结他的"养生之道"是"抽烟、喝酒、不锻炼"，他听后哈哈大笑，予以认同，后来此说流传甚广，还被纽约一家报纸引用。当然，吴先生生性活泼，对世界充满好奇心，每到一地，总是徒步游览风景名胜，市井民俗，自得其乐。他虽然自称不锻炼，但实际上到了晚年，不仅每日到公园散步，而且还自编"诗操"，按照诗句配以动作。北京卫视曾采访他，编出《吴承明老先生养生之道》，于2009年2月3日在北京卫视生活频道播出。

最足以表现吴先生内心世界的，应当是他1992年自己印行的诗文集《濯足偶谈》。这些诗文虽非经济史研究著作，但是细把玩之，不仅可以从中窥见他兴趣之广、修养之深和品味之雅，而且可以使人得以看到感情世界的丰富多彩。一位友人读了这些诗文之后，感慨地说："此其吴承明之所以为吴承明也。"

"九派末梢路难行，雨也泥泞，雪也飘零，一年难得半年晴，才罢南风，又是西风"，吴先生1971年11月作于固安干校的这首《一剪梅》，从某种意义上来说，正是他那一代中国学者坎坷生涯的写照。但是吴先生生性豁达，世间荣誉一笑置之；努力探索，追求真理而终生不渝。他之留洋、归国、从政、教书，都是为了找到一条最适合于自己的报国道路。经过这一曲折的过程，最后断定自己的事业是经济史。而他所经历的一切，又恰恰为他的经济史研究奠定了最坚实的基础。历史本是一个时间的延续，一个内外因素共同作用的产物，一个包罗万象的多面结晶体，所以要真正懂得历史，理解过去，绝非易事。而他丰富的人生阅历，深厚的中西学术功底，加上本人的资质禀赋，使得他在中国经济史研究中，能够独树一帜，不论在

"史"与"论"、"中"与"西"还是"古"与"今"的结合方面,都具有特色。

　　吴先生在四十五岁生日时,曾赋诗总结半生经历,并以这样的诗句自明其志:"四十尚云壮,五十犹未迟。垦辛无老幼,执杖亦耘籽。春来多娇丽,江山在一麾。"吴先生的一生,又何尝不是如此。他实现了昔日老师陈寅恪先生的理想,"以求学之故,奔走东西洋数万里",学到最好的知识,做出最好的学问;他经历了各种政治运动的磨难,经历了物质极端匮缺的年月,还经历了悼亡、丧子等人生不幸,但他在精神上却永远年轻,充满为追求真理而献身的热情。正是因为他的这种人格和志向,使他成为经济史学史上的传奇人物,也成为经济史学研究中一座难以逾越的高峰。

　　附言:本文是在作者的《吴承明先生学术小传》(收入《市场·近代化·经济史论》,云南大学出版社,1996)的基础上增补修改而成的。在此次增补修改过程中,参考并引用了叶坦教授的文章。读者倘若希望更多地了解吴承明先生,请参阅方行先生撰《吴承明传略》(载《中国当代经济学家传略》第5辑,1990)、吴柏均先生撰《吴承明先生传略》(载《近代中国》第2辑)、叶坦教授撰《学贯中西古今　德泽桃李同仁——吴承明先生的生平与学术》(载《经济学动态》2011年第9期)等。

　　　　　　　　　　　　　　　　　　　　　　　　　2017年7月

吴承明著述目录

余清良

说明： 自 20 世纪 30 年代 "中国经济史" 这一学科诞生以来，在从事这一领域研究的众多学者中，迄今为止，吴承明先生无疑是最具权威者之一，其造诣之深、影响之广，少有人能出其右。同时，由于先生自幼天赋异常，秉承家学，一生用力颇勤，笔耕不辍，加之又颐年鲐背，故其治学之时长（前后长达 70 余年）、著述之丰厚，亦非一般学者所能望其项背。为了能使后世学人全面了解先生之著述，以及便于具体的检索与查阅，特编撰本目录，拟对先生之著述做一全面、系统地搜集与整理。然而，面对时间跨度这么长、数量又这么庞大的著述，如何尽所能地搜集齐全、不致遗漏，以及对其目录如何进行著录与编排，都是极为困难的事情。为了叙述和编排的方便起见，同时也为了便于后人能够清晰掌握先生生前著述的时间脉络，本目录拟采取以下体例（凡例）进行编排：总体原则是先分类，再按年代进行编排，并对相关信息进行说明和考订；先是，根据著述的实际形态，将先生的著述划分为著作、论文两大类，有关学界介绍、纪念及追忆吴承明生平与学术的文章则另行附录；然后，在每大类之下，再依照一般常用的目录编撰体例进行，即依据各论著的具体发表（出版）时间（非实际撰写的时间）先后，按序进行分类、编排，其中同一书目或文目有多个版本的，则著以时间最早的版本，其他版本（包括译本和各种集子收录本）则放入注释中，标注顺序为书名或文章名、出版社或发表期刊、出版年月或发表年份及期数。

本目录对所收录的"著作"和"论文"的范围作了专门的界定。所谓的著作，在著作形态上，既包括先生独著或与他人合著的专著，以及独自主编或与他人联合主编的编著，也包括先生相关论文汇编的论文集；在版本形态上，既包括已正式出版的各种印刷本，也包括未公开出版的自印本和手稿本，但不包括其他语言的译本，对于译本是以注释的方式将其补注在原著书目之下，不单独著目。所谓的论文，在内容上，既包括先生在各种期刊、报纸上发表的专题论文，也包括其在各种座谈会、讲座和学术会议上的发言稿和讲话稿，以及为学界同仁的著作所做的书序或书评，此外还包括了先生在美国所获的硕士学位论文和写给同事方行研究员的学术书信等。

需要予以特别指出的是，本目录是一个考述目录，即不是一个单纯罗列书名或文名的目录，在编目的同时，通过加注的方式，对书目中的作者、书名（文名）、出版者（出版社、期刊、报纸）、出版（发表）时间等书目内容中所出现的相关史实及容易引起混淆的问题，如个别书中（文中）出现的署名作者与实际作者两者不符、同人而不同名或同名而不同人等情况，或进行补充说明，或进行具体考订。

此外，为了节省篇幅和叙述流畅起见，本目录对具体的行文作以下几个方面的处理：1. 在正文和注释的中，凡是笔者行文之语中，涉及"吴承明"之名的，均以"先生"之称代之，仅个别特殊之处另行著录本名；2. 对于正文书目中的作者，凡是署以"吴承明"之名且是独立撰著的，则直接予以省略，如是署以其他别名、笔名的，或与他人合著的，以及是主编而非著的，则都专门加以注明；3. 注释中凡是需要注明作者"吴承明"之名的，均以"氏著"代称；4. 书目的出版信息中，除了国外及台湾、香港出版的著作都加以注明出版地外，国内大陆出版的著作对出版地都加以省略；5. 对于注释考述中引用到的其他相关文献，仅于首次出现时著录其详细书目信息，之后均只简著其书名（文名）。

一　著作

1.《古代云南与中土关系之研究》，手稿本，1940 年。[①]

2.《帝国主义在华投资》，人民出版社，1951 年 1 月。[②]

3.《美帝在华经济侵略》，人民出版社，1951 年 3 月。[③]

4.《英国在华企业及其利润》，人民出版社，1951 年 6 月。[④]

5.《帝国主义与开滦煤矿》，神州国光社，1954 年 1 月。[⑤]

6.《过渡时期的国家资本主义》，人民出版社，1954 年 10 月、1956 年 1 月。[⑥]

7.《帝国主义在旧中国的投资》，人民出版社，1955 年 10 月。[⑦]

[①] 本著为先生手稿，著于 1940 年的昆明，从未正式出版，现为先生女公子北京邮电大学吴洪教授所藏，其中的第 1 章第 3 节、第 2 章第 3 节和第 3 章内容，在进行了部分改写和文字修订后分别以《庄蹻王滇考》、《百濮考》和《哀牢考》之题，在《益世报》史学副刊（昆明）第 21 期（1939 年 10 月 7 日）、《益世报》边疆研究周刊（重庆）第 19、20、24 期（1941 年 4 月 3 日、10 日、5 月 8 日）和第 26 期（1941 年 5 月 22 日）上刊发。

[②] 本著署名"魏子初"（即"外资处"的谐音）；又，本著后有三联书店修订版《帝国主义在华投资》（三联书店，1954 年 1 月）；另有俄译本 *Капиталовложения империалистов в Китае*（1902–1945），莫斯科：苏联科学院，1956 年。另，"魏子初"为先生所用的笔名。新中国成立后，先生在当时的中央人民政府政务院财政经济委员会私人企业局工作，任该局外资处副处长，自 1951 年起，先生即以笔名"魏子初"（谐音"外资处"）开始发表了一些成果，详见叶坦《学贯中西古今　德泽桃李同仁——吴承明先生的生平与学术》（《经济学动态》2011 年第 9 期）、《史实·史法·史观——吴承明先生的生平与学述》（载吴承明《经济史：历史观与方法论》，商务印书馆，2014 年 4 月、2017 年 5 月）。

[③] 本著署名"魏子初"。

[④] 本著署名"魏子初"。

[⑤] 本著署名"魏子初"；又，本著另有香港繁体版《帝國主義與開灤煤礦》（香港：大東圖書公司，1978 年 12 月）。

[⑥] 本著署名"同明"，即管大同与吴承明，系两人合著。

[⑦] 本著署名"吴承明编"，但实为著；另，本著是在《帝国主义在华投资》（署名"魏子初"）一书的基础上增补、扩充、修订基础上形成的。

8. 《北京瑞蚨祥》（典型企业调查资料），三联书店，1959 年 3 月。[①]

9. 《中国资本主义工商业的社会主义改造》，人民出版社，1962 年 11 月。[②]

10. 《中国资本主义工商业史料丛刊》（7 种），中华书局，1963～1979 年。[③]

[①] 本著署名"中国科学院经济研究所、中央工商行政管理局资本主义经济改造研究室编"，但由于对北京瑞蚨祥商店的调查是由先生主持进行的（参见汪敬虞《〈中国资本主义发展史〉第二卷读后》，《经济研究》1991 年第 1 期），是 20 世纪 50 年代对"资本主义工商业的社会主义改造"（简称"对资改造"）中所得之典型企业调查资料，氏著《从一家商店看商业资本的一种特殊形态》（《经济研究》1958 年第 5 期）也是据该调查的一部分资料所写，因此本著的实际执笔人就是先生，这也得到先生生前同事方行研究员（亦为该研究室成员，现已过世）的证实，其言本著实由先生和汪士信两人编写〔详见方行《关于中国资本主义发展史组的由来》，手稿本（此文乃应中国社会科学院经济研究所封越健研究员的请求所写），现为封越健所藏〕；又，本著另有《中国资本主义工商业史料丛刊》科学出版社重版本，2018 年即将出版。

又，当年"对资改造"运动的领导之一许涤新（著名的马克思主义经济学家，中国广义政治经济学的先驱，曾长期担任中央工商行政管理局局长）、先生自己及方行研究员等都将该著误列为是《中国资本主义工商业史料丛刊》中的第一种，详见许涤新《〈中国资本主义发展史〉总序》（载许涤新、吴承明主编《中国资本主义发展史》第 1 卷《中国资本主义的萌芽》，人民出版社，1985 年 3 月，第 2～3 页）、氏著《〈新民主主义革命时期的中国资本主义〉前言》（载《中国资本主义发展史》第 3 卷《新民主主义革命时期的中国资本主义》，人民出版社，1993 年 8 月，第 1、2 页）、《企业史和中国近代化道路研究：序〈大兴纱厂史稿〉》（载《中国的现代化：市场与社会》，三联书店，2001 年 9 月，第 369 页）、《学术成就·论著篇目》〔实为吴承明生前所填的一个表格，亲笔手迹，见孔夫子网魏榆古旧书店（山西省晋中市榆次区）〕和方行《倾注心力，探讨中国经济史——吴承明传略·吴承明主要著作目录》（载《经济日报》主编《中国当代经济学家传略》第 5 辑，辽宁人民出版社，1990 年 4 月，第 184 页）、《关于中国资本主义发展史组的由来》，正因于此，学界后来常据此以讹传讹，特予以订正。不过从中也可以看出，在先生和大多数学者的心目中，本著是与《中国资本主义工商业史料丛刊》性质一样的资料书。

[②] 本著署名"中央工商行政管理局、中国科学院经济研究所资本主义经济改造研究室（原系中央工商局调研处，1957 年改此名，由经济所和中央工商局双重领导，简称'对资改造研究室'或'资改室'）编"，先生为该室主任，承担着主要的编写任务，据先生生前所拟个人著作目录，本著实为先生主编；又，凡是当时（1958～1966）以"资改室"名义编写的著作，实际上均是先生主编，之所以会出现上述现象，是那个时代特殊历史背景下的产物，在"文革"及其前后的较长一段时期内，我国不太重视著作的个人署名权，尤其是集体编著类的，都不兴个人署名，一般都署单位名或集体名；另，本著另有日译本《中国资本主义の变革过程》（上、下），〔日〕江副敏生、加贺美嘉译，东京：日本中央大学出版部，1972 年。

[③] 本《丛刊》是在 1956 年开始整理的"对资改造"资料基础上，根据 1958 年 4 月由中央工商行政管理局和中国科学院经济研究所联合拟定的《资本主义经济社会主义改造研究工作五年规划（草案）》这一决定进行编辑、出版的，是为编写《中国资本主义发展史》（受周恩来总理之命）作的资料准备，具体由"资改室"组织有关单位和人员集体编写，是一套资料性的书，但并不是纯粹的资料汇编，有一定著的成分，是研究中国近代经济史的重要资料。

11.《旧中国的资本主义生产关系》，人民出版社，1977 年 3 月。①

12.《中国资本主义工商业的社会主义改造》，人民出版社，1978 年 10 月。②

13.《上海民族橡胶工业》，中华书局，1979 年 6 月。③

又，尽管本《丛刊》中的每一种资料上都只署单位或集体名，但从编辑方针、具体内容，乃至文字、数字、附注格式，先生都提出了具体详细意见，有的甚至完全改写（详见《1965 年 4 月 27 日吴承明致徐新吾函》），故实际上是由先生负责主编〔参见方行《倾注心力，探讨中国经济史——吴承明传略·吴承明主要著作目录》、吴柏均《吴承明先生传略》（载丁日初主编《近代中国》第 2 辑，上海社会科学院出版社，1991 年 11 月，第 308 页）、李伯重《吴承明先生学术小传》（载吴承明《市场·近代化·经济史论》，云南大学出版社，1996 年 6 月，第 298 页）、吴文川《博学勤思通古今——记荣誉学部委员、中国经济史专家吴承明》（载中国社会科学院老专家协会编《学问人生：中国社会科学院名家谈》，高等教育出版社，2007 年 5 月，第 90 页）、叶坦《学贯中西古今　德泽桃李同仁——吴承明先生的生平与学术》和《史实·史法·史观——吴承明先生的生平与学述》（第 393 页）〕，先生生前自己亦说他是这套《丛刊》的主编（参见氏著《企业史和中国近代化道路研究：序〈大兴纱厂史稿〉》，载《中国的现代化：市场与社会》，第 369 页）。不过，尽管是由先生主编，但并非每一种书都由先生编写，各书都各自有实际执笔者，先生实际执笔编著的只有其中的《上海民族橡胶工业》和《上海市棉布商业》两种。

另，本《丛刊》所收书目的数量，实际上只有 7 种，但先生与许涤新、方行等都将前述的《北京瑞蚨祥》一书纳入，误记为 8 种（详见许涤新《〈中国资本主义发展史〉总序》、氏著《〈新民主主义革命时期的中国资本主义〉前言》和《企业史和中国近代化道路研究：序〈大兴纱厂史稿〉》及《学术成就·论著篇目》、方行《倾注心力，探讨中国经济史——吴承明传略·吴承明主要著作目录》和《关于中国资本主义发展史组的由来》）；其科学出版社重版本（2018 年即将出版）更是收录有 22 种。关于该《丛刊》的历史由来及不同版本的具体书目等相关问题，可详见封越健《关于〈中国资本主义工商业史料丛刊〉出版及其学术价值的考察》（载《产业与科技史研究》第 2 辑，科学出版社，2017 年 11 月；该文稍作修改后又作为《中国资本主义工商业史料丛刊》重版本的"前言"）。

① 本著署名"《旧中国的资本主义生产关系》编写组编"，据先生生前所拟个人著作目录，本著实为先生主编。

② 本著署名"中国社会科学院经济研究所著"，同 1962 年版的前同名著一样，本著实际上是由先生主编。又，本著与 1962 年版的前同名著相比，书名相同，且是根据前著进行修订，但在内容上有大幅度的增补和改动，可以说是一个扩展版的重写本，故本目录将其认定为是两种不同的论著，而非前著简单的修订版，因而各自进行编目（本意见由封越健研究员提出，笔者仔细阅读、核对两部原著后，认为其所言在理，故予以采纳，特此注明并致谢）。

③ 本著为《中国资本主义工商业史料丛刊》中的一种；署名"上海市工商行政管理局、上海市橡胶工业公司'史料工作组'编"，但在该著前言中明确提到该著的实际编写者是先生与上海市工商行政管理局的徐新吾、黄琦以及上海市橡胶公司的沈邦梁，加上先生又是该《丛刊》的主编，故予以著目；又，本著早在 1966 年就编写完成，但一直迟迟未予出版；另，本著另有《中国资本主义工商业史料丛刊》科学出版社重版本，2018 年即将出版。

14. 《上海市棉布商业》，中华书局，1979 年 7 月。①

15. 《中国资本主义与国内市场》（论文集），中国社会科学出版社，1985 年 3 月。

16. 《中国资本主义发展史》第 1 卷《中国资本主义的萌芽》，人民出版社，1985 年 3 月、2003 年 6 月、2005 年 1 月（"中国文库"版）。②

17. 《中国资本主义发展史》第 2 卷《旧民主主义革命时期的中国资本主义》，人民出版社，1990 年 9 月、2003 年 6 月、2005 年 1 月（"中国文库"版）。③

18. 《中国资本主义发展史》第 3 卷《新民主主义革命时期的中国资本主义》，人民出版社，1993 年 8 月、2003 年 6 月、2005 年 1 月（"中国文库"版）。④

19. 《濯足偶谈》（诗话及诗集），自印本，1992 年。⑤

20. 《市场·近代化·经济史论》（论文集），云南大学出版社，1996 年 6 月。

---

① 本著为《中国资本主义工商业史料丛刊》中的一种；署名"上海市工商行政管理局、上海市纺织品公司'棉布商业史料组'编"，但在该著前言中明确提到该著的实际编写者是先生与上海市工商行政管理局的徐新吾、黄琦及上海市纺织品公司的曹世军、高杰，加上先生又是该《丛刊》的主编，故予以著目；又，本著早于 1966 年就完成初稿，但直至 1978 年才修改出版；另，本著另有《中国资本主义工商业史料丛刊》科学出版社重版本，2018 年即将出版。

② 本著署名"许涤新、吴承明主编"；又，本著除人民出版社多次重印外，又有"中国社会科学院文库·经济研究系列——中国社会科学院建院 30 周年纪念"版（社会科学文献出版社，2007 年 4 月）、臺灣繁體版《中國資本主義發展史》（臺北：谷風出版社，1987年）。另，本著另有英译本 Chinese Capitalism, 1522 – 1840，〔英〕C. A. Curwen（柯文南）译，London, The MacMillan Press Ltd, 2000.

③ 本著署名"许涤新、吴承明主编"；又，本著除人民出版社多次重印外，又有"中国社会科学院文库·经济研究系列——中国社会科学院建院 30 周年纪念"版（社会科学文献出版社，2007 年 4 月）。

④ 本著署名"许涤新、吴承明主编"；又，本著除人民出版社多次重印外，又有"中国社会科学院文库·经济研究系列——中国社会科学院建院 30 周年纪念"版（社会科学文献出版社，2007 年 4 月）。

⑤ "文革"开始后，"资改室"被解散，吴承明和千家驹、方行、汪士信等一道被下放到辽宁盘锦"干校"劳动，他们都雅好诗词，每日劳动归来，"濯足"（赤足种稻后必浸泡双足）登炕后，常评诗品词或海阔天空漫谈，1973 年底，吴承明返京后，将自己在干校期间的所记、所忆诗文自印成集，并分赠干校同窗老友，这就是该集的来源，1992 年又将其汇编成册，自印出版，详见吴文川《博学勤思通古今——记荣誉学部委员、中国经济史专家吴承明》、叶坦《学贯中西古今　德泽桃李同仁——吴承明先生的生平与学术》、《史实·史法·史观——吴承明先生的生平与学述》。又，该集实际包含了两部分内容，除了上述干校老友之间品谈的诗词外，据先生女公子吴洪教授所述，该集还收录了先生写给妻子洪达琳女士（原中央音乐学院教授，著名音乐家）的私人诗词《一锄集》（手稿本，为吴洪教授所藏）；另，该集与下文的《濯足二谈》《濯足三谈》《濯足四谈》均未正式出版过。

21.《中国的现代化：市场与社会》（论文集），三联书店，2001 年 9 月。

22.《中华人民共和国经济史》第一卷（1949～1952），中国财政经济出版社，2001 年 12 月。①

23.《濯足二谈》（诗话及诗集），自印本，2002 年 1 月。②

24.《吴承明集》（论文集），中国社会科学出版社，2002 年 12 月。

25.《中国企业史·近代卷》，企业管理出版社，2004 年 1 月。③

26.《经济史：历史观与方法论》，上海财经大学出版社，2006 年 12 月。④

27.《濯足三谈》（诗话及诗集），自印本，2008 年 5 月。⑤

28.《经济史理论与实证：吴承明文集》（论文集），浙江大学出版社，2012 年 8 月。⑥

29.《濯足四谈》（诗话及诗集，一首），自印本，2009 年 11 月。⑦

二　论文

1.《中国土地问题》，载姚依林、杨述主编《东方既白》（北京）创刊号，1935 年 3 月。⑧

---

① 本著署名"吴承明、董志凯主编"。

② 该集实为《濯足偶谈》的重印、修订版，修改了其中几首诗，并增加了几首后作的新诗，书名仍署为《濯足偶谈》，但据其内容应是《濯足二谈》，故改之。

③ 本著署名"吴承明、江泰新（即江太新）主编"。

④ 本著除上海财经大学版之外，商务印书馆又于 2014 年 4 月对其进行了修订、再版，并于 2017 年 5 月重印，在修订版中，除了对该著进行个别文字上的修订外，还补入了先生女公子吴洪教授整理的《吴承明先生学术年表》和叶坦教授所著的《史实·史法·史观——吴承明先生的学术与生平》二文。

⑤ 本集又常被名为《濯足偶谈续集》，详见吴文川《博学勤思通古今——记荣誉学部委员、中国经济史专家吴承明》。

⑥ 本著署名"吴承明著，刘兰兮整理"，是在 2011 年先生过世后，由其弟子刘兰兮研究员整理、出版的。

⑦ 本集仅有先生诗文 1 篇，为未完成之作，且从未以任何形式印刷、面世过，系先生之遗著，现为吴洪教授所藏。

⑧ 本文为先生的首篇学术论文，时年先生刚年满 18 岁；《东方既白》杂志由姚依林（克广）、杨述、黄诚等于 1935 年 3 月在清华校内联合创刊，详见叶坦《学贯中西古今　德泽桃李同仁——吴承明先生的生平与学术》、《史实·史法·史观——吴承明先生的生平与学述》、《吴承明为"经济救国"理想而奋斗》（载《抗战时期的中国经济学家》，《人民日报》2015 年 7 月 27 日第 16 版）。

2. 《五四告今日青年》，《北大周刊》第 1 卷第 1 期，1936 年 5 月 4 日。

3. 《一二九之话》，《清华副刊》（周刊）第 45 卷第 8、9 期合刊，1936 年 12 月。

4. 《内地的工作经验》，《战时青年》（半月刊，武汉）第 1 卷第 6 期，1938 年 4 月 10 日。①

5. 《一星期的士兵工作——经验谈》，《战时青年》（半月刊，武汉）第 1 卷第 7 期，1938 年 4 月 25 日。②

6. 《庄蹻王滇考》，《益世报》史学副刊（昆明）第 21 期，1939 年 10 月 7 日。③

7. 《百濮考》，《益世报》边疆研究周刊（重庆）第 19、20、24 期，1941 年 4 月 3 日、10 日、5 月 8 日。④

8. 《哀牢考——历史上中国境内之泰族》，《益世报》边疆研究周刊（重庆）第 26 期，1941 年 5 月 22 日。⑤

---

① 本文署名"吴之光"；《战时青年》1938 年 1 月 10 日创刊于武汉，为中国共产党南方局青年委员会以"战时青年社"名义主办，为半月刊，自 1939 年 7 月第 2 卷第 1 期开始迁往重庆，并改为月刊，1940 年 9 月又改为半月刊，至是年 12 月停刊；1937 年卢沟桥事变后，先生曾一度"投笔从戎"，参加了由平津学生及医护人员组成的战地服务团，在国民党第一军随军服务团中随军服务，从事医护和宣传动员工作，先生任该团政治部主任，至 1938 年冬随军服务团解散后，先生经越南辗转回到昆明，入西南联大社会历史系复学，详见李为扬、赵继昌、吴承明编《清华大学第十级简史》、氏著《我的简况》（载《清华十级纪念刊》编辑组编《清华十级纪念刊：1934~1938~1988》，油印本，1988 年，第 84、184 页），方行《倾注心力，探讨中国经济史——吴承明传略·吴承明主要著作目录》（第 184 页），吴柏均《吴承明先生传略》（第 305 页），李伯重《吴承明先生学术小传》（第 295 页），吴文川《博学勤思通古今——记荣誉学部委员、中国经济史专家吴承明》（第 88~89 页），苏金花《吴承明 求知不懈 笔耕不辍》〔载中国社会科学院青年人文社会科学研究中心编《学问有道——学部委员访谈录·荣誉学部委员》（下），方志出版社，2007 年 8 月，第 848 页〕，叶坦《学贯中西古今 德泽桃李同仁——吴承明先生的生平与学术》、《史实·史法·史观——吴承明先生的生平与学述》、《吴承明 为"经济救国"理想而奋斗》。本文与下文《一星期的士兵工作——谈经验》均是先生根据这一经历所写。

② 本文署名"吴之光"。

③ 本文为氏著《古代云南与中土关系之研究》（未刊手稿本，1940 年）第 3 章的内容，进行了部分改写和文字修订。

④ 本文署名"吴之光"；本文为氏著《古代云南与中土关系之研究》第 1 章第 3 节的内容，进行了部分改写和文字修订。

⑤ 本文署名"吴之光"；本文为氏著《古代云南与中土关系之研究》第 2 章第 2 节的内容，进行部分改写和文字修订。

9. 《法币问题之一——货币政策的意义》，《银行界》（月刊，重庆）第 1 卷第 1 期（创刊号），1941 年 11 月。[1]

10. 《法币问题之二——对数量说的认识》，《银行界》（月刊，重庆）第 1 卷第 2 期，1942 年 3 月。[2]

11. 《利润之谜》，《经济新闻周报》（重庆）第 13 期，1942 年 3 月。

12. 《论当前生产政策》，《时事新报》（月刊，重庆）1942 年 4 月 12 日。[3]

13. 《法币问题之三——战时的通货膨胀》，《银行界》（月刊，重庆）第 1 卷第 3 期，1942 年 4 月。[4]

14. 《论管理银行》，《银行界》（月刊，重庆）第 1 卷第 3 期，1942 年 4 月。

15. 《论大小生产——再论当前生产政策》，《时事新报》（月刊，重庆）1942 年 6 月 8 日。

16. 《利息与利息政策》，《银行界》（月刊，重庆）第 1 卷第 4 期，1942 年 6 月。

17. 《金融讲座：利息》，《银行界》（月刊，重庆）第 1 卷第 4 期，1942 年 6 月。[5]

18. 《论生产调整》，《中国工业》（月刊，桂林）第 7 期，1942 年 7 月。

19. 《如何收缩通货》，《银行界》（月刊，重庆）第 1 卷第 5 期，1942 年 7 月。

20. 《商业银行资金运用问题》，《银行界》（月刊，重庆）第 1 卷第 8 期，1942 年 12 月。

21. 《生产资金之困难及其解决》，《西南实业通讯》（月刊，重庆）第 7 卷第 1 期，1943 年 1 月。

22. 《产业资金问题之检讨》，《金融知识》（双月刊，重庆）第 2 卷第 5 期，

---

[1] 本文署名"吴之光"。

[2] 本文署名"吴之光"。

[3] 本文另转载于《财政评论》（月刊，重庆）第 7 卷第 4 期，1942 年 4 月；后又修订、改题为《论当前的生产政策：几个具体的建议》，刊发于《半月文萃》（半月刊，桂林）第 1 卷第 2 期，1942 年 6 月。

[4] 本文署名"吴之光"。

[5] 本文署名"吴之光"。

1943 年 9 月。

23. 《理想利率》，《金融知识》（双月刊，重庆）第 3 卷第 2 期，1944 年
3 月。

24. *War Borrowing Under the Federal Reserve System*，MS，New York，Columbia
University，October 1946. ①

25. "Manufacturing Industries in China，a Preliminary Report，" Mimeograph，
New York，1946. ②

26. "A Preliminary Report on Industries in Free China，" Mimeograph，New York，
1946.

27. "A Preliminary Report on Saving in Modern Saving Institutions，" Mimeograph，
New York，1946.

28. 《我国资本构成之初步估计》《中央银行月报》（上海）新 1 卷第 11 期，
1946 年 11 月。③

29. 《美国战时公债与金融政策评述》，《财政评论》（月刊，上海）第 16 卷
第 1、2 期，1947 年 1 月、2 月。④

30. 《认股权、股票股利及股票分裂与扩充公司之投资理论》，《证券市场》

---

① 本文为吴承明在美国哥伦比亚大学的经济学硕士学位论文（MS），中文名为《美国的战时
公债与金融政策》。

② 先生于 1946 年 6 月被国民政府聘为美国著名经济学家西蒙·库兹涅茨〔S. S. Kuznets，被誉
为 "GNP"（后改用 "GDP"）之父，1971 年诺贝尔经济学奖金获得者〕的助手，陪同库氏
到南京国民政府资源委员会工作，主要是辅助库氏工作，由于库氏对中国的 GNP 有兴趣，
要求助手（有吴承明、张培刚和丁忱）为其提供相关资料〔最为主要的就是巫宝三主编的
《中国国民所得（一九三三）》，中华书局，1947 年 1 月〕，并摘译成英文供库氏参用，本
文与后列其他两篇英文文章就是当时先生根据为库氏所准备的资料写成的，详见叶坦《学
贯中西古今 德泽桃李同仁——吴承明先生的生平与学术》、《史实·史法·史观——吴承
明先生的生平与学述》。

③ 本文刊发后，随即产生很大的反响，被译成英文在香港发表（由于诸多原因，笔者未能查
阅到这一英文译文的原文，书目信息也无从著录，特此说明），详见叶坦《学贯中西古今
德泽桃李同仁——吴承明先生的生平与学术》、《史实·史法·史观——吴承明先生的生
平与学述》。又，本文后修订、改题为《我国资本构成之初步估计（1931～1936）》，打印
本，1950 年；另，本文以后者为题，相继收录于氏著《吴承明集》（2002）、《经济史理论
与实证：吴承明文集》（2012）。

④ 本文系根据先生在哥伦比亚大学的经济学硕士学位论文（MS）*War Borrowing Under the
Federal Reserve System*（New York，Columbia University，October 1945）改写、修订而成，是
其中译概要本。

（半月刊，上海）第 2 卷第 2 期（总第 14 号），1947 年 5 月。[①]

31. 《近代征信事业之发展》，《中央银行月报》（上海）新 2 卷第 9 期，1947 年 9 月。

32. 《经济政策对于政治的辅助力量》，《经济评论》（周刊，上海）第 2 卷第 1 期，1947 年 10 月。[②]

33. 《财务报告析之理论与方法方法：附：证交上市股票发行公司之财务报告分析》（上）、（下），《资本市场》（月刊，上海）第 1 卷第 3、4 期，1948 年 3 月、4 月。

34. 《不宜征收法人财产税——在临时财产税问题座谈会上的发言》，《财政评论》（月刊，上海）第 18 卷第 6 期，1948 年 6 月。[③]

35. 《外汇转移证缺点多 提出三点来供商讨》，《经济通讯》（周刊，香港）第 3 卷第 47、48 期合刊，1948 年。

36. 《新民主主义经济与个性发展》，《新语》（半月刊，上海）第 14 卷第 15 期，1949 年 8 月。

---

① 本文初为先生于 1945 年在哥伦比亚大学商学院研究生部（主修货币理论）选修多德（D. L. Dodd）的金融市场课程后所撰写的论文，获得当时美国的贝塔－西格玛－伽马（ΒΣΓ）荣誉学会的"金钥匙奖"，本文为其中译概要本，详见叶世《学贯中西古今 德泽桃李同仁——吴承明先生的生平与学术》、《史实·史法·史观——吴承明先生的生平与学述》、《吴承明 为"经济救国"理想而奋斗》。

又，关于先生获得"金钥匙奖"的文章，在先生晚年的访谈中，或说是《论美国战时的货币政策》〔杲文川《博学勤思通古今——记荣誉学部委员、中国经济史专家吴承明》（第 89 页）〕，或说是《货币数量分析》〔苏金花《吴承明 求知不懈 笔耕不辍》（第 848 页）〕。其中前者所说的《论美国战时的货币政策》一文，应指的是先生在美国哥伦比亚大学的经济学硕士学位论文（MS）《美国的战时公债与金融政策》（两者文名也不完全能对应上）；至于后者所说的《货币数量分析》估计指的是其《法币问题之二——对数量说的认识》〔《银行界》（月刊，重庆）第 1 卷第 2 期，1942 年 3 月〕一文（两者文名也不完全相符）。笔者以为，先生的这两条忆述，显然是因时间久远的原因弄混或记错了，故特予以订正，以免以讹传讹。

② 本文实为一个笔谈讨论稿，是当时《经济评论》社所组织编写的《经济与政治的相互关系——兼论当前经济学人的责任》三《经济可以影响政治，从经济和行政的改善，政治亦可望好转》中先生的讨论发言内容。

③ 本文实为先生在当时由《财政评论》杂志社资料室所组织的"临时财产税问题座谈会"上的发言内容，该杂志社在编辑《临时财产税座谈会记录》时，曾将先生的发言与盛穆杰、丘汉平两位的发言归纳后合在一起，定题名为《法人不应课征财产税 筹措战费另想他法》，但笔者以为该题名不能完全切合先生发言内容的意思，故本目录该文文名系笔者根据其发言内容要点重拟的，并非真正意义上的文章题目。

37. 《中国工业资本的估计和分析》（上、下），《经济周报》（上海），第 9 卷第 8、9 期，1949 年 8 月。①

38. 《中国工业资本的初步估计》（上、下），《中国工业》（月刊，上海）新 1 卷第 5、6 期，1949 年 9 月、10 月。②

39. 《关于帝国主义在华工业资本》，《中国工业》（月刊，上海）新 1 卷第 12 期，1949 年 11 月。

40. 《美帝在中国的宗教文化侵略》，《新华月报》（北京）第 3 卷第 3 期，1951 年 1 月。③

41. 《美帝在华企业及其利润》，《经济周报》（上海）第 12 卷第 2 期，1951 年 1 月。

42. 《美帝资本输出及其利润榨取的特点》，《新中华》（半月刊，上海）第 14 卷第 8 期，1951 年 4 月。

43. 《中国企业资本的特点和重估财产调整的资本问题》，《经济周报》（上海）第 13 卷第 1 期，1951 年 1 月。

44. 《帝国主义在华企业及其利润》，《中国工业》（月刊，上海）新 2 卷第 10 期，1951 年 10 月。

45. 《开展私营工业改进品质、革新技术的工作》，《工商界》（月刊，上海）1955 年第 1 期。

46. 《关于帝国主义在旧中国资本的估计》，见《帝国主义在旧中国的投资》附录，人民出版社，1955 年 10 月。④

47. 《中国民族资本的特点》，《经济研究》1956 年第 6 期。⑤

---

① 本文另合稿转载于《新华月报》（北京）第 1 卷第 1 期（创刊号），1949 年 11 月；后又进一步修订，改以《旧中国工业资本的估计和分析》为题，收录于氏著《中国资本主义与国内市场》（1985）。

② 本文后又进一步修订，改以《中国工业资本的估计（1936～1946）》为题（打印本，1950 年），并相继收录于氏著《吴承明集》（2002）、《经济史理论与实证：吴承明文集》（2012）。

③ 本文署名"魏子初"。

④ 本文未曾单独刊发，仅见于氏著《帝国主义在旧中国的投资》（1955）一书的附录。

⑤ 本文后来又作了删改和补充（打印本，1964 年），并相继收录于黄逸平编《中国近代经济史论文选集》（上海师范大学历史系，打印本，1979 年 4 月）、《中国近代经济史论文选》（上海人民出版社，1985 年 4 月）、氏著《中国资本主义与国内市场》（1985）、中国社会科学院近代史研究所经济史研究室编《中国近代经济史论著目录提要（1949.10～1985）》（摘要，上海社会科学院出版社，1989 年 12 月）。

48. 《我国对资产阶级的赎买形式》，《大公报》1956 年 12 月 13 日版。①

49. 《从一家商店看商业资本的一种特殊形态》，《经济研究》1958 年第 5 期。②

50. 《中国资产阶级的产生问题——从影片〈不夜城〉谈起》，《经济研究》1965 年第 9 期。③

51. 《对旧中国商业资本剥削问题的一些看法》，《光明日报》经济学副刊，1965 年 9 月 27 日版。④

52. 《帝国主义在旧中国的资本扩张》，载黄逸平编《中国近代经济史论文选集》二，上海师范大学历史系，打印本，1979 年 4 月；《中国近代经济史论文选》，上海人民出版社，1985 年 4 月。⑤

53. 《中国经济の社会主義改造と四つの现代化建设》（1980 年 3 月 1 日在日本福冈西日本新闻会馆的演讲），福冈：中国研究中心，1980 年专刊。

54. 《中国近代经济史の史料工作の近况について》，东京：東京大学東洋文化研究所附属东洋学文献中心《東洋学文献セソター通信》第 19 期，1980 年 5 月。

55. 《中国の社会主義改造と现代化》（1980 年 3 月 15 日在日本东京中国研究所的报告），东京：東京大学中国研究所《中国研究月报》1980 年 6 月号。

56. 《日本研究中国近代经济史概况》，《经济学动态》1980 年第 7 期。

57. 《八十年来中国经济发展和变化》，载《香港中华总商会八十周年纪念特刊》，香港：中华总商会，1980 年 11 月。

58. 《论男耕女织》，载山西省社会科学研究所编《中国社会经济史论丛》第 1 辑，山西人民出版社，1981 年 7 月。⑥

59. 《资本主义工商业的社会主义改造是马克思主义在中国的胜利》，《经济

---

① 本文另转载于《新华半月刊》1957 年第 1 期。

② 本文是专门分析、研究北京瑞蚨祥商店的，实为前著《北京瑞蚨祥》内容的一部分，由此可以证明先生是《北京瑞蚨祥》一著的主要执笔人之一。

③ 本文后略作删节、修改后，以《中国资产阶级的产生问题》为题，另收录于《中国近代经济史论文集》三、《中国近代经济史论文选》、《中国近代经济史论著目录提要（1949.10 ~ 1985）》（摘要）。

④ 本文收录于《中国近代经济史论著目录提要（1949.10 ~ 1985）》（摘要）。

⑤ 本文是氏著《帝国主义在旧中国的投资》（人民出版社，1955 年 10 月）的摘要；另收录于黄逸平编《中国近代经济史文选》，上海人民出版社，1985 年 4 月。

⑥ 本文收录于氏著《中国资本主义与国内市场》（1985）。

研究》1981 年第 7 期。①

60. 《毛泽东同志对中国资产阶级的深刻分析丰富和发展了马克思列宁主义》，《经济研究》1981 年第 8 期。②

61. 《评外国学者对旧中国经济不发达原因的分析》，《经济学动态》，1981年第 9 期。③

62. 《关于中国资本主义萌芽的几个问题》，《文史哲》1981 年第 5 期。④

63. 《中国资本主义的发展述略》，载中华书局编辑部编《中华学术论文集》（中华书局 70 周年纪念刊），中华书局，1981 年 11 月。⑤

64. 《关于研究中国近代经济史的意见》，《晋阳学刊》1982 年第 1 期。⑥

65. 《"爱国犯"的呼声》，《一二九运动资料》第 2 辑，人民出版社，1982 年4 月。⑦

66. 《关于旧中国二三十年代的市场危机》，《历史研究》1982 年第 4 期"论文摘要"。⑧

67. 《论明代国内市场和商人资本》，载中国社会科学院经济研究所学术委

---

① 本文收录于氏著《中国资本主义与国内市场》（1985）；另，本文有英文本 "The Socialist Transformation of Capitalist Industry and Commerce Was a Victory of Marxism in China," *Selected Writings on Studies of Marxism*，Nos. 16，中国社会科学院，1981 年 6 月。

② 本文是当时中国社会科学院经济研究所所组织的一个政治学习——《认真学习〈决议〉加强经济理论研究——中国社会科学院经济研究所部分研究人员座谈学习〈决议〉发言摘登》中先生的学习发言内容。

③ 本文系先生与侯方合著。

④ 本文收录于南京大学历史系明清史研究室编《中国资本主义萌芽问题论文集》，江苏人民出版社，1983 年 4 月。

⑤ 本文收录于复旦大学历史系、《历史研究》编辑部、《复旦学报》编辑部合编《近代中国资产阶级研究》（复旦大学出版社，1984 年 2 月）、氏著《中国资本主义与国内市场》（1985）、《中国近代经济史论著目录提要（1949. 10～1985）》（摘要）；又，本文有日译本《中国における資本主義の発展略述》（〔日〕池田诚监译，京都：立命馆大学法学部《立命馆法学》第 163 号，1982 年 3 月）和英译本 "A Brief Account of the Development of Capitalism in China," in Tim Wright eds. , *The Chinese Economy in Early Twentieth Century*，London：The MacMillan Press Ltd，1992。

⑥ 本文中有关数量概念的内容另行摘录、改写，以《中国近代经济史的研究要加强数量概念》为题，刊于《经济学文摘》1982 年第 4 期；又，本文收录于《中国近代经济史论著目录提要（1949. 10～1985）》（摘要）。

⑦ 本文由陈元、刘毓珩、黄诚与先生等四人合著。

⑧ 本文为阮方纪摘录《中国资本主义的发展述略》第五部分 "20 年代和 30 年代的经济危机"的部分内容而成，并改题名为《关于旧中国二三十年代的市场危机》。

员会编《中国社会科学院经济研究所集刊》第 5 集，中国社会科学出版社，1983 年 2 月。①

68. 《论清代前期我国国内市场》，《历史研究》1983 年第 1 期。②

69. 《我国手工棉纺织业为什么长期停留在家庭手工业阶段?》，《文史哲》1983 年第 1 期。③

70. 《什么是自然经济?》，《经济研究》1983 年第 9 期。④

71. 《我国半殖民地半封建国内市场》，《历史研究》1984 年第 2 期。⑤

72. 《国外研究中国经济史的学派和方法》，《经济学动态》，1985 年第 2 期。

73. 《中国资本主义的萌芽概论》，载《中国资本主义与国内市场》（论文集），中国社会科学出版社，1985 年 3 月。⑥

74. 《帝国主义在旧中国的投资》，载《中国资本主义与国内市场》（论文

① 本文相继收录于氏著《中国资本主义与国内市场》（1985）、《中国的现代化：市场与社会》（2001）；又，1986 年法国著名汉学家贾永吉（Michel Cartier）将本文及后文《论清代前期我国国内市场》和《我国半殖民地半封建国内市场》三文进行摘要，写成《吴承明的国内统一市场形成观》，刊于《年鉴：经济 社会 文明》（*Annales, Économies Sociétés Civilisations*）1986 年 11~12 月号，详见叶坦《学贯中西古今 德泽桃李同仁——吴承明先生的生平与学术》、《史实·史法·史观——吴承明先生的生平与学述》。

② 本文刊出后，旋即于 1984 年引起了美国著名历史学家费维凯（Albert Feuerwerker）的注意，阅读此文后，费维凯立即邀请先生到意大利参加于是年召开的中国经济史研讨会（Internaational Conference on Spacial and Temporal Trends and Cycles in Chinese Economic History，980 - 1980），详见叶坦《学贯中西古今 德泽桃李同仁——吴承明先生的生平与学术》、《史实·史法·史观——吴承明先生的生平与学述》。

本文的部分内容另行摘录、改写、以《我国封建社会的各级市场》为题，刊于《经济学文摘》1983 年第 5 期；本文在经改写、修订后，相继收录于〔法〕贾永吉（Michel Cartier）《吴承明的国内统一市场形成观》、氏著《中国资本主义与国内市场》（1985）、《中国的现代化：市场与社会》（2001）（增加了"附记"）。

③ 本文收录于氏著《中国资本主义与国内市场》（1985）。

④ 本文收录于氏著《中国资本主义与国内市场》（1985）；另，本文的部分内容另行摘录、改写，以《自然经济的四层含义》为题，刊于《经济学文摘》1983 年第 12 期。

⑤ 本文实是对氏著《旧中国的资本主义生产关系》（1977）中第 6 章"资本家对农民和其他小生产者的剥削"的内容进行摘录、改写而成，后收录于《历史研究》编辑部编《〈历史研究〉五十年论文选》（近代中国·上），社会科学文献出版社，2005 年 7 月；又，本文后进一步修订、改以《论我国半殖民地半封建国内市场》为题，相继收录于氏著《中国资本主义与国内市场》（1985）、《中国的现代化：市场与社会》（2001）、《中国近代经济史论著目录提要（1949.10~1985）》（摘要）；另，本文另有日译本《近代中国にぉける半殖民地·半封建的国内市场》，〔日〕池田诚监（时任日本中国现代史研究会会长）译，京都：立命舘大学法学部《立命舘法学》第 5、6 号，1984 年。

⑥ 本文未曾单独刊发。

集），中国社会科学出版社，1985 年 3 月。[1]

75. 《市场理论和市场史》，载商业部经济研究所编《调研资料》第 46 期，1985 年 4 月。[2]

76. 《许涤新〈广义政治经济学〉一书评介》，《经济研究》1985 年第 11 期。

77. 《黄诚传》，中共党史人物研究会编《中共党史人物传》第 27 卷，陕西人民出版社，1986 年 5 月。[3]

78. 《试论交换经济史》，《中国经济史研究》1987 年第 1 期。[4]

79. 《中国民族资本主义的几个问题》，载孙健编《中国经济史论文集》，中国人民大学出版社，1987 年 8 月。[5]

80. 《吴承明同志讲话——广义政治经济学的先驱》，载中国社会科学院经济研究所《到老犹磅礴》编辑小组编《到老犹磅礴——许涤新同志从事学术活动五十五周年纪念文集》，经济科学出版社，1987 年 10 月。

81. 《中国经济史研究方法杂谈》，载上海社会科学院经济研究所编《中国近代经济史资料》第 6 辑，1987 年 4 月。[6]

82. 《早期中国近代化过程中的内部和外部因素》，载章开沅、朱英主编《对外经济关系与中国近代化》，华中师范大学出版社，1990 年 12 月。[7]

---

[1] 本文实是对氏著《帝国主义在旧中国的投资》（1955）中第 1、2 章的内容进行摘录、改写，并增补了"附记"内容而成；又，另有节选自先生该著第 1、3 章内容的同名文，刊于王振中总主编、剧锦文主编《中国经济学百年经典》中卷（1949～1978），广东经济出版社，2005 年 12 月。

[2] 本文相继收录于《平准学刊》编辑委员会编《平准学刊：中国社会经济史研究论集》第 3 辑（下）（中国商业出版社，1986 年 5 月）、氏著《市场·近代化·经济史论》（1996）、《经济史理论与实证：吴承明文集》（2012）。

[3] 本文署名"蔡水泉、张铭洽等"，但其中黄诚在清华的经历，主要由先生撰稿；又，本文后又经先生改写、题为《黄诚小传》，单独署名刊发于《清华十级纪念刊》编辑组编《清华十级纪念刊：1934～1938～1988》，油印本，1988 年。

[4] 本文相继收录于乌杰主编《中国经济文库：综合理论卷》4（中央编译出版社，1995 年 10 月）、氏著《市场·近代化·经济史论》（1996）、《经济史理论与实证：吴承明文集》（2012）。

[5] 1984 年暑假，人民大学孙健教授受教育部委托举办了一个"中国经济史暑期讲习班"，讲习班结束后孙健教授将期间各位学者的讲稿汇编成《中国经济史论文集》，本文就是先生在该讲习班上的讲稿。

[6] 本文又相继刊于《红旗·内部文稿》，1987 年第 8 期；《轻工业经济研究》，1987 年第 3 期。

[7] 本文原为先生于 1987 年参加由华中师范大学主办的"对外经济关系与中国近代化国际学术会议"（武汉）所提交的会议论文。

83. 《早期中国近代化过程中的外部和内部因素——兼论张謇的实业路线》，《教学与研究》1987 年第 5 期。①

84. 《历史的回顾与祝愿》，《工商行政管理》1988 年第 1 期（创刊 35 周年纪念刊）。

85. 《中国近代经济史若干问题的思考》，《中国经济史研究》1988 年第 2 期。②

86. 《中国经济史》，《中国大百科全书·经济学》，长词条，中国大百科全书出版社，1988 年 9 月。

87. 《〈发展与制约：明清江南生产力研究〉序》，载李伯重《发展与制约：明清江南生产力研究》，台北：联经出版事业股份有限公司，2002 年 12 月。③

88. 《清华大学第十级简史》，《清华十级纪念刊》编辑组编《清华十级纪念刊：1934～1938～1988》，油印本，1988 年。④

89. 《中国近代农业生产力的考察》，《中国经济史研究》1989 年第 2 期。⑤

90. 《许涤新传略》，载刘启林主编《当代社会科学名家》，社会科学文献出版社，1989 年 6 月。⑥

91. 《谈封建主义二题》，《中国经济史研究》1989 年第 4 期。⑦

92. 《〈大兴纱厂史稿〉序》，载杨俊科、梁勇《大兴纱厂史稿》，中国人民政治协商会议石家庄市委员会编《石家庄文史资料》第 10 辑，1989 年

---

① 本文原为先生 1987 年于参加由南京大学"张謇研究中心"主办的"（首届）张謇国际学术研讨会"（南京）所提交的会议论文；本文另收入严学熙主编的会议论文集《论张謇——张謇国际学术讨论会论文集》（江苏人民出版社，1993 年 6 月）；另，后吴承明又将本文与前文——《早期中国近代化过程中的内部和外部因素》两文一道进行综合、改写，以《早期中国近代化过程中的内部和外部因素》为题，收录于氏著《市场·近代化·经济史论》（1996）。

② 本文相继收录于乌杰主编《中国经济文库：综合理论卷》4（中央编译出版社，1995 年 10 月）和氏著《市场·近代化·经济史论》（1996）、《吴承明集》（2002）、《经济史理论与实证：吴承明文集》（2012）。

③ 本文另以《生产力经济史和区域研究：序〈发展与制约：明清江南生产力经济史研究〉》为题，收录于氏著《中国的现代化：市场与社会》（2001）。

④ 本文署名"李为扬、赵继昌、吴承明"。

⑤ 本文收录于氏著《市场·近代化·经济史论》（1996）。

⑥ 本文另收录于薛暮桥等编《傲霜集》，中国展望出版社，1989 年 11 月。

⑦ 本文收录于氏著《市场·近代化·经济史论》（1996），但漏注了原稿的刊发出处。

12 月。①

93. 《忆蒋南翔同志在清华园的几件事》，载清华大学《蒋南翔纪念文集》
    编辑小组编《蒋南翔纪念文集》，清华大学出版社，1990 年 4 月。

94. 《世潮·传统·近代化——在第五届洋务运动史学术讨论会上的发言》，
    《近代史研究》1990 年第 3 期。

95. 《近代中国工业化的道路》，《文史哲》1991 年第 6 期。②

96. 《中国经济史研究的回顾与前瞻——在中国经济史学会首届学术年会上
    的开幕词》，《中国经济史研究》1991 年第 3 期。

97. 《中国近代资本集成和工农业及交通运输业产值的估计》，《中国经济史
    研究》1991 年第 4 期。③

98. 《近代中国经济现代化水平的估计》，载《中国的现代化：市场与社会》
    （论文集），三联书店，2001 年 9 月。④

99. 《总结鸦片战争的历史教训是我们世代相传的任务——在鸦片战争 150
    周年国际学术讨论会上的讲话》，载张海峰等主编《鸦片战争与中国现
    代化》，中国社会出版社，1991 年 8 月。

100.《中国经济史研究的方法论问题》，《中国经济史研究》1992 年第 1 期。⑤

101.《中国封建经济史和广义政治经济学》，载云南大学历史系编《史学论
    文集——纪念李埏教授从事学术活动五十周年》，云南大学出版社，

---

① 杨俊科、梁勇著《大兴纱厂史稿》又作为《石家庄地方史志研究丛书》之一，另行出版
（中国展望出版社，1990 年 5 月）；本文另刊发于河北《史志文丛》编辑部编《史志文丛》
1989 年第 1 期（创刊号）；另，又以《企业史和中国近代化道路研究：序〈大兴纱厂史
稿〉》为题，收录于氏著《中国的现代化：市场与社会》（2001）。

② 本文相继收录于氏著《市场·近代化·经济史论》（1996）、《吴承明集》（2002）、《经济
史理论与实证：吴承明文集》（2012）。

③ 本文是对前著《中国资本主义的发展述略》一文中有关"中国资本集成和工农业及交通运
输业产值的估计"这部分内容的、重新估算、修订并进行改写而成，无论是内容和体例都
有了大幅度的增补和变动，故本目录认定其是一篇独立的、新的文章；另，本文收录于氏
著《市场·近代化·经济史论》（1996），并又进一步修订、改以《近代中国资本集成和工
农业与交通运输业总产值的估计》为题，收录于氏著《吴承明集》（2002）。

④ 本文又收录于氏著《经济史理论与实证：吴承明文集》（2012），但该集将本文的原始刊发
出处误注为《中国经济史研究》1991 年第 4 期，这是与上述《中国近代资本集成和工农业
及交通运输业产值的估计》一文混同了，二者的主题有一定的关联，但其内容完全不同，
是各自独立的两篇文章。

⑤ 本文收录于氏著《市场·近代化·经济史论》（1996）。

1992 年 9 月。

102. 《论广义政治经济学》，《经济研究》1992 年第 11 期。①

103. 《论历史主义》，《中国经济史研究》1993 年第 2 期。②

104. 《经济史的研究要上一个新台阶——在中国经济史学会第二届年会上
    的开幕词》，《中国经济史研究》1993 年第 4 期。

105. 《论工场手工业》，《中国经济史研究》1993 年第 4 期。③

106. 《论二元经济》，《历史研究》1994 年第 2 期。④

107. 《从社会主义市场经济的角度研究私营经济》，载中华全国工商业联合
    会、香港经济导报社、中国民（私）营经济研究会联合编辑，张绪武、
    谢明幹、李定主编《中国私营经济年鉴》（1978～1993 中文繁体字
    版），香港：香港经济导报社，1994 年 8 月。

108. 《功在开拓　遗范长存》，载本书编辑组编《管大同纪念文集》，工商
    出版社，1994 年 10 月。⑤

109. 《近代国内市场商品量的估计》，《中国经济史研究》1994 年第 4 期。⑥

110. 《洋务运动与国内市场》，《文史哲》1994 年第 6 期。⑦

111. 《经济学理论与经济史研究》，《经济研究》1995 年第 4 期。⑧

112. 《要重视商品流通在传统经济向市场经济转换中的作用》，《中国经济
    史研究》1995 年第 2 期。

---

① 本文收录于氏著《市场·近代化·经济史论》（1996）。

② 本文相继收录于氏著《市场·近代化·经济史论》（1996）、《吴承明集》（2002）、《经济
史理论与实证：吴承明文集》（2012）。

③ 本文相继收录于氏著《市场·近代化·经济史论》（1996）、《中国的现代化：市场与社会》
（2001）、《吴承明集》（2002）、《经济史理论与实证：吴承明文集》（2012）。

④ 本文相继收录于氏著《市场·近代化·经济史论》（1996）、《中国的现代化：市场与社会》
（2001）、《吴承明集》（2002）、《经济史理论与实证：吴承明文集》（2012）。

⑤ 本文系吴承明与方行合著；又，"本书编辑组"成员有左平、陆永阳、方行、葛兰（管大同
夫人）等四人；另，"工商出版社"自 2002 年起更名为"中国工商出版社"。

⑥ 本文收录于氏著《市场·近代化·经济史论》（1996）。

⑦ 本文收录于氏著《市场·近代化·经济史论》（1996）。

⑧ 本文另刊发于《中国经济史研究》1995 年第 1 期；又，本文相继收录于氏著《市场·近代
化·经济史论》（1996）、《吴承明集》（2002）、《经济史理论与实证：吴承明文集》
（2012）和孙冶方经济科学基金会编《孙冶方经济科学基金获奖文集》（1990·1994·
1996）（山西经济出版社，1998 年 10 月）、中国社会科学院经济研究所编《纪念中国社会
科学院建院三十周年学术论文集·经济研究所卷》（经济管理出版社，2007 年 1 月）。

113. 《〈中国经济发展的区域研究〉序》，载吴柏均《中国经济发展的区域研究》，上海远东出版社，1995 年 6 月。①

114. 《评〈清代皇族人口行为和社会环境〉》，《历史研究》1995 年第 4 期。②

115. 《16 世纪与 17 世纪的中国市场》，载中国商业史学会编《货殖：商业与市场研究》第 1 辑，中国财政经济出版社，1995 年 9 月。③

116. 《市场经济和商业史研究》，《中国商业史学会通讯》第 7 期，1996 年 1 月。④

117. 《谈创新》，《中国经济史研究》1996 年第 1 期。

118. 《〈1949～1952 年中国经济分析〉序》，载董志凯主编《1949～1952 年中国经济分析》，中国社会科学出版社，1996 年 4 月。⑤

119. 《利用粮价变动研究清代的市场整合》，《中国经济史研究》1996 年第 2 期。⑥

120. 《市场经济和经济史研究》，载《市场·近代化·经济史论》（论文集），云南大学出版社，1996 年 6 月。⑦

121. 《传统经济·市场经济·现代化》，《中国经济史研究》1997 年第 2 期。⑧

122. 《市场机制的演变》，《中国商业史学会通讯》第 8、9 期，1997 年 4 月。

---

① 本文又以《二元经济理论与区域经济史研究：序〈中国经济发展的区域研究〉》为题，收录于氏著《中国的现代化：市场与社会》（2001）。

② 《清代皇族人口行为和社会环境》，〔美〕李中清、郭松义主编，北京大学出版社，1994 年 9 月；本文另收录于氏著《中国的现代化：市场与社会》（2001）。

③ 本文后以《十六与十七世纪的中国市场》为题，收录于中国会计学会编《1993 年会计学论文选·古代商业与市场》（中国财政经济出版社，1995 年 12 月）、氏著《市场·近代化·经济史论》（1996）；以《16 与 17 世纪的中国市场》为题，收录于氏著《中国的现代化：市场与社会》（2001）、《吴承明集》（2002）、《经济史理论与实证：吴承明文集》（2012）。

④ 本文为先生在 1996 年 1 月于中国商业史学会成立十周年庆典会议（绍兴）上的一个发言稿。

⑤ 本文以《新民主主义经济的实践分析：序〈1949～1952 年中国经济分析〉》为题，收录于氏著《中国的现代化：市场与社会》（2001）。

⑥ 本文收录于氏著《中国的现代化：市场与社会》（2001）。

⑦ 本文是由先生在 1995 年参加的两次经济史研讨会上的发言进行综合和改写而来，未曾单独刊发。

⑧ 本文相继收录于氏著《中国的现代化：市场与社会》（2001）、《吴承明集》（2002）、《经济史理论与实证：吴承明文集》（2012）。

123. 《〈近代中国价格结构研究〉序》，载王玉茹《近代中国价格结构研究》，陕西人民出版社，1997 年 5 月。①

124. 《吴承明自述》，载国务院学位委员会办公室编《中国社会科学家自述》，上海教育出版社，1997 年 12 月。

125. 《发挥大运河的运输潜力》，《中国商业史学会通讯》第 10 期，1998 年 6 月。

126. 《近代中国国内市场商品量的估计》，载《中国的现代化：市场与社会》（论文集），三联书店，2001 年 9 月。②

127. 《从经济理论和历史上看社会主义市场经济》，载张世英、张学仁主编《中国著名经济学家论社会主义市场经济》，河南人民出版社，1995 年 1 月。

128. 《令仁教授八秩华诞》，载王育济主编《岁月有情》，山东大学出版社，2004 年 10 月。③

129. 《〈明代黄册制度研究〉序》，载栾成显《明代黄册研究》，中国社会科学出版社，1998 年 7 月、2007 年 10 月（增订本）。④

130. 《要从社会整体性发展来考察中国社会近代化进程——在"纪念傅衣凌逝世十周年学术座谈会"上的讲话》，《北京商学院学报》1998 年第 5 期。⑤

131. 《对研究明清商业史的几点看法》，载中国商业史学会明清商业史专业委员会编《明清商业史研究》第 1 辑，中国财政经济出版社，1998 年 11 月。

132. 《现代化与中国十六、十七世纪的现代化因素》，《中国经济史研究》

---

① 本文以《价格研究——经济史与经济理论：序〈近代中国价格结构研究〉》为题，收录于氏著《中国的现代化：市场与社会》（2001）。

② 本文未曾单独刊发，与前文《近代国内市场商品量的估计》是内容不同的两文；另，本文相继收录于氏著《吴承明集》（2002）、《经济史理论与实证：吴承明文集》（2012，内容又略有修订）。

③ 即原山东大学历史系孔令仁教授（1924.11~2016.7），孔子的第 76 代孙女。

④ 本文转载于《新华文摘》1998 年第 12 期；又，以《档案资料与微观分析：序〈明代黄册研究〉》为题，收录于氏著《中国的现代化：市场与社会》（2001）。

⑤ 本文另刊发于《经济研究资料》1999 年第 1 期。

1998 年第 4 期。①

133. 《〈转变的中国——历史变迁与欧洲经验的局限〉序》，载〔美〕R. Bin Wong（王国斌）著《转变的中国——历史变迁与欧洲经验的局限》，李伯重、连玲玲译，江苏人民出版社，1998 年 12 月、2010 年 7 月。②

134. "Forward to Agriculture Development in Jiangnan, 1620 – 1850," Li Bozhong, *Agriculture Development in Jiangnan, 1620 – 1850*, London：The MacMillan Press Ltd, 1998.③

135. 《市场史、现代化和经济运行：吴承明教授访谈录（1998 年 12 月 25 日）》，《中国经济史研究》1999 年第 1 期。④

136. 《经济史学的理论与方法》，《中国经济史研究》1999 年第 1 期。

137. 《18 世纪与 19 世纪上叶的中国市场》，载中国商业史学会编《货殖：商业与市场研究》第 3 辑，中国财政经济出版社，1999 年 3 月。⑤

138. 《〈中国经济史料考证与研究〉序》，载徐新吾编《中国经济史料考证与研究》，上海社会科学院出版社，1999 年 5 月。⑥

139. 《许涤新治学录》，载中国社会科学院科研局编《中国社会科学院学术

---

① 本文以《现代化与中国 16、17 世纪的现代化因素》为题，相继收录于叶显恩、卞恩才主编《中国传统社会经济与现代化：从不同的角度探索中国传统社会的底蕴及其与现代化的关系》（广州：广东人民出版社，2001 年 9 月）、氏著《吴承明集》（2002）、《经济史理论与实证：吴承明文集》（2012）。

② 本文另以《中西历史比较研究的新思维》为题，刊发于《读书》1998 年第 12 期；以《中西历史比较研究的新思维：序〈转变的中国——历史变迁与欧洲经验的局限〉》为题，相继收录于氏著《中国的现代化：市场与社会》（2001）、《吴承明集》（2002）。

③ 本文的中文本为《〈江南农业的发展，1620～1850〉序》〔载李伯重著，王湘云译《江南农业的发展（1620～1850）》，上海古籍出版社，2007 年 6 月〕；另以《李伯重：〈江南农业的发展（1620～1850）〉（Li Bozhong, *Agriculture Development in Jiangnan, 1620 – 1850*）》为题，刊发于刘东主编《中国学术》2001 年第 1 辑，总第 5 辑，商务印书馆，2001 年 1 月；以 "Spatial and Temporal Study：Forward to Agriculture Development in Jiangnan, 1620 – 1850" 为题，收录于氏著《中国的现代化：市场与社会》（2001）。

④ 本文署名 "《中国经济史研究》编辑部"。

⑤ 本文相继收录于氏著《中国的现代化：市场与社会》（2001，但在该论文集中漏注了原稿的刊发出处）、《吴承明集》（2002）、《经济史理论与实证：吴承明文集》（2012）。

⑥ 本文以《治史要从考证开始：序〈中国近代经济史考证和探索〉》为题，收录于氏著《中国的现代化：市场与社会》（2001）；另，由于本文撰写在徐著出版之前的 1998 年 3 月，而徐著原拟书名为《中国近代经济史考证和探索》，在正式出版时改为现名，在收入该论文集时，先生未对其作相应的变更，故导致本文文名中所题的徐著书名与实际书名不符，特此说明。

大师治学录》，中国社会科学出版社，1999 年 9 月。

140. 《经济发展、制度变迁和社会与文化思想变迁的关系》，载张伟保、黎华标主编《近代中国经济史研讨会 1999 年论文集》，香港：香港新亚研究所，1999 年 9 月。①

141. 《读〈中国近代经济史简编〉》，《中国经济史研究》1999 年第 4 期。②

142. 《李文治先生论中国地主制经济的启示》，《中国经济史研究》1999 年增刊。

143. 《现代化：历史观与方法论》，《经济研究资料》2000 年第 5 期。③

144. 《究天人之际，通古今之变》，《中国经济史研究》2000 年第 2 期。④

145. 《〈中国经济通史〉总序》，载《中国经济通史》（九卷本），经济日报出版社，2000 年 8 月、2007 年 10 月；中国社会科学出版社，2007 年 4 月。⑤

146. 《经济史研究的实证主义和有关问题》，《南开经济研究》2000 年第 6 期。

147. 《〈宋代江南经济史研究〉序》，载〔日〕斯波义信著，方健、何忠礼译《宋代江南经济史研究》，江苏人民出版社，2001 年 1 月、2012 年 1 月。⑥

148. 《一部金字塔式的中国经济史新著——〈中国近代经济史，1895 ~

---

① 本文相继收录于氏著《吴承明集》（2002）、《经济史理论与实证：吴承明文集》（2012）。

② 《中国近代经济史简编》，刘克祥、陈争平著，浙江人民出版社，1999 年 8 月。

③ 本文另收录于中国社会科学院近代史研究所编《近代中国与世界：第二届近代中国与世界学术讨论会论文集》第一卷，社会科学文献出版社，2005 年 1 月。

④ 本文相继收录于李根蟠、〔日〕原宗子、曹幸穗编《中国经济史上的天人关系》（中国农业出版社，2002 年 12 月）和氏著《吴承明集》（2002）、《经济史理论与实证：吴承明文集》（2012）。

⑤ 本文另刊发于《中国史学会通讯》2000 年第 6 期、《中国社会科学院院报》2001 年 1 月 9 日；又，以《中国经济史研究的系统工程——序九卷本〈中国古代经济史〉》为题，收录于氏著《中国的现代化：市场与社会》（2001）；以《历史实证主义与经济分析——九卷本〈中国经济通史〉总序》为题，收录于氏著《吴承明集》（2002）。本文诸文本的内容并不完全一致，相互之间略有差异和出入。

⑥ 本文另以《斯波义信：〈宋代江南经济史研究〉》为题，刊发于刘东主编《中国学术》第 4 辑，商务印书馆，2000 年 10 月；以《经济史理论与方法论的创造性运用——序斯波义信〈宋代江南经济史研究〉中文版》为题，收录于氏著《吴承明集》（2002）。

1927〉评介》，《经济研究》2001 年第 1 期。①

149. 《经济史：历史观与方法论》（在中国社会科学院研究生院讲座的讲稿，2001 年 9、10 月），《中国经济史研究》2001 年第 3 期。②

150. 《中国的现代化：市场与社会（代序）》，载《中国的现代化：市场与社会》（论文集），三联书店，2001 年 9 月。

151. 《16、17 世纪中国的经济现代化因素与社会思想变迁》，载《中国的现代化：市场与社会》（论文集），三联书店，2001 年 9 月。③

152. 《中国 GDP 的故事》，载金明善主编《经济学家茶座》第 10 辑，山东人民出版社，2002 年 10 月。

153. 《从传统经济到现代经济的转变》，《中国经济史研究》2003 年第 1 期。④

154. 《〈百年工农产品比价与农村经济〉序》，载陈其广《百年工农产品比价与农村经济》，社会科学文献出版社，2003 年 4 月。

155. 《〈大分流〉对比较研究方法的贡献》，载刘东主编《中国学术》2003 年第 1 辑，总第 13 辑，商务印书馆，2003 年 6 月。⑤

156. 《西方史学界关于中西比较研究的新思维》，《中国经济史研究》2003 年第 3 期。⑥

---

① 该著的书目信息为汪敬虞主编《中国近代经济史（1895～1927）》（上、中、下），人民出版社，2000 年 5 月、2012 年 1 月（"中国文库"版）、2012 年 4 月/经济管理出版社，2007 年 3 月（中国社会科学院文库·经济研究系列——中国社会科学院建院 30 周年纪念版）；本文另刊发于《中国社会科学院院报》（摘要）2000 年 12 月 26 日、《中国经济史研究》2001 年第 1 期。

② 本文相继收录于氏著《吴承明集》（2002）、《经济史理论与实证：吴承明文集》（2012）。

③ 本文未曾另行单独刊发。

④ 本文为《中国经济史研究》编辑部组织、编辑的《"传统经济的再评价"笔谈》中先生的发言内容。

⑤ 《大分流》的英文原著书目信息为〔美〕Kenneth Pomeranz, *The Great Divergence*：*Europe*, *China*, *and the making of the Modern World Economy*, Princeton：Princeton University Press Ltd.，2000；中译简体版为〔美〕彭慕兰（Kenneth Pomeranz）著，史建云译《大分流：欧洲、中国及现代世界经济的发展》，江苏人民出版社，2003 年、2008 年、2010 年、2014 年、2016 年；中譯繁體版為〔美〕彭慕蘭（Kenneth Pomeranz）著，邱澎生等譯，"國立編譯館"主譯《大分流：中國、歐洲與現代世界經濟的形成》，臺北：巨流圖書公司，2004 年 6 月。

⑥ 本文收录于云南大学中国经济史研究所、云南大学历史系编《李埏教授九十华诞纪念文集》，云南大学出版社，2003 年 11 月。

157. 《〈增长、发展与变迁——中国近代经济发展研究〉序》，载王玉茹《增长、发展与变迁——中国近代经济发展研究》，中国物资出版社，2004 年 1 月。

158. 《多视角看历史：地域经济史研究的新方向（代序）》（在中国东南区域史第二次国际学术讨论会上的讲话），载李伯重、周生春主编《江南的城市工业与地方文化（960~1850）》，清华大学出版社，2004 年 2 月。

159. 《关于清史编纂体例的四点意见》，载国家清史编纂委员会体裁体例工作小组编《清史编纂体裁体例讨论集》（上、下），中国人民大学出版社，2004 年 4 月。

160. 《回忆郝诒纯同志在"一二·九"运动中二三事》，载中国地质大学（北京）郝诒纯院士纪念文集编委会编《大地的女儿：郝诒纯院士纪念文集》，地质出版社，2004 年 9 月。①

161. 《谈谈经济史研究方法问题》，《中国经济史研究》2005 年第 1 期。

162. 《研究经济史的一些体会》，《近代史研究》2005 年第 3 期。

163. 《〈中国社会经济史研究：独特的"食货"之路〉序》，载萧国亮《中国社会经济史研究：独特的"食货"之路》，北京大学出版社，2005 年 9 月。

164. 《〈中国现代化过程中的企业发展〉序》，载刘兰兮主编《中国现代化过程中的企业发展》，福建人民出版社，2006 年 1 月。

165. 《中外历史上"天人"观和"主客"观的演变——在"环境史视野与经济史研究"学术研讨会上的发言》，《中国经济史研究》2006 年第 1 期。②

166. 《谈百家争鸣》，《中国经济史研究》2006 年第 2 期。

167. 《〈经济全球化与文化全球化：历史的思考与求证〉序》，载王述祖《经济全球化与文化全球化：历史的思考与求证》，中国财政经济出版社，2006 年 6 月。

168. 《对〈中国十个五年计划研究报告〉的简要评论》，《当代中国史研究》2006 年第 4 期。

---

① 本文系先生与文铭（先生继室）合著。

② 本文收录于中国社会科学院学部工作局经济学部工作室编《中国社会科学院经济学部学部委员与荣誉学部委员文集（2007）》，经济管理出版社，2008 年 1 月。

169. 《生命不息　奋斗不止——纪念许涤新同志诞辰一百周年》，《经济研究》2006 年第 10 期。①

170. 《学习和治学的一些体会》，载中国社会科学院老专家协会编《学问人生：中国社会科学院名家谈》（上、下），高等教育出版社，2007 年 5 月。

171. 《史学方法和历史实证主义》，载杜恂诚、陈争平、朱荫贵、林刚等著《汪敬虞教授九十华诞纪念文集》，人民出版社，2007 年 7 月。

172. 《〈南开经济丛书〉总序》，首载王玉茹、燕红忠《世界市场价格变动与近代中国产业结构模式研究》，人民出版社，2007 年 10 月。

173. 《秦以后的中国是有中国特色的封建社会》（在"封建译名与马列主义封建观"学术研讨会上的发言），《史学月刊》2008 年第 3 期。

174. 《在清代经济宏观趋势与总体评价学术研讨会上的发言》，《清史研究》2008 年第 3 期。

175. 《悼王永兴教授》（诗一首），《王永兴先生纪念文集》编委会编《通向义宁之学：王永兴先生纪念文集》，中华书局，2010 年 6 月。

176. 《一部承前启后的中国经济史杰作：〈中国近代经济史，1927～1937〉评介》，《经济研究》2011 年第 2 期。②

177. 《全要素分析方法与中国经济史研究》，载武建国、林文勋、吴晓亮主编《永久的思念：李埏教授逝世周年纪念文集》，云南大学出版社，2011 年 5 月。

178. 《关于传统经济的通信》，《中国经济史研究》2012 年第 2 期。③

---

① 本文系先生与方行合著；另以《纪念许涤新同志诞生一百周年》为题，刊发于《中国经济史研究》2006 年第 4 期。

② 本文系先生与叶坦合著；该著的书目信息为刘克祥、吴太昌主编《中国近代经济史（1927～1937）》，人民出版社，2010 年、2012 年。

③ 本文系先生与同事方行研究员的学术信函，由方行研究员生前整理、提供（原件现为方行家人所藏），共有 22 封，可以说是先生的遗著，具体依次为《对讨论商人支配生产问题的来信》（1982 年 2 月）、《对〈清代前期农村市场的发展〉（载〈历史研究〉1987 年第 6 期）的意见》（1987 年 3 月 19 日）、《对我（即方行，下同）一个讨论提纲的意见》（1987 年 11 月 12 日）、《对〈封建社会的自然经济与商品经济〉（载〈中国经济史研究〉1988 年第 1 期）所提意见》（1987 年 10 月 25 日）、《对〈封建社会地主的自给经济〉（载〈中国经济史研究〉1988 年第 4 期）所提意见》（1988 年 2 月 15 日）、《对〈清代前期湖南四川的小农经济〉（载〈中国史研究〉1991 年第 2 期）所提意见》（1990 年 8 月 1 日）、《对

179. 《〈中国经济学术史研究——以经济思想为中心〉序》，载叶坦《中国经济学术史研究——以经济思想为中心》，商务印书馆即将出版。①

编后记： 关于吴承明先生著述的整理和编目，本目录并非首创，之前学界已有多个目录存世，最早的是由方行先生所撰的《吴承明主要著作目录》，② 其后相继有吴承明自撰的《吴承明集·作者主要著作目录》③ 和《吴承明著作目录》、④ 吴太昌等整理的《吴承明文存目录》和《吴承明学术著作目录》、⑤ 苏金花的《吴承明主要论著》、⑥ 吴太昌等主编的《影响新

〈中国封建地租率〉（载〈中国经济史研究〉1992 年第 2 期）所提意见》（1992 年 2 月 14 日）、《对〈中国封建社会农民的经营独立性〉（载〈中国经济史研究〉1995 年第 1 期）所提意见》（1994 年 10 月 23 日）、《对〈应当重视对流通的研究〉（载〈中国经济史研究〉1997 年第 1 期）所提意见》（1996 年 11 月 16 日）、《对我地主制经济论文提纲的意见》（1997 年）、《对拙作〈清代商人对农民产品的预买〉（载〈中国农史〉1998 年第 1 期）所提意见》（1997 年 4 月 28 日）、《对我关于地主制经济讨论提纲所提意见》（1997 年 12 月 8 日）、《对我一篇未刊稿的意见》（1998 年 10 月 20 日）、《讨论对希克斯"命令经济"一词的看法》（1999 年 1 月 25 日）、《对〈中国封建经济发展阶段述略〉（载〈漆侠先生纪念文集〉，河北大学出版社，2002 年）所提意见》（1994 年 4 月 26 日）、《对〈清代江南市镇的劳动力市场〉（载〈中国经济史研究〉2004 年第 2 期）所提意见》（2003 年 2 月 20 日）、《对〈中国封建经济发展阶段述略〉定稿的意见》（2000 年 8 月 25 日）、《对〈中国封建赋税与商品经济〉（载〈中国社会经济史研究〉2002 年第 1 期）所提意见》（2001 年 5 月 21 日）、《对〈中国封建地租与商品经济〉（载〈中国经济史研究〉2002 年第 2 期）所提意见》（2002 年 1 月 6 日）、《对我一个讨论提纲的意见》（2003 年 5 月 4 日）、《对我一个论文提纲的意见》（2004 年 10 月 25 日）、《对我一个未刊稿的意见》（2004 年 11 月 26 日）；本文后改题为《关于传统经济的若干论述——与方行先生的通信》，收录于氏著《经济史理论与实证：吴承明文集》（2002）。

又，本文在收入《吴承明全集》后，先生女公子吴洪教授又增补了一封先生与方行研究员的学术信函《对我关于"江浙与湖南、四川农民收入研究"所提的意见》（1995 年 6 月 10 日，编号"九"），故共为 23 篇。

① 该序作于 2004 年 7 月 31 日（由先生女公子吴洪教授提供），但不知何故，叶坦教授的这本书迄今尚未正式出版，故该序文也迟迟未能公之于世。

② 载方行《倾注心力，探讨中国经济史——吴承明传略》，《经济日报》主编《中国当代经济学家传略》第 5 辑，辽宁人民出版社，1990 年 4 月，第 184 页。

③ 载氏著《吴承明集》，中国社会科学出版社，2002 年 12 月，第 406~410 页。

④ 自印本，2010 年。

⑤ 载吴太昌等编《吴承明文存》及附录，内部打印本，2001 年。

⑥ 载苏金花《吴承明 求知不懈 笔耕不辍》，中国社会科学院青年人文社会科学研究中心编《学问有道——学部委员访谈录·荣誉学部委员》（下），方志出版社，2007 年 8 月，第847 页。

中国60年经济建设的100位经济学家·吴承明主要著作》、① 刘兰兮整理的《经济史理论与实证：吴承明文集·作者论著一览表》、② 吴洪整理的《吴承明学术年表》③ 等。然而，这些目录均收录不全，尤其是对1949年前先生的著述，多有遗漏，个别还存在舛误，但无疑都是本目录编撰的重要基础和线索，本目录就是在这些已有的目录基础上，再充分利用当前便利的网络技术条件，广泛检索各类相关数据库，增补以往缺漏的书目（文目），接着对所有目录进行一一比对、逐条稽查、考订有关目录的信息内容，然后对其进行统一梳理、综合和完善，最终编撰而成。

本目录的撰拟、修订，前后历时三月有余，易稿二十余次，是在不断地增补、辑考和修订中逐步完善起来的。在编撰过程中，得到了诸多师长的鼓励和帮助。业师李伯重教授在获悉笔者的初步工作后，即给予了充分的赞赏和鼓励，并介绍、结识了先生之女公子吴洪教授。吴洪老师在看到笔者的初稿目录后，不仅对笔者的"冒犯"未加任何责语，而且还屡加鼓励，不仅赐下其所藏的先生生前所亲自整理、撰拟的手稿目录及其父亲当年在美国哥伦比亚大学的硕士学位论文目录，而且还就目录的部分细节内容多次、不厌其烦地和笔者进行了讨论和交流，指出了初稿目录中的个别编撰错误，提出了许多具体的修改意见。社科院经济所的王砚峰、常旭两位老师在得知笔者在编撰先生的著述目录后，亦都先后联系上笔者，分别赐予之前由经济所前辈吴太昌教授牵头整理之《吴承明文存》的内部电子文稿。首都师范大学的张天虹教授则据其所掌握的信息和资料，针对本目录初稿内容的缺漏，帮助增补了十余条目录。《中国经济史研究》副主编高超群研究员对本目录的编撰给予了极大的关心和帮助，不仅对目录的所有内容都进行了逐条、逐句、逐字地进行了审定和修润，使得本目录的行文大为增色，而且还就目录中所出现的部分问题，如个别论著的署名并非是先生本人名字等，进行了批评指正，并给出了其自己的看法，本目录充

---

① 载吴太昌等主编《影响新中国60年经济建设的100位经济学家》6，广东经济出版社，2009年9月，第502页；该目录原无目录名，乃编者所拟加。
② 载氏著《经济史理论与实证：吴承明文集》（刘兰兮整理），浙江大学出版社，2012年8月，第423~430页。
③ 载氏著《经济史：历史观与方法论》，商务印书馆，2014年4月、2017年5月，第381~387页。

分汲取了高老师的相关批评意见；尤要着重感谢的是，社科院经济研究所的封越健研究员，对本目录的编撰和最终完善，给予了极为认真、细心的热情帮助，付诸了相当多的心血，贡献良多。封越健老师先是对本目录的内容进行了数次辑补，增补了十余篇笔者所无法查到的遗漏目录，尤其是收录在部分稀见文集中的文章，与此同时还提供了数条笔者之前严重疏漏的线索，如发现吴承明曾以其别名"吴之光"之名刊发过多篇文章，学界长期以来都误将《北京瑞蚨祥》一著作为《中国资本主义工商业史料丛刊》的一种等；接着，封老师又对本目录的体例和内容，以及文字措辞上都进行了全面审定，修订了部分笔者原先所疏忽的错误和不严谨的措辞，尤其是对《中国资本主义工商业史料丛刊》书目的著录费力良多。幸得其批评和指正，才得以避免考述错误，也使得本目录的整体内容能够最终得以修订得更为严谨和完善。

需要说明的是，尽管笔者在编撰本目录的过程中，力图尽自己最大所能将先生的著述都搜集齐全，力求编制成一个完整的《吴承明著述目录》，然而，主观上由于笔者的学识和学力所限，客观上也由于各种条件所限、无法查找齐全，因此难免会出现挂一漏万情况，其中最为明显之处，就是先生在 1940 年任职于重庆中央银行经济研究处时，曾兼任《新蜀报》（重庆）主笔一职，[①] 照一般常理，其肯定在该报上发表过相关文章，但由于笔者目前一时无法查阅到该报纸，故对先生可能在该报上刊发的文章也无法进行搜集和编目，甚为遗憾。但不管怎样，本目录的编撰是对先生学术史的一次重要梳理，相信其在公诸学林之后，对于从事中国经济史研究的后进全面阅读、学习先生的著述定大有裨益。由于笔者才疏学浅，学力不深，学识浅薄，因此本目录内容定有诸多疏漏、舛误之处，敬请诸方家批评指正。

---

① 详见方行《倾注心力，探讨中国经济史——吴承明传略·吴承明主要著作目录》（第184页）、吴柏均《吴承明先生传略》（第305页）、李伯重《吴承明先生学术小传》（第296页）、吴文川《博学勤思通古今——记荣誉学部委员、中国经济史专家吴承明》（第89页）、叶坦《学贯中西古今 德泽桃李同仁——吴承明先生的生平与学术》、《史实·史法·史观——吴承明先生的生平与学述》、《吴承明为"经济救国"理想而奋斗》。

附录 学界介绍、纪念及追忆吴承明
生平与学术的文章①

1. 林其锬：《吴承明教授谈国外对不发达国家经济的研究情况》，《上海经济研究》1981 年第 7 期。

2. 朱秀琴：《吴承明研究员谈中国近代的封建经济》，《南开经济研究所季刊》1983 年第 1 期。

3. 〔法〕贾永吉（Michel Carrier）：《吴承明的国内统一市场形成观》，载〔法〕《年鉴：经济 社会 文明》（*Annales，Économies Sociétés Civilisations*）1986 年 11～12 月号。②

4. 方行：《倾注心力，探讨中国经济史——吴承明传略》，载《经济日报》编《中国当代经济学家传略》第 5 辑，辽宁人民出版社，1990 年 4 月。

5. 吴柏均：《吴承明先生传略》，载丁日初主编《近代中国》第 2 辑，上海社会科学院出版社，1991 年 11 月。

6. 李伯重：《吴承明先生学术小传》，载吴承明《市场·近代化·经济史论》（论文集），云南大学出版社，1996 年 6 月。

7. 刘佛丁：《新时期中国经济史学理论的探索——吴承明〈市场·近代化·经济史论〉读后》，《经济研究》1997 年第 5 期。

---

① 由于吴承明先生是中国经济史学界最具权威的学者之一，有着极为崇高的学术声望，他人难以望其项背，在其晚年学术声誉达到顶峰时，其部分同事、晚学乃至媒体都纷纷撰文，或介绍先生之学术思想和治学方法，或撰写其生平学术传略，乃至对其进行学术访谈；先生仙逝后，其生前在学术上所指教、提挈过的同事、弟子、晚学以及其家人，都各自从不同角度撰写了纪念、追忆先生生平与学术的文章。这些文章既有阐释吴承明学术理论和治学方法的，又有崇敬先生之人品与和学术品德的，也有怀念、追忆先生教诲和提挈恩泽的，尽管这些文章并不属于先生自身著述的内容，但无疑应是先生学术精神的一个重要组成部分，故本目录亦将其收集、编目附录于后。

② 本文实为贾永吉（Michel Carrier）对先生《论明代国内市场和商人资本》（载中国社会科学院经济研究所学术委员会编《中国社会科学院经济研究所集刊》第 5 集，中国社会科学出版社，1983 年 2 月）、《论清代前期我国国内市场》（载《历史研究》1983 年第 1 期）及《我国半殖民地半封建国内市场》（载《历史研究》1984 年第 2 期）三文的摘要、综合及介绍。

8. 叶坦：《吴承明教授的经济史研究》，载台北中研院近代史研究所编《近代中国史研究通讯》第 26 期，1998 年 9 月。

9. 叶坦：《经济学不老人——吴承明》，载金明善主编《经济学家茶座》第 7 辑，山东人民出版社，2002 年 1 月。①

10. 刘兰兮：《吴承明》，载中国社会科学院研究生院教务处编《名师荟萃中国社会科学院研究生院博士生导师简介》二，中国经济出版社，2005 年 9 月。

11. 赵德馨：《高山仰止》，载方行主编《中国社会经济史论丛：吴承明教授九十华诞纪念》，中国社会科学出版社，2006 年 12 月。②

12. 刘福寿：《珍贵的一课》，载方行主编《中国社会经济史论丛：吴承明教授九十华诞纪念》。

13. 昃文川：《博学勤思通古今——记荣誉学部委员、中国经济史专家吴承明》，载中国社会科学院老专家协会编《学问人生：中国社会科学院名家谈》（上、下），高等教育出版社，2007 年 5 月。③

14. 方行：《仁者寿 智者寿》，《中国经济史研究》2007 年第 2 期。④

15. 林甘泉：《〈南山〉之诗，"眉寿"之颂》，《中国经济史研究》2007 年第 2 期。

16. 经君健：《哲人其康——敬贺吴承明先生、汪敬虞先生九秩华诞》，《中国经济史研究》2007 年第 2 期。

17. 丁长清：《学习大家风范，开创经济史研究新局面——吴承明先生、汪敬虞先生九秩华诞学术研讨会笔谈》，《中国经济史研究》2007 年

---

① 本文另收录于金明善主编，詹小洪执行主编《经济学家茶座》（精华本），山东人民出版社出版，2004 年 1 月。

② 本文又以《高山仰止——记吴承明教授二三事》为题，刊发于金明善主编《经济学家茶座》第 26 辑，山东人民出版社，2006 年 12 月；后又另收录于金明善主编《经济学人》，山东人民出版社，2008 年 12 月。

③ 本文另刊发于《中国社会科学院院报》2007 年 1 月 25 日第 4 版（摘要）；本文另收录于王俊义主编《炎黄文化研究》第 7 辑，大象出版社，2008 年 4 月。

④ 2007 年 4 月 15 日中国社科院在北京主办了"吴承明、汪敬虞先生九十华诞学术研讨会"，来自中国社科院、北京大学、清华大学、复旦大学、南开大学、南京大学、云南大学、上海财经大学等单位的 60 余位专家学者出席了学术研讨会并发言，本文及下列同期所刊发的诸文均为选登的在此次研讨会上的发言或发言稿。

第 2 期。

18. 李根蟠：《开拓创新　永葆青春——庆贺吴、汪二老九十华诞，兼谈经济所经济史学科的学术传统》，《中国经济史研究》2007 年第 2 期。

19. 董志凯：《大师风范　楷模长存——贺吴老、汪老九十寿辰》，《中国经济史研究》2007 年第 2 期。

20. 朱荫贵：《汪老吴老九十寿诞感言》，《中国经济史研究》2007 年第 2 期。

21. 陈争平：《两位老师给后学的教益》，《中国经济史研究》2007 年第 2 期。

22. 王玉茹：《博学笃志　惠泽百家》，《中国经济史研究》2007 年第 2 期。

23. 苏金花：《吴承明　求知不懈　笔耕不辍》，载中国社会科学院青年人文社会科学研究中心编《学问有道——学部委员访谈录·荣誉学部委员》（下），方志出版社，2007 年 8 月。

24. 魏明孔：《"吴承明、汪敬虞先生九十华诞学术研讨会"在京隆重举行》，《清华大学学报》（哲学社会科学版）2007 年第 4 期。

25. 牛贯杰：《20 世纪 80 年代：吴承明及其清代国内市场研究》，载牛贯杰著《17～19 世纪中国的市场与经济发展》，黄山书社，2008 年 3 月。

26. 隋福民：《吴承明：新经济史方法论的良窳》，载隋福民著《创新与融合——美国新经济史革命及对中国的影响（1957～2004）》，天津古籍出版社，2009 年 11 月，第 300～302 页。

27. 刘维维：《经济史应当成为经济学之源——访中国经济史学专家吴承明》，《中国社会科学报》2010 年 11 月 11 日第 6 版。

28. 王玉茹：《如父亦友　人生导师》，《中国社会科学报》2011 年 07 月 28 日。

29. 叶坦：《学贯中西古今　德泽桃李同仁——吴承明先生的生平与学术》，《经济学动态》2011 年第 9 期。①

30. 《中国经济史研究》编辑部：《沉重悼念吴承明先生》，《中国经济史研究》2011 年第 3 期。

31. 武力：《吴承明先生的经济史观》，《中国社会科学报》2011 年 12 月 15 日。

32. 郭松义：《纪念吴老》，《中国经济史研究》2012 年第 2 期。

---

①　本文作为附录另收录于氏著《经济史理论与实证：吴承明文集》（刘兰兮整理），浙江大学出版社，2012 年 8 月。

33. 丁长清：《纪念吴承明》，《中国经济史研究》2012 年第 2 期。

34. 董志凯：《洞晓与践行"包容"理念的睿智大师——缅怀吴承明先生》，《中国经济史研究》2012 年第 2 期。

35. 李伯重：《良师难遇——回忆吴承明先生》，《中国经济史研究》2012 年第 2 期。①

36. 萧国亮：《与时俱进，老当益壮——深切怀念吴承明先生》，《中国经济史研究》2012 年第 2 期。

37. 方健：《高山仰止　景行行之——深切悼念吴老归道山一周年》，《中国经济史研究》2012 年第 2 期。

38. 武力：《学贵在通，识之于变——忆向吴承明先生讨教的几点收获》，《中国经济史研究》2012 年第 2 期。②

39. 朱荫贵：《怀念吴老》，《中国经济史研究》2012 年第 2 期。

40. 陈争平：《吴老教诲追忆》，《中国经济史研究》2012 年第 2 期。

41. 王玉茹：《忆恩师吴承明先生》，《中国经济史研究》2012 年第 2 期。

42. 叶坦：《史无定法　识人唯长——吴承明先生的治学与为人》，《中国经济史研究》2012 年第 2 期。

43. 李根蟠：《吴承明先生与中国经济史论坛——缅怀经济史界的智慧之星》，《中国经济史研究》2012 年第 2 期。

44. 龙登高：《清华园里忆吴老》，《中国经济史研究》2012 年第 2 期。③

45. 袁为鹏：《经济史理论与研究——纪念吴承明先生逝世一周年学术研讨会述要》，《中国经济史研究》2012 年第 4 期。

46. 张天虹：《吴承明先生与清华学生运动——以"一二·九"运动为中心》，载李越主编《世纪清华——学人、学术与教育》，清华大学出版社，2013 年 11 月。

47. 吴洪整理《吴承明学术年表》，载吴承明《经济史：历史观与方法论》，

---

① 本文收录于李埏、李伯重《良史与良师：学生眼中的八位著名学者》，清华大学出版社，2012 年 1 月。

② 本文收录于王玉茹、吴柏均、刘兰兮编《经济发展与市场变迁——吴承明先生百年诞辰纪念文集》下篇《回忆与缅怀》，南开大学出版社，2016 年 12 月。

③ 本文收录于《经济发展与市场变迁——吴承明先生百年诞辰纪念文集》下篇《回忆与缅怀》。

商务印书馆，2014 年 4 月、2017 年 5 月。①

48. 叶坦：《史实·史法·史观——吴承明先生的生平与学述》，载吴承明《经济史：历史观与方法论》。②

49. 刘巍：《对"经济史应当成为经济学之源"理念的思考——谨以此文纪念吴承明先生》，《广东外语外贸大学学报》2015 年第 2 期。③

50. 叶坦：《吴承明为"经济救国"理想而奋斗》，见《抗战时期的中国经济学家》，《人民日报》2015 年 7 月 27 日第 16 版。

51. 林刚：《从国情出发以长时段的基本规律把握中国问题——略谈吴承明先生关于中国传统与现代化道路关系的研究》，《中国经济史研究》2015 年第 4 期。④

52. 陈争平：《"史无定法"与重视计量分析——吴承明学术思想讨论》，载王玉茹、吴柏均、刘兰兮编《经济发展与市场变迁——吴承明先生百年诞辰纪念文集》上篇《学术论文》，南开大学出版社，2016 年 12 月。

53. 董志凯：《如何认识经济史研究中的"史无定法"——缅怀吴承明先生》，载《经济发展与市场变迁——吴承明先生百年诞辰纪念文集》上篇《学术论文》。

54. 任放：《历史观与方法论——吴承明先生晚年学术思想蠡测》，载《经济发展与市场变迁——吴承明先生百年诞辰纪念文集》上篇《学术论文》。

55. 张耕：《深切缅怀恩师吴承明先生》，载《经济发展与市场变迁——吴承

---

① 本文收录于《经济发展与市场变迁——吴承明先生百年诞辰纪念文集》下篇《回忆与缅怀》；在该著第 1 版（上海财经大学出版社，2006 年 12 月）中并未收录该文，是在该书商务印书馆修订版中补收的。

② 本文是叶坦在前文《学贯中西古今 德泽桃李同仁——吴承明先生的生平与学术》（载《经济学动态》2011 年第 9 期；吴承明著，刘兰兮整理《经济史理论与实证：吴承明文集》（论文集），浙江大学出版社，2012 年 8 月）的基础上再次补充、改写、修订而成，内容已经有了重大的变动，题名也进行了更改，故不是一个简单的修订和再刊，而是已成相互独立的两篇论文，特此注明；本文另收录于《经济发展与市场变迁——吴承明先生百年诞辰纪念文集》下篇《回忆与缅怀》。在该著第一版（上海财经大学出版社，2006 年 12 月）中，并未收录该文，是在商务印书馆修订版中补收的。

③ 本文另收录于《经济发展与市场变迁——吴承明先生百年诞辰纪念文集》上篇《学术论文》，南开大学出版社，2016 年 12 月。

④ 本文后略作修改，以《以长时段的基本规律把握中国问题——略谈吴老关于中国传统与现代化道路关系的研究》为题，收录于《经济发展与市场变迁——吴承明先生百年诞辰纪念文集》上篇《学术论文》。

明先生百年诞辰纪念文集》下篇《回忆与缅怀》。

56. 魏明孔：《"学派"与学术杂志：追记吴承明先生关于经济史期刊的点滴教诲》，载《经济发展与市场变迁——吴承明先生百年诞辰纪念文集》下篇《回忆与缅怀》。

57. 吴明煌：《论市场经济的文化——为纪念吴承明教授》，载《经济发展与市场变迁——吴承明先生百年诞辰纪念文集》下篇《回忆与缅怀》。

58. 吴洪：《不泯的记忆：怀念父亲吴承明》，载《经济发展与市场变迁——吴承明先生百年诞辰纪念文集》下篇《回忆与缅怀》。

59. 吴承光：《回忆大哥吴承明》，载《经济发展与市场变迁——吴承明先生百年诞辰纪念文集》下篇《回忆与缅怀》。

60. 吴承康：《怀念承明哥》，载《经济发展与市场变迁——吴承明先生百年诞辰纪念文集》下篇《回忆与缅怀》。

61. 汪新：《家常话念吾舅》，载《经济发展与市场变迁——吴承明先生百年诞辰纪念文集》下篇《回忆与缅怀》。

62. 刘兰兮：《吴承明与〈中国资本主义发展史〉》，《近代史研究》2017 年第 5 期。

63. 叶坦：《吴承明》，载中国史学会《中国历史学年鉴》编委会编《中国历史学年鉴·现代史学家》（2012～），待版。①

---

① 本文作者早于 2012 年 3 月时就《吴承明》的内容交稿，但该《年鉴》何时能出版，目前尚不得缞而知。

后　记

吴　洪

终于赶在父亲百年诞辰的 2017 年结束之前完成了全部稿子的搜集、整理。这套《吴承明全集》将先父的著述划分为"专著""经济史研究""经济评论""研究与创新""书评与序言""会议发言""未发表的论述""通信""诗话""外文论著""附录"等部分。

全集共分为六卷：第一卷、第二卷共收入九部专著，其中第一本《古代云南与中土关系之研究》为手稿形式，是父亲的本科毕业论文，其余八本都曾经出版过。列入专著的仅限父亲独著、一本与人合著及一本明确他为主要执笔人的著作，而仅作为主编的著作均未收入其中。全集所收录的论文，主要按其内容又分为"经济史研究""经济评论""研究与创新"三个部分。其中经济史是父亲毕生的主攻领域，八十多篇研究成果收入在全集的第三卷、第四卷中。第五卷是除经济史研究论文之外的一些内容，分为"经济评论"与"研究与创新"；第五卷还包括了"书评与序言"与"会议发言"。"书评与序言"中除了一本即将出版的书籍的序言外，其余各篇所做序言的书籍都已经出版面世。"会议发言"基本上没有公开发表。第六卷包括"未发表的论述"、"通信"、"诗话"、"外文论著"以及"附录"。本卷内容除了父亲与方行先生"关于传统经济的若干论述"的 22 封通信，以及两篇日文文章外，其余均未曾公开发表，"诗话"父亲虽然几次打印装订成册，但也只是送给亲朋好友。

　　到目前为止，我们所能够了解到的父亲的主要的文章，仅以下两篇未能包括在本套书中，一是《中国土地问题》，载姚依林、杨述主编《东方既白》（北京）创刊号，1935 年；二是《庄蹻王滇考》，载《益世报·史学副刊》第 21 期，发表在《益世报》（昆明）1939 年 10 月 7 日。这两篇文章，父亲在自己的著作中曾经提起，但是几经努力仍然没能找到刊发的刊物。其余的都尽可能地纳入了全集中的某个部分，也没有刻意滤掉某些今日看来有着一些历史局限性的文章。

　　限于专业，更限于水平和能力，我深知靠一己之力是无法完成全集的主编工作的。所幸整个过程中一直遇到各位学者、老师、朋友们的鼎力相助。当得知出版父亲全集的信息后，社科院经济研究所的刘兰兮老师首先带着我去见了著名的经济史学家、父亲半个多世纪的挚友方行先生，那时方先生已经身体虚弱，但还是为全集的章节安排出谋划策，并提供了序言，又将仔细保留装订的父亲的 20 多封信件交到我手中。中国社会科学院经济研究所的叶坦研究员和清华大学的李伯重教授，几乎我每隔一段时间都会因各种各样的问题打搅两位先生，每次求教，他们都给予了认真、耐心的答复。两位先生还分别为全集撰写了序言和父亲的小传。苏州学者方健先生，我打电话询问是否可以当面请教一些问题，方先生满口答应。但我一进他家门不禁愣住，他不仅自己正在胃癌手术后的恢复期，且夫人几天前刚刚突发疾病去世。但是方先生仍然热情的帮助我解答问题和看稿子。方行先生的研究生、我的大学同学蔡湘汉先生，大半年来一直帮助校对文稿，修订表格，核算数据，为了赶时间，放弃了自己的许多事情，为全集的出版付出了巨大的心血。

　　最初，我们主要根据父亲在世时自己整理的一份目录来准备全集的内容，由于那时的数据库建设不完善以及没有找到科学的检索方式，那份目录仅限于父亲自己当时能够收集到的文章，是很不完整的。感谢杭州师范大学历史系余清良教授，他耗费了大量时间精力做出父亲的著述目录，又根据随时发现的信息多次仔细修订补充，终于完成这份最为完整的著述目录（见附录），多篇父亲在 20 世纪三四十年代的文章，我都是从余教授的目录中找到的。父亲曾经在清华大学读书和作为学生领袖参加抗日救国运动，有着浓浓的清华情结，他关于清华的文字很多是首都师范大学的张天虹老师向我提供的。中国社会科学院经济研究所的封越健先生，不仅帮助找到多篇父亲的文章和信件，还发现了父亲在撰写文章时曾经使用过的另一笔名"吴之光"，且找到多个证据，就在我写这篇《后记》的现在，小封（他坚持不容许我叫他老师）还在为两篇新发现的父亲的文章忙碌。此外，我还要感激首都经济贸易大学的朱月教授，他帮助认真校对了日文稿件，美国匹茨堡大学的罗斯基（Thomas G. Rawski）教授帮助我找到了父亲在美国念书时的文章。国家图书馆的张超亚先生和朱庆华女士为我们寻找那些半个多世纪前的文献和缩微胶片提供方便，张先生还多次帮助看稿子和解答问题。最后，我还要感谢认真负责、兢兢业业的出版社编辑，由于不断有新发现的文章，其间还有发现与父亲同名但最后证实不是父亲的文章，导致一直在稿子的安排上不断增减变化，无形中给编辑工作增加了一些麻烦。还有许多这里没提到名字的曾经给予过帮助的朋友，我都将铭记于心，谨在此表示诚挚的谢意和敬意。而书中的任何缺陷和问题都是由于自己的能力所限，应由自己负责，希望大家指正。

2017 年 10 月 15 日

图书在版编目（CIP）数据

吴承明全集：全六册 / 吴承明著. -- 北京：社会
科学文献出版社，2018.4
ISBN 978 - 7 - 5201 - 2444 - 7

Ⅰ.①吴… Ⅱ.①吴… Ⅲ.①吴承明（1917 - 2011）
- 文集②经济史 - 文集 Ⅳ.①F1 - 53

中国版本图书馆 CIP 数据核字（2018）第 047161 号

吴承明全集

著　　者 / 吴承明

出 版 人 / 谢寿光
项目统筹 / 宋荣欣
责任编辑 / 宋　超

出　　版 / 社会科学文献出版社·近代史编辑室（010）59367256
　　　　　地址：北京市北三环中路甲 29 号院华龙大厦　邮编：100029
　　　　　网址：www.ssap.com.cn
发　　行 / 市场营销中心（010）59367081　59367018
印　　装 / 三河市东方印刷有限公司

规　　格 / 开　本：787mm × 1092mm　1/16
　　　　　印　张：238.25　插　页：0.5　字　数：3862 千字
版　　次 / 2018 年 4 月第 1 版　2018 年 4 月第 1 次印刷
书　　号 / ISBN 978 - 7 - 5201 - 2444 - 7
定　　价 / 1980.00 元（全六卷）